The International Dimensions
of Internal Conflict

CSIA Studies in International Security

Michael E. Brown, Sean M. Lynn-Jones, and Steven E. Miller, series editors
Karen Motley, executive editor
Center for Science and International Affairs (CSIA)
John F. Kennedy School of Government, Harvard University

Published by The MIT Press:

Allison, Graham T., Owen R. Coté, Jr., Richard A. Falkenrath, and Steven E. Miller, *Avoiding Nuclear Anarchy: Containing the Threat of Loose Russian Nuclear Weapons and Fissile Material* (1996)

Allison, Graham T., and Kalypso Nicolaïdis, eds., *The Greek Paradox: Promise vs. Performance* (1996)

Brown, Michael E., ed., *The International Dimensions of Internal Conflict* (1996)

Falkenrath, Richard A., *Shaping Europe's Military Order: The Origins and Consequences of the CFE Treaty* (1994)

Feldman, Shai, *Nuclear Weapons and Arms Control in the Middle East* (1996)

Forsberg, Randall, ed., *The Arms Production Dilemma: Contraction and Restraint in the World Combat Aircraft Industry* (1994)

Shields, John M., and William C. Potter, eds., *Dismantling the Cold War: U.S. and NIS Perspectives on the Nunn-Lugar Cooperative Threat Reduction Program* (1997)

Published by Brassey's, Inc.:

Blackwill, Robert D., and Sergei A. Karaganov, eds., *Damage Limitation or Crisis? Russia and the Outside World* (1994)

Johnson, Teresa Pelton, and Steven E. Miller, eds., *Russian Security After the Cold War: Seven Views from Moscow* (1994)

Mussington, David, *Arms Unbound: The Globalization of Defense Production* (1994)

Published by CSIA:

Allison, Graham, Ashton B. Carter, Steven E. Miller, and Philip Zelikow, eds., *Cooperative Denuclearization: From Pledges to Deeds* (1993)

Campbell, Kurt M., Ashton B. Carter, Steven E. Miller, and Charles A. Zraket, *Soviet Nuclear Fission: Control of the Nuclear Arsenal in a Disintegrating Soviet Union* (1991)

The International Dimensions of Internal Conflict

Editor
Michael E. Brown

CSIA Studies in International Security

The MIT Press
Cambridge, Massachusetts
London, England

Copyright © 1996 by the Center for Science and International Affairs
John F. Kennedy School of Government
Harvard University
Cambridge, Massachusetts 02138
(617) 495-1400

All rights reserved. No part of this book may be reproduced, stored in a retrieval system,
or transmitted in any form or by any means — electronic, electrostatic, magnetic tape,
mechanical, photocopying, recording, or otherwise — without permission in writing from
the Center for Science and International Affairs, 79 John F. Kennedy Street,
Cambridge, MA 02138.

Library of Congress Cataloging-in-Publication Data

The international dimensions of internal conflict / Michael E. Brown, editor.
p.   cm. — (CSIA studies in international security; no. 10)
Includes bibliographical references and index.
ISBN 0-262-02397-0 (hardcover: alk. paper). — ISBN 0-262-52209-8 (pbk.: alk. paper)
1. Civil war. 2. Guerrilla warfare. 3. Security, International. I. Brown, Michael E.
(Michael Edward), 1954–   . II. Series.
JX4541.I57   1996
341.6′8—dc20   96-3428
                                                                                CIP

10 9 8 7 6 5 4 3
Printed in the United States of America

Contents

Preface

Internal conflict is the most pervasive form of armed conflict in the world today. Civil wars rage in dozens of countries, and are responsible for killing and displacing literally millions of people. Internal conflicts destabilize regions, undermine respect for international law and norms of behavior, and can affect the national interests of distant powers. Scholars who care about war and peace issues, political and economic development, and political and social justice should care about the causes and consequences of internal conflict. Policymakers who have responsibilities for national and international security should care deeply about these problems as well.

Unfortunately, the causes and consequences of internal conflict are not well understood. The conventional wisdom is that these conflicts are driven by "ancient hatreds" and that they "spill over" from one place to another in a process that is largely beyond human control. Scholarly studies of these issues are more sophisticated but, in the end, still unsatisfying.

In this book, we focus on three main issues. First, we analyze the causes of internal conflicts, identifying different types of conflicts along the way. Second, we examine the different ways in which neighboring states become involved in domestic disputes. Third, we assess efforts to prevent, manage, and resolve internal conflicts, with the goal of developing concrete recommendations for policymakers at the national level and in regional and international security organizations.

The academic world rightly places great emphasis on individual scholarship, but some subjects can be analyzed most effectively by groups of dedicated researchers and analysts. This is one of those subjects. It would be difficult if not impossible for any one individual, in a short period of time, to develop the expertise needed to comment intelligently on many different kinds of developments in many widely scattered parts of the world. I was most fortunate to find over two dozen people who were willing to share their time generously and to pool their expertise in a joint investigation of a complex problem.

The project that led to the production of this book was launched in September 1994, when Steven Miller, Director of the International Security Program at Harvard University's Center for Science and International Affairs (CSIA), and I decided to form a CSIA Working Group on Internal Conflict. The Working Group, which I chaired, was comprised mainly of CSIA Research Fellows, but it also included experts from other research centers at Harvard, as well as scholars from other universities and research institutes. We met as a group for a one-day workshop in November 1994 to sharpen the intellectual focus of our enterprise and to go over outlines of book chapters. Those of us who were based in Cambridge met several times a month thereafter. The entire Working Group re-assembled for three days in March 1995 to go over first drafts of chapters. Final drafts were delivered over the summer, and we subsequently began editing and production work. The book was sent to the publishers in January 1996, roughly sixteen months after the project got under way.

The fact that such a massive book was produced in a comparatively short period of time can be traced to the efforts of a great many people. Steven Miller was present at the creation, and deserves at least half of the credit for zeroing in on this topic. He gave me good advice whenever I asked for it, encouragement whenever I needed it, and a helping hand at many critical junctures along the way. One could not ask for a better colleague or friend.

The fourteen contributors to this volume made extraordinary efforts to focus on a common set of questions and produce first-rate research and analysis in a remarkably short period of time. They deserve the lion's share of the credit for whatever substantive and analytic contributions this volume might make. Richard Falkenrath, John Matthews, Colin Scott, Katherine Tucker, and Barbara Walter, who were also active members of the CSIA Working Group, contributed to our thinking and to this book in important ways. Five distinguished scholars and international affairs experts — John Chipman, William Durch, Brian Mandell, John Mearsheimer, and Stephen Van Evera — took several days out of their busy schedules and helped us review first drafts at our March 1995 workshop. We are very grateful to them for their invaluable advice and guidance.

I would also like to thank Chantal de Jonge Oudraat, Dan Lindley, Sean Lynn-Jones, Steven Miller, and Stephen Stedman for their comments on my contributions to this volume, and those who gave me feedback on talks given at the Australian National University, Brown University, the University of Calcutta, CSIA, Fudan University in Shanghai, the University of Indonesia in Jakarta, the Institute for Defence Studies and Analyses in New Delhi, Jawaharlal Nehru University in New Delhi, and McGill University in Montreal.

Karen Motley handled the monumental task of copy-editing and producing this book with consummate professionalism and unflagging good cheer. Karen spent many late nights and long weekends turning our murky prose into pristine copy. Teresa Lawson, Senior Editor at CSIA, gave us sage advice and graciously took on other editorial burdens so that Karen could concentrate on this book. These efforts went above and beyond the call of duty, and are much appreciated. Meara Keegan, Editorial Assistant at CSIA, helped to prepare the bibliography, list of contributors, and index, and aided in other ways too numerous to mention. Stephen Zisk, Joshua Levitt, and Celes Eckerman produced the maps that appear in the first part of this book; I am especially grateful to Stephen for jumping in at the last minute and helping us out. Interns Daniel Alexandre, Celes Eckerman, Deborah Kamen, Leigh Miller, and Spencer Rascoff provided research, editorial, and administrative assistance at important points along the way. Mera Kachgal and Graceann Todaro helped to organize our two workshops. Marie Allitto and Peggy Scannell made everything run smoothly on the financial front. Tom D'Espinosa and his staff at Wellington Graphics handled a massive typesetting job with extraordinary skill and dexterity. Ann Callahan, Lynne Meyer-Gay, Dawn Opstad, and Helen Snively helped with proofreading. To one and all, my sincere thanks.

Finally, I would like to thank Graham Allison, who took over as Director of CSIA in January 1995 and who has supported this project enthusiastically. His advice and encouragement have been greatly appreciated. The Carnegie Corporation of New York provided generous grants to CSIA that enabled us to undertake this project. We are most grateful to David Hamburg, David Speedie, and Astrid Tuminez of the Carnegie Corporation and to Jane Holl, Esther Brimmer, and Thomas Leney of the Carnegie Commission on Preventing Deadly Conflict for their support of our endeavors.

CSIA is known for bringing scholarly weight and analytical rigor to bear on problems of great importance to the international community. I hope that we have lived up to those standards.

Michael E. Brown
Cambridge, January 1996

List of Maps

List of Tables

The International Dimensions
of Internal Conflict

Introduction

Michael E. Brown

This is a book about internal conflict. In it, we analyze three main sets of issues: the causes of internal conflict; the regional dimensions of internal conflict; and international efforts to deal with the problems posed by internal conflict. Our aim is to advance understanding of how internal conflict begins, how it involves neighboring states, and what distant powers and international organizations can do about it.

By "internal conflict," we mean violent or potentially violent political disputes whose origins can be traced primarily to domestic rather than systemic factors, and where armed violence takes place or threatens to take place primarily within the borders of a single state.[1] Examples include violent power struggles involving civilian or military leaders; armed ethnic conflicts and secessionist campaigns; challenges by criminal organizations to state sovereignty; armed ideological struggles; and revolutions. The level of violence can range from low-level terrorist campaigns to sustained guerilla insurgencies to all-out civil war or genocide. In most cases, the key actors are governments and rebel groups, but when state structures are weak or non-existent, groups of various kinds fight among themselves in a Hobbesian universe of their own.[2]

Many types of deadly conflict are beyond the scope of this study,

---

1. Of course, conflict is a fact of life in every society and political system. Our concern, however, is with violent conflict.

2. For a thoughtful discussion of definitional conundrums, see Harry Eckstein, "Introduction: Toward the Theoretical Study of Internal War," in Harry Eckstein, ed., *Internal War: Problems and Approaches* (New York: Free Press, 1964), especially pp. 8–21. See also James B. Rule, *Theories of Civil Violence* (Berkeley: University of California Press, 1988), pp. 9–13; Lori Fisler Damrosch, "Introduction," in Lori Fisler Damrosch, ed., *Enforcing Restraint: Collective Intervention in Internal Conflicts* (New York: Council on Foreign Relations, 1993), pp. 4–5.

including inter-state wars caused by systemic factors such as changing patterns of alliance relationships or breakthroughs in military technology. Nor will we examine colonial wars and anti-colonial struggles, which have unique features that merit special attention elsewhere.[3] Mob violence and riots that lack political agendas or the organizational capacity for sustained action are also beyond the scope of this study, as is non-political criminal activity. Political disputes of a non-violent nature are left for others to contemplate, although we are interested in disputes that have the potential to escalate and generate sustained violence.

This book begins with an examination of internal conflict in eight regions of the world: the Balkans; East-Central Europe; the former Soviet Union; South and Southwest Asia; Southeast Asia; the Middle East and North Africa; sub-Saharan Africa; and Latin America. We then direct our attention to the track record of international efforts to deal with internal conflicts, focusing on key policy instruments and prominent international actors. The three main tasks that confront international peacemakers are conflict prevention, conflict management, and conflict resolution. The main instruments at their disposal are humanitarian assistance; fact-finding; mediation; confidence-building measures; traditional and multi-functional peacekeeping; arms embargoes and arms transfers; economic sanctions and economic inducements; judicial enforcement measures; and the use of military force. The main international actors engaged in the prevention, management, and resolution of internal conflicts are states, operating either unilaterally or multilaterally; international organizations; and nongovernmental organizations (NGOs). Our analysis of international efforts that have been made through 1995 provides us with a solid foundation for generating policy recommendations about the problems posed by internal conflicts and about the conditions under which different kinds of international action are most likely to be effective.

To make this enterprise more manageable and to make our analysis more relevant to current concerns, this book focuses on the post–Cold War era. The scholarly rationale for this is that the dynamics of many internal conflicts and the patterns of regional and international involvement in internal conflict have changed with the end of the global competition between Washington and Moscow.

---

3. The line between anti-colonial struggles and internal conflict is not always easy to draw. For example, we are interested in the war in Chechnya and would define it as an internal conflict even though many Chechens would describe their struggle in anti-colonial terms. However, we will not examine the conflicts between European powers and their former colonies in Africa, Asia, and elsewhere.

The Importance of Internal Conflict

Internal conflict is important for five main reasons: it is widespread; it causes tremendous suffering; it almost always affects and involves neighboring states, thereby undermining regional stability; it often engages the interests of distant powers and international organizations; and efforts to deal with the problems posed by internal conflict are in the process of being reassessed by policymakers at the national level and in regional and international organizations.

First, internal conflict is widespread. As of late 1995, major armed conflicts — that is, conflicts in which at least 1,000 people have been killed — raged in over thirty-five locations around the world. (See Table 1.) Although many of these conflicts involved cross-border activities of one kind or another, all were fundamentally intra-state in character. Internal conflict is the most pervasive form of armed conflict in the international system today.

Second, internal conflict is important because it usually causes tremendous suffering. In most internal conflicts, the stakes are high and fighting is vicious. Internal conflict often involves direct, deliberate attacks on civilians. Conflicts over control of territory frequently escalate into military campaigns designed to drive out or kill civilians from rival groups. Intimidation, assassination, rape, forced expulsion, and systematic slaughter are commonly employed instruments. The numbers of people displaced or killed in such conflicts are often counted in tens and hundreds of thousands, and sometimes even in millions. (See Table 1.) In the most extreme cases — in Bosnia since 1992 and in Rwanda in 1994, for example — genocide is carried out.[4]

Third, internal conflict is important because it often affects and involves neighboring states. Refugees, for example, often flee across international borders in large numbers: at the height of the genocidal slaughter in Rwanda in 1994, 250,000 Rwandans fled into Tanzania in a single day.[5] Over the course of just a few months, an estimated 2 million people fled from Rwanda to Tanzania, Zaire, and Burundi; none of these countries was in a position to provide adequately for a sudden influx of needy

---

4. According to Article 2 of the Genocide Convention of 1948, genocide is defined as "acts committed with intent to destroy, in whole or in part, a national, ethnical, racial, or religious group." Although the term "ethnic cleansing" is new, the practice is not; see Andrew Bell-Fialkoff, "A Brief History of Ethnic Cleansing," *Foreign Affairs*, Vol. 72, No. 3 (Summer 1993), pp. 110–121.

5. Julia Preston, "250,000 Rwandans Flee to Tanzania in One Day," *Boston Globe*, April 30, 1994, p. 1.

Table 1. Major Internal Conflicts (as of 1995).

Country[a]	Current Hostilities Began[b]	Warring Parties[c]	Number of People Displaced[d]	Number of People Killed[d]
Afghanistan	1978	Government of Afghanistan Government of USSR National Islamic Movement Hezb-I-Islami Hezb-I-Wahdat Taliban Militia	5,200,000	1,200,000
Algeria	1992	Government of Algeria Islamic Salvation Front Armed Islamic Group	40,000	30,000
Angola	1975	Government of Angola UNITA	2,000,000	300,000
	1992	Government of Angola UNITA	2,300,000	100,000–500,000
Azerbaijan	1990	Government of Azerbaijan Government of Armenia Republic of Nagorno-Karabakh	1,700,000	55,000
Bangladesh	1982	Government of Bangladesh Chittagong Hill Insurgents	50,000	3,000–3,500
Bosnia-Herzegovina	1992	Government of Bosnia-Herzegovina Government of Croatia Government of Serbia Bosnian Croatians, Bosnian Serbs	2,500,000	140,000–250,000
Burma	1948	Government of Burma Karen National Union Mong Tai Army	290,000	14,000–17,500
Burundi	1972	Government of Burundi Hutu and Tutsi Militia	300,000	100,000
	1993	Government of Burundi Hutu and Tutsi Militia	700,000	100,000
Cambodia	1975	Government of Cambodia Khmer Rouge	500,000	1,000,000
Colombia	1964	Government of Colombia Revolutionary Armed Forces of Colombia National Liberation Army Popular Liberation Army Grupo Jaime Bateman Cayon Paramilitary Groups Cocaine Cartels	600,000	30,000–70,000

Table 1. *continued*

Country[a]	Current Hostilities Began[b]	Warring Parties[c]	Number of People Displaced[d]	Number of People Killed[d]
Croatia	1991	Government of Croatia Government of Serbia Serb Secessionists	320,000	10,000– 25,000
Egypt	1992	Government of Egypt Gamaat Islamiya	1,500	1,000
Georgia	1991	Government of Georgia Republic of Abkhazia South Ossetians	475,000	17,500
Guatemala	1965	Government of Guatemala Guatemalan National Revolutionary Union	120,000– 170,000	46,000
India	1979	Government of India Assamese Insurgents	50,000	5,000
	1981	Government of India Sikh Insurgents	30,000	20,000
	1989	Government of India Kashmiri Insurgents	250,000	15,000
Indonesia	1975	Government of Indonesia East Timorese Insurgents		100,000– 200,000
	1984	Government of Indonesia Irian Jaya Insurgents		10,000– 30,000
Iran	1979	Government of Iran Mujahideen e-Khalq Kurdish Democratic Party of Iran	200,000	5,500
Iraq	1980	Government of Iraq Kurdish Democratic Party Popular Union of Kurdistan Shi'ite Rebels	1,300,000	600,000
Israel	1948	Government of Israel Palestinians Palestinian Liberation Organization Hamas, Hezbollah, Islamic Jihad	3,000,000	
Kenya	1992	Government of Kenya Kikuyu, Luhya, Luo Tribes	300,000	1,500

Table 1. *continued*

Country[a]	Current Hostilities Began[b]	Warring Parties[c]	Number of People Displaced[d]	Number of People Killed[d]
Liberia	1989	Government of Liberia ECOWAS Monitoring Group National Patriotic Forces of 　Liberia Various Splinter Factions	1,700,000	150,000
Moldova	1992	Government of Moldova Government of Russia Dniester Separatists Cossack Forces	105,000	1,000
Pakistan	1994	Government of Pakistan Mujahir National Movement		1,600
Peru	1980	Government of Peru Sendero Luminoso Tupac Amaru Revolutionary 　Movement	600,000	28,000
Philippines	1986	Government of the Philippines New People's Army Revolutionary Alliances of the 　Masses Moro National Liberation Front	900,000	30,000
Russia	1994	Government of Russia Chechen Rebels	400,000	20,000– 30,000
Rwanda	1990	Government of Rwanda Rwandan Patriotic Front Hutu Militia	2,000,000	800,000
Somalia	1990	United Somali Congress Various Warring Factions	1,000,000	400,000
Sierra Leone	1991	Government of Sierra Leone Revolutionary United Front	660,000	10,000
Sri Lanka	1983	Government of Sri Lanka Liberation Tigers of Tamil Eelam	1,200,000	36,000
Sudan	1983	Government of Sudan Sudanese People's Liberation 　Army (two factions)	4,500,000	1,200,000
Tajikistan	1992	Governments of Tajikistan, 　Russia, Uzbekistan Popular Democratic Army	320,000	70,000
Turkey	1984	Government of Turkey Kurdish Workers' Party	2,000,000	13,000

Table 1. *continued*

Country[a]	Current Hostilities Began[b]	Warring Parties[c]	Number of People Displaced[d]	Number of People Killed[d]
United Kingdom	1969	Government of the United Kingdom and Northern Ireland Irish Republican Army		3,200

SOURCES: Primary sources used to compile these figures are: Margareta Sollenberg and Peter Wallensteen, "Major Armed Conflicts, 1994," in Stockholm International Peace Research Institute [SIPRI], *SIPRI Yearbook 1995* (Oxford: Oxford University Press, 1995), pp. 21–35; U.S. Committee for Refugees, *1995 World Refugee Survey* (New York: Immigration and Refugee Services of America, 1995); Human Rights Watch, *Human Rights Watch World Report 1995* (New York: Human Rights Watch, December 1994); Gil Loescher, *Refugee Movements and International Security*, Adelphi Paper No. 268 (London: International Institute for Strategic Studies, 1992), pp. 70–71.

NOTES:
[a] Only countries with active, major conflicts are listed in this table; the ongoing conflicts in Cyprus and Lebanon, for example, which produced little sustained bloodshed in 1995, are not listed. A "major" conflict is one in which at least 1,000 people have been killed.
[b] These dates refer to the onset of armed hostilities as opposed to the origins of underlying political disputes, which are harder to pinpoint. When two dates are given, two rounds of hostilities are being noted.
[c] Only the main antagonists are listed. In some cases, many splinter groups are also active.
[d] Casualty and refugee estimates vary widely; the most authoritative estimates available in the public domain are listed here.

people.[6] At a minimum, refugees impose heavy economic burdens on host states, and they can pose political and security problems as well.[7]

Internal conflict can also affect neighboring states at a military level. The territory of neighboring states can be used to ship arms and supplies to insurgent groups, which can lead to interdiction campaigns. Outlying regions of neighboring states can also be used as bases from which terrorist assaults or more conventional attacks can be launched. This can lead to hot-pursuit operations across borders and reprisals. Military forces from neighboring states often become involved in internal conflicts. In the 1970s and 1980s, Israeli and Syrian forces fought both local militia and each other in Lebanon; Indian military forces intervened in Bangladesh and Sri Lanka; Vietnamese forces fought in Cambodia; and Soviet forces

6. For details on the genocide in Rwanda, see Human Rights Watch, *Human Rights Watch World Report 1995* (New York: Human Rights Watch, December 1994), pp. 39–48.

7. See Gil Loescher, *Refugee Movements and International Security*, Adelphi Paper No. 268 (London: International Institute for Strategic Studies [IISS], 1992).

invaded Afghanistan. Since the end of the Cold War, Armenian troops have fought in Nagorno-Karabakh and elsewhere in Azerbaijan; Serbian and Croatian troops have fought in Bosnia; and Russian troops have been involved in conflicts in Georgia, Moldova, and Tajikistan. Many analysts and policymakers worry that turmoil in Macedonia could lead to Serbian, Albanian, Greek, and Bulgarian military intervention — and a regional Balkan war.

Neighboring states are not always the innocent victims of turmoil in their regions. In some cases, neighboring states are responsible for sparking internal conflict. In many cases, they meddle in conflicts that are already under way, making bad situations worse. In most cases, internal conflict has important implications for regional stability.

Fourth, internal conflict is important because it can affect the interests and engage the attention of distant powers and international organizations. In some cases, the national interests of distant powers can be directly threatened by internal conflict. For starters, internal conflict can endanger foreign nationals who happen to be in the wrong place at the wrong time; U.S. Marines had to rescue U.S. citizens trapped in Liberia during its civil war, for example. Internal conflict can also threaten political and ideological allies, and under some circumstances it can activate alliance commitments; Turkey's assault on Kurdish bases in northern Iraq in 1995 was sensitive for these reasons. In addition, internal conflict can disrupt or threaten to disrupt access to strategic resources such as oil, and it can threaten to disrupt political stability in strategically important areas. These are two reasons why the stability of Saudi Arabia, for example, is considered by many states to be important.

When internal conflicts become regional conflicts due to the involvement of neighboring states, as discussed above, the likelihood that the interests of distant powers will be engaged increases. Internal conflicts can have particularly ominous implications if command and control of weapons of mass destruction are in jeopardy or are about to change hands, perhaps to an unsavory regime. More generally, internal conflicts can undercut the international credibility and standing of distant powers if the latter fail to take timely and effective action to deal with conflicts that jeopardize their interests.

Internal conflict can also threaten the interests of distant states indirectly, by undermining regional and international organizations, international law, international norms of behavior, and international order in general. Failures to stop internal conflict can do great damage to regional and international organizations, such as the Organization of African Unity (OAU), the Organization for Security and Cooperation in Europe (OSCE, formerly CSCE, the Conference on Security and Cooperation in Europe), and the United Nations (UN), whose stated purpose is the promotion of peace and security. Casual defiance of international law and international norms of behavior will undercut principles that the international community would like to maintain and perhaps even extend. For example, the international community has tried to distinguish between combatants and non-combatants in formulating rules and laws about the conduct of war. It will find its distinctions and norms hard to sustain in the long run if it allows them to be trampled in ethnic conflicts in which civilians are attacked deliberately and systematically. The breakup of a state, even a small one, also has implications for international law and order. In short, conflicts in remote, isolated places can have important implications for international order and the interests of distant powers.[8]

Finally, internal conflict is important because the international community is currently reassessing its efforts to deal with it. In the early 1990s, following the end of the Cold War and in the immediate aftermath of the Gulf War, many people were decidedly optimistic about the international community's ability to address both intra-state and inter-state conflicts and to create a stable, peaceful international order. In 1991, U.S. President George Bush spoke of creating a "new world order" that would be characterized by peaceful settlement of disputes, solidarity against aggression, reduced and controlled military arsenals, and just treatment of all people.[9] In January 1992, for the first time in history, a meeting of the UN Security Council took place at the level of heads of state and government. The Security Council invited the UN Secretary-General, Boutros Boutros-Ghali, to prepare recommendations for strengthening the UN collective security system. His June 1992 report, *An Agenda for Peace*, began with the declaration that, with the end of the Cold War, "an opportunity has been regained to achieve the great objectives of the [UN] Charter — a United Nations capable of maintaining international peace and security."[10]

Since the end of the Cold War, actions approved by the UN Security Council have increased in number and widened in scope. Only five peacekeeping operations were under way in early 1988, but twenty-one have been undertaken since then. Thirteen of these twenty-one and nine

---

8. For a discussion of the interests great powers have with respect to their "milieu," see Arnold Wolfers, *Discord and Collaboration* (Baltimore, Md.: Johns Hopkins University Press, 1962).

9. See Nancy Dunne, "Bush Spells Out Vision of 'New World Order'," *Financial Times*, April 15, 1991, p. 4.

10. Boutros Boutros-Ghali, *An Agenda for Peace: Preventive Diplomacy, Peacemaking, and Peacekeeping* (New York: United Nations, June 1992), p. 1.

of the most recent eleven operations were directed at internal conflicts. The number of personnel assigned to UN peacekeeping operations has increased by a factor of ten since 1988: from around 7,500 to 75,000. Many of these new operations are multifunctional undertakings, involving not just the supervision of cease-fires, but also the demobilization of military forces, the return of refugees, the provision of humanitarian assistance, the establishment of new police forces, the design and supervision of political and institutional reforms, the organization and supervision of elections, and the coordination of support for economic reconstruction and development.[11] In some cases, UN military operations went beyond traditional peacekeeping, which required the consent of the warring parties, and involved coercive action. Many people believed and still more hoped that the United Nations was developing into an effective instrument for worldwide conflict prevention, conflict management, and conflict resolution.

Great expectations were not limited to the United Nations. Many believed that regional organizations — such as the European Union (EU), the North Atlantic Treaty Organization (NATO), the OSCE, and the OAU — would deal effectively with many types of regional security problems. NATO's leaders stated in November 1991, for example, that one of the alliance's fundamental tasks, given the end of the Cold War, was "to provide one of the indispensable foundations for a stable security environment in Europe . . . in which *no* country would be able to intimidate or coerce *any* European nation."[12] Many hoped that the United States, as the only remaining superpower, would build on the active, effective role it played in standing up to Iraqi aggression against Kuwait, and lead the world into a new, more peaceful era.

Those who had high hopes in the early 1990s for the international community's conflict prevention, conflict management, and conflict resolution capabilities have been chagrined by the international community's inability to prevent, stop, or resolve most of the violent internal conflicts that raged in the early to mid-1990s: in Afghanistan, Angola, Azerbaijan, Bosnia, Burma, Georgia, Liberia, Rwanda, Somalia, Sri Lanka, Sudan, and Tajikistan. Some of these conflicts — in the former Soviet Union and in Burma and Rwanda, for example, were never addressed in a serious way

---

11. Boutros Boutros-Ghali, *Supplement to "An Agenda for Peace": Position Paper of the Secretary-General on the Occasion of the Fiftieth Anniversary of the United Nations,* January 3, 1995, pp. 3–7.

12. "The Alliance's New Strategic Concept," Agreed by the Heads of State and Government Participating in the Meeting of the North Atlantic Council in Rome, November 7–8, 1991; emphasis added.

by the international community as a whole. This failure was particularly striking in Rwanda, where about 800,000 Tutsi were killed in a four-month period between April and July 1994; distant powers did next to nothing while one of the worst genocides the world had seen in five decades was carried out. Multilateral actions were taken in Bosnia and Somalia, but they failed to bring the armed conflicts in these countries to a speedy end. More than three years of slaughter in Bosnia made a mockery of international efforts through the EU, NATO, and the United Nations to bring fighting to an end. The UN force in Somalia was withdrawn in March 1995; the struggle for power among warlords continued. The credibility of the world's major powers, the multilateral organizations through which they often operate, and the international community in general has suffered.

As a result, the euphoria of the early 1990s has given way to frustration and, for some, disillusionment in the mid-1990s. Hopes for vigorous international efforts to deal with internal conflicts in many parts of the globe have given way to a more limited view of what individual states, multilateral organizations, and the international community can and should do. Many in the U.S. Congress, for example, would like to cut U.S. financial support for UN peacekeeping operations. In 1995, UN member states as a group were over $2 billion behind in their contributions to the UN peacekeeping account, a significant sum given that the annual cost of UN peacekeeping operations is around $3.5 billion.[13] Military personnel for all UN operations must come from member states, since the United Nations does not have standing, independent military forces, and "donor fatigue" is a growing problem. Boutros-Ghali acknowledged in January 1995 that "we are still in a time of transition . . . unforeseen or only partly foreseen difficulties have arisen . . . the different world that emerged when the Cold War ceased is still a world not fully understood."[14]

How far the pendulum will swing is unclear. It is certainly true that distant powers and, through them, international organizations have failed to prevent or resolve internal conflicts in many parts of the world. But there have been notable successes — in El Salvador, Nicaragua, Mozambique, Cambodia, and Haiti, for example. The challenge for scholars, analysts, and policymakers is to identify the circumstances under which effective action can be taken and the kinds of actions most appropriate to different kinds of situations. This will require a sophisticated understanding of the causes and dynamics of internal conflicts, and of the track

---

13. See Chantal de Jonge Oudraat's chapter on the United Nations in this volume.

14. Boutros-Ghali, *Supplement to "An Agenda for Peace,"* pp. 2, 3, 24.

record of international efforts to prevent, manage, and resolve internal conflicts.

The Causes of Internal Conflicts

Many policymakers and journalists believe that the causes of internal conflicts are simple and straightforward. The driving forces behind these violent conflicts, it is said, are the "ancient hatreds" that many ethnic and religious groups have for each other. In Eastern Europe, the former Soviet Union, and elsewhere, these deep-seated animosities were held in check for years by authoritarian rule. The collapse of authoritarian rule, it is argued, has taken the "lid" off of these ancient rivalries, allowing long-suppressed grievances to come to the surface and to escalate into armed conflict.

George Bush maintained that the war in Bosnia between Serbs, Croats, and Muslims grew out of "age-old animosities."[15] His successor, Bill Clinton, argued that the end of the Cold War "lifted the lid from a cauldron of long-simmering hatreds. Now, the entire global terrain is bloody with such conflicts."[16] Writing about the Balkans, U.S. political commentator Richard Cohen declared:

Bosnia is a formidable, scary place of high mountains, brutish people, and tribal grievances rooted in history and myth born of boozy nights by the fire. It's the place where World War I began and where the wars of Europe persist, an ember of hate still glowing for reasons that defy reason itself. At the Pentagon, my view was confirmed. Mention Bosnia, and men with stars shuddered.[17]

Serious scholars reject this explanation of internal conflict.[18] This simple but widely held view cannot explain why violent conflicts have broken out in some places, but not in others, and it cannot explain why some disputes are more violent and harder to resolve than others. It is

---

15. Bush is quoted in Jack Snyder, "Nationalism and the Crisis of the Post-Soviet State," in Michael E. Brown, ed., *Ethnic Conflict and International Security* (Princeton, N.J.: Princeton University Press, 1993), p. 79.

16. Clinton is quoted in Ann Devroy, "President Cautions Congress on 'Simplistic Ideas' in Foreign Policy," *Washington Post*, May 26, 1994, p. A31.

17. Richard Cohen, "Send in the Troops," *Washington Post*, November 28, 1995, p. 17.

18. See, for example, Snyder, "Nationalism and the Crisis of the Post-Soviet State"; Barry Posen, "The Security Dilemma and Ethnic Conflict," in Brown, *Ethnic Conflict and International Security*, pp. 103–124; Susanne Hoeber Rudolph and Lloyd I. Rudolph, "Modern Hate," *New Republic*, March 22, 1993, pp. 24–29.

undeniably true that Serbs, Croats, and Bosnian Muslims have many historical grievances against each other and that these grievances have played a role in the Balkan conflicts that have raged since 1991. But it is also true that other groups, such as Czechs and Slovaks, Ukrainians and Russians, French-speaking and English-speaking Canadians, and the Flemish and the Walloons have historical grievances of various kinds that have not led to violent conflict in the 1990s. This single-factor explanation, in short, cannot account for significant variation in the incidence and intensity of internal conflict.

The scholarly literature on this subject is massive because the subject itself is so broad. If we define "internal conflict" to include violent civilian power struggles, military coups, ethnic conflicts, militarized ideological campaigns, insurgencies, civil wars, and revolutions, then the literatures on all of these topics are relevant to our concerns. In addition, the problem of "internal conflict" is related to the development of civil society, political order, and state-society relations, problems that have attracted the attention of great thinkers "throughout the history of social and political thought."[19]

Trying to summarize the collected wisdom of the ages in a few paragraphs is perhaps a fool's errand. At a minimum, one should approach the task with considerable trepidation and humility. With these caveats on the record, I would suggest that the scholarly literature on internal conflict has identified four main clusters of factors that make some places more predisposed to violence than others: structural factors; political factors; economic/social factors; and cultural/perceptual factors. (See Table 2.)

STRUCTURAL FACTORS

Three main structural factors have drawn scholarly attention: weak states; intra-state security concerns; and ethnic geography.

Weak state structures are the starting point for many analyses of internal conflict.[20] Some states are born weak. Many of the states that were carved out of colonial empires in Africa and Southeast Asia, for example, were artificial constructs. They lacked political legitimacy, politically sensible borders, and political institutions capable of exercising meaningful control over the territory placed under their nominal supervision. The

---

19. Rule, *Theories of Civil Violence*, p. 9.

20. See I. William Zartman, "Introduction: Posing the Problem of State Collapse," in I. William Zartman, ed., *Collapsed States: The Disintegration and Restoration of Legitimate Authority* (Boulder, Colo.: Lynne Rienner, 1995), pp. 1–11; Gerald B. Helman and Steven R. Ratner, "Saving Failed States," *Foreign Policy*, No. 89 (Winter 1992–93), pp. 3–20.

Table 2. Underlying Causes of Internal Conflict.

Structural Factors	Economic/Social Factors
Weak states	Economic problems
Intra-state security concerns	Discriminatory economic systems
Ethnic geography	Modernization
Political Factors	Cultural/Perceptual Factors
Discriminatory political institutions	Patterns of cultural discrimination
Exclusionary national ideologies	Problematic group histories
Inter-group politics	
Elite politics	

---

same can be said of many of the states created out of the rubble of the Soviet Union and Yugoslavia. The vast majority of these new entities came into existence with only the most rudimentary political institutions in place.

In many parts of the world, Africa perhaps most notably, states have become weaker over time. In some cases, external developments, such as reductions in foreign aid from major powers and international financial institutions and drops in commodity prices, played key roles in bringing about institutional decline. In other areas, states have been weakened by internal problems such as endemic corruption, administrative incompetence, and an inability to promote economic development. Numerous countries have suffered from several of these problems.

When state structures weaken, violent conflict often follows. Power struggles between politicians and would-be leaders intensify. Regional leaders become increasingly independent and, if they consolidate control over military assets, virtual warlords. Ethnic groups which had been oppressed by central authorities are more able to assert themselves politically, perhaps by seeking more administrative autonomy or their own states. Ethnic groups which had been protected by central authorities or which had exercised power through the state find themselves more vulnerable. Criminal organizations become more powerful and pervasive, as we have seen in the Caucasus, Afghanistan, and elsewhere. Borders are controlled less effectively. Cross-border movements of militia, arms, drugs, smuggled goods, refugees, and migrants therefore increase. Massive humanitarian problems, such as famines and epidemics, can develop. Widespread human rights violations often take place. The state in question might ultimately fragment or simply cease to exist as a political entity.

Second, when states are weak, individual groups within these states feel compelled to provide for their own defense; they have to worry about whether other groups pose security threats.[21] If the state in question is very weak or if it is expected to become weaker with time, the incentives for groups to make independent military preparations grow. The problem is that, in taking steps to defend themselves, groups often threaten the security of others. This can lead neighboring groups to take steps that will diminish the security of the first group: this is the security dilemma. These problems are especially acute when empires or multiethnic states collapse and ethnic groups suddenly have to provide for their own security. One group's rush to deploy defensive forces will appear threatening to other groups. Moreover, the kinds of forces most commonly deployed — militia and infantry equipped with light arms — have inherent offensive capabilities even if they are mobilized for defensive purposes; this inevitably intensifies the security concerns of neighboring groups.

The third structural factor that has received attention is ethnic geography.[22] More specifically, states with ethnic minorities are more prone to conflict than others, and certain kinds of ethnic demographics are more problematic than others. Some states are ethnically homogeneous, and therefore face few problems of this type. However, of the more than 180 states in existence today, fewer than 20 are ethnically homogeneous, in the sense that ethnic minorities account for less than five percent of the population.[23] Some of these states, such as Japan and Sweden, have had a uniform ethnic composition for some time. Others — Poland, Hungary, the Czech Republic — have few minorities in the 1990s because of the population transfers and genocide that took place during World War II, and the way borders were drawn after the war. One of the reasons why Poland, Hungary, and the Czech Republic are relatively stable in the mid-1990s is their lack of contentious minorities.[24] It is important to note, however, that ethnic homogeneity is no guarantee of internal harmony: Somalia is the most ethnically homogeneous state in sub-Saharan Africa, yet it has been torn apart by clan warfare and a competition for power among local warlords.

---

21. See Posen, "The Security Dilemma and Ethnic Conflict." See also Milton J. Esman, *Ethnic Politics* (Ithaca, N.Y.: Cornell University Press, 1994), pp. 244–245.

22. See Stephen Van Evera, "Hypotheses on Nationalism and War," *International Security*, Vol. 18, No. 4 (Spring 1994), pp. 5–39; Posen, "The Security Dilemma and Ethnic Conflict." See also Stephen Stedman's chapter on sub-Saharan Africa in this volume.

23. See David Welsh, "Domestic Politics and Ethnic Conflict," in Brown, *Ethnic Conflict and International Security*, p. 45.

24. See Milada Vachudová's chapter on East-Central Europe in this volume.

In some states with ethnic minorities, ethnic groups are intermingled; in other states, minorities tend to live in separate provinces or regions of the country. Countries with different kinds of ethnic geography are likely to experience different kinds of internal problems.[25] Countries with highly intermingled populations are less likely to face secessionist demands because ethnic groups are not distributed in ways that lend themselves to partition. However, if secessionist demands develop in countries with intermingled populations, ethnic groups will seek to establish control over specific tracts of territory. Direct attacks on civilians, intense guerilla warfare, ethnic cleansing, and genocide may result. Countries with groups distributed along regional lines are more likely to face secessionist demands, but if warfare develops, it will generally be more conventional in character.

Most states, particularly those carved out of former empires, have complex ethnic demographics and face serious ethnic problems of one kind or another. In Africa, for example, arbitrary borders have divided some ethnic groups and situated them in two or more countries. Most African countries contain large numbers of ethnic groups, some of which are historic enemies.[26] Many of the states of the former Soviet Union inherited borders that were deliberately designed to maximize ethnic complications and to cripple the political effectiveness of local leaders with respect to what used to be the center.[27]

POLITICAL FACTORS

Four main political factors have attracted attention in the scholarly literature on internal conflict: discriminatory political institutions; exclusionary national ideologies; inter-group politics; and elite politics.

First, many argue that the prospects for conflict in a country depend to a significant degree on the type and fairness of its political system. Closed, authoritarian systems are likely to generate considerable resentment over time, especially if the interests of some ethnic groups are served while others are trampled. Even in more democratic settings, resentment can build if some groups are inadequately represented in the government, the courts, the military, the police, political parties, and other state and political institutions. The legitimacy of the system as a whole can, over time, be called into question. Internal conflict is especially likely if oppression and violence are commonly employed by the state or if a

---

25. See Alicia Levine's chapter on secessionist violence in this volume.

26. See Stephen Stedman's chapter on sub-Saharan Africa in this volume.

27. See Matthew Evangelista's chapter on the former Soviet Union in this volume.

political transition is under way. The latter can take many forms, including democratization, which can be destabilizing in the short run even if it promises stability in the long run.[28]

Second, it is said that much depends on the nature of the prevailing national ideology in the country in question. In some places, nationalism and citizenship are based on ethnic distinctions, rather than on the idea that everyone who lives in a country is entitled to the same rights and privileges. Although the existence of civic conceptions of nationalism is no guarantee of stability — civic nationalism prevails in Indonesia — conflict is more likely when ethnic conceptions of nationalism predominate. Under what conditions are these two conceptions of nationalism likely to emerge? According to Jack Snyder:

Civic nationalism normally appears in well-institutionalized democracies. Ethnic nationalism, in contrast, appears spontaneously when an institutional vacuum occurs. By its nature, nationalism based on equal and universal citizenship rights within a territory depends on a supporting framework of laws to guarantee those rights, as well as effective institutions to allow citizens to give voice to their views. Ethnic nationalism, in contrast, depends not on institutions, but on culture. Therefore, ethnic nationalism is the default option: it predominates when institutions collapse, when existing institutions are not fulfilling people's basic needs, and when satisfactory alternative structures are not readily available.[29]

It is not surprising, therefore, that there are strong currents of ethnic nationalism in parts of the Balkans, East-Central Europe, and the former Soviet Union, where state structures and political institutions have diminished capacities, and in those parts of the developing world where state structures and political institutions are weak.

It is important to keep in mind that exclusionary national ideologies do not have be based on ethnicity. Religious fundamentalists committed to establishing theocratic states divide societies into two groups: those who subscribe to a theologically derived political, economic, and social order; and those who do not.

Third, many scholars argue that the prospects for violence in a

28. See, for example, Ted Robert Gurr and Barbara Harff, *Ethnic Conflict and World Politics* (Boulder, Colo.: Westview, 1994), chap. 5; Arend Lijphart, *Democracy in Plural Societies* (New Haven, Conn.: Yale University Press, 1977); Edward D. Mansfield and Jack Snyder, "Democratization and the Danger of War," *International Security*, Vol. 20, No. 1 (Summer 1995), pp. 5–38.

29. Snyder, "Nationalism and the Crisis of the Post-Soviet State," p. 86. See also William Pfaff, "Revive Secular Citizenship Above 'Ethnic' Nationality," *International Herald Tribune*, July 20, 1993, p. 5.

country depend to a significant degree on the dynamics of domestic, inter-group politics.[30] The prospects for violence are great, it is said, if groups — whether they are based on political, ideological, religious, or ethnic affinities — have ambitious objectives, strong senses of identity, and confrontational strategies. Conflict is especially likely if objectives are incompatible, groups are strong and determined, action is feasible, success is possible, and if inter-group comparisons lead to competition, anxiety, and fears of being dominated. The emergence of new groups and changes in the inter-group balance of power can be particularly destabilizing.

Fourth, some scholars have emphasized elite politics and, more specifically, the tactics employed by desperate and opportunistic politicians in times of political and economic turmoil. According to this line of thinking, ethnic conflict is often provoked by elites in times of political and economic trouble in order to fend off domestic challengers. Ethnic bashing and scapegoating are tools of the trade, and the mass media are employed in partisan and propagandistic ways that further aggravate interethnic tensions. The actions of Slobodan Milosevic in Serbia and Franjo Tudjman in Croatia stand out as cases in point.[31]

ECONOMIC/SOCIAL FACTORS

Three broad economic and social factors have been identified as potential sources of internal conflict: economic problems; discriminatory economic systems; and the trials and tribulations of economic development and modernization.

First, most countries experience economic problems of one kind or another sooner or later, and these problems can contribute to intra-state

---

30. See Joseph Rothschild, *Ethnopolitics: A Conceptual Framework* (New York: Columbia University Press, 1981); Donald L. Horowitz, *Ethnic Groups in Conflict* (Berkeley: University of California Press, 1985); Charles Tilly, *From Mobilization to Revolution* (Reading, Mass.: Addison-Wesley, 1978); Charles Tilly, "Does Modernization Breed Revolution?" *Comparative Politics*, Vol. 5, No. 3 (April 1973), pp. 425–447; Lewis Coser, *The Functions of Social Conflict* (Glencoe, Ill.: Free Press, 1956); Gurr and Harff, *Ethnic Conflict and World Politics;* Van Evera, "Hypotheses on Nationalism and War." For an overview, see Saul Newman, "Does Modernization Breed Ethnic Conflict?" *World Politics*, Vol. 43, No. 3 (April 1991), pp. 451–478; Jack A. Goldstone, "Theories of Revolution: The Third Generation," *World Politics*, Vol. 32, No. 3 (April 1980), pp. 425–453.

31. See V.P. Gagnon, Jr., "Ethnic Nationalism and International Conflict: The Case of Serbia," *International Security*, Vol. 19, No. 3 (Winter 1994/95), pp. 130–166; Human Rights Watch, *Playing the "Communal Card": Communal Violence and Human Rights* (New York: Human Rights Watch, 1995); Warren Zimmermann, "The Last Ambassador: A Memoir of the Collapse of Yugoslavia," *Foreign Affairs*, Vol. 74, No. 2 (March–April 1995), pp. 2–20.

tensions. In the industrialized world, problems can emerge even if a country's economy is growing, if it is not growing as fast as it once was or fast enough to keep pace with societal demands. In Eastern Europe, the former Soviet Union, parts of Africa, and elsewhere, transitions from centrally planned to market-based economic systems have created a host of economic problems, ranging from historically high levels of unemployment to rampant inflation. Many countries in what we would like to think of as the developing world seem to be in a semi-permanent state of economic shambles. Others are in an economic free-fall. Unemployment, inflation, and resource competitions, especially for land, contribute to societal frustrations and tensions, and can provide the breeding ground for conflict. Economic reforms do not always help and can contribute to the problem in the short term, especially if economic shocks are severe and state subsidies for food and other basic goods, services, and social welfare are cut. In short, economic slowdowns, stagnation, deterioration, and collapse can be deeply destabilizing.[32]

Second, discriminatory economic systems, whether they discriminate on the basis of class or ethnicity, can generate feelings of resentment and levels of frustration prone to the generation of violence.[33] Unequal economic opportunities, unequal access to resources such as land and capital, and vast differences in standards of living are all signs of economic systems that disadvantaged members of society will see as unfair and perhaps illegitimate. This has certainly been the case in Sri Lanka, for example, where Tamils have been discriminated against in recent decades by the Sinhalese majority. Economic development is not necessarily the solution. Indeed, it can aggravate the situation: economic growth always benefits some individuals, groups, and regions more than others, and those who are on top to begin with are likely to be in a better position to take advantage of new economic opportunities than the downtrodden.

---

32. For a general discussion and several case studies, see S.W.R. de A. Samarasinghe and Reed Coughlan, eds., *Economic Dimensions of Ethnic Conflict* (London: Pinter, 1991). For a detailed discussion of the economic roots of the wars in the former Yugoslavia, see Susan L. Woodward, *Balkan Tragedy: Chaos and Dissolution After the Cold War* (Washington, D.C.: Brookings Institution, 1995), especially chap. 3. For a discussion of the economic sources of turmoil in South Asia, see Gordon, "Resources and Instability in South Asia."

33. For an overview of Marxist thinking on this question, see Rule, *Theories of Civil Violence*, chap. 2; A.S. Cohan, *Theories of Revolution* (New York: Wiley, 1975), chaps. 4–5. For a discussion of how this applies to the developing world in particular, see Sandy Gordon, "Resources and Instability in South Asia," *Survival*, Vol. 35, No. 2 (Summer 1993), pp. 66–87.

Even if a country's overall economic picture is improving, growing inequities and gaps can aggravate intra-state tensions.

Third, many scholars have pointed to economic development and modernization as taproots of instability and internal conflict.[34] The process of economic development, the advent of industrialization, and the introduction of new technologies, it is said, bring about a wide variety of profound social changes: migration and urbanization disrupt existing family and social systems and undermine traditional political institutions; better education, higher literacy rates, and improved access to growing mass media raise awareness of where different people stand in society. At a minimum, this places strains on existing social and political systems.[35] It also raises economic and political expectations, and can lead to mounting frustration when these expectations are not met. This can be particularly problematic in the political realm, because demands for political participation usually outpace the ability of the system to respond. According to Samuel Huntington, "The result is instability and disorder. The primary problem . . . is the lag in the development of political institutions behind social and economic change."[36]

CULTURAL/PERCEPTUAL FACTORS

Two cultural and perceptual factors have been identified in the scholarly literature as sources of internal conflict. The first is cultural discrimination against minorities. Problems include inequitable educational opportunities, legal and political constraints on the use and teaching of minority languages, and constraints on religious freedom. In extreme cases, draconian efforts to assimilate minority populations combined with programs to bring large numbers of other ethnic groups into minority areas

---

34. See Samuel P. Huntington, *Political Order in Changing Societies* (New Haven, Conn.: Yale University Press, 1968); Samuel P. Huntington, "Civil Violence and the Process of Development," in *Civil Violence and the International System*, Adelphi Paper No. 83 (London: IISS, 1971), pp. 1–15; Ted Robert Gurr, *Why Men Rebel* (Princeton, N.J.: Princeton University Press, 1970); Walker Conner, "Nation-Building or Nation-Destroying?" *World Politics*, Vol. 24, No. 3 (April 1972), pp. 319–355; Walker Conner, *Ethnonationalism: The Quest for Understanding* (Princeton, N.J.: Princeton University Press, 1994). For an overview of this literature, see Newman, "Does Modernization Breed Ethnic Conflict?" For critiques of this approach, see Rod Aya, "Theories of Revolution Reconsidered: Contrasting Models of Collective Violence," *Theory and Society*, Vol. 8, No. 1 (July 1979), pp. 1–38; Tilly, "Does Modernization Breed Revolution?"

35. See Chalmers Johnson, *Revolutionary Change* (Boston: Little, Brown, 1966); Mark Hagopian, *The Phenomenon of Revolution* (New York: Dodd, Mead, 1974). For an overview, see Cohan, *Theories of Revolution*, chap. 6; Goldstone, "Theories of Revolution," pp. 425–434.

36. Huntington, *Political Order in Changing Societies*, p. 5.

constitute a form of cultural genocide. Aggressive forms of these policies were implemented by Josef Stalin in the Soviet Union in the 1930s and 1940s, particularly in the Caucasus. Similar policies have been pursued by China in Tibet since the 1950s. Somewhat less vicious forms of assimilationist policies have been pursued in Bulgaria with respect to ethnic Turks, in Slovakia with respect to ethnic Hungarians, and in Thailand with respect to members of northern and western hill tribes, for example.[37]

The second factor that falls under this broad heading has to do with group histories and group perceptions of themselves and others.[38] It is certainly true that many groups have legitimate grievances against others for crimes of one kind or another committed at some point in the distant or recent past. Some "ancient hatreds" have legitimate historical bases. However, it is also true that groups tend to whitewash and glorify their own histories, and they often demonize their neighbors, rivals, and adversaries. Explaining away the Hutu slaughter of 800,000 Tutsi in Rwanda in 1994, one Hutu who had been training for the priesthood insisted, "It wasn't genocide. It was self-defense."[39] Stories that are passed down from generation to generation by word of mouth become part of a group's lore. They often become distorted and exaggerated with time, and are treated as received wisdom by group members.

These ethnic mythologies are particularly problematic if rival groups have mirror images of each other, which is often the case. Serbs, for example, see themselves as heroic defenders of Europe and Croats as fascist, genocidal thugs. Croats see themselves as valiant victims of Serbian hegemonic aggression. When two groups in close proximity have mutually exclusive, incendiary perceptions of each other, the slightest provocation on either side confirms deeply held beliefs and provides the

37. Many argue that formal minority rights safeguards are the solution. See, for example, Jonathan Eyal, "Eastern Europe: What About the Minorities?" *World Today,* Vol. 45, No. 12 (December 1989), pp. 205–208; Wiktor Osiatynski, "Needed Now: Bills of Rights," *Time,* December 24, 1990, p. 41. L. Michael Hager, "To Get More Peace, Try More Justice," *International Herald Tribune,* July 30, 1992, p. 6. Stephen S. Rosenfeld, "Serbs Are the Problem, Minority Rights the Solution," *International Herald Tribune,* September 26–27, 1992, p. 4.

38. See Van Evera, "Hypotheses on Nationalism and War," pp. 8–9; Posen, "The Security Dilemma and Ethnic Conflict," p. 107; Snyder, "Nationalism and the Crisis of the Post-Soviet State," pp. 92–93; Donald Rothchild and Alexander J. Groth, "Pathological Dimensions of Domestic and International Ethnicity," *Political Science Quarterly,* Vol. 110, No. 1 (Spring 1995), pp. 69–82.

39. This Hutu apologist is quoted in "You're Saying We Did It?" *Economist,* June 3, 1995, p. 38.

justification for a retaliatory response. Under conditions such as these, conflict is hard to avoid and even harder to limit once started.

EXPLAINING THE CAUSES OF INTERNAL CONFLICT

The existing literature on internal conflict has three great strengths and three corresponding weaknesses. First, it does a commendable job of surveying the underlying factors, or permissive conditions, that make some situations particularly prone to violence, but it is weak when it comes to identifying the catalytic factors — the triggers or proximate causes — of internal conflict. As James Rule put it in his review of the literature on civil violence, "We know a lot of things that are true about civil violence, but we do not know when they are going to be true."[40] Jack Goldstone came to a similar conclusion in his assessment of the literature on revolutions, noting that it is "incapable of denoting exactly when a potentially revolutionary situation has arisen."[41] The result is that we know a lot less about the causes of internal conflict than one would guess from looking at the size of the literature on the subject.

Second, the literature is strong in its examination of structural, political, economic, social, and cultural forces that operate at a mass level, and indeed, it places great emphasis on mass-level factors, but it is weak in its understanding of the roles played by elites and leaders in instigating violence. The latter problem has received comparatively little attention. The result is "no-fault" history that leaves out the pernicious effects of influential individuals — an important set of factors in the overall equation.

Third, the literature is strong when it comes to examining the forces at work within countries, but weak in its analysis of the roles played by external forces in triggering internal conflict. A great deal of emphasis has been placed on "contagion" and "diffusion" effects, but their causal mechanisms are shrouded in mystery.[42] Little attention has been paid to the actions and activities of neighboring states in instigating violent conflict.

40. Rule, *Theories of Civil Violence*, p. 265.

41. Goldstone, "Theories of Revolution," p. 433.

42. See, for example, John A. Vasquez, "Factors Related to the Contagion and Diffusion of International Violence," in Manus I. Midlarsky, ed., *The Internationalization of Communal Strife*, (London: Routledge, 1992), pp. 149–172; Ted Robert Gurr, *Minorities at Risk: A Global View of Ethnopolitical Conflicts* (Washington, D.C.: U.S. Institute of Peace, 1993), pp. 132–135. For an excellent overview of this literature, see Stuart Hill and Donald Rothchild, "The Contagion of Political Conflict in Africa and the World," *Journal of Conflict Resolution*, Vol. 30, No. 4 (December 1986), pp. 716–735.

In my contributions to this book, I will attempt to advance thinking in each of these three areas. First, drawing on the chapters that examine internal conflicts in various parts of the world, I will try to integrate our collective assessments of permissive conditions and proximate causes into a more comprehensive framework for understanding the causes of internal conflict.

Second, I will try to integrate discussions of elite-level and mass-level factors into what I hope will be a more comprehensive explanation of how internal conflicts begin. To paraphrase Donald Horowitz, we need a theory that links elite-level and mass-level factors and answers two questions: how do the leaders lead? And why do the followers follow?[43]

Third, I will try to develop a more nuanced understanding of how external developments and the actions of neighboring states can trigger internal conflict. Here, too, I will endeavor to integrate our discussions of external and internal factors into a more robust framework for analyzing the origins of internal conflict.

My main argument with respect to the causes of internal conflict is that most major conflicts are triggered by internal, elite-level activities — to put it simply, bad leaders — contrary to what one would gather from reviewing the scholarly literature on the subject. Elite decisions and actions are usually the catalysts that turn potentially volatile situations into violent confrontations. External forces are occasionally the proximate causes of internal conflicts, but the discrete actions of some neighboring states — bad neighbors — are more important than mysterious, mass-level "contagion" or "diffusion" effects. This is also contrary to what one would gather from a review of the scholarly literature on the subject.

Having a clear understanding of the proximate causes of internal conflict is extremely important, because a critical threshold is crossed when blood is shed and political disputes become deadly clashes. Conflict management and conflict resolution become much more difficult once this happens.

The Regional Dimensions of Internal Conflict

Internal conflict frequently involves neighboring states in one way or another. Many policymakers and journalists, however, have simplistic and mechanistic views of how this can come about: they frequently rely on crude analogies to diseases, fires, floods, and other forces of nature.

For example, in explaining why the United States needed to send

---

43. Horowitz, *Ethnic Groups in Conflict*, p. 140.

troops to Bosnia as part of the NATO peacekeeping mission there, Clinton explained that, if the United States failed to act, "the conflict that already has claimed so many people could spread like poison throughout the entire region."[44] His Secretary of State, Warren Christopher, argued that "if this best hope for peace fails, the war will re-ignite and spread."[45] Earlier in the war, Christopher explained why it was important for the United States to become "actively engaged" in Bosnia: if the West failed to stop the fighting there, he argued, "you may well have the entire Balkans involved . . . it could draw in Greece and Turkey . . . the United States has a stake in preventing the world from going up in flames."[46] Many think of conflicts "spilling over" from one place to another in hydraulic fashion. Writing about Bosnia, for example, the journalist Misha Glenny worries about "the spillover of this struggle into the Aegean Sea."[47] Scholars can get caught up in this kind of thinking as well. Ralph Premdas frets about "ethnically-ignited strifes becoming contagious and uncontrollable . . . threatening world stability and mankind's future."[48] There is, as noted above, a sizable scholarly literature that frames this problem as a "contagion" problem.[49]

This way of thinking about the regional dimensions of internal conflict is both simplistic and mechanistic. It is simplistic because it sees things moving in one direction only — from the place where the conflict began to neighboring states, which are characterized as the passive, innocent victims of epidemics, firestorms, floods, and rivers of refugees. This line of thinking is mechanistic, moreover, because it sees things happening in an uncontrolled and uncontrollable fashion. Problems are blamed on forces of nature or on "conflict" itself, rather than on the decisions and acts of men and governments. "No-fault" history is again the rule, and the implication is that little can be done to control these inanimate forces.

---

44. Clinton is quoted in "Clinton's Words: 'The Promise of Peace'," *New York Times*, November 22, 1995, p. A11.

45. Warren Christopher, "No Troops, No Peace," *New York Times*, November 27, 1995, p. 15.

46. Christopher is quoted in Mats R. Berdal, "Fateful Encounter: The United States and UN Peacekeeping," *Survival*, Vol. 36, No. 1 (Spring 1994), pp. 36–37.

47. Misha Glenny, "Heading Off War in the South Balkans," *Foreign Affairs*, Vol. 74, No. 3 (May–June 1995), p. 103.

48. Ralph R. Premdas, "The Internationalization of Ethnic Conflict: Some Theoretical Explorations," in K.M. de Silva and R.J. May, eds., *The Internationalization of Ethnic Conflict* (London: Pinter, 1991), p. 10.

49. See note 42 for further reading on the "contagion problem."

The regional dynamics of internal conflict are poorly understood. No systematic study exists of the ways in which internal conflict engages and involves neighboring states.[50] In my contributions to this book, I will endeavor to advance our understanding of these issues. I will start by suggesting that we distinguish between the effects of internal conflict on neighboring states and on the actions that neighboring states take with respect to these conflicts.

The effects of internal conflict on neighboring states include refugee problems and military entanglements, as touched on at the beginning of this chapter. The effects of internal conflict also include economic repercussions, because the economies of contiguous states are often interconnected, and political instability. As noted above, scholars often refer to these instability problems as "contagion effects" and "diffusion effects." The use of bacteriological and mechanical analogies is unfortunate and confusing, and the confusion in the literature is compounded by the fact that different scholars use these terms in different ways.

I believe that we also need to distinguish between the different kinds of actions that neighboring states have taken and can take with respect to internal conflict. The most useful way to analyze this problem, I argue, is to dissect the different motivations that neighboring states have in these situations. One can therefore distinguish between comparatively benign interventions aimed at relieving humanitarian suffering and restoring regional peace and security; defensive interventions aimed at safeguarding national security interests; protective interventions designed to shield ethnic brethren who are being persecuted; opportunistic meddling designed to further political, economic, or military interests; and opportunistic invasions. Of course, many interventions are driven by a combination of considerations, and states always try to characterize their actions in benign terms, regardless of their true motivations. This complicates matters, but is not a barrier to analysis.

In sum, there are many different ways in which neighboring states

---

50. Several studies touch on aspects of this problem. See James N. Rosenau, ed., *International Aspects of Civil Strife* (Princeton, N.J.: Princeton University Press, 1964); Karl W. Deutsch, "External Involvement in Internal War," in Eckstein, *Internal War*, pp. 100–110; Hedley Bull, "Civil Violence and International Order," in *Civil Violence and the International System*, Adelphi Paper No. 83 (London: IISS, 1971), pp. 27–36; Evan Luard, *The International Regulation of Civil Wars* (London: Thames and Hudson, 1972); Alexis Heraclides, "Secessionist Minorities and External Involvement," *International Organization*, Vol. 44, No. 3 (Summer 1990), pp. 341–378; Midlarsky, *The Internationalization of Communal Strife*; de Silva and May, *Internationalization of Ethnic Conflict*; Brown, *Ethnic Conflict and International Security*.

can be affected by and become involved in internal conflict, and it is important to differentiate between and among these different kinds of problems.

My main argument with respect to the regional dimensions of internal conflict is that, although neighboring states can be the passive victims of turmoil in their regions, they are often active contributors to military escalation and regional instability: opportunistic interventions are quite common. It is therefore a mistake to think of internal conflicts "spilling over" from one place to another through a process that is always beyond human control. This is not to say that all of the regional aspects of internal conflicts are controllable, but some are: some are the products of discrete decisions taken by identifiable individuals and by nearby governments not necessarily immune to international pressure.

This is extremely important, because another critical threshold is crossed when internal conflicts begin to involve neighboring states. Violence then becomes much more difficult to control and resolve.

Implications for International Action

As noted above, the international community is now in the process of reassessing its efforts to deal with the problems posed by internal conflict. Two main schools of thought exist on what distant powers and, through them, international organizations, can and should do in this regard.

Although the great expectations of the early 1990s have clearly been dampened, many analysts remain cautiously optimistic about the ability of distant powers to deal with the problems posed by internal conflicts. Tony Smith, for example, argues:

Much suffering could be spared if the United States, working with other countries through multilateral institutions like the United Nations, the Organization of American States, or NATO, took a clear position on what is not tolerable in world affairs and then moved decisively to enforce the collective will in areas where such efforts could produce results. A historically critical opportunity to give structure and meaning to the post–Cold War world is being missed and will be even more difficult to recover later.[51]

Some contend that even the most vicious outbursts of genocidal slaughter can be quelled by timely international action. Two weeks after the massacre of the Tutsi began in Rwanda in April 1994, General Romeo Dallaire, the Canadian commander of the UN force in the country, insisted that he

---

51. Tony Smith, "In Defense of Intervention," *Foreign Affairs*, Vol. 73, No. 6 (November–December 1994), p. 35.

could end the carnage if given 5,000–8,000 troops. The UN Security Council responded by cutting Dallaire's force of 2,500 to 270.[52]

Others take a radically different view of what international powers can and should do with respect to internal conflicts. Those who subscribe to "ancient hatreds" explanations of internal conflict believe that outside powers can do nothing to prevent these kinds of conflicts, or to influence the course of events when violence does break out. Implicit in this line of thinking is a policy recommendation — do not get involved if it is at all possible to avoid doing so. Political commentator Thomas Friedman puts it bluntly:

To try to extinguish one of these ethnic conflicts when it is raging at full force is futile. When the call of the tribe beckons an ethnic group into battle, get out of the way. The tribal impulse for survival and revenge is like a political blowtorch. No amount of rational argument can tone it down, and if you try to smother it with your own body, or army, it will burn a hole right through you.[53]

One retired U.S. admiral summed up the view of many on the question of international intervention in internal conflicts: "Let them fight. They've been fighting for a thousand years."[54]

It is undoubtedly the case that many policymakers who profess to subscribe to "ancient hatreds" explanations of internal conflict have cynically embraced this line of argumentation because it provides an intellectual rationale for non-interventionist policies, which they favor for domestic reasons. It is also undoubtedly true that many oppose interventionist policies on straightforward national interest grounds, believing that important national security interests are rarely engaged by internal conflicts in distant lands.

To make sense of this debate, it is important to recognize that it is framed by two related but distinct questions: first, what *can* international powers and international organizations do to prevent, manage, and resolve internal conflicts? Second, what *should* international powers and international organizations do with respect to these problems? Our primary focus in this book is on the first of these questions. With that in mind, we will review and assess the track record of international efforts

---

52. See Philip Gourevitch, "After the Genocide," *New Yorker*, December 18, 1995, pp. 91–92.

53. Thomas L. Friedman, "Lift, Lift, Contain," *New York Times*, June 4, 1995, p. E15.

54. Rear Admiral James W. Nance (ret.), is quoted in Tom Ashbrook, "U.S. Weighs Solo Role, Multilateral Efforts," *Boston Globe*, May 3, 1995, p. 1.

in this area, focusing on the post–Cold War era. Our goal is to identify the conditions under which key international actors — individual states, the international organizations through which they often operate, and nongovernmental organizations — can take effective action, and the conditions under which different kinds of policy instruments — humanitarian assistance, fact-finding, mediation, confidence-building measures, traditional and multifunctional peacekeeping, arms embargoes and arms transfers, economic sanctions and economic inducements, judicial enforcement measures, and the use of military force — work most effectively.

Three tasks have to be considered: conflict prevention, conflict management, and conflict resolution. Conflict prevention will always be challenging because disputes are an inherent part of political, economic, and social discourse and because a comprehensive strategy for conflict prevention will have to be preceded by the development of a comprehensive theory of the causes of internal conflict — a distant prospect.[55] However, the framework that I will develop for analyzing the causes of internal conflict provides a corresponding framework for action. If the causes of internal conflict can be categorized as permissive conditions and proximate causes, it follows that one should adopt a two-track approach to conflict prevention: one track should be a series of broad-based, long-term efforts to address the underlying structural, political, economic, social, cultural, and perceptual problems that predispose some countries to violence; the other should be a series of focused, aggressive efforts to neutralize the catalytic factors that transform potentially volatile situations into bloodbaths. The proximate causes of internal conflicts are key, and they can take several forms: internal as well as external factors; elite-led as well as mass-led factors. Different kinds of efforts will have to be undertaken to deal with each of these types of conflict: no single formula will do. However, since internal, elite-level forces are usually the catalysts of internal conflict, those interested in conflict prevention should direct their attention accordingly.

Conflict management is also difficult when one is dealing with internal conflicts. Once violence breaks out in domestic settings, escalation is easy and de-escalation is hard. Internal conflicts often involve weak states. This means that groups and troops will often be difficult to control. This, in turn, means that negotiations will be difficult, and agreements will be difficult to implement. Internal conflicts are almost always high-stakes competitions where the survival of political and ethnic groups hangs in

---

55. See Stephen John Stedman, "Alchemy for a New World Order: Overselling 'Preventive Diplomacy'," *Foreign Affairs*, Vol. 74, No. 3 (May–June 1995), pp. 14–20.

the balance. Warring groups are consequently highly motivated and determined to achieve their objectives; they are always more strongly motivated than outside powers contemplating intervention. Because combat situations are often highly fluid, involving no front lines, it is difficult for outside powers to intervene at the point of attack. Civilians are almost always deeply involved in internal conflicts both as fighters and as targets. Because internal conflicts often involve horrifying attacks on civilian populations, warring parties often find it increasingly difficult to compromise as time goes by. As bad as this picture is, it gets even worse if the conflict in question escalates either vertically, to higher levels of violence, or horizontally, involving neighboring states.

Two broad policy guidelines flow from this. First, if distant powers or international organizations are going to take action to manage conflicts, they should act sooner rather than later; probabilities of success are higher and costs are lower. Second, if preventive actions fail and violence does break out, the next key act is keeping opportunistic neighboring states out of the conflict. The involvement of nearby powers adds other interests and resources to the equation, and makes settlements more difficult to reach.[56]

Conflict resolution is far from easy — the persistence of violence in Afghanistan and Sudan and the periodic re-emergence of armed conflict in Burundi and Kashmir, for example, prove that. However, distant powers working through the United Nations have had some notable success in helping to resolve conflicts in places where warring parties were ready to lay down their arms and reconstruct their countries. Nicaragua, El Salvador, Mozambique, Namibia, and Cambodia stand out in the post–Cold War pantheon in this regard. This suggests that, when the conditions for conflict resolution are ripe, there is much the international community can do to facilitate the peace process.

The main argument in this book with respect to international action is that, although internal conflicts pose formidable policy problems for distant powers and international organizations, options do exist. It is certainly true that policy instruments have not always been used effectively in the past; it does not follow that every action is doomed to fail in the future. The key is understanding the problems that internal conflict poses for different kinds of policy instruments and the conditions under which different instruments can be used effectively.

---

56. See I. William Zartman, "Internationalization of Communal Strife: Temptations and Opportunities of Triangulation," in Midlarsky, *The Internationalization of Communal Strife*, pp. 27–42.

Organization of the Study

This book is divided into three main parts. In the first part, chapters are organized along regional lines. Authors analyze the reasons why internal conflicts have or have not developed, the ways in which these conflicts have involved neighboring states, and both regional and international efforts to prevent, manage, and resolve the conflicts that have developed. Particular attention is paid to the impact of the end of the Cold War and the prospects for internal conflict in the region in the future. Because eight important regions of the world are examined, this study has a strong empirical foundation and a broad comparative perspective on the problem.

In Chapter 1, Ivo Daalder analyzes the former Yugoslavia and the Balkans, focusing in particular on the evolution of the war in the Balkans since 1991, and the many failed international efforts to bring the war to an end. In Chapter 2, Milada Vachudová examines East-Central Europe, a part of the world that has experienced considerable political and economic turmoil in the 1990s but, unlike the Balkans a few hundred miles away, little to no armed conflict. In Chapter 3, Matthew Evangelista looks at developments in the former Soviet Union and the reasons why armed conflict has broken out in some regions, but not others. In Chapter 4, Sumit Ganguly identifies and dissects different patterns of internal conflict in South and Southwest Asia. In Chapter 5, Trevor Findlay studies Southeast Asia, a region consumed by internal conflicts and outside interventions during the Cold War but moving toward stability in the 1990s. In Chapter 6, Rachel Bronson assesses developments in the Middle East and North Africa, where internal conflicts and opportunistic interventions were common in the past and where religious fundamentalism has become a potential source of instability. In Chapter 7, Stephen Stedman analyzes different patterns of internal conflict and outside engagement in sub-Saharan Africa, a region encompassing several dozen states. In Chapter 8, Mark Chernick reviews developments in Central and South America, a part of the world, like East-Central Europe and Southeast Asia, that has seen some encouraging developments in recent years.[57]

The second part of the book focuses more directly on the policy instruments that have been employed in efforts to deal with these problems, and on several key actors. In addition to providing background analysis, chapters in this part of the book aim to develop concrete

---

57. North America, Western Europe, and the Asia-Pacific region will not be given chapter-length treatment because they have experienced comparatively few internal conflicts in the recent past.

recommendations and guidelines for policymakers involved in conflict prevention, conflict management, and conflict resolution efforts.

In Chapter 9, Alicia Levine outlines ways of preventing secessionist violence through political accommodation. In Chapter 10, Stephen Stedman examines the conditions under which negotiation and mediation can be effective tools for conflict prevention, management, and resolution. In Chapter 11, Joanna Spear evaluates the role that arms limitation measures and confidence-building measures can play in international efforts to deal with internal conflict. In Chapter 12, Elizabeth Rogers analyzes the enhanced opportunities that exist, given the demise of the U.S.-Soviet strategic competition, for employing economic sanctions.

In Chapter 13, Thomas Weiss appraises the important roles played by different kinds of nongovernmental organizations. Ivo Daalder investigates the changing U.S. attitude towards international intervention in general and internal conflict in particular in Chapter 14. In Chapter 15, Chantal de Jonge Oudraat assesses the evolution of UN efforts to address internal conflict. Dan Lindley wraps up Part II of the book in Chapter 16, where he discusses the roles collective security organizations have played and can play effectively in this area.

In the third part of this book, I contribute two chapters and develop some broad arguments about the causes of internal conflict, its regional dimensions, and what distant powers and the international community can reasonably expect to do about it.

Part I
Internal Conflict:
Causes and Implications

Chapter 1

Fear and Loathing in the Former Yugoslavia

Ivo H. Daalder

The conflict in the former Yugoslavia represented a brutal awakening for a Europe slumbering in a supposed post–Cold War peace. It was a reminder to everyone that the quiet, non-violent revolutions of 1989 which freed Eastern Europe from Soviet domination might not have a quiet, non-violent aftermath. Not only had communism failed to deliver on its promise to fulfill people's basic needs, but it also proved unable to erase national sentiment and ethnic loyalties. These had been submerged by years of totalitarian rule, but they reappeared in the aftermath of totalitarianism's collapse. It was soon discovered that nationalism was a powerful political tool used by the unscrupulous few to retain the power the defeat of communism threatened to take away. Nowhere in post-revolutionary Europe was this tool exploited more skillfully than in Yugoslavia, an ethnically mixed federal state that had escaped Soviet, but not communist, rule. The resurgence of nationalism was not inevitable, nor was the violence it was to spawn throughout much of Yugoslavia. But resurge it did, and with a vehemence that made war all but inevitable.

Yugoslavia was born in 1918 out of the remnants of the defeated Ottoman and Austro-Hungarian Empires, which had fought over its territory for centuries. However, the Yugoslav Kingdom was no less artificial than the empires that preceded it, neither creating a new nation-state nor uniting all members of different ethnic groups within one country. Instead, the Kingdom contained, under Serbian royal hegemony, a

This chapter was written before the author joined the U.S. National Security Council staff in August 1995. It represents his personal views, not those of the Clinton administration. The author would like to thank William Durch, Brian Mandell, John Mearsheimer, Jim Schear, Warren Zimmermann, and participants in the workshop on "The International Dimensions of Internal Conflict," held at Harvard University's Center for Science and International Affairs in March 1995, for their many useful comments.

disparate mixture of nationalities, many of whose brethren enjoyed majority status in neighboring countries. Hence, not only would a nationalist explosion convulse Yugoslavia itself, it would also invariably affect neighboring states. Situated in the heart of the volatile Balkans — a region where conflict had already triggered one world war — a Yugoslavia torn asunder by ethnic conflict would be of concern to the international community at large.

In this chapter, I analyze the sources of conflict in the former Yugoslavia and examine its international implications. Of the latter, three were crucial: the fear that conflict might spread beyond the confines of the former Yugoslavia; the humanitarian consequences of the war that the disintegration of Yugoslavia produced; and the threat posed by unchecked Serb aggression. International involvement in the conflict was driven by these concerns: to contain the conflict within Yugoslavia proper; to minimize the human costs of war; and to set an example that aggression does not pay. Through 1995, international involvement in the conflict produced decidedly mixed results. The conflict did not spread beyond the territory of Yugoslavia, although international efforts contributed only marginally to its containment. More important was the remarkable degree of forbearance shown by neighboring states, although Serbia did not challenge the interests that most directly affected those states. Moreover, unlike in the past, the differences among the major powers regarding developments within the former Yugoslavia were muted to a large extent by their overriding common interest in containing the conflict. As far as the human costs of the conflict were concerned, many thousands of people labored valiantly to relieve the worst suffering, saving many tens of thousands of innocent people from what otherwise would have been sure starvation. However, this admirable humanitarian effort came into direct conflict with international efforts to punish Serb aggression. Indeed, the major powers singularly failed to stand up to Serb aggression. This failure could undermine their ability to prevent the spread of conflict in the future. The United States did weigh in diplomatically in the summer and autumn of 1995, leading a mediation effort that led to the signing of a peace agreement in Paris in December 1995, but the ultimate impact of this peace initiative will not be known for some time.

The Causes of Conflict

The breakup of the former Yugoslavia was driven by specific historical experiences, political developments, and economic conditions that combined to produce a virulent nationalism. The result was vicious conflict, with untold destruction, on the territory of two of the six constituent republics of the former Yugoslavia. Despite the Paris agreements, the possibility remains that conflict might re-ignite and spread to other parts of the former Yugoslavia and beyond. Understanding the causes of the conflict is critical to any examination of its international implications and to efforts to permanently resolve outstanding differences.

The immediate cause of the breakup of the former Yugoslavia was the rise of virulent nationalism, especially in Serbia, in the late 1980s and early 1990s. By itself, hypernationalism need not be the cause of conflict or war.[1] Set against the specific historical background of Yugoslavia, however, the probability that Serb nationalism would produce the breakup of the federation and end in violence was very high indeed. This is not to say that the brutality and long duration of the resulting wars were inevitable, for effective international action was possible; but conflict was highly likely, and attempts at peaceful resolution of political differences were fraught with difficulties.

If hypernationalism was the immediate cause of the Yugoslav conflict, what accounts for its emergence in the late 1980s? Many if not most journalistic accounts attribute the rise of nationalism to the presence within Yugoslavia of different ethnic minorities, many with a history of mutual animosity. However, this is a simplistic view. Taken to its logical conclusion, it suggests that all states with people of different ethnic, tribal, religious, or national backgrounds are unstable and prone to violent disintegration, especially if these differences have at one time or another been the cause of violent conflict.[2] Clearly, the presence of diverse ethnic groups within a state and a history of conflict among them are not sufficient to explain either the rise of nationalism or the violent breakup of a state. The ethnic geography of a country and a legacy of ethnic conflict may become the focal points of nationalist appeals, as, indeed, happened in Yugoslavia. But why, how, and at what specific point in time this happens cannot be explained simply by observing that ethnic differences exist. In other words, while these differences and historical animosities may have been permissive conditions for the outbreak of ethnic conflict in the former Yugoslavia, they were not the sole, or even its main, cause.

To understand why the Yugoslav conflict occurred when it did, we

---

1. See Stephen Van Evera, "Hypotheses on Nationalism and War," *International Security*, Vol. 18, No. 4 (Spring 1994), pp. 5–39.

2. John Mearsheimer and Robert Pape have made this argument explicitly, arguing that multiethnic states are inherently unstable. See John J. Mearsheimer and Robert A. Pape, "The Answer," *New Republic*, June 14, 1993, pp. 22–29. Of course, since very few states are ethnically homogeneous, this argument would predict the violent disintegration of nearly every state in the world.

must examine the proximate causes of the rise of virulent nationalism in the late 1980s. Three distinct, though interrelated, factors can be identified. First, in the 1980s, Yugoslavia witnessed a sharp deterioration in its economic conditions, produced in part by demands from its foreign creditors and Western governments for a transformation of its economy to increased reliance on the market. Second, this economic transformation was undertaken by an increasingly weak state, riven by internal divisions, both within the central government and among the increasingly powerful and independent regional governments, about the shape of the new political order. Finally, this economic and political transformation occurred at a time of rapid international change, when many of Yugoslavia's neighbors chose to make the leap from totalitarian communist rule to democracy and a reliance on market economics.

This economic and political context enabled nationalism in Yugoslavia to arise and assume its virulent form. Economic decline and political conflict helped produce growing uncertainty and insecurity among the citizenry of Yugoslavia, thus laying the foundation for successful ethnic scapegoating and nationalist appeals. Opportunistic Serb politicians, incapable of meeting the pressing needs of the people, skillfully exploited the appeal of nationalism in order to maintain the power that the collapse of communism within and outside Yugoslavia threatened to deny them. The success of nationalism as a political strategy within Serbia led to a surge in nationalism in other parts of Yugoslavia (notably in Slovenia and Croatia), where equally unscrupulous politicians followed the Serb example and used nationalist appeals for their own political ends. The result was that the opportunity for political compromise narrowed over time until, by 1991, it had disappeared altogether, thus producing the breakup of the Yugoslav state. Given the specific ethnic geography of Yugoslavia — with minority ethnic populations living throughout most republics — and the incompatible nationalist sentiments that had arisen, it was not surprising that the breakup of the state became a violent one.

PERMISSIVE CONDITIONS OF CONFLICT — ETHNIC GEOGRAPHY AND HISTORY

Of all the states created in the name of ethnic justice after World War I, Yugoslavia was the most ill-conceived.[3] Established in 1918, it encompassed a disparate mixture of ethnic groups, each with distinctive histori-

---

3. On the origins of Yugoslavia, see Ivo Banac, *The National Question in Yugoslavia* (Ithaca, N.Y.: Cornell University Press, 1985). For an overview of the history of Yugoslavia, including its disintegration, see Lenard Cohen, *Broken Bonds: The Disintegration of Yugoslavia* (Boulder, Colo.: Westview, 1993). See also John Zametica, *The Yugoslav Conflict*, Adelphi Paper No. 270 (London: International Institute for Strategic Studies [IISS], 1992); Henry Wijnaendts, *Joegoslavische Kroniek: Juli 1991–Augustus 1992* (Amster-

The Former Yugoslavia and the Balkans.

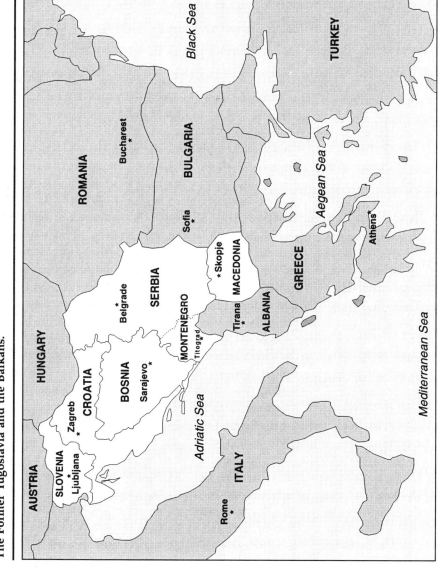

cal backgrounds and experiences. The new kingdom included Serbia and Montenegro, which had been independent since 1878; Macedonia, which had been ruled by Turkey until 1912 and by Serbia thereafter; Austrian-controlled Slovenia and Dalmatia; Hungarian-governed Vojvodina, Croatia, and Slavonia; and Bosnia-Herzegovina, which had been under the Dual Monarchy's tutelage since 1878 and ruled directly from Vienna since 1908. This ethnically mixed constellation was also divided along religious lines between Eastern Orthodox, Roman Catholic, and Muslim communities.

The new Kingdom of the Serbs, Croats, and Slovenes was, in essence, a "Greater Serbia," and its Serb rulers governed with little regard for the interests of other nationalities. A centralized, unitary state was established, with power concentrated in Belgrade. This generated resentment in other parts of the Kingdom, notably in Croatia, where a more decentralized political system was desired. As resentment grew, the central authorities in Belgrade responded not by granting greater regional autonomy, but by suspending efforts to establish parliamentary rule. In 1929, the ruling Serb monarch Alexander I suspended the constitution, assumed all legislative power, and renamed the country Yugoslavia in the name of national unity. These acts did little to resolve the underlying problems of the country and, instead, sowed the seeds of its eventual destruction.

That destruction arrived with the Nazi invasion of Yugoslavia in 1941. The country was divided among the Axis powers — with Germany and Italy taking parts of Slovenia, Italy establishing a protectorate in Montenegro, Albania annexing Kosovo, Hungary grabbing the northern parts (including Vojvodina), and Bulgaria absorbing Macedonia. A nominally independent, fascist puppet state was established in Croatia, which also included most of Bosnia-Herzegovina. What was left of Serbia was occupied by Germany. The war was a calamity for most inhabitants of Yugoslavia, but especially for the Serbs. Of those living outside Serbia proper, one third were murdered by the Croatian *Ustashe*, one third were forced to convert to Catholicism, and one third were deported to Serbia. Irregular Serbian forces, known as *Chetniks*, retaliated in a similarly brutal fashion, and after the war exacted their revenge on tens of thousands of Croatians. The one political force uniting many of Yugoslavia's disparate groups was the Communist Party, led by Josip Broz Tito. With help from the Allied Powers, Tito's partisans liberated the country toward the end of the war, and it fell to the communists to unify a bitterly divided state.

---

dam: Thomas Rap, 1993); Susan Woodward, *Balkan Tragedy: Chaos and Dissolution after the Cold War* (Washington, D.C.: Brookings Institution, 1995), chaps. 2–5. I have relied heavily on these accounts in my review of the history of Yugoslavia.

Tito sought to make good on his wartime slogan of "Brotherhood and Unity" by creating a federal state composed of six republics: Bosnia-Herzegovina, Croatia, Macedonia, Montenegro, Serbia, and Slovenia. The federation satisfied the desires of most ethnic groups — except the Serbs. Although Serbs had made claims on Macedonia and Montenegro, the latter were set up as constituent republics. Moreover, within Serbia proper, two provinces — Vojvodina and Kosovo — were granted a degree of autonomy. Finally, Croatia's borders were drawn along the lines established during the Dual Monarchy, leaving the Krajina Serbs, who had suffered tremendously during the war, under at least partial Croatian control.

The federal experiment was at first successful in promoting economic growth and ameliorating ethnic conflict. By the late 1960s, however, nationalist sentiment was again on the rise as the wealthier republics (notably Croatia and Slovenia) increasingly resented having to carry the economic burdens of the more economically backward parts of the federation. In response, a new constitutional arrangement was adopted in 1974, granting considerably more autonomy to the republics. The new constitution also gave the two provinces in Serbia, Vojvodina and Kosovo, a vote in the federal system, which was to rule by consensus after Tito's death in 1980.

Decentralization allayed demands for more local autonomy, but once it was combined with the imperative of consensus decision-making at the top, it resulted not in greater inter-regional cooperation but in an increasingly weak central state. Even the communist party became fragmented along regional lines, leaving only the Yugoslav National Army (JNA) as a manifestation of national unity and a mechanism for central control. Throughout the 1980s, these problems were aggravated by a collapsing economy and increasingly fractious political order. In the end, Yugoslavia was little more than a confederation consisting of eight separate units; the basis of political legitimacy had shifted from the federal state to the local level, laying the foundation for Yugoslavia's eventual disintegration.

PROXIMATE CAUSES OF CONFLICT — THE COLLAPSE OF ECONOMIC AND POLITICAL ORDER

The 1980s witnessed a sharp economic decline and increased political conflict between and within republics and regions over the future of the political order in Yugoslavia. These problems laid the foundation for a surge of nationalism, first in Serbia and subsequently in other republics. The economic downturn aggravated inequalities within and between republics, and fostered resentment on the part of the less well-off toward those better able to cope. Growing insecurity combined with increasing political conflict created fertile ground for a deliberate strategy of ethnic scapegoating and a nationalist rallying of the discontented and dispossessed. Historical animosities, combined with the presence of ethnic minorities within the republics, rendered nationalist appeals both possible and credible. With nationalism rising in Serbia, nationalist counterreactions arose in other parts of Yugoslavia until the conflict exploded into violence.

A major cause of the surge in nationalism was a decade of precipitous economic decline, combining rising unemployment, growing foreign indebtedness, and sky-high inflation. Unemployment in Yugoslavia averaged 15 percent throughout the 1980s, but the burden was not distributed equally. Whereas Slovenia enjoyed full employment and Croatia experienced a single-digit unemployment rate, unemployment reached 50 percent in Kosovo, 27 percent in Macedonia, 23 percent in Bosnia-Herzegovina, and over 20 percent in Serbia. Inflation soared, climbing to 50 percent in the early 1980s and then sky-rocketing to 1,200 percent in the late 1980s. Per capita income dropped by almost 50 percent between 1979 and 1988.[4]

This economic crisis stimulated political conflicts over how to respond to the crisis and how to organize political power more generally. By the late 1980s, both Croatia and Slovenia believed that a rapid shift to market economics was warranted, a step other provinces were not prepared to take. Differences over the management of the economy amplified growing differences about future political arrangements within and between the republics. The power and legitimacy of the Communist Party, already fragmented along regional lines, was increasingly undermined by the growing political decay of the federal state. Political pluralism was on the rise in a number of republics — notably Slovenia, Croatia, and Bosnia — echoing developments taking place in other parts of Eastern Europe. The federal government, operating on the basis of a rotating presidency, proved unable to mediate the differences among the republics about the future of constitutional arrangements. Slovenia and Croatia insisted on both greater political pluralism and further decentralization. Serbia and Montenegro favored increased centralization under one-party rule. Bosnia-Herzegovina and Macedonia were primarily worried about keeping the federal state together.

Growing political conflict within Yugoslavia provided fertile ground for ethnic polarization. This polarization was a direct consequence of a deliberate political strategy on the part of hardliners within the Serb Communist Party, led by Slobodan Milosevic and supported by the JNA,

---

4. Economic data are from Woodward, *Balkan Tragedy*, pp. 50–57.

to use the appeal of Serb nationalism to keep and extend their power.[5] The initial target of Serb nationalism was the Albanian population in Kosovo, which, following riots in 1981, became the object of continuing Serb derision and physical attack. But Kosovo was only the beginning. By the mid-1980s, a campaign to paint the Serbs as the aggrieved party in Titoist Yugoslavia was gaining popular backing. In March 1986, the Serb Academy of Arts and Sciences released a memorandum that called for immediate recentralization of the Yugoslav state and blamed Tito for all Serb problems. The establishment of Macedonia as an independent republic after it had been part of Serbia in the interwar years and the granting of political rights and autonomy to the provinces of Kosovo and Vojvodina were depicted as direct affronts to the Serb nation. Tito's decision in 1966 to declare the Muslims a nation was derided, and the centrality of the Serbs, as Yugoslavia's original and only constituent nation, was repeatedly emphasized. Although the memorandum was meant to buttress Serbia's demand for the recentralization of the federal state, its argument that Serbs throughout Yugoslavia should live in a single state laid the intellectual foundations for later calls to establish a Greater Serbia. Against the backdrop of economic crisis, political conflict, and growing insecurity, these arguments had great appeal among the Serbs, and Milosevic exploited them skillfully to strengthen his political base.

The original aims of Serb nationalism were to reverse Yugoslavia's fragmentation by recentralizing power in Belgrade and to exert central, Serbian control over the state apparatus. These objectives failed for two reasons. First, the movement toward recentralization and authoritarianism went against the prevailing view in other parts of Yugoslavia and much of Eastern Europe. Second, Serb nationalism provoked a powerful nationalist reaction in other republics. By 1989, Milosevic had succeeded in toppling the governments in Vojvodina, Montenegro, and Kosovo, replacing them with his supporters. With Milosevic in control of four out of the eight votes in Yugoslavia's federal council, the other republics had quite a few incentives to chart an independent course, and little choice but to do so.

Having failed to recentralize Yugoslavia, Milosevic embarked on the creation of Greater Serbia. Serb communities living outside Serbia — particularly in Croatia, but also in Bosnia — became increasingly radicalized, in part through Belgrade's propaganda and in part because of

---

5. On the political basis of Serb nationalism, see V.P. Gagnon, Jr., "Ethnic Nationalism and International Conflict: The Case of Serbia," *International Security*, Vol. 19, No. 3 (Winter 1994/95), pp. 130–166. On Milosevic, see Aleksa Djilas, "A Profile of Slobodan Milosevic," *Foreign Affairs*, Vol. 72, No. 3 (Summer 1993), pp. 81–96.

growing nationalism within the republics, especially in Croatia, where the newly elected, pro-independence government did much to antagonize the Serb community. In August 1990, Serbs around Knin launched an uprising, demanding autonomy for Serb-dominated areas in Croatia. In December 1990, Slovenia and Croatia declared that they would secede in six months unless a more acceptable federal arrangement was negotiated, a promise both provinces fulfilled in June of 1991. This step inevitably led to conflict with Serbia, where Milosevic a year earlier had warned that Yugoslavia's internal borders were inextricably linked to the integrity of Yugoslavia itself — any change in the latter would call into question the sanctity of the former.

THE BREAKUP OF YUGOSLAVIA — THE INTERNATIONALIZATION OF INTERNAL CONFLICT

Slovenia's declaration of independence in June 1991 received only *pro forma* opposition from Belgrade, a strong indication that Serbia's interests lay in defending Serbs (of whom there were only a few in Slovenia) rather than in maintaining Yugoslavia's territorial integrity. Some 3,000 JNA troops were deployed in Slovenia in the hope that a show of force might bring Ljubljana to its senses. It did not. The Slovenian territorial army had retained a large stock of weapons and put up stiff resistance against a not-very-determined JNA. The war lasted all of ten days and ended with a ceasefire agreement mediated by the European Community (EC), in which Slovenia agreed to suspend implementation of its independence declaration for three months. Belgrade's *de facto* recognition of Slovenia's secession was understood a few weeks later when all JNA forces were withdrawn to concentrate their efforts on the real objective: creating a Greater Serbia.

Unlike Slovenia, Croatia had a large Serbian population, about half of which lived in the Croatian border region with Bosnia and in parts of eastern Croatia. Zagreb's declaration of independence, combined with its celebration of nationalist images (including not-so-subtle reminders of the *Ustashe* period), posed a perceived danger to Croatian Serbs, if only because Croatia's claim to independence on the basis of self-determination took no account of the rights and aspirations of the Serb minority. Spurred by a demand for ethnic justice and with full backing from Belgrade (including the JNA), Croatian Serbs launched an all-out effort to deny Croatian sovereignty over Serb-inhabited territories. The campaign was swift and brutal. Within weeks, Serb/JNA forces had captured nearly one-third of Croatian territory, expelled non-Serbs from much of the territory, and commenced large-scale bombardment of key cities, including the historically picturesque coastal town of Dubrovnik and the eastern city of Vukovar. After months of fighting, a UN-brokered cease-fire was accepted by all sides in January 1992.

The Serb-Croatian agreement was followed by German-led EC recognition of Croatia and Slovenia as independent states. The extension of diplomatic recognition, which transformed the internal Yugoslav conflict into an international one, had profound implications for developments elsewhere in the former Yugoslavia. Macedonia and Bosnia, both of which had been offered conditional EC recognition, concluded that they had little choice but to follow Slovenia and Croatia, lest they be subjugated within a Yugoslavia dominated by Milosevic. A referendum on Bosnian independence was held in February 1992, which, though boycotted by Serbs, showed overwhelming support for independence. International recognition was extended on April 5, which set the stage for a well-prepared Serb onslaught on Sarajevo and on Muslim towns in eastern Bosnia.[6] Macedonia was spared a similar fate when the JNA withdrew its forces in early 1992 to concentrate on military operations elsewhere. Although international recognition was held up because of an esoteric dispute with Greece concerning the new country's formal name, the EC extended qualified recognition in late 1992. The Former Yugoslav Republic of Macedonia was admitted to the United Nations in April 1993.

The breakup of Yugoslavia was confirmed on April 27, 1992, when a new Federal Republic of Yugoslavia, consisting of Serbia and Montenegro, was proclaimed in Belgrade. Although the Serb leadership argued that Yugoslavia was only being restructured, this action implied *de facto* recognition of the other republics' independence, if not of their territorial integrity. From that point on, intervention by the new "Yugoslavia" in Croatia, Bosnia, and elsewhere had an unmistakable international character.

International Implications and Responses

The violent breakup of Yugoslavia had three principal implications for the major powers, including the United States, Russia, and members of the European Community. First, there was a threat to regional stability, with the possibility that the conflict might spread beyond Yugoslavia to

---

6. As early as August 1991, the JNA was preparing to make arms deliveries to Bosnian Serbs, who the previous May had declared three regions in Bosnia "Serb Autonomous Regions." The JNA itself intervened to establish these borders in September and, following the Serb-Croatian cease-fire in January, poured more armaments into Bosnia while forcefully disarming Bosnia's national guard. See Warren Zimmermann, "A Pavane for Bosnia," *National Interest*, No. 37 (Fall 1994), p. 78.

involve neighboring states and perhaps the Balkans as a whole. Such a development would pose a threat to European security and could, as in the past, involve the major powers on opposite sides in the conflict. Second, the violence accompanying the breakup created a humanitarian crisis, with millions of refugees, hundreds of thousands of casualties, and the threat of widespread starvation appearing at a time when many had assumed that, with the end of the Cold War, peace in Europe was at hand. Third, international powers had a strategic interest in countering aggression; if the Serbs could demonstrate that they could secure their aims through forceful means, assertive nationalists in other parts of the world (including the former Soviet Union) would be more likely to conclude that they could implement aggressive designs with impunity.

International involvement in the Yugoslav conflict was propelled by the need to address these problems. Accordingly, the major powers sought to respond to the breakup of Yugoslavia by attempting to prevent the spread of war, mitigate the humanitarian consequences of the conflict, and demonstrate that aggression does not pay. Through 1995, their actions helped to prevent the spread of war beyond the confines of the former Yugoslavia and were marginally effective in addressing the worst humanitarian consequences of the conflict. But the major powers failed to send a clear signal that aggression does not pay. They failed to do so for two reasons. First, the United States, Russia, and the major European powers believed that effective containment of the conflict within the areas where war had broken out required unity of purpose, a purpose that found expression in the establishment of the five-nation Contact Group. Since there was no agreement on what action was appropriate to punish Serb aggression — with the United States generally taking a tough stance, Russia a conciliatory position, and Europeans a middle course — the perceived need for five-power unity led to paralysis. Second, the use of force to punish Serb aggression was in direct conflict with efforts by the United Nations to deal with the conflict's humanitarian consequences.

PREVENTING THE SPREAD OF CONFLICT

The most immediate implication of the conflict in the former Yugoslavia was the possibility that the war could spread throughout the Balkans. For both historical and ethnic reasons, nearly all of its neighbors had a direct interest in the developments taking place in the former Yugoslavia. The breakup provided the occasion for asserting old territorial demands that most had thought settled with Yugoslavia's creation in 1918. Moreover, the status of minorities within the former Yugoslavia, many of whom had ethnic brethren in neighboring states, was of direct interest. The danger was that if one neighboring state sought to intervene in or exploit the consequences of the conflict for its own gain, others might follow suit. War could rapidly spread throughout the Balkans. Preventing this was the primary motive for international involvement in the Yugoslav conflict.

REGIONAL INTERESTS AND ASPIRATIONS. Of Yugoslavia's seven neighbors, four (Hungary, Bulgaria, Greece, and Albania) had direct and compelling interests in the developments taking place there.[7] The direct involvement of any one state in the conflict probably would have propelled others to follow suit. Because of its long-standing involvement in the region, Turkey could have become involved as well.

Hungary's primary concern was the status of the Hungarian minority in Vojvodina, although early in the Croat-Serb war it was also concerned about repeated violations of its airspace by the JNA air force. At times, Budapest has made veiled irredentist claims, suggesting that the territorial revisions accompanying the Yugoslav breakup called into question the settlement of 1918, which broke up the Austro-Hungarian Empire. It also clearly sided with Croatia in its war with Serbia, but it has otherwise refrained from direct intervention in the conflict.[8]

Bulgaria's principal interest in the Yugoslav conflict revolved around Macedonia, whose inhabitants are closely linked to Bulgaria. Indeed, much of the region was ruled by Sofia from 1878 to 1918 and again during World War II.[9] Although Bulgaria was one of the first states to recognize Skopje's declaration of independence, it has refused to recognize Macedonians as a distinct nationality, claiming that they are Bulgarians. Its minimal aim has been to support the independence of the new state as a way of expressing its opposition to Serbia (with whom, together with Greece, it fought two wars over the region in 1912–13). Bulgaria would ultimately like to absorb Macedonia into its sphere of influence.

Macedonia was also of great interest to Greece; it was part of the historic Macedonia of Philip and Alexander. Athens refused to recognize Macedonia's independence, arguing that its name, flag, and coinage reflected expansionist designs on Greek parts of historic Macedonia. It

---

7. The other three countries — Austria, Italy, and Romania — also had interests in Yugoslavia, but none were of a sufficiently compelling character to lead to intervention and war. On their interests, as well as those of the remaining four, see Zametica, *The Yugoslav Conflict*, pp. 47–58.

8. George Schöpflin, *Hungary and its Neighbors*, Chaillot Paper No. 7 (Paris: Western European Union [WEU] Institute for Security Studies, 1993), pp. 18–22.

9. See Gabriel Munuera, *Preventing Armed Conflict in Europe: Lessons from Recent Experience*, Chaillot Papers Nos. 15–16 (Paris: WEU Institute for Security Studies, 1994), pp. 39–61.

successfully opposed international recognition of the new state for more than two years, and only reluctantly accepted Macedonia's membership in international organizations as the "Former Yugoslav Republic of Macedonia." Greece only recognized Macedonia in 1995, when it lifted a two-year-old embargo that had prohibited cross-border trade with this desperately poor, land-locked country. Greece's exaggerated fears about Macedonia's purported expansionist designs hide a greater Greek concern: regional isolation. Athens sees Bulgaria, Albania, and Turkey as potential foes, and Macedonian independence would isolate Greece by cutting it off from its longstanding orthodox ally, Serbia.

Albanian interests in the former Yugoslavia were a function of the Albanian nationals living in Kosovo (whose population is 90 percent Albanian), Montenegro, and Macedonia. Even with the breakup of Yugoslavia, Albanians remain a minority in each of the three new states in which they live. Moreover, their minority status has not been recognized by any of these republics, nor have their demands for greater autonomy been met. This has led to growing political radicalization, often with open support from Tirana. Of all the potential ethnic flash points involving the former Yugoslavia and its neighbors, the ones involving Albanians are possibly the most dangerous.

The disintegration of Yugoslavia has reawakened the historical and ethnic interests of important neighboring states. So far, none has exploited the situation and seized a unilateral advantage, fearing that doing so might spark a wider Balkan war as well as isolation from the West, on whose continued economic and political support their prosperity depends. Nevertheless, the Balkans are a powder keg, and with the breakup of Yugoslavia the powder is drier than it has been in years.

THE INTERNATIONAL RESPONSE. The involvement of the major powers in the former Yugoslavia has been driven by the need to keep the conflict from spreading beyond the confines of the former Yugoslavia. Working through institutions such as the United Nations, the European Community, the Conference (later Organization) on Security and Cooperation in Europe (CSCE/OSCE), and the five-nation Contact Group, the major powers sought to prevent the spread of the conflict within that country. They did so by working to halt the war in Slovenia, seeking a quick end to the war in Croatia, preventing its spread to Bosnia, and, failing that, attempting to negotiate an end to conflict there. In addition, they sought to forestall the spread of conflict to other parts of the former Yugoslavia by placing monitors in Vojvodina, Kosovo, and Sandzak within Serbia, and deploying military forces in Macedonia. These efforts met with some success; the conflict has largely been confined to Croatia and Bosnia, even though it did spread from Slovenia to Croatia and Bosnia. However, it did not spread to Macedonia or within Serbia proper, which would affect the latent interests of neighboring states and make containment that much more difficult.

Ending the wars that broke out after Slovenia's and Croatia's declarations of independence in June 1991 was the first imperative.[10] Unless these wars could be brought to a rapid conclusion and a new *modus vivendi* worked out among the constituent republics of Yugoslavia, conflict was bound to spread. With this in mind, international powers focused first on halting the fighting in Slovenia. The European Community took the lead and succeeded in brokering an agreement in early July among the six Yugoslav republics and Yugoslavia's federal government. Under the Brioni Agreement, a cease-fire was established, Slovenia and Croatia agreed to suspend their declaration of independence for three months, all parties pledged to enter into negotiations on Yugoslavia's future, Slovenian territorial forces were disarmed, and Slovenia's siege of JNA barracks was lifted. The agreement also called for the deployment of thirty (later fifty) EC observers to monitor the agreement.

The conflict nonetheless spread to Croatia, where a vicious war between the Croatian government and Serb separatists (directly supported by Belgrade and the JNA) had broken out. The EC again took the lead in mediating an end to the conflict, adopting a two-pronged strategy to impose a cease-fire and negotiate a political settlement of Yugoslavia's future.[11] Neither proved successful. The first track foundered over intra-European disagreements on whether to send a large "interposition" force of some 30,000 troops under the auspices of the Western European Union (WEU), a proposal supported by France, Germany, Italy, and the Netherlands but strongly opposed by Britain. Some twelve cease-fires were signed among the warring parties, but, lacking enforcement, each was broken.

Attempts to reach a political settlement were conducted under the

---

10. The following account draws on Woodward, *Balkan Tragedy*, chaps. 6–9; James Steinberg, "Yugoslavia," in Lori Fisler Damrosch, ed., *Enforcing Restraint: Collective Intervention in Internal Conflicts* (New York: Council on Foreign Relations, 1993), pp. 27–76; James E. Goodby, "Peacekeeping in the New Europe," *Washington Quarterly*, Vol. 15, No. 2 (Spring 1992); Marc Weller, "The International Response to the Dissolution of the Socialist Federal Republic of Yugoslavia," *American Journal of International Law*, Vol. 86, No. 3 (1992); John Newhouse, "Dodging the Problem," *New Yorker*, August 24, 1992, pp. 60–71; John Newhouse, "No Exit, No Entrance," *New Yorker*, June 28, 1993, pp. 44–51.

11. The best account of these efforts is Wijnaendts, *Joegoslavische Kroniek*. Ambassador Winjaendts was the chief EC mediator in Yugoslavia during the last half of 1991.

EC-sponsored Conference on Yugoslavia. The main obstacle in these ne-gotiations was the inherent incompatibility of Serb and Croatian de-mands: Belgrade insisted that all Serbs should live in one state, while Zagreb sought nothing less than full independence for all areas of Croatia. A proposal by Lord Carrington, the EC mediator, to recognize the inde-pendence of any republic if the new state granted considerable autonomy to ethnic minorities and agreed to a "special status" arrangement for their territories, was clearly responsive to a main cause of the conflict, but ultimately failed to overcome these incompatible positions.

Even if these inherent contradictions and difficulties had not been present, a political settlement was doomed by Germany's oft-repeated intention to recognize the independence of Slovenia and Croatia uncon-ditionally, which left neither Zagreb nor Belgrade any incentive to settle underlying political issues. Throughout the second half of 1991, Bonn pressed for the recognition of Croatia in particular, even though it for-mally agreed with its EC partners that recognition would be extended only in the context of a general political settlement. In early December, it finally succeeded in persuading its partners to drop this proviso. Against the advice of Lord Carrington, the UN Secretary-General, and the United States, the EC agreed to recognize the independence of any republic that met certain standards set out by the European arbitration commission, including respect for the rule of law, democracy, human rights, and rights of minority populations, as well as acceptance of Lord Carrington's pro-posal for granting "special status" to certain areas in which minorities lived. In late December, Germany moved to recognize the independence of Slovenia and Croatia without waiting to find out if these conditions had been met. (Croatia, the commission later found, did so only partially.)

Once Croatian independence became a *fait accompli*, all sides in the war decided to accept, at least temporarily, the status quo. In early January 1992, the UN's representative to Yugoslavia, Cyrus Vance, suc-ceeded in negotiating an agreement among the warring sides. The Vance plan called for the withdrawal of JNA forces from Croatia, the estab-lishment of three UN Protected Areas (UNPA) in Krajina and eastern and western Slavonia where Serbs lived, the complete withdrawal or demo-bilization of all forces within the UNPA and the return of all refugees, many of whom had been expelled by the Serbs, to their homes.[12] Imple-mentation of the plan was to be supervised by a 14,000-strong UN Pro-tection Force (UNPROFOR) in Croatia. While the plan addressed the

---

12.   UN Security Council, "Concept for a United Nations Peace-keeping Operation in Yugoslavia," *Report of the Secretary-General Pursuant to Security Council Resolution 721 (1991)*, S/23280 (December 11, 1991), annex III.

military problems raised by the conflict, it deliberately left the political questions for later negotiations. In doing so, it effectively froze the status quo, leaving about 30 percent of Croatian territory outside of Zagreb's political control and in local Serbian hands. The shooting might have ended, but the conflict had not been solved.

With international efforts in late 1991 and early 1992 concentrated on halting the war in Croatia, little attention was devoted to other parts of the former Yugoslavia. Notably absent from German and EC calculations about speedy recognition of Croatia and Slovenia was proper considera-tion of the impact of this act on the fate of Bosnia and Macedonia.[13] Bosnia's president, Alija Izetbegovic, had tried without success to keep Yugoslavia together within a loose federation, realizing that Bosnian independence would have to follow if Croatia and Slovenia were to depart. The German push for recognition therefore had fateful conse-quences for Bosnia (and Macedonia). Once Croatian and Slovenian inde-pendence were *faits accomplis,* Bosnia had no choice but to try to meet the criteria established by the arbitration commission for recognition, includ-ing holding a referendum on independence. In April 1992, the EC (this time joined by the United States) recognized Bosnia's independence, providing Serbia with an excuse to contest Bosnia's territorial integrity openly and secure the two-thirds of Bosnian territory that the Serbs claimed as their own.

The ensuing war was particularly brutal — involving concentration camps, massive expulsions of Muslims and Croats from their homes in a self-described Serb campaign of "ethnic cleansing," widespread inci-dences of rape, and the unrelenting shelling of cities, including the capital, Sarajevo. The international response to these developments was three-fold: a complete economic embargo was imposed on Serbia and Monte-negro to force an end to their involvement in the Bosnian war; UN peacekeeping forces were deployed to bring humanitarian relief to af-fected communities; and diplomats scurried to negotiate a peaceful solu-tion to the war. The embargo succeeded in devastating the economies of Serbia and Montenegro, but not in ending Belgrade's support for Bosnian (and Croatian) Serbs. The relief effort reached millions of people and may indeed have prevented a worse humanitarian disaster, but at the cost of

---

13.   UN Secretary-General Javier Perez de Cuellar wrote the European Community on December 10, 1991, warning against extending diplomatic recognition, noting that doing so could "light the powder keg, especially in Bosnia-Herzegovina." The EC nonetheless decided to extend recognition five days later. Cited in Wijnaendts, *Joe-goslavische Kroniek,* p. 162.

holding hostage the option of using military intervention to bring the conflict to an end. Although diplomatic efforts produced a variety of plans for a political settlement and brought about an uneasy rapprochement between the Muslim and Croatian communities, they foundered over the fact that whereas Bosnian Muslims wanted to maintain the state's territorial integrity and independence, Bosnian Serbs insisted on an independent state. As a result, while the intensity of the war waxed and waned, the fighting never fully stopped.

The continuation of fighting in Croatia and Bosnia posed a major challenge to international efforts to prevent the spread of conflict to other areas of the former Yugoslavia. By 1995, the war had not spread to Serbia proper, where Hungarians in Vojvodina, Albanians in Kosovo, and Muslims in Sandzak face Serb oppression.[14] The constant barrage of Serb nationalist propaganda promulgated by media under the near-total control of Milosevic has naturally troubled these minority populations. Frightened in part by Belgrade's discriminatory behavior and in part by the brutal example of Bosnia, the Muslims of Sandzak have followed the example of the Serbs in Croatia and Bosnia by declaring their desire for independence — the difference being that the Muslims of Sandzak have neither the arms nor the outside support to act on that desire. The Albanians in Kosovo share a similar sentiment, and though they too lack military capabilities, they could receive outside support from Albania should Serbia move to suppress the call for independence through force. Many Hungarians in Vojvodina have already left for Hungary; those who remain realize that even within Vojvodina they constitute a minority, leaving them little choice but to leave or to submit to Belgrade's rule.

International involvement to prevent Serb repression of these minorities has been very limited. In August 1992, twenty CSCE observers were sent to the three regions to collect and report on information about local conditions and to facilitate a dialogue between the Serb authorities and the local populations. Though intended as "a mission of long duration," the observers were ousted in July 1993 by Belgrade, effectively ending their information-gathering and mediating role.[15] Given tight control over the local media, it is no longer possible to obtain good information about developments in these areas.

---

14. It is noteworthy, and brutally ironic, that the Serbs, who have championed the rights of Serb minorities in Bosnia and Croatia to choose their own destiny, have never accepted similar claims by non-Serb minorities living within Serbia.

15. Ambassador Tore Bøgh, "Some Comments on the Operation of the CSCE Missions of Long Duration to Kosovo, Sandzak, and Vojvodina," unpublished paper by the Head of Missions, CSCE, September 1993.

The one other instance of international involvement in support of minorities within Serbia relates to the warning, first issued by the Bush administration and later explicitly repeated by the Clinton administration, that the United States would respond with force if Serbia were to take military action in Kosovo.[16] This threat was designed to help prevent the spread of conflict beyond Yugoslavia. Fearing that Serb military action against the Albanian population would compel Albania and other countries to become involved, the United States meant not only to deter Belgrade but also to reassure Tirana (as well as Athens and Sofia).

A similar concern led to the deployment of a small UN force in Macedonia in December 1992. Initially composed of some 700 Scandinavian soldiers, the UN mission in Macedonia was designed to monitor the borders with Serbia and Albania. In mid-1993, the United States decided to deploy some 300 soldiers as part of the mission, thus providing the first U.S. combat troop presence in the former Yugoslavia. The operation has since been enlarged somewhat, with more than 1,000 troops (about half of which come from the United States) deployed in Macedonia in 1995. As a tripwire presence, the force serves both to reassure Macedonia and to deter its neighbors (mainly Serbia, but also Greece and Albania) from intervening. Although its effect is impossible to know, its presence makes more credible the threat of U.S. military action in case of Serb aggression.

International efforts to prevent the spread of conflict have only partially succeeded. The conflict has been effectively contained within the borders of the former Yugoslavia, and, given the historical record of the Balkans, that is no mean achievement. On the other hand, the flames that could light the Balkan powder keg have only been contained, not put out: unresolved differences in Croatia could rapidly escalate once again; war in Bosnia remains a possibility; and minorities within Serbia still lack rudimentary political rights, creating potential new sources of conflict. Much international effort has been expended to deal with the symptoms of conflict — the humanitarian consequences of war — but not with the underlying causes.

DEALING WITH THE HUMANITARIAN CONSEQUENCES OF WAR
War, by its very nature, has horrendous humanitarian consequences — refugees, injuries, death. What made the consequences of war in the former Yugoslavia especially horrifying was their scale and brutality, as

---

16. John M. Goshko, "Bush Threatens 'Military Action' If Serbs Attack Ethnic Albanians," *Washington Post*, December 29, 1992, p. A10; "Clinton Warns Serbian Leaders on Military Action in Kosovo," *Washington Post*, March 2, 1993, p. A14.

well as the fact that they occurred in a region of the world where many had thought that such developments could never again take place. By late 1993, the United Nations estimated that 140,000–250,000 people had been killed or were missing in the former Yugoslavia, and another 60,000–150,000 were seriously wounded. One-fifth of the former Yugoslavia's prewar population of 22 million had been displaced, including 2.25 million people in Bosnia alone.[17] Much of this displacement was not simply the "normal" consequence of armed conflict, but the product of a deliberate strategy by the belligerents, especially the Serbs, to "cleanse" villages, towns, and cities of people belonging to different ethnic groups. "Ethnic cleansing" consisted of forced expulsions, murder, rape, and internment in concentration camps. The wars in Croatia and Bosnia also exacted a high civilian toll because the Serb tactic of choice was to exploit their advantage in heavy weapons by shelling urban areas relentlessly from a distance. Finally, deliberate interference with and obstruction of humanitarian relief efforts became part of a strategy to force the "voluntary" departure of non-Serb peoples, many of whom faced an unpalatable choice between flight and starvation.

Aside from diplomatic efforts designed to end the conflict, the international response was to mitigate its humanitarian consequences through a two-pronged strategy of delivering aid to those in need and protecting highly vulnerable populations. These efforts were massive in scope, involving tens of thousands of people, hundreds of thousands of tons of supplies, and billions of dollars. There is little doubt that these efforts saved many lives and alleviated the suffering of many civilians.[18] At the same time, there can be no doubt that humanitarian relief efforts proceeded at the expense of efforts to address the underlying causes of the wars in the former Yugoslavia. Indeed, the sad irony is that international humanitarian efforts held hostage (or provided a convenient excuse for

---

17. Figures are from Richard D. Caplan, "Yugoslavia," in John Tessitore and Susan Woolfson, eds., *A Global Agenda: Issues before the 49th General Assembly of the United Nations* (Lanham, Md.: University Press of America, 1994), p. 11. There is considerable uncertainty about the number of Bosnian fatalities. The high ratio of deaths to wounded is particularly puzzling, suggesting that fatalities may well be significantly lower than the generally accepted figure of 100,000 to 200,000. See George Kenney, "The Bosnian Calculation," *New York Times Magazine*, April 23, 1995, pp. 42–43. Kenney estimates Bosnian fatalities at 25,000–60,000.

18. A thorough investigation of UN efforts from 1991–93 concluded that the civilian population was better off as a result of the UN effort, which "provided relief to many, protection to some, resettlement and asylum to a few." Larry Minear et al., *Humanitarian Action in the Former Yugoslavia: The U.N.'s Role 1991–1993*, Occasional Paper No. 18 (Providence, R.I.: Watson Institute for International Studies, 1994), p. 9.

forgoing) forceful international action designed to end the conflict. As Rosalyn Higgins has argued, "we have chosen to respond to unlawful violence not by stopping that violence, but by trying to provide relief to the suffering. But our choice of policy allows the suffering to continue."[19]

By late 1994, the United Nations High Commission for Refugees (UNHCR), the lead agency for providing relief in the former Yugoslavia, estimated that 3.8 million people required food and other assistance, 2.7 million of whom lived in Bosnia.[20] Through September 1994, UNHCR supervised the delivery of more than 600,000 metric tons of food at a total cost of $1.2 billion. The bulk of the assistance was delivered to areas in Bosnia, although significant assistance was also provided to other parts of the former Yugoslavia. Overall, this relief effort succeeded in preventing widespread starvation among large numbers of people.

The assistance effort was complicated by the fact that UNHCR had no experience in delivering humanitarian assistance to people in war zones. In June 1992, this effort focused on Sarajevo, and UNPROFOR's mandate was extended to include opening and securing the airport and ensuring the safe movement of aid and relief workers from the airport into the city.[21] In subsequent months, UNPROFOR's mandate and size were enlarged to provide protection of humanitarian aid convoys throughout Bosnia. UN Security Council resolutions included a provision to use "all necessary means" to carry out this new mandate.[22]

The humanitarian mission in Bosnia nonetheless continued to be plagued by a number of problems, each of which hampered the relief effort.[23] First, UNPROFOR troop deployments in Bosnia never reached authorized levels. Moreover, the authorized levels constituted what UNPROFOR commanders in Bosnia believed to be a "light option." To protect convoys and safe areas, an additional 25,000 troops were believed to be necessary. Second, coordination between UNPROFOR (which was responsible for security operations) and UNHCR (which had responsibility for humanitarian efforts) was weak during the initial eighteen months

---

19. Rosalyn Higgins, "The New United Nations and Former Yugoslavia," *International Affairs*, Vol. 69, No. 3 (1993), p. 469.

20. UNHCR, *Information Notes on Former Yugoslavia*, No. 10/94 (Zagreb: Office of the Special Envoy for Former Yugoslavia, October 1994), p. 5. Unless otherwise stated, figures on humanitarian assistance are from this source.

21. S/RES/758 (1992), June 8, 1992; S/RES/761 (1992), June 29, 1992.

22. S/RES/110 (1992), August 13, 1992; S/RES/776 (1992); September 14, 1992.

23. U.S. General Accounting Office [U.S. GAO], *Humanitarian Intervention: Effectiveness of UN Operations in Bosnia*, GAO/NSIAD-94-156BR (Washington, D.C.: U.S. GAO, April 1994), appendix IV.

of the operation. It was not until January 1994 that a special representative arrived in the former Yugoslavia to take full control over the entire UN operation. Third, the operation lacked an overall plan for integrating humanitarian objectives with military support functions. As a result, UNHCR and UNPROFOR often worked at cross purposes.

Finally, the operation suffered from the fact that humanitarian assistance was regarded by the Serbs as a weapon in the ongoing war. This confronted UNPROFOR with a dilemma: on the one hand, strict neutrality was necessary to protect the convoys and UN forces; on the other hand, neutrality often meant acquiescence in the face of deliberate attempts to hold up convoys as a way of exerting pressure on besieged populations. Thus, UNPROFOR's commitment to impartiality often ended up aiding the strongest side in the conflict against the weaker.

A similar dilemma confronted the international community's second major effort to mitigate the humanitarian consequences of the conflict — providing protection to besieged populations. Protection came in two specific forms. The first consisted of the imposition of a no-fly zone over Bosnian airspace in October 1992 and coordination with NATO with respect to its enforcement; this was agreed upon in March 1993.[24] The second related to the protection of six safe areas around the cities of Sarajevo, Tuzla, Zepa, Gorazde, Bihac, and Srebrenica.[25] In both instances, the objective was to protect the civilian populations from direct air or heavy weapons attack. In principle, this should not have interfered with UNPROFOR's requirement to remain neutral in the conflict, a requirement imposed by its role as a protector of humanitarian convoys and other relief efforts. In practice, however, the protection function brought UN forces into direct conflict with Bosnian Serbs, for it was the latter who possessed the aircraft and heavy weapons that were being used against the (mostly Muslim) civilian population.

This significantly hampered and eventually undermined completely UNPROFOR's ability to implement its mandate. Although the no-fly zone was largely successful in halting direct attacks by fixed-wing aircraft, numerous violations occurred when Bosnian Serbs or JNA forces in Serbia used helicopters to resupply belligerent forces or transport troops to different battle fronts.[26] More problematic was the defense of safe areas. Even when not attacked directly, most safe areas remained surrounded by Bosnian Serb forces which allowed only a trickle of humanitarian aid

---

24. S/RES/781 (1992), October 9, 1992; S/RES/816 (1993), March 31, 1993.

25. S/RES/824 (1993), May 6, 1993; S/RES/836 (1993), June 3, 1993.

26. John Pomfret, "NATO, UN Squabble Over Bosnia," *Washington Post*, February 21, 1995, pp. A1, A12.

to reach civilians. And when safe areas were attacked directly, the United Nations had to choose between calling in NATO air strikes and thus in essence becoming a party to the war, and attempting to maintain its neutrality and the safety of the peacekeeping force by acquiescing and seeking to mediate an end to the attack.

At the outset, the United Nations, prodded by the North Atlantic Treaty Organization (NATO), took a stern approach, hoping to demonstrate the viability of the safe areas. In February 1994, NATO issued a stern ultimatum demanding the establishment of a 20-kilometer heavy weapons exclusion zone around Sarajevo. The threat of NATO airpower worked: within weeks, heavy weapons were withdrawn from the exclusion zone or placed in collection sites under UN control. However, similar action was not forthcoming in November 1994, when Bosnian and Croatian Serbs challenged the Bihac safe area. Following limited NATO airstrikes, the Serbs called UNPROFOR's and NATO's bluff by threatening retaliation against UN forces (hundreds of whom were taken hostage) and deploying sophisticated air defense systems designed to deter NATO airstrikes. Having learned a lesson in Bihac, Bosnian Serbs moved five months later to challenge the UN's authority in Sarajevo by removing weapons from the UN collection sites and recommencing the shelling of the Bosnian capital. NATO airstrikes were followed by the taking of UN hostages, which led the United Nations and NATO to desist. Although additional British, French, and Dutch peacekeepers were deployed in Bosnia, the United Nations made explicit what had been implicit for months: it would not act with force to protect the safe areas, and it would operate in Bosnia only with the consent of all warring parties, including the Serbs, or else it would withdraw all forces from the country.[27] Consequently, the Bosnian Serbs attacked and captured the Eastern Bosnian enclaves of Srebrenica and Zepa in July 1995.

The failure to protect the safe areas was a clear demonstration of the fundamental contradiction underlying international involvement in the former Yugoslavia. Its principal aim was to mitigate the very real and terrible human consequences of the wars in the former Yugoslavia. But these efforts inevitably clashed with the requirements to stand up to aggression and the virulent nationalism that was the driving force behind

---

27. In late May 1995, UN Secretary-General Boutros Boutros-Ghali expressed his preference for revising the UNPROFOR mandate, to include "maintaining a presence in the safe areas, after negotiating appropriate regimes for them but without any actual or implied commitment to use force to deter attacks against them." UN Security Council, *Report of the Secretary-General Pursuant to Security Council Resolutions 982 (1995) and 987 (1995)*, S/1195/444 (May 30, 1995), para. 78. See also John Pomfret, "U.N. Restricts Troops' Enforcement in Bosnia," *Washington Post*, June 11, 1995, p. A27.

these wars. In a very real sense, efforts to mitigate the humanitarian consequences of the war in Bosnia prevented effective international efforts to deal with Serb aggression. The conflict therefore continued unabated, leaving more human suffering in its wake.

COUNTERING AGGRESSION

Aggression that succeeds has at least two pernicious consequences. First, it denies the victims of aggression their legitimate rights. Second, it sets an example that others with similarly aggressive designs are more inclined to follow. Even when the interest in averting the first of these consequences is not vital, the major powers have a strategic interest in ensuring that the second does not happen. This is why distant powers have an overriding interest in ensuring that aggression does not pay. With respect to the former Yugoslavia, the point was well stated by U.S. Secretary of State Warren Christopher in the Clinton administration's first formal pronouncement on the crisis in February 1995:

The continuing destruction of a new UN member state challenges the principle that internationally recognized borders should not be altered by force. . . . Bold tyrants and fearful minorities are watching to see whether 'ethnic cleansing' is a policy the world will tolerate. If we hope to promote the spread of freedom or if we hope to encourage the emergence of peaceful multi-ethnic democracies, our answer must be a resounding no.[28]

Identifying the interests at stake is one thing, acting on them is quite another. That is where the international community as a whole — and its major members in particular — have utterly failed. Except for intensive diplomatic efforts, no steps were taken to address the causes of the conflict until nearly a year after the breakup of Yugoslavia. Admittedly, as long as Yugoslavia was still formally recognized as a single, independent state, international law placed constraints on international action. But Serb actions were an undeniable threat to international peace and security, with refugees flowing across borders, aircraft violating the airspace of neighbors (and even bombing foreign territory), the imminent possibility of outside involvement in support of ethnic minorities, and gross violations of international humanitarian law. Yet, international action was limited to placing an arms embargo on Yugoslavia and urging a diplomatic settlement. When the Croat-Serb cease-fire was negotiated,

---

28. Warren Christopher, "New Steps Toward Conflict Resolution in the Former Yugoslavia," opening statement at a news conference, Washington, D.C., February 10, 1992. Reprinted in *Dispatch*, Vol. 4, No. 7 (February 15, 1993), p. 81.

a UN peacekeeping force was deployed with the consent of all parties concerned.

It was only after the war had spread to Bosnia, and three new member states (Slovenia, Croatia, and Bosnia) had been admitted to the United Nations, that the international community took its first and only action to punish Serbia. On May 30, 1992, the UN Security Council passed Resolution 757, imposing a complete economic embargo on Serbia and Montenegro. Thereafter, the Security Council passed numerous resolutions designed to counter specific Serb actions, including mandating the protection of aid convoys by UNPROFOR, using "all necessary means" if needed; establishing a no-fly zone over Bosnia's airspace and authorizing its enforcement by NATO; and deterring attacks on six safe areas, also to be enforced by NATO. But, as the earlier discussion made clear, the effectiveness of these measures was highly questionable, and the Bosnia Serbs (with full support from Belgrade) flouted each at will.

INSTITUTIONAL BUCK-PASSING.   Instead of a concerted international response to Serb aggression, international powers engaged in an elaborate game of institutional buck-passing. With no one country willing to take the lead, it was left to security institutions to try to prove their worth in Europe's first post–Cold War crisis. The CSCE, which only months before the outbreak of the crisis in Yugoslavia had boldly proclaimed, "A New Era of Democracy, Peace, and Unity" at its Paris summit meeting, was prevented by its requirement to make decisions by consensus to take any effective action.[29] As a result, the CSCE was quickly relegated to the sidelines, having to satisfy itself with a minor monitoring role.

The European Community eagerly seized on the crisis to prove its new-found relevance, boldly proclaiming at the outset that "this is the hour of Europe."[30] The moment was short-lived. Some success was achieved in Slovenia, where the EC brokered the Brioni Agreement, though this reflected Belgrade's disinterest in restraining Ljubljana rather

---

29. *The Charter of Paris for a New Europe*, adopted by the Heads of State and Government of the Conference on Security and Cooperation in Europe, Paris, November 1990. In response to the Yugoslav crisis, the CSCE adopted a "consensus minus-one" policy in which the organization could act against any state that had engaged in gross violations of CSCE principles. Even so, effective CSCE action was continually frustrated by Russian support for the Serb position.

30. Statement by Luxembourg's Foreign Minister, Jacques Poos, chairman of the EC Council of Foreign Ministers following a meeting on the Yugoslav crisis. Cited in Alan Riding, "European Leaders Seek Common Line on Crisis," *New York Times*, June 29, 1991, p. 4.

than European diplomatic clout. The same could not be said for EC actions in Croatia, where it failed to halt the fighting. Lacking a credible military capability (and being divided over whether national forces should be employed), the EC's diplomatic efforts accomplished little.[31]

The United Nations only reluctantly interceded in late 1991 in a conflict its Secretary-General was to characterize as a "rich man's war."[32] In Croatia, the United Nations succeeded in brokering a cease-fire, but not a permanent settlement to the conflict. The deployment of UN troops therefore did little more than freeze the territorial status quo. And like the European Community, the United Nations ignored developments in Bosnia in early 1992. When war erupted there in April, it was slow to respond; once it did, the emphasis was on humanitarian relief rather than peace enforcement. By 1995, UNPROFOR had been largely discredited.

NATO was the one institutional actor that could have intervened forcefully at any time in the conflict. Some had urged it to do so well before the crisis erupted in the summer of 1991.[33] But without strong U.S. engagement, NATO was little more than a larger and less-united European Community, and for the first time in four decades Washington decided not to play an active role in a European crisis. It was a fateful decision, leaving the one organization with real clout completely on the sidelines.[34] Only when the United States showed an interest in the conflict did NATO accept a role — primarily as the means to enforce a number of Security Council resolutions. But the U.S. absence from the scene, combined with the very tentative nature of the Clinton administration's engagement, ensured that NATO's role would be subordinated to that of the United Nations. The result was tactical confusion and inaction.

The involvement of regional and other security institutions in the former Yugoslavia was driven by a desire to demonstrate their relevance and credibility. But their involvement did precisely the opposite: it

---

31. See the conclusion of Dutch Foreign Minister Hans van den Broek, who led the EC's efforts in the second half of 1991, in the preface to Wijnaendts, *Joegoslavische Kroniek.*

32. This quote is cited in David Rieff, *Slaughterhouse: Bosnia and the Failure of the West* (New York: Simon and Schuster, 1995), p. 24.

33. See Jonathan Dean, *Ending Europe's Wars: The Continuing Search for Peace and Security* (New York: Twentieth Century Fund, 1994), pp. 132–133.

34. David Gompert, Senior Director for European Affairs on the National Security Council staff in the Bush administration, admitted that this decision totally contradicted the administration's insistence that NATO should stand at the center of European security. See Gompert, "How to Defeat Serbia," *Foreign Affairs,* Vol. 73, No. 4 (July/August 1994), p. 36.

showed how utterly irrelevant and devoid of credibility each had become. However, this was not a failure of institutions, which merely reflect the wishes of their members. The one common thread running through all international efforts in the former Yugoslavia was the refusal of the major Western powers to take the steps necessary to deal with this conflict in a decisive manner. It is the United States, Britain, France, and Germany — not the EC, UN, or NATO — that were reluctant to use force, and they must bear the blame for the failure to stand up to Serb aggression.

THE RELUCTANCE TO USE FORCE. Because of the profound changes in the international environment that have taken place since the end of the Cold War, the United States bears disproportionate responsibility for international decisions about the use of force because it possesses disproportionate power. Nowhere has the reluctance to resort to military means in the former Yugoslavia been greater than in the United States. The reasons for this can be found in two widely shared assumptions: first, that the United States does not have vital strategic interests at stake in the conflict; and, second, that the use of force in resolving internal conflicts is unlikely to be successful or at the very least too costly and risky to contemplate.

With the end of the Cold War, Yugoslavia's strategic importance to the United States had indeed been significantly reduced. Although it was once a symbol of independence in Eastern Europe, by the late 1980s Washington's principal concern was to urge Belgrade to reform and open up its political and economic systems as many of its neighbors were beginning to do. It was a message that the United States communicated directly to Belgrade as the crisis in Yugoslavia began to unfold.[35] Though internal developments in the Balkans remained a concern, they were not seen in Washington as being as vital as developments in other parts of Eastern Europe, which was being released from the Soviet yoke. Yugoslavia would remain important, but it no longer was of strategic interest to the United States. Therefore, when developments turned sour, the United States was reluctant to get involved.

This reluctance was strengthened by the prevailing dogma in Washington concerning the use of force.[36] The Vietnam experience, reinforced by the military misadventure in Lebanon in 1982–84, had left many U.S. citizens uneasy about using force in internal conflicts. The prevailing military doctrine emphasized decisive use of overwhelming force, clear

---

35. Warren Zimmermann, "The Last Ambassador," *Foreign Affairs*, Vol. 74, No. 2 (March/April 1995), p. 2.

36. For further discussion of these issues, see my chapter on the United States and military intervention in this volume.

and attainable military objectives, agreed measures of success to allow for an early exit, and the overriding importance of public support. The first three of these requirements were difficult to achieve in the confusing circumstances of internal war, while the last underlined the importance of using force only when vital interests were at stake. The 1991 war in the Persian Gulf was a textbook confirmation of the doctrine's apparent soundness. Few in the Bush administration or, indeed, elsewhere in Washington, were willing to become involved in a Balkan conflict that was unlikely to be decisive or where casualties could not be easily held to a minimum. Still fewer advocated the deployment of hundreds of thousands of troops, which the U.S. military deemed necessary to bring an end to the fighting in Yugoslavia. Nor was there much support for relying on air strikes, which were judged to be ineffective and the first step towards a long-term engagement involving U.S. ground forces.

Without U.S. military involvement, Western Europeans were unwilling to use force on their own. Indeed, the absence of a U.S. ground presence in the former Yugoslavia undermined Washington's ability to forge agreement with its allies on the limited use of air power. At the same time, Washington's lack of engagement provided many European countries with a convenient excuse to eschew measures they themselves did not want to take.

Britain's experience in Cyprus and, more important, in Northern Ireland, made London extremely reluctant to deploy forces in Yugoslavia. British opposition squelched a plan, proposed by France, Germany, and the Netherlands, to deploy a 30,000-strong interposition force in Croatia in the fall of 1991. Britain only agreed to deploy forces as part of UNPROFOR on the condition that the United States would not call for air strikes.[37]

On a rhetorical level, France was more willing to contemplate forceful military action than Britain, but it had few allies once Britain and the United States refused to go along. Once French troops were actually on the ground as part of UNPROFOR, concern for their safety came to dominate Paris's strategic calculations. With its forces essentially held hostage, France, like Britain, opposed air strikes to punish Serb behavior. France accepted a NATO enforcement role only because the decision to use air power was shared under a dual arrangement with the UN command in the former Yugoslavia, which France and Britain, as UNPROFOR's largest contributors, effectively dominated.

---

37. Gompert, "How to Defeat Serbia," p. 38.

Germany dodged responsibility by erecting constitutional barriers to military involvement and hiding behind its historical guilt.

THE CONSEQUENCES OF INACTION. Given the risks and costs associated with the use of military force, a reluctance to use force is understandable. However, inaction also involves risks and costs, and it is not clear that these were weighed equally in this case. The most important and immediate consequence of not using force in the former Yugoslavia was the unintended encouragement of the Serbs to continue with their aggressive behavior. While no one knows for certain whether a credible threat to use force at an early stage in the conflict might have deterred Belgrade and its regional allies, its absence can only have encouraged them to continue forcefully acquiring large swaths of territory. It is also clear in retrospect — and it was evident to many at the time — that the occasions for threatening or using force during the first year of the conflict were numerous, and that the failure to act firmly left precious few options for resolving the conflict in a manner that did not reward Serb gains.

The best, although the most unlikely, moment to act was before the breakup of Yugoslavia in early 1991. At the time, the shared Western goal was to promote both unity and democracy in Yugoslavia, and the United States was well aware that the disintegration of Yugoslavia would probably be violent.[38] Throughout the first half of 1991, the United States clearly told all parties concerned that it would oppose both unilateral secession and the use of force, a message that U.S. Secretary of State James Baker delivered personally in June. But the consequences of taking either action were never spelled out.

The result was an ambiguous policy that encouraged Serbia to oppose the Slovenian and Croatian declarations of independence.[39] Although the European Community eagerly sought to play a central role in the Yugoslav drama, it emphasized Yugoslav unity and political solutions in its initial discussions with the parties and ignored efforts to counter the brazen use of force. Lawrence Eagleburger (then Baker's deputy) and Brent Scowcroft (then Bush's national security adviser) have come to

---

38. An October 1990 Central Intelligence Agency estimate predicted the violent breakup of Yugoslavia within the next eighteen months and pointed to Milosevic as the main culprit. The estimate was widely read within the Bush administration and shared with the European allies, most of whom dismissed it. See David Binder, "Yugoslavia Seen Breaking Up Soon," *New York Times*, November 28, 1990, p. A7; Don Oberdorfer, "A Bloody Failure in the Balkans," *Washington Post*, February 8, 1993, pp. A1, A14; Gompert, "How to Defeat Serbia," pp. 32–34.

39. Zimmermann, "The Last Ambassador," p. 11.

believe that this focus was misplaced. Both now maintain that a clear threat to use force might have pushed the republics to come to a political solution.[40] However, it was Eagleburger and Scowcroft — the administration's experts on Yugoslavia — who strongly opposed any U.S. involvement at the time.

The second opportunity for using force came during the Serb siege of Vukovar and the offshore bombardment of Dubrovnik. Starting in August 1991 and for three months thereafter, the JNA surrounded the city of Vukovar and shelled it from a safe distance. Some 2,000 civilians were killed as a result. In October, the ancient town of Dubrovnik was shelled from the surrounding hills and ships at sea, flattening whole sections of the town. These were war crimes, yet no international power proposed to intervene. NATO's Supreme Commander, General John Galvin, had prepared contingency plans for NATO action and, following his retirement, stated that NATO intervention could have succeeded in silencing the Serb guns.[41] The failure to intervene, however, further emboldened the Serbs. Having set the precedent in Croatia, the Serbs mercilessly shelled cities in Bosnia, including Sarajevo, where in less than two years 9,000 people were killed and 57,000 wounded.[42]

If outside intervention in the Serb-Croatian war was unlikely, given the EC's lead role and the U.S. decision to abstain from involvement, the same cannot be said for the war in Bosnia. In fact, the failure to intervene in the early stages of the war in Bosnia may well have been the major powers' greatest mistake. Preoccupied with negotiating a cease-fire in Croatia in late 1991 and early 1992, the Western countries failed to act when the EC's recognition of Croatian and Slovenian independence in early 1992 placed Bosnia in jeopardy. That recognition was a mistake is now evident to all, except Germany, which forced the diplomatic pace.[43] But once recognition was extended the consequences of this act should have been clearly understood. Bosnian President Izetbegovic had repeatedly warned that Croatia's independence would inevitably be followed

---

40. Michael Kelly, "Surrender and Blame," *New Yorker*, December 19, 1994, p. 45.

41. Statement by General John Galvin (Ret.) in U.S. House Armed Services Committee, *The Policy Implications of U.S. Involvement in Bosnia*, 103d Cong., 1st sess., May 25, 1993, pp. 5, 19–20.

42. General John Shalikashvili in U.S. Senate Armed Services Committee, *Briefing on Bosnia and Other Current Military Operations*, 103d Cong., 2nd sess., February 23, 1994, p. 11.

43. For a defense of German policy, see German Foreign Ministry, "Recognition of the Yugoslav Successor States," *Statements and Speeches*, German Information Center, New York, Vol. 16, No. 10 (March 10, 1993).

by a Bosnian decision to secede from Yugoslavia. He also repeatedly asked for the deployment of UN troops in Bosnia as a preventive measure. Even after recognition was extended to Croatia, the United Nations rejected his request.[44] But the failure was not the UN's alone. The United States, while opposing the EC's move toward recognition of Croatia and Slovenia in part because of its consequences for Bosnia, did not support a UN deployment and neither did any of the other permanent members of the UN Security Council. This was a tragic mistake. Although a deployment might not have prevented the war that followed, its absence virtually guaranteed that fighting would occur.[45]

A final moment when force could have and should have been used came after the August 1992 EC International Conference on the Former Yugoslavia in London, which took place following the first published reports that concentration camps had been established in Bosnia. The conference produced a series of documents and pledges, all signed by the Serb delegation, that included agreements to end the siege of cities, place heavy weapons under international control, disarm regular and irregular forces, halt military flights, deploy monitors along Bosnia's borders with Serbia and Montenegro, allow unhindered passage for humanitarian relief convoys, return refugees to their own homes, and close detention camps. In the days and weeks following the conference, however, the Serbs ignored every commitment they had made. The Western response was to intensify the negotiations in Geneva and to extend the mandate of UNPROFOR to include protection of humanitarian relief efforts. There was no threat, implied or otherwise, to deter Serb violations. Washington continued to resist military involvement in the region, in part because of the 1992 election campaign and in part because the political leadership deferred to its military advisers, who cautioned that limited air strikes would inevitably drag the United States further into the conflict.[46] Other countries were willing to deploy military forces as part of the UNPRO-

---

44. Wijnaendts, *Joegoslavische Kroniek*, p. 153; Zimmerman, "The Last Ambassador," p. 15.

45. Although the United Nations rejected preventive deployments in early 1992, in part because peacekeepers had traditionally been deployed only after, not before, a conflict, the Secretary-General identified preventive deployments as important components of his newly formulated belief in preventive diplomacy in June 1992. See Boutros Boutros-Ghali, *An Agenda for Peace: Preventive Diplomacy, Peacemaking, and Peace-Keeping* (New York: United Nations, 1992).

46. Some military officials even thought it necessary to go public with their arguments. See, for example, Michael R. Gordon, "Powell Delivers a Resounding No On Using Limited Force in Bosnia," *New York Times*, September 28, 1992, pp. A1, A5; Colin Powell, "Why Generals Get Nervous," *New York Times*, October 8, 1992, p. A35.

FOR, but only to help deliver humanitarian assistance. When British, French and other troops arrived to carry out the UN mandate, the opportunity to use force against the Serbs had effectively passed. Fearing for the safety of their troops, the contributing countries vetoed any attempt to use force. They had become hostages and the Serbs had gotten away with their ill-begotten gains.

Aside from allowing the Serbs to achieve their objectives, the Western failure to use force had other negative consequences. First, this failure reduced the credibility of subsequent threats to use force. This became evident in November 1994, when the Serbs blatantly defied NATO and UN threats to use air power in defense of the Bihac safe area. Six months later, the Serbs responded to NATO air strikes by taking hundreds of UN peacekeepers hostage and shooting down a U.S. aircraft. Rather than responding with greater force, the United Nations abandoned enforcement as a means of fulfilling its mandate. This led to the Serb takeover of Srebrenica and Zepa in July 1995.

Finally, the failure to counter Serb aggression may have implications for conflicts in other parts of the world. If Western powers were unwilling to stand up to aggression in the middle of Europe despite the immense carnage the war caused, are aggressors elsewhere likely to be deterred in the future by the threat of international intervention? Although one should not carry this argument too far, it is equally unwise to discount the perceptions of others regarding U.S., European, and international willingness to act. If action speaks louder than words, so does inaction. Indeed, it was concerns about creating such a perception that propelled the Clinton administration to intervene in Haiti.[47] It is also the reason why the administration finally did move, in August 1995, to seek an end to the conflict in Bosnia.

Conclusions

International involvement in the former Yugoslavia has been marked by considerable confusion, reflecting a lack of will to take the steps necessary to address the underlying causes of the conflict and significant disagree-

---

47. Among the reasons for the Haitian intervention in September 1994, Anthony Lake listed first "the essential reliability of the United States and the international community. Having exhausted all other remedies, we must make it clear that we mean what we say. Our actions in Haiti will send a message far beyond our region — to all who seriously threaten our interests." Anthony Lake, "The Purpose of American Power," address to the Council on Foreign Relations, Washington, D.C., September 12, 1994, reprinted in *Dispatch*, Vol. 5, No. 38, September 19, 1994, p. 623.

ment on which goal — containment, meeting humanitarian needs, or punishing aggression — should have priority. As a result, the major powers adopted a minimalist approach to the conflict, emphasizing short-term humanitarian assistance over long-term strategic considerations. Indeed, the deployment of UN peacekeeping forces in Croatia and Bosnia was characterized more by a sense that the international community needed to "do something" than by a clear strategy for resolving the conflict.

Yugoslavia has broken apart; it cannot be put back together again. Although this certainly was not inevitable, once nationalism rather than the search for accommodation became the main form of political discourse among ambitious political leaders, keeping the country together became all but impossible. The violence that ensued was aggravated by specific historical experiences, occurring most notably during World War II, which became readily understood sources of motivation for engaging in the worst forms of behavior. Healing the wounds of war will take time, but there is nothing in Balkan history to suggest that these wounds cannot be healed in ways that recognize the distinctive political desires of different ethnic groups. That is why, when all is said and done, a *modus vivendi* will have to be found that combines independence for the constituent republics of the former Yugoslavia with a large degree of political autonomy for minority populations within these newly independent states.

Chapter 2

Peaceful Transformations in East-Central Europe

Milada Anna Vachudová

East-Central Europe has been a peaceful region in the post–Cold War era, despite the tremendous political, economic, and social changes that followed the overthrow of communist regimes in 1989.[1] Some internal problems, which might have led to violent conflict, have been resolved through political means; others, although unresolved, have not led to violence. The greatest threats to regional stability are attempts by former communists to turn nationalist sentiments against minorities. The extent and character of this risk vary widely from country to country.

An appreciation of three factors helps to explain why nationalism has played a dominant role in the politics of some states in the region, but not others: the prospects for economic prosperity, the nature of the regime change, and ethnic geography. One should distinguish between Poland, Hungary, and the Czech Republic — where aggressive nationalism has been marginalized — and Slovakia, Bulgaria and, most notably, Romania — where former communists have used nationalist appeals to win elections.

First, the level of economic prosperity in 1989, and the fate of economic reform since, are keys to explaining the appeal of nationalist politicians. The Czech Republic and Hungary, blessed with relative prosperity in 1989, are on the path toward steady economic growth thanks to marketizing reforms. Poland, despite very serious economic problems in

The author would like to thank Matthew Evangelista, Sharon Fisher, Charles King, John Matthews, Tim Snyder, Stephen Van Evera, and Kieran Williams for their insightful and helpful comments on an earlier draft.

1. For the purposes of this chapter, East-Central Europe is said to include Poland, the Czech Republic, Hungary, Slovakia, Bulgaria, and Romania, although the latter two are traditionally considered part of Southeastern Europe or the Balkans.

1989, has managed through radical reform to join the Czech Republic and Hungary in the region's economic vanguard. Romania and Bulgaria, by contrast, struggled in 1989 with the most impoverished economies of the region; since 1989, incomplete and halting reforms have brought great hardship without accomplishing a systematic transition to the free market. Slovakia sits between these two groups: its economy is growing, but its commitment to reform wavers.

Second, the nature of the regime changes that took place during and after 1989 determined in large measure whether nationalists were blocked from politics, and whether comprehensive economic reforms were implemented. In Poland, Hungary, and the Czech lands, opposition leaders took power in 1989, and effected a fundamental economic and political transformation. Their governments set the parameters of political debate, marginalizing nationalist and extremist parties. They initiated comprehensive economic reforms which were legitimized by their association with the democratic revolution. The election of former communist parties in Poland (1993) and Hungary (1994) did not change this basic equation. These parties had been forced to reform by the weight of opposition before 1989 and by the need to compete with strong post-opposition parties since 1989. In states which had lacked a strong opposition to communist rule — Slovakia, Bulgaria, and Romania — moderate democrats were shunted aside by former communists, who were able to use nationalism to forge new political identities and thereby convince voters that they were legitimate participants in the new democratic polity. These post-communist nationalists lacked both the will and the political capital to implement ambitious economic reforms.

Third, although history has simplified the ethnic geography of East-Central Europe, large minority populations remain in several states. While Poland, the Czech Republic, and Hungary are relatively homogeneous, a cohesive ethnic minority forms about ten percent of the populations of Slovakia, Bulgaria, and Romania. In these latter three states, post-communist nationalists have manipulated popular prejudices against minorities to bolster their political positions. They have been successful because minorities are large; because history lends credibility to assertions that minorities harbor separatist agendas; and because minorities have formed effective political organizations. These organizations have responded by seeking to define and protect their collective rights. When this response takes the form of calls for territorial autonomy, minorities become easy targets for nationalists and difficult allies for moderates.

Despite the importance of ethnic politics in some states, there has as yet been no large-scale, violent conflict in East-Central Europe. The peacefulness of the region stands in sharp contrast to the violence which has accompanied the dissolution of Yugoslavia. Nevertheless, external powers have become substantially implicated in the internal affairs of these six states in two ways. First, the rights of minorities have been championed both by neighboring states and by European institutions. Second, Western states and institutions have provided various forms of concrete assistance (financial and advisory), new markets for trade (if limited by protectionism), models to imitate (prosperous constitutional democracies), and goals to strive for (membership in Western institutions).

As East-Central European states depend upon trade with the West, and as they seek membership in Western institutions, Western influence in the region has been considerable. It is beginning to wane, however, as a result of continuing Western protectionism and the lack of timetables for admission to the North Atlantic Treaty Organization (NATO) and the European Union (EU). Western institutions such as the Council of Europe and the Organization for Security and Cooperation in Europe (OSCE, formerly CSCE, Conference on Security and Cooperation in Europe) have exerted a positive influence on East-Central European governments with respect to democratic standards and minority rights, but both organizations must be more consistent in their attention to abuses. The influence of the West on this question has been limited by a lack of agreement among Western states as to the character of minority rights.

After exploring the potential sources of conflict within East-Central Europe, I will evaluate their regional and international implications, and provide recommendations for regional and international actors.

Potential Sources of Internal Conflict

The potential sources of conflict in East-Central Europe have their roots in nationalism, particularly in the exploitation of national feeling by former communists. Differences in the regime changes in the region after 1989, the region's economies, and the region's ethnic geography help to explain why nationalism has dominated politics in some states but not in others.

ECONOMIC REFORM AND DEMOCRATIC LEGITIMACY

Since 1989, the six states of East-Central Europe have begun two fundamental transformations: from one-party states to pluralist democracies, and from centrally planned economies to free-market capitalism. Why has this difficult dual transition proceeded peacefully? The absence of social unrest and political violence is especially striking since many of the political conditions in these countries — weak state structures, immature party systems, uninformed electorates, ineffectual bureaucracies — have led to internal conflict in other states.

In post-revolutionary Poland, Hungary, and Czechoslovakia (and later in Bulgaria), power was transferred to pro-democracy organizations formed from groups which had opposed communist rule. After 1989, these opposition groups split, and numerous new parties joined post-communist parties in a burgeoning political spectrum. Romania was also flooded by new parties, as well as by groups that split from the major post-communist party. Despite the fragmentation of the former opposition, on the one hand, and the communist past of some parties, on the other, all important political parties have generally followed the rules of the democratic process. In all six countries, democratically elected presidents have at times risen above the fray of parliamentary politics to act as a stabilizing influence. A consensus prevails throughout the region that democracy, in conjunction with the free market, provides the only path to economic prosperity, symbolized by membership in the European Union.

After 1989, some Western analysts feared that authoritarian political forces would threaten the new democracies, as politicians responded to popular demands for state protection from the economic difficulties brought by marketizing reforms.[2] By this reasoning, economic depression would undermine democracy as populations called for a strong hand to shield them from the market. Although economic conditions have varied dramatically in East-Central Europe, widespread unrest resulting from economic hardship has been averted. Military elites, moreover, have accepted the authority of the new democratic regime in all six states. The consensus in favor of democracy and the free market has rendered important elements of these societies willing to endure the penury and insecurity of the transition. At the same time, post-communist state institutions have, to varying degrees, been effective in managing the process of economic adjustment to prevent destabilizing economic shocks.[3]

Nevertheless, important political risks remain, which demand a closer investigation of the region's economies. The nature of each state's economic problems provides the first indication that its polity will be dominated by nationalism. Poland, the Czech Republic, and Hungary are the

---

2. See, for example, Ralf Dahrendorf, *Reflections on the Revolutions in Europe* (London: Chatto and Windus, 1990); J.F. Brown, *Hopes and Shadows: Eastern Europe After Communism* (Durham, N.C.: Duke University Press, 1994), pp. 7–9.

3. Jack Snyder, "Nationalism and the Crisis of the Post-Soviet State," in Michael E. Brown, ed., *Ethnic Conflict and International Security* (Princeton, N.J.: Princeton University Press, 1993), p. 90.

East-Central Europe.

region's economic success stories, while Bulgaria and Romania are struggling to end steep declines in production. Slovakia lies in between. The character of economic reform in these states has depended on the legitimacy of the first post-communist government; the distinct economic problems of each state; and the attributes of the left-wing alternative available to populations disillusioned with the market.

In 1989, Poland had been in a state of economic crisis for over a decade. The first post-communist government therefore believed it had no alternative but to embrace radical economic reform. Political leaders were able to implement arduous reforms only because they had strong democratic credibility. Poland's partially free elections in spring 1989 made possible the formation of a mixed Solidarity-communist government that August. Solidarity had been by far the largest and most effective opposition group in Eastern Europe, and its ministers were able to persuade the public to accept painful economic changes. Although Solidarity had originally been formed in response to price increases by the communist regime, Poles generally accepted the new democratic leaders even as they freed prices and presided over a sharp drop in the standard of living. Economic reform was legitimized by its association with the democratic revolution.

The Czechs and the Hungarians were in a more favorable position in 1989: their small but vital anti-communist movements produced respected leaders with solid democratic credentials, who could convince the population of the need for economic reform. Meanwhile, their economies were sufficiently prosperous to allow for gradual reform, rather than shock therapy. Romania, Bulgaria, and Slovakia (after its creation on January 1, 1993) fared worse on both fronts. Their relatively weak economies demanded radical reform, but they lacked opposition movements with either the will or the credentials to push through a Polish-style marketizing program.

PROSPERITY AND PENURY. Although East-Central Europe passed through a period of declining production and consumption between 1990 and 1993, in 1994 all six states experienced some economic growth. As a result of two broad factors — the level of economic prosperity in 1989 and the implementation and success of comprehensive marketizing reforms — some states are faring much better than others. The Czech Republic has managed to keep unemployment and inflation down while balancing its budget and preserving its relatively high gross national product (GNP) per capita ($2,800 in 1994). Poland, with a GNP per capita of $2,400 in 1994, has been propelled into the region's first rank by its early embrace of radical reforms: in 1993, Poland's growth rate of 5 percent was the highest in Europe, and the Polish economy grew by about the same rate in 1994. Hungary (with a GNP per capita of $3,450) is relatively prosperous, but like Poland, it has experienced high unemployment (about 16 percent and 11 percent, respectively). Hungary is also the region's most profligate state; its large budget deficits cost it the favor of the International Monetary Fund (IMF) and forced it to adopt an austerity program in 1994. The Czech Republic, Poland, and Hungary have had the most success in reorienting their foreign trade from east to west.

Slovakia, with a GNP per capita of $1,950, has fared much better than expected during the first two years of its existence, and its 12 percent inflation and 4 percent growth in 1994 are encouraging. Still, Slovakia joins Bulgaria and Romania as the states which have yet to implement large-scale privatization. Both Bulgaria ($1,180 GNP per capita) and Romania ($1,100 GNP per capita), which are the region's poorest countries, saw their economies shrink by about 10 percent per year from 1989 to 1992. Both economies are now growing at a very modest rate. Inflation was high in 1994: 70 percent in Romania, and 120 percent in Bulgaria.[4]

COMMUNISTS, REFORMED AND OTHERWISE. In 1993 and 1994 left-wing parties were elected in Poland, Hungary, Slovakia, and Bulgaria, with a mandate to check the social repercussions of the free market (though not to reverse the course of economic reforms). One must, however, distinguish among these post-communist parties in order to appreciate the importance of this development for the future of reform.

The character of the communist party during communism's last decade is the key to explaining the nature of the left-wing alternative available to electorates weary of economic reform. The Polish and Hungarian communist parties had made attempts at internal reform in the 1980s, and a few modernizers had sought to move their comrades in the direction of Western European social democracy. This internal debate was both a response to and a catalyst for strong domestic opposition to communist rule. By 1989, these communist parties had groomed future social democrats and even conservative liberals: politicians who — despite their communist pasts — had become constructive and credible actors on the democratic political scene. This helps to explain the relative ease with which certain post-communist parties have become social democratic parties akin to those of Western Europe.[5]

4. Philippe Lemarchand, ed., *L'Europe Centrale et Balkanique* (Paris: Editions Complex, 1995); Ben Slay, "East European Economies," *Transition*, Vol. 1, No. 1 (January 30, 1995), pp. 68–72.

5. See Timothy Garton Ash, "Neo-Pagan Poland," *New York Review of Books*, Vol. 43,

The Romanian, Bulgarian, and Czechoslovak communist parties, however, allowed virtually no internal debate and undertook no internal reform in the 1980s. This partly explains why the Czech communist party has played an insignificant role on the Czech political scene since 1989. The success of Czechoslovak (and, after 1992, Czech) economic reforms has also helped to marginalize the communists. In any event, Czechs who seek to slow the pace of economic reform have a non-communist alternative in the Social Democrats. This also helps to explain why the former communist parties in power in Romania and Bulgaria in 1995 tend to have less respect for democracy and less interest in economic reform. Unlike the Czechs, Romanian and Bulgarian voters who seek protection from the market have no strong left-wing alternative to post-communist nationalists. In Bulgaria and Romania, economic problems have helped the least reconstructed of the region's post-communist parties to gain power, and it is these parties which seek to blame economic problems on ethnic minorities.

POST-COMMUNIST PARTIES AND NATIONALIST POLITICS

The advent of democracy in East-Central Europe has created an upsurge of nationalist appeals: democratic political competition accompanied by difficult economic restructuring created a tempting opportunity to use nationalism in a bid for legitimacy and political power.

Whether the nationalist ticket to power was successful depended in large measure on the presence or absence of a strong pro-democracy movement. In the first democratic elections, electorates sought to vote against the communist regime. In places where a strong pro-democracy movement had existed (Poland, Hungary, and the Czech lands), umbrella pro-democracy groups were elected. Although their leaders were patriots who appealed to national symbols, they generally governed without recourse to intolerance or chauvinism. Typically, these new politicians had spent years as dissidents, contemplating the transformation of their state into a democracy and its reintegration into the West. Once in power, they hastened to create democratic institutions and to reshape the parameters of political discourse to Western standards. Extremist parties did appear, but were marginalized.

In states where no effective opposition movement existed (Romania, Bulgaria, and Slovakia), electorates voted for former communists who sought to distinguish themselves from the communist regime by way of

No. 1 (January 11, 1996), pp. 10–14; Thomas W. Simons, Jr., *Eastern Europe in the Postwar World* (New York: St. Martin's, 1991), pp. 193–200.

nationalist gestures. Nationalism served as a political shortcut: former communist parties offering nationalist rhetoric rather than coherent reform programs succeeded in attracting uninformed voters who felt threatened by political and economic change. This is not as strange as it may appear: Slovak communism was associated with emancipation from Czech tutelage, and the Romanian and Bulgarian communist parties tried to promote national unity by discriminating against ethnic minorities. By using a more openly articulated nationalism to forge a new image and thus to manipulate the electorate after 1989, traditional elites in these three states remained in or regained power. Even though former communists behaved more or less like democratic politicians, they had neither the vision nor the will to transform the state, and they lacked the political capital to launch intensive economic reform. Instead, as they drew on nationalist rhetoric to re-legitimize themselves as political actors, they infused the political culture of the state with nationalism. Opposition parties had to take up nationalist rhetoric in order to compete on the emerging political scene.

Six years after the collapse of communist regimes, a clear connection is visible between states where members of the communist establishment never (or only briefly) relinquished control, and the prevalence of ethnic nationalism. The democratic redefinition of the state, which took place under the aegis of former dissidents, conferred on state institutions a new legitimacy and marginalized extreme nationalism. The former communists who govern in Hungary and Poland in 1995 are different in one essential respect from their Bulgarian and Romanian counterparts: they do not need to resort to ethnic nationalism to establish their new political identity. In fact, they are the alternatives to more patriotic parties in the former opposition. They won elections not on the issue of nationalism, but on the defining issue of Western political competition: the economy. This distinction is not absolute: Romanian, Bulgarian, and Slovak elections are also fought on economic issues, but in these states nationalist overtones are far more audible. Lacking the experience of intra-party debate and of competition with democratic oppositions both before and after 1989, former communists in Romania, Bulgaria, and Slovakia have relied on the language of national unity. Precisely because their break with the communist past is less pronounced, former communists in these states are forced to justify their renewed rule in explicitly nationalist terms. In Slovakia and Romania, post-communist leaders have accepted alliances with extreme nationalists in order to retain power. In the context of economic difficulties, the election of post-communist nationalists has caused problems for ethnic minorities in Slovakia, Bulgaria, and Romania.

NATIONS AND STATES

The potential problems created by nationalist politics in East-Central Europe are for the most part limited to relations between national governments and minority ethnic groups. The inter-state boundaries inherited in 1989 are considered legitimate and inviolable by East-Central European governments, which are generally unmoved by territorial claims based on history or myth. Ethnic minorities in the region have not struggled for independence, and national diasporas have not sought inclusion in a neighboring co-ethnic state. In sum, the acceptance of existing political boundaries by governments and ethnic minorities alike has greatly diminished the scope for nationalist confrontation in East-Central Europe. This attitude, so different from the revanchism and petty imperialism which characterized the region between the world wars, deserves an explanation.

RESPECT FOR BORDERS. The interwar period is well and truly buried in East-Central Europe — or rather, it is as buried in Poland, Romania, and Hungary as it is in France, Italy, and Germany. The postwar era brought the notion of "Western Europe" — a collection of interwar democracies, fascist dictatorships, and authoritarian regimes which, by way of U.S. aid and unprecedented cooperation, have become robust democracies — as well as "Eastern Europe" — a collection of one interwar democracy and several authoritarian regimes which were subjected to wholesale changes in borders, massive migrations of populations, and two generations of Stalinist social engineering. "Eastern Europe's" traditional social structures were transformed after World War II: aristocracies were flattened, peasant populations were educated and urbanized, and new working classes and technical intelligentsias were created. At the same time, a growing awareness (especially in the 1970s and 1980s) of the success of "Western Europe" led to an incomplete but nevertheless important assimilation of certain "Western" values.

Since East-Central European societies have been so thoroughly transformed, one must not assume that interwar political preoccupations (such as revanchism) will reappear now that communist rule has ended. There are several other reasons why the general attitude towards the legitimacy of borders has changed. First, the origins of World War II taught Europe a searing lesson about the dangers of territorial revanchism. East-Central European leaders understand that a "favorable" change in the postwar settlement could create an "unfavorable" one. Poles who look nostalgically towards Wilno (Vilnius) know that they have German counterparts who dream of Breslau (Wroclaw). East-Central European leaders are also sensitive to changed attitudes in the West. No contemporary revanchist leader would find a champion, as interwar Hungary and Bulgaria found in Nazi Germany and fascist Italy. Instead, Western aid and support are now linked to respect for existing borders.

There are some partial exceptions, but these tend to confirm the general rule. Romanians believe that merger with Moldova is inevitable, but no Romanian government has challenged the Moldovan state's right to exist. Similarly, although most Bulgarians do not believe that Macedonians constitute a separate nationality, the Bulgarian state recognized the Macedonian state and Bulgarian leaders have disavowed any territorial claims on Macedonia.[6] The Slovaks are the only true exception, in that they have obtained independence from the Czechs. The peaceful dissolution of Czechoslovakia removed the only pressing border question in the region.

HISTORY AND ETHNIC GEOGRAPHY. The final reason why contemporary borders are generally accepted in East-Central Europe is that World War II and the postwar settlements profoundly simplified the ethnic geography of the region. After World War I, Poland was recreated from formerly German, Austrian, and Russian territories. A new state, Czechoslovakia, was formed from the Czech lands (Bohemia and Moravia), Slovakia, and part of Ruthenia; a Czechoslovak "nationality" was needed to create a unitary state in which 3 million ethnic Germans would clearly be in the minority.[7] Romania gained lands ceded by Austria, Russia, Bulgaria, and Hungary. Bulgaria lost access to the Aegean Sea. Hungary was forced to cede two-thirds of its territory to Romania, Czechoslovakia, and Yugoslavia. One-third of all Hungarians, some 5 million in all, suddenly found themselves outside of Hungary's borders. On the eve of World War II, Hungary seized much of its lost territory with the assistance of Germany and Italy; yet at the close of the war, it was reduced to its interwar borders. Five million ethnic Hungarians have lived under the rule of others ever since.

The ethnic composition of all East-Central European states was dramatically and tragically simplified during World War II and its aftermath. Jews and Germans had once played an integral role in the cultural, economic, and political life of multicultural cities such as Warsaw, Prague, and Bratislava. Most of the 6 million Jews who perished in the Holocaust came from East-Central Europe, 3 million from Poland alone. Of those

---

6. On ethnic issues in Eastern Europe, see Janusz Bugajski, *Nations in Turmoil* (Boulder, Colo.: Westview, 1993).

7. Rudolf Kucera, *Kapitoly z Dejin Stredni Evropy* (Prague: Institute for Central European Culture and Politics, 1992), pp. 80–89.

who survived, most emigrated. Hundreds of thousands of Roma also died in Nazi concentration camps. After the war, 2.8 million Germans were expelled from Czechoslovakia, and 2.3 million from Poland. Voluntary emigration and expulsion also substantially reduced the size of the German communities in Hungary and Romania. When Poland's borders were shifted westward at the close of the war, its large Ukrainian and Belarussian minorities all but vanished into the Soviet Union. Despite population exchanges of some 2 million persons with the Soviet Union, 4 million Poles remained beyond Poland's eastern border.[8]

The communists who took power after the war denounced "bourgeois nationalism," but continued the process of national homogenization through expulsions and population exchanges. As the years passed, communist parties "felt compelled, in proportion to the decay of the communist ideas, to employ nationalism increasingly as a tool of self-legitimacy."[9] By the 1970s and 1980s, communists (especially in Romania and Bulgaria) had turned to greater repression of minority groups in a nationalist campaign to bolster the legitimacy of their regime. The resulting grievances ensured that ethnic problems would be on the agenda when communist rule ended.[10]

MAJORITY NATIONALISTS AND ETHNIC MINORITIES

I have advanced the claim that the importance of nationalism in postcommunist political discourse varies inversely with, first, the democratic credentials of early governments and, second, with the success of economic reforms and general levels of economic prosperity. The third factor in the equation is ethnic geography: Poland, Hungary, and the Czech Republic are almost ethnically homogeneous. Minorities are very small relative to the population as a whole, and have not called for territorial autonomy. It would thus be difficult for majorities to view these groups as a threat to the integrity of their state.

Poland and Hungary do have substantial co-ethnic populations beyond their borders. Still, the plight of ethnic brethren in neighboring states is a less powerful political tool than the "threat" posed by an ethnic minority within one's own state. First, voters concerned about their eco-

---

8. Ivo Banac, "Political Change and National Diversity," in Stephen Graubard, ed., *Eastern Europe . . . Central Europe . . . Europe* (Boulder, Colo.: Westview, 1991), pp. 148–150; George Schöpflin, *Politics in Eastern Europe* (Oxford: Blackwell, 1993), pp. 60–62.

9. Leszek Kolakowski, "Amidst Moving Ruins," *Daedalus*, Vol. 121, No. 2 (Spring 1992), p. 52.

10. Renée de Nevers, "Democratization and Ethnic Conflict," *Survival*, Vol. 35, No. 2 (Summer 1993), pp. 37–38.

nomic welfare can be told that it is threatened by a minority. Second, bullying minorities within the state is cheap and easy compared to coming to the rescue of co-ethnics in a neighboring state, or seeking to absorb another state.

In Slovakia, Bulgaria, and Romania, the ethnic majority must coexist with a politically and culturally cohesive minority which constitutes nearly ten percent of the population.[11] The character of ethnic politics in these three states have much in common. In Slovakia and especially in Romania, nationalist parties have capitalized on perceptions that the Hungarian minority poses a threat to the political and cultural integrity of the state; Bulgarian nationalist parties have similarly exploited fears of the Turks. Three factors have enabled politicians to use nationalism in this way. First, minorities form a significant portion of the total population — eleven percent in Slovakia, eight percent in Romania, and ten percent in Bulgaria — but are still overwhelmingly outnumbered by the majority. Politicians can stir up ethnic tensions to win office, knowing that they will be able to keep minorities under control. Second, history lends credibility to assertions that the minority community harbors an irredentist agenda. In all three cases, all or part of today's majority nation was once ruled by a state run by the nationality that is now in the minority. Finally, the fact that the minorities have organized themselves politically and culturally lends credibility to the nationalists' claims.

THE HUNGARIAN MINORITY IN SLOVAKIA. The Slovak people lived under Hungarian rule for nearly one thousand years. When Hungary gained control over its domestic affairs within the Habsburg empire in 1867, it systematically repressed Slovak cultural, political, and economic life. Consequently, the Slovaks had virtually no intelligentsia or middle class when the Czechoslovak state was formed in 1918. Hungary's reannexation of ethnically-Hungarian southern Slovakia after the First Vienna Arbitration of 1938 reinforced the Slovak perception of Hungarians as a threat. Two waves of repression against Slovakia's remaining Hungarians ensued. After the proclamation of Slovak independence in March 1939, the Slovak fascist puppet state of Father Jozef Tiso persecuted the country's Hungarians. After 1945, when Hungarian-occupied southern Slovakia reverted to Czechoslovak control, ethnic Hungarians were subjected to discrimination and expulsions.

In the mid-1990s, Slovakia's total population stands at 5.3 million, of

---

11. Unless otherwise noted, all statistics on ethnic demographies are from Janusz Bugajski, *Ethnic Politics in Eastern Europe: A Guide to Nationality Policies, Organizations, and Parties* (Armonk, N.Y.: M.E. Sharpe, 1994).

which 86 percent are ethnic Slovaks. The Hungarian minority numbers 600,000, comprising 11 percent of the population. Ethnic Hungarians often live near the border, in areas where they represent a decided majority. Hungarian political parties have formed an electoral coalition, which has consistently received a high percentage of the ethnic Hungarian vote. It won 10.4 percent of total votes in the June 1992 and 10.2 percent in the October 1994 parliamentary elections.

Vladimir Meciar, the leading Slovak politician, created his political base by rallying Slovak nationalism behind the cause of an autonomous Slovakia in a loose confederal structure with the Czech Republic. Meciar's party, the Movement for a Democratic Slovakia (MDS), includes numerous former communists; its democratic credentials are compromised by its extreme intolerance to criticism and blatant attempts to control the media. Meciar has relied heavily on ethnic nationalism as a source of political support. He found that the call to rally the Slovak nation was especially effective if the nation was said to be in danger, and hinted at various times that Czechs, Hungarians, and Roma posed a threat. The rise of Slovak nationalism resulted in a growing climate of intolerance toward the Hungarian minority.

From the outset, the Meciar government (June 1992–March 1994) was unreceptive to Hungarian initiatives to strengthen minority rights, and rejected changes to the draft Slovak constitution, which would have codified a civic definition of the state.[12] The most intolerant measures taken by the Meciar government involved the removal of bilingual road signs, and certain restrictions on the official use of Hungarian names.

In response to Meciar's discriminatory measures, Hungarian groups proposed in December 1993 the creation of a territorially autonomous district uniting Hungarian areas, situated along the Slovak-Hungarian border. In addition to promoting political and cultural goals, Hungarians hoped that autonomy would accelerate economic growth: in 1993 the unemployment rate in several Hungarian-dominated regions reached nineteen percent, compared to the national average of thirteen percent. The Hungarian call for territorial autonomy was immediately condemned by all Slovak political parties, including those sympathetic to strengthening minority rights. Hungarian representatives subsequently backed away from proposals for territorial autonomy.[13] At a gathering in January

---

12. Commission on Security and Cooperation in Europe, *Human Rights and Democratization in Slovakia* (Washington, D.C.: Commission on Security and Cooperation in Europe, September 1993), pp. 8–10.

13. Definitions of the various forms of autonomy sought by minorities remain vague.

1994, they called only for cultural and educational autonomy, expanded language rights, and a greater role in local administration.[14]

The Hungarians' brief call for territorial autonomy nonetheless exacerbated ethnic tensions in Slovakia. Slovak nationalists raised the specter of a "Magyarization" of southern Slovakia, and renewed charges that the Hungarians threatened the integrity of the Slovak state. No Hungarian group has in fact advocated the secession of southern Slovakia. Even so, Slovak nationalists have found that the threat of Hungarian secession is an effective political rallying cry, given Slovak resentment of the Hungarian nation. In addition to providing ammunition to Slovak nationalists, calls for territorial autonomy isolated the Hungarian coalition from their Slovak political allies. Slovak opposition parties opposed Hungarian territorial autonomy, and, more importantly, feared losing electoral support through association with Hungarian parties, which were increasingly seen as radical.

In March 1994, the Meciar government was ousted by a no-confidence vote. Five moderate rightist, centrist, and leftist parties formed a new government, which relied on the tacit support of the ethnic Hungarian parties. The new government, led by Jozef Moravcik, made considerable progress in privatization and economic reform, and passed legislation to conform with Council of Europe recommendations on the protection of ethnic minorities. Meciar's discriminatory policies were reversed.

This enlightened Slovak government was short-lived: the October 1994 elections brought to power Slovakia's most nationalist government yet. Meciar's MDS received a plurality of thirty-five percent of the vote. None of the political parties from the outgoing governing coalition were willing to share power with the MDS, so Meciar formed a coalition with the extreme right-wing Slovak National Party (SNP) and the neo-communist Association for Slovak Workers (ASW), which received five percent

---

One clear distinction, however, is possible: "cultural autonomy" includes only self-administered schools, universities, churches, and social organizations, funded in part from the state budget; while "territorial autonomy" involves self-government in a territorially-defined district. The concept of autonomy itself is controversial, as it is based on the principle of collective rights which, unlike the principle of individual rights, has not been codified or embraced by Western European states. Council of Europe Recommendation 1201 asks Eastern (but not Western) European states to grant some autonomy to minorities, but its language does not clearly specify what kinds of autonomy it is advocating.

14. In 1995, one of the three Hungarian parties in the Slovak parliament, Coexistence, reopened the issue of territorial autonomy. Sharon Fisher, "Meeting of Slovakia's Hungarians Causes Stir," *RFE/RL Research Report*, Vol. 3, No. 4 (January 28, 1994), pp. 42–47.

and seven percent of the vote, respectively.[15] Jan Slota, the leader of the SNP, advocates restricting Hungarian-language education and requiring the exclusive use of the Slovak language in official communications. His party was given control of the ministry of education; the Trotskyite ASW was given control of the ministry of privatization. Members of the ruling coalition have taken complete control of all parliamentary committees, replaced radio and television directors, threatened critical newspapers with higher taxes, stalled privatization, and reintroduced to politics an atmosphere of fear and intimidation.[16]

THE HUNGARIAN MINORITY IN ROMANIA. The lands of Transylvania were also under Hungarian rule between 1867 and 1918, when they were incorporated into Romania. When Hungary reclaimed two-fifths of Transylvania after the Second Vienna Arbitration of 1940, it confirmed Romanian suspicions that the Hungarians posed a threat to the Romanian state. Romania regained this territory after the war, and today its Hungarians number as many as 2 million (or 8 percent of Romania's population of 22.8 million), and comprise about 24 percent of the population of the Transylvanian region.[17] However, areas of Hungarian settlement are not contiguous; most Hungarians do not live near the border; and in no sizable region do Hungarians constitute a majority.

Transylvanian Hungarians have historically had greater educational and economic success than Romanians, which has fueled Romanian feelings of inferiority and, hence, animosity. In the 1970s and 1980s, the Romanian leader, Nicolai Ceausescu, persecuted Hungarians in order to strengthen his eroding position. Thousands of Romanians were resettled in Transylvania, and hundreds of Hungarian villages were emptied and then bulldozed. This left Hungarians in the minority in districts where hitherto they had been in the majority. Ceausescu also closed Hungarian-language schools and removed Hungarians from administrative posts. After Ceausescu fell, Hungarians hoped that democracy would allow them to rebuild their organizations, restore Hungarian-language schools,

---

15. Sharon Fisher, "Slovakia: Turning Back?" *Transition*, Vol. 1, No. 1 (January 1995), pp. 60–63.

16. Martin Butora and Zora Butorova, seminar at the Center for European Studies, Harvard University, April 10, 1995.

17. Hungarians also comprise 21 percent of the population of the Crisana Maramures region and 7 percent of the Banat region. George Schöpflin, *Hungary and Its Neighbors*, Chaillot Paper No. 7 (Paris: Western European Union [WEU] Institute for Security Studies, May 1993), p. 37; Bugajski, *Ethnic Politics in Eastern Europe*, p. 197.

and run local governments. The Hungarian Democratic Federation of Romania (HDFR) was formed, and has consistently won a high percentage of the ethnic Hungarian vote. It won about 7.5 percent of the total vote in the May 1990 and September 1992 parliamentary elections.

The ethnic cohesion of the Transylvanian Hungarians since 1990 has been perceived as threatening by Romanians, who see cultural pluralism as territorial fragmentation, and educational autonomy as political separatism. But since the Hungarians have not armed themselves and do not seek separation from Romania, they threaten "the state" only insofar as they threaten the cultural and political hegemony of Romanians in Transylvania. Even so, Romanian nationalists have been able to capitalize on this sense of threat, gathering popular support with charges that Transylvanian Hungarians seek to secede and that Budapest may intervene militarily on their behalf.

The popular extremist group, Vatra Romaneasca (Romanian Cradle), which draws much of its support from Transylvanian Romanians, advocates forced assimilation of Hungarians. In March 1990, Vatra Romaneasca incited anti-Hungarian riots in Tirgu-Mures. An unknown number of Hungarians and Romanians were killed in what has so far been the only instance of large-scale ethnic violence in East-Central Europe since 1989. In view of Vatra Romaneasca's popularity and the approaching election, the National Salvation Front (NSF) government did not condemn the group, instead blaming Hungarian "extremists" and their purported patrons in Budapest. Media coverage of the events was astonishingly anti-Hungarian. Weeks later the NSF affirmed the "unitary" character of the "Romanian national state" and deplored Hungarian "chauvinism, irredentism, and extremism." NSF Prime Minister Petre Roman claimed to have discovered a Hungarian-Transylvanian government-in-exile. In the run-up to the first parliamentary and presidential elections in May 1990, the NSF warned of the "dangers" of voting for Hungarian parties.[18]

After winning the presidency (with eighty-five percent of the vote for Ion Iliescu, a former lieutenant of Ceausescu) and a majority in both chambers of the parliament (with sixty-six percent of the vote), the NSF became "a party devoted to the protection of Romanians in their own nation-state."[19] Though its name has changed twice, Iliescu's party is the

---

18. Martyn Rady, *Romania in Turmoil* (New York: St. Martin's, 1992), pp. 145–159, 198.

19. Jonathan Eyal, "Romania," in Stephen Whitefield, ed., *The New Institutional Architecture of Eastern Europe* (London: St. Martin's, 1993), pp. 136–137.

only one in East-Central Europe to have held power continuously since the revolutions of 1989. Its offshoot, the Democratic National Salvation Front (DNSF), won the parliamentary elections in 1992 with twenty-seven percent of the vote, and formed a minority government with the support of three extremist parties.[20] In July 1993, the DNSF merged with several small parties and renamed itself the Party of Social Democracy in Romania (PSDR).

After the 1990 elections, the HDFR was the largest opposition party to the NSF in parliament. In 1992, the HDFR campaigned in a coalition within the Democratic Convention, which brought together the principal opposition parties. The increasing influence of Romanian extremist parties and organizations, combined with the refusal of the government to meet minimal Hungarian demands in the spheres of education and local administration (often combined with accusations of "treason" in parliament), have radicalized the HDFR. After years of consciously moderating its agenda, the HDFR decided in December 1994 to work for territorial autonomy. In January 1995, the HDFR set up a council on local administration, comprised of Hungarian mayors and councilors. The council was declared illegal by the government and denounced by virtually all Romanian political parties. The chauvinist Greater Romanian Party, which formally joined the governing coalition in January 1995 along with two other extremist parties, set out to ban the Hungarian party. The PSDR and President Iliescu strongly criticized the HDFR, but blocked these extremist attempts. The Romanian opposition parties, which had previously sought to promote Hungarian-Romanian dialogue, expelled the HDFR from the Democratic Convention in February 1995.[21]

The dynamic of ethnic animosity and the political isolation of minorities, visible in Slovakia, has taken a more extreme turn in Romania. The climate created by the nationalist post-communist party during its five unbroken years of power has forced even moderate opposition parties to embrace nationalist rhetoric. At the same time, the Hungarian minority's moves toward self-administration and calls for territorial autonomy have made it an easy target for Romanian nationalists and an impossible ally for Romanian moderates.

---

20. See Matei Calinescu and Vladimir Tismaneanu, "The 1989 Revolution and Romania's Future," *Problems of Communism*, Vol. 40 (January–April 1991), pp. 42–59; Rady, *Romania in Turmoil*, pp. 191–192; Eyal, "Romania," pp. 121–127.

21. Michael Shafir, "Ruling Party Formalizes Relationship with Extremists," *Transition*, Vol. 1, No. 5 (April 14, 1995), pp. 41–46; Michael Shafir, "Agony and Death of an Opposition Alliance," *Transition*, Vol. 1, No. 8 (May 26, 1995), p. 23.

THE HUNGARIAN MINORITY IN VOJVODINA. Hungarians in Vojvodina, a region of northern Serbia bordering Hungary and Romania, number about 350,000 (or just under one-fifth of Vojvodina's 2 million inhabitants). This group has suffered much more than its counterparts in Slovakia and Romania. The Vojvodina region itself has a long history of ethnic tolerance, and most local Serbs did not take up the call of Serbian President Slobodan Milosevic to repress ethnic minorities. The Milosevic government then brought in thousands of Serb refugees from outside of Vojvodina. These refugees were encouraged to occupy abandoned Hungarian houses, and massive demonstrations were organized to intimidate Hungarians and other minorities into leaving the region. Furthermore, the Milosevic government greatly curtailed Hungarian-language education, prohibited the use of Hungarian in official business, and removed most Hungarians from local administration. By 1994, about 50,000 Hungarians had fled the region to escape harassment, economic privation, and military conscription.[22]

The Democratic Community of Hungarians in Vojvodina (DCHV) has cooperated with numerous local groups, including Serb opposition parties. But the Hungarians have at times called for territorial autonomy, thereby alienating non-Hungarian members of Vojvodina's ethnically diverse community. The DCHV's ambitious plan, a predictable reaction to its precarious political situation, envisages a territorially autonomous district. It would be comprised of areas where Hungarians form the majority; have jurisdiction over the judiciary, education, police, local administration, and economic affairs; and take as its emblem the Hungarian tricolor of red, white, and green.[23] This plan has of course been denounced by the Milosevic government, and has no chance of being implemented. Meanwhile, the Vojvodina Hungarians have made the same mistake as Hungarian minorities in Slovakia and Romania: by calling for territorial autonomy, they have alienated valuable political allies.

THE TURKISH MINORITY IN BULGARIA. The Turkish minority settled in Bulgaria during the five hundred years of Ottoman occupation. The postwar communist government in Sofia eliminated the Turkish minority's educational and cultural privileges, and pressured the least assimilable Turks to emigrate. Communist policy varied from spates of repression to periods of indifference until 1984, when the Bulgarian government forced

---

22. Stan Markotich, "Vojvodina: A Potential Powder Keg," *RFE/RL Research Report*, Vol. 2, No. 46 (November 19, 1993), pp. 13–18.

23. Edith Oltay, "Hungarians under Political Pressure in Vojvodina," *RFE/RL Research Report*, Vol. 2, No. 48 (December 3, 1993), pp. 43–48.

Turks to adopt Slavic names and took brutal measures against Islam and the Turkish language. Over 1,000 Turks were detained in prison camps, and over one hundred were killed. In the spring and summer of 1989, over 300,000 Turks fled to Turkey, but by the end of 1990, over half had returned to their homes in Bulgaria.

In the mid-1990s, ethnic Turks number about 820,000, or nearly 10 percent of Bulgaria's population of 8.5 million. Relations between the Bulgarian government and the Turkish minority were relatively harmonious after the collapse of the communist regime. The predominantly Turkish Movement for Rights and Freedoms (MRF) enjoyed significant political power after the 1991 elections (in which it won 7.6 percent of the vote), since one of the two major parties had to form a coalition with it in order to govern. The MRF became a coalition partner of the Union of Democratic Forces (UDF) in Bulgaria's first non-communist government, but agreed not to take up any ministerial posts in order to prevent an anti-Turkish backlash. Near the end of 1992, the MRF sided with the Bulgarian Socialist Party (BSP) — the former communist party — and toppled the UDF government, apparently to cater to constituents suffering from economic reforms. This alienated the UDF, the natural coalition partner for the Turks, and led some UDF leaders to adopt a more nationalist stance.[24] Still, the MRF has generally been a responsible political force: it has succeeded in curbing its radical elements and has never called for territorial autonomy.[25]

The BSP has increasingly connived with minor chauvinist parties and employed nationalist rhetoric to bolster its position, linking the Turks with the hardships of reform and reviving fears of a Turkish threat.[26] In 1994, the BSP's electoral campaign promoted Bulgarian ethnic nationalism, and promised economic recovery with few social costs. In the December 1994 parliamentary elections, the coalition led by the BSP won a resounding victory with 43.5 percent of the vote; the UDF won only 24.2 percent, and the MRF only 5.4 percent. The new BSP government has appointed as education minister Ilcho Dimitrov, an extremist politician who took part in the assimilation campaign in the 1980s, and who has

---

24. Kjell Engelbrekt, "Bulgaria," *RFE/RL Research Reports*, Vol. 3, No. 16 (April 22, 1994), p. 79.

25. Ivanka Nedeva, "Democracy Building in Ethnically Diverse Societies: The Cases of Bulgaria and Romania," in Ian Cuthbertson and Jane Liebowitz, eds., *Minorities: The New Europe's Old Issue* (Boulder, Colo.: Westview, 1993), pp. 123–150.

26. Plamen S. Tzvetkov, "The Politics of Transition in Bulgaria: Back to the Future?" *Problems of Communism*, Vol. 41 (May–June 1992), pp. 40–41.

vowed to restrict Turkish language education. In March 1995, the new BSP government released the "White Book," purportedly an objective assessment of the country's situation. It is in fact a propaganda document which blames the UDF for most of Bulgaria's problems, while making virtually no mention of the consequences of forty-five years of rule by the BSP's antecedent, the Bulgarian Communist Party.[27]

THE ROMA AND OTHER MINORITIES. The Roma, Jews, and other minority groups have been persecuted by right-wing groups and skinheads throughout East-Central Europe. However, violence has been minimal, and certainly not higher than in Western Europe. The Roma remain the poorest, most disadvantaged, and most despised of Eastern Europeans, with very low levels of education and very high rates of unemployment.[28] Racism against the Roma population remains a significant problem in all six countries. The Czech Republic, for example, has come under intense criticism for its citizenship law, which in effect strips perhaps 100,000 Roma of their citizenship.[29] Intolerance of the Roma, manifested most clearly in racist attacks and in the behavior of local officials, was largely ignored by the Czech government until a set of policies to counter racist violence was designed in 1995. Polish and Hungarian governments have also taken official stands against racism toward the Roma, while Bulgarian and especially Romanian governments have remained aloof. The situation is most alarming in Romania, where attacks against Roma have become commonplace.

Roma minorities are politically disorganized and lack an outside champion. Mistreatment of Roma is thus very unlikely to cause internal conflict with international implications, unless the international community chooses to act on their behalf.[30]

---

27. Stefan Krause, "The White Book," *Transition*, Vol. 1, No. 10 (June 23, 1995), pp. 32–37.

28. Zoltan D. Barany, "Nobody's Children: The Resurgence of Nationalism and the Status of Gypsies in Post-Communist Eastern Europe," in Joan Serafin, ed., *East Central Europe in the 1990s* (Boulder, Colo.: Westview, 1994).

29. Commission on Security and Cooperation in Europe, *Human Rights and Democratization in the Czech Republic* (Washington, D.C.: Commission on Security and Cooperation in Europe, September 1994), pp. 18–27.

30. Max van der Stoel, CSCE High Commissioner on National Minorities, speech at CSCE Human Dimension Seminar on "Roma in the CSCE Region," Warsaw, Poland, September 20, 1994.

THE DISSOLUTION OF CZECHOSLOVAKIA

Although secessionist struggles have often turned violent — in the Caucasus and in the former Yugoslavia, for example — East-Central Europe has been peaceful in this regard. Indeed, the dissolution of the Czechoslovak federation provides an example of a national dispute which was resolved in an exemplary and harmonious fashion. Unlike virtually every other secession in history, in this case the leaders of the national group seeking greater autonomy created a political situation in which the dominant national group was willing — indeed, preferred — to see the state dissolve. This extraordinary sequence of events requires some explanation.[31]

At the founding of the Czechoslovak state in 1918, the Slovaks came into union with the Czechs as unequal partners. The Czechs outnumbered the Slovaks two to one. Moreover, the Czechs had a large intelligentsia and middle class, while much of Slovak society was agrarian and poorly educated. As a result, the Czechs dominated the government and the professions in the interwar period. The leaders of the Slovak Nazi puppet state, followed by the leaders of communist Czechoslovakia, manipulated Slovak resentment of the Czechs in order to gain popular support. By 1989, the feeling that Slovaks were second-class citizens had been building for seventy years, and state institutions were widely seen as Czech, not Czechoslovak.[32]

As democratic competition unfolded in Czechoslovakia after 1989, most political parties were identified as either Czech or Slovak, and met with little success when they tried to bridge the Czech-Slovak border in federal elections. Under the communist regime, democratic opposition groups had been much stronger in the Czech lands than in Slovakia. While Vaclav Havel and his entourage emerged from the Czech opposition to dominate politics in Prague, the Slovak opposition yielded fewer democrats, who proved unable to play the same role in Bratislava. The parameters of political debate had diverged: while Czech parties opposed each other along a spectrum defined by the speed of economic reform, Slovak parties competed primarily on the question of autonomy for the Slovak nation.

Slovak nationalist politicians exploited Slovak resentment of Czechs to fill the power vacuum created in Bratislava by the lack of a strong pro-democracy group. Once the idea of an independent Slovakia entered

31. For more discussion of secessionist movements and the causes of secessionist violence, see Alicia Levine's chapter in this volume.

32. Jiri Musil, "Czechoslovakia in the Middle of Transition," *Daedalus*, Vol. 121, No. 2 (Spring 1992), p. 184.

the political debate, nationalist parties gained political capital from the efforts of moderate parties to seek an accommodation with the Czechs and to preserve the federation.[33] The powerful personality of Vladimir Meciar was decisive in radicalizing this debate. A former communist with tenuous democratic credentials, Meciar's political legitimacy rested entirely on his claim that he was a staunch defender of the Slovak nation. By 1992, nationalist Slovak politicians had disabled the federal parliament with demands for Slovak autonomy, blocking Czech efforts to consolidate democratic institutions and create a free market.

Many Slovaks genuinely believed themselves to be second-class citizens of the Czechoslovak federation, and therefore supported more autonomy for the government in Bratislava. The transition to the free market contributed significantly to the perception that Czech and Slovak interests had diverged: the economic downturn was much steeper in Slovakia, where the communist regime had located much of Czechoslovakia's armament factories and heavy industry. Much of this industry proved to be obsolete, pushing unemployment in 1991 to eleven percent in Slovakia, while it reached only four percent in the Czech lands. Moreover, due to the kinds of goods it produced, Slovakia was more dependent on trade with the former communist bloc, and suffered accordingly when intra-regional trade collapsed in 1990. At the same time, most new foreign investment in Czechoslovakia flowed to the Czech lands, and especially to Prague.[34]

Although a clear majority of Slovaks opposed the dissolution of Czechoslovakia, Meciar's nationalist, economically leftist, pro-autonomy party won the June 1992 elections with thirty-seven percent of the vote. Meanwhile, the Czechs elected Vaclav Klaus's conservative, economically liberal, pro-reform party. That Meciar and Klaus would never be able to agree on fundamental political and economic matters effectively sealed Czechoslovakia's fate. It remains unclear whether Meciar really wanted independence, for while he was pushing for greater autonomy, he was also trying to secure larger Czech subsidies. In any case, after two years of fruitless confrontation and constitutional impasse, Klaus's Czech government was prepared to dissolve the federation. Again, economic reform played a critical role: Slovak politicians were hindering the implementation of reform measures, and foreign investors were deterred by the Czech-Slovak confrontation from investing in Czechoslovakia. An inde-

---

33. David Welsh, "Domestic Politics and Ethnic Conflict," in Brown, *Ethnic Conflict and International Security*, p. 48.

34. Otto Ulc, "The Bumpy Road of Czechoslovakia's Velvet Revolution," *Problems of Communism*, Vol. 41 (May–June 1992), pp. 28–33.

pendent Czech Republic promised the Klaus government easier reform, greater prosperity, and a more Western geopolitical position.

The division of Czechoslovakia into two sovereign states, which formally began on January 1, 1993, proceeded peacefully. The Czech and Slovak governments, albeit for different reasons, both agreed to the dissolution of the federation. The insignificant territorial disputes were resolved through negotiation. Minorities were not a contentious issue: although there is a substantial Slovak population in the new Czech Republic, it is well-integrated and suffers no discrimination. Negotiations on the division of federal property were long and at times acrimonious, but both sides compromised and emerged satisfied with the results. At no time was there any mention of resorting to arms to resolve contentious issues. Since the divorce, relations between the Czech and Slovak governments have generally been good.

The Role of International and Regional Actors

How does the prospect of joining the European Union affect state behavior in East-Central Europe? Offers of EU membership are conventionally thought to depend on the democratic behavior and economic performance of prospective members. While this is to some extent true, it is also the case that the behavior of prospective members depends on their perceptions of whether the EU will expand and, if so, of their place in the membership queue. Polish, Czech, Hungarian, and even Slovak governments are more attentive to Western, especially EU, expectations than are their Bulgarian and Romanian counterparts.

The four Visegrad states — the Czech Republic, Hungary, Poland, and Slovakia — considered to be the "first tier" of eastern applicants to the EU, are careful not to endanger their position. This is perhaps most striking in the case of Slovakia, where the Meciar government has been torn between its domestic agenda, which includes ethnic intolerance and undemocratic maneuvers, and its foreign policy agenda, which centers on riding the first wave of an eastern enlargement of the EU.

WESTERN INSTITUTIONS, MINORITY RIGHTS, AND DEMOCRATIC STANDARDS
The considerable influence of the Council of Europe and the OSCE High Commissioner on National Minorities on the treatment of ethnic minorities stems from the desire of East-Central European states to join "Europe." While neither organization can directly influence domestic policies or impose meaningful sanctions, both play a pivotal role in forming Western impressions of East-Central European states. Western impressions in turn shape relations with the EU and NATO, and influence

the decisions of foreign investors. It is impossible to assess how democratic standards and minority rights would be treated in the absence of this dynamic, but it seems likely that politicians in power in Romania, Bulgaria and Slovakia would go much farther in the direction of nationalist excesses.[35]

The treatment of the Hungarian minority in Slovakia appears to have been particularly subject to outside influence. In 1993, the Council of Europe recommended the revision of laws restricting the official use of non-Slovak names and ordering road signs to be posted only in Slovak. This gave the opposition political leverage, and both measures were reversed within two months of Meciar's ouster in March 1994. The OSCE High Commissioner on National Minorities has sent representatives to report on the situation of the Hungarian minority in Slovakia, and has advocated the creation of minority roundtables and the provision of Hungarian-language education to all Hungarians in Slovakia.[36]

The EU has played an important role by criticizing serious democratic lapses on the part of the Slovak government. When Meciar's governing coalition consolidated power using undemocratic measures after the October 1994 elections, the EU sent a critical demarche which helped prevent certain coalition maneuvers, including the attempt to expel former Prime Minister Moravcik's party from parliament. In late October 1995, the EU sent Slovakia a second demarche, denouncing coalition attacks on Slovak President Michael Kovac which were designed to force him out of office. The coalition accused Kovac of treason for criticizing the Slovak government at home and abroad.[37] Finally, the European Parliament approved a resolution on November 16, 1995, warning the Slovak government to respect democratic principles and to guarantee that all citizens have the right to free expression in the media and public life. The parliament warned that it might close its office in Slovakia and stop its assistance programs. Meciar's party, the MDS, responded by comparing the resolu-

35. For a discussion on the role of regional organizations in Europe, see Jenonne Walker, "European regional organizations and ethnic conflict," in Regina Cowen Karp, ed., *Central and Eastern Europe: The Challenge of Transition* (Oxford: Oxford University Press, 1993), pp. 45–66.

36. Max van der Stoel, CSCE High Commissioner on National Minorities, "Controlling Ethnic Tensions in Europe," Address to the Oxford University Civil Liberties Society, October 28, 1994; on the work of the High Commissioner, see Konrad Huber, "Preventing Ethnic Conflict in the New Europe: The OSCE High Commissioner," in Cuthbertson and Liebowitz, *Minorities*, pp. 273–284.

37. Sharon Fisher, "EU Worried about Slovakia," *OMRI Digest*, October 27, 1995.

tion to demarches sent by Nazi Germany and the Soviet Union on the eve of military invasions of East-Central Europe.[38]

The European Union has also exercised considerable leverage over the treatment of the Hungarian minority by the Slovak government. In 1993 it forced Slovakia to sign a clause on the protection of minority rights as part of its Europe Agreement; this demonstrably reduced Meciar's anti-Hungarian rhetoric. In March 1995, due to strong words from Brussels, Meciar signed a bilateral treaty with Hungary which includes ambitious provisions concerning minority rights. As long as Slovakia seeks to remain in the first tier of eastern applicants to the EU, the West will retain substantial leverage over the Slovak government.

The oppression of the Hungarian minority by the Romanian government appears to be deepening as external pressure decreases. The Council of Europe waited four years before admitting Romania in 1993. Although it had serious reservations about Romania's commitment to democracy and minority rights, the Council decided that it would be better able to influence Romania as a member. In 1993 and 1994, the Romanian government did make some efforts to implement Council recommendations, but by 1995, many of these had been reversed. Oddly, now that the danger of minority rights violations is greater, the Council of Europe has "decided to abandon its practice of monitoring Romania's performance on minority rights."[39] With extremists in power, Council of Europe membership in hand, and EU membership clearly a distant prospect, Western leverage has diminished.

WESTERN INSTITUTIONS AND EASTERN REFORMS

The West played an integral role in the collapse of communism by providing, for forty years, a spectacular model for the East, a convincing passive case that democracy and capitalism bring security and economic prosperity. Since 1989, Western European democracies have provided not only a model, but also a tangible goal for reform: membership in European institutions. The belief that NATO and EU membership would be forthcoming if transitions were successful has provided a strong motivation for sticking to difficult restructuring programs.

NATO and the EU expect a considerable asymmetry of commitment: while offering no criteria or timetable for admitting new states, both

---

38. Sharon Fisher, "EU Parliament Passes Resolution on Slovakia," *OMRI Digest*, November 17, 1995.

39. Michael Shafir and Dan Ionescu, "The Tangled Path Toward Democracy," *Transition*, Vol. 1, No. 1 (January 30, 1995), p. 53.

institutions expect East-Central European states to move as rapidly as possible to emulate certain existing members. Also, East-Central European states are expected to accept EU competition and intellectual property laws, and encouraged to adopt the bulk of EU legislation and practices. The growing disillusionment brought about by these inequalities has had repercussions for political parties which support the laborious and economically painful process of integration with the West. As Tony Judt observes, "the alacrity with which Western Europeans (notably the French) backed away from their earlier enthusiasm for a liberated Eastern Europe has seriously weakened the position of those in the former communist lands who are pro-Europe."[40]

Most troubling to pro-Western politicians in East-Central Europe has been EU trade policy. East-Central European economies — contrary to some predictions — have competed very effectively in Western European markets when they have been allowed to compete on equal terms. Trade between the EU and East-Central Europe was liberalized by the Europe Agreements in 1993, but the EU has retained a substantial degree of protection. Formidable trade barriers are to remain in place indefinitely for agricultural goods; tariffs and quotas on steel and textiles will be phased out over a number of years. Any sector in which East-Central European states become successful may be targeted for contingent protection. East-Central European exports also confront layers of non-tariff barriers.[41] Thus, although the Europe Agreements were ostensibly designed to aid East-Central European economies, the EU trade balance with these countries has improved since 1993. Remarkably, this holds true even for many of the "sensitive" products where East-Central European economies have a comparative advantage. The myriad EU protectionist measures which remain after the implementation of the Europe Agreements have made full membership in the EU an imperative for reasons of market access.

Other external actors have been drawn into East-Central Europe since 1989. Western states and international organizations have implemented various programs to support democratic institutions and to build democratic skills and attitudes. Economic reforms have been underpinned by Western loans, debt forgiveness, trade concessions, and some grants. The

---

40. Tony Judt, "The End of Which European Era?" *Daedalus*, Vol. 123, No. 3 (Summer 1994), pp. 5–6.

41. See Andras Inotai, "Central and Eastern Europe," in C. Randall Henning et al., eds., *Reviving the European Union* (Washington, D.C.: Institute for International Economics, 1994), pp. 139–164.

International Monetary Fund, the World Bank, the European Union, and other international organizations have tied economic assistance and loans to continued steps toward the free market. This has been instrumental in sustaining the political commitment to difficult economic measures, particularly when economic leftists have succeeded economic liberals in power. The IMF has threatened to suspend and has actually suspended loans when particular economic reforms were under threat, and when specific IMF economic criteria, such as exceeding targets for budget deficit as percentage of GNP, were not met. Still, the discipline imposed by the IMF is at most a necessary, and certainly not a sufficient, condition for the success of reforms. Austerity sometimes breeds austerity. A moderate government could lose support while seeking to meet IMF criteria, and be replaced by an extremist government.

OUTSIDE ACTORS AND THE CZECH–SLOVAK SPLIT

There was no concerted pressure from any outside actor to prevent the dissolution of Czechoslovakia. European institutions did not take an active role in the conflict, realizing that if a split did occur, it would be carried out in an orderly, consensual manner. The international community did play a role in convincing Slovak politicians to negotiate a constitutional end to the Czechoslovak state.[42] As expected, the international repercussions of the split were minimal. The Czech and Slovak Republics had to apply individually for membership in international organizations, and had to renegotiate previous agreements with the European Union and the Council of Europe.

The division of Czechoslovakia had some regional repercussions beyond the creation of the more nationalist, less democratic, and economically weaker Slovak state. The creation of a Czech state allowed Prague to take a self-centered foreign policy stance toward its neighbors. Prime Minister Klaus believes that the Czech Republic, as a small and relatively prosperous democracy, has little to gain from close association with its East-Central European neighbors. Cooperation among the Visegrad states has been scaled back considerably, on the rationale that close relations with Poland, Hungary, and Slovakia could only impede Czech entry into the EU.

This reduction in regional cooperation has increased the risk of conflict in three ways. First, Visegrad cooperation helped to keep Slovakia

42. For example, Slovak Prime Minister Jan Carnogursky observed in 1991 that "no state would be willing to recognize Slovakia if it gained its independence through unconstitutional means." Carnogursky is quoted in Jiri Pehe, "Bid for Slovak Sovereignty Causes Political Upheaval," *Report on Eastern Europe*, October 11, 1991, p. 24.

among the first tier of eastern applicants to the EU. If Slovakia slips from this tier, it will lose some of its incentive to respect democratic standards and minority rights. Second, Romania's desire to join the Visegrad group could have been used to improve the Romanian government's treatment of its Hungarian minority and to expand relations between Romania and Hungary. Third, communication and understanding among the four have been weakened. This could render the resolution of future disputes more difficult.

PROTECTOR STATES AND CO-ETHNICS

Hungary has tempered its activism as the protector state of Hungarians beyond its borders. Hungarian leaders and diplomats have become more adroit; the EU and NATO have pushed Hungarian foreign policy towards a more conciliatory posture; and the Hungarian people elected a less patriotic parliament in 1994. Nevertheless, the fundamental dilemma of Hungarian foreign policy remains: on the one hand, Hungary can expect to be admitted to the EU and NATO only if it resolves its disputes with Slovakia and Romania; on the other hand, for domestic political reasons, no Hungarian government can ignore the plight of Hungarian minorities abroad.

Hungary's first post-communist government, led by Jozsef Antall of the conservative Hungarian Democratic Forum (HDF), adopted an activist approach to the problems of Hungarian minorities in neighboring states. The Antall government was persistent in bringing these problems to the attention of international fora. Another important component of Antall's campaign was the adoption of a liberal law on national minorities, intended to serve as a model for neighboring states. Provisions of the law include cultural autonomy, minority language education, the use of the minority language in all spheres of public life, parliamentary representation, and unrestricted relations with the "ethnic homeland."[43] The right to state-financed self-government, the most ambitious provision of the law, enabled a dozen minorities to elect a total of 787 minority councils in December 1994.

In 1990, Antall declared that he would like to be the prime minister of all 15 million Hungarians, and set up a special department to oversee the affairs of Hungarian minorities abroad. However, the Antall government never advocated revision of Hungary's borders, and pursued exclusively political channels in its efforts to protect Hungarian minorities. Nevertheless, Hungarian speculation about the possibility of peaceful

---

43. Istvan Ijgyarto, "Codification of Minority Rights," in Cuthbertson and Liebowitz, *Minorities*, pp. 273–284.

border changes provided ammunition for Slovak and Romanian nationalists eager to portray Hungary as an aggressive neighbor and to condemn Hungarian minorities as threats to national integrity. Neighboring nationalists (and Western observers) often blurred the distinction between the policy of the Hungarian government and the rhetoric of Hungarian extremists who called for the creation of a "greater Hungary." After a period of damaging silence, in June 1993 the HDF expelled its extremist faction, led by Istvan Csurka.[44]

The Hungarian citizenry has in fact become increasingly disinterested in the fate of Hungarians abroad, especially as the arrival of Hungarian refugees from Vojvodina and Romania strains the Hungarian economy. There is no political will in Hungary for military intervention on behalf of Hungarians abroad. This was underscored by the election of 1994, which brought a substantially less nationalist government to power. Led by Prime Minister Gyula Horn, the government of the Hungarian Socialist Party (HSP) took office in July 1994. In contrast to the Antall government, the Horn government declared that Hungarian minorities would no longer be the focal point of relations with Romania and Slovakia. It also encouraged Hungarians in Slovakia and Romania to moderate their demands for autonomy. Horn's party charged that, by making the minority issue the centerpiece of its policy toward its neighbors, the Antall government had exacerbated relations with Slovakia and Romania and had thus damaged Hungary's chances of early entry into NATO and the EU.

In 1995, NATO and the EU emphasized to Hungary, Slovakia, and Romania the importance of concluding bilateral treaties that would resolve outstanding ethnic issues. The Horn government had already entered into serious negotiations with both Slovakia and Romania during the summer of 1994.[45] Political extremists subsequently became more influential in both Slovakia and Romania. A Slovak-Hungarian treaty guaranteeing both borders and minority rights was nevertheless signed in March 1995. Negotiation of a Romanian-Hungarian treaty, however, was compromised in 1995 by political attacks on the HDFR in Romania; even the Horn government, conciliatory by nature, was compelled to react strongly to these attacks.

Like Hungary, Poland has shown a consistent interest in its co-ethnics abroad. Although large numbers of Poles live in Lithuania, Belarus, and

---

44. Pál Dunay, "Hungary: Defining the Boundaries of Security," in Karp, *Central and Eastern Europe*, p. 129.

45. Alfred Reisch, "The New Hungarian Government's Foreign Policy," *RFE/RL Research Report*, Vol. 3, No. 33 (August 26, 1994), pp. 46–57.

Ukraine, Poland has succeeded in regulating its relations with all three states. Lithuania was by far the most difficult case, partly because Lithuania overreacted to the provocative demands of Polish minority leaders and partly because of Lithuania's traditional fear of Polish cultural and political domination. Throughout the Polish-Lithuanian negotiations, which were concluded in 1994, Polish governments urged the Polish minority in Lithuania to abandon its territorial claims. With only occasional exceptions, Polish parties did not exploit this issue for political ends.[46]

Turkey has, naturally enough, followed with interest the fate of Bulgarian Turks. Yet Turkish politicians consistently renounce pan-Turkism, and follow a tradition of restraint which dates from Ataturk's choice of the modern nation-state as Turkey's destiny. Even the most nationalist factions in Turkish politics are not seeking a pretext to intervene in Bulgaria.[47]

Potential Problems

Oppression of ethnic minorities is the most likely cause of instability and conflict in East-Central Europe, and oppression is most likely when post-communist nationalist governments in states with large ethnic minorities face severe economic problems. Slovakia, Romania, and Bulgaria therefore stand out as the states that are most likely to engage in provocative behavior. Problems could also develop in the Czech Republic, Poland, and Hungary if Western indifference were to deepen and if economies were to take a sudden turn for the worse. In the near future, however, Slovakia, Romania, and Bulgaria demand the greatest attention and concern.

Of these three, the picture is brightest in Slovakia. Despite its extremist coalition partners, Meciar's MDS cannot fairly be described as an extremist party; it is a populist party whose rhetoric has at times embraced ethnic nationalism. Although the prospects for sound government and economic reform are bleak, in 1995 Meciar at times adopted a conciliatory approach toward Slovakia's Hungarian minority, if only on the international stage. Meciar apparently took heed of EU warnings regarding the consequences of a Slovak failure to sign a bilateral treaty with Hungary. Such a treaty was signed in March 1995 and ratified by the

---

46. Tim Snyder, "National Myths and International Relations: Poland and Lithuania, 1989–1994," *East European Politics and Societies*, Vol. 9, No. 2 (Spring 1995), pp. 317–344.

47. Gareth Winrow, *Where East Meets West: Turkey and the Balkans*, European Security Study No. 18 (London: Institute for European Defence and Strategic Studies, 1992), pp. 23–24.

Hungarian parliament in June 1995. The Slovak parliament, however, has yet to ratify it. The treaty's opponents are making much of the well-founded argument that the treaty would require Slovakia to accept standards which the Council of Europe has recommended but which many Western European states would not accept. Meanwhile, on the domestic stage, the Meciar government has again attacked the rights of the Hungarian minority by passing a discriminatory language law and centralizing control of education.

Although populist and extremist parties control the Slovak parliament with eighty-three seats, the remaining sixty-seven are held by the moderate leftist, centrist, and rightist parties which governed Slovakia very effectively from March to September of 1994. (This distinguishes Slovakia from Romania, where the weak and divided opposition has virtually no experience in government.) In short, Slovakia has a credible and moderate opposition; its economy is in better shape than those of Bulgaria and Romania; and Slovaks want to maintain their place in the front rank of eastern applicants to the EU.

In Romania, the picture is much bleaker. The Hungarian party was expelled from the opposition coalition and the coalition itself collapsed in early 1995. The ruling PSDR, moreover, has entered into a formal coalition with three extremist parties. Tensions between Romanians and Hungarians in Transylvania are rising and, with the apparent decline of Western influence on the Romanian government, unpunished violence by Romanian extremists is becoming more and more likely. Meanwhile, Hungary and Romania remain far apart in negotiations on a bilateral treaty, which is to include provisions on minority rights.

The present level of occasional violence and the denial of minority rights in Romania are far from sufficient to provoke a Hungarian military intervention. The Hungarian minority in Transylvania does not seek to provoke such an intervention, no Hungarian government has sought a pretext to intervene, and the Hungarian public is increasingly indifferent to the fate of compatriots abroad. Further, Hungarians are fully aware that any military action on their part would torpedo their chances of joining NATO and the EU. Finally, Hungary's military forces are inferior to Romania's. This is especially important, because an intervention on behalf of ethnic Hungarians would involve a deep penetration of Romanian territory, not a simple border raid.

Only a massive repression of Hungarians in Romania or Slovakia could provoke Hungarian military action. A provocation from the Serbs in Vojvodina is more likely, but Serb oppression would probably spark a mass exodus to Hungary rather than a military response from Budapest.

It is difficult to imagine extremists coming to power in Hungary: as of 1995, Hungarians have endured eight consecutive years of declining living standards without opting to support extremists. In this very unlikely scenario, the Hungarian government would still face the constraints on military action enumerated above.

Although the ruling Bulgarian Socialist Party is relying more and more on nationalist rhetoric, it is nevertheless difficult to imagine an ethnic conflict in Bulgaria drawing in an outside power. The Turkish minority is well-organized but politically moderate, and has a solid chance of regaining its kingmaker role in Bulgarian politics. This simple political fact should restrain the hand of the Socialists, even those who took part in the ethnic persecutions of the 1980s. Even if such campaigns were repeated, it is very unlikely that the response of the Turkish government would extend beyond diplomatic or economic measures. The experience of the 1980s suggests that repression of Bulgarian Turks does not bring a strong response from Ankara. Since the collapse of the Soviet Union, Turkey's attention has been divided among several Turkish states and minorities abroad; the Bulgarian Turks are not seen as having special importance. Both Turkey and Bulgaria seek EU membership, and this would play a further restraining role in their relations.

According to present trends, the types of provocation necessary to trigger a Hungarian intervention in Romania and Slovakia or a Turkish intervention in Bulgaria seem quite improbable. Should Slovakia's economy deteriorate drastically, or should the dramatic decline of Bulgarian and Romanian industry since 1989 recommence, such a provocation would become more likely. The risks are greatest in Bulgaria and Romania, where large parts of the population are on the edge of desperate poverty. In all three states, the post-communist parties in power have already demonstrated their ability to seek ethnic scapegoats for economic problems, and there are even more radical nationalist formations waiting in the wings (or already in governing coalitions). Of the three factors which allow such a situation — the presence of a large ethnic minority, governance by relatively unreconstructed post-communists, and economic decline — Western actors can do nothing about the first, something about the second, and much about the third.

Recommendations

Seven main recommendations flow from the forgoing analysis of developments in East-Central Europe.

First, EU member states should allow complete market access to

East-Central European producers in all sectors.[48] Unrestricted access to EU markets could have substantially accelerated economic recovery and facilitated economic restructuring in the first half of the 1990s; in the years ahead, it would be an invaluable tool for consolidating economic transitions. Access to EU markets would also increase foreign investment in East-Central Europe: Western European firms would set up shop in order to supply home markets. Income generated by free trade would be substantially greater than any likely inflow of aid.[49] In addition, trade policy will have a significant impact — for good or ill — on perceptions in East-Central Europe about the benefits of pursuing economic reform. A dramatic change in EU trade policy is therefore sorely needed.

Economists agree that while the welfare benefits of free trade with the EU would be substantial for East-Central Europe, the effects on EU producers would be modest. Rollo and Smith conclude that "no rational economic explanation for the EC's sensitivity with respect to trade with Eastern Europe emerges: the shock of competition from Eastern Europe is not insignificant, but it is well within the range of the normal experience of economic change. The scale of the adjustments required by liberalized trade with Eastern Europe seem quite manageable, even making no allowance for the growing Eastern European market for Western European products."[50]

Second, the European Union and NATO should begin to admit East-Central European states as full members. Because the central cultural idea of reform is the "return to Europe," reform is at risk if this idea continues to be undermined by policy choices in the West. Both the EU and NATO encouraged East-Central European politicians to believe that membership would reward political and economic reform. These politicians in turn promised their electorates that if certain difficult steps were taken, NATO and the EU would open their doors. The continued denial of membership is beginning to have a detrimental effect on electoral outcomes: moderate parties discredited by their past commitment to "Europe" are being replaced by more extreme parties, and pro-Western politicians are losing

---

48. Helen Wallace and Alasdair Smith, "The European Union: towards a Policy for Europe," *International Affairs*, Vol. 70, No. 3 (1994), p. 438.

49. Alan Winters, "The Europe Agreements: With a Little Help from Our Friends," *The Association Process: Making it Work, Central Europe and the European Community*, Occasional Paper No. 11 (London: Centre for Economic Policy Research (CEPR), November 1992), pp. 18–28.

50. Jim Rollo and Alasdair Smith, "EC Trade with Eastern Europe," *Economic Policy*, No. 16 (April 1993), p. 165.

influence within their parties.[51] NATO and EU membership would restore the credibility of moderate, pro-Western politicians.

NATO membership would encourage the EU to formulate a list of membership criteria and a timetable for admission. This timetable should allow Poland, Hungary, the Czech Republic, and possibly Slovakia to join by the end of this century. The European Union should take care not to isolate other eastern candidates. This should not be a problem: if some states are admitted, it should be easy to convince others that membership is an attainable goal.

Third, European institutions should adopt a clear policy on the rights of ethnic minorities, especially in the spheres of education, local administration, and linguistic freedom. Thus far, European states have failed to reach a consensus on codifying minority rights. In November 1994, twenty-one of the thirty-three members of the Council of Europe — including Hungary, Romania, and Slovakia, — agreed to develop a framework for protecting national minorities. Several Western European states have not signed, fearing that it would strengthen separatist movements in their own countries.[52] Western European states cannot hold Eastern Europeans to standards which they themselves are not prepared to explicitly and consistently embrace.

Fourth, minority groups should be encouraged to abandon calls for territorial autonomy. Territorial autonomy would only deepen the ethnic definition of the state, and is unacceptable even to centrist political forces. Its advocacy isolates ethnic parties from potential political allies, and provides rhetorical ammunition for nationalist extremists. Minority organizations should limit their demands to cultural and local political autonomy, which are more attainable by nature and which may be, as the debate continues, derived from emerging European standards. The West, through the mediation of "protector states" and OSCE missions, should try to dissuade minorities from seeking territorial autonomy.

Fifth, moderate Western political parties should be encouraged to help their ideological counterparts in Eastern Europe. (Extremist parties seem to form ties without any encouragement.) The German Christian Democratic Union (CDU) provides a promising example: it helped the center-right Civic Democratic Party of Czech Prime Minister Vaclav Klaus design campaign and recruitment strategies.

Sixth, European states and organizations should educate East-Central

---

51. George Kolankiewicz, "Consensus and Competition in the Eastern Enlargement of the EU," *International Affairs*, Vol. 70, No. 3 (1994), p. 479.

52. Marcel Scotto, "Paris rechigne à signer la convention européenne sur les minorités," *Le Monde*, February 23, 1995.

Europeans about the distinction between ethnic and civic definitions of the state, and they should strongly encourage states to adopt the civic option. Although it would be naive to think outsiders can determine the character of East-Central European nationalism, the exceptional influence of Western models at this particular moment in history has opened a small window of opportunity. If Western states succeed in introducing the conception that the political nation is defined by choice rather than ethnicity, this notion of the civic state can at least serve as another pole in the debate. In particular, if East-Central European states can be persuaded to use the language of civic rather than ethnic nationalism in their constitutions, their constitutions may serve at some future time as a refuge for oppressed minorities and as legal and moral support for those who wish to protect them.

To this end, Germany should change its citizenship laws, which clearly embrace an ethnic definition of citizenship and therefore set a terrible example for its eastern neighbors. Under German law, ethnic Germans whose parents have never lived in Germany can be granted citizenship, while Turkish children born in Germany are not automatically made citizens. The methods used to prove German ethnicity can be scandalous: Poles have qualified for German citizenship by proving that their fathers or other relatives served the Third Reich. Germany should also reconsider its postwar role as protector of ethnic Germans abroad. This precedent could lead to trouble elsewhere on the continent.[53]

Seventh, the Council of Europe should be diligent in criticizing lapses in democratic practice by its new members, singling out legislation or statements which it finds objectionable. In the first half of the 1990s, the Council had the most impact on East-Central European states while the merits of their applications for membership were under consideration.[54] When the Council admitted states with democratic shortcomings, it did so in the hope of supporting the reform process and improving minority rights through inclusion. Once states have been admitted, however, the Council has generally been circumspect in criticizing their behavior, and the unlikelihood of suspension has compromised its deterrent value. Similarly, the OSCE High Commissioner on National Minorities has adopted a cautious approach to criticizing state behavior. The influence and leverage of the Council and the OSCE have thus not been fully utilized.

---

53. Timothy Garton Ash, *In Europe's Name* (London: Jonathan Cape, 1993), pp. 236, 402–403.

54. Walker, "European Regional Organizations," in Karp, *Central and Eastern Europe*, p. 52.

Conclusions

East-Central Europe is one of the few regions in the world where violent conflict is almost completely absent, and where a general respect for human rights prevails. Ethnic groups living beyond the borders of their ethnic homeland have refrained from any form of armed action, and co-ethnic governments have not supplied arms, incited violence, or advocated border changes. No government has pursued a foreign policy of economic or political coercion toward a neighboring state. Indeed, relations among the region's states, despite disputes over minorities, have probably never been better.

It is striking that the region has remained peaceful while the six states have embarked on a fundamental transformation of their polities and economies with neither substantial financial assistance nor security guarantees from outside powers. For the moment, the West continues to have an extraordinary influence over the course of events in the region: it is thus more striking still that the West has not done more to remove the potential causes of conflict which remain, more to recognize the achievements of these new democracies, and more to anchor them in the European civilization to which states East and West both aspire.

Chapter 3

Historical Legacies and the Politics of Intervention in the Former Soviet Union

Matthew Evangelista

The former Soviet Union is rife with cases of domestic turmoil spilling over international borders, as well as external actors becoming involved in internal conflicts. Because the fifteen independent successor states of the Soviet Union were part of one country until just a few years ago, in late 1991 — and most are members of the Commonwealth of Independent States (CIS) — the dynamics of external involvement in the region are rather distinctive. Three features in particular stand out.

First, the boundaries of the new states, and the regions within them, are often artificial or arbitrary. The territorial legacy of the Soviet Union — many groups with common linguistic and ethnic identities now divided by international borders — enhances the likelihood that internal conflicts will involve external actors in one way or another.

Second, Moscow's role as the military, political, and economic center of the Soviet empire, and Russia's position as the indisputably preponderant power in the region, mean that Russian external interference in the affairs of the other Soviet successor states is, and will continue to be, common. This is reinforced by Russia's pretensions to continued great-power or even superpower status, which incline its leaders to view any internal conflict in the "near abroad" as engaging Russian national interests.

Third, many influential political leaders in the Soviet successor states, including Russia, seem determined to reverse the Soviet legacy of isolation from international political and economic institutions. Their desire to make their countries members in good standing of the international community increases the opportunities for involvement by international

For comments on an earlier draft of this chapter, I am grateful to Stuart Kaufman, Celeste Wallander, and the participants in the CSIA workshop on internal conflict, especially John Mearsheimer and Steven Miller.

institutions and outside powers in the resolution of internal conflicts. At the same time, however, some leaders in the former Soviet Union are preoccupied with acquiring, maintaining, and extending their personal power; they show little regard for the views of international organizations or other states. Only by diminishing the power of such political opportunists can international actors hope to influence the policies of the Soviet successor states.

Those who would attempt to influence the states of the former Soviet Union — to prevent or resolve internal conflicts and keep them from spreading — must recognize two fundamental facts. The first is that more than seven decades of Soviet rule have left a legacy of ethnic division, economic disparity, and political uncertainty that creates powerful preconditions for internal conflict. The second is that efforts to resolve conflicts anywhere in the former Soviet Union must give due weight to Russia's power and interests. That does not mean allowing the region to become a Russian sphere of influence. It does, however, mean that strategies for influencing developments in the region must take into account Russia's involvement and try to shift Russian policy in benign directions.

In the first section of this chapter, I describe the historical legacy that provides the pre-conditions for violent conflict in the former Soviet Union. I then analyze the causes of the conflicts that broke out during the last years of the Soviet Union and the first few years of the post-Soviet era. Next, I discuss the involvement of international actors — states and organizations — in internal, post-Soviet conflicts, with particular attention to the role played by Russia. Finally, I look to the future to consider the kinds of violent conflicts that could erupt in Russia and elsewhere in the former Soviet Union, their likely causes, and what outside powers and international institutions might be able to do about them.

Historical Legacies and Changing Conditions

The situation in the former Soviet Union is the product of a historical legacy that includes features common to other major powers, as well as features peculiar to the Soviet experience. As with other large, multiethnic empires, Russia's imperial expansion over several centuries entailed violent conquest of indigenous peoples and wars against neighboring states. Many of these conflicts — in the Caucasus, the Crimea, the Far East, and elsewhere — brought tsarist Russia into conflict with other major powers. The sources of internal conflict in the tsarist empire and factors that contributed to involvement by other powers were not unique to Russia: economic grievances, secessionist campaigns, ethnic strife, political opportunism, power politics.

The early years of the Bolshevik regime were also marked by considerable violence: first, a civil war that involved more than a dozen foreign states; then, reconstitution and expansion of the tsarist empire into Central Asia and the Caucasus — actions that, by contrast, did not occasion much international response.[1] Violent internal conflict was rare throughout most of the rest of the Soviet Union's history — until its last few years. Occasional manifestations of discontent, such as workers' protests against poor living conditions, were quickly and brutally suppressed and therefore had few international, or even local, repercussions. Even military invasions of nominally independent states of the Soviet Union's "external empire" in Eastern Europe — Hungary in 1956 and Czechoslovakia in 1968 — met with rhetorical opprobrium from the international community, but little else.

In the decades following World War II, the Soviet Union's possession of nuclear weapons and the bipolar nature of the international system, particularly the antagonistic relationship between Washington and Moscow, undoubtedly contributed to a cautious attitude on the part of states that might have considered taking advantage of any internal Soviet strife. But the nature of the Soviet domestic political system — highly centralized, authoritarian, repressive — restrained potential sources of internal conflict in any case. What has changed with the end of the Cold War — indeed, what in many respects we mean by the end of the Cold War — are two structural conditions: the change in the international system away from bipolarity and represented by U.S.-Russian rapprochement, and the change in the domestic system of Russia, a process that began before, and contributed to, the breakup of the Soviet Union. These structural changes are the permissive conditions that have allowed internal conflicts to erupt in the former Soviet Union and have made external involvement of other states and international organizations possible.

Sources and Types of Internal Conflict

The legacy of the Soviet domestic system, in combination with changes instituted by Mikhail Gorbachev, go a long way toward explaining the outburst of internal conflict in the former Soviet Union, starting in the late 1980s. Many conflicts have been driven by a combination of ethnic

---

1. On Bolshevik expansion into Central Asia, see Marie Bennigsen Broxup, "Comrade Muslims!" *Washington Quarterly*, Vol. 15, No. 3 (Summer 1992), pp. 40–47; on the Caucasus, see Ronald Grigor Suny, *The Revenge of the Past: Nationalism, Revolution, and the Collapse of the Soviet Union* (Stanford, Calif.: Stanford University Press, 1993).

strife, political and economic discontent, and opportunism on the part of political leaders.

LEGACIES OF THE SOVIET POLITICAL SYSTEM

Russia has inherited key features of the Soviet political system — in particular, the contradictory relationship between political-economic power centralized in Moscow and the regional organization of political units based on ethnic or national criteria. These structural features contributed to the disintegration of the Soviet Union and to the violence that erupted in its wake. They are worth reviewing for what they tell us about the context in which events in the region continue to unfold.

The Soviet Union was nominally organized as a federation of republics, each identified with a titular nationality which did not necessarily constitute a majority of the republic's population. In practice, however, the Soviet Union was a highly centralized state in both political and economic affairs. Hypercentralization of the economy contributed to economic stagnation and decline. Political centralization left many local concerns unmet and focused popular anger on Moscow for its high-handed and arbitrary rule. When a reformist leadership came into power in the mid-1980s, it favored timid economic decentralization and a political liberalization intended to give people a stake in the system. The result was the opposite of what the reformers intended. People took advantage of the political opening to criticize the economic results of half-hearted reforms — and much else as well. Ultimately the legitimacy of the Soviet system itself came into question, and along with it, the right of politicians sitting in Moscow's Kremlin to rule over 285 million people spread across eleven time zones.

The peculiar structure of the Soviet Union provided the impetus and opportunity for political action.[2] The Soviet state was organized into a hierarchy of territorial units, comprised of union republics, autonomous republics, and autonomous provinces (oblasti), each identified with a particular ethnic group. As Jessica Stern points out, "the establishment of a federal state based on ethnic divisions gave ethnic groups the expectation, and in some cases the administrative infrastructure, of national

---

2. This discussion draws on Stephen D. Shenfield, "Armed Conflict in Eastern Europe and the Former Soviet Union," in Thomas G. Weiss, ed., *The United Nations and Civil Wars* (Boulder, Colo.: Lynne Rienner, 1995), pp. 31–50. For background on the relationship between Soviet domestic structure and ethnic mobilization, see Philip G. Roeder, "Soviet Federalism and Ethnic Mobilization," *World Politics*, Vol. 43, No. 2 (January 1991), pp. 196–232; David D. Laitin, "The National Uprisings in the Soviet Union," *World Politics*, Vol. 44, No. 1 (October 1991), pp. 139–177.

Russia and the Former Soviet Union.

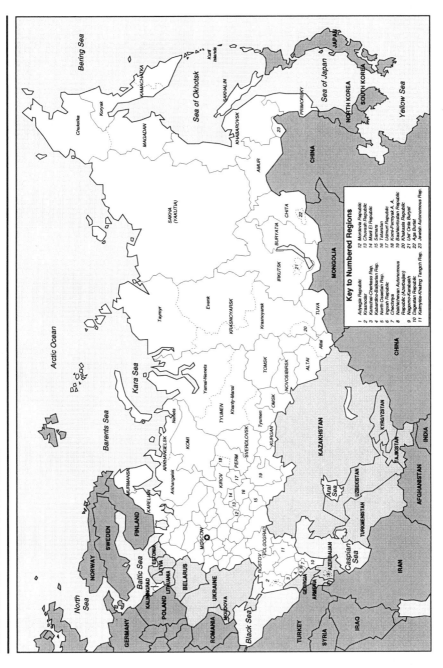

Key to Numbered Regions

1 Adygeia Republic
2 Krasnodar
3 Karachai-Cherkess Rep.
4 Kabardino-Balkarian Rep.
5 North Ossetian Rep.
6 Ingush Republic
7 Chechnya
8 Nakhichevan Autonomous Republic (Azerbaijan)
9 Nagorno-Karabakh
10 Dagestan Republic
11 Kalmykia-Khalmg Tangch Rep.
12 Mordovia Republic
13 Chuvash Republic
14 Mari El Republic
15 Samara
16 Tatarstan
17 Udmurt Republic
18 Komi-Permyak A. A.
19 Bashkortostan Republic
20 Khakasia Republic
21 Ust Orda Buryat
22 Aga Buriat
23 Jewish Autonomous Rep.

statehood."[3] Each of the fifteen union republics had, for example, its own parliament and other institutions of government. These became ready vehicles for expression of anti-Moscow sentiments, once Gorbachev's political reforms permitted open discussion of politics and free elections. The most striking examples of this phenomenon were the three Baltic republics of Estonia, Latvia, and Lithuania, whose ties to the Soviet Union were always tenuous, given their forced incorporation into the union during World War II. Beginning in 1987, new political organizations and politicians arose in the Baltic region, demanding and ultimately achieving independence from Moscow — with very little bloodshed.

Elsewhere in the Soviet Union, and later in Russia as well, the same peculiar political structures contributed to intense violence. As Stephen Shenfield has described, the organization of the Soviet state and the Russian Federation into ethnically-based territorial units created "many anomalies that one or another ethnic group perceived as unjust," and thereby fostered interethnic tension: "many titular groups (Tatars, Bashkirs, Yakuts, Abkhazis, etc.) constituted a minority in their territories; in some cases (for example, Tatars, Jews), most of the titular group was dispersed outside 'its' territory."[4]

The war between Armenia and Azerbaijan provides the starkest example of the possibility for conflict inherent in such a system. It was triggered by the grievances of the Armenian majority in the Nagorno-Karabakh region of Azerbaijan, who complained that the central government in Baku denied them their rights as an autonomous province. A similar situation developed in Abkhazia, which sought independence from Georgia even though ethnic Abkhazis made up only 17 percent of the region's population (and 1.7 percent of Georgia as a whole). As Shenfield points out, "were it not for the Soviet tradition of ethnic autonomies, it is doubtful whether the Abkhaz political leadership could have rationalized giving precedence to Abkhaz 'self-determination' over the rights of the Georgian majority" in Abkhazia.[5]

The case of the self-proclaimed "Dniester Republic," or Transdniestria, illustrates the hold of the Soviet legacy on post-Soviet politics. The Moldavian Soviet Socialist Republic was created in 1940 when a formerly autonomous republic of Ukraine — a narrow strip of land along

---

3. Jessica Eve Stern, "Moscow Meltdown: Can Russia Survive?" *International Security*, Vol. 18, No. 4 (Spring 1994), p. 40.

4. Shenfield, "Armed Conflict in Eastern Europe and the Former Soviet Union," pp. 36–37.

5. Ibid., p. 37.

the left bank of the Dniester River — was combined with Bessarabia, the province seized from Romania under the terms of the Molotov–von Ribbentrop agreement of 1939. As he did elsewhere in the Soviet Union (particularly in the Baltic republics), Stalin sought to dilute the local Moldovan population by fostering immigration of Russian-speakers. Five decades later, when the newly named Republic of Moldova declared its independence from the Soviet Union, the Russian-speaking population of the left bank seceded from the new republic and formed the Dniester Republic. They did so ostensibly to protect the rights of Russians and Ukrainians living there against anticipated discrimination by the Moldovan government, which had announced plans, since downplayed, to reunite with Romania. During the spring and summer of 1992, armed clashes broke out between the Moldovan authorities and the leaders of the breakaway Dniester Republic. The Dniester forces were backed by the Russian (formerly Soviet) 14th Army, based in Tiraspol, the capital of the secessionist republic.[6]

Ethnic Moldovans make up 40 percent of the roughly 740,000 people in the left-bank region, with Ukrainians comprising 28 percent and Russians 25 percent. There are actually more Russians and Ukrainians living in Moldova proper than in the secessionist region.[7] They have not supported the secession; nor, by and large, have they been mistreated by the Moldovan government. The Dniester Republic government, by contrast, has violated the rights of ethnic Moldovans in the region, for example, by forcing Moldovan schools to adopt the Cyrillic alphabet over the Latin one.[8] Yet the conflict in Moldova is not strictly or even essentially an

---

6. For background, see Vladimir Baranovsky, "Conflict Development on the Territory of the Former Soviet Union," *SIPRI Yearbook 1994* (New York: Oxford University Press, 1994), pp. 188–190; Bruce D. Porter and Carol R. Saivetz, "The Once and Future Empire: Russia and the 'Near Abroad'," *Washington Quarterly*, Vol. 17, No. 3 (Summer 1994), pp. 83–85; Fiona Hill and Pamela Jewett, *Back in the USSR: Russia's Intervention in the Internal Affairs of the Former Soviet Republics and the Implications for United States Policy toward Russia* (Cambridge, Mass.: Strengthening Democratic Institutions Project, John F. Kennedy School of Government, Harvard University, January 1994), pp. 61–65.

7. According to the 1989 Soviet census, some 564,000 Russians and 598,000 Ukrainians lived in the Moldavian Soviet Socialist Republic, out of a total population of 4,335,000. See Elizabeth Teague, "Russians Outside Russia and Russian Security Policy," in Leon Aron and Kenneth M. Jensen, eds., *The Emergence of Russian Foreign Policy* (Washington, D.C.: U.S. Institute of Peace, 1994), pp. 81–106.

8. The "Moldovan" language is essentially Romanian, a Romance language written in the Latin script until the Russians imposed their alphabet after taking over in 1940. See Vladimir Socor, "Dniester School Conflict," *RFE/RL Daily Report*, No. 210 (November 4, 1994). All citations to the *RFE/RL Daily Report*, and its successor, the Open Media Research Institute's *OMRI Daily Digest*, refer to the electronic versions.

interethnic one — indeed, both sides deny that it is. Rather, it pits sup-porters of the old Soviet way of life against proponents of change. Jour-nalists who have visited the Dniester Republic describe it as "a living museum of the old USSR" and "a microcosm of the Soviet Union" domi-nated by "Russians filled with Soviet nostalgia."[9] It is the peculiar Soviet legacy that provided the pre-conditions for the conflict — including arbitrary territorial demarcations and the presence of the pro-Russian armed forces on the left bank.

Other arbitrary political divisions and combustible agglomerations of ethnic groups — such as Nikita Khrushchev's 1954 "gift" of the histori-cally Russian Crimean peninsula to Ukraine — could yet produce violent conflict.

Many of the dynamics of interethnic strife that accompanied the breakup of the Soviet Union have been repeated in Russia, where the structure of autonomous regions mirrors the Soviet one. More than a third of the 89 administrative-territorial units that now comprise the Russian Federation are ethnically identified. These include 21 "republics," such as Chechnya, Tatarstan, Dagestan, and North Ossetia, and 10 autonomous "areas" (*okrugi*). Out of a total population of 150 million, Russia contains 30 million non-ethnic Russians representing more than 100 ethnic groups.[10]

Ethnic groups within the Russian Federation, as in the rest of the Soviet Union, were subjected to Stalin's strategy of divide and rule. Many groups thus remain separated by artificial borders, including inter-state ones. Ossetians, for example, are divided between the Russian Federation (the Republic of North Ossetia) and Georgia (the South Ossetian Autono-mous Region). Attempts by the Ossetians of Georgia to gain greater autonomy and unite with their ethnic brethren in the north led in January 1991 to violent repression by Georgian armed forces. Refugees sub-sequently fled over the border into Russia.

Many ethnic groups still live with the consequences of Stalin's whole-sale deportations of native peoples, particularly Chechens, Ingush, Bal-kars, and others from the Caucasus, and with subsequent laws (in 1956 and 1991) that sought to reverse the Stalinist legacy by permitting de-ported peoples to return to their former territories. The Ingush, for exam-

---

9. The first quote is from a Reuters dispatch of November 1, 1994; the second is from the *Frankfurter Allgemeine Zeitung* of November 2, 1994. Both are quoted in Vladimir Socor, "A Rare Close-up View of 'Dniester Republic'," *RFE/RL Daily Report*, No. 212 (November 8, 1994).

10. Stern, "Moscow Meltdown," pp. 47–48. Much of the rest of this section draws on this article.

ple, had been expelled during World War II from an area of North Ossetia known as the *prigorodnyi raion* or "suburban district." Their lands were occupied by Ossetians. When Ingush deportees and their relatives sought to resettle the area during the Gorbachev period, the Ossetians resisted. In autumn 1992, with Russian support, they massacred some ten to twenty thousand Ingush residents of the *raion*.[11]

Evidence of Russian discrimination against a particular ethnic group, combined with historic grievances, contributes in important ways to instability and violence. The most striking example is Chechnya, whose declaration of independence from Russia in 1991 provoked a delayed but extraordinarily violent response from Moscow during the winter of 1994–95. The lessons of Russia's brutal but unexpectedly difficult war against Chechnya may serve to dampen demands for autonomy elsewhere, but the initial reaction from the Caucasus and beyond was, instead, a renewal of suspicion of and opposition to Boris Yeltsin's regime.[12]

One may hope that the Russian army's disastrously inept military performance may have a chastening effect on Moscow, leading to more serious attempts at peaceful resolution of future conflicts, but such an outcome is far from certain. In any case, the preconditions for further ethnic conflict abound throughout the Russian Federation. In combination with other economic and political factors, they could yet produce more violent conflicts of the character, if not magnitude, of the one in Chechnya.

ECONOMIC COMPETITION AND POLITICAL OPPORTUNISM

The territorial-governmental structure of the Soviet Union and Russia, with its arbitrary divisions of ethnic groups and promotion of sometimes artificially constructed national identities, provided only some of the pre-conditions for violent conflict. Other factors that contributed to the outbreak of violence in the former Soviet Union included economic concerns and political opportunism.

---

11. Shenfield, "Armed Conflict in Eastern Europe and the Former Soviet Union," pp. 33, 40; Peter Jarman, "Ethnic Cleansing in the Northern Caucasus," *Moscow News*, No. 6 (February 11–17, 1994), p. 13.

12. Vladimir Socor, "Spillover Effect in Caucasus," *RFE/RL Daily Report*, No. 236 (December 15, 1994); Vladimir Socor, "Ingushetia, Dagestan: Resistance to Russian Advance Reported," *RFE/RL Daily Report*, No. 233 (December 12, 1994); Liz Fuller, "Abkhaz, North Caucasians, Crimean Tatars Support Dudaev," *RFE/RL Daily Report*, No. 233 (December 12, 1994); Vladimir Socor, "More from the Region," *RFE/RL Daily Report*, No. 235 (December 14, 1994); Bess Brown, "Reaction in Kazakhstan to Situation in Chechnya," *RFE/RL Daily Report*, No. 235 (December 14, 1994); Vladimir Socor, "Resistance in Ingushetia . . . and in Dagestan," *RFE/RL Daily Report*, No. 234 (December 13, 1994); Vladimir Socor, "Regional Reverberations," *RFE/RL Daily Report*, No. 235 (December 14, 1994.)

REGIONAL ECONOMIC DISPARITIES. Many of the conflicts in the former Soviet Union are fueled, at least in part, by economic discontent. Although the entire region has suffered dramatic drops in production and economic growth, poverty and declining standards of living are not the main economic factors giving rise to conflict. Even the growing disparities between the poor and the recently rich do not figure prominently among explanations for internal violence — at least not yet.[13] More important are regional disparities, the breakdown of the administrative-command economy, and the attendant scramble for control of economic resources, especially by former members of the Soviet *nomenklatura* or administrative elite.

Many of the conflicts that ultimately take on ethnic dimensions are disputes over control of economic resources that pit a given region against the "center." Nature has endowed some regions of Russia and the former Soviet Union with greater natural resources than others, especially in the energy sector.[14] Many of the richest endowments are located in autonomous republics and areas identified with particular ethnic groups. Sakha (formerly Yakutia), Tatarstan, and Chechnya are prime examples.

Although many of these regions bear historical grievances against Moscow, the more immediate source of discontent during the late Soviet period was the perceived disparity between what the regions contributed to the Soviet economy and what they received back in funds for education, culture, health care, and other services.[15] The initial demands of the

---

13. For background on the economic disparities and decline, see Rustam Arifdzhanov, "The Middle Class is Turning into the Poor, as More and More Mercedes and Beggars Appear," *Izvestiia*, September 15, 1993, trans. in *Current Digest*, Vol. 45, No. 36 (1993), p. 16; Alastair McAuley, "Poverty and Underprivileged Groups," in David Lane, ed., *Russia in Flux: The Political and Social Consequences of Reform* (Brookfield, Vt.: Edward Elgar, 1992), pp. 196–209; Mary Buckley, "The Politics of Social Issues," in Stephen White, Alex Pravda, and Zvi Gitelman, eds., *Developments in Russian and Post-Soviet Politics* (Durham, N.C.: Duke University Press, 1994), pp. 187–207.

14. James P. Dorian and Vitaly P. Borisovich, "Energy and Minerals in the Former Soviet Republics," *Resource Policy*, Vol. 18 (September 1992), pp. 205–229; Gertrude E. Schroeder, "Regional Economic Disparities, Gorbachev's Policies, and the Disintegration of the Soviet Union," pp. 121–145, and Jeffrey W. Schneider, "Republic Energy Sectors and Inter-state Dependencies of the Commonwealth of Independent States and Georgia," pp. 475–489, both in Richard F. Kaufman and John P. Hardt, eds., *The Former Soviet Union in Transition*, papers prepared for the U.S. Congress Joint Economic Committee (Armonk, N.Y.: M.E. Sharpe, 1993).

15. See Roeder, "Soviet Federalism and Ethnic Mobilization"; Donna Bahry, "*Perestroika* and the Debate over Territorial Decentralization," *Harriman Institute Forum*, Vol. 2, No. 5 (May 1989), pp. 1–10.

various regions of the Soviet Union to correct perceived economic disparities were relatively moderate. They became more radical as they
encountered resistance from Moscow.

The Baltic republics, for example, initially sought changes within the
existing Soviet system. In the mid-1980s they sought to implement Gorbachev's policy of *perestroika* and economic decentralization and to reduce
Moscow's economic tutelage. Failing that, they issued formal declarations
of economic autonomy or "sovereignty" in 1988 and 1989. In 1990, they
demanded full independence.[16] In the Tatar Autonomous Soviet Socialist
Republic (ASSR), initial demands were also rather modest. In 1989, the
consensus position of Tatar political activists was to demand an "up-
grade" of their region to the level of Union Republic. In 1991, Tatarstan
declared its independence — a claim as yet unrecognized by any other
country.

POLITICAL OPPORTUNISM AND RADICALIZATION.   Many of the demands for
more economic autonomy from Moscow were understandable responses
to the hypercentralization of the Soviet economy, and, as such, probably
represented a consensus view of the people who lived in these regions.
In many cases, though, economic and political grievances provided opportunities for political figures to gain (or retain) power. Their escalation
and radicalization of demands, in combination with Moscow's recalci-
trance, often inflamed conflicts and made compromise solutions difficult.

In some cases, pressure for radicalization has come "from below," as
in 1989, when Tatar activists declared a prominent writer an "enemy of
the Tatar people" because he opposed making Kazan Tatar the official
language of the Tatar autonomous republic. (Given that Tatars and Tatar-
speakers constituted a minority in the Tatar ASSR, his position was not
unreasonable.[17]) Many activists adopted such radical stances as a means
of launching their political careers. Some embraced extreme positions in
order to discredit their opponents; this was true, for example, of Zviad
Gamsakhurdia in Georgia and Abulfez Elchibey in Azerbaijan.

Many of the most radical nationalist views were espoused not only
by former dissidents such as Gamsakhurdia and Elchibey, but by former

---

16. Edward Walker, "Appendix: A Chronology of Nationality-Related Events, 1985–
1991," in Charles F. Furtado, Jr. and Andrea Chandler, eds., *Perestroika in the Soviet
Republics: Documents on the National Question* (Boulder, Colo.: Westview, 1992). I am
grateful to Sharon Werning for research on these declarations of sovereignty and
independence.

17. Uli Schamiloglu, "The Tatar Public Center and Current Tatar Concerns," *Report
on the USSR,* December 12, 1989, pp. 11–15; see p. 15.

Communist Party officials who sought new identities and bases of support in the post-Soviet world. Prominent examples include Leonid Kravchuk, the former Communist Party leader of the Ukrainian Soviet Socialist Republic, who was elected president of Ukraine on a nationalist platform, and then worked hard to learn to speak Ukrainian as well as he spoke Russian; and Dzhokhar Dudaev, the highly Russified former Soviet air force general who served most of his career outside his native Chechnya, but returned in time to lead its disastrous independence drive from Moscow. Significantly, however, some former communist officials have not embraced radical nationalism. Eduard Shevardnadze of Georgia and Nursultan Nazarbaev of Kazakhstan are notable in this regard. So, too, is Heidar Aliev, former KGB official, Soviet Politburo member, and communist leader of Azerbaijan, whose interest in improving relations with Russia apparently led Moscow to support him and help depose his predecessor Elchibey in a coup.[18]

In addition, non-communists who were new to politics often adopted increasingly radical positions in order to distance themselves from their previously apolitical accommodation to Soviet rule. A journalist captured the essence of this transformation in describing his 1991 interview with Vytautus Landsbergis, the professor of musicology who became the first post-Soviet president of Lithuania: "his once elegant Russian had become gradually more accented; now it seemed almost painfully halting, or pointedly tentative, as if he was carefully shedding any traces of the Soviet past."[19]

The radicalization of political views between the regions and Moscow or between ethnic groups within a region makes peaceful compromise difficult. Politicians interested more in furthering their own political and economic ambitions than in providing for the security and welfare of their constituencies are sometimes prone to incite ethnic hatred and violence in order to attain or maintain power.

International Implications and Involvement

The end of the Cold War increased the scope for non-Russian international involvement in the internal affairs of the Soviet successor states in a number of ways — including the participation of international organi-

---

18. Ilja Dadashidze, "Geidar Aliev Has Become President of Azerbaijan," *Moscow News*, No. 41 (October 8, 1993), p. 8; Thomas Goltz, "Letter from Eurasia: The Hidden Russian Hand," *Foreign Policy*, No. 92 (Fall 1993), pp. 92–116; Hill and Jewett, *Back in the USSR*, pp. 10–17.

19. Paul Quinn-Judge, "Do Svidaniya," *Boston Globe Magazine*, October 4, 1992, p. 43.

zations in conflict resolution, peacekeeping, and monitoring, and the possibility of unilateral action, such as making aid contingent on maintaining certain standards of internal behavior. The possibility for such international involvement is the legacy of Gorbachev's foreign policy reforms. Under Gorbachev, the Soviet Union sought to improve its relations with and become better integrated into the international community. Soviet foreign policy increasingly took into account the legitimate interests of other states. Soviet support for, and involvement in, international institutions grew.

Boris Yeltsin continued the trend, to the point where at least some portion of the Russian foreign policy community came to advocate multilateralism and reliance on international institutions as an alternative (or supplement) to traditional, unilateral, power politics.[20] Although the attachment to international institutions is tenuous in some cases and merely rhetorical in others, the fact that leaders in Russia and the other former Soviet republics have explicitly expressed their intention to participate actively in international institutions gives those institutions wider scope for involving themselves in conflicts in the region.

The end of the Cold War has also transformed the role that other states can play in post-Soviet affairs. Whereas external criticism of Soviet internal policy — and Soviet rejection of that criticism — were the common currency of the Cold War, the situation has changed. The Soviet successor states' rhetorical embrace of human rights, individual freedoms, and democracy means that they can less readily dismiss criticism of their behavior. The fact that the United States and the advanced industrialized countries of Europe provide economic aid to Russia and the other states gives them more standing to comment on these matters. For example, the French foreign minister, German chancellor, and North Atlantic Treaty Organization (NATO) secretary-general have all criticized Russia for its invasion of Chechnya.[21] At the same time, Western governments often seem reluctant to criticize the practices of the Soviet successor states — particularly Russia — for fear of undermining leaders whom they support. This was clearly the thinking behind the weak U.S. response to Russia's war on Chechnya.[22]

---

20. Celeste Wallander, "International Institutions and Modern Security Strategies," *Problems of Communism*, Vol. 41, No. 1–2 (January–April 1992), pp. 44–62.

21. Liz Fuller, "International Reaction," *OMRI Daily Digest*, Vol. 1, No. 5 (January 6, 1995); Liz Fuller, "International Diplomatic Responses," *OMRI Daily Digest*, Vol. 1, No. 7 (January 10, 1995).

22. Elaine Sciolino, "Administration Sees No Choice but to Support Yeltsin," *New York Times*, January 7, 1995, p. 4.

Although substantial changes in Soviet and post-Soviet policies toward the international community have taken place, in crucial respects the prospects for international involvement in internal conflicts depend, as in the past, on considerations of relative state power. As far as Russia is concerned, international involvement in the former Soviet Union is "by invitation only." Formally, Russia can veto any international intervention conducted under the auspices of the United Nations (UN) by virtue of its permanent seat on the Security Council. In practical terms, it has the military power to deter unwanted interventions. Russia can also reject outside economic assistance to which unacceptable strings are attached — as can the other post-Soviet states. Finally, Russia can simply break the constraints imposed by international institutions when it so chooses. In its invasion of Chechnya in December 1994, for example, Russia violated the provisions established by the Conference on Security and Cooperation in Europe (CSCE, now OSCE, Organization for Security and Cooperation in Europe) for prior notification of large troop movements.

To the extent that we characterize Russia's own involvement in the conflicts along its periphery as "external," "regional," or "international," considerations of relative power are again crucial. Because of its predominant position, Russia needs no invitation to intervene in the affairs of its weaker neighbors. The situation is more ambiguous with regard to the intervention of other states in the affairs of Russia's neighbors in the "near abroad." Turkey, Iran, and Afghanistan have sought in various ways to increase their influence in several former Soviet republics, at Russia's expense. There is not much that Russia can do about this without explicitly raising the prospect of military conflict.

REGIONAL INVOLVEMENT

The most prominent regional actor involved in the conflicts on the territory of the former Soviet Union is Russia. Acting independently, as well as through the Commonwealth of Independent States (CIS) — the regional organization that nominally succeeded the Union of Soviet Socialist Republics — Russia has interfered in some way in every conflict of consequence. Other former Soviet states, such as Ukraine and Uzbekistan, have sought to act mainly through the CIS to assert their influence in conflicts that affected their interests. They have also sought to use the CIS collective decision-making procedures to temper whatever imperial ambitions Russia might harbor. Finally, neighboring states to the west, such as the Baltic countries and Poland, and to the south, such as Iran, Turkey, and Afghanistan, have expressed concern about conflicts on former Soviet territory; the latter three states have become directly involved in some of these conflicts — sometimes as partisans of one side, sometimes as mediators.

RUSSIA'S ROLE. Because of Russia's predominant position among the Soviet successor states and the great-power sensibilities of Russia's leaders, few violent conflicts of any consequence in the former Soviet Union have failed to engage Russia in one way or another. In social-science jargon, Russian intervention is "overdetermined." One can adduce various motivations for Russian involvement: strategic requirements for a system of military bases along Russia's periphery; protection of Russian nationals in the "near abroad"; the need to restore stability to conflict-ridden areas; the desire to gain or retain control of resources, particularly energy; a preference for "friendly" leaders in neighboring states; even the need to stop organized crime, as Yeltsin suggested in demonizing Chechnya as a "criminal republic." Removing one or several of these motivations might still not remove the impetus for intervention. It may be that Russian activity in the "near abroad" is mainly a function of a hypertrophied security establishment, or it may be that prominent members of the Russian foreign policy establishment are determined to reconstitute the Soviet Union — something that cannot be done by peaceful means.

In any case, Russia has managed to involve itself indirectly in all of the civil wars along its periphery.[23] Shenfield has offered this "rough generalization" of Moscow's role:

Russia first helps the side it favors up to the point at which a politico-military result that it considers satisfactory has been achieved. It then shifts to the role of an impartial peacekeeper, prepared to use force even against those maverick extremist elements of the previously favored side who are determined to fight for a result better than the one secured for them by Moscow.[24]

The conflicts in Georgia, Moldova, Tajikistan, and Azerbaijan fit this generalization quite well.

In Georgia, Russian military forces intervened twice in conflicts between the central government and regional minorities. The secession movements in South Ossetia and Abkhazia mobilized in response to the

---

23. A detailed overview of these conflicts is found in Hill and Jewett, *Back in the USSR.* The Russian "peacekeeping" role is discussed in Roy Allison, *Peacekeeping in the Soviet Successor States,* Chaillot Paper 18 (Paris: Western European Union (WEU) Institute for Security Studies, November 1994), especially pp. 2–11, and in Porter and Saivetz, "The Once and Future Empire."

24. Shenfield, "Armed Conflict in Eastern Europe and the Former Soviet Union," p. 43.

nationalist rhetoric and policies of Zviad Gamsakhurdia, elected chair of the Georgian Supreme Soviet (in effect, the president of Georgia) in October 1990, more than a year before the breakup of the Soviet Union. Russia took advantage of the conflicts in Georgia to support the secessionists and to put pressure on the central government in Tbilisi. Its main objective, following the dissolution of the Soviet Union in December 1991, was to blackmail Georgia into joining the CIS and permitting the permanent basing of Russian military forces on Georgian territory.

In January 1991, efforts by the South Ossetian Autonomous Region (*oblast'*) to secede from Georgia and unite with neighboring North Ossetia, a republic within the Russian Federation, resulted in violence when Gamsakhurdia ordered the Georgian army to crush the secessionists. The ensuing fight led to a mass exodus of thousands of South Ossetian refugees across the border into North Ossetia. They exacerbated an already tense situation in the region, where Ossetians were resisting the return of deported Ingush settlers seeking to reclaim their land. Russian troops became involved in the conflict in two ways. First, in October and November 1992, they supported the operations of Ossetian special forces in their massacre of Ingush civilians.[25] Second, in July 1992, the Russian army intervened in South Ossetia as "peacekeepers," providing a foothold for further operations in Georgia.[26]

In August 1992, Abkhazia's attempt to secede from Georgia led to warfare with the central government, headed by Eduard Shevardnadze following the ouster of Gamsakhurdia in December 1991. While the Russian government formally professed neutrality, Russian military forces provided the Abkhaz separatists with arms, equipment, personnel, and training as they fought to gain control of the Abkhaz capital of Sukhumi. Russian Su-27 aircraft bombed the city, on behalf of the secessionists, even as President Shevardnadze traveled to the city to organize its defense and attempt — unsuccessfully, as it turned out — to keep it under Georgian control. With Shevardnadze preoccupied with the war against Abkhazia, Gamsakhurdia returned from exile in September 1993 to launch an attack from the western region of Mingrelia. Not until the Abkhazis had taken Sukhumi and Gamsakhurdia's forces were pressing their offensive did Russia come to Shevardnadze's aid, even though he had already acceded to all of Russia's demands. Georgia was to join the CIS, grant Russia

---

25. Shenfield, "Armed Conflict in Eastern Europe and the Former Soviet Union," pp. 33, 40; Jarman, "Ethnic Cleansing in the Northern Caucasus," p. 13.

26. Hill and Jewett, *Back in the USSR*, p. 48; Porter and Saivetz, "The Once and Future Empire," p. 85.

long-term military basing rights on the Black Sea, and agree to an indefinite Russian military presence in Georgia.

Russia's approach to the conflict between Moldova and the secessionist Dniester Republic followed the same pattern. Like Georgia, Moldova initially refused to join the CIS. The Moldovan government in Chisinau demanded the withdrawal of the Russian 14th Army from its territory. Instead, Moscow sided with the Russian-speakers in their conflict with the Moldovan authorities. It allowed Russian Cossack forces from throughout the Russian Federation to travel to Moldova to support the Dniester secessionists. It directed the 14th Army, led by Lieutenant-General Aleksandr Lebed, to support the breakaway republic (Lebed himself was elected to its parliament), and it provided massive subsidies of energy and raw materials to Tiraspol. Only when Moldova capitulated to Russia's demands — CIS membership, economic and security integration — did Moscow take a more evenhanded approach to the conflict, including promises, as yet unfulfilled, to withdraw the 14th Army.[27]

In 1992, Russia became involved in a full-scale civil war in Tajikistan. To simplify an extremely complicated situation, the war pitted stalwarts of the old Soviet *nomenklatura*, supported by an array of organized criminals largely drawn from the province of Kulob, plus Tajikistan's ethnic Uzbek minority, against a loose coalition of Muslims, democrats, nationalists, and residents of the Gharm and Pamir regions that have long been Kulob's rivals. The opposition coalition claimed the 1991 election of President Rakhmon Nabiev was fraudulent, and agitated for new elections in March 1992. Nabiev responded by forming a paramilitary presidential security force, led by Yakub Salimov, a "notorious racketeer," to disperse the opposition by force.[28] His opponents rebuffed Nabiev's attack and he was obliged to form a coalition government, granting the opposition eight ministerial portfolios. Nabiev's pro-communist allies refused to accept the new arrangement, however, and managed to depose the coalition government by seizing the capital, Dushanbe, in December 1992. The communists were backed by the so-called Popular Front, an armed band led by Sangak Safarov, an ex-felon recently freed after twenty-three years in prison. In taking Dushanbe, the Front carried out an "ethnic cleansing" of opposition sympathizers (mainly people from the regions of Gharm and Badakhshon). Tens of thousands of people were

---

27. This account draws mainly on Hill and Jewett, *Back in the USSR*, pp. 61–65.

28. Vladimir Klimenko, "A Tale of Two Countries," *Mother Jones* (July/August 1993), pp. 54–57; Shahrbanou Tadjbakhsh, "The Bloody Path of Change: The Case of Post-Soviet Tajikistan," *Harriman Institute Forum*, Vol. 6, No. 11 (July 1993), pp. 1–10.

killed between October 1992 and March 1993, more than in any other conflict in the former Soviet Union.[29]

The Russian military role in the conflict is somewhat uncertain, but hardly inconsequential. Many reports indicate that Russia's 201st Motorized Rifle Division, stationed in Tajikistan, armed both sides in the early stages of the conflict, either deliberately or by negligence (for example, by allowing the theft or sale of Kalashnikov rifles, armored vehicles, and tanks).[30] In autumn 1993, Russia accused Afghan groups of smuggling weapons across the Afghan-Tajik border to the opposition forces. In late September, Russian troops seized control of the Dushanbe airport and reinforced their deployments along the border. In October, the CIS deployed "peacekeeping" forces to Tajikistan — mainly Russian units, with some Uzbek troops, all under Russian command. The substantial Russian military presence in Tajikistan has helped keep the country in Russia's sphere of influence and insure that the Tajik government continues to pursue pro-Moscow policies.

The conflict between Armenia and Azerbaijan over Nagorno-Karabakh combines elements of civil war with inter-state war. Russia has manipulated both aspects of the conflict, seeking mainly to secure the integration of Armenia and Azerbaijan into the CIS and the deployment of Russian troops on their territories. Unlike the Soviet government, which tended to support Baku's position by denying Nagorno Karabakh's right to secede from Azerbaijan, Yeltsin's government has favored the Armenians. The Republic of Armenia depends on Russia for protection against its historic enemies, Turkey and Azerbaijan, and has allowed the stationing of Russian troops on its territory. Azerbaijan, by contrast, refused to join the CIS or adhere to its economic and military accords, as Armenia had done.

Russia's actions seem to have been calculated to undermine Azerbaijan's intransigence. On May 17, 1992, the day after Azerbaijan refused to sign the CIS Mutual Security Pact, troops from Nagorno-Karabakh launched a successful offensive on the Azeri town of Lachin, creating a land bridge between the breakaway province and Armenia. With Russian troops patrolling Armenia's borders during the attack, few considered the timing coincidental. Russia subsequently contributed to the downfall of the recalcitrant government of Abulfez Elchibey in Baku by backing Surat Huseinov, a renegade Azeri military commander who inherited much of

---

29. Tadjbakhsh, "The Bloody Path of Change," pp. 1–3; Klimenko, "A Tale of Two Countries."

30. Porter and Saivetz, "The Once and Future Empire," p. 86; Tadjbakhsh, "The Bloody Path of Change," p. 7.

the weaponry of the Russian 104th Airborne Division when it withdrew unexpectedly in May 1993. Huseinov, who supported the return of Heidar Aliev to power, conducted an assault on the Elchibey government; this coup attempt, which followed another military victory for the Karabakh Armenians, contributed to the collapse of the Elchibey government in July.[31]

Ironically, Azerbaijan had been close to an agreement with Armenia on the conflict over Nagorno-Karabakh. Indeed, Baku had announced a unilateral cease-fire just two weeks before the Karabakh forces attacked. The Elchibey government had, however, resisted Russia's demand to deploy its troops as peacekeepers to secure the agreement. Russia seems to have encouraged the Karabakh offensive to persuade Azerbaijan to agree to its conditions for a settlement.

When Heidar Aliev took over from Elchibey, Azerbaijan still faced intense military pressure from the Armenians as well as from Turkish and Iranian forces which had mobilized along the border. Russian tanks were reported to be supporting the Armenian offensive. In desperation, Aliev made a play for Russian support by securing a mandate from the Azeri parliament to have Azerbaijan join the CIS and accept Russian troop deployments. Russia consequently switched sides in November 1993 and sent 200 military officers to help train the Azeri military. At the same time, the Russian foreign minister threatened Armenia with "something other than persuasion" if it did not cease its support for the Karabakh forces.[32]

Not only did Russia's actions *vis-à-vis* Armenia and Azerbaijan support its strategic objectives in maintaining a CIS security zone, but they also demonstrated that these objectives took precedence over resolving the Azeri-Armenian conflict. Indeed, Russia was willing, in this case as in others, to escalate and prolong the conflict in order to secure its own ends.

COMMONWEALTH OF INDEPENDENT STATES. The involvement of the Commonwealth of Independent States in internal conflicts in the former Soviet Union is controversial. Many critics suspect that it is merely an extension of Russian foreign policy, another instrument of Russia's domination of its neighbors. Is there any reason to consider the CIS, as Russia claims, an international organization that should be officially endorsed as such by the United Nations?[33]

---

31. Hill and Jewett, *Back in the USSR*, pp. 10–12.

32. This quote comes from ibid., pp. 14–17.

33. For background, see Elizabeth Teague, "The CIS: An Unpredictable Future,"

There is no doubt that many Russian political figures consider the territory of the former Soviet Union "a sphere of vital Russian interests," as Yeltsin put it in an address to the UN General Assembly in September 1994. Yeltsin claimed that "the main burden of peacemaking [there] rests on the Russian Federation's shoulders."[34] There is also little doubt that senior Russian military leaders see "peacekeeping" deployments in strategic terms. By maintaining bases and troops in states on Russia's periphery, the Russian army can defend the country at the old Soviet borders rather than develop new defensive lines at the Russian Federation's actual international borders. Considerable evidence supports this conclusion, from Yeltsin's description of the Tajik-Afghan border as "in essence the border of Russia" to a Russian Security Council decision to defend the former Soviet borders, at least in Central Asia, but possibly in the Caucasus as well.[35]

Although Russia is undoubtedly inclined to use the CIS for its own purposes, one can argue that the presence of CIS forces does help to preserve peace and stability in some cases. It is unrealistic to assume that, were Russia not directly involved in peacekeeping in the former Soviet Union, an impartial, multilateral force sponsored by the United Nations would step in to take its place. Many of the conflicts in the former Soviet Union do not meet the UN's criteria for launching a peacekeeping mission — the existence of a cease-fire in place, and the acceptance by all parties of the peacekeeping force, for example. Russian "peacekeepers," as Roy Allison describes, "are ready forcefully to separate the opposing sides before a cease-fire has come into effect." Their duties, according to a Russian military commander, include "the pursuit, apprehension or destruction by fire of groups and individuals who are not following the rules of a given situation."[36] This is far more ambitious than anything the

RFE/RL Research Report, Vol. 3, No. 1 (January 7, 1994), pp. 9–12; Suzanne Crow, "Russia Promotes the CIS as an International Organization," *RFE/RL Research Report*, Vol. 3, No. 11 (March 18, 1994), pp. 33–38; Vladimir Socor, "Conflict-Resolution Groups Created," *RFE/RL Daily Report*, No. 209 (November 3, 1994); Susan L. Clark, "Russia in a Peacekeeping Role," in Aron and Jensen, *The Emergence of Russian Foreign Policy*, pp. 119–147.

34. Vladimir Socor, "Yeltsin at UN on CIS Affairs," *RFE/RL Daily Report*, No. 184 (September 27, 1994); Vladimir Socor, "'Yeltsin Doctrine,' 'Kozyrev Doctrine'," *RFE/RL Daily Report*, No. 190 (October 6, 1994).

35. Pavel Felgengauer, "Starye granitsy i 'novye bazy'" [Old borders and "new bases"], *Segodnia* [Today], September 16, 1993, and the discussion in Allison, *Peacekeeping in the Soviet Successor States*, pp. 54–55.

36. This quote comes from Allison, *Peacekeeping in the Soviet Successor States*, pp. 26–27.

United Nations would undertake. In some cases, Russian actions have probably saved lives and brought stability to dangerous situations.

Unfortunately, in too many cases Russia appears to have deliberately provoked, prolonged, or intensified regional conflicts in order to secure "invitations" to intervene. In return for playing the role of peacemaker, Russia has extracted concessions, such as membership in the CIS from republics that had initially resisted (Moldova, Georgia, Azerbaijan), and agreements to long-term basing of Russian forces.

One might have more enthusiasm for the use of CIS peacekeeping forces in the future if they had adhered in the past to the set of principles upon which Russian Foreign Minister Andrei Kozyrev and his British counterpart, Douglas Hurd, agreed at the end of 1993: "strict respect for the sovereignty of the countries involved; an invitation from the government concerned, and the consent of the parties to the conflict; the use of multinational peacekeeping forces wherever possible; and an exit strategy for the peacekeeping forces."[37] There may be emergency situations where these conditions need not be met, but Russia has violated these principles on a regular basis.

OTHER REGIONAL POWERS. Russia's neighbors to the west take a great interest in the conflicts in the former Soviet Union, but have so far avoided direct involvement. The Baltic states, in particular, are concerned that Russia's behavior in Chechnya and Tajikistan, for example, could set precedents for actions directed against them. Russian leaders have made no secret of the issue (or pretext) that could lead to military intervention in the Baltic area: protection of Russian speakers living there.

Other states that have manifested interest in the conflicts along Russia's periphery include Turkey, Iran, and Afghanistan. Turkey seems to be motivated primarily by a desire to expand its influence in Central Asia — a region populated mainly by Turkic-speaking peoples (in Kazakhstan, Turkmenistan, Uzbekistan, Azerbaijan, and Kyrgyzstan). It is also interested in the economic benefits to be derived by helping to export Azerbaijan's oil.[38] Iran and Afghanistan seem to view conflicts along Russia's southern border as opportunities to promote their versions of Islam in regions where there are also people of related ethnic background. Tajiks, for example, are related to the Iranians and speak a Persian language; Azeris live in northern Iran.

---

37. Joint article published simultaneously in *Izvestiia* and the *Financial Times*, December 14, 1993, quoted in Allison, *Peacekeeping in the Soviet Successor States*, p. 62.

38. Liz Fuller, "Russia, Turkey, Azerbaijan, and Oil," *RFE/RL Daily Report*, No. 209 (November 3, 1994).

All three states are also undoubtedly motivated by concerns for their security — but this does not tell us much about their preferences. Presumably they would feel most secure if they dominated the regions along their borders. Short of that, it is not clear if they would prefer prolonged instability to a Russian-imposed stability. To avoid that choice, they might prefer the more neutral involvement of international organizations. Turkey, in particular, has endorsed international efforts at peaceful resolution of the conflicts in Nagorno-Karabakh and Chechnya, and Iran has sponsored talks between the Tajik government and opposition.[39]

INTERNATIONAL INVOLVEMENT

Given the importance of traditional power politics in the former Soviet Union — especially evident in Russia's behavior — it is somewhat surprising how little the major powers have become involved in the region's conflicts. Their involvement has taken indirect forms, as reflected in their support for participation by international institutions, such as NATO, the OSCE (formerly CSCE), and the United Nations, in sponsoring negotiations and monitoring cease-fires.

THE UNITED STATES.   The United States has had little involvement in conflicts in the former Soviet Union. To the extent that one can identify U.S. interests at stake there, they revolve around concerns that nuclear weapons and fissile material remain secure and under Russian control. There is also a rhetorical commitment to the territorial integrity of the three Baltic states and Ukraine. Kazakhstan also seems to engage U.S. interests because of its size, its vast natural resources, its place in the Soviet nuclear legacy, and its large Russian population.

However, the United States has not sought to invoke, for example, humanitarian concerns as a reason to involve itself in post-Soviet affairs — despite cases of ethnic cleansing (in Tajikistan and North Ossetia-Ingushetia), massive refugee crises (Abkhazia, Tajikistan), and deliberate aerial attacks on civilian homes, hospitals, and orphanages (Chechnya). Nor has the United States upheld the norm of sovereignty when Russia has intervened in its neighbors' civil wars.

EUROPE.   The major European powers have tended to involve themselves in the internal conflicts of the Soviet successor states mainly through the

39.   Ibid. Also, Liz Fuller, "Dudaev Appeals to Turkey for Help," *RFE/RL Daily Report*, No. 238 (December 19, 1994); Bess Brown, "Tajik Government-Opposition Commission Meets," *RFE/RL Daily Report*, No. 217 (November 15, 1994); Bess Brown, "Tajik Cease-Fire Extended," *RFE/RL Daily Report*, No. 216 (November 14, 1994).

actions of the international organizations of which they are the leading members. Beyond that, Western European political leaders have made public pronouncements about various conflicts in the former Soviet Union, and have occasionally linked economic aid programs to the peaceful resolution of these conflicts — as Alain Juppé, then France's foreign minister and head of the Western European Union, did in reaction to Russia's attack on Chechnya.

NATO. The North Atlantic Treaty Organization has become involved in conflicts on the territory of the former Soviet Union in two ways. First, at a rhetorical level, NATO officials express the views of the alliance's leading members in response to particular developments, such as the indiscriminate killing of civilians during Russia's bombardment of Grozny, the capital of Chechnya. Second, NATO's Partnership for Peace program provides a mechanism for bringing former Soviet republics — including Russia itself — closer to NATO. (Of the fifteen former Soviet republics, only Tajikistan has not joined the Partnership program.) What that means in terms of a NATO, and, therefore, a U.S. commitment to the security of these states is unclear, but it does imply a greater level of involvement and interest. Russia's uneasiness about an eastward expansion of NATO, and the use of NATO forces in Bosnia, has probably made some of the new "partners" in the "near abroad" reluctant to provoke their powerful Russian neighbor by developing close ties with NATO. Armenia, for example, upon signing a Partnership for Peace agreement, explicitly ruled out direct NATO participation in efforts to resolve the conflict in Nagorno-Karabakh.[40]

CSCE/OSCE. The CSCE, now the OSCE, has become involved in the resolution of several disputes in the former Soviet Union. In particular, it has worked to reach a settlement of the conflict between Armenia and Azerbaijan over Nagorno-Karabakh. It has also sent observers to South Ossetia, the Dniester Republic, and Abkhazia. The OSCE maintains a permanent mission in Moldova and has made recommendations, endorsed by the Moldovan president, for resolving the conflict there by granting the Dniester Republic a special administrative status.[41] Finally, it has sought to end the Russian war against Chechnya by sponsoring

---

40. Liz Fuller, "Armenia Joins Partnership for Peace," *RFE/RL Daily Report*, No. 190 (October 6, 1994).

41. Allison, *Peacekeeping in the Soviet Successor States*, pp. 49–50; Dan Ionescu, "Moldovan President Says Russia Has Special Role in Dniester Region," *OMRI Daily Digest*, No. 110, Part II (June 7, 1995).

negotiations between the Russian government and the forces of Chechen president Dudaev.[42]

The OSCE's involvement in the Nagorno-Karabakh dispute initially created friction with Russia, which was conducting its own negotiations with Armenia and Azerbaijan. In October 1994, Russia's negotiator charged that "some countries are trying to use the CSCE as a cover for their geopolitical interests, rather than as a conflict resolution mechanism. Some people would like to minimize Russia's role and exclude the CIS from the process." The CSCE's Committee of Senior Officials, in turn, criticized Russia for undermining its mediation efforts.[43] Since then relations between the OSCE and Russia have improved. In December 1994, the OSCE decided, with Russia's approval, to dispatch a multinational peacekeeping force to Nagorno-Karabakh.[44] By June 1995, Russia had fully joined the OSCE effort as co-chair of the mediation effort and appeared to be exerting a positive influence on the parties involved.[45]

UNITED NATIONS. The United Nations has played a fairly active role in several conflicts in the former Soviet Union, although its effectiveness has often been overshadowed by Russian and CIS involvement. The UN's main activities have consisted of sponsoring negotiations to resolve the civil war in Tajikistan and monitoring the conflicts there and in Abkhazia.

In August 1993, the UN Security Council approved the deployment of 88 observers to monitor a cease-fire between Georgia and Abkhazia. When the United Nations failed to get the two sides to agree to deployment of UN peacekeepers, the Russian army stepped in to play that role.[46] In November 1994, the Abkhaz parliament adopted a new constitution characterizing Abkhazia as an independent country. Arguing that the Abkhaz action threatened to undermine the basis for a negotiated solution to the conflict, Shevardnadze appealed unsuccessfully to the UN

---

42. Liz Fuller, "OSCE Chechnya Talks Collapse," *OMRI Daily Digest*, No. 102, Part I (May 26, 1995).

43. Vladimir Socor, "Russia Challenges CSCE over Karabakh," *RFE/RL Daily Report*, No. 190 (October 6, 1994).

44. Liz Fuller, "Karabakh Mediation Update," *RFE/RL Daily Report*, No. 216 (November 14, 1994); Liz Fuller, "Reaction to CSCE Karabakh Decision," *RFE/RL Daily Report*, No. 232 (December 9, 1994).

45. Lowell Bezanis, "Armenia to Participate in Talks," *OMRI Daily Digest*, No. 108, Part I (June 5, 1995).

46. Allison, *Peacekeeping in the Soviet Successor States*, pp. 46–47; Clark, "Russia in a Peacekeeping Role."

Security Council to convene an emergency session and discuss the issue.[47] Nodar Natadze, a leading Georgian opposition politician, asserted that "the UN is incapable of exerting any practical influence on the settlement of the conflict."[48] Nevertheless, the UN Security Council extended the mandate of its observer force, expanded to 136 members, until January 1996. The CIS followed suit by agreeing to maintain its peacekeeping force in Georgia until 1996 as well.[49]

During 1994 and 1995, the United Nations sponsored a series of negotiations between the Tajik government and opposition forces in an effort to secure a cease-fire and work out a longer-term settlement. The fourth round of talks, held in Kazakhstan in May 1995, produced a three-month extension of the cease-fire, but efforts to establish a coalition government and revise the constitution to meet the concerns of the opposition were adamantly resisted by the Tajik government.[50]

In the meantime, Russia had convinced the other members of the CIS to send a Russian-dominated peacekeeping force to Tajikistan. Russia's 201st Motorized Rifle Division has maintained an uneasy truce between the communist government and the opposition, although it is generally understood to favor the former. It has been particularly preoccupied with securing the Tajik-Afghan border, where nine Russian border guards were killed in January 1995.[51] The United Nations sent a six-person mission to Tajikistan to monitor the CIS peacekeepers, but most observers have been disappointed with the UN mission's performance.[52]

International organizations have achieved their greatest successes when they have worked with Russia rather than against it — a truism that reflects the importance of Russian power in resolving disputes in the region. Despite the primacy of Russia's role, however, international organizations bring to the conflicts qualities that the Russians often lack — impartiality, prestige, and good offices. Moreover, they are sources of new

---

47. Liz Fuller, "Abkhaz-UN Talks Deadlocked," *RFE/RL Daily Report*, No. 219 (November 18, 1994); Liz Fuller, "Georgia Calls for UN Security Council Meeting on Abkhazia," *RFE/RL Daily Report*, No. 227 (December 2, 1994).

48. Nodar Natadze is quoted in Liz Fuller, "Boutros-Ghali on Abkhaz Refugees," *RFE/RL Daily Report*, No. 209 (November 3, 1994).

49. Liz Fuller, "CIS Peacekeeping Force to Remain in Abkhazia?" *OMRI Daily Digest*, No. 94, Part I (May 16, 1995).

50. Bruce Pannier, "Tajik Talks Yield Results," *OMRI Daily Digest*, No. 105, Part I (May 31, 1995).

51. Liz Fuller, "Tajik Opposition Will Not Attend Next Round of Peace Talks," *OMRI Daily Digest*, Vol. 1, No. 5 (January 6, 1995).

52. Clark, "Russia in a Peacekeeping Role," p. 135.

ideas and proposals for conflict resolution. Even if Russia must ultimately endorse international proposals for them to be implemented, the fact that they are put forward adds a new element to the internal Russian debates over policies towards the "near abroad." International engagement opens up possibilities for Moscow to adopt a less self-interested approach than it might have done, left to its own devices.

Conclusions

The economic and political legacy of the Soviet period has sown the seeds of future conflicts, much as it contributed to the breakup of the union itself. Such conflicts are likely to stem from unresolved irredentist claims and problems of diaspora populations, combined with economic discontent and inflamed by opportunistic politicians. The result in many regions will be violent conflict, including the possibility of civil war among Russians. The role for outside powers and international organizations in preventing or resolving such conflicts will not be a large one, especially given the preponderance of Russian power in the region. External actors will exert a positive influence, however, if they can bolster the position of internal proponents of moderation and undercut extremists. Such efforts promise better results than ceding the region to a Russian sphere of influence.

THE OUTLOOK FOR CONFLICT
Because violent conflict on the territory of the former Soviet Union is a recent phenomenon, it is impossible to make confident assessments of which situations are likely to turn violent, and which are likely to engage other states and international organizations. Situations which have not yet turned violent or involved regional powers may yet do so.

PROBLEMS OF ECONOMIC TRANSITION.   The fundamental political and economic transformations that have been taking place in the former Soviet Union have set the stage for free-for-all competitions for control of economic resources. The collapse of central planning and state ownership has left property rights up for grabs. As Shenfield describes, "the prospect of privatization greatly raises the stakes in struggles for power and makes it much more urgent to win. If the coming to power of some group is delayed by a few years, privatization may have been completed already in a fashion detrimental to the interests of that group."[53]

---

53. Shenfield, "Armed Conflict in Eastern Europe and the Former Soviet Union," p. 35.

Many regions within Russia have appealed to the Soviet legacy of "autonomies" to assert control over local resources, thereby creating potential conflict situations.[54] In 1993, for example, Russia's Constitutional Court recognized as legal the separation of the autonomous area of Chukotka (okrug) from Magadan (oblast'). The Chukchi people represented only 7.3 percent of the population, whereas Russians and Ukrainians made up 83 percent (according to the 1989 census). The motives were clearly not "ethnic," but rather economic. Separation from Magadan would give Chukotka control over its valuable mineral resources (mainly tin and coal).[55] With the same goal in mind, the autonomous areas of Khanty-Mansi and Iamalo-Nenets sought to secede from Tiumen oblast'. In doing so, they would have taken most of the region's oil wealth with them.[56] In the Komi Republic of Siberia, some local activists have sought to "put the natural resources exclusively to the use of the indigenes," even though only 290,000 of the republic's 1.3 million residents are ethnic Komi. Their proposals have provoked residents of the Russian-dominated energy-producing towns, such as Vorkuta, to threaten to declare themselves free economic zones.[57]

Do these kinds of potential conflicts have any international repercussions? Two possibilities come to mind. First, the divisive tendencies inherent in the "battle of the autonomies" could cause Russia to break apart, with uncertain but potentially destabilizing consequences for the international system. Second, international interests could become directly involved in the struggle for economic resources. As investors negotiate joint ventures with localities, they could come into conflict with Moscow; then the host countries of the foreign firms would have to decide whether and how to support their companies against the Russian government.

There are already worrisome precedents. When Azerbaijan negotiated a deal with foreign firms and countries (Iran and Turkey) for development of oil in the Caspian Sea, Russia strongly objected and was ultimately cut in; Azerbaijan's objectives were patently political rather than economic.[58]

---

54. Andrei Neshchadin, "Russia's Regions Oppose the Government on Economic Reforms, *Moscow News*, No. 26 (June 28, 1992), p. 9; Valery Lavsky, "Russian Regions Use the Threat of Self-Isolation," *Moscow News*, No. 41 (October 8, 1993), p. 8.

55. Ann Sheehy, "Chukotka's Separation from Magadan Oblast Legal," *RFE/RL Daily Report*, No. 91 (May 13, 1993); Dorian and Borisovich, "Energy and Minerals in the Former Soviet Republics," pp. 218–219.

56. Sheehy, "Chukotka's Separation."

57. Dmitrii Ukhlin, "Road toward Vorkuta's Freedom," *Moscow News*, No. 15 (April 9, 1993), p. 1.

58. Vladimir Socor, "Russia Insists on Sharing Other Caspian States' Resources,"

It stands to reason that if Russia is willing to assert its *droit de regard* over the resources of a nominally independent neighboring country, it would do so with even greater energy with respect to its own regions. One cannot be confident that regional leaders will be willing or able to make the political compromises that the Azeri leadership made or that foreign investors and their host countries will tolerate Moscow's interference in their business transactions. Conflict cannot be ruled out in such situations.

PROBLEMS OF IRREDENTA AND DIASPORA.   There are several outstanding problems left over from the breakup of the Soviet Union that could erupt into violence and involve international actors. Ukraine and Russia have not yet resolved the status of Crimea or the disposition of the Black Sea fleet. Failure to do so could lead to violent conflict between troops of the Crimean militia and the Ukrainian army, or between units of the fleet. The dispute between Ukraine and Russia over the former's nuclear status seems closer to resolution. In return for signing the Nuclear Nonproliferation Treaty, Ukraine received assurances that the United States, Britain, and Russia would "respect Ukraine's independence, sovereignty, and integrity within its existing borders." Belarus and Kazakhstan, the other two former Soviet republics "born nuclear" but committed to denuclearization, have apparently been given similar guarantees.[59]

These assurances could involve Western powers in conflicts between Russia and its three neighbors. Ukraine and Kazakhstan both have large populations of Russians living in border regions. That in itself is not enough to provoke violence, but combined with factors that have operated in other post-Soviet conflicts, differences between Russia and its neighbors could turn violent. Economic disparities between Ukraine and Russia could come into play. Russia's economic reforms, a failure by most standards, are a model of success compared to those of Ukraine. The continuing decline of the Ukrainian economy has led many Russian citizens of Ukraine, especially in Crimea, to seek closer affiliation with Russia. Separatist movements in Ukraine and Kazakhstan, combined with annexationist impulses on the part of Russian politicians, could ignite conflicts fueled largely by economic discontent.

The potential for conflict between Russia and the Baltic states also merits serious concern. Latvia, Lithuania, and Estonia all have border

---

RFE/RL Daily Report, No. 213 (November 9, 1994); Vladimir Socor, "Russia Seeks World Bank Oil Credits," *RFE/RL Daily Report*, No. 181 (September 22, 1994); Liz Fuller, "Russia and the Caspian," *RFE/RL Daily Report*, No. 211 (November 7, 1994); Liz Fuller, "Russia, Turkey, Azerbaijan, and Oil."

59.   Doug Clarke and Ustina Markus, "Ukraine Accedes to NPT," *RFE/RL Daily Report*, No. 218 (November 17, 1994).

disputes with Russia; Estonia's is probably the most serious, owing to the large concentration of Russians in the northeastern part of the country. The anomalous situation of Russia's Kaliningrad *oblast'* has also led to friction and could worsen. The region around the former Koenigsberg was absorbed into the Soviet Union after World War II as a discontiguous province of the Russian Federation. It became a key western outpost of Soviet military power during the Cold War. With the breakup of the Soviet Union, Russia has come into conflict with Lithuania over transit rights for military personnel and equipment.[60] All three Baltic states and Poland have expressed concern about the high level of Russian military deployments in the Kaliningrad region. Russia has responded mainly with intemperate statements and threats.[61] The situation could become worse if NATO proceeds with its plans to expand to include countries such as Poland. The NATO alliance would then share a border with one of the most heavily armed regions of Russia.

Arbitrary borders could contribute to conflicts with Russia's other neighbors as well. One particularly worrisome case concerns the Lezgis, "a North Caucasian people divided by the interstate border between the multiethnic Republic of Dagestan of the Russian Federation and the contiguous area of Azerbaijan."[62] Since every ethnic group in the former Soviet Union has easy access to weapons, the Lezgis have had no trouble forming an armed movement dedicated to the unification of "Lezgistan." Its efforts could destabilize the already tense interethnic balance in Dagestan and contribute to conflict within and between Russia and Azerbaijan.

Within the Russian Federation itself, problems of irredenta and diaspora could combine with economic discontent and political opportunism to produce violent conflicts. As with many potential problems in the former Soviet Union, these owe much to the country's Stalinist legacy. In 1937, for example, Stalin divided the former Mongolian Buriat Autonomous Republic into three separate entities: the republic of Buriatia; the

60. Saulius Girnius, "Military Transit through Lithuania," *RFE/RL Daily Report*, No. 220 (November 21, 1994).

61. Vladimir Gubarev, "Kaliningrad: Living without Moscow Supervision," *Moscow News*, No. 6 (February 4, 1993), p. 11; Dzintra Bungs, "Moscow Blasts Baltic Statement on Kaliningrad," *RFE/RL Daily Report*, No. 218 (November 17, 1994); Victor Yasmann, "Baltic Resolution on Kaliningrad Criticized," *RFE/RL Daily Report*, No. 219 (November 18, 1994); Dzintra Bungs, "More Russian Criticism of Baltic Resolution on Kaliningrad," *RFE/RL Daily Report*, No. 220 (November 21, 1994).

62. Shenfield, "Armed Conflict in Eastern Europe and the Former Soviet Union," p. 34.

Aga Buriat area within Chita *oblast'*; and the Ust' Orda area within Irkutsk *oblast'*. The economic resources of the former Mongolian Buriat republic were likewise divided up, with rich farms and cattle lands ceded to Chita and valuable lead mines controlled by Irkutsk. The Buriat people consequently have serious economic grievances that opportunistic politicians could use to foster ethnic conflict in order to promote their personal positions. With these possibilities in mind, one Russian official called the situation in the Buriat regions as explosive as Nagorno-Karabakh.[63] Unfortunately, this is not a rare situation in contemporary Russia.

CIVIL WAR AMONG RUSSIANS. Violent conflict in the former Soviet Union has frequently included an ethnic dimension. As we have seen, however, many disputes are more fundamentally about political power and control over economic resources. The ethnic dimensions of conflict should not, therefore, distract our attention from the possibility of violence among Russians. The Russian political spectrum is as wide as any, with violent extremists at both ends and a government demonstrably willing to use force to achieve domestic political objectives. In October 1993, Yeltsin called out the army to settle his conflict with the Russian parliament by bombing the parliament building. In December 1994, Yeltsin ordered an attack on Grozny, the Chechen capital, that resulted in indiscriminate killing of Russian as well as Chechen residents — not to mention the needless sacrifice of hundreds of Russian soldiers.

Disputes over control of resources could also pit Russian regions against the central government. Some regions may well have renegade armed forces of their own. Not surprisingly, separatist sentiments are strongest in areas rich in resources, such as Krasnoiarsk territory (*krai*), whereas heavily subsidized regions such as the Altai territory are more loyal to Moscow. Leaders of many parts of the Russian Federation have sought control of local economic resources by declaring that their own laws take precedence over federal laws. At least eleven republics have staked such claims: Bashkortostan, Buratia, Chechnya, Ingushetia, Kalmykia, Karelia, Mordova, Sakha, Tatarstan, Tuva, and Udmurtia.[64]

Struggles for control of major economic assets could lead to the breakup of the federation itself. Jessica Stern has called attention to the possibility that an independent "Volga-Urals Federation," encompassing six of Russia's republics, could be formed with Tatarstan and Bashkortostan at its core. Such an entity would clearly be viable. As Stern points

---

63. Stern, "Moscow Meltdown," p. 53.

64. Ibid., pp. 45, 57.

out, Tatarstan's gross national product exceeds that of many of the former Soviet republics that became independent states: Armenia, Estonia, Latvia, Lithuania, Moldova, Tajikistan, and Turkmenistan. Bashkortostan alone possesses more oil reserves than Kuwait. Not only would a Volga-Urals Federation control much of Russia's automobile manufacturing, oil refining, and machine building, it would contain major facilities for the production of aircraft and missiles, as well as nuclear weapons research and manufacturing centers.[65] Clearly, Moscow would not give up such assets without a fight. The violence that such a struggle would provoke almost defies the imagination.

POLICY RECOMMENDATIONS

The main policy advice for fostering the peaceful resolution of conflicts in the former Soviet Union is, unfortunately, the same as that offered to the proverbial lost traveler: "I wouldn't start from here if I were you." The Soviet legacy of arbitrary ethnic divisions, sharp economic disparities, and political tension has made violent conflict in the region highly likely in the future.

Outside powers and international institutions interested in preventing or resolving internal conflicts in the former Soviet Union must recognize that their ability to operate effectively in the Soviet successor states will be heavily influenced by the dominant role that Russia plays in the region. Even if its army is corrupt and inept and its economy is a shambles, Russia remains a powerful country. It would be naive to think that any international organization or state could exert a great deal of influence, against Russia's interests, in matters that Russian leaders consider vital to national security.

One might think, therefore, that the most reliable way to keep conflicts in the former Soviet Union from spilling over or drawing in other states would be to cede the region to Russia as a sphere of influence. Then, presumably, one would only have to worry about the moral implications of endorsing Russian domination over millions of non-Russians, or perhaps the long-term international consequences of giving Russia an opportunity to regain superpower status. The recent tragedy in Chechnya suggests, however, that Russian leaders are not capable of maintaining stability, let alone peace, in their own federation, let alone in the "near abroad." Rather than containing conflict, they have provoked it by antagonizing peoples throughout the Caucasus and inspiring calls for the formation of a regional alliance "from the Caspian to the Black Sea" to

---

65. Ibid., pp. 62–63.

resist Russian military intervention;[66] by spreading exaggerated claims of outside interference (especially from Islamic countries) and thereby creating self-fulfilling prophecies;[67] and by fostering unrest and opposition in Russia,[68] including within the military itself.[69] It is difficult not to wonder about the competence of Russia's leaders.

One should also recognize that the Russian leadership is hardly united in its views. Even during the Soviet era, political figures disagreed about how best to pursue security or what constitutes the national interest. Outside actors could occasionally affect internal debates.[70] The behavior of other states or international organizations could influence Russian policy in the future, at least at the margins and possibly even more fundamentally, by strengthening the position of one side or another in Russian debates over security policy. Fundamental disagreements over national interests, security policy, even national identity are rife in Russia today.[71] No one argues that international institutions influence foreign

---

66. Socor, "Spillover Effect in Caucasus"; Socor, "Ingushetia, Dagestan: Resistance to Russian Advance Reported"; Fuller, "Abkhaz, North Caucasians, Crimean Tatars Support Dudaev"; Socor, "More from the Region"; Brown, "Reaction in Kazakhstan to Situation in Chechnya"; Socor, "Resistance in Ingushetia . . . and in Dagestan"; Socor, "Regional Reverberations."

67. Liz Fuller, "Chechnya Considers Playing the Islamic Card," *RFE/RL Daily Report*, No. 221 (November 22, 1994). Several Russian leaders, including the prime minister, claimed that "thousands" of fighters from Afghanistan, Pakistan, Tajikistan, Azerbaijan, Ukraine, and the Baltic States had joined the Chechen forces. See Vladimir Socor, "Russian Government Broadens Warnings Beyond Chechnya," *RFE/RL Daily Report*, No. 236 (December 15, 1994); Liz Fuller, "Dudaev Appeals to Turkey for Help," *RFE/RL Daily Report*, No. 238 (December 19, 1994); Lowell Bezanis, "Turkish Spy Spills Beans?" *OMRI Daily Digest*, No. 107, Part I (June 2, 1995).

68. Vladimir Socor, "Critical Voices," *RFE/RL Daily Report*, No. 236 (December 15, 1994); Julia Wishnevsky, "Invasion of Chechnya Unpopular in Russia," *RFE/RL Daily Report*, No. 233 (December 12, 1994); Julia Wishnevsky, "Polls on Russian-Chechen Conflict," *RFE/RL Daily Report*, No. 236 (December 15, 1994).

69. Vladimir Socor, "Russian General: Law and Humanity above Orders," *RFE/RL Daily Report*, No. 238 (December 19, 1994); Doug Clarke, "Commander of Elite Unit Resigns over Covert Operations," *RFE/RL Daily Report*, No. 228 (December 5, 1994); Vladimir Socor, "Hardline Generals Soft on Chechnya," *RFE/RL Daily Report*, No. 235 (December 14, 1994); Vladimir Socor, "Army Demoralized," *RFE/RL Daily Report*, No. 239 (December 20, 1994).

70. See Jack Snyder, "International Leverage on Soviet Domestic Change," *World Politics*, Vol. 42, No. 1 (October 1989), pp. 1–30; Matthew Evangelista, "Internal and External Constraints on Grand Strategy: The Soviet Case," in Richard Rosecrance and Arthur Stein, eds., *The Domestic Bases of Grand Strategy* (Ithaca, N.Y.: Cornell University Press, 1993), pp. 154–178.

71. For an outline of general debates on security policy, see Alexei G. Arbatov,

policies independently of politics and power, but their activities could lend support to certain domestic actors and produce comparatively benign outcomes.

There is some evidence that international organizations have successfully supported the position of some domestic Russian actors over others. Consider, for example, the case of Russian "peacekeeping" efforts in Tajikistan. Russian Foreign Minister Andrei Kozyrev proposed that United Nations observers be stationed on the Tajik border and that they supervise the disarmament of government and opposition forces — an operation that would nominally be carried out under the auspices of the CIS but mainly by the Russian army. Russian military leaders opposed any introduction of UN observers. The foreign ministry, with UN support, nevertheless carried the day. Although no wide-scale disarmament took place, a UN mission was established, a ten-member commission of government and opposition representatives was set up, and a cease-fire went into effect in November 1994 and was extended several times. The UN observer mission and the Russian/CIS peacekeeping forces were subsequently successful in coordinating their efforts effectively. When the balance of internal power in Russia's foreign policy debates is close, external actors can make a difference in shifting the agenda and broadening the scope of possible policy options.

Intervention by international institutions can play an important role in relieving the suffering of innocent civilians caught in violent conflicts in the former Soviet Union, but again the domestic balance of power in Russia will determine how such humanitarian efforts will fare. During Russia's war against Chechnya, for example, the Russian government invited the International Committee of the Red Cross to aid civilians in distress, but the Russian military blocked the relief convoys' access to the area.[72] The same fate befell relief efforts organized by the United Nations, prompting one UN official to wonder "Why, when we were invited in at the highest level, are we not allowed to do our task?"[73] The answer lies in the delicate balance between Russian proponents and opponents of international involvement. A strong statement condemning such actions from the U.S. president or the UN secretary-general could have shifted the balance in favor of those who would allow international organizations

---

"Russia's Foreign Policy Alternatives," *International Security*, Vol. 18, No. 2 (Fall 1993), pp. 5–43; for debates specifically about peacekeeping, see Allison, *Peacekeeping in the Soviet Successor States*.

72. Report on National Public Radio, January 13, 1995.

73. Quoted in "UN Official Says Russia Blocking Aid to Refugees," *Boston Globe*, January 15, 1995, p. 16.

to operate. By contrast, statements to the effect that Russia's attack on Chechnya is an "internal matter" (U.S. President Bill Clinton), that Yeltsin is in full control of his military, that "Russia is operating in a democratic context" and therefore the United States should "not rush to judgment" (U.S. Secretary of State Warren Christopher) could cost lives by undermining those policymakers in Russia who appeal to international demands for adherence to humanitarian norms.[74]

Another way of trying to moderate Russia's behavior towards its neighbors would be, as Shenfield suggests, "to take the CIS seriously as a multilateral institution." In other words, international support for greater participation by the other CIS members — especially Ukraine and Kazakhstan — in CIS peacekeeping and mediation efforts might help keep in check Russia's hegemonic ambitions.[75]

The wisest approach to the former Soviet Union must be founded on a realistic assessment of Russia's aims — that many influential leaders do harbor desires to reconstitute the Soviet empire in some form, if only because their conceptions of reliable security dictate it, but that other political figures have more modest views of the requirements of security. At least some of the neo-imperialists within the Russian foreign policy community recognize a role for international institutions, even if that role is mainly to legitimize Russia's "peacekeeping" operations along its periphery. That grudging acceptance of international organizations gives international actors an opening to monitor Russian behavior and perhaps to influence internal debates in support of moderate leaders. The brief record of international operations in the former Soviet Union is mixed so far. They nevertheless offer more hopeful prospects for containing conflicts in that part of the world than Russia's unconstrained pursuit of a neo-imperialist agenda.

---

74. Elaine Sciolino, "Administration Sees No Choice but to Support Yeltsin."

75. Shenfield, "Armed Conflict in Eastern Europe and the Former Soviet Union," p. 45.

Chapter 4

Conflict and Crisis in South and Southwest Asia

Sumit Ganguly

South and Southwest Asia are fraught with a range of conflicts.[1] The central inter-state conflict in the region is, of course, the Indo-Pakistani dispute over Kashmir. Virtually all the other conflicts in the region are intra-state conflicts, but with important regional dimensions. They are, starting from the western periphery of South and Southwest Asia, the impact of the disintegration of Afghanistan on Pakistan and the Sindhi-*muhajir* conflict in Sindh. Conflicts within India include the separatist insurgencies in Kashmir and Punjab, and problems caused by the Uttar-khand movement in Uttar Pradesh, the Naxalite movement in Andhra Pradesh, the Jharkhand movement in Bihar and West Bengal, the Gork-haland movement in West Bengal, the Bodo tribal movement in Assam, the nativist movement in Assam, and the Naga-Kuki conflict in Nagaland. In addition to these regionally based movements and conflicts, India is also contending with Hindu-Muslim religious and caste-based conflicts. In Bangladesh, the Chakma hill tribes movement in the Chittagong Hill Tracts is the focal point of the country's principal internal conflict. Hindu-Muslim tensions have also resulted in violence in Bangladesh. In Sri Lanka, the principal conflict is a particularly violent one revolving around Tamil-Sinhalese differences.

The myriad conflicts in South Asia arise from four major sources. Pre-colonial and colonial historic legacies underlie a number of the

The author thanks Traci Nagle for substantial assistance in the preparation of this chapter. Stephen P. Cohen and Robert L. Hardgrave, Jr., provided extensive comments on an earlier draft.

1. For purposes of my discussion, South and Southwest Asia are comprised of Afghanistan, Bangladesh, Bhutan, India, Iran, Maldives, Nepal, Pakistan, and Sri Lanka.

conflicts; the British colonial government often found it expedient to amplify existing differences between ethnic and religious groups in order to further its own objectives. Since independence, the exigencies of politics within the region have helped exacerbate these schisms. Although their origins lie deep in the demographics of the subcontinent, the two most intractable conflicts in the region, Hindu-Muslim animosity and the Indo-Pakistani contest over Kashmir, were brought to the fore by the vagaries and subsequent vacation of British rule.

The intersecting trends of modernization, social change, and institutional decline explain a second set of conflicts in the region. Modernization opens up both social and economic opportunities. Simultaneously, it undermines existing norms, tears the bonds between communities, and sharpens class and ethnic differences. The existence of robust political institutions can provide mechanisms for limiting the social upheavals that the forces of social change generate. Rapid social and political mobilization taking place against a background of institutional decay can result in violent conflict. The secessionist movement in the Indian state of Punjab falls in this category. To some extent, the Tamil-Sinhalese conflict in Sri Lanka and the current unrest in Kashmir can also be placed within this cluster.

The third source of conflict in the region stems from problems with resources, such as employment and land. Cross-border movements have produced major demographic shifts, which in turn have produced ethnically-based political mobilizations among indigenous populations. Given acutely scarce resources, ethnic mobilization frequently culminates in violence. The internecine political wars in Sindh and the clashes between the Chakmas and ethnic Bengalis in Bangladesh reflect these problems. The track record of the Indian state of West Bengal, however, suggests that these problems can be resolved peacefully under certain conditions.

A fourth and final source of conflict in the region is the intrusion of external powers, the most notable recent case being the Soviet invasion of Afghanistan in 1979. Despite the Soviet withdrawal from Afghanistan in February 1989, the legacies of this invasion still haunt not only Afghanistan but much of Pakistan and parts of India. These legacies include the proliferation of small arms through much of Pakistan and northern India, drug trafficking through much of the same areas, and the continued presence of Afghans within Pakistan.

In this chapter, I analyze each of these regional conflicts, focusing in particular on the ways in which regional powers have been involved in and affected by internal conflicts in others. I conclude with a discussion of the prospects for resolution of internal conflict in South and Southwest

Asia, patterns of regional involvement in the internal conflicts of others, and the prognosis for international engagement in the region.

Colonial Legacies and Ethnoreligious Conflicts

Ethnoreligious conflicts have wracked South and Southwest Asia throughout much of modern history. The most salient, and one of the principal sources of violence in the region, is the Hindu-Muslim conflict, the roots of which can be traced to the pre-colonial period. There is no doubt that the proselytizing zeal of Islamic conquerors contributed to an early rift between the Hindu and Muslim communities on the subcontinent.[2] It is important to note, however, that the history of Hindu-Muslim relations in the pre-colonial era was not one of uninterrupted discord and violence. There were important periods of collaboration and forms of religious synthesis, including the syncretistic Sufi movement. In the nineteenth century, British colonial scholarship nonetheless fashioned a historical perspective that emphasized enduring religious and communal discord on the subcontinent.[3] Through a range of practices, the most important of which was the 1909 creation of separate electorates for Hindus and Muslims, the British colonial government contributed significantly to the rise of Muslim separatism.

In the twentieth century, one of the principal figures of the Indian nationalist movement, Mohandas Gandhi, made a number of ultimately unsuccessful attempts to foster Hindu-Muslim amity, particularly in the wake of World War I and the collapse of the Ottoman empire. The ideology of the principal Indian nationalist organization, the Indian National Congress Party, also known as the Congress(I) Party, was also decidedly secular and inclusive; the Congress(I) Party had a number of prominent Muslims among its ranks.[4] Yet despite its commitment to a secular ideal, the Congress(I) Party was frequently unable to implement its ideological commitments at the local level. The necessity of obtaining support from local Hindu notables for political patronage often diluted secular ideals.[5] It was in part the Congress(I) Party's failure to reassure

---

2. Peter Hardy, *The Muslims of British India* (Cambridge, U.K.: Cambridge University Press, 1972).

3. See Thomas R. Metcalf, *Ideologies of the Raj* (Cambridge, U.K.: Cambridge University Press, 1994).

4. On this point, see Hardy, *The Muslims of British India*.

5. John Gallagher, *Locality, Province, and Nation* (Cambridge, U.K.: Cambridge University Press, 1973).

all segments of the Muslim populace, coupled with the rise of the extremely ambitious Muslim politician Mohammed Ali Jinnah, that ultimately caused the creation of two separate states — India and Pakistan.[6]

The Hindu-Muslim problem continued to haunt the region after partition. Despite enormous and violent population transfers between the two nascent countries, a Muslim community amounting to nearly 11 percent of the population remained within India's domain. In the mid-1990s, sporadic Hindu-Muslim communal violence broke out across the subcontinent. The renewal of Hindu-Muslim violence, unless managed effectively through political negotiations and institutions, has a range of adverse ramifications for the long-term political stability of the subcontinent.

My discussion of these issues will focus, first, on ethnoreligious turmoil in India and, second, on the conflict in Kashmir in particular.

POLITICAL MOBILIZATION AND ETHNIC CONFLICT: INDIA

Paradoxically, ethnoreligious discord and violence in the region have been exacerbated in part by the success of India's democratic institutions. Increased access to education, growing media exposure, and the growth of grass-roots power through local and state elections have all contributed to an extraordinary level of political mobilization in India. Long-disenfranchised groups, most notably Muslims and "untouchables," have become increasingly assertive in Indian politics. This assertiveness, in turn, has generated a tremendous backlash from sections of the Hindu community, many of whose leaders have exploited the growing sense of unease about the erosion of the majority's privileged status. Hindu religious notables, for example, have attacked the government's putative "pampering" of Muslims as contrary to the principle of secularism. They claim that legislative directives such as the Hindu Religious Endowments Act (which permits the national government to obtain property from Hindu religious institutions) are biased because no similar legislation permits the acquisition of mosque or church property.[7]

Other, far-flung events have given rise to a powerful, albeit inaccurate, image of Hindus as a beleaguered minority. In February 1981, for example, some 180 low-caste families in the remote village of Meenakshipuram in the south Indian state of Tamil Nadu converted to Islam. These conversions, not unlike others that took place during previous

---

6. Ayesha Jalal, *The Sole Spokesman: Jinnah, the Muslim League, and the Demand for Pakistan* (New York: Cambridge University Press, 1985).

7. Inderjit Badhwar, Prabhu Chawla, and Farzand Ahmed, "Militant Revivalism," *India Today*, May 31, 1986, pp. 30–39.

South and Southwest Asia.

historical epochs, were principally reactions to high-caste maltreatment of low-caste Hindus. Shrewd political leaders, intent on deriving political benefit, suggested more sinister explanations, including allegations that monetary incentives from the oil-rich Arab world had prompted the conversions.[8] The veracity of such claims is largely immaterial; the notion of external involvement, once asserted, quickly seized the popular imagi-nation. Despite the fact that 80 percent of India's population remains Hindu, zealous activists portrayed Hindus as fast becoming an endan-gered minority; they painted an image of India being buffeted in a sea of Muslim nations stretching from Algeria to Indonesia.

These sentiments were further fueled by Sikh secessionist move-ments, such as that for the creation of a separate state of Khalistan (literally, "the land of the pure") in the northern Indian state of Punjab. In an attempt to create a Hindu-Sikh divide, Sikh terrorists started to target Hindus systematically.[9] The widely reported massacres of Hindus in Punjab, along with the central government's seeming inability to stop the terrorism, wreaked considerable havoc on both the Hindu and Sikh communities and contributed to the sense of Hindu anxiety.[10]

Religious leaders have not been alone in seizing upon and exploiting misgivings within the Hindu community. The right-wing, Hindu-chau-vinist Bharatiya Janata Party (BJP) has capitalized on the growing discon-tent within the majority community and has moved the issue to the forefront of national politics. A political party once relegated to the fringes of Indian political life, the BJP subsequently surged at the polls in the last two general elections: in 1989 and 1991, it expanded its electoral strength in the parliament from 2 to 119 seats in a parliament of 535 seats. Its electoral success has enabled the BJP to shift the terms of political dis-course in India. And indeed, it has significantly legitimized the expression of blatant anti-Muslim sentiment in India.

After December 1992, however, the BJP juggernaut briefly stumbled. In December 1992, members of the Vishwa Hindu Parishad (VHP) and the Rashtriya Swayam Sevak (RSS), two organizations known to be linked with the BJP, attacked and destroyed the Babri mosque in the town of Ayodhya in the northern Indian state of Uttar Pradesh. The founder of the Mughal dynasty, Babur, is believed to have constructed the mosque

---

8. Arthur Bonner, *Averting the Apocalypse* (Durham, N.C.: Duke University Press, 1990), pp. 344–351.

9. Paul Wallace, "Political Violence and Terrorism in India: The Crisis of Identity," in Martha Crenshaw, ed., *Terrorism in Context* (State College, Penn.: Pennsylvania State University Press, 1995).

10. "Punjab: What Can Be Done?" *India Today*, December 31, 1986, pp. 28–36.

on the ruins of a Hindu temple in 1528. That temple, in turn, was supposed to have consecrated the birthplace of Lord Rama, one of the principal deities in the Hindu pantheon.[11] In the wake of the destruction of the mosque, widespread Hindu-Muslim riots broke out across much of India. The spate of nationwide violence that was unleashed damaged the BJP's image and gave many of its supporters pause. Subsequently, the BJP restrained its blatantly anti-Muslim rhetoric, focusing instead on more purely political issues, such as corruption within the principal political party, the Congress(I) Party, and the shortcomings of the government's economic liberalization program.[12]

The BJP's anti-incumbent strategy paid handsomely in a series of state-level elections in March 1995. The BJP swept the polls in the western states of Gujarat and Maharashtra. In the latter, it forged an electoral coalition with a virulently nativist party, the Shiv Sena, and formed a government.

Two other interrelated factors have also widened the Hindu-Muslim divide. The Congress(I) Party's commitment to secularism has eroded significantly since the early years of India's independence. Admittedly, Jawaharlal Nehru's vision of secularism may have been somewhat extreme. Instead of promoting religious tolerance, Nehruvian secularism reviled the display of any form of religiosity in public life. India's first president, Rajendra Prasad, for example, was criticized for offering Hindu prayers at Rastrapati Bhavan, his official residence. At another time, efforts were made to drop the word "Hindu" from the name of Benaras Hindu University, then a well-known center of higher learning. Such measures may have needlessly irritated the majority community.

Nevertheless, Nehru's successors, although secular in terms of their personal beliefs, have undermined the Indian secular state in their quest for short-term electoral gains. Cognizant of the significance of the Muslim vote in India, the Congress(I) Party and the breakaway Janata Dal (literally, "people's party") have made important concessions to certain vocal elements of the Muslim population. A few examples will suffice. After the Congress(I) Party's electoral debacle in 1977, when her party suffered its worst defeat, Indira Gandhi shifted the party's orientation away from its traditional adherence to secular principles and its concerns about the protection of minority interests. In an effort to establish a foothold for her party in the Muslim-majority states of Jammu and Kashmir, she cam-

---

11. Peter van der Veer, "Ayodhya and Somnath: Eternal Shrines, Contested Histories," *Social Research*, Vol. 59, No. 1 (Spring 1992), p. 97.

12. Y. Ghimire, "Changing Tack," *India Today*, December 31, 1994, p. 15.

paigned vigorously in the predominantly Hindu area of Jammu, making veiled appeals to communal sentiments.[13] Her son and successor, Rajiv Gandhi, was far less subtle in his quest for electoral gains. In a transparent attempt to court the conservative Muslim vote, the Congress(I) Party under his leadership introduced legislation that overturned a 1986 Supreme Court decision that had awarded alimony payments to Shah Bano, an indigent Muslim woman; the Supreme Court verdict had been protested by the Muslim community, which claimed it was a violation of their rights as a community.[14] Both BJP stalwarts and Indian secularists reacted with dismay to Congress(I) Party's decision to overturn the Supreme Court decision. The former asserted that the decision amounted to yet another sign of the party's "pseudo-secularism," the latter that the legislation moved the country away from a uniform civil code.

The present political configuration in India does not offer significant hope for the resurrection of the Nehruvian version of secularism, nor for prospects of Hindu-Muslim amity. India's recent economic liberalization program will probably contribute to further social dislocation, which will worsen communal relations, at least in the short run. Nevertheless, the institutional structures of the Indian state and its vast coercive powers should successfully limit the scope of potential conflict. Two other factors will also restrain escalatory tendencies. First, Muslims do not constitute a monolithic bloc within India. Substantial sections of the Muslim community have prospered and have assimilated into the mainstream of Indian life. Second, with the singular exception of Kashmir, Muslims are geographically dispersed across India and, consequently, geographically based Muslim separatism simply cannot arise. Hence, despite collective Muslim grievances, there is little danger that Hindu-Muslim discord will result in India's disintegration.

KASHMIR

The Hindu-Muslim rift in India, despite its bloody history, has little prospect of contributing to inter-state conflict. The issue of Kashmir, in marked contrast, has contributed to two wars and even in the 1990s remains one of the key flash points of inter-state conflict in the region. Since 1989, a secessionist insurgency in the Indian states of Jammu and Kashmir has propelled the nearly fifty-year-old conflict to the forefront of politics on the subcontinent.

Although the roots of the Kashmir problem are located in the colonial

---

13. Manju Parikh, "The Debacle at Ayodhya: Why Militant Hinduism Met a Weak Response," *Asian Survey*, Vol. 33, No. 7 (July 1993), p. 679.

14. Ajay Kumar, "The Gathering Storm," *India Today*, March 31, 1986, pp. 14–17.

history of the subcontinent, the more immediate precipitants of the crisis in Kashmir can be traced to three key forces: the political mobilization of an emergent generation of Kashmiri Muslims, the deinstitutionalization of Indian politics, and efforts by Pakistan to exploit incipient political discontent within Indian Kashmir.

THE WEIGHT OF HISTORY: KASHMIR 1947–71. When Britain disengaged from the subcontinent in 1947, the rulers of the "princely states," including Kashmir, were given two choices: they could join either India or Pakistan, subject to demographic composition and geographic constraints. Independence was ruled out as an option, as it would have led to the fragmentation of the entire subcontinent.

Kashmir and states such as Junagadh, Hyderabad, and Khairpur posed a peculiar problem: they had Hindu populations and Muslim monarchs, or Muslim populations and Hindu monarchs. According to the British plan, the monarch would choose to which nascent state he would accede. Kashmir, which had a Hindu monarch and a predominantly Muslim population, abutted both India and Pakistan. Both states attached considerable significance to Kashmir for diametrically opposite reasons. For India, the absorption of Kashmir into the Indian Union would be a critical demonstration of its secular credentials. Pakistan's claim to Kashmir was irredentist; its leadership contended that Pakistan could not be "complete" unless it incorporated a Muslim-majority population that abutted its borders. Thus, from its very onset the Kashmir dispute has had enormous significance for both sides.

As the maharajah of Kashmir vacillated, a tribal rebellion broke out in Poonch, along the western reaches of Kashmir. Taking advantage of this rebellion, Pakistani leaders sent in army troops disguised as local tribesmen to force Kashmir's accession to Pakistan.[15] As the rebels approached the capital city of Srinagar, the maharajah panicked and appealed to New Delhi for assistance. Prime Minister Jawaharlal Nehru agreed to provide assistance only after two conditions were met: Kashmir would have to accede to India, and the accession would have to have the imprimatur of Sheikh Mohammed Abdullah, the leader of the largest popular and secular organization within the state. The latter condition would, in the absence of a referendum, confer a degree of legitimacy on Kashmir's accession to India.

These conditions were accepted, an Instrument of Accession was

---

15. Major General Akbar Khan, *Raiders in Kashmir* (Karachi: Pak Publishers, 1970); H.V. Hodson, *The Great Divide* (London: Oxford University Press, 1969).

signed, and Indian troops landed in Srinagar on October 27, 1947, moving rapidly to halt the invading forces. By this time, however, the invaders had occupied about one-third of the state. The fighting continued through much of the autumn, with neither side making appreciable gains.

The case was referred to the United Nations (UN) on January 1, 1948, and after one year a cease-fire was negotiated between the two warring parties. Initially, India succeeded in obtaining a sympathetic hearing of its position in the UN Security Council. Eventually, the UN discussions stalled on two key issues: Pakistan insisted on a plebiscite to determine the wishes of the Kashmiris, while India insisted on the "vacation of Pakistan's aggression" before a plebiscite could be held.

In 1962 and 1963, an attempt was made to resolve the stalemate through bilateral negotiations. These talks were destined to fail; India had just suffered a humiliating military defeat at Chinese hands and, under such circumstances, could not afford to make meaningful concessions to Pakistan on the Kashmir question.[16]

The failure of both multilateral and bilateral attempts at conflict resolution, India's steady attempts to integrate Kashmir into the Indian Union, and the armament program that India embarked on in the wake of the 1962 border war with China led Pakistani decision-makers to an inexorable conclusion: the window of opportunity to seize Kashmir by force was rapidly closing. Anti-Indian riots in the Kashmir valley in December 1963 and January 1964 convinced the Pakistani leadership that there was widespread support for them in the valley.

To test Indian military preparedness, the military leadership of President Ayub Khan conducted a "limited probe" in January 1965 in the Rann of Kutch along a poorly demarcated border in the Indian state of Gujarat. When India did not respond vigorously, the Pakistani military decided to seize Kashmir. Their strategy involved Pakistani troops disguised as local tribesmen infiltrating the Kashmir valley, making contact with disaffected Kashmiris, and fomenting an internal uprising. Then, taking advantage of the prevailing conditions, Pakistan would attempt to seize Kashmir in a short, sharp incursion.

This audacious plan went awry from the very outset. To the Pakistani's surprise and dismay, the local populace did not respond favorably; instead, the locals alerted the Indian authorities. Despite the loss of the element of surprise, Pakistan persisted, and, throughout the summer, border skirmishes took place along the Cease Fire Line (CFL) in Kashmir.

In further contrast to Pakistani expectations, the Indian leadership

---

16. Denis Wright, *India-Pakistan Relations, 1962–1969* (New Delhi: Sterling, 1989).

dramatically escalated the conflict; their forces crossed the CFL, as well as the international border in Punjab, and moved toward the Pakistani city of Lahore. However, the war lasted less than two weeks. The onset of full-scale hostilities in September led to an Anglo-American arms embargo on both of the warring parties, and UN mediation brought the war to a close on September 23, 1965.[17] The Soviet Union mediated a settlement in Tashkent on January 4, 1966. Under the terms of the Tashkent Agreement, both sides agreed to return to the *status quo ante.*

After the Tashkent Agreement, the Kashmir problem lay dormant for over two decades. A third conflict between India and Pakistan in 1971 culminated in Indian intervention in East Pakistan and led to the creation of Bangladesh. During the 1971 war, military action was mainly confined to the eastern theater; India's objectives in the west (i.e., Kashmir) were clearly limited to the prevention of territorial gains by Pakistan, destroying Pakistani armor and other military hardware, and seizing a few strategic enclaves along the border.[18]

KASHMIR REDUX. The distribution of power that emerged on the subcontinent after 1971 effectively foreclosed Pakistan's ability to wrest Kashmir from India. Pakistan's claim to Kashmir eroded after its loss in the 1971 war: if the bonds of Islam could not hold the two wings of Pakistan together, Indian commentators argued, on what basis could Pakistan assert a legitimate claim to Kashmir?[19]

But what, then, explains the abrupt rise of violent, secessionist sentiment in Kashmir since 1989? Like the resurgence of Hindu-Muslim violence elsewhere in India, this latest manifestation of the Kashmir problem can also be seen as a paradox of Indian democracy. On the one hand, since 1947, the Indian state has made extensive investments in educational infrastructure, communications, and social welfare in Kashmir. These investments have contributed to the creation of a far better-educated, more informed, and more politically astute younger generation of Kashmiris. On the other hand, however, the Indian state has systematically undermined the growth of honest political opposition within the state. Various forms of political skullduggery, including intimidation of voters, tampering with ballot boxes, and abuse of state resources in electioneer-

---

17. Russell Brines, *The Indo-Pakistani Conflict* (London: Pall Mall, 1968).

18. The best description and analysis of Indian war plans can be found in Pran Chopra, *India's Second Liberation* (Delhi: Vikas Publications, 1973). Also see Richard Sisson and Leo Rose, *War and Secession* (Berkeley: University of California Press, 1990).

19. Chopra, *India's Second Liberation.*

ing have been common in Kashmir. Consequently, virtually all state-level elections in Kashmir, with the possible exceptions of those in 1977 and 1983, were corrupt.

Whereas previous generations of Kashmiris largely tolerated the political chicanery of both the Congress(I) Party in New Delhi and the state-level party, the Kashmir National Conference, the new generation of Kashmiris has proven unwilling to countenance the central government's reckless disregard for established democratic procedures.

In 1987, the Congress(I) Party and the Kashmir National Conference formed an alliance to win the state-level elections in Kashmir, in which there was significant electoral fraud. Candidates and likely voters for the combined opposition, the Muslim United Front (MUF), were harassed and intimidated. The Congress(I) Party/National Conference alliance won the election, but their corruption of the electoral process blocked the final avenue of legitimate dissent. Large numbers of young, disaffected Kashmiris resorted to violence.

With discontent seething in the Kashmir valley, the Pakistani military regime under General Zia ul-Haq saw a long-awaited opportunity to exploit anti-Indian sentiment once again. This time significant numbers of Kashmiris welcomed Pakistani support, which came in the form of sanctuaries, weaponry, and training. Thus, although the causes of the current insurgency in Kashmir are internal, systematic external assistance from Pakistanis has significantly escalated the level of violence.[20]

The situation in Kashmir has reached a stalemate. The Indian forces cannot prevail militarily; the depth of disaffection in Kashmir against India is far too great. The insurgents, even with Pakistani support, cannot defeat the Indian army and paramilitary forces. And no militant group is publicly willing to start negotiations with the government of India; to do so would be political suicide. Consequently, despite the government's release of two prominent insurgent leaders, Yaseen Malik and Shabir Shah, in 1994, there is little hope for a quick end to the conflict.

As of 1995, 400,000 Indian army troops and paramilitary forces were deployed in Kashmir. The bulk of these forces, however, was deployed against the Pakistani army along the CFL and against Chinese forces across the border from Ladakh. Nevertheless, some of these Indian army units have been increasingly drawn in to assist the Border Security Force and the Central Reserve Police Force in counterinsurgency operations. Reliable estimates of the numbers of insurgents involved are hard to ascertain. Some estimates suggest that the various insurgent groups com-

---

20. Anthony Davis, "The Conflict in Kashmir," *Jane's Intelligence Review*, Vol. 7, No. 1 (January 1, 1995), pp. 40–47.

bined would amount to 6,000–8,000 active combatants.[21] Of these, anywhere from 1,000–2,000 are Islamic militants, mainly from Afghanistan but also from as far away as Sudan.

Despite their common opposition to Indian rule, Kashmiri insurgents have been unsuccessful in forging a unified strategy. They range from the notionally secular and pro-independence Jammu and Kashmir Liberation Front to the pro-Pakistani, Islamic fundamentalist Hizb-ul-Mujahideen and the Harkat-ul-Ansar. Ideological and programmatic differences have hindered the formation of a concerted opposition, and the fragmented structure of the insurgent movement has often led to internecine conflict.

Kashmir remains a flash point in Indo-Pakistani relations and has drawn the attention of the international community because of its potential to escalate into a wider inter-state conflict. Specifically, the United States has urged both India and Pakistan to exercise restraint over this issue. The dangers of a deliberate resort to war are small. However, war can result from inadvertence and misperception. Indeed, in 1990, India and Pakistan nearly stumbled into a conflict over Kashmir when the insurgency threatened to spin out of control. Some U.S. intelligence analysts believe that Pakistani decision-makers had contemplated using nuclear weapons upon learning that India was planning cross-border attacks against insurgent training camps.[22] Prompt U.S. intervention, which involved the visit of the deputy national security adviser, Robert Gates, to both Islamabad and New Delhi, helped prevent a further escalation of tensions. In the wake of Gates's visit, India and Pakistan have agreed to institute a number of confidence and security building measures. According to most accounts, however, these agreements have been violated fairly routinely by both sides.[23]

Modernization and Its Discontents

Conflicts generated by the socioeconomic changes that are sweeping South and Southwest Asia also have the potential for provoking inter-state conflict. Contrary to the expectations of both Marx and Weber,

---

21. Harinder Baweja, "The Hostage Crisis," *India Today*, September 15, 1995, pp. 19–25.

22. Michael Krepon and Mishi Faruqee, eds., *Conflict Prevention and Confidence Building Measures in South Asia: The 1990 Crisis*, Occasional Paper No. 17 (Washington, D.C.: Henry L. Stimson Center, April 1994).

23. John H. Sandrock and Michael Maldony, *The History and Future of Confidence-Building Measures in South Asia* (McLean, Va.: Science Applications International Corporation, 1994).

the forces of modernization do not efface ethnic identities. The evidence from both India and elsewhere overwhelmingly suggests a different conclusion. Modernization often tends to homogenize communities; the development of literacy, mass media, and common standards of education creates similar tastes, mores, and expectations. As a consequence, particularly in ethnically plural societies, minority ethnic groups often fear that their unique cultural features will be stripped away. This concern, in turn, leads to what anthropologists have termed "revitalistic movements."[24] In the face of the inexorable forces of social change, these movements seek to restore the ostensibly pristine and original features of the culture that have been or are in the process of being effaced.

My discussion of these issues will examine the cases of Punjab and Sri Lanka, in turn.

POLITICAL DECAY AND ETHNIC CONFLICT: PUNJAB

The Sikh insurgency in Punjab has an important "revitalistic" component.[25] The long-term origins of the Sikh insurgency are complex.[26] Its proximate causes, however, are rooted in the transformation of the socioeconomic landscape of Punjab in the early 1970s. The "green revolution," which involved the introduction of hybrid seeds, petrochemical fertilizers, and large-scale farm machinery, completely altered the agricultural economy of Punjab and had a number of unforeseen social and political consequences.[27] As small tracts of land were consolidated to promote large-scale commercial agriculture, segments of the Sikh peasantry were rendered landless. Increasing numbers of dispossessed Jat Sikh farmers flocked to cities in Punjab in search of alternative employment. Equipped with few skills appropriate to an urban setting, these migrants were often employed as day laborers, performing a range of menial tasks. Relocation from close-knit rural and agricultural communities to cold and alien urban landscapes led to a rupturing of norms and social bonds.

24. The two best statements of this process are Ralph Linton, "Nativistic Movements," *American Anthropologist*, Vol. 45 (January–March 1943), pp. 231–241, and Anthony C.F. Wallace, "Revitalistic Movements," *American Anthropologist*, Vol. 58, No. 2 (April 1956), pp. 264–281.

25. On the "revitalistic" aspects of the Punjab crisis, see Wallace, "Political Violence and Terrorism in India: The Crisis of Identity." On Kashmir, see Sumit Ganguly and Kanti Bajpai, "India and the Crisis in Kashmir," *Asian Survey*, Vol. 34, No. 5 (May 1994), pp. 401–416.

26. Hamish Telford, "The Political Economy of the Punjab: Creating Space for Sikh Militancy," *Asian Survey*, Vol. 32, No. 11 (November 1992), pp. 969–987.

27. Francine Frankel, *India's Green Revolution: Economic Gains and Political Costs* (Princeton, N.J.: Princeton University Press, 1971).

Furthermore, this process of modernization transformed the social and religious mores among educated Sikhs. As larger numbers of Sikhs obtained university educations, courtesy of increased prosperity and the expansion of the university system in Punjab, they started to dispense with their unique cultural markers — turbans, beards, and abstinence from alcohol, for example. This awoke in more traditional Sikhs long-held fears of being assimilated into the Hindu majority.[28]

An itinerant Sikh preacher, Sant Jarnail Singh Bhindranwale, started a movement in Punjab in the 1980s that fed on precisely these misgivings, focusing on the disaffection of rural Jat Sikhs whose lives had been uprooted by the forces of the "green revolution." Bhindranwale's message was embraced by this group for two reasons: it promised to reconstruct a Sikh *quam* (community), and it directed the ire of the community towards an external enemy.

The rise of Bhindranwale's movement in Punjab took place against a backdrop of institutional decline and political decay in India as a whole.[29] Prime Minister Indira Gandhi, famous for generating an extraordinary level of political mobilization through various populist measures, found to her dismay that this mobilized population would no longer vote in expected ways. As Gandhi grasped at the vestiges of her declining political position, political mobilization proceeded apace and local political parties came to the fore. Unwilling to countenance the growth of any challenge to the writ of the Congress(I) Party, Gandhi sought to undermine legitimately elected state and local governments throughout India.

In an attempt to undermine the Akali Dal, a regional party in Punjab, the Congress(I) Party boosted Bhindranwale's political fortunes. Despite being arrested for his involvement in the murder of several members of a heretical Sikh sect, the Nirankaris, Bhindranwale was released at the behest of the central government.[30] Upon his release, Bhindranwale rapidly expanded his political base in Punjab through a strategy of terror, intimidation, and violence, with an ultimate goal of ridding Punjab of all non-Sikhs. Although the violence of his followers was primarily directed against Hindus in Punjab, Sikhs failing to conform to Bhindranwale's

---

28. M.J. Akbar, *India: The Siege Within: Challenges to A Nation's Unity* (London: Penguin, 1985).

29. The dangers that these two opposing tendencies posed were first highlighted in Samuel P. Huntington, *Political Order in Changing Societies* (New Haven, Conn.: Yale University Press, 1968).

30. Mark Tully and Satish Jacob, *Amritsar: Mrs. Gandhi's Last Battle* (London: Jonathan Cape, 1985).

dictates also suffered.[31] Ultimately, he and his followers met a fiery end in June 1984. The Indian army launched a military operation that sealed off Amritsar and led to an attack on Bhindranwale's lair in the Golden Temple.

This, however, did not bring the Sikh problem to an end. Indeed, the violence in Punjab continued unabated. Many Sikhs who had not been particularly sympathetic to Bhindranwale nevertheless deeply resented the attack on Sikhism's holiest shrine.[32] Later that year, their disaffection erupted. On the morning of November 30, Indira Gandhi's Sikh body-guards assassinated her as she walked out to the garden of her official residence. Following her assassination, a spate of violence swept through New Delhi. Considerable evidence suggests that this violence was care-fully orchestrated by members of the Congress(I) Party against the city's Sikh population. According to one source, nearly 3,000 Sikhs were sys-tematically killed in this pogrom.[33]

Terrorist violence continued unabated in Punjab through much of the 1980s but tapered off substantially by the mid-1990s for four main rea-sons. First, as is often the case with violent ethnoreligious movements, the Sikh secessionist movement lost its pristine features as it evolved over time; it became increasingly criminalized and thereby lost much of its legitimacy and potency. Second, internecine violence within the move-ment also undermined its power.[34] Third, the Indian paramilitary forces' sealing of the Indo-Pakistani border, persistent cordon-and-search opera-tions, and widespread use of force against the terrorists broke the will of many to fight. Fourth, after a hiatus of nearly five years, the government held state and local elections in Punjab. Although the voter turnout for the state-level election of March 1992 was low, turnout for the subsequent *panchayat* (local self-government) elections in February 1993 was simply overwhelming; it is estimated that close to 83 percent of the eligible electorate voted in this election.[35] The installation of an elected govern-ment dissolved much of the pent-up hostility of the secessionist move-ment.

---

31. Wallace, "Political Violence and Terrorism in India: The Crisis of Identity."

32. Amrik Singh, "An Approach to the Problem," in Amrik Singh, ed., *Punjab in Indian Politics* (Delhi: Ajanta, 1985).

33. Amiya Rao, Aurobindo Ghose, and N.D. Pancholi, *Report to the Nation: Truth About Delhi Violence* (Delhi: Citizens for Democracy, 1985), pp. 1–54.

34. Chandan Mitra, "Anatomy of the Terrorist Challenge in Punjab," *Hindustan Times*, May 26, 1992.

35. Much of this analysis has been drawn from Sumit Ganguly, "Ethno-Religious Conflict in South Asia," *Survival*, Vol. 35, No. 2 (Summer 1993), pp. 88–109.

The widespread instability within Punjab made it an attractive target for external intervention. There is evidence that the Pakistani military systematically aided the Sikh insurgents, providing them with sanctuaries, weapons, and training.[36] Not surprisingly, Indo-Pakistani relations plummeted during much of the 1980s and, at one point, in part as a consequence of the Punjab crisis, the two nations teetered on the brink of war. This crisis was precipitated by a spiral of perceptions and misperceptions generated by the 1987 Indian "Brasstacks" military exercise, which was designed to serve notice on Pakistan with respect to its involvement in the Sikh insurgency. The size, complexity, and location of the exercise alarmed Pakistani leaders, who interpreted Indian motivations in the worst possible way: India was preparing to invade Pakistan. Although General K.M. Arif, the Pakistani vice-chief of staff, took a more restrained view of potential Indian intentions, he nevertheless moved the Pakistani army's Southern Reserve in combat-ready formations to an area near the Indo-Pakistani border in Punjab. This precautionary movement alarmed Indian decision-makers, who feared a Pakistani cross-border assault designed to link up with Sikh militants. Given the turbulent conditions in Punjab, this could not be dismissed as improbable.[37] The escalatory spiral caused by Brasstacks alarmed political leaders on both sides. Arun Singh, the Indian minister of state for defense, in a meeting with U.S. Ambassador to India John Gunther Dean, expressed his concerns about the Pakistani troop movements near an acutely sensitive border area. Dean, in turn, contacted the Pakistanis and urged them to communicate directly with the Indians to address these fears. The influential intermediary role of the United States and its sharing of U.S. intelligence on troop deployments with both sides helped to defuse the crisis.[38] Nevertheless, this incident brought India and Pakistan close to war with each other.

Regional conflicts such as Punjab, though precipitated by internal forces, can nevertheless affect the security and stability of the subcontinent. The crisis of 1987, for example, threatened to escalate into full-scale war. Prompt external intervention, in this case, helped de-escalate tensions.

---

36. Shekhar Gupta, "Darra Adam Khel: Arms for the Asking," *India Today*, July 31, 1989, pp. 42–47.

37. Kanti P. Bajpai, P.R. Chari, Pervaiz Iqbal Cheema, Stephen P. Cohen, and Sumit Ganguly, *Brasstacks and Beyond: Perception and Management of Crisis in South Asia* (New Delhi: Manohar, 1995).

38. Ibid., p. 60.

ETHNIC PREFERENCES AND POLITICAL VIOLENCE: SRI LANKA

The failure to accommodate legitimate political demands in ethnically plural societies frequently results in widespread ethnic violence, which can spill, and in South Asia has spilled, across national borders. One conflict that has had adverse consequences for regional stability is the Tamil-Sinhalese rift in Sri Lanka.[39]

This conflict began in the nineteenth century, when British entrepreneurs developed a plantation economy in Sri Lanka. When the dispossessed local farmers refused to work as plantation laborers, the British brought in a large Tamil immigrant work force from southern India. Successive generations of immigrant Tamils acquired a degree of Western education, primarily from British missionary schools, and entered professional life in significant numbers. At the time of Sri Lanka's independence in 1948, Tamils were disproportionately represented in the professional classes. In an attempt to appease native sentiment, Sinhalese politicians passed legislation that disenfranchised the so-called plantation Tamils. Furthermore, Sinhala was made the official state language in 1956, impinging on Tamil access to public employment and government agencies. A government-sponsored attempt to encourage Sinhalese settlement in north-central and northeastern lands, long considered the Tamil homeland, generated further Tamil resentment.[40] In 1972, Sri Lanka adopted a new constitution, which contained few federalist provisions and which conferred a special status on Buddhism, the religion of the Sinhalese majority. The progressive alienation of the Tamil community was intensified by the constriction of university admission for Tamils. For a community that had long viewed education as the pathway to social and economic mobility, this proved to be a particularly harsh setback. Tamil youth, who had already become disenchanted with the political process, resorted to violence.

Perceptions and beliefs play a strikingly important role in the Tamil-Sinhalese conflict. Sinhalese apologists insist that their community finds itself adrift in a Tamil sea. Objectively, however, this argument is largely groundless; ethnic Sinhalese constitute about 70 percent of the population of Sri Lanka, whereas the Tamils make up only about 18 percent. A closer examination of this argument reveals that it has much in common with

---

39. It is important to clarify that there are two segments in the Tamil population of Sri Lanka. The original Tamil inhabitants of Sri Lanka trace their origins to a kingdom of the thirteenth century A.D.; Sinhalese nationalists, understandably, contest this historical claim. See Mohan Ram, *Sri Lanka: The Fractured Island* (New Delhi: Penguin, 1989).

40. Ibid., p. 58.

the BJP view of Hindus trapped in a sea of Muslims. Sinhalese chauvinists attribute an irredentist outlook to the 55 million Tamils in the southern Indian state of Tamil Nadu. Growing clandestine Indian support for various Tamil insurgent groups, most notably the Liberation Tigers of Tamil Eelam (LTTE), followed by the disastrous involvement of the Indian Peace-Keeping Force (IPKF) in Sri Lanka in 1987, did much to reinforce these Sinhalese beliefs.[41]

The primary task of the IPKF was to supervise the disarming of the LTTE in the northern and eastern provinces of Sri Lanka, thereby helping to implement the terms of the Indo–Sri Lankan Accord. Although sent to act as a neutral force between the Sri Lankan armed forces and the LTTE, the IPKF quickly became embroiled in the civil war as the LTTE, for a variety of complex reasons, refused to abide with the terms of the accord.

At the insistence of the Sri Lankan government, the IPKF agreed to a phased withdrawal starting in July 1989. As the IPKF withdrew from Sri Lanka, the government in Colombo entered into negotiations with the LTTE, and it assisted the LTTE so much that it was able to dominate other Tamil groups. The negotiations followed a desultory course for about a year, but broke down following an outbreak of violence in June 1990.

After the breakdown of negotiations, the Sri Lankan army began to both literally and figuratively direct its fire at the LTTE. After a number of brutal sieges, most prominently at the Elephant Pass entrance to the Jaffna peninsula in July 1991, the Sri Lankan army was able to restrict the LTTE's activities to the northern province. In 1992, the LTTE again extended its activities to the eastern province, killing large numbers of Sinhalese and assassinating the Sri Lankan naval chief in a suicide-bomb attack.[42] The spiral of violence escalated in 1993 as Sri Lankan opposition leader Lalith Athulathmudali was shot by a lone gunman and another suicide bomber took the life of the Sri Lankan president, Ranasinghe Premadasa. In 1994, opposition leader Gamini Dissanayake was assassinated; suspicion inevitably focused on the LTTE. Shortly after assuming office, Chandrika Kumaratunga, the winner of the 1994 presidential elections, expressed a willingness to start negotiations with the LTTE, despite opposition from Sinhalese nationalists. In January 1995, the LTTE agreed to a cease-fire, to be monitored by external observers from Norway and the Netherlands.[43] The cease-fire and the subsequent negotiations were

41. For an excellent discussion of the Indian involvement in Sri Lanka, see S.D. Muni, *The Pangs of Proximity* (New Delhi: Sage, 1994).

42. Mervyn de Silva, "Sri Lanka Violence Kills 105," *Financial Times*, April 30, 1992.

43. V. Jayanth, "Foreign Observers to Monitor Ceasefire in Sri Lanka," *Hindu*, January 7, 1995.

hopeful portents. Any optimism they inspired did not last long, however. In May 1995, the LTTE attacked and sank two Sri Lankan gunboats, killing sixty military personnel. The government promised to retaliate. Faced with the continuing intransigence of the LTTE, on October 17, 1995, the Sri Lankan government launched a major military offensive against the LTTE stronghold in the Jaffna peninsula. On December 5, 1995, after heavy fighting and substantial casualties on both sides, the Sri Lankan armed forces successfully re-took Jaffna. In the wake of the military victory, President Kumaratunga sought to pursue a two-pronged strategy: maintaining the military pressure on the LTTE to bring it to the negotiating table while simultaneously ensuring that the Sinhalese population did not turn against the Tamil minority.

Clearly, Sri Lanka is not out of the woods. After twelve years of civil war, finding an amicable settlement with the LTTE that will also be politically acceptable to the Sinhalese will be no easy task.

Demographic Shifts and Institutional Failures

Movements of populations, both within national borders and across international boundaries, have often, but not always, spawned ethnopolitical unrest in South and Southwest Asia. To develop a better understanding of the conditions most conducive to peace and violence, we will examine developments in the Indian state of West Bengal, where population movements have by and large been managed effectively, and Sindh and Bangladesh, where violent confrontations have unfolded.

IMMIGRATION AND ACCOMMODATION IN WEST BENGAL

Prior to independence, unified Bengal had its share of communal violence. However, in the post-independence era West Bengal has been largely free of communal violence, despite a continuing influx of both Hindus and Muslims from East Pakistan and, subsequently, Bangladesh.[44] What accounts for this? For a variety of historical reasons, caste consciousness is not nearly as great in West Bengal as in other parts of northern India. As a consequence, political mobilization, which in other parts of India was driven along caste lines, took place in West Bengal along linguistic and regional lines. The Bengali elite, the *bhadralok,* found solidarity in their linguistic and cultural pride, and on occasion through their religious traditions.

Until 1992, the Communist Party of India (Marxist), which has ruled

---

44. On this point, see Atul Kohli, *Democracy and Discontent* (Cambridge, U.K.: Cambridge University Press, 1990).

West Bengal since 1977, had succeeded in maintaining political order. Two factors contributed to its success. First, owing to its ideological predilections, it did not resort to communally based political appeals. Second, as a cadre-based political party, it was able to maintain contact with local community leaders and thereby prevent outbreaks of violence during troubled times.

The party's ability to maintain communal harmony, however, appears to be breaking down. For example, in the wake of the Ayodhya crisis of December 1992, widespread communal rioting swept through the capital city of Calcutta. The continuing influx of Bangladeshi illegal migrants against a backdrop of economic stagnation and widespread unemployment is generating ethnic tensions. Furthermore, the Communist Party apparatus is starting to show signs of wear. The cadres' loyalty to the party ideology and their commitment to social reform is starting to wane. Consequently, West Bengal's relative peacefulness may well erode in the late 1990's

THE SORROWS OF SINDH

The Pakistani province of Sindh, which has over time absorbed waves of non-Sindhi migrants, has experienced waves of interethnic violence as well. The first wave of migration into Sindh occurred at the time of independence and partition in 1947; the immigrant *muhajirs* (migrants) were well-educated, Urdu-speaking, and had considerable entrepreneurial skills. Before long, they dominated major sectors of Sindh's economy and, more importantly, they quickly grew to outnumber native Sindhis in urban areas.[45] More recently, the province has seen internal migration from the other provinces of Pakistan, mostly by Punjabis and Pathans.

Pakistani government policies favored the *muhajir* community over the Sindhis in a number of key areas, including the adoption of Urdu as the national language shortly after independence in 1947, a decision made in large part because the Pakistani elite had been dominated by either Punjabis or *muhajirs*. Problems arising from the east-west Pakistani divide greatly overshadowed the issue of Sindhi subnationalism until 1971. After the breakup of Pakistan in 1971 and the election of Zulfiquar Ali Bhutto, a powerful Sindhi landowner, as prime minister, Sindhi interests found a powerful political voice. In an effort to undermine the popularity of G.M. Syed's Jiye Sindh Mahaz (Long Live Sindh) movement, Bhutto embarked on two important populist measures. First, his Pakistan People's Party

---

45. Charles H. Kennedy, "The Politics of Ethnicity in Sindh," *Asian Survey*, Vol. 31, No. 10 (October 1991), p. 942.

(PPP) sought to make Sindhi the sole official language of the province. Faced with violent and concerted opposition from the *muhajir* community, however, the PPP eventually amended its position, making both Urdu and Sindhi official languages. Second, Bhutto undertook plans to change the ethnic quotas for recruitment to the federal bureaucracy. This strategy was explicitly directed against the *muhajir* community.

General Zia ul-Haq, who deposed Bhutto in a military coup in 1977, did not immediately move to eliminate Bhutto's federal quota system, but added his own criteria; he established a military quota for the recruitment of non-Sindhis. This decision effectively enhanced the privileges of the Punjabis and the Pathans — two ethnic groups already over-represented in the military and the civil services.

Bhutto's death at the hands of the military regime reignited Sindhi nationalism, which in turn provoked a political response from the *muhajir* community. Its initial manifestation as a student political organization, the All-Pakistan Muhajir Students Organization, metamorphosed into the Muhajir Quami Mahaz (MQM) Party when General Zia banned the student organization in 1984. Tensions between the *muhajirs* and the Sindhis flared in 1985–86, when the ethnic composition of Sindh changed appreciably with an influx of Afghans escaping the war and of economic migrants from other provinces of Pakistan. Initially confined to the Pathan and *muhajir* communities, ethnic unrest rapidly engulfed the Sindhis as well. The *muhajirs*, under the leadership of Altaf Husain, issued a series of demands that sought to protect their interests from the encroachment of the Punjabis and Pathans.

After General Zia's death in 1988 and in the face of upcoming elections, Altaf Husain chose to fashion an accord with the PPP, now run by Benazir Bhutto. The PPP accepted many of Altaf Husain's demands, finding them to be politically expedient. Once in office, however, the PPP reneged on the vast majority of their agreements with Husain. Not surprisingly, the accord unraveled and widespread disturbances broke out through much of Sindh. President Ghulam Ishaq Khan, who along with the military was hostile towards the Bhutto government, used the regime's failure to maintain order in Sindh as a pretext for dismissing the Bhutto regime in 1990. In the next national election, the PPP was routed in Punjab, the North West Frontier Province (NWFP), and Baluchistan. In Sindh, although the MQM dominated urban areas, the PPP formed an alliance with the Pakistan Democratic Alliance and fared reasonably well in rural areas. Nevertheless, it was unable to cobble together a coalition in the Sindh Assembly, in large part due to the efforts of a PPP dissident, Jam Sadiq Ali, who was supported by the military and who blocked PPP attempts to forge a coalition government. Eventually, an MQM coalition government came to power in Sindh with the army's support. But this coalition proved unable to contain the ethnic violence in the province, and in June 1992, the army was again deployed to maintain public order.[46]

The situation did not significantly improve under the Nawaz Sharif regime, particularly after differences between Nawaz and the military began to surface. After Benazir Bhutto's return to power in October 1993, the Pakistani military's hostility toward Altaf Husain and the MQM prevented the PPP from reaching a power-sharing agreement with the MQM. Unable to articulate its political demands in a legislative context, the MQM again resorted to extra-constitutional measures such as strikes and political demonstrations. The continued failure to reach a political accommodation within an institutional framework bodes ill for the future of ethnic politics in Sindh.

THE CHAKMAS OF BANGLADESH

Demographic pressures of a more extreme variety are responsible for the continuing clashes between the Chakmas of the Chittagong Hill Tracts and the ethnic Bengalis of Bangladesh.

The Chakmas are a Buddhist tribal community. They had largely been left to their own devices during British colonial rule. Indeed, after 1900 the British prohibited the settlement of non-tribals in the region. After the creation of Pakistan, however, the British regulations governing the Chittagong Hill Tracts were repealed and ethnic Bengalis were encouraged to settle there. After the breakup of Pakistan and the creation of Bangladesh in 1971, the new Bengali government did little to reverse old Pakistani policies. In fact, faced with increasing population pressures, various Bangladeshi regimes provided incentives to settlers to move into tribal areas.

The increasing encroachment of ethnic Bengalis into tribal areas fueled resentment among the Chakmas. As early as 1966, they created an underground organization, the Chakma Hill Tracts Welfare Association, which sought to protect tribal rights. The Pakistani government responded with violent repression, and the government of Bangladesh failed to adopt more conciliatory policies towards the Chakmas. This led to the creation of the Parbottya Chattagram Jana Sanghati Samiti (PCJSS) — the Hill Tracts People's Solidarity Association. This organization has a militant wing, the Shanti Bahini.

The Shanti Bahini has fought with the Bangladeshi army since the

---

46. Samina Ahmed, "The Military and Ethnic Politics in Sind," in Charles H. Kennedy and Rasul B. Rais, eds., *Pakistan Briefing, 1995* (Boulder, Colo.: Westview, 1995).

early 1970s. The Bangladeshi government has alleged that India has aided the activities of the Shanti Bahini. India, for its part, has routinely denied any involvement.[47] Bangladesh's repressive policies have resulted in an influx of Chakmas into the neighboring Indian state of Arunachal Pradesh. By the 1990s, there were perhaps 70,000 Chakmas in Arunachal Pradesh — close to eight percent of the population of the state. The presence of the Chakmas in Arunachal Pradesh has generated considerable resentment among the local populace, who insist that the Chakmas must be made to return to Bangladesh. Leading the charge against the Chakmas are the members of the All-Arunachal Pradesh Students Union. The Chakmas, in turn, have appealed to the Indian National Human Rights Commission. Thus far, the government in New Delhi has responded sympathetically, sending in paramilitary forces to protect the Chakmas.[48]

In the long run, New Delhi's ability to provide continued refuge to the Chakmas is limited. Anti-foreigner resentment runs high in Arunachal Pradesh, and indeed throughout many of India's northeastern states. Eventually, India will have to negotiate with Bangladesh if it is to deal effectively with the Chakma issue. The international community can play an important role in resolving this growing problem. For example, both bilateral and multilateral assistance to Bangladesh can be explicitly linked to better treatment of its tribal communities.

The Lingering Costs of External Intrusion: Afghanistan

In the post–World War II era, no other external intrusion into the subcontinent has proved as costly as the Soviet invasion of Afghanistan. Since the Soviet withdrawal in February 1989, Afghanistan has been caught in a vortex of bloody, internecine conflict despite the formal restoration of political authority in 1992. The continuing civil war in Afghanistan has had important repercussions for Pakistan and, to a lesser extent, India.

Following the Soviet withdrawal, there was a widespread belief in Western political and intelligence circles that the Soviet-supported regime of Najibullah would collapse.[49] However, Soviet-supplied weaponry and

---

47. For a careful analysis of the Chakma insurgency, see Partha S. Ghosh, *Cooperation and Conflict in South Asia* (New Delhi: Manohar, 1989), pp. 74–85.

48. Jayanta Sarkar, "No Refuge," *Far Eastern Economic Review,* November 17, 1994, p. 20.

49. Riaz M. Khan, *Untying the Afghan Knot: Negotiating Soviet Withdrawal* (Durham, N.C.: Duke University Press, 1991).

internal divisions within the various *mujahidin* factions enabled the regime to endure. In September 1991, both the United States and the Soviet Union agreed to cut off military assistance to their respective clients in Afghanistan. They also declared their support for a UN-sponsored interim government that would replace Najibullah.[50]

The UN-sponsored proposal broke down even though an agreement among the seven Pakistan-based *mujahidin* groups and Najibullah was forged in early April 1992. At the very last moment, a Tajik leader, Burhanuddin Rabbani, whose forces were on the outskirts of Kabul, expressed reservations about the accord. He was joined by the son of Sibghatullah Mujaddidi, another *mujahidin* leader, who harbored aspirations for the presidency.[51]

After Kabul fell and Najibullah took refuge in the UN offices in the city, the *mujahidin* leaders reached an accord in Peshawar, Pakistan, in late April 1992. Under the terms of the this accord, after two years of interim governments, elections would be held.

Those plans proved premature, however. Fratricidal conflicts among four ethnic groups — Uzbeks, Pashtuns, Shi'ites, and Tajiks — prevented national consolidation and reconciliation. As fighting continued into 1993, yet another externally sponsored accord in Islamabad was reached. This accord established an interim government, which was enjoined to call a constituent assembly within eight months and hold elections within eighteen.[52] Under the terms of the Islamabad Accord, Rabbani would serve as president and Gulbuddin Hikmatyar, a Pashtun Sunni leader long supported by Pakistan's Inter-Services Intelligence agency, would become prime minister. Difficulties surfaced almost immediately, as the two disagreed about the choice of a defense minister.

Since then, internecine violence and civil war have plagued Afghanistan. Throughout 1994, the various *mujahidin* factions continued to fight, and renewed UN-sponsored attempts to negotiate a cease-fire proved ineffective. In a peculiar shift of loyalties, a former communist general, Abdul Rashid Dostum, who had broken with the Najibullah government in 1992, formed an alliance of convenience with Hikmatyar against Rabbani. The Dostum-Hikmatyar group launched a vicious attack on Kabul in January 1994. The attack was repulsed by Rabbani's military support-

---

50. Barnett R. Rubin, *The Fragmentation of Afghanistan: State Formation and Collapse in the International System* (New Haven, Conn.: Yale University Press, 1995), p. 265.

51. Ibid., p. 269.

52. Ibid., p. 274.

ers, principally the forces of Ahmed Shah Massoud, a battle-hardened Tajik military commander.[53]

In 1995, President Rabbani's regime came under attack from several sides. One of the more serious challenges emerged from the Taliban movement. This movement, composed primarily of students from *madrassas* (Islamic schools), has a following of about 25,000 members. Largely Sunni and Pashtun in composition, it is also believed to be tacitly supported by Pakistan.[54] After some initial military successes, the Taliban forces suffered a major defeat in June 1995 at the hands of Massoud.

Despite Rabbani's success in beating back the Taliban forces, little semblance of political authority exists in Afghanistan. One of the principal challenges to his regime remains the forces of Abdul Rashid Dostum. In late May 1995, discussions about a cease-fire were held between Rabbani and Dostum. No settlement was forthcoming.[55]

The continuing unrest in Afghanistan has significant implications for the stability of South and Southwest Asia. Turmoil within Afghanistan affects Pakistan in a number of different ways, three of which are significant to this discussion. First, the unsettled conditions within Afghanistan make it exceedingly difficult for Pakistan to forge significant ties with the newly emergent states of Central Asia.[56] As long as Afghanistan remains caught in the throes of civil war, Pakistan's ability to pursue its economic and political interests in Central Asia will be hampered.

Second, the virtual collapse of state authority in Afghanistan has, in the early and mid-1990s, revived the cultivation and trade of illicit drugs. During the Afghan war, the drug trade received a boost, as many of the *mujahidin* groups relied on the drug trade to finance their operations. In the absence of easily marketable and lucrative crops, many returning Afghan refugees have revived the cultivation of the opium poppy. Pakistan has consequently become a major highway for the transshipment of drugs. Islamabad's tenuous hold on political authority in Pakistan's North West Frontier Province, which abuts Afghanistan, has only exacerbated the problem.

In 1994, the findings of a UN study of the drug trade caused considerable consternation within Pakistan's official circles. The study reported that the drug trade accounted for as much as 5 percent of Pakistan's gross

---

53. Jefferson Penberthy, "Up Against Starvation," *Time*, March 25, 1994.

54. Ahmed Rashid, "Foiled Again," *Far Eastern Economic Review*, March 2, 1995, p. 20.

55. Reuters, June 1, 1995.

56. Marvin G. Weinbaum, *Pakistan and Afghanistan* (Boulder, Colo.: Westview, 1994).

domestic product in 1992–93.[57] Pakistan also faces a major drug addiction problem — an estimated 1.9 million addicts threaten to tear apart its social fabric. The seriousness of the situation forced the government of Prime Minister Benazir Bhutto to create a Special Anti-Narcotics Task Force led by the military; existing drug enforcement agencies have proven to be corrupt or inept.[58]

A third legacy of the Afghan war is the proliferation of small arms in both Pakistan and northern India. Precise statistics on the availability and spread of small arms are notoriously unreliable.[59] However, the dramatically increased firepower that local *condotierri* wield from Sindh to Kashmir attests to the growing dispersion of light weaponry. The availability of such weaponry is both a symptom and a cause of political instability. It is a symptom in that it reflects the growing inability of local authorities to exert effective political control. It is a cause in that disaffected groups can easily obtain sophisticated weaponry; their ability to inflict violence and create havoc consequently increases. State authorities, in turn, respond with greater force, thereby escalating the level of violence.

A political settlement in Afghanistan is unlikely in the near future. Afghanistan has no tradition of political pluralism or power-sharing. It is unlikely that traditional forms of political organization like the *loya jirga,* a tribal assembly, can be easily resurrected. The various ethnoreligious groups vying for power were brutalized by Soviet invasion forces, and consequently lack the instinct for political negotiation and compromise. Furthermore, guerilla organizations are rarely well-equipped to be nation-builders. Consequently, Afghanistan will most likely remain a strife-torn land — another piece of detritus on the Cold War's periphery. Further political disintegration could impinge even more on the stability of Iran, Pakistan, and Tajikistan.

Conclusions

What are the prospects for internal conflict in South and Southwest Asia? How are these conflicts likely to involve or engage regional powers and affect regional stability? To what extent and in what ways might conflicts

---

57. Ahmed Rashid, "Drug Overdose," *Far Eastern Economic Review,* December 15, 1994, pp. 23–24.

58. Ibid., p. 26.

59. Chris Smith, "The Diffusion of Small Arms and Light Weapons in Pakistan and Northern India," Centre for Defence Studies, University of London, 1993.

in the region engage more distant international powers and the international community in general?

PROSPECTS FOR INTERNAL CONFLICT

On the basis of the forgoing analysis it is perhaps easier to spell out the *least* likely outcomes before turning to a discussion of possible conflicts and their consequences. To begin with, like Mark Twain's death, the dangers of India's disintegration have been greatly exaggerated. Comparisons with the Soviet Union's collapse are essentially fatuous. The Soviet Union was a totalitarian empire with a significant disincentive to adapt, to progress, or to democratize. Despite India's institutional decline and decay, it remains a democratic polity. As long as the fundamental structures of Indian democracy (a free press, an independent judiciary, the regular conduct of free elections, and some semblance of the rule of law) persist, there is little danger of India's collapse. Furthermore, the degree of social and economic integration that has been accomplished in India should not be underestimated. These bonds are virtually indissoluble.

The civil war in Kashmir is the one exception that could break apart the Indian Union. The secession of Kashmir from India could set off an internal domino effect. Thus, limiting the scope of the Kashmir crisis is of inestimable importance, both to the countries of the region and to the international community. Given Kashmir's tortured history, however, it is unlikely that multilateral initiatives to resolve the Kashmir conflict will yield better results today than they did in 1949 or 1965. A regional and bilateral solution will have to be found to this continuing crisis. The international community, and especially the United States, can nevertheless play an important role in helping to resolve this conflict. The United States possesses sufficient leverage over both India and Pakistan to nudge the parties to the bargaining table. Specifically, the United States needs to inform Pakistan that support for terrorism in Kashmir is unacceptable, and simultaneously, to urge India to restore both law and order in Kashmir. To accomplish this, India will have to rein in its security forces, open negotiations with the insurgents and with Pakistan, and restore the now-fractured rule of law to Kashmir. None of these tasks will be easy, but they nevertheless still remain within the scope of skillful leadership and diplomacy.

The Punjab problem has, at one level, been all but solved. A combination of widespread repression and the rekindling of the electoral process has returned a large measure of normalcy to Punjab. The secessionist movement has been marginalized, and it is unlikely to pose a significant challenge to governance. However, one strand of Sikh grievances persists.

Namely, well over a decade since the pogrom against the Sikhs in New Delhi, which occurred after Indira Gandhi's assassination in November 1984, none of the perpetrators has been brought to justice. The national government's continued failure to punish the guilty has created misgivings amongst the Sikh community about the fairness of India's judicial system.

Pakistan's crisis of governance is far more complex than that of India. The continuing preeminent position of the Pakistani military in government affairs will hobble Pakistan's ability to evolve into a genuinely democratic polity. Coercive strategies of governance, such as those applied in Sindh, cannot work indefinitely in a polyethnic and multilingual society like Pakistan. Consequently, Pakistan's long-term unity cannot be taken for granted. Its collapse would have serious consequences for regional stability and security; virtually endless streams of refugees would percolate across the porous borders into India and possibly Iran and Afghanistan. Such a prospect should give India's policymakers a significant stake in Pakistan's stability. Indeed, on occasion, senior Indian policymakers have publicly expressed such concerns. These gestures need to be translated into concrete proposals for addressing Pakistan's problems.

The other conflicts in the region, such as the Tamil-Sinhalese conflict, though costly in human terms, are unlikely to affect regional stability in a fundamental way. India, the main regional power, is unlikely to directly involve itself in the Tamil-Sinhalese conflict a second time. Nevertheless, the intransigence of the LTTE and the inability of the Sri Lankan armed forces to prevail on the battlefield bode poorly for the future of Sri Lanka's stability. In December 1995, the Sri Lankan armed forces successfully concluded their fifty-day offensive, Operation Riviresa (Sunshine), against the LTTE and recaptured Jaffna. Nevertheless, the LTTE is far from a spent force. The Sri Lankan government will have to maintain military pressure on the LTTE while holding out the promise of autonomy and a more just political dispensation for the Tamil minority.

In Bangladesh, the small Hindu minority will, in all likelihood, remain hostage to the vagaries of Hindu-Muslim conflict in India. Violence against Muslims will beget violence against Hindus in Bangladesh. At another level, the persistent scarcity of land and other natural resources will contribute to illegal migration into India. Such illegal immigration is likely to generate interethnic tensions along India's northeastern border states.

The further disintegration of Afghanistan is unlikely. However, a total collapse of state authority and increasing violence could inundate Pakistan with refugees, thereby undermining its stability. Such political disarray could also draw in Iran and Tajikistan, thereby significantly expanding the scope and dimensions of the conflict. To prevent this outcome, the continuing UN-sponsored efforts to broker peace between the Rabbani regime and its challengers remain important.

PROSPECTS FOR REGIONAL INVOLVEMENT

One area of concern for both India and Pakistan is the incipient nuclearization of the region. A form of Glenn Snyder's "stability-instability" paradox has already arisen in South and Southwest Asia;[60] neither side can resort to war for fear of nuclear escalation. Despite this, both sides have covertly and overtly supported indigenous conflicts using clandestine means. The risks associated with these strategies may prove to be neither controllable nor calculable.

The stability that nuclear weapons appear to have provided in the region may well prove to be illusory for at least two reasons. First, command, control, and communications in both countries remain poorly developed. Evidence drawn from the superpower context certainly points to the dangers of organizational failure and inadvertent nuclear alerts.[61]

Second, nuclear war may result from misperception and inadvertent escalation. Although both sides exercised some degree of circumspection during the 1987 and 1990 crises, the rapid pace of the escalation in both those instances gives pause; in a future crisis similar levels of caution may not prevail.

This brief survey of the major conflicts in the region does reveal a number of identifiable pathways through which external powers are either drawn into or intervene in domestic turmoil. The first type of engagement involves benign victims. The illegal migrants from Bangladesh who are percolating into India's northeastern states fall into this category. They are fleeing from Bangladesh because of land pressures, unemployment, and consequent poverty. The majority of the Afghans who took refuge in Pakistan during the Soviet invasion and occupation were also hapless victims. Though most of these migrants and refugees had no strong political affiliations, they nevertheless became embroiled in the local politics of their respective host nations. The continuing presence of Afghans in Pakistan and the continued flow of illegal migrants into India raise the potential for local conflict along ethnoreligious lines.

Second, conflicts can also spread along more active pathways. For

---

60. For a discussion of this paradox, see Glenn Snyder, *Deterrence and Defense* (Westport, Conn.: Greenwood, 1975).

61. Scott Sagan, *The Limits of Safety* (Princeton, N.J.: Princeton University Press, 1993).

example, states can provide sanctuaries for groups involved in conflicts elsewhere. India has long accused Pakistan of providing safe havens and training grounds for Sikh and Kashmiri separatists.

A third variety of intervention may encompass defensive motivations. For example, India intervened in East Pakistan in 1971 for a variety of complex motives. One of them was to ease the colossal refugee burden in West Bengal that India could ill afford to shoulder indefinitely.

A fourth category of intervention may involve protective action. These interventions are usually undertaken on behalf of ethnic brethren. Pakistan's support for the Kashmiri insurgents, to some degree, falls into this category. Pakistan will continue its support for the insurgents as long as its leaders believe that the costs of potential risks involved with such assistance are both controllable and calculable.

Finally, South and Southwest Asia have seen their share of opportunistic interventions. These interventions seek to exploit existing internal discontent in an adversary's midst. Pakistan's involvement with the Sikh insurgents and India's support for Sindhi separatism are both examples of opportunistic interventions. As long as weak regimes persist in both states, the temptation to engage in this form of covert intervention will not abate.

SOUTH AND SOUTHWEST ASIA AND THE INTERNATIONAL COMMUNITY

South and Southwest Asia never played an integral role in the Cold War; India and Pakistan were marginal actors in most conflicts between the superpowers. Three critical factors limited the impact of the Cold War competition on the security and stability of South and Southwest Asia. First, India's policy of non-alignment, begun under the leadership of Prime Minister Jawaharlal Nehru, was explicitly designed to limit the role of external actors in the region. Second, notwithstanding the U.S. military pact concluded with Pakistan in 1954, the impact of the U.S.-Soviet competition was limited in the region, for neither the Soviet Union nor the United States saw South and Southwest Asia as a region of great geostrategic importance.[62] Apart from promoting various multilateral solutions to the Kashmir problem, neither superpower devoted substantial resources to conflict resolution in the region. Finally and perhaps most importantly, the Kashmir issue, the central conflict on the subcontinent, was not an artifact of the Cold War. It was and remains rooted in the region's dynamics. Understandably, therefore, although the Cold War has

---

62. Robert J. McMahon, *The Cold War on the Periphery: The United States, India and Pakistan* (New York: Columbia University Press, 1994).

drawn to a close, the intractable Kashmir conflict shows little or no sign of abating.

International efforts have been made to resolve some of the conflicts that have developed on the subcontinent since the end of British rule. These efforts failed because they did not address the underlying sources of conflict in the region. Furthermore, because the superpowers were never deeply involved in the persistent conflicts of South and Southwest Asia, the end of the Cold War and the emergence of a new world power structure have had little effect on the resolution of these problems.

Russia, the successor state to the Soviet Union, has only a limited interest in the region. It is too preoccupied with its domestic transformation and its relations with the Western world and Japan to devote substantial attention to South and Southwest Asia. The United States, for its part, will remain fitfully involved in South and Southwest Asia. Its principal security concern in the region is the prevention of an escalating arms race in South and Southwest Asia. To that end, it will seek to thwart the further acquisition of weapons of mass destruction by the two principal adversaries in the region, India and Pakistan. It will undoubtedly continue to urge them to pursue an arms control and confidence-building regime in the region. However, it is highly unlikely that the United States will contribute greater resources to the resolution of conflicts in South and Southwest Asia.

In the final analysis, only concerted efforts by the countries of the region to recognize and resolve the roots of their problems will be able to put an end to the seemingly endemic problems of the region.

Chapter 5

Turning the Corner in Southeast Asia

Trevor Findlay

Unlike most of the other regions considered in this volume, Southeast Asia is, as of the mid-1990s, relatively unaffected by internal armed conflict.[1] It is booming economically, relatively stable politically, and involved in constructing regional political and economic relationships on a scale unknown outside of Europe. Since 1945, Southeast Asia has transformed itself from a decolonizing backwater, where internal armed conflict was endemic and external involvement the norm, into the fastest growing region in the world, where internal armed conflicts are few and external intervention, at least by more distant powers, almost inconceivable. The sources of conflict in the region have also changed profoundly. While ideology was once a primary engine of internal conflict in the region, the causes of conflict in mid-1995 are much more prosaic, among them ethnicity, religion, and secessionism. The pivotal period of change in this respect was not the end of the Cold War, as in other regions, but the mid-1970s.

This chapter addresses the question of why this great transformation has come about. I first consider the sources of internal conflict and the nature of external intervention in Southeast Asia in the early Cold War years. I continue with an examination of the region's long-term decline in internal conflict and the reduction in foreign intervention, and the proximate and underlying causes of these trends. In the following section, I examine the relatively limited effects of the end of the Cold War on internal conflict and external intervention in the region. I conclude with a discussion of the region's prospects and an assessment of the lessons that might be drawn from the Southeast Asian experience.

---

1. Southeast Asia is comprised of Burma, Laos, Cambodia, Vietnam, Thailand, the Philippines, Malaysia, Singapore, Brunei, and Indonesia.

Sources of Internal Conflict During the Cold War

After achieving independence from the colonial powers immediately after World War II, the states of Southeast Asia typically faced internal conflicts that were ideological in nature. Compared with other regions, where ethnic, religious, and secessionist conflicts were prominent, in Southeast Asia these problems were often subordinated to or overshadowed by ideological struggles. The first generation of Southeast Asian nationalist leaders, who headed conservative or moderately reformist governments and in some cases were democratically elected, were challenged in almost every instance by left-wing or communist opposition parties. While undoubtedly motivated by genuine local economic, political, and anti-colonial grievances, these parties utilized an essentially foreign ideology, Marxism-Leninism, to define their goals. In almost every case they initially operated openly, but, faced with government repression, soon moved underground and began terrorist and guerrilla operations. Governments typically sought military solutions to such challenges, resulting in a series of guerrilla wars throughout Southeast Asia. This was the pattern in Burma, Cambodia, Laos, Malaysia (and one of its pre-federation components, Malaya), Thailand, the Philippines, and South Vietnam. Singapore, the island state which broke out of a three-year federation with Malaysia in 1965, was able, through draconian policing methods, to contain a political challenge from the communists.

Exceptions to this general pattern were Indonesia, North Vietnam, East Timor, and Brunei. In Indonesia, the Indonesian Communist Party was legal and influential, having been an integral part of the independence struggle against Dutch rule. There was, however, a mass purge of the party in the mid-1960s that involved widespread killings. North Vietnam declared itself a communist state at independence. Neither East Timor, under Portuguese rule until 1975, nor Brunei, under British suzerainty until independence in 1984, faced a communist insurgency. Indeed, Brunei, blessed with oil wealth, has faced no significant internal conflict since independence.

Other types of internal conflicts aside from ideological ones did occur in Southeast Asia during the Cold War, but they tended to be overshadowed by the more dramatic ideological struggles going on around them. Burma, in addition to hosting a communist insurgency, has been plagued since independence in 1948 by several ethnic secessionist conflicts in its frontier regions, particularly by the Shan, Karen, and Kachin minorities. In the southern Philippines, Moro secessionists began fighting for a separate Muslim state long before the country became independent in 1946. They have continued the struggle, through both political and military means, almost uninterruptedly since then. The Moro National Liberation Front (MNLF) was founded in the 1960s for this purpose. Brunei experienced an insurrection in 1962, led by those opposed to its planned integration into Malaysia. This was short-lived and was ultimately resolved when Britain granted Brunei independence as a separate state.

Other ethnic conflicts simmered in Southeast Asia during the Cold War, but did not lead to sustained violence. These included tensions between the ethnic Chinese communities spread throughout the region and the majority populations of their host countries (the most violent clash occurred in Indonesia when ethnic Chinese were targeted during anti-communist purges in the 1960s), and racial animosity in Malaysia between Malays, ethnic Chinese, and ethnic Indian communities (the most violent expression of which occurred during race riots in 1969).[2] These conflicts tended to be grounded in economic and social inequalities rather than racial hatred. In contrast, racial animosities between Thais, Cambodians, and Vietnamese, while not erupting into widespread violence, have deeper historical roots and have exacerbated other types of conflict between and among Thailand, Cambodia, and Vietnam.

The underlying factors behind internal conflict in Southeast Asia during the early Cold War years included the inexperience of the newly installed indigenous governments, the weakness of the fledgling bureaucracies left behind by the departing colonial powers, a poorly developed concept of the nation-state, and rising expectations created by the struggle for independence and the beginnings of modernization. The populations of these new states were especially receptive to the appeal of communism, an ideology that promised order, equality, and modernity, in contrast to the vagaries of the democratic systems which the colonial powers had, in most cases, bequeathed them. As Seymour Martin Lipset has pointed out, the newly independent governments of Asia and Africa faced "the thorny problem of winning the loyalties of the masses to democratic states which [could] do little to meet the utopian objectives set by nationalist movements during the period of colonialism and the transitional struggle to independence."[3]

---

2. There was intermittent intercommunal violence in the 1950s and 1960s. See Harold Crouch, "Malaysia," in Kevin Hewison, Richard Robison, and Garry Rodan, eds., *Southeast Asia in the 1990s: Authoritarianism, Democracy and Capitalism* (Sydney: Allen & Unwin, 1993), p. 152.

3. Seymour Martin Lipset, *Political Man: The Social Bases of Politics* (New York: Anchor Books, 1963), p. 67.

External Intervention During the Cold War

The ideological conflicts in Southeast Asian states during the Cold War almost invariably had consequences for other countries, and often led to active intervention, both from within the immediate region and more widely. To the extent that conditions after World War II were the legacy of colonialism and that imported ideologies provided the language of dissent, external interference in internal conflicts in the region was inherent in the conflicts themselves. To varying degrees, left-wing opposition forces (the various communist parties) and governments (most notably, those of North Vietnam and Indonesia) were influenced or manipulated by outside communist powers, especially the Soviet Union and China, while most of the new post-colonial governments had similar dependent relationships with Western powers and their former colonial masters, France, the United Kingdom, and the United States. Both the Western countries and the Socialist bloc were drawn in not by the particular merits of the conflicts, but because of the ideological and strategic contexts in which the conflicts were viewed.

After the French defeat at Dien Bien Phu in 1954 and the end of French colonial power in the region, Indochina continued to be a particular focus of external engagement because of its strategic location next to China; the existence in the region of a homegrown communist state, North Vietnam; and the West's containment doctrine and domino theory. Each Indochinese state was drawn into the internal conflicts of the other, either inadvertently or deliberately, followed by their non-Indochinese neighbors, China and Thailand.[4] One means of involvement was ideology itself. The civil wars in Laos and Cambodia fed off the Vietnam War, as North Vietnam guided and influenced the Viet Cong, the Viet Minh, and the Khmer Rouge. A second means of involvement was material assistance. While North Vietnam assisted insurgents in all neighboring states, the Cambodian government allowed the transit of war matériel from the port of Sihanoukville to the National Liberation Front in South Vietnam. A third means was the flight of refugees, such as Vietnamese refugees moving into Cambodia and vice versa. These population movements often created ill will between the Indochinese states and even caused

---

4. Cross-border intervention in Southeast Asia after World War II did not have the same connotations it had in Europe or North America, where borders are carefully delineated, border regions are firmly under government control, nationality is clearly defined, and there is a long history of diplomatic interaction between governments. Even today, the governments of Cambodia, Laos, and Burma do not have control over all of their territory, and their borders remain either unclear or contested.

Southeast Asia.

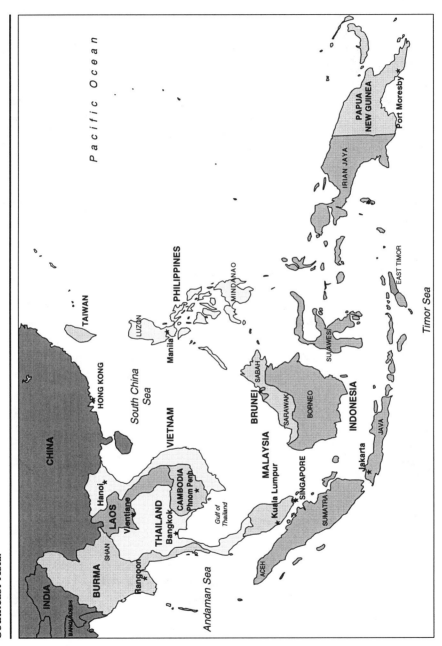

armed clashes between them. Thousands of Cambodian, Laotian, and Vietnamese refugees fled to Thailand, Malaysia, Indonesia, Hong Kong, and other countries by land and sea. A fourth means, more deliberate and opportunistic, was the use by one state of another state's territory to conduct military operations. The Vietnam War deeply affected Cambodia as a result of North Vietnamese and Viet Cong use of supply routes through Cambodian territory.

Depending on one's view of the legitimacy of the two Vietnamese states established by the Geneva Accords of 1954, the Vietnam War can be regarded as either an internal conflict, in the sense that there was genuine opposition to the series of right-wing governments that ruled South Vietnam, or as an inter-state conflict between North Vietnam and South Vietnam. Some observers would argue that it was both. In any event, the Vietnam War illustrates cogently the difficulty of attempting to distinguish in some cases between intra-state and inter-state conflicts.

Because of their ideological nature, the Indochinese conflicts also drew in, and were fostered by, the two main protagonists in the Cold War, the United States and the Soviet Union, and their allies (Australia, New Zealand, the Philippines, Taiwan, and South Korea on the U.S. side; the Warsaw Pact states on the Soviet side). A chain reaction took place: North Vietnam became involved in the South Vietnamese civil war with the assistance of China, the Soviet Union, and the Warsaw Pact, while the United States, concerned over the global spread of communism, intervened on the side of the South, followed by its allies. U.S. involvement was incremental but ultimately massive, involving deployment of U.S. sea, air, and land forces and large-scale economic and military assistance. In Cambodia, the use by North Vietnam and the Viet Cong of Cambodian territory for infiltration and supply led to intervention by the United States in the form of a secret bombing campaign.[5] This became one of the most tragic interventions in modern history, since it destabilized the Sihanouk government, and led to the Pol Pot takeover, a Vietnamese invasion, and civil war that continues in the mid-1990s.

U.S. intervention in Indochina failed spectacularly, and all three Indochinese states ultimately fell to communism. While an analysis of this failure is beyond the scope of this chapter, what can be said is that successive South Vietnamese governments were either not dictatorial enough or not popular enough to withstand communist subversion and aggression alone, and that U.S. intervention, given the political and mili-

---

5. William Shawcross, *Sideshow: Nixon, Kissinger and the Destruction of Cambodia* (New York: Simon and Schuster, 1987).

tary constraints under which it operated, was insufficient to make the difference over the long haul.[6]

Beyond Indochina, Britain, as the colonial power, was drawn into helping defend Malaya from a communist insurgency, both before and after independence, in what was called the Malayan Emergency (1948–60). The insurgency continued in the new Federation of Malaysia after 1963, but was confined to the Thai-Malaysian border and the border areas of Sarawak adjoining Indonesia.[7] The campaign against the Malaysian communists met with greater success than did its counterpart in Vietnam, because the central government was stronger and had more popular support; there was unity of command and tight coordination between the military, police, and civilian elements of the campaign; there was no communist state with contiguous borders; there were no extensive infiltration routes through purportedly neutral neighbors; and foreign involvement was less prominent and less controversial. Also, the membership of the Malaysian Communist Party was mostly ethnic Chinese, which helped isolate it from the Malay population. Civic action and relocation programs were consequently successful, unlike those attempted in Vietnam.

The intensity of the ideological conflicts and the level of external involvement in Southeast Asia led to a seemingly permanent presence in the region by outside powers, in the form of U.S. bases in the Philippines; mutual defense treaties between the U.S. and Thailand and the U.S. and the Philippines; the establishment of the South East Asia Treaty Organization (SEATO); the establishment of the Five-Power Defense Arrangement between Australia, Singapore, Malaysia, New Zealand, and the United Kingdom; and, on the Soviet side, the Soviet-Vietnamese Treaty of Friendship, and later a Soviet naval presence at Cam Ranh Bay.

Foreign powers were, perhaps surprisingly, not drawn into helping suppress communist movements in the Philippines and Burma. Nor did the non-ideological conflicts in these states draw them in, since such conflicts were not seen by foreign powers as threatening to their fundamental interests. The Philippines, despite the presence of U.S. forces on its soil, deliberately avoided seeking help from its former colonial master against either its communist Hukbalahap or its Muslim rebels, in order to preserve its sovereign independence. Under General Ne Win's "Burmese Way to Socialism," Burma adopted a policy of autarchy and isola-

---

6. For an account of the proximate cause of the fall of South Vietnam, see Frank Snepp, *Decent Interval* (Harmondsworth: Penguin, 1977).

7. Indonesia's three-year "confrontation" with Malaysia (1962–65) will not be considered here since it was an inter-state conflict.

tionism that totally precluded external assistance in dealing with its various internal conflicts.

Whether any of the Western interventions helped prevent the spread of internal conflict throughout Southeast Asia is a moot point. The domino theory, which posited that communist insurgencies in one country would spread throughout the region unless checked, has since been largely discredited. Former U.S. Defense Secretary Robert McNamara, one of the architects of U.S. intervention in Vietnam, claims that he had begun to disbelieve the domino theory even while helping to escalate U.S. involvement.[8] The contention of the theory's remaining supporters, that intervention in Indochina helped create a shield behind which the rest of Southeast Asia could stabilize itself and prosper (as argued for many years by Singaporean Prime Minister Lee Kuan Yew), is debatable. This is especially so given that the prolonging of the war through foreign intervention had negative consequences for the region in the form of large refugee flows, the militarization of Thailand, the damaging social effects of a large U.S. presence in Thailand and the Philippines, and a legacy of bitterness throughout the region that is only twenty years later, in the mid-1990s, being overcome. These costs are quite apart from the human and physical damage done to Vietnam and Laos, and the utter destruction of Cambodia.

Because of their global implications, internal conflicts in Indochina during the Cold War also triggered relatively benign forms of multilateral intervention aimed at conflict management and resolution, in the form of peace conferences, peace agreements, and implementation mechanisms. Following the negotiation of the 1954 Geneva Accords on Indochina, an International Control Commission comprising Poland, Canada, and India was established to monitor implementation of the agreement. This was singularly unsuccessful. The 1962 Agreement on the Neutralization of Laos similarly failed. The 1973 Paris Peace Accords, negotiated by Henry Kissinger and Le Duc Tho putatively to end the Vietnam War (but in fact to ensure an orderly U.S. exit), collapsed soon after their signature, along with the international mechanism intended to monitor their implementation, the International Commission of Control and Supervision.[9] These attempts at peace settlements were unsuccessful because they reflected neither a genuine commitment to a settlement (especially on the part of

---

8. Robert S. McNamara, *In Retrospect: The Tragedy and Lessons of Vietnam* (New York: Random House, 1995).

9. The International Commission of Control and Supervision consisted of representatives from Hungary, Poland, Indonesia, and Canada; Canada was later replaced by Iran.

the great powers) nor political and military realities on the ground, nor were they backed by sufficient implementation and verification capabilities vested in an international authority.

Another benign international intervention occurred between 1962 and 1963, when the United Nations Temporary Executive Authority (UNTEA) supervised the transition of Irian Jaya (West Papua) from Dutch to Indonesian administration.[10] The people of Irian Jaya subsequently participated in a so-called "Act of Free Choice" in regard to Indonesian rule, although in effect they had little choice but to accept the *fait accompli*. From the perspective of the United Nations (UN) and the international community, this was a successful case of multilateral intervention to resolve an inter-state conflict. Its success was due to the weight of international opinion on the Dutch (especially from Australia and the United States), the Dutch unwillingness to sustain a prolonged armed conflict on the other side of the world, and the UN's ability to smooth the transition. However, the principle of self-determination lost out badly to that of the territorial integrity of the nation-state, in this case Indonesia's. The potential for internal conflict, represented by the foiled aspirations of the people of Irian Jaya, would return to haunt Indonesia in later years.

The Long-Term Decline in Internal Conflict

In the 1970s, a long-term decline began in the number of armed conflicts in Southeast Asia as ideological struggles began to wane. One obvious reason was that in two cases — South Vietnam and Laos — the communists won in 1975 and the conflicts ended.[11] A further key factor was that China, in pursuit of international recognition and acceptance after U.S. President Richard Nixon's 1971 visit to Beijing, gradually reduced its support for local communist parties, most significantly in Burma, Malaysia, the Philippines, and Thailand. (The exception was its continued support for Cambodia's Khmer Rouge into the 1990s.) From the 1970s onward, Thailand and Malaysia successfully kept their communist insurgencies at bay and eventually defeated them; they also avoided new internal armed conflicts.

---

10. For an account of this mission, see William J. Durch, "The Temporary Executive Authority," in William J. Durch, ed., *The Evolution of UN Peacekeeping: Case Studies and Comparative Analysis* (Washington, D.C.: Henry L. Stimson Center, 1993), pp. 285–298.

11. In Laos, an anti-communist group attempted to continue the conflict from Thailand, but sporadic guerrilla raids appear to have ended. See Paul Handley, "Laos: Making Connections," *Far Eastern Economic Review*, Vol. 156, No. 44 (November 4, 1993), p. 30.

As for Indonesia, the centrifugal forces which many feared would tear the sprawling republic apart were not unleashed, and no serious threat to Indonesia's overall integrity developed. However, two outbreaks of internal conflict did occur, in East Timor and Irian Jaya. Both are special cases that illustrate the difficulties of classifying some conflicts as "internal." The conflicts in East Timor and Irian Jaya were "acquired" rather than "internal" in the sense that neither territory was part of the original Republic of Indonesia granted independence in 1949. Both were absorbed later, and this led to conflict. In East Timor, the Frente Revolucionára Timorense de Libertacao e Independencia (Revolutionary Front for an Independent East Timor, or Fretilin) began fighting for independence after Indonesia invaded the former Portuguese colony in 1975. In 1984, the Organisasi Papua Merdeka (Free Papua Movement) began an armed struggle for independence for Irian Jaya. The latter conflict spilled over into neighboring Papua New Guinea (PNG) as guerrillas sought shelter there and Indonesian forces pursued them into PNG territory.

Only in the Philippines and Burma did classic communist insurgencies persist after the 1970s. Having seriously threatened the Philippine government in the late 1940s, the Hukbalahap movement was successfully suppressed until the Marcos era (1965–86), when first the Huks and then a revived communist movement, the New People's Army, once more threatened the stability of the country. After the declaration of martial law in 1972, the Muslim insurgents' MNLF also engaged the Marcos government in full-scale armed conflict, resulting in over 10,000 deaths and the forcible evacuation and exile of about 500,000 people.[12] Armed conflict by the MNLF was suspended by the 1976 Tripoli Agreement which promised autonomy to thirteen largely Muslim provinces. However, the follow-up negotiations to settle the details of political devolution repeatedly failed. As for Burma, it also continued to struggle with both its low-level communist insurgency and its various ethnic conflicts.

The most serious internal conflict in Southeast Asia in the late 1970s and early 1980s was the one in Cambodia. It led to the deaths of more than 1 million Cambodians (out of an estimated population of 7.3 million), created significant problems for its neighbors, and actively involved external powers. This war between two types of communist regimes was by this stage less about ideology than about political survival and, on the Khmer Rouge side, a passionate hatred of the Vietnamese. Although the communists had come to power in Phnom Penh in 1974, thereby ending

---

12. Temario C. Rivera, "Armed Challenges to the Philippine Government: Protracted War or Political Settlement?" in Daljit Singh, ed., *Southeast Asian Affairs 1994* (Singapore: Institute of Southeast Asian Studies, 1994), p. 260.

that phase of the ideological conflict, internal upheaval continued after their victory, as the Khmer Rouge's Democratic Kampuchea sought to return Cambodia to "Year Zero," a primitive, autarchic, xenophobic, rural-based form of communism involving depopulation of Cambodia's cities and the decimation of its former intellectual, bureaucratic, and technocratic elite. Vietnam, motivated by opportunism, Khmer Rouge provocations, threats to ethnic Vietnamese, and general instability across its borders, invaded Democratic Kampuchea in late 1978 and overthrew the Khmer Rouge regime. Civil war then began between the Hun Sen government installed by Vietnam on one side, and the Khmer Rouge and two non-communist opposition factions on the other side, who had formed an uneasy anti-Vietnam coalition, the so-called Coalition Government of Democratic Kampuchea (CGDK).

The Cambodian conflict inevitably drew in outsiders. China and Thailand supported the Khmer Rouge, while the Soviet Union and its allies supported the Hun Sen government. Vietnam was punished by China for its invasion of Cambodia in a series of attacks across northern Vietnam in 1979. The non-Indochinese states of Southeast Asia formed the Association of Southeast Asian Nations (ASEAN), and the West did not intervene militarily, but attempted to isolate Vietnam and its puppet regime in Phnom Penh and provided political and military support to the non-communist elements of the CGDK.[13]

One of the most intriguing questions about internal conflict in Southeast Asia from the 1970s onward is why four key states in the region — Indonesia, Malaysia, Singapore, and Thailand — began to enjoy increasing stability, managing both to end existing armed conflicts within their borders and to ward off new ones, while others, such as Burma and the Philippines, did not.[14] Thailand and Malaysia certainly used their military forces in attempts to crush active insurgencies, and received considerable external assistance (from the United States and Britain respectively) in doing so. But although the communist threat was contained and isolated by military means, it was never defeated militarily. Decades passed before the insurgencies' leaders finally surrendered (in Malaysia this occurred as late as 1989). As the cases of Vietnam, Cambodia, Burma, and the Philippines graphically illustrate, military force, with or without outside assistance, is by itself rarely decisive in internal armed conflicts. Furthermore,

---

13.   ASEAN's current members are Brunei, Indonesia, Malaysia, the Philippines, Singapore, Thailand, and Vietnam.

14.   For Vietnam and Laos, the reason for their success in ending internal conflicts is clear. Their communist governments used draconian methods of political control and centrally planned economies to stifle dissent and "unify" their populations.

military factors do not explain why no new internal conflicts have erupted in Indonesia, Malaysia, Singapore, and Thailand, and why general instability has declined so much.[15]

The Four Southeast Asian "Tigers"

Four Southeast Asian states — Indonesia, Malaysia, Singapore, and Thailand — have enjoyed increasing stability since the 1970s for reasons that are complex and structural in nature. They include growing economic prosperity and modernization, effective governance, and deepening political and economic regionalism.

ECONOMIC PROSPERITY AND MODERNIZATION

The conventional wisdom is that growing economic prosperity and modernization, under conditions of free-market capitalism, have been responsible for the decline in internal armed conflicts in the four Southeast Asian "tigers." Indeed, all four began to achieve astounding economic growth from the 1960s onward, joining a select group in North Asia (Japan, South Korea, Taiwan, and Hong Kong) as the fastest growing region in the world, collectively lauded as the "East Asian economic miracle."[16] Real income per capita more than doubled in the four states, exports soared, and all began to take on characteristics of developed countries.

If it is assumed that genuine economic grievances lay behind the spread of communist insurgencies in the 1950s and 1960s, so it might be supposed that increasing economic prosperity helped reduce popular support for communist ideology. Other types of dissent, whether political, ethnic, or secessionist, might be similarly "bought off" with increasingly large slices of a growing economic pie. Economic prosperity in the early years of independence, as in Malaysia and Singapore in the 1960s, also

---

15. Moreover, one could argue that at least in the Thai case, it is the military which has often been most threatening to stability by staging periodic coups against more or less democratically elected governments.

16. The World Bank records that since 1960, the high-performing Asian economies (South Korea, Japan, Taiwan, Hong Kong, Indonesia, Malaysia, Singapore, Thailand, and Vietnam), of which the four Southeast Asian states are a part, have grown twice as fast as the rest of East Asia (China, North Korea, Vietnam, the Philippines, Brunei, Laos, and Cambodia), roughly three times as fast as Latin America and South Asia (Bangladesh, Bhutan, Burma, India, Nepal, Pakistan, and Sri Lanka), and five times as fast as sub-Saharan Africa. They also outperformed the industrial economies and the oil-rich Middle East–North Africa region. See World Bank, *The East Asian Miracle: Economic Growth and Public Policy* (Oxford: Oxford University Press for the World Bank, 1993), p. 2.

permitted states to improve their anti-insurgency forces, sustain expensive "civic action" programs targeted at rural communities vulnerable to communist influence, strengthen the military and governmental presence in formerly wayward frontier areas, and generally improve administrative control.

Economic growth and modernization do not, however, necessarily cause a decline in internal conflict. Samuel Huntington has argued that, on the contrary, they may lead to a dramatic increase in internal conflict.[17] According to Huntington, "urbanization, literacy, education, mass media, all expose the traditional man [sic] to new forms of life, new standards of enjoyment, new possibilities of satisfaction. These experiences break the cognitive and attitudinal barriers of the traditional culture and promote new levels of aspirations and wants."[18] The more rapid the pace of modernization, in his view, the greater the prospects for instability.

The cases of Indonesia, Malaysia, Singapore, and Thailand would appear to challenge Huntington's thesis. These countries have become more stable while experiencing what may be the fastest rate of modernization in history. Part of the explanation may lie in the fact that, as the World Bank puts it, these states have been "unusually successful in sharing the fruits of growth" among their people, achieving "rapid growth with equity."[19] For instance, the proportion of people living in absolute poverty in Indonesia dropped from 58 percent in 1960 to 17 percent in 1990, and in Malaysia from 37 percent to less than 5 percent during the same period.[20] To establish their legitimacy and win the support of their societies at large, East Asian leaders pursued, through carefully targeted policies, the principle of shared growth, promising that as economies expanded all groups would benefit.[21] Indonesia used rice and fertilizer price policies to raise rural incomes, and Malaysia introduced explicit wealth-sharing programs to improve the lot of ethnic Malays relative to the wealthier Chinese, while Singapore launched massive public housing programs. Governments assisted workers' cooperatives and established programs to encourage small and medium-size enterprises. Educational policies were targeted at building "human capital" as rapidly as possible, focusing first on primary education and later on secondary

---

17. Samuel P. Huntington, *Political Order in Changing Societies* (New Haven, Conn.: Yale University Press, 1968), p. 6.

18. Ibid., p. 53.

19. World Bank, *The East Asian Miracle*, p. 2.

20. Ibid., pp. 2–3.

education. Declining fertility and rapid economic growth meant that even though education spending declined as a percentage of gross domestic product, more money could be spent per child. In societies where education is highly valued, this made good political as well as economic sense.

GOVERNANCE AND INSTITUTIONS

Along with economic prosperity, governance must also be taken into account. All four states quickly developed moderately authoritarian political systems in which dissent was absorbed within strictly controlled umbrella movements or parties. Other elements of democratic governance, such as elections, parliaments, and a popular press with varying degrees of freedom also accommodated and relieved moderate political dissent. In Malaysia the electoral system was designed to give the economically poorer Malays the edge in political power.[22] Radical dissent, such as that represented by the communist parties, was suppressed ruthlessly. Perhaps most significantly, leaders in all four states were willing to grant both a voice and genuine authority to a technocratic elite and to key leaders of the private sector. The types of policies that helped to create their economic miracles — a judicious and pragmatic mix of state direction and coordination, and free-market principles — were thus replicated in the political field, reinforcing the trend toward internal stability.[23]

Particular national characteristics must also be considered. Thailand is ethnically homogeneous by Southeast Asian standards, it was never colonized, and it has a monarchy that serves as a unifying force in political life. All of these factors contributed to its ability to stay comparatively peaceful. Malaysia also has a monarchical system, and it was lucky to have valuable export commodities, especially natural rubber and tin (of which it has the world's largest holdings). Singapore, a city-state, is small and relatively easy to govern. Britain left both Malaysia and Singa-

---

21. Ibid., p. 13.

22. Although this prevented dissatisfaction among the Malays, it led to dissatisfaction among the Chinese and Indian populations, which was presumably only assuaged by the spectacular rise in general living standards.

23. According to Robert Wade, the successful East Asian capitalist countries have combined the "advantages of markets (decentralization, rivalry, diversity, and multiple experiments)" with "the advantages of partially insulating producers from the instabilities of free markets and of stimulating investment in certain industries selected by government as important for the economy's future growth." See Robert Wade, *Governing the Market: Economic Theory and the Role of Government in East Asian Industrialization* (Princeton, N.J.: Princeton University Press, 1990), p. 5.

pore with relatively efficient and effective bureaucracies. Indonesia, although it inherited neither an efficient bureaucracy nor a well-developed infrastructure, did have substantial oil deposits. In both Thailand and Indonesia, the military played decisive roles in governance, providing institutional coherence and organizational effectiveness.

A key factor in preventing secessionism in the Federation of Malaysia was the flexibility with which it was assembled, including the decision not to incorporate Brunei against its will and a willingness to let the mainly Chinese island of Singapore secede. This was easier to do in Malaysia, a post-colonial creation, than in the Philippines, Burma, and Indonesia, which had been ruled by their colonial masters as single entities.

The cases of the Philippines and Burma tend to support the thesis that economic growth and effective governance have led to a decline in internal conflict in the four "tigers." With its poor economic growth rate and relatively chaotic governance, the Philippines has managed only to hold its insurgencies at bay without defeating them outright. The Marcos regime was both repressive and unable to deliver economic growth or redistribution of wealth; this resulted in more rather than less internal conflict. During its democratic periods before and after Ferdinand Marcos, the Philippines lacked the determined government policies that would have propelled it ahead economically. In the field of education, the Philippines has traditionally favored liberal arts, while its ASEAN partners favored technical and vocational skills. It has also had the highest birthrate in the region.

After a fourteen-year flirtation with democracy, Burma fell under the authoritarian rule of Ne Win as a result of a military coup in 1962. His autarchic "Burmese Way to Socialism" led to the nationalization of industry; the growth of a bloated, inefficient public sector; a ban on investment; and the stifling of contacts with the outside world. These policies left Burma among the most backward countries of the region, and one where internal conflict has been endemic.

REGIONALISM

Another reason why internal conflicts have declined in Southeast Asia is the growth of regionalism, in particular the establishment of ASEAN in 1967. ASEAN was envisaged as an organization for economic cooperation, rather than a defense alliance or one that would involve itself in the domestic affairs of its members. Indeed, it was based on the principles of sovereignty, territorial integrity, and non-interference in domestic affairs. This, as Muthiah Alagappa notes, "precludes any formal role . . . in domestic conflicts except with the consent of participating states."[24] Such regional organizations, moreover, are geared towards supporting states rather than peoples; this makes it difficult for ASEAN to deal with domestic conflicts involving political identity and legitimacy issues, or to draw opposition parties into the regional enterprise. However, ASEAN did contribute to the growth of regional confidence and self-reliance, which in turn strengthened the ability of member states to deal with internal conflicts themselves and made external intervention, both from inside and outside the region, less likely. The establishment of joint border committees, for example, helped Thailand and Malaysia to control their communist insurgencies.

The Decline in Foreign Intervention

Along with the decline in internal conflict, large-scale foreign intervention in Southeast Asia also declined over the course of the 1970s, after the withdrawal of the United States and its allies from South Vietnam, the fall of Cambodia, Laos, and South Vietnam to communist forces, and the promulgation of the Nixon Doctrine, which obliged regional powers to be responsible for their own security. So traumatized by the Vietnam experience was the United States that Southeast Asia was almost the last region in which it would have considered intervening militarily. This was true despite the existence of alliances with Thailand and the Philippines and the retention of major U.S. bases in the latter at Subic Bay and Clark Field. The benign neglect of Southeast Asia by the United States after the Vietnam War helped lower the international profile of Southeast Asia's continuing internal conflicts.

The only instance of direct U.S. military involvement in an internal conflict in Southeast Asia after Vietnam came in December 1989, at the very end of the Cold War, when President Bush responded to requests for assistance from the government of Corazon Aquino in heading off a military coup attempt. Although the Philippine government requested that the U.S. bomb airfields and bases controlled by the rebels, the U.S. responded less provocatively by having two F-4s, based in the Philippines, fly over the captured facilities. They did not open fire, nor were they fired upon. The coup leaders were intimidated and the coup failed.

---

24. Muthiah Alagappa, "Regionalism and Security," in Andrew Mack and John Ravenhill, eds., *Pacific Cooperation: Building Economic and Security Regimes in the Asia-Pacific Region* (Sydney: Allen & Unwin, 1994), p. 174.

This was a carefully calibrated, non-violent, and successful U.S. intervention.[25]

The End of the Cold War

The end of the Cold War did not unleash suppressed internal conflicts in Southeast Asia. On the contrary, it helped produce a major breakthrough in the region's most intractable internal conflict, the struggle in Cambodia. It was, in fact, only when outside powers decided that their interests were no longer served by a continuation of the conflict that the basis for a Cambodian settlement emerged in the form of the 1991 Paris Peace Accords.[26] Vietnam withdrew its troops from Cambodia in September 1989, more than ten years after their arrival, leading to an improvement of relations with China. The dissolving Soviet Union and Warsaw Pact ended aid to both their long-standing ally, Vietnam, and the Hun Sen government, while Thailand and other members of ASEAN concluded that Indochina was more lucrative as a marketplace than as a battlefield. China, the Khmer Rouge's principal foreign supporter, and the Soviet Union began a slow rapprochement, hastened by Soviet withdrawal from Afghanistan. The United States stepped up pressure on China and Thailand to end their support for the Khmer Rouge, began overtures to Vietnam and the Hun Sen government, and withdrew support for the occupation of Cambodia's UN seat by the CGDK. All these moves, like the unblocking of a giant gridlock, were made possible by the end of the Cold War.

The end of the Cold War also created a consensus in the UN Security Council, which permitted the five permanent members to collaborate in securing agreement to the 1991 Paris Peace Accords and in deploying an expensive, intrusive, and comprehensive multilateral peacekeeping operation. Known as the UN Transitional Authority in Cambodia (UNTAC), this operation, deployed in Cambodia between March 1992 and May 1993, was at that time the largest and most complex UN peacekeeping operation ever established.[27] Although it was unable to bring about an end to

---

25. Richard N. Haass, *Intervention: The Uses of American Military Force in the Post–Cold War World* (Washington, D.C.: Carnegie Endowment for International Peace, 1994), p. 29.

26. Muthiah Alagappa, "The Cambodian Conflict: Changing Interests of External Actors and Implications for Conflict Resolution," *Pacific Review,* Vol. 3, No. 3 (Fall 1990), pp. 266–271.

27. For a detailed analysis of the performance of UNTAC, see Trevor Findlay, *Cambodia: The Legacy and Lessons of UNTAC* (Oxford: Oxford University Press, 1995).

the Cambodian civil war as intended by the Paris Accords, UNTAC did help end foreign intervention in the conflict, isolate the Khmer Rouge, begin the tortuous process of national reconciliation, and permit the Cambodian people for the first time in almost forty years to choose their government in a comparatively free, fair, and democratic manner.

Aside from Cambodia, though, seemingly none of Southeast Asia's existing internal conflicts were affected one way or the other by the passing of the Cold War. The fortunes of the communist New People's Army in the Philippines continued to decline, but this was part of a long-term trend due to other factors, such as the reinstitution of democracy after the fall of the Marcos regime. In Burma, where the communists had been forced to compete with the country's numerous ethnic secessionist movements, their highly fractured enterprise collapsed after an internal mutiny in 1989. This also had little to do with the end of the Cold War.

The end of the Cold War did, however, strengthen existing trends towards greater military self-reliance and political and economic regionalism in Southeast Asia. The continued advancement and institutionalization of ASEAN, the establishment of the ASEAN Regional Forum (ARF)[28] in 1993, and the institutionalization of the loosely organized consultative forum called the Asia Pacific Economic Cooperation (APEC),[29] in which the Southeast Asian countries play key roles, are all evidence of these favorable trends. The end of the Cold War and the Cambodia settlement, moreover, permitted the reintegration of the Indochinese states into the region. Vietnam has joined ASEAN, and Laos and Cambodia will not be far behind. Because of its harsh internal policies, Burma is likely to be the last to be admitted, but probably will be by 2000.

Given the sensitivity of all Southeast Asian states to any hint of outside interference in their internal affairs, ASEAN will probably remain extremely reluctant to become involved in preventing, managing, or resolving internal conflicts in the region. Although it did intervene in the Cambodian conflict, this was possible because Cambodia was not a mem-

---

28.   ARF comprises all the members of ASEAN plus Australia, Canada, China, the European Union, Japan, Laos, New Zealand, Papua New Guinea, Russia, South Korea, the United States, and Vietnam. For details, see Trevor Findlay, "South-East Asia and the New Asia Pacific Security Dialogue," *SIPRI Yearbook 1994* (Oxford: Oxford University Press for the Stockholm International Peace Research Institute [SIPRI], 1994), pp. 125–147.

29.   The participating countries are Australia, Brunei, Canada, China, Hong Kong, Indonesia, Japan, South Korea, Malaysia, New Zealand, Philippines, Singapore, Chinese Taipei, Thailand, and the United States. For details, see *U.S. Department of State Dispatch*, Vol. 4, No. 38 (September 20, 1993), pp. 642–644.

ber (and could not veto ASEAN involvement); Vietnam was a regional pariah; and ASEAN member Thailand, Cambodia's next door neighbor, wanted a settlement. It is notable, in contrast, that negotiations to end the armed conflict in the Philippines between the government and the National Democratic Front are taking place not in the region but in the Netherlands. Moreover, for assistance in negotiating with its Muslim secessionists, the Philippines turned not to ASEAN but to Indonesia and a non-regional organization, the Organization of the Islamic Conference. The case of Burma is also instructive. ASEAN's so-called "constructive engagement" with the Burmese government may have only served to strengthen the regime, to the detriment of groups seeking political change in that country.

The end of the Cold War reduced even further the already low likelihood of foreign intervention in internal conflicts (or indeed any conflicts) in Southeast Asia. In concrete terms it led to the physical disengagement of the United States from the region, including withdrawal from its bases in the Philippines, with a resulting inability to intervene quickly and substantially even if it wished to. Concomitantly, the Soviet Union and then Russia withdrew from Vietnam. China cut its links with the Khmer Rouge (but retains them with Thailand and has increased them with Burma). Vietnam, one of the region's most interventionist powers in the past, is interested in economic prosperity and reconciliation with the United States, and is unlikely to be interventionist in the future, except perhaps in Cambodia in the unlikely event that the Khmer Rouge manage to return to power and threaten Vietnamese interests. None of the conflicts in Southeast Asia has warranted new outside involvement or spilled over since the end of the Cold War; rather, de-escalation and contraction have been the rule.

Trends and Prospects

Some internal armed conflicts remain active in Southeast Asia in the mid-1990s. These include ethnic or territorial conflicts in Indonesia, Burma, and the Philippines. But none of these is likely to have major effects on neighboring states or lead to foreign intervention. Most pose no threat to central governments; some are petering out or being repressed militarily, while others are being resolved through negotiations.

Rapid economic growth in Southeast Asia is likely to continue and spread throughout the region, especially to the Philippines and Vietnam. It should not be assumed, however, that economic growth will necessarily favor political stability in every case. Those countries which have begun economic liberalization, with or without political liberalization (Vietnam,

Laos, and Cambodia are in the former camp, Burma in the latter), may not be as adept as the Southeast Asian "tigers" in managing the stresses and strains of the modernization process; nor might the democratic Philippines, where internal conflicts could yet erupt over distribution of national wealth and the aspirations of ethnic minorities.

The four "tigers" themselves are not necessarily immune to internal problems. Possible causes of turmoil include rural-urban disparities in wealth and opportunity, especially in Indonesia and Thailand; high-level corruption; major environmental degradation (especially in huge metropolitan areas like Bangkok and Manila); and the depletion of forest, agricultural, and marine resources.[30] While these problems may lead to internal political instability (and perhaps in some cases to disputes between neighboring states), they are not, given current indications, likely to lead to organized armed conflict.

THE GROWTH OF DEMOCRACY

As Southeast Asian polities have become more educated and sophisticated and a strong middle class has emerged, there have been greater pressures for democratization. In 1995, although their systems are far from perfect, almost all the states of Southeast Asia have some form of democratic governance (Laos, Burma, and Vietnam were the exceptions). Since it is one of the tenets of democratic theory that a democracy permits societal conflict to be managed below the level of armed conflict, it might be expected that democratization will provide a hedge against the outbreak of internal conflict in the region, and that the growth of democracy should therefore be encouraged.

However, clearly democracy is by itself not enough to prevent internal conflict.[31] The Philippines and Burma are among the Southeast Asian countries with the longest experiences of real democracy, where democratic norms and practices were presumed to be most deeply imbedded in the popular psyche; however, they are also the countries in the region with the most active and persistent armed conflicts on their territories.

---

30. Linda Y.C. Lim and Pang Eng Fong, "The Southeast Asian Economies: Resilient Growth and Expanding Linkages," in Singh, *Southeast Asian Affairs 1994*, p. 28.

31. There is a large and complex literature on the relationship between economic development, democracy, and domestic conflict in Southeast Asia which cannot be detailed here. For an excellent short treatment see Richard Robison, Kevin Hewison, and Garry Rodan, "Political Power in Industrializing Capitalist Societies: Theoretical Approaches," in Hewison, Robison, and Rodan, *Southeast Asia in the 1990s*, pp. 9–38; see also Bruce M. Koppel, "The Prospects for Democratization in Southeast Asia: Local Perspectives and International Roles," *Journal of Northeast Asian Studies*, Vol. 12, No. 3 (Fall 1993), pp. 3–33.

Both also succumbed relatively easily, despite their democratic traditions, to authoritarian regimes, under Ne Win in Burma and Marcos in the Philippines.

It would appear instead that rising equitable economic prosperity and democratic governance together provide the best guarantee against the rise of internal conflict. The question is how this can be achieved. It may be that rising and equitable economic prosperity produces both a decline in internal conflict and pressure towards democracy. Once they take root, these trends may begin to reinforce each other, with continued economic growth supporting democracy and increasing democracy sustaining equitable economic growth, leading to a decline in internal conflict. This would confirm traditional democratic theory, which posits that the growth of democracy is "encouraged" by, *inter alia,* the widespread distribution of property, particularly landed property; economic achievement generally consonant with economic aspirations; widespread social and geographic mobility; minimal social alienation; cultural tendencies to generalize and extend the application of moral principles to others; high participation rates in voluntary organizations; an open class system; literacy; an effective bureaucracy; and urbanization.[32] However, as democratic theorist Lipset pointed out, the complex characteristics of a socioeconomic system have multivariate causes and consequences, so that while the growth of democracy may be encouraged by economic wealth, literacy, bureaucracy, and urbanization, as in Thailand, these can also be consequences of democracy, as in the United States.[33]

The establishment of the institutional trappings of democracy, as in Southeast Asia, may be useful in encouraging the growth of true democracy. Robert Putnam has revealed, however, in his careful study of democratization in Italy, that social context and history profoundly condition the effectiveness of institutions associated with democracy, and that although new institutions can change political practices, such changes may take decades to bear fruit.[34]

The loosening of authoritarian controls in Southeast Asia is occurring long after modernization first began. This process, moreover, is sometimes excruciatingly slow, almost completely controlled by the governments themselves, and subject to periodic regression, as military coups in

---

32. Robert E. Lane, *Political Man* (New York: Free Press, 1959), pp. 39–40; Lipset, *Political Man: The Social Bases of Politics,* p. 61.

33. Lipset, *Political Man: The Social Basis of Politics,* p. 61.

34. Robert D. Putnam, *Making Democracy Work: Civic Traditions in Modern Italy* (Princeton, N.J.: Princeton University Press, 1993), pp. 182, 184.

Thailand and the ebb and flow of press controls in Indonesia attest. As Robert Wade argues in relation to Taiwan (although it could be equally applicable to the Southeast Asian states), "no regime with a tight control apparatus lets up until the volume of disaffection generated by the controls begins to exceed the probable volume of disaffection which the controls suppress."[35] A continually rising standard of living, shared equitably, can presumably help attenuate the difficulties of managing this balance by buying off disaffection.

THE EXTERNAL ENVIRONMENT

The growth of regionalism, both economic and political, will continue to be a barrier to external intervention in Southeast Asia. States in the region are now viewed by both the states themselves and by external powers such as the United States, Australia, and the European powers as having the maturity, stability, and economic strength to manage their own internal affairs. This has rendered external intervention politically unacceptable. In any event, it is difficult to determine who would be inclined to intervene in the region, especially militarily. The end of the Cold War has removed much of the motivation for intervention, whether in Southeast Asia (where it has been low since the Vietnam War) or elsewhere. Russia does not have the military or economic reach of the former Soviet Union, and is preoccupied with its domestic affairs and its so-called "near abroad." The United States has staged a retreat from Southeast Asia which is unlikely to be reversed. Although the United States has signed visiting and basing rights for its navy with all the ASEAN states except Vietnam, the United States is unlikely to use these to intervene in an internal Southeast Asian conflict. Isolationist sentiment in the U.S. Congress and among the general public is likely to constrain future administrations, regardless of party affiliation.

China is a wild card. Although in the UN Security Council it defends the principals of non-interference in internal affairs, it has not vetoed the deployment of UN peacekeepers and multilateral forces to conflict areas, even in cases where the permission of the states or conflicting parties involved was not given. It played a constructive role in Cambodia, deploying its first peacekeepers; it has mended its relations with Vietnam; and it has joined the Asia-Pacific regional dialogue on both economic and political issues. It has, on the other hand, aggressively asserted its claims over the entire South China Sea, and it is extending its influence in Burma.

---

35. Wade, *Governing the Market*, p. 254.

It is also beginning to oppose some of the more ambitious plans for regional cooperation in the Asia-Pacific region, especially in regard to military transparency.[36]

China's internal stability is uncertain, as its economic boom, in contrast to those of the Southeast Asian "tigers," creates staggering regional variations in wealth and opportunity. While Deng Xiaoping has already effectively handed power to his chosen successor Jiang Zemin, this does not constitute either a generational or an ideological change and may be insufficient to ward off threats to China's long-term stability. The way in which China handles these difficulties will affect the internal stability of its neighbors in Southeast Asia, especially Thailand, Burma, Laos, Vietnam, and Cambodia. A major faltering in the Chinese economy, widespread civil unrest, an outflow of refugees, or secessionist conflict in China's southern provinces could also affect the internal stability of China's neighbors. Vietnam, newly modernizing and dependent on outside investment, is particularly vulnerable, especially in view of the long-standing and ill-concealed Chinese-Vietnamese hostility.

POTENTIAL TROUBLE SPOTS
Burma, Cambodia, the Philippines, and Indonesia are the places in Southeast Asia where internal conflicts are most likely to endure or flare up in the future.

BURMA. Burma not only has had more active ethnic conflicts than any other Southeast Asian state, but now also has the most repressive government. The State Law and Order Restoration Council (SLORC) gained power in 1988 after the military violently suppressed pro-democracy demonstrations. Despite democratic elections in 1990 which were won in a landslide victory by the main opposition party, the National League for Democracy, the SLORC refused to step aside. It has ruled by decree since then, crushing democratic opposition, violating human rights, and imprisoning the Prime Minister–elect, Aung San Suu Kyi, for almost six years. The political opposition retreated to the border areas and, in league with ethnic secessionist movements, began its own armed struggle against the government.

Burma's internal conflicts have had a significant impact on neighboring Bangladesh and Thailand as streams of refugees have fled the country. The Rohingya, a minority Muslim group numbering 300,000, was delib-

---

36. *Jane's Defence Weekly*, August 12, 1995, p. 20.

erately forced over the border into impoverished Bangladesh by the military in 1992; they are slowly being repatriated under UN auspices.[37] There are more than 70,000 Karen, Mon, and Karenni refugees in Thailand. In early 1995, fighting spilled over into Thailand as Burma's military forces pursued rebel forces across the border and the rebels themselves engaged in internecine warfare. Military engagements between Thai and Burmese forces have also occurred.

In addition to spilling across its borders, Burma's internal conflicts have drawn in outside powers, with mixed results. Burma has sought closer relations with China, which has supplied it with $1.4 billion worth of weaponry and training.[38] On the other hand, China has pressured some of the minorities in its border areas to make peace with Rangoon. There have also been reports that China is constructing a major naval base near the Irrawaddy River delta and a maritime reconnaissance facility on Burma's Great Coco island, just thirty nautical miles north of India's Andaman group. This has created anxiety in India, which has traditionally regarded Burma as a buffer between it and China. Establishment of such facilities should be seen not just as a reaction to Burma's internal conflicts, although they would be useful to Burma in that context, but also as a Chinese move to increase its influence and military presence in the Indian Ocean region. This illustrates how internal conflict can attract outside involvement which can then feed on itself to create even greater regional security problems. Thailand has also been drawn into Burma's internal conflicts, having long given at least tacit support to ethnic secessionists and offered sanctuary to both political and ethnic refugees.

In 1993 the SLORC began an attempt to end Burma's isolation through a public relations campaign in the West, a liberalization of foreign investment laws, and a showcase, jury-rigged National Convention to write a new constitution. But no real dialogue with the political opposition has begun, and the National Convention has proven to be a fiasco. Although Aung San Suu Kyi was released in July 1995, she has refused to participation in the convention. Thousands of other political prisoners remain in jail. However, the economy has begun to expand as liberalization measures take effect.

Surprising success has also been achieved in reaching peace accords with a number of ethnic secessionist groups, including the Kachin Independent Organization, the ex-communist Wa and Kokang ethnic groups,

---

37. *Far Eastern Economic Review Asia 1994 Yearbook* (Hong Kong: Review Publishing Company, 1993), p. 99.

38. Ibid., p. 98.

and several other smaller groups.[39] In early 1995, government forces scored an important military victory against one of the largest and most persistent secessionist groups, the Karen National Union, which has been isolated to the Thai border area. The last significant secessionist area in the country — the self-declared Shan state ruled by heroin drug lord Khun Sa — came under government control in January 1996, when troops entered the region without resistance following a peace agreement signed in December 1995. The accord grants considerable autonomy to this area. This leaves only small pro-democracy opposition groups and Karen remnants along the Thai border as minor irritants. The SLORC has therefore apparently succeeded in gaining more real control over the country's territory than any government since independence.

It is not clear, however, how permanent the relative peace in Burma will be. The combination of strict authoritarian military rule and inequitable distribution of wealth resulting from the partial liberalization of the economy is more likely to lead to the "Latin American or Philippine road to stagnation and social inequity than the East Asian model of prosperity for all."[40] Moreover, the informal semi-autonomy granted to various ethnic minorities may not endure should they develop faster economically than the country as a whole, which is quite possible given their proximity to Burma's rapidly developing neighbors. Burma may therefore experience further secessionist conflicts in the future. Major external intervention is unlikely, however, simply because Burma is not strategically important. While Thailand may meddle on the margins and China may supply arms, neither is likely to make the same mistake they made with the Khmer Rouge and become too deeply involved.

CAMBODIA. The continuing civil war in Cambodia, which now pits the Khmer Rouge against all its erstwhile allies combined in a coalition Royal Cambodian government, is unlikely to end in the foreseeable future and may flare up under certain conditions. For its part, the Khmer Rouge is weaker than it has been for many years. After the UN-organized elections in May 1993, it was outmaneuvered politically and confined largely to its jungle bastions in western Cambodia without Chinese support, the international recognition that came with its previous membership in the anti-Hun Sen coalition, and its captive population base in the border refugee

---

39. Khin Maung Kyi, "Myanmar: Will Forever Flow the Ayeyarwady?" in Singh, *Southeast Asian Affairs 1994*, pp. 221–222.

40. Ibid., p. 227.

camps. Under strong pressure from the United States and other nations, Thailand eventually cut its assistance to the Khmer Rouge, further isolating the guerrillas, although some sanctuary in Thailand is still available. The Cambodian government's amnesty program finally appears to be working, and defections are reportedly increasing.

The new government is in no position, however, to defeat the Khmer Rouge militarily. The Royal Cambodian Armed Forces, comprising the combined forces of the non-communist former resistance factions and the Hun Sen regime's army, is corrupt, poorly equipped, badly led, and bloated with phantom soldiers and too many officers. Reform is slow and foreign countries which have been invited to provide military aid — in particular, Australia, France, and the United States — have been reluctant to do so until substantial reform is carried out.

The Cambodian government has adopted a strategy of containment and harassment of the Khmer Rouge, affording the country breathing space to pursue economic and social development, which ultimately hold the key to undermining residual popular support for the rebels. Success on the battlefield has seesawed between the Khmer Rouge and the government, with ritual dry-season offensives being conducted by both sides.

There are, however, troubling weaknesses within the government which threaten to overwhelm it. The structure of the coalition government, a forced union of two erstwhile enemy parties of vastly different organization, experience and motivation, is itself a threat to political stability. There is also concern among human rights organizations that the peace settlement and the presence of UNTAC have had little effect on the traditional arbitrariness, secretiveness, and lack of accountability of the Cambodian government. Press restrictions and government attacks on parliamentary procedure and immunity are troubling. Lawlessness, corruption, the illegal drug trade, and the widespread availability of weapons also threaten stability. The role of the Cambodian monarchy is increasingly in doubt because of King Sihanouk's poor health. The coalition arrangement is due to end in 1998, when general elections are scheduled. On the positive side, the Cambodian economy shows signs of genuine growth, foreign investment is increasing, and significant economic reforms have been carried out. The international donor community continues to keep an open mind about the government's performance.

The most dangerous scenarios for Cambodia revolve around a resurgence of the Khmer Rouge and a resumption of large-scale civil war. These would inevitably re-create a large refugee problem, signal a loss of confidence in the new Cambodian government, and, if Khmer Rouge forces threaten Vietnam, invite renewed military intervention by that country. Expanded Khmer Rouge use of Thai sanctuaries could provoke conflict between Thailand and Cambodia. China is unlikely to intervene on the Khmer Rouge's behalf, having already won so much international approbation for cutting off support to its erstwhile allies. A resurgence of the Khmer Rouge is unlikely in view of its lack of external support, its past reputation, and its waning numerical strength. The more likely scenario is a continuing low-level guerrilla war, perhaps for another decade, along the lines of those in Burma and the Philippines.

Even without Khmer Rouge help, Cambodia could experience a prolonged period of political instability if current political and constitutional arrangements collapse, perhaps triggered by the death of King Sihanouk or a military coup. The result could be the emergence of an authoritarian but largely non-ideological government comprising various elements of the current government but not structured along existing party lines. None of these developments is likely to trigger international intervention, although the human rights record of such a regime would be closely watched and the regime would come under international pressure if its record deteriorated significantly.

THE PHILIPPINES.   There are indications that, under the government of General Fidel Ramos, the Philippines is finally undertaking necessary political and economic reforms to achieve high economic growth rates, and that, particularly if it can control its high birthrate, it will be propelled before long into the ranks of its rapidly developing neighbors.[41] This may ultimately help dampen dissent. The withering of external assistance to the Communist Party of the Philippines and internal splits within the party render it a declining threat. Membership in the Party's New People's Army has fallen from a peak of 25,000 in the 1980s to well under 10,000 in mid-1994.[42] The threat of a military coup, which bedeviled the Aquino administration, also appears to have receded now that former General Ramos is in power.

The issue of Muslim secessionism on the southern island of Mindanao is a more intractable problem. While the MNLF has suspended armed conflict since the Tripoli Agreement of 1976, splinter groups have continued the struggle. In this case foreign "intervention," in the form of support for the MNLF by the Organization of the Islamic Conference and

---

41. Philippine officials started using the term "tiger cub" in 1993 to refer to the Philippine economy, and a growing number of investors appeared to believe them. See *Far Eastern Economic Review Asia 1995 Yearbook* (Hong Kong: Review Publishing Company, 1995), p. 196.

42. Research Institute for Peace and Security, *Asian Security 1994–95* (Washington, D.C.: Brassey's, 1994), p. 169.

the Indonesian government, has served to modify the movement's aims from seeking full independence to accepting more autonomy within the existing constitutional framework. Continuing negotiations have failed to produce a satisfactory settlement, however. Militarily, as it has in the past, the Philippine government will probably be able to contain a major flare-up of armed conflict using its own resources. Since the Philippines has no contiguous land border with another state, the likelihood of conflict involving neighboring states is minimal, although the centuries-old links between the southern Philippines and the Malaysian state of Sabah still permit the smuggling of weaponry and other supplies.

After the signing of the Tripoli Agreement, the most significant elements of external involvement in the conflict — Libya's supply of arms to the MNLF and its threat of an oil embargo against the Philippines — ended. However, one renegade group, Abu Sayyaf (Bearer of the Sword), which carried out a devastating attack on the town of Ipil in April 1995, is alleged to have links with the Islamic fundamentalists who were charged with the 1993 bombing of the World Trade Center in New York and is thought to have received arms, money, and training from Libya and from Islamic groups in the Middle East, Pakistan, and Malaysia. A training camp for Abu Sayyaf was reported to have been established in Malaysia, Syria had reportedly promised support, and some of the rebels were allegedly Afghan war veterans.[43] While it is difficult to test the veracity of these reports, it is worrying that for the first time, Muslim secessionists in the Philippines are being linked with international terrorist groups. As an unruly democracy, the Philippines is vulnerable to such groups and, along with its other problems, such as a high birthrate and enduring poverty, it can ill afford the measures needed to deal with such a development. It also illustrates the relatively new phenomenon of non-state actors being able to interfere, across great distances, in internal conflicts in seemingly remote locations.

INDONESIA. One conflict with the potential for affecting neighboring states is the independence movement in Irian Jaya. In the past, it has spilled over across the long land border that Irian Jaya shares with Papua New Guinea. Were the conflict to flare up, it would likely happen again. In the unlikely event that such a development seriously threatened Papua New Guinea, Australia, which has a defense agreement with PNG, could be drawn in. Australia's security treaty with Indonesia, signed in late

---

43. Anthony Spaeth, "A Mad Dream of Global Terror," *Time*, April 10, 1995, p. 31; Anthony Spaeth, "Death in the Afternoon," *Time*, April 17, 1995, pp. 32–33; "Manila Dubious on Muslim Rebels," *International Herald Tribune*, April 19, 1995, p. 4.

1995, commits both parties merely to consult each other in such a situation.

The armed conflict involving Indonesia's other independence movement, in East Timor, appears to be ending. Although occasional military clashes occur, the number of Fretilin guerrillas is now estimated to have fallen to the low hundreds. As a reflection of this trend, the six Indonesian army battalions in East Timor were reduced to one by the end of 1993.[44] On the political front, however, the Indonesian government has not done well; it has been continually embarrassed by allegations of human rights violations in the territory, and has been unable to prevent Fretilin from acquiring political capital at its expense. Talks mediated by the United Nations have been taking place between the Timorese parties themselves (in 1995) and between Indonesia and Portugal, the former colonial power (over several years), but little progress is expected in view of the power imbalance between the Indonesians and the rebels and the fact that the Indonesians are winning the battle on the ground. The conflict is likely to remain mostly in the political sphere, and to be confined to East Timor itself and to international fora such as the United Nations. Since East Timor is an island in the heart of the Indonesian archipelago, there are few opportunities or incentives for external intervention. The United Nations and other international bodies will continue to monitor the situation, but a peace settlement is unlikely. The conflict will not be resolved until the Indonesian government at the very least ends its heavy-handed treatment of the Timorese, improves its human rights record substantially, opens the territory completely to outsiders, and engages in a genuine dialogue with all sectors of Timorese society. The Timorese leadership is unlikely to settle for anything less than substantial autonomy within the Indonesian state.

One other separatist movement is operating on Indonesian territory, in the region of Aceh. Although persistent, it is comparatively tiny, involving less than 1,000 insurgents. There is always the possibility of Indonesia breaking apart due to economic stresses if economic growth stalls and if prosperity is not shared more equitably. Low-level secessionist movements, as in Aceh, could take advantage of such developments. The succession to the long rule of President Suharto is unclear — another potential destabilizing factor, both within the country and in Indonesia's relations with other states, notably Australia and Malaysia. No outside powers are likely to intervene in a collapsing Indonesia, however, except perhaps to rescue their nationals from a chaotic situation.

---

44. Harold Crouch, "Indonesia: An Uncertain Outlook," in Singh, *Southeast Asian Affairs 1994*, p. 136.

Lessons from the Southeast Asian Experience

It is tempting to draw lessons for other regions from the success of the Southeast Asian "tigers" in enhancing their internal stability. One such lesson is that once traditional societies begin to modernize, the best prospects for maintaining internal social peace and harmony are obtained if economic growth is rapid enough to ensure a relatively equitable and constantly rising standard of living, and if government policies are deliberately targeted towards such goals. Education should be widely available, the bureaucracy relatively efficient, and opportunities afforded to minority and disaffected groups. The Southeast Asian experience strongly suggests that the type of government that produces such economic outcomes — moderately authoritarian administrations whose policies combine a judicious and pragmatic mix of state direction and coordination with free markets — are also most likely to handle political dissent by permitting sufficient opportunities within the system for innovative thinking and political advancement.

However, one should be extremely wary of extrapolating lessons from one region to another. All of the success stories of Southeast Asia, although based on broadly similar economic and social policies, have unique roots. The differences in history, culture, language, and religion between Thailand and Indonesia alone should give pause. Simple transplantation of their development policies to Africa or Latin America, or even other parts of Asia, should be avoided. Just as there is no single East Asian economic model of growth with equity, neither is there a model for the reduction of internal conflict through such means. Solutions must be adapted to particular circumstances.

The Southeast Asian experience also suggests that while regional economic and political cooperation can strengthen the ability of states to meet internal threats themselves, regional organizations can be reluctant to intervene in the internal affairs of any member state. Indeed, a conspiracy of silence about internal conflicts often exists in such organizations, mostly out of fear that once interference is brooked in one case it will become endemic. This leaves the United Nations — the one international organization with the requisite political clout, financial resources (however stretched), credibility, and impartiality (however tarnished) — as the only agency capable of multilateral interventions in most internal conflicts. However, Cambodia, Southeast Asia's UN success story, is unlikely to be easily replicated elsewhere, if only because of the enormous resources involved in such an operation.

As for intervention by one state or a coalition of states, the history of Southeast Asia since World War II strongly confirms the obvious: that foreign intervention in support of unpopular and poorly motivated governments is doomed to failure. Similarly, as the Cambodian experience demonstrated, multilateral peacemaking or peacekeeping operations are unlikely to succeed unless they reflect political realities on the ground, are strongly supported by the international community, and are well-funded and efficiently organized.

A final lesson is that internal and inter-state conflicts are often inextricably linked and difficult to disentangle. What began as a conflict between Indonesia and Portugal over the future of East Timor became an "internal" conflict once Indonesia absorbed the Portuguese colony by force. Similarly, Cambodia's tragic history has shown how external powers can initiate, stimulate, manipulate, and take advantage of internal conflicts. Attempts to deal with the causes and implications of internal conflict must take such external realities into account.

Conclusions

The level and nature of internal conflict and the possible triggers for external intervention in Southeast Asia have changed dramatically since the beginning of the Cold War. The era of ideological conflict has passed. Economic prosperity has increased the capacity of many Southeast Asian governments to end or successfully manage internal conflict. The end of the Cold War strengthened these trends but had only one dramatic effect on the region — the peace settlement in Cambodia.

Southeast Asia is likely to be increasingly prosperous economically and to remain politically stable into the next century. Although the region will undoubtedly face great challenges as a result of continued modernization and rapid development, the pursuit of policies that strengthen political and social equity, combined with greater democracy and the growth of economic and political regionalism, should help to avoid the escalation of internal disputes into armed conflict. Vietnam, Laos, Cambodia, and Burma are all moving to modernize and liberalize their economies, and to involve themselves in cooperative regional relationships. Every country in the region, with the possible exception of Laos, has the potential, given the right mix of government policies, to experience the rapid economic growth and increasing integration that has characterized most of the member states of ASEAN.

Burma and Cambodia remain the most likely exceptions to these continuing trends. Despite the 1991 Paris Peace Accords and the relatively successful UN mission, Cambodia's civil war with the Khmer Rouge continues and could escalate if certain conditions prevail, such as a collapse of the government. Burma, wracked by ethnic secessionism since gaining independence and with an authoritarian government that shows few signs of relinquishing or genuinely sharing power, is also a potential trouble spot. The most plausible armed conflict scenario in Southeast Asia, however, involves not intra-state issues but competing claims between regional powers and China over possession of the islands of the South China Sea.

For external powers, the best policy towards Southeast Asia would appear to be encouragement of continued economic growth along with political liberalization. Otherwise, they should leave the region to its own devices. Intervention should come only at the behest of the region itself.

Chapter 6

Cycles of Conflict in the Middle East and North Africa

Rachel Bronson

The Middle East and North Africa contain tremendous ethnic and religious diversity. Because of its location, the region has historically been at the heart of international trade, linking Europe, Asia, and Africa, and bringing together a wide variety of linguistic, ethnic, and racial groups. The region has also been the birthplace of many of the world's religions, and continues to be a spiritual center. Kurds, Berbers, Shi'ites, Sunnis, Baha'is, Turkomens, Druze, Greek Orthodox, Jews, and Copts represent only a portion of the ethnic and religious mosaic that characterizes the Middle East and North Africa.

The main argument of this chapter is that, contrary to what one might suspect, ethnic and religious cleavages do not necessarily lead to conflict. These cleavages present problems for states, to be sure, but whether or not they lead to political turmoil and armed conflict depends on a host of other political and economic factors. More specifically, when states are weak and undemocratic, and when they lack the economic and financial wherewithal to address domestic problems effectively, internal conflict is likely. So is regional meddling in the affairs of neighboring states. This was the case in the Middle East and North Africa in the 1950s and 1960s: economic and financial resources were limited, internal conflicts were common, and regional meddling was the rule. Conversely, when states are strong and when they have significant economic and financial resources at their disposal, internal conflicts and pernicious regional interventions are less likely. This was the case in the Middle East and North Africa in the 1970s and 1980s, when oil revenues and foreign aid provided many states with sufficient resources to dampen internal conflicts and discourage external meddling.

The collapse in oil prices in the mid-1980s and the sharp reductions in foreign aid from Washington and Moscow in the late 1980s and early 1990s do not bode well for the region. Many Middle Eastern and North

African states will be less able to keep domestic problems and opportunistic neighbors under control in the future.

I begin with an overview of the region's historical, religious, ethnic, and political context. I continue with a comparative analysis of developments in the 1950s and 1960s, on the one hand, and the 1970s and 1980s, on the other. This leads to a discussion of the region's prospects for the future, focusing on the challenges posed by decreasing resources, Islamic fundamentalism, ethnic and refugee problems, and leadership succession. The impact of the Arab-Israeli peace process on the region's prospects is also analyzed. I conclude with recommendations for regional and international actors interested in preventing and mitigating the effects of internal conflicts in this part of the world.

The Historical and Political Context

I begin with a discussion of the region's Ottoman and colonial legacy, and the ways in which religious and ethnic diversity has been managed and exploited by different occupying powers. I then proceed with an examination of the region's potential for religious and ethnic turmoil, and its lack of strong democratic traditions.

THE OTTOMAN LEGACY

The religious and ethnic diversity of the Middle East was addressed by the Ottoman Empire through what became known as the millet system. Millets were communities of non-Muslim groups that received considerable autonomy in return for subservience to Istanbul.[1] Although the official religion of the Ottoman Empire was Islam, minority groups were allowed to maintain control over most spiritual and some administrative and juridical matters.[2]

The decline of the Ottoman Empire was accompanied by the breakdown of the millet system. European states seized upon this and continued to make inroads into the region by claiming to be protectors of different religious and ethnic groups. In Lebanon, France sought to protect Maronite Christians from Ottoman rule. Britain responded by defending the rights of the Druze, and Russia developed closer ties with the Orthodox community elsewhere in the region. Trade subsequently flour-

---

1. Shi'ites and other non-Sunni Muslims did not have their own millets and were treated worse than other groups.

2. A.H. Hourani, *Minorities in the Arab World* (London: Oxford University Press, 1947), p. 19.

ished between European states and their regional associates. Catholic and Protestant schools were established, conferring educational benefits to select societal groups. This disrupted the social fabric of Middle Eastern society; the traditional social and economic positions of privileged groups were challenged by these new elites.

THE COLONIAL LEGACY

Following the collapse of the Ottoman Empire after World War I, European powers carved the region into explicit spheres of influence. This was done to facilitate European rule rather than for indigenous economic or political reasons. Areas that had previously been considered indivisible were partitioned. Lebanon was separated from Syria, which was separated from Palestine and cut off from Iraq. As a result, Aleppo, for instance, was obligated to regard Damascus as its main economic partner and political hub, rather than Baghdad, to which it had many important ties. In areas where ethnic and religious groups had been previously separated, groups were suddenly expected to coexist peacefully. The French creation of greater Lebanon, for example, altered the demographic and political balance between Druze and Maronite communities. This affected the ethnic and religious organization of societies and created new sources of conflict.

With few exceptions, the new borders did not correspond with local loyalties[3] that were both smaller (e.g., tribal, family) and larger (e.g., pan-Arabism) than the imposed borders. The concept of the nation-state, so central to European political organization, did not find its natural counterpart in the Middle East. The imposition of these newly constituted borders meant that leaders had to create, rather than reflect, societal loyalties. This obviously limited the role of state-based nationalism as a political force in the region.

Colonial policies also tended to undercut existing patterns of politics. Over an extended period of rule, both France and Britain systematically undermined local political structures and relationships. In an effort to facilitate their rule, both France and Britain favored particular ethnic and religious groups over others, pursuing a strategy of divide and rule. No area was left unaffected. France, for instance, played the Druze and Alewites against the urban Sunni elite in Syria, and the Berbers against the Moroccan aristocracy. F. Gregory Gause describes the similar steps Britain took to consolidate control over what became South Yemen:

---

3. Egypt, Iran, Saudi Arabia, and Turkey are exceptions.

British measures served to cut the rulers off from the sources of their power. . . . The British openly interfered in the selection of local rulers, deposing those who opposed their plans and forcing the election of more pliable successors . . . British-sponsored "reforms" also isolated the rulers from the tribes they claimed to rule. . . . In the name of "good government," many of the tenuous ties that had bound ruler to ruled in the protectorates were severed.[4]

Even relatively homogeneous societies were subjected to variants of this strategy. In Egypt, Britain transferred powers from village chiefs and sheikhs to local landlords, creating new institutions — village councils and local probate courts — which facilitated colonial rule.[5]

THE POTENTIAL FOR RELIGIOUS TURMOIL

Although ethnic and religious diversity has long been a significant feature of Middle Eastern politics, religious activism has been more important politically at certain times than at others. Religious activism has also varied from place to place, and different movements have pursued different political agendas. The content of the message has also changed, paralleling economic and political developments.[6]

Even in Egypt, the birthplace of the Muslim Brotherhood, differences among groups exist, particularly between the Brotherhood and splinter groups. The Muslim Brotherhood is generally comprised of older activists who protested against President Gamal 'Abd al-Nasser and flourished under President Anwar al-Sadat. Many participated in government coalitions in the 1980s. Groups that seceded from the Muslim Brotherhood are generally comprised of younger, university-educated activists. They are often more militant, and they therefore receive a great deal of international attention.

It is important to emphasize that in 1995, a variety of Islamic groups operate in the region and, indeed, in most states. These groups are not guided by a single set of leaders. A well-organized, monolithic "green

---

4. F. Gregory Gause III, *Saudi-Yemeni Relations* (New York: Columbia University Press, 1990), pp. 36–37.

5. See Joel Migdal, *Strong Societies and Weak States: State-Society Relations and State Capabilities in the Third World* (Princeton, N.J.: Princeton University Press, 1988), p. 129.

6. There have always been conflicts, for instance, between *ijtihad* (independent reasoning or judgment) and *taqlid* (imitation, strict adherence to legal precedent). The former has been emphasized when innovation and creativity were required, and the latter when rulers were intolerant and when people looked for certainty and predictability. See Nazih Ayubi, *Political Islam: Religion and Politics in the Arab World* (New York: Routledge, 1991), chap. 3.

The Middle East.

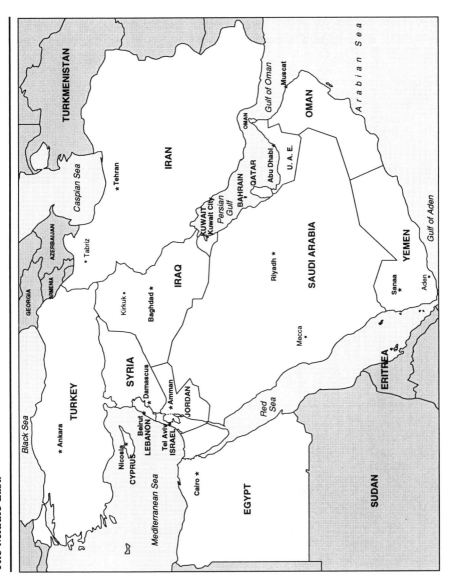

peril" does not threaten the region or, more generally, the West.[7] If anything unites these groups it is a belief that there should be a reintroduction of the Shari'a (Islamic law) at the state level and thus a reestablishment of an Islamic community. However, even this is quite vague, since the Shari'a can be interpreted in many ways.[8]

THE POTENTIAL FOR ETHNIC TURMOIL

Like religion, ethnicity has played an important role in Middle Eastern politics. But like the religious communities discussed above, the goals of the ethnic communities "have differed, depending on the objective circumstances they encountered and the ideologies and assessments of their often competing aspirants for leadership."[9] Like religious conflict, ethnic strife has been a variable rather than a constant force in the region.

Ethnic differences do not necessarily cause unresolvable difficulties for local leaders. The Berbers of North Africa, for example, have had a somewhat easier time than the Kurds in Iraq, Syria, Turkey, and Iran. Although groups of Berbers have rebelled on occasion (in Morocco there were five armed rebellions between 1956 and 1973), the 1970s and 1980s have been relatively calm. Many of their cultural demands have been met, which has helped to defuse tensions.[10] Algerian Berbers were previously well-represented in the bureaucracy, and the Moroccan Berbers have been allowed to join the army, particularly as members of the officer class. The Moroccan government has been relatively receptive to Berber cultural demands, such as leniency regarding spoken Berber and the establishment of institutes for the study of Berber culture. In part because of these overtures by the government, there has been no widespread

---

7. For a discussion of the "green peril," see Judith Miller, "The Challenge of Radical Islam," *Foreign Affairs,* Vol. 72, No. 2 (Spring 1993), pp. 43–55; Samuel P. Huntington, "The Clash of Civilizations?" *Foreign Affairs,* Vol. 72, No. 3 (Summer 1993), pp. 22–49. For the competing argument that the "green peril" is not a unified threat to the West, see, among others, Fouad Ajami, "The Summoning," *Foreign Affairs,* Vol. 72, No. 4 (September/October 1993); and Leon T. Hadar, "What Green Peril?" *Foreign Affairs,* Vol. 72, No. 2 (Spring 1993), pp. 27–42.

8. See James P. Piscatori, *Islam in a World of Nation-States* (Cambridge, U.K.: Cambridge University Press, 1986).

9. Milton J. Esman and Itamar Rabinovich, "The Study of Ethnic Politics in the Middle East," in Milton J. Esman and Itamar Rabinovich, eds., *Ethnicity, Pluralism, and the State in the Middle East* (Ithaca, NY: Cornell University Press, 1988), pp. 23–24.

10. Barbara Harff, "Minorities, Rebellion, and Repression in North Africa and the Middle East," in Ted Robert Gurr, ed., *Minorities at Risk: A Global View of Ethnopolitical Conflicts* (Washington, D.C.: U.S. Institute of Peace, 1993), pp. 217–251.

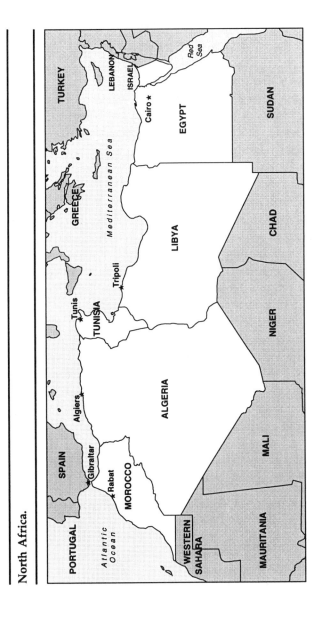

North Africa.

rebellion in the 1990s.[11] In the past, the Algerians tried to woo Berbers into government by increasing their presence to reflect their numbers in society. Significant government funds were also devoted to agricultural and industrial development in Berber regions.[12] Protests in Algeria in 1995, however, indicate that this pattern might be changing.

WEAK, UNDEMOCRATIC STATES

Ethnic and religious diversity does not in and of itself precipitate domestic conflict. In weak, undemocratic states, however, the likelihood of conflict increases. State strength can be measured by a state's ability to regulate social relationships, extract resources, and appropriate or use resources in determined ways. Strong states have formidable capabilities in these areas; weak states do not.[13] Until the 1970s, most Middle Eastern states could be classified as weak.

In addition, the absence of democratic traditions calls into question the legitimacy of most Middle Eastern governments. In a democracy, the process of participating in elections and contesting candidates confers legitimacy on a leader. In the absence of such processes, nationalism, ethnicity, or religion tend to be relied on. Until the late 1960s, however, state-based nationalism was a dangerous card to play in the Middle East because it opposed the prevailing ideology — Arab nationalism — which mandated that states were subordinate to the Arab nation as a whole. Many Middle Eastern leaders have consequently relied on religion and ethnicity to legitimize their regimes. This, however, has often antagonized and alienated unfavored ethnic and religious groups.

This deep-seated legitimacy problem largely accounts for the volatile nature of Arab politics.[14] As Max Weber observed,

without legitimacy, a ruler, regime or governmental system is hard-pressed to attain the conflict-management capability essential for long-run stability and good government. While the stability of an order may be maintained for a time through fear or expediency or custom, the optimal or most harmonious

---

11. Ibid., pp. 232–233.

12. William E. Hazen, "Minorities in Assimilation: The Berbers of North Africa," in R.D. McLaurin, ed., *The Political Role of Minority Groups in the Middle East* (New York: Praeger, 1979), pp. 146–147.

13. Migdal, *Strong Societies*, p. 4.

14. Michael C. Hudson, *Arab Politics: The Search for Legitimacy* (New Haven, Conn.: Yale University Press, 1977), p. 2.

relationship between the ruler and the ruled is that in which the ruled accept the rightness of the ruler's superior power.[15]

In the Middle East, few have accepted the rightness of the ruler's superior power.

As a result, ethnic and religious relations have often degenerated into zero-sum games where some ethnic or religious groups are privileged at the expense of others. In Syria, for example, the Alawi area of Latakia has benefited under the Ba'ath at the expense of non-Alawi areas of the country. Leaders have managed these potential conflicts more effectively at some times than others. Their ability to manage these problems well is mainly a function of the resources available to co-opt and control different groups rather than actually meeting the political needs of the disenfranchised.

The Historical Record

How well leaders prevent and manage political turmoil is to a great degree dependent on the resources available to them. A leader's ability to co-opt and coerce various groups affects the likelihood of rebellion and the prospects for its success. It also affects the calculations neighbors make with respect to meddling and intervention. This section focuses on developments in the Middle East during two periods: 1950–69 and 1970–89.

THE 1950S AND 1960S

The period of the 1950s and 1960s was a time of intense conflict in the Middle East. Many of these conflicts developed because of weak states and artificial borders. While a few states, such as Egypt, had both strong institutions and a well-defined national identity, the region as a whole was not as fortunate. Because of the weaknesses of their states, many leaders had difficulty managing domestic conflict and resisting regional interventions. This had important effects on the region's stability.

One positive effect of this was that many Middle Eastern leaders did not have the same motivations for intervening on behalf of co-nationalists as did their counterparts in other areas of the world. Because national identity in many cases was formed after international borders were set, there were no pockets of ethnic Lebanese living in Syria or ethnic Libyans

---

15. Max Weber, *The Theory of Social and Economic Organization*, trans. A.M. Henderson and Talcott Parsons (New York: Oxford University Press, 1947), pp. 124–126; Hudson, *Arab Politics*, p. 1.

living in Algeria whose defense would garner public support. Unlike Eastern Europe, for example, where leaders have routinely used threats to co-nationalists in neighboring states as a *casus belli,* the notion of being Syrian or Libyan followed the construction of national borders and thus spared the region this source of tension.

At the same time, though, the lack of strong national identities made it more difficult for Middle Eastern leaders to rebuff interventions by neighboring states. In other parts of the world, nationalism provided a power base for leaders to draw on and generated a certain level of loyalty from the population. Because the level of state-based nationalism in the Middle East was relatively low in the 1950s and 1960s (except in Egypt and Iran), outside powers could easily interfere in the domestic politics of neighboring states.

Along with low levels of nationalism, weak domestic political institutions hampered the ability of states to withstand aggression. President Nasser of Egypt, for instance, was able to bring down regimes in Syria and threaten others in Iraq and Jordan by promoting Arab nationalism and supporting dissenting societal groups. Iraq also engaged in regional meddling; it attempted to counter Egyptian successes by manipulating Syrian and Lebanese politics. In 1958, the Iraqi Prince, Abdul Illah, told the United States that he was "very disturbed" by developments in Lebanon and suggested that if Egyptian pressure on Lebanon continued, a "diversionary revolutionary movement should be started in Northern Syria to take UAR [Egyptian and Syrian] pressure off Lebanon."[16] Saudi Arabia was able to intervene in North Yemen more easily than in South Yemen because of the comparative weakness of the former's state institutions.[17]

In most parts of the world, intervention is usually said to be undertaken on behalf of societal groups that need the protection of an outside power. In the Middle East, outside powers intervened opportunistically when they determined that supporting one faction over another would improve their regional positions. Until the late 1960s, intervention was easy and relatively cheap. The pattern began to change, however, in the following decades.

---

16. Telegram, U.S. Embassy in Turkey to U.S. Secretary of State, No. 3130, June 18, 1958, Records of the Department of State, Record Group Number 783.00/6-1858, National Archives, Washington, D.C..

17. Gause, *Saudi-Yemeni Relations;* see especially chap. 1, pp. 1–15.

THE 1970S AND 1980S

Important changes in the region since the late 1960s have affected both the national identity and institutional problems discussed above. This, in turn, has affected the dynamics of internal conflict and patterns of intervention in the region.

From the late 1960s through the mid-1980s, vast resources poured into the Middle East. With few exceptions, most states in the region benefited from either increased oil revenues (especially since 1973) or more foreign aid (most significantly since 1967).[18] By coincidence, many states which benefited little from oil revenues were confrontation states (Egypt, Israel, Jordan, Lebanon, and Syria), and therefore received large sums of foreign aid and beneficial arms and trade packages.[19] (See Tables 6.1 and 6.2.)

What foreign aid and oil revenues have in common is that both flow directly into state coffers. In the Middle East, all resources found beneath the ground are owned by the government. Any profits derived from oil or minerals therefore accrue directly to the state.[20]

Oil revenues and foreign aid have strengthened states *vis-à-vis* their populations. They have underpinned bureaucratization and centralization efforts, which have improved state abilities to monitor and co-opt groups in society. This has helped states to manage domestic problems and resist outside interventions. It is unlikely that the cost-of-living riots that erupted in Tunisia (1978, 1984), Egypt (1977), Algeria (1988), and Morocco (1981) would have been dealt with as decisively in the 1950s and 1960s as they were in the 1970s and 1980s.

Throughout the region, levels of government expenditure and public wages rose steadily during the 1970s and 1980s. Governments became increasingly important features in Middle Eastern society. In Saudi Arabia, the number of civil servants increased from a few hundred in 1950 to 37,000 in 1962–63, to 85,000 in 1970–71, and to over 245,000 in 1979–80. In the 1940s, Syria and Jordan each had fewer than ten ministries. By the 1980s, Jordan had twenty-two and Syria had twenty-four. In 1978, the

---

18. Some may argue that North Africa was an exception. But even here, France has been an active supporter of Morocco and Tunisia. Algeria has also benefited from Soviet assistance and income from indigenous sources of natural gas.

19. Lebanon has not benefited as significantly as the others. For a good example of how much one confrontation state has benefited from regional and international involvement, see Patrick Clawson, *Unaffordable Ambitions: Syria's Military Build-Up and Economic Crisis* (Washington, D.C.: Washington Institute for Near East Policy, 1989).

20. Hazem Beblawi, "The Rentier State in the Arab World," in Giacomo Luciani, ed., *The Arab State* (Berkeley: University of California Press, 1990), chap. 4.

Table 6.1. Foreign Aid (in Millions of 1987 U.S. Dollars).

Country	1960	1965	1970	1975	1980	1985	1990	1993
Confrontation states								
Egypt	1.54	34.01	863.64	1409.76	–	837.92	987.64	1082.26
Israel	345.38	74.83	–68.18	918.43	1655.62	4419.49	3360.11	3140.32
Jordan	35.00	32.55	310.80	617.72	1102.29	783.47	518.62	287.58
Syria	39.62	–	8.52	935.79	1277.25	1283.90*	70.61	32.26
Oil and gas states								
Algeria	–	–	34.09	–17.36	19.68	10.61	0.88	–
Iran	143.08	27.21	11.36	–24.31	–	–	–	–
Iraq	–2.58	–0.14	2.84	–380.22	–	–	–	–
Kuwait	–	–	–	–1133.72	–745.79	–557.20	–3700.00	–104.03
Libya	1956.31	1.02	–321.02	–234.39	–38.27	–47.67	–30.89	–
Saudi Arabia	–	149.66	–230.11	–4472.34	–4958.10	–3441.74	–3884.38	–758.06
Others								
Morocco	98.80	61.17	11.36	–6.95	94.04	115.47	282.44	124.19
Tunisia	168.04	148.36	88.07	53.82	85.30	50.85	198.59	90.32
North Yemen	–	–	–	167.20	122.48	97.41	–	–
South Yemen	–	–	–	–	66.71	28.14*	–	–

SOURCES: Information about central government transfer payments was taken from International Monetary Fund (IMF), *Balance of Payments Yearbook*, Vols. 15, 20, 29, 37, 43, 45 (Washington, D.C.: IMF, 1964, 1969, 1978, 1986, 1992, and 1994). Exchange rates were taken from Robert Summers and Alan Heston, *Penn World Tables* (Cambridge, Mass.: National Bureau of Economic Research, 1994) and IMF, *International Financial Statistics Yearbook* (Washington, D.C.: IMF, 1993). Information about implicit price deflators was taken from *Economic Report of the President* (Washington, D.C.: U.S. Government Printing Office [U.S. GPO], 1995).

NOTES: The variable used is central government transfer payments. This includes some small non-aid transfers such as pensions. However, it is most significantly an indicator of aid. Because this variable does not include barter or other preferential trading arrangements, it actually under-represents the amount of aid flowing to any given state. However, it serves as a useful proxy to determine trends in aid flow. Negative signs mean that countries give more than they receive. It is therefore not surprising that after 1973, oil states tend to have negative totals. The fact that the values move closer to zero in 1990 for oil states is an indicator that resources are becoming more scarce, and foreign aid is more in demand.

* 1984 statistic

Table 6.2. Government Oil Revenue (in Billions of 1987 U.S. Dollars).

	1970	1973	1975	1978	1980	1983	1985	1988	1990	1993
Algeria	1.95	3.71	8.77	9.76	17.57	10.88	9.76	4.80	7.84	6.43
Iran	6.74	13.70	40.07	36.14	18.45	22.13	13.95	8.86	12.92	11.48
Iraq	2.25	2.50	13.33	15.93	36.52	11.38	12.10	8.95	8.37	0.29
Kuwait	4.56	5.78	17.19	15.70	24.55	11.43	10.35	6.58	5.65	8.05
Libya	6.73	9.56	19.18	16.14	29.72	13.68	11.19	6.15	8.67	6.13
Qatar	0.65	1.47	3.59	3.83	7.54	3.60	3.57	1.64	2.62	2.09
Saudi Arabia	6.91	21.84	60.15	67.22	150.24	51.53	27.59	19.43	35.51	33.34
United Arab Emirates	1.36	4.24	13.89	14.46	27.08	15.87	14.25	7.07	13.81	10.92

SOURCE: Organization of the Petroleum Exporting Countries (OPEC), *Annual Statistical Bulletin* (Vienna: OPEC, 1986, 1993), Table 5. Information for 1970–86 was taken from the volume issued in 1986. All other data were taken from the volume issed in 1993.

Egyptian bureaucracy employed 1,900,000 people; at the beginning of the 1980s it employed 2,876,000.[21] These growing state bureaucracies allowed leaders to monitor and control domestic groups effectively because people were increasingly dependent on the state for their well-being. Economic benefits and employment opportunities were distributed to loyal citizens. State penetration into the periphery rewarded those whose agricultural decisions corresponded with state policies.

In addition to providing funds for various state ventures, increased revenues allowed states to devote additional resources to domestic policing. Throughout the 1970s and 1980s, there were large increases in the budgets and staffing levels of military and paramilitary organizations. (See Table 6.3.) These increases enhanced state abilities to co-opt and coerce their populations.

Growing capabilities made it more difficult for groups to rebel. As Esman and Rabinovich noted:

As a rule, the weak regimes of the 1950s and 1960s were replaced by more powerful regimes that have survived challenges and crises through coercion and dexterity (Lebanon and the Shah's Iran are two obvious exceptions). This has enabled minority groups in Syria and Iraq to use the state for their purposes and to stifle the discontent of the majority. In other countries, minority groups encountered state power that had been conspicuously absent twenty years earlier.[22]

Although the presence of relatively successful Islamic groups showed that dissent could still be a political force, these groups were also challenged by the developments of the 1970s and 1980s.

In addition to making it more difficult to rebel against the state, strengthened state institutions made it harder for outside powers to intervene on behalf of disadvantaged groups. In the 1950s and 1960s, successful intervention in the domestic affairs of neighbors was increasingly more difficult than in the 1970s and 1980s. There is evidence, for example, that Nasser had an easier time affecting internal developments in neighboring states than did Ayatollah Khomeini, even though both were purportedly leaders of pan-regional movements. The Middle Eastern state, since the 1970s, has also had more tools at its disposal to control its own domestic critics, as the management of the food riots discussed above implies. Increases in domestic police forces, government

---

21. Nazih Ayubi, "Arab Bureaucracies: Expanding Size, Changing Roles," in Luciani, *The Arab State*, chap. 6.

22. Esman and Rabinovich, *Ethnicity*, p. 8.

Table 6.3. Middle East Armed Forces, 1966–92.

	Active Military Duty Forces (in 1,000s)			
	1966	1975	1984	1992
Algeria	65.0	63.0	130.0	139.0
Egypt	180.0	298.0	460.0	410.0
Iran	221.0*	250.0	550.0	528.0
Iraq	80.0	101.0	640.0	382.5
Israel	40.0*	156.0	141.0	175.0
Jordan	35.0	37.0	68.0	99.4
Lebanon	10.8	15.2	20.3	36.8
Libya	5.0	25.0	73.0	85.0
Morocco	35.0	56.0	144.0	195.5
Saudi Arabia	30.0	43.0	51.0	157.0
Syria	60.0	137.0	362.0	408.0
Tunisia	20.0	24.0	35.0	35.0
North Yemen	–	20.9	36.5	–
South Yemen	10.0	9.5	27.0	–

	Paramilitary Forces (in 1,000s)			
	1966	1975	1984	1992
Algeria	8.0	10.0	25.0	52.2
Egypt	90.0	100.0	140.0	374.0
Iran	25.0*	74.0	2500.0	57.0
Iraq	10.0	19.0	650.0	24.8
Israel	–	9.5	4.5	6.0
Jordan	8.5	22.0	20.0	9.0
Lebanon	2.5	5.0	7.5	7.0
Libya	–	23.0	10.0	5.5
Morocco	3.0	23.0	30.0	40.0
Saudi Arabia	20.0	32.0	45.0	11.0
Syria	8.0	9.5	38.5	12.5
Tunisia	5.0	10.0	8.5	13.5
North Yemen	–	–	25.0	–
South Yemen	–	–	45.0	–

SOURCES: Elizabeth Picard, "Arab Military in Politics: From Revolutionary Plot to Authoritarian State," in Giacomo Luciani, ed., *The Arab State* (Berkeley: University of California Press, 1990) pp. 189–219, esp. p. 192. Data for 1992 come from International Institute for Strategic Studies [IISS], *The Military Balance 1993–94* (London: IISS, 1994). Data for Israel and Iran come from *The Military Balance 1968–69, 1978–79, 1984–85* and *1993–94.*

* 1968 data

Table 6.4. Number of Successful Coups.

1950–69		1970–89	
Egypt	3	Iraq	1
Iraq	4	South Yemen	2
Syria	7	North Yemen	3
North Yemen	2		
South Yemen	1		
Iran	2		
Algeria	1		
Libya	1		

NOTE: The Lebanese civil war and the Iranian revolution do not appear in this table because they were not coups in the traditional sense. However, they were both major governmental changes. Their absence should not be taken as an indication that they were not important.

SOURCES: Eliezer Be'eri, *Army Officers in Arab Politics and Society* (New York: Praeger, 1970), pp. 246–248; David E. Long and Bernard Reich, eds., *The Government and Politics of the Middle East and North Africa* (Boulder, Colo.: Westview, 1986).

bureaucracies, and security apparatuses throughout the region have affected the ability of Middle Eastern states to repel international and domestic threats. Table 6.4 outlines some of these developments.

It should be noted that five of the six coups that occurred in the later period took place in North and South Yemen, which did not benefit to a great degree from growing oil income and foreign aid. It is also important to remember that the Gulf states did not receive full independence until 1971. Had they become independent earlier, they might have experienced more turbulence in the 1950s and 1960s.

Resources clearly do not explain everything. Morocco and Tunisia did not witness the same windfalls as the rest of the region, but they nonetheless built strong states and have experienced no coups. Iran's 1979 revolution came at a time when oil revenues should have been strengthening the tools at the Shah's disposal. Nonetheless, there is no doubt that resources and state capacities have significant effects on political stability.

They also have significant effects on the prospects for regional meddling. Aggressive Iranian policies toward Gulf states would probably have been more successful in the 1950s and 1960s than they were later on. As one scholar has argued, "changes over the last three decades in domestic political structures have made the Arab regimes more capable of resisting hostile ideological pressure."[23] This is not to say that Arab

23. F. Gregory Gause III, "Revolutionary Fevers and Regional Contagion: Domestic Structures and the 'Export' of Revolution in the Middle East," *Journal of South Asian and Middle Eastern Studies*, Vol. 14, No. 3 (Spring 1991), p. 2.

states have had an easy time rebuffing Iranian claims since the 1970s. The Iranian revolution affected and continues to affect domestic stability throughout the region. For instance, the Sunni government in Bahrain has been battling sporadically with the Shi'ite population since the Iranian revolution in 1979. The most recent incidents were mass arrests in January 1995; an Amnesty International report published in 1993 chronicled evidence of governmental abuse of the minority population.[24]

Similarly, Syrian President Hafez al-Assad is better able to control Syrian society than were his predecessors. This has made regional involvement in Syrian politics more difficult. From independence in the 1940s to Assad's ascension to power in 1970, Syria was little more than a pawn in the game of regional power politics. Assad's focus on domestic institutions, particularly the Ba'ath party, and a surge in foreign aid allowed him to discourage outside intervention more effectively than any previous Syrian leader.

Lebanon, however, has clearly not been so lucky. The collapse of the Lebanese state, which began in 1958, preceded the influx of resources that bolstered other states in the region. If it had possessed more resources to draw on, the government might have been able to shore up domestic support and check outside intervention. As it turned out, weaknesses in Lebanon's domestic institutions allowed for an internationalization of the conflict. In the 1970s and 1980s, virtually every state in the region has been involved in the Lebanese civil war at one time or another.

Prospects for the Future

What will happen as external sources of revenue dry up? While Table 6.1 showed that the 1970s and early 1980s were profitable for oil-producing states, the trend has not been maintained into the 1990s. Although it is true that the Arab world's share of oil production and export has increased in relation to the rest of the world, it has not increased enough to overcome the significant drop in oil prices. Evidence of this downward trend in prices, and thus revenues, began after the 1986 oil price wars. While prices showed some signs of increasing in the latter half of the 1980s, they never fully recovered and again began decreasing at the beginning of the 1990s. In addition, increases in consumer taxes placed on oil and gas in Western countries do not provide an encouraging picture for oil producers. Nicolas Sarkis, director of the Arab Petroleum Research Center, nicely illustrates this point:

---

24. This report is cited in "Bahrain: Introductory Survey," *Europa World Yearbook 1995*, Vol. 1 (London: Europa Publications 1995), p. 476.

Nominal oil prices, which rose from $2.70/b [barrel] in 1973 to $11.20/b in 1974, reached a peak of $34.30/b in 1981, before falling to $13.70/b in 1986. From 1989 until 1993, the average annual price of OPEC crude basket rose from $17.31/b in 1989 to $22.26/b in 1990, but then fell to $18.66/b in 1991 and $18.31/b in 1992. Expressed in real terms, and taking 1974 as the base, prices rose from $11.20/b in 1974 to $19.30/b in 1981, before dropping to $6.40/b in 1989 and $5.80/b in 1992, only half the 1974 level.

The sharp drop in the revenues of Arab states and other oil-producing countries shatters the myth propagated since 1973 about the financial clout of these countries.[25]

The end of the Cold War and declining oil revenues mean that financial sources of support for Middle Eastern states are declining. Wealthy oil states, such as Saudi Arabia, are being forced to scale back development programs and retrench. Former Soviet allies have seen foreign aid virtually disappear. State institutions and bureaucracies, dependent on international sources of income, are being dealt a serious blow. Not only are financial resources drying up, but previous donors have become competitors for foreign aid. Moscow, previously one of the region's most important patrons, is trying to attract Arab money to promote its economic renewal.[26] This dramatic shift illustrates the monumental changes occurring in both the international system and the region.

As a result, internal conflict in the Middle East is increasingly likely. The trouble that Algeria has experienced in the 1990s was preceded by a reduction in Soviet aid. Syrian, Jordanian, and Israeli foreign policy shifts are bids to attract Western financial support. Governments throughout the region are attempting to deal with the sudden changes that have taken place in the international system. These changes have the potential to generate domestic instability.[27]

In the following section, I examine the near-term threats to political stability in the Middle East and North Africa. I focus in particular on the potential for ethnic and religious conflict in the region. I conclude with a

---

25. Nicolas Sarkis, "Arab Oil 20 Years After the 1973 Crisis: Production Has Increased but . . . Revenues Have Plummeted," in *Arab Oil and Gas Directory 1993* (Paris: Arab Petroleum Research Center, 1994), pp. 557–559.

26. See interview with Aleksandr Zotov, cited in Richard K. Herrmann, "Russian Policy in the Middle East: Strategic Change and Tactical Contradictions," *Middle East Journal*, Vol. 48, No. 3 (Summer 1994), p. 462. See also, Alvin Z. Rubinstein, "Moscow and the Gulf War: Decisions and Consequences," *International Journal*, Vol. 49, No. 2 (Spring 1994), pp. 301–327.

27. For a discussion of how North African states are dealing with these problems, see Lisa Anderson, "Liberalism in Northern Africa," *Current History*, Vol. 89, No. 546 (April 1990), pp. 145–148.

discussion on how influxes of refugees, possible changes in leadership, and the potential collapse of the Arab-Israeli peace process could endanger already-weakened states and thus threaten the region as a whole.

THE RISE OF ISLAMIC FUNDAMENTALISM

Fundamentalism will remain a pressing problem for the region, especially as state resources dwindle. What is surprising about the resurgence of Islamic political movements is that they began in the early 1970s, just as state resources began to grow. Why were several groups successful at organizing and opposing governments under these conditions? Understanding the sources of these Islamic movements will help to illuminate appropriate ways of dealing with them.

There are many explanations for the Islamic revival. First, the dramatic loss of Arab territory during the 1967 War led many Arabs to question their secular governments. Second, failed modernization plans led others to question the merit of Western-inspired programs. Third, frustrated by their inability to participate in politics, political challengers believed that they could safely confront governments by cloaking their opposition in religious terms.

What all of these explanations overlook is the role of the state. A careful look at state policy in the region shows that state action was taken to encourage Islamic political movements. This was done in order to diffuse other societal tensions. In the 1970s, Sadat came under pressure from those who believed that he was ill-suited to follow in Nasser's footsteps as the president of Egypt. Instead of co-opting them, Sadat funneled resources into mosques and religious schools in order to create an alternative opposition movement and divide the government's critics. The policy worked, at least as a short-term tactical maneuver. Banks and other institutions were established to support the Islamic movement. Religious relief organizations were encouraged to help the state care for needy people. The Egyptian government's ability to create such a movement was predicated on increased state resources and its ability to set up organizations and mobilize society.

This pattern was repeated in other states throughout the region. In Tunisia, the Ministry of Religion established the Quranic Preservation Society in order to counter the left. In the West Bank and Gaza Strip, the Israeli government favored Islamic organizations over the Palestinian Liberation Organization (PLO). It was much more lenient in its responses to protests couched in religious terms than to those initiated by the PLO.[28]

---

28. Emile Sahliyeh, *In Search of Leadership: West Bank Politics since 1967* (Washington, D.C.: Brookings Institution, 1988), pp. 142–144.

Once religious organizations served governmental purposes, however, the states in question tried to disband them. This has not been as easy as anticipated. When resources are in decline, the ability of states to combat opposition groups — even groups they once supported — decreases, because they have created a situation in which opposition now has a voice and organizational structures to support it. Rather than co-opting dissenters in the 1980s, states attempted to marginalize them. The capabilities of Middle Eastern states to dampen dissent are limited in the 1990s. Ironically, strong states gave voice to opposition movements that threaten them now that the tables have turned.

It is important to stress that Islamic movements in the Middle East and North Africa vary in form and content from place to place. They are dialogues, albeit sometimes violent, between individual states and society. There is a tendency, for instance, to see the Algerian situation as a simple conflict between revolutionary Islamic militants and a secular army. This is certainly how the French see it, as their policy of arming the Algerian army suggests.[29] But such a position is naive and short-sighted. Indeed, upon closer investigation there appears to be a marked diversity in the views of both camps on democracy, political integration, and political rule. While the Armed Islamic Group has been steadfast in its unwillingness to negotiate with the current regime, its main religious opposition, the Islamic Salvation Front (FIS), along with the Islamic Salvation Army, have been more willing.[30] There is also evidence that Abassi Medani and his FIS followers are ready and willing for some type of dialogue with the regime and have accepted the notion of alternation of power through universal suffrage.[31] Thus, while it might be true that Washington can do little in Algeria, especially since openly embracing certain groups may only hurt their legitimacy, there are some things that the French government can do.[32] France's policy of viewing the situation as black or white forces it into the position of supporting the Algerian army. Contrary to the official French position, however, there does seem to be room to maneuver between the National Liberation Front (FLN), the previous ruling political party, and FIS. Thus, France could back away from the army and support both the state (FLN) and democracy (FIS).

---

29. al-Tahir Hammad, "Military Containment Campaign Described," *Foreign Broadcast Information Service; Near East and South Asia,* January 18, 1995, p. 16.

30. Hugh Roberts, "Algeria's Ruinous Impasse and the Honourable Way Out," *International Affairs,* Vol. 71, No. 2 (April 1995), pp. 247–267.

31. See Roberts, "Algeria's Ruinous Impasse," pp. 257–263.

32. Edward G. Shirley, "Is Iran's Present Algeria's Future?" *Foreign Affairs,* Vol. 74, No. 3 (May/June 1995), pp. 28–44.

Unfortunately, it is not just Western regimes that tend to view Islamic oppositionists as a homogeneous group. Egyptian President Hosni Mubarak does the same. Islamic groups in Egypt have targeted foreigners and Egyptian cultural and political figures. They have wreaked havoc on revenue from tourism, a main source of income for the Egyptian state. As discussed above, however, Islamic groups vary in terms of their use of violence and their political agenda. Like Western leaders, Mubarak has tended to overlook this. He has recently imposed heavy regulations on political activity that has heretofore been considered to be the province of "civil society," such as legal associations and engineering unions.[33] He has done this because figures sympathizing with Islamic political platforms have won elections in such organizations. As a result, he has alienated members of society who had previously been potential allies. He has generated much resentment without being able to co-opt such groups. While the Egyptian state is responsible for the strength of many contemporary Islamic parties, it has not been able to easily control them.

These movements threaten Middle Eastern regimes far more than they do Western interests.[34] However, this is not to say that there is nothing for Western powers to worry about. Domestic instability may create windows of opportunity that other states can exploit. For example, in the late 1980s, Sudan actively supported various Islamic groups in Egypt. It cut back on this assistance when Egypt mobilized its troops on the Egyptian-Sudanese border.

A victory in one state can embolden radical factions in neighboring states. Algerian militants, for instance, have already warned neighbors against siding with the Algerian government.[35] The Algerian government, for its part, has set fire to forests near the Tunisian border in order to root out the opposition's safe havens. Although an Islamic victory in Algeria could strengthen movements in Morocco and Tunisia, it cannot substitute for them: too much of the Tunisian Islamic opposition, for example, is focused on country-specific issues for a victory in Algeria to propel it to power.

How — and how well — have states in the region dealt with this Islamic resurgence? Most have been more successful than Algeria. Syria, for instance, has been relatively successful in crushing religious

---

33. See Ahmad Abdalla, "Egypt's Islamists and the State: From Complicity to Confrontation," *Middle East Report*, Vol. 23, No. 4 (July/August 1993), pp. 28–31.

34. Graham E. Fuller and Ian O. Lesser, *A Sense of Siege: The Geopolitics of Islam and the West* (Boulder, Colo.: Westview, 1995) p. 119.

35. Youssef M. Ibrahim, "Algeria Rebels Said to Attack Post in Tunisia," *New York Times*, February 17, 1995, p. A6.

opposition.[36] In 1980 and 1982, Syria embarked on extraordinary campaigns to liquidate Islamic opposition. As a general rule, however, suppression has not been effective in this regard. With state resources becoming more limited, repressive policies may be becoming less feasible.

Unlike Syria, Jordan has dealt with its fundamentalist movement through democratic means. In a 1989 election for the lower parliament, Muslim Brotherhood members won twenty-two of the eighty available seats, which Jordan allowed them to assume. In 1992, Jordan officially legalized political parties. During the succeeding election in 1993, however, many representatives from Islamic opposition groups were voted out of power because it was believed that they were as, if not more, ineffective in dealing with the country's problems. King Hussein is widely considered to be one of the most successful Middle Eastern leaders in dealing with Islamic militants. His popularity as a leader increased dramatically after he showed at least some respect for popular opinion regarding the political process. In pursuing such a strategy, Hussein simultaneously reduced the appeal of the government's opposition and increased his own legitimacy.

Jordan's success in managing Islamic fundamentalism suggests that the international community should push for some types of democratic elections as an effort to combat radical forces. Part of the problem in Algeria was that all seats in the parliament were openly contested. Rather than supporting such sweeping changes, the regime should have begun modification of the process by beginning reforms with municipal elections and choosing something other than a winner-take-all system. Once part of a governing structure, radicals in other states will be forced to accept some responsibility for many of the region's intractable problems, as in Jordan.[37]

ETHNIC AND REFUGEE PROBLEMS

Although religious conflict in the Middle East and North Africa receives much attention in the international press, some ethnic conflicts in the region have the potential to erupt or re-erupt in the near future.

---

36. Umar F. Abd-Allah, *The Islamic Struggle in Syria* (Berkeley, Calif.: Mizan Press, 1983), and Itamar Rabinovich, "Arab Political Parties: Ideology and Ethnicity," in Esman and Rabinovich, *Ethnicity.*

37. Some fear that rather than successfully managing dissent, King Hussein's tactics have actually forced opposition groups underground, which will only come back to haunt the kingdom. See, for instance, Ben Wedeman, "The King's Loyal Opposition? The Muslim Brotherhood's Foray into Jordanian Politics," *Middle East Insight,* Vol. 11, No. 2 (January–February 1995), pp. 15–19.

Collapsing states are exacerbating many underlying ethnic problems, which will inevitably have consequences for the region as a whole.

The 1991 Gulf War has exacerbated ethnic tensions in the region in a variety of ways. First, the near-collapse of the Iraqi state allowed many ethnic divisions in Iraq to become more visible. The Shi'ite uprising in the south and the Kurdish uprising in the north resulted from the collapse of the Iraqi state. Interestingly enough, Turkey and Syria have not aided the Iraqi Kurds as much as they have in the past: it is one thing to aid a neighbor's opposition to weaken a strong adversary; it is another to hasten the collapse of a regime and destabilize the region. In a departure from traditional practice in the region, Turkey crossed into Iraqi territory and established military outposts in March 1995 in an attempt to neutralize the Kurdistan Worker's Party (PKK); countering a threat to Turkish security was seen as more important than continuing to assist Iraqi Kurds in their campaign to overthrow the Iraqi regime.

The Turkish offensive into Iraq highlights the influence that state strength has on regional meddling. Iraq is not the only state harboring the PKK. Syria, while officially banning the group, allows the PKK to operate from Syrian territory. Syria is in fact using the PKK to pressure Turkey into reconsidering its water reallocation projects, which will affect the amount of water flowing into Syria.[38] Turkey invaded northern Iraq because it was easy to do so; a window of opportunity was created by the collapse of the Iraqi state. No such window exists with respect to Syria.

The Kurds are likely to remain a problem for the region as long as states continue to abuse them. This could lead to an interesting policy twist. Although states like Turkey have seized an opportunity to root out the PKK, they could be supporting various Kurdish factions in a few years time — if Iraq begins to reassert itself in the region. This would be consistent with past policy.

In addition to reigniting Kurdish and Shi'ite nationalism, the 1991 Gulf War has had a significant impact on the region's ethnic geography. Iraq expelled 500,000 Egyptians, and Saudi Arabia expelled 700,000 Yemenis. Some 400,000 Iraqi refugees are said to have crossed the border into Turkey.[39] Only 40,000 of 250,000–300,000 Palestinians are left in

38. Mehmet Ali Birand, "Al-Shar' on Linking Water, PKK Issues," *Foreign Broadcast Information Service; Near East and South Asia*, January 17, 1995, p. 84.

39. Jane E. Stromseth, "Iraq's Repression of Its Civilian Population: Collective Responses and Continuing Challenges," in Lori Fisler Damrosch, ed., *Enforcing Restraint: Collective Intervention in Internal Conflicts* (New York: Council on Foreign Relations, 1993), pp. 77–117; see n. 45.

Kuwait.[40] Jordan has been hit hard by this flood of refugees, absorbing much of the Palestinian diaspora. About 350,000 Palestinians poured into Jordan's labor market as a result of the Gulf War.[41] The arrival of these refugees at a time when Jordan is not capable of fully absorbing them is likely to have serious ramifications for the region. Regardless of whether dissatisfaction takes the form of Palestinian nationalism or religious fundamentalism, these newly dispossessed citizens are likely to demand the attention of their new governments. Jordan, in particular, will require the help of the international community.

The potential collapse of the Algerian state would provide not only Islamic groups with an opportunity to mobilize, but Berbers as well. As noted earlier, Berbers have had a much easier time in Algerian society than Kurds in Iraq, Syria, Turkey, and Iran. In the past, they have had access to bureaucratic and some other economic and social opportunities. The Algerian government, however, has been committed to eliminating the Berber language and culture from the country's life. The Berbers have also been generally discouraged from participating in politics. Although it is unlikely that the Berbers will mobilize to the same extent that the Kurds in Iraq have, it is not surprising that with the collapse of the Algerian state, Berber protest marches have begun to surface in Algeria.

Political and economic troubles in Iran have the potential to spark conflict in its northern Azeri territories. Some twelve to twenty million Iranians consider themselves Azeri, or claim Azeri as their mother tongue.[42] This Azeri minority has become increasingly worrisome to Tehran as the Azeri-Armenian conflict has continued. Tehran is worried that an Azeri victory will embolden ethnic Azeris in Iran. Rather than trying to co-opt Azeri groups, Iran has moved industry from Tabriz, inhabited mostly by Azeris, to southern cities in an effort to reduce the concentration of Azeris in northern areas.[43] It does not seem that the Iranians have formulated a coherent long-term plan regarding the Azeris; however, although the Azeris have made important contributions to Iranian culture and politics and are represented throughout domestic

---

40. Andrew Whitley, "Minorities and the Stateless in the Persian Gulf," *Survival*, Vol. 35, No. 4 (Winter 1993), pp. 39–40.

41. Alan Cowell, "Jordan's King is Betting on a 'Peace Dividend'," *New York Times*, October 19, 1994, p. A10.

42. Sharam Chubin and Charles Tripp, "Domestic Politics and Territorial Disputes in the Persian Gulf and the Arabian Peninsula," *Survival*, Vol. 35, No. 4 (Winter 1993), p. 10. See also Whitley, "Minorities and the Stateless."

43. "Embassy in Baku Reports Problems in Tabriz," *Foreign Broadcast Information Service; Near East and South Asia*, January 18, 1995, p. 58.

institutions, Iran is watching developments with some concern. Iran's current economic and political difficulties do not bode well for its Azeri minority.[44] Nor do they bode well for the Kurds, Baluchs, and Afghani refugees currently living in Iran.[45]

TURMOIL OVER LEADERSHIP SUCCESSION

Changes in leadership could also unleash domestic turmoil in the Middle East and North Africa. Many leaders have remained in power for years by manipulating ethnic and religious balances in their countries. When changes in leadership do take place, as they eventually must, ethnic or religious conflict could erupt in several states.

In Iraq, the dangers associated with ill-prepared leadership succession are obvious. After the 1991 Gulf war, it was unclear whether or not it was in the interest of the region or the international community to force the downfall of Saddam Hussein. His treatment of the Kurds, Shi'ites, and other minority groups notwithstanding, it was feared that Saddam's fall would precipitate domestic turmoil because it was not clear who would succeed him. These concerns recall the earlier discussion of legitimacy. In many states in the Middle East and North Africa, it is not clear who legitimate successors might be. Changes in leadership have the potential to set off periods of intense domestic conflict, as groups mobilize to fill power vacuums and secure resources.

In addition to Iraq, this could be a problem in Jordan, Syria, and Saudi Arabia. In Syria, many years of Alawi privilege over other groups is likely to become an issue when Assad leaves the scene. There is no love lost between the Sunni urban bourgeoisie and the Alawi establishment. Although Sunni opposition has not been effectively organized in the past, the passing of Assad will bring grievances to the surface and present opposition groups with an opportunity to mobilize and press their demands.

Similar problems exist in Jordan between the Palestinians and Bedouin. In 1970, Palestinian groups threatened to take over the Jordanian government. Their failure led to the expulsion of large numbers of Palestinians to Lebanon. Divisions still exist between Bedouin Jordanians

---

44. The Iranians would prefer an Azerbaijan strong enough to keep Turkey out of the region, but not strong enough to infuse Iran's Azeri minority with nationalist feelings. William Ward Maggs, "Armenia and Azerbaijan: Looking Toward the Middle East," *Current History*, Vol. 92, No. 570 (January 1993), pp. 6–11.

45. While its own minorities are causing Iran concern, it is also fair to say that, in the post–Cold War era, Iran is much more preoccupied by the possibility of political unraveling in neighboring states. For more on this viewpoint, see Chubin and Tripp, "Domestic Politics and Territorial Disputes," especially p. 10.

and the Palestinians who remained. If an easy transition does not occur between the King and Crown Prince Hassan and especially if the Arab-Israeli peace process comes to an end, the polarization between the two groups will increase.

The situation does not look much better in Saudi Arabia. There is much speculation about who will take control of the reins of government when King Fahd gives up the throne.[46] Although the process might be orderly, there are several contenders for power. If fratricidal conflict develops, the contenders could mobilize different factions in support of their aspirations.

IMPACT OF THE ARAB-ISRAELI PEACE PROCESS

Although some states in the region can still garner popular domestic support by championing radical Palestinian groups, the costs of doing so are beginning to outweigh the benefits.[47] With the end of the Cold War, U.S. foreign aid has unprecedented clout. Syria and Jordan will be better positioned to receive U.S. assistance if they make strides toward peace. U.S. President George Bush's willingness to delay the extension of loan guarantees impressed upon Israel the need to choose between expanding Jewish settlements in the West Bank and receiving U.S. assistance. The United States is now in a position to force leaders in the region to make these kinds of choices.

The success of the Arab-Israeli peace process is essential for regional stability, both economically and politically. Important progress has been made, especially between Israel and Jordan, but support must be maintained for further agreements. Jordan's economic livelihood is dependent on increased trade with Israel, as are the West Bank's and Gaza's

---

46. See "The Cracks in the Kingdom," *Economist*, March 18–24, 1995, pp. 21–25; Thomas L. Friedman, "Before It's Too Late," *New York Times*, December 10, 1995, p. E13; Eliyahu Kanovsky, *The Economy of Saudi Arabia: Troubled Present, Grim Future*, Policy Paper No. 38 (Washington, D.C.: Washington Institute for Near East Policy, 1994). For a dissenting viewpoint on the political instability of Saudi Arabia, see Michael Collins Dunn, "Is the Sky Falling? Saudi Arabia's Economic Problems and Political Stability," *Middle East Policy*, Vol. 3, No. 4 (April 1995), pp. 29–39. In early December 1995, King Fahd temporarily passed the leadership to his half-brother Crown Prince Abdullah after being hospitalized for what many speculated to be either a stroke or a heart attack. Even if power is permanently transferred to Crown Prince Abdullah in a peaceful fashion, the question of succession will soon be revisited when power is passed from this generation of Saudi leaders, the sons of the founder of the Saudi state, to the next generation, the grandsons.

47. Syria's recent cut in aid to the Popular Front for the Liberation of Palestine (PFLP) supports this point. See "PFLP-GC Disbands 30% of Fighters with Less Than 8 Years," *Foreign Broadcast Information Service; Near East and South Asia*, January 24, 1995, p. 11.

livelihoods. The failure of the talks would send a message to radical groups on all sides that resistance is the best path to victory. This would increase the power and prestige of opposition groups.

An Arab-Israeli peace settlement is one of the keys to the region's political stability. With the Palestinians nearing eighty percent of the Jordanian population, a breakdown in negotiations could lead to the collapse of the Jordanian state.[48] As Mary Morris has observed, "it is ironic that a stable and secure Jordan is of little intrinsic political interest to the security of the region as a whole, while a destabilized or hostile Jordan could be of profound significance . . . such a state could threaten the security of all its neighbors, [and] conflict would almost certainly not be confined within its borders."[49]

What also makes the peace process important politically is that it is a case of state formation rather than state deterioration. In the mid-1990s, a relatively authoritarian regime has begun trying to develop some sort of state structures in the West Bank and Gaza. The question has become whether international aid should be used to encourage a move toward democracy, and which countries should provide this aid.

Continued support must be given to Yasser Arafat and to the developing Palestinian state. Without a state there will be no democracy, and resources are the most sorely needed commodity. Without political representation, it is likely that radical opposition parties will become even more prevalent, following a well-established regional pattern. It is therefore preferable that international donors tie aid and diplomatic assistance to Palestinian democratization.[50]

Even if it is possible to encourage international assistance and democratization, some may argue that this is not the optimal strategy. As Edward Mansfield and Jack Snyder show, democratizing states are clearly a risky bet if one wants to promote regional stability.[51] However, many of the conditions that cause democratizing states to be more belligerent than authoritarian or democratic states are absent in the case of Palestine,

---

48. The figure of eighty percent includes Palestinians arriving after the Gulf War. Previously, Palestinians made up only sixty percent of Jordanian population.

49. Mary E. Morris, *New Political Realities and the Gulf: Egypt, Syria and Jordan* (Santa Monica, Calif.: RAND, 1993), p. 37.

50. William Quandt, "The Urge for Democracy," *Foreign Affairs*, Vol. 73, No. 4 (July/August 1994), pp. 2–7.

51. Edward D. Mansfield and Jack Snyder, "Democratization and War," *Foreign Affairs*, Vol. 74, No. 3 (May/June 1995), pp. 79–97; Edward D. Mansfield and Jack Snyder, "Democratization and the Danger of War," *International Security*, Vol. 20, No. 1 (Summer 1995), pp. 5–38.

and some of the conditions that make democratizing states less belligerent exist.

For instance, Mansfield and Snyder argue that existing elites may pose a problem for democratizing states, because they have no incentive to share power. However, this is not as problematic in Palestine as in other areas of the world. Because a state is being created, rather than reconstructed, there are few established, entrenched elites. Israel has held political power for so long that few Palestinians have much to lose by experimenting with democracy. It is true that the PLO has more to lose than some of the opposition. But in the current situation, it seems that the PLO would probably garner many of the votes anyway, as long as security and economic concerns continue to be met.

Mansfield and Snyder also argue that certain kinds of international environments are conducive to peaceful democratizers. They point to the examples of Japan and Germany, which democratized peacefully due to "the favorable international setting provided by the Marshall Plan, the Bretton Woods economic system, and the democratic military alliance against the Soviet threat."[52] The Marshall Plan provided economic assistance and the Bretton Woods system provided financial stability that the international community could replicate in the Middle East through aid and reliance on the International Monetary Fund (IMF) and the World Bank.

Finally, the war-weariness of the Palestinian population needs to be considered. After six years of the Intifada, which followed five Arab-Israeli wars and decades of turmoil, aggressive nationalism is unlikely to appeal to the masses. There is ample evidence, for instance, that terrorist attacks against Israelis do not generate the same wave of support from Palestinians as they once did. Thus, aggressive nationalism and war do not seem as likely in the case of Palestine as in other democratizing states. Thus, there are reasons to be hopeful about the prospects for democracy and stability in a Palestinian state.

Conclusions

This chapter has analyzed some of the changes that have occurred in the Middle East since the collapse of the Ottoman Empire. Changes in social organization have had profound effects on regional politics. Since independence, Middle Eastern leaders have faced extraordinary difficulties in organizing societies to facilitate their rule. Ethnic and religious cleavages continue to challenge leaders throughout the region.

---

52. Mansfield and Snyder, "Democratization and War," p. 95.

In the 1970s and 1980s, revenue from foreign aid and oil exports helped overcome many of these problems by providing the resources necessary to co-opt and coerce various societal groups. Obviously, co-optation and coercion are not perfect substitutes for political participation. However, financial resources have helped leaders in the region manage political life in their countries and maintain domestic stability.

The problem comes, of course, when financial sources dry up. Recent declines in oil prices and foreign aid will inevitably allow societal grievances to bubble to the surface. It is therefore likely that there will be an increase in the level of domestic instability in the Middle East in years to come. Many of the problems witnessed in the 1950s and 1960s could re-emerge in the late 1990s and beyond.

I conclude that the recent debates in the United States about its commitment to foreign aid and United Nations (UN) membership are disturbing. At a time when aid is most crucial, its utility is being questioned. It has long been argued that deterrence is easier, and often cheaper, than compellence.[53] By the same token, conflict prevention is easier, and often cheaper, than conflict resolution.

There are many places in the Middle East and North Africa where foreign aid could make a big difference. Instability in Algeria puts pressure on North Africa as a whole. The United States and Western powers should be involved in strengthening Tunisian and Moroccan borders and ensuring that economic crises do not affect either government at such a propitious moment. This would cost much less than rebuilding a collapsed state after the fact.

More broadly, the international community should support elections at local and municipal levels, accepting fundamentalist victories if they occur in order to foster more states like Jordan and fewer states like Algeria. It is simplistic to view each Islamic group in each state as a threat to regional stability and Western interests, as the French are currently doing in Algeria. My discussion of the Muslim Brotherhood's involvement in Egyptian politics and differing goals within Algeria's religious community underscores this point. Increased participation may be the only answer to the difficult times ahead.

As far as Arab-Israeli relations are concerned, the United States must remain involved in the peace process. The United States and the international community must be willing to underwrite peace settlements, as they did at Camp David. Syria, in particular, is expecting to receive a substantial aid package if it signs a peace treaty with Israel. If the peace

---

53. Thomas Schelling, *Arms and Influence* (New Haven, Conn.: Yale University Press, 1966), chap. 3.

process collapses, radical groups on all sides will be the only beneficiaries. President Bush's and Secretary of State James Baker's commitment to the region played an important role in getting the parties to the table. The Clinton administration would do well to follow their lead.

By itself, U.S. engagement cannot solve the many problems the region will face in the future. Ethnic and religious conflicts have their origins in state-society relationships that have deep roots. However, the United States can influence the costs and benefits of adopting various policies. Its presence thus remains crucial.

I thus conclude on both pessimistic and optimistic notes. Trends in the international system suggest that conflict in the Middle East and North Africa will increase. Reductions in foreign aid and oil revenue will revive many of the patterns of conflict witnessed in the 1950s and 1960s. However, there are ways of dealing with conflicts that will help lessen their effects. These include supporting certain types of democratization, distinguishing between different types of Islamic groups, and supporting those regimes most in need. Failure to do so will only exacerbate current political difficulties.

Chapter 7

Conflict and Conciliation in Sub-Saharan Africa

Stephen John Stedman

Between 1991 and 1994, Africa became synonymous with chaos. Images from the continent mostly consisted of civil war, famine, and anarchy. To a large extent, these images conformed to reality; in the early 1990s Africa was the location of the most deadly conflicts in the world. Between 1991 and 1993, 400,000 Somalis died from war-induced famine. In a little over two months in 1994, approximately 800,000 Rwandans fell victim to genocide. When the civil war in Angola resumed in late 1992, the death toll reached one thousand people per day. In four years of civil war, Liberia has seen nearly half of its population of 2.5 million die or flee. In Sudan, nearly 1.2 million people have died from famine and civil war since 1984. In October 1993, over 100,000 people lost their lives in Burundi during a one-month ethnic bloodletting.

The bad news from Africa has crowded out the good news. If Africa is home to the collapsed state (Liberia, Somalia, and Sierra Leone), it is also home to the negotiated settlement (Zimbabwe, Namibia, South Africa, and Mozambique) and the reconstructed state (Uganda and Ghana). Africa has displayed a range of responses to economic decay, state collapse, environmental degradation, and the violent conflicts such calamities can engender. Although anarchy is endemic to Central Africa and parts of West Africa, there are signs of hope that the Horn of Africa may be starting to come out of chaos. And in Southern Africa, a region that could easily have gone the way of the rest of the continent, one can speak of national and regional institutions that seem capable of managing conflict and mitigating the regional effects of domestic conflict.

Africa's divergent trends raise obvious questions. What combination of causes led to the violence and misery that Angola, Rwanda, Somalia, and Sudan have experienced? What enabled Mozambique and South Africa to end their civil wars and begin the slow process of reconstruction and reconciliation? Why have some states in Africa collapsed, while others have prospered? Why has Southern Africa been able to create institutions capable of conflict management and resolution? How have internal conflicts engaged neighboring states and fostered regional instability? What policies should the international community pursue toward African conflicts?

In this chapter, I argue that Africa's recent internal conflicts have arisen from long-term permissive conditions and more immediate proximate causes. Legacies from colonialism predisposed much of Africa to violent conflicts over the distribution of resources in societies, access to political power, and basic political identities. Such legacies helped to create a pattern of state and class formation in which African political leaders relied on external support to reward internal allies and ignored the needs of their citizens. By the early 1980s, the survival of many African regimes depended on external, not internal, legitimacy.[1] Two precipitating events in the 1980s — the triumph of free market ideas in international financial institutions (the World Bank and International Monetary Fund) and the end of the Cold War — undermined the external sources of support for Africa's patrimonial regimes and left some with no legs to stand on.

Africa's crisis of state legitimacy prompted different responses. Some regimes found themselves under armed attack from old political rivals and new insurgencies. In many African countries, leaders accepted multiparty elections and attempted for the first time to seek the consent of their people. Other embattled leaders spewed ethnic hatred and pursued divide-and-rule tactics against nascent opposition movements in order to forestall political change. Still others have sought to create single party populist dictatorships.

Africa's internal conflicts have had profound effects on neighbors, sub-regions, the continent as a whole, and the international community writ large. But Africa's diverse experiences caution against sweeping generalizations about the regional and international effects of internal violence. In many cases, domestic violence has indeed destabilized neighbors. But in some cases, leaders in nearby states have taken advantage of a neighbor's internal troubles, intervened for selfish reasons, and made matters worse. And in a few cases, well-planned regional and international responses have confined the spread of violence.

Africa's conflicts have triggered a near-hysterical response among those who fail to differentiate among African countries, and conclude that

---

1. Robert H. Jackson and Carl G. Rosberg, "Why Africa's Weak States Persist: The Empirical and the Juridical in Statehood," in Atul Kohli, ed., *The State and Development in the Third World* (Princeton, N.J.: Princeton University Press, 1986), pp. 259–282.

the political and economic collapse of the state due to civil war in Sierra Leone is characteristic of all of Africa and that Africa's condition may foreshadow collapses of states and societies elsewhere in the world.[2] This undifferentiated view of Africa has contributed to donor and compassion fatigue among international actors: if Rwanda or Sierra Leone or Somalia is indicative of all of Africa, then the task of assisting the continent seems hopeless.

Paradoxically, however, the international community continues to focus the bulk of its attention on Africa's complex humanitarian tragedies — the Liberias, Rwandas, and Somalias, — which, clearly, will be exceedingly difficult to resolve. Peace enforcement and humanitarian intervention, which are expensive, risky, and thus far ineffective, have drawn attention and resources away from assisting countries in Africa that have a chance to develop in benign directions.

The humanitarian tragedies of the 1990s have taken place at a time when international aid resources have become scarce. Dollars spent on humanitarian relief now come at the expense of dollars available for sustainable development. If the international community is unwilling to increase dramatically the overall amount of aid for Africa, then it should explicitly adopt a policy of triage and provide aid only to those countries that have a chance to achieve sustainable development. The present policy of responding to a few crises at the expense of the needs of the many is both unethical and untenable. It is a policy doomed to produce more, not fewer, humanitarian disasters.

Africa's Deadly Conflicts

Since the 1970s, Africa has been the site of many of the world's most deadly conflicts. Seven wars — in Angola, Ethiopia, Mozambique, Rwanda, Somalia, Sudan, and Uganda — took between 500,000 and 1,000,000 lives each, either directly through battlefield casualties or indirectly through war-induced famine and disease. Two other conflicts, in Burundi and Liberia, took over 100,000 lives each. In 1995, there were five ongoing wars (in Angola, Liberia, Sierra Leone, Somalia, and Sudan), several countries that were candidates for state collapse or civil war (Burundi, Cameroon, Kenya, Nigeria, Rwanda, Togo, and Zaire), and a host of other countries where low-level ethnic and political conflict remained contained, but unresolved (Chad, Congo, Djibouti, Ethiopia, Malawi, Mali, Mozambique, Senegal, South Africa, and Uganda).

---

2. Robert Kaplan, "The Coming Anarchy," *Atlantic Monthly,* Vol. 273, No. 2 (February 1994), pp. 44–76.

The violent internal conflicts of the 1990s must be put into historical context. Political instability has plagued Africa since most of its countries became independent in the 1960s. Between 1960 and 1980, eight civil wars took place on the continent; ten more occurred over the next decade.[3] Almost one-third of the world's genocides between 1960 and 1988 (eleven of thirty-five) took place in Africa.[4] Between 1963 and 1985, sixty-one coups d'état occurred in Africa — an average of almost three coups per year.[5] Between 1960 and 1990, Africa's conflicts accounted for more than 6.5 million deaths.[6]

Some of these numbers can be attributed to the peculiarities of Southern Africa. Between 1960 and 1994, war was endemic there, the result of three interlocking conflicts — wars for independence in Angola, Mozambique, Namibia, and Zimbabwe; the attempt by South Africa's National Party to maintain white supremacy in South Africa; and South Africa's destabilization of its neighbors in the 1980s, which was a direct extension of its own civil war. Between 1980 and 1988 alone, between 1.2 and 1.9 million people died in Angola and Mozambique.[7]

The roots of Africa's violence lie principally with the political and economic conditions that existed after independence and the policies pursued by elites to gain and consolidate power. Common patterns of state and class formation in Africa have led to endemic, intense internal conflict. Even in Southern Africa, where wars of independence and majority rule continued into the 1990s, violence was exacerbated by conditions inherited from colonialism and the policy choices of new elites.

PERMISSIVE CONDITIONS OF AFRICA'S CRISIS

Africa's internal conflicts have roots that extend to various conditions present at independence. Colonial powers established borders that corre-

---

3. This figure is cited in Ted Robert Gurr, "Theories of Political Violence and Revolution in the Third World," in Francis M. Deng and I. William Zartman, eds., *Conflict Resolution in Africa* (Washington, D.C.: Brookings Institution, 1991), p. 153.

4. Barbara Harff and Ted Robert Gurr, "Toward an Empirical Theory of Genocides and Politicides: Identification and Measurement of Cases Since 1945," *International Studies Quarterly*, Vol. 32, No. 3 (September 1988), pp. 359–371.

5. Samuel Decalo, *Coups and Army Rule in Africa*, 2nd ed. (New Haven, Conn.: Yale University Press, 1990), pp. 1–2.

6. Ruth Leger Sivard, *World Military and Social Expenditures 1993*, 15th ed. (Washington, D.C.: World Priorities, 1993), p. 21.

7. Thomas Ohlson and Stephen John Stedman, with Robert Davies, *The New is Not Yet Born: Conflict Resolution in Southern Africa* (Washington, D.C.: Brookings Institution, 1994), p. 4.

Africa.

sponded little to African political, cultural, and economic life. Colonial governments were primarily policing and taxing organizations with few representative functions. Colonial economies exported primary products — agricultural goods and minerals — to their respective metropoles and possessed little industrial capability. Colonial governments neglected the cultivation of Africa's human capital; when independence came, few Africans were trained to step in and operate large state bureaucracies. The first generation of African leaders compounded Africa's political and economic underdevelopment by emphasizing the state as the leading engine for economic growth and insisting on national unity at the expense of sub-national ethnic and political identities.[8]

The first generation of African independence leaders accepted colonial borders rather than entering into the arduous and politically volatile process of redrawing them. Indeed, the charter of the Organization of African Unity (OAU) places great emphasis on the permanence of existing borders and the principle of territorial integrity. Although many analysts attribute Africa's lack of inter-state wars to this commitment, it guaranteed that internal instability would be rife throughout Africa.[9] A few examples suffice to indicate the depth of the problem. Nigeria's territory included 3 major religions (Islam, Christianity, and Animism) and 250 ethnic groups, the largest three (Hausa Fulani, Yoruba, and Igbo) possessing "vastly different political values and institutions."[10] Zambia contained 72 ethnolinguistic groups, Tanzania 120.[11] Some states contained historical enemies. In Sudan, Arabs in the north had enslaved Nuer and Dinka in the south; in Rwanda and Burundi, Hutu lived under near-feudal submission to Tutsi. The borders of Ethiopia, Kenya, and Somalia divided ethnic and clan groups, thus prompting periodic irredentist struggles.

If Africa's borders generated intense domestic conflicts over political identity, the lack of domestic economic capital ensured that states would be important sources of resources and would become the subjects of intense distributional conflicts. As Larry Diamond observes, the state structures established by the colonial powers "dwarfed in wealth and power both existing social institutions and various new fragments of

---

8. Basil Davidson, *The Black Man's Burden* (New York: Times Books, 1993).

9. See, for example, William Foltz, "The Organization of African Unity and the Resolution of Africa's Conflicts," in Deng and Zartman, *Conflict Resolution in Africa,* pp. 347–366.

10. Richard Sandbrook, *The Politics of Africa's Economic Recovery* (Cambridge, U.K.: Cambridge University Press, 1993), p. 93

11. Ohlson and Stedman, *The New is Not Yet Born,* p. 53.

modern organization."[12] At independence, Africa's new elites sought to harness the power of their states to be the lead instruments in their economies. Regulatory and other state-sponsored bodies and widespread nationalization of foreign industries provided income opportunities for state officials. The state soon became the largest employer in these new countries: for example, 47.2 percent of Senegal's budget in 1964–65 was spent on administrative salaries, and 81 percent of the budget in the Central African Republic went to the civil service.[13]

As the state became the main source of employment and capital in the new countries of Africa, a pattern of patrimonial politics soon crystallized. Groups organized to ensure access to state largesse — the only way to accumulate wealth. Office holders appropriated state resources to consolidate their power bases and reward their networks of clients. National interests were subordinated to the interests of politicians and their supporters, who viewed public office as private property.[14]

The rapidity of Africa's decolonization and the weakness of colonial efforts to prepare Africans for independence created an enduring paradox. As Africans rushed to take advantage of the resources and rewards that their new states could confer, and as African leaders expanded state bureaucracies to consolidate their patron-client networks, states became large, omnipresent bureaucracies. At the same time, a shortage of human capital assured that bureaucracies would lack skilled civil servants and technicians. The result, in Thomas Callaghy's memorable phrase, was the creation of "lame leviathans."[15]

Colonial neglect of education posed nearly intractable problems for Africa's new states. There were, for example, no more than 1,200 university graduates in all of sub-Saharan Africa in 1960.[16] In Zaire, there were fewer than 20 college graduates at independence; in Zambia, only 108

---

12. Larry Diamond, "Class Formation in the Swollen African State," *Journal of Modern African Studies*, Vol. 25, No. 4 (December 1987), p. 570.

13. Ibid., p. 574.

14. Ibid., p. 581. See also Richard Joseph, *Democracy and Prebendal Politics in Nigeria: The Rise and Fall of the Second Republic* (New York: Cambridge University Press, 1987); Thomas Callaghy, *The State-Society Struggle: Zaire in Comparative Perspective* (New York: Columbia University Press, 1984). For an analysis of the prospects for democratic change in patrimonial African regimes, see Michael Bratton and Nicolas Van De Walle, "Neopatrimonial Regimes and Political Transitions in Africa," *World Politics*, Vol. 46, No. 4 (July 1994), pp. 453–489.

15. Thomas M. Callaghy, "The State as Lame Leviathan: The Patrimonial Administrative State in Africa," in Zaki Ergas, ed., *The African State in Transition* (London: Macmillan, 1987), pp. 87–116.

16. Sandbrook, *The Politics of Africa's Economic Recovery*, p. 25.

Africans had received university education.[17] In Tanzania, "there were only twelve African civil engineers, eight African telecommunication engineers, nine African veterinarians and five African chemists. No Africans had been trained as geologists or mechanical or electrical engineers."[18] When the Portuguese left Angola in 1974, there were no African civil servants.[19] When Mozambique became independent, there were three African doctors and one African lawyer; ninety percent of the population was illiterate.[20]

Africa's new leaders consolidated their rule through access to state coffers. Some leaders, fearing potential ethnic conflicts, created inclusive coalitions that provided rewards for many societal groups. In other cases, one ethnic group succeeded in capturing the state and shutting other groups out. In still other cases, political leaders chose to ignore ethnicity and insist on establishment of a national identity as a unifying principle for the country.[21]

Patrimonial politics eventually had devastating economic consequences. Most states were organized to redistribute wealth: existing resources were divided to buy and maintain political support. The production of wealth received short shrift. Domestic investment dried up, and foreign investment was transferred to more profitable regions of the world. The result was that most African countries suffered economic declines; in many African countries, standards of living were worse in the 1980s than in the 1960s. To cope with the reduction in economic production and lack of investment capital, African states borrowed heavily from international financial institutions. African countries found themselves simultaneously marginalized from the international economy and dependent on international loans and assistance.[22] State formation became based on ties to international financial institutions or external patrons,

---

17. Ibid., p. 25; Naomi Chazan et al., *Politics and Society in Contemporary Africa* (Boulder, Colo.: Lynne Rienner, 1988), p. 228.

18. Chazan et al., *Politics and Society in Contemporary Africa*, p. 228.

19. Gerald J. Bender, *Angola Under the Portuguese: The Myth and the Reality* (Berkeley: University of California Press, 1978), p. 201.

20. Per Wastberg, *Assignments in Africa: Reflections, Descriptions, Guesses*, trans. Joan Tate (New York: Farrar, Straus, and Giroux, 1986), p. 115.

21. For a fuller discussion of various policies towards ethnic groups in Africa, see Donald Rothchild, "Ethnic Bargaining and State Breakdown in Africa," *Nationalism and Ethnic Politics*, Vol. 1, No. 1 (Spring 1995), pp. 54–72.

22. Thomas Callaghy, "Africa and the World Economy: Caught Between a Rock and Hard Place," in John Harbeson and Donald Rothchild, eds., *Africa in World Politics* (Boulder, Colo.: Westview, 1991), pp. 39–68.

either the superpowers or former colonial masters. Regime stability came to depend on the support of the few in society with access to state largesse and on the coercive force of the military and police. In time, the state became the biggest threat to individual security in Africa.

PROXIMATE CAUSES OF AFRICA'S CRISIS

Two factors contributed to Africa's wave of political instability in the late 1980s. At the end of the 1970s, an ideological revolution took place in international financial institutions; neoclassical theories of economic growth overtook models that emphasized state action. As international financial institutions grew impatient with the waste and corruption of African governments, they began to impose strict economic conditions on access to international aid. In order to maintain the flow of international loans and assistance, African leaders were forced to cut state employment, liberalize prices, sell off state-run businesses, and eliminate state regulation of markets. Economic conditionality cut at the heart of the patrimonial state. If African leaders followed the dictates of international financial institutions, they would divest themselves of the resources necessary to maintain the support of their clients. If leaders chose to defy these financial institutions, they would lose access to badly needed international capital. Either way, the patrimonial state was in jeopardy.

Some African states, however, could rely on superpower patronage and sidestep the dilemma posed by economic conditionality. But as the 1980s ended, the end of the Cold War closed off this economic lifeline. The only regimes able to sustain shrinking internal patronage networks were those that oversaw economies that exported natural resources in world demand — for example, Gabon, Nigeria, and Zaire.

NATIONAL RESPONSES TO CRISIS

As Africa entered the 1990s, many regimes found themselves in a crisis of state legitimacy and under pressure to institute democratic reforms. African leaders responded in four ways.

In the first category were countries such as Liberia and Somalia, where dictators refused to give up political power in the face of armed challenges. When no quick victory was forthcoming, the armed factions splintered into smaller camps. The result was state collapse and the proliferation of armed warlords who controlled small pieces of territory and who were sustained by plunder.

In the second category were countries such as Cameroon, Kenya, Nigeria, Togo, and Zaire, where despots initially conceded to demands for democratic participation, but then manipulated the process to retain power through corruption, coercion, ethnic mobilization, and other divisive tactics. Given diminishing resources to buy internal support, leaders in these countries focused their patronage on smaller segments of society and politicized ethnicity as a means of maintaining their hold on power.

In the third category were countries such as Ghana and Uganda, where authoritarian leaders tried to build regime legitimacy from the top down. In both of these countries, for example, dictators invoked populist rhetoric, insisted on citizen participation in rebuilding the nation, implemented the structural reforms mandated by international financial institutions, and used coercion against internal dissidents. These regimes claimed that their countries were in chaos and that political and economic discipline, not democracy, were needed — a claim largely accepted by donor nations and international financial institutions.

In the fourth category were countries such as Benin, Malawi, and Zambia, where authoritarian leaders ceded power to democratically elected forces. In these countries, civil society, emboldened by democratic successes in Eastern Europe and elsewhere in Africa, asserted itself. This led to multiparty elections and political freedoms. In these cases, former dictators did not have private sources of wealth that could be used to manipulate elections. Instead, they faced united opposition, which rendered the politics of ethnic hatred ineffective.

The three types of countries that have avoided collapse are precariously balanced. Where dictators have manipulated democratic processes to retain power, the potential for violence is high; countries such as Cameroon, Kenya, Nigeria, and Zaire are candidates for collapse. In countries that have pursued state-led reform, such as Ghana and Uganda, it remains to be seen whether leaders can avoid the fate of all of Africa's previous experiments in authoritarianism, where dictatorships become corrupt, fossilized, and ultimately brittle when confronted by strong populist challenges.[23] Finally, the countries that have embarked on democratic transitions lack the basic economic, social, and cultural conditions that facilitate the consolidation of democracy.[24] These countries are attempting to establish multiparty political processes and implement tough economic reforms at the same time. Simultaneous economic and political liberalization may result in the failure of both.

---

23. Even in terms of political stability, these regimes have not completely delivered. In Ghana, ethnic conflicts have periodically erupted into violence. In Uganda, the regime was still fighting a low-level insurgency in the north in 1995.

24. For a discussion of factors that assist the creation of democracy, see Larry Diamond, "Economic Development and Democracy Reconsidered," *American Behavioral Scientist*, Vol. 35, No. 2 (March/June 1992), pp. 450–499.

The Regional Effects of Africa's Internal Conflicts

Africa's internal conflicts have had wide-ranging, costly effects on their sub-regions.[25] The need for protection has led some rebel groups to cross borders in search of sanctuary. The existence of rebel bases in neighboring countries has prompted some countries to cross borders when carrying out search-and-destroy missions. And although there have been few inter-state wars in Africa, regimes have often been willing to support rebels who threaten and weaken their rivals. Africa's wars have created millions of refugees and a thriving illegal market in small arms, both of which can destabilize neighboring countries. Finally, in some cases it is possible to speak of internal conflicts having contagion effects, whereby conflict in one country produces similar problems in neighboring countries.

THE TACTICAL AND STRATEGIC SPREAD OF INTERNAL CONFLICT
Violent conflict in one country can spread to a neighboring country because combatants judge that they have something to gain by taking this step. First, rebel groups may establish bases or seize territory across borders in order to gain access to resources or sanctuary from state security forces. Often this is done with the approval of the neighboring country. For example, Mozambique and Tanzania provided bases and supplies to Zimbabwean guerrillas in the 1970s. Angola and Tanzania provided bases for African National Congress (ANC) guerrillas from South Africa. Uganda willingly hosted rebels of the Rwandan Patriotic Front (RPF). In some cases, however, neighboring countries are unwilling hosts of marauding rebel forces. In 1991, soldiers of Liberian rebel leader Charles Taylor invaded Sierra Leone and plundered diamond mines there in order to fund his war in Liberia. When the government of Sierra Leone attempted to stop the invasion, Taylor formed alliances with local villagers and armed them to fight their government. In order to improve his odds in Liberia, Taylor sparked a civil war in Sierra Leone.

Second, civil wars have spread across borders when government forces have attacked neighboring states in the hope of eliminating rebel bases and supply lines and intimidating countries which gave sanctuary to rebels. Throughout the 1980s, South African defense forces attacked Botswana, Mozambique, and Zimbabwe in order to kill members or supporters of the ANC. South Africa actively aided and abetted parties

---

25. For an excellent extended analysis of the interplay between internal conflicts, sub-regional effects, and state rivalries for regional power and status, see Terrence Lyons, "Regional Dynamics," in Francis Deng et al., *Sovereignty as Responsibility: Conflict Management in Africa* (Washington, D.C.: Brookings Institution, forthcoming).

such as the Mozambican National Resistance (RENAMO) and the National Union for the Total Independence of Angola (UNITA) as a way of punishing and undermining their respective governments.

Third, violent conflict has spread when neighboring governments have used insurgencies to weaken and destabilize regional rivals. In Africa, support for rebel movements has been a common substitute for direct inter-state war. In this sense, the OAU's prohibition on external interference in the domestic affairs of others has been routinely violated. Violent conflict can spread when a state that has been weakened by a neighbor's meddling responds by supporting rebel groups in the offending country. For instance, Zairean assistance, training, and leadership of the Front for the National Liberation of Angola (FNLA) in 1975 prompted the Angolan government to sponsor the rebels who invaded Zaire's Shaba province in 1978. Ugandan support for the Sudanese People's Liberation Army (SPLA) has led the Sudanese government to train and support rebels in northern Uganda.

REFUGEES AND THE SPREAD OF INTERNAL CONFLICT

At the beginning of 1995 there were an estimated 6.7 million refugees in Africa.[26] Although the international community views refugees as a humanitarian problem, host and home governments often view them as a security problem. First, refugee camps are potential pools for rebel recruitment. Home countries may respond with direct attacks against camps in host countries, as Rhodesia did in Mozambique in the late 1970s. Second, refugee flows can overwhelm communities and cause intense conflicts over food, water, and shelter. If local governmental authorities are ill-equipped to cope with such conflicts, their own legitimacy can be weakened. Third, camps often impose economic burdens and health dangers to nearby communities and can easily provoke resentment in the host country. Outbreaks of infectious diseases in Mozambican camps in Zimbabwe led to violent protests by Zimbabweans in surrounding communities. Tanzanian resentment of the destruction wrought by Rwandan refugees became a heated political issue in Tanzania.

Although refugees are sometimes destabilizing political forces, this is not a forgone conclusion. Much depends on the capabilities of the host governments, as well as the policies and actions of the international community. For example, the government of Botswana strictly prohibited South African and Zimbabwean refugees from engaging in political and

---

26. United Nations High Commission for Refugees, *Statistical Overview, 1994* (New York: United Nations, 1995).

military activity. International aid and assistance depended on the neutrality of the camps. However, in the Goma camps in Zaire, international relief agencies supplied food, water, medicine, and shelter to Rwandan refugees, many of whom were armed and some of whom dressed in military fatigues. Since humanitarian assistance was not predicated on the demilitarization of the camps and because the Zairean armed forces were unwilling to disarm the Rwandans, the refugee camps sheltered former units of the Rwandan military and members of the government who were implicated in the genocide of 1994. Not only has humanitarian assistance protected gross violators of human rights, it has enabled the Rwandan military to regroup and retrain in order to prosecute the war anew.

SMALL ARMS TRAFFIC AND THE SPREAD OF CONFLICT
Africa's wars have created a booming cross-border traffic in small arms. This leads to political instability in several ways. In collapsed states such as Liberia and Somalia, easy access to weaponry has led groups to fragment, making negotiated settlements next to impossible to reach. The easy availability of arms and the porousness of borders will intensify civil conflicts in several African states where dictators have fanned ethnic hatred in order to stay in power. Countries that are trying to manage democratic transitions find that disgruntled groups have access to weapons and can challenge the viability of new governments. Violence in Mali, for instance, prompted the newly elected president, Alpha Oumar Konaré, to request help from the United Nations (UN) in ascertaining the source of illegal arms in his country. Banditry and insurrectionist groups there have pushed the new government to its limits.[27]

In many of Africa's fledgling democracies, the supply of small arms has exacerbated violent crime. This undermines popular confidence in new regimes and scares off foreign investment, which is crucial for the economic turnarounds needed to sustain democratic transitions. In South Africa, for example, where leaders are trying to create a government that for the first time in that nation's history is viewed by the black majority as legitimate, widespread criminal violence and lingering political violence continue to create insecurity. Criminal violence is carried out by youth gangs who have access to black market AK-47s — guns that were used in the civil war in Mozambique that are smuggled through Swaziland and sold for the equivalent of $6 each.[28] In 1993, over 17,000 murders

---

27. See the UN Mali Advisory Mission, Draft Report, October 10, 1994.

28. Ohlson and Stedman, *The New Is Not Yet Born*, p. 259.

took place in South Africa; Johannesburg and Cape Town have among the highest murder rates in the world.[29]

CONFLICT AND CONTAGION

Conflicts in Africa have also spread across borders through contagion or demonstration effects. They raise fears that similar violence could erupt and provide opportunities for leaders to learn the costs and benefits of violence and the likely responses of the international community. One must be careful, however, about ascribing too much explanatory power to demonstration effects. This implies that conflicts spread through a natural or automatic process, or at least one unmediated by the choices of leaders. Second, it is often asserted, without evidence, that leaders in one conflict base their behavior on lessons learned and expectations formed by conflicts elsewhere.[30]

In Africa it is possible to point to at least one case where contagion effects mattered a great deal: in Rwanda and Burundi, countries that share a common border, a similar colonial history, and a similar ethnic composition. In both countries, Hutu constitute about eighty-five percent of the population and Tutsi constitute about fifteen percent. After independence, both countries experienced large-scale ethnic massacres and established political regimes based on ethnic domination. In Burundi, the Tutsi minority ruled through control of the army. In Rwanda, the Hutu majority systematically oppressed and excluded the Tutsi minority from politics. Many Tutsi fled Rwanda in the 1970s and 1980s; some formed the RPF in Uganda, which invaded Rwanda in 1990.

As 1993 began, politicians in both countries attempted to foster ethnic accommodation. In Burundi, the Tutsi agreed to institute a system of majoritarian democracy, but held on to their monopoly over the army. A successful election in June 1993 led to a change of government there, which led the international community to encourage Rwandans to negotiate a settlement to their civil war. In August, the RPF and the government of Rwanda signed an agreement to end their civil war and create a power-sharing government.

In October 1993, Tutsi military extremists in Burundi assassinated the

29. "Political Violence Drops, But Not Crime," *Frontiers of Freedom*, November 1994, p. 10.

30. For a sophisticated attempt to test the conditions under which contagion is a factor in the spread of conflicts, see Stuart Hill and Donald Rothchild, "The Contagion of Political Conflict in Africa and the World," *Journal of Conflict Resolution*, Vol. 30, No. 4 (December 1986), pp. 716–735.

Hutu president, which led to a one month-long ethnic slaughter. Hutu hardliners in the Rwandan military drew two lessons from what happened in Burundi: that accommodation between the two ethnic groups was impossible and that genocide would not necessarily trigger an international response. These lessons galvanized the Rwandan Presidential Guard, which organized and directed the 1994 genocide of hundreds of thousands of Tutsi and moderate Hutu.

Although contagion was a factor in this case, one must not lose sight of the fact that the spread of Burundi's violence to Rwanda was the result of decisions made by the Rwandan Presidential Guard.

"No-fault" history should not be embraced here. One should also consider the cases of Angola and Mozambique, two structurally similar conflicts where a violent development in one country ameliorated violence in the other. Jonas Savimbi's rejection of the peace process in Angola in October 1992 could have led to a rejection of political compromise in Mozambique, where warring parties had just concluded an agreement to end their civil war. Instead, the intensification of violence in Angola sobered the parties in Mozambique. The Mozambican government reversed its longstanding insistence on a limited role for the United Nations in implementing any agreement. Afonso Dhlakama, the leader of the Mozambican National Resistance, could see that Savimbi's return to war was leading to his defeat. Dhlakama concluded that peaceful compromise would ultimately be preferable to a return to war.

Responses to Africa's Internal Conflicts

Africa's conflicts have prompted six different sub-regional, continental, and international responses. These include military support or intervention to aid one side; peace enforcement, to impose a settlement on the warring parties; humanitarian intervention, to ameliorate the effects of war; mediation, to bring conflicts to a negotiated end; preventive diplomacy, to keep incipient conflicts from becoming violent; and regional institution-building, to manage conflicts.

MILITARY INTERVENTION OR ASSISTANCE TO ONE SIDE
During the Cold War, it was common for international powers to supply weapons, training, and assistance to clients and friends in Africa in the hope that they would prevail in civil conflicts. U.S. military assistance was provided to Liberia, Somalia, Sudan, and UNITA in Angola. Soviet and East European assistance was given to Ethiopia, the Mozambican government, and the Popular Movement for the Liberation of Angola (MPLA),

among others. On numerous occasions, Belgium and France sent troops to assist friendly regimes in their former colonies.[31]

There was a widespread hope that African and European countries would become responsible peacemakers in Africa in the post–Cold War era. This has not yet happened. South Africa, France, Egypt, and nine other countries supplied the Rwandan government with weapons for its civil war against the RPF.[32] It has been alleged that the Chinese, French, and South African governments continue to supply Rwandan soldiers in the refugee camps of Zaire.[33] China and Iran have sold weapons to the Sudanese government. Burkina Faso, Côte d'Ivoire, and Libya have provided military assistance to Charles Taylor's forces in Liberia. Portugal and Russia supplied military hardware to the Angolan government after civil war resumed in 1992. Uganda has hosted representatives of seven different rebel movements in Africa and has supplied arms and equipment to the RPF in Rwanda and the SPLA in Sudan.

PEACE ENFORCEMENT: THE ECOWAS INTERVENTION IN LIBERIA

Unlike traditional peacekeeping, peace enforcement operations lack the consent of the relevant warring parties. And unlike mediation, peace enforcement operations use military muscle on the ground in attempts to force parties to reach political settlements, including defeating recalcitrant armies deemed to be enemies of peace.

There were two attempts between 1990 and 1995 at peace enforcement in African civil wars: a sub-regional effort by West African countries operating under the aegis of the Economic Community of West African States (ECOWAS) to impose a peace settlement in Liberia, and the intervention by the United States and United Nations to establish peace in Somalia. Since the latter was driven to a very large degree by humanitarian concerns, the discussion in this section will focus on the former.

The intervention by West African states into Liberia's civil war illustrates the difficulties of peace enforcement in civil war and demonstrates the limitations of sub-regional organizations with respect to such operations. The West African intervention in the Liberian civil war took place

31. Alain Rouvez, "French, British, and Belgian Military Involvement," in David R. Smock, ed., *Making War and Waging Peace: Foreign Intervention in Africa* (Washington, D.C.: U.S. Institute of Peace, 1993), pp. 27–51.

32. Stephen D. Goose and Frank Smyth, "Arming Genocide in Rwanda," *Foreign Affairs*, Vol. 73, No. 5 (September/October 1994), p. 89.

33. Human Rights Watch Arms Project, "Rwanda/Zaire: Rearming With Impunity, International Support for the Perpetrators of the Rwandan Genocide," May 1995.

in August 1990, eight months after the war began. By that time, the forces of Charles Taylor's National People's Liberation Front (NPLF) controlled almost all of Liberia and were laying siege to Monrovia, the capital city and redoubt of President Samuel Doe. A small faction commanded by Prince Johnson had broken away from Taylor in July 1990, creating a three-sided war.

Nigeria, the largest and most powerful country in West Africa, argued that the ECOWAS charter provided a mandate and rationale for military intervention in the Liberian war. The purported reason for military intervention was that the civil war endangered the security of the entire community. The fighting was said to have reached a military stalemate; with little chance of one side winning, anarchy would continue indefinitely. The original mandate of the intervening force was peacekeeping or "cease-fire monitoring." Since there was no cease-fire to monitor, mediation efforts sought to bring about a cease-fire and set up elections to end the conflict. The proposal for the military force, the Economic Community of West African States Monitoring Group (ECOMOG), was contested by the Francophone members of the community, who saw it as a tool for furthering Nigerian interests in the region.

Almost every aspect of ECOWAS reasoning about the intervention was suspect. It was premature to conclude that the war had become a military stalemate; the fight for Monrovia had been going on for only a month. The Doe government had almost completely collapsed, Johnson's troops were far outnumbered by Taylor's forces, and most impartial observers believed that it was only a matter of time before Taylor triumphed. Although the first eight months of war had forced Liberian refugees into neighboring countries, the fighting had not spread outside the borders of Liberia. That a civil war was taking place in Liberia was not in and of itself a threat to peace and stability in the region; Taylor was in fact receiving assistance from two neighboring states. The architects of intervention assumed that ECOMOG would be seen as an impartial peacekeeping force; in fact, Taylor immediately recognized it as a belligerent intent on denying him victory. The architects of intervention believed that they could impose a peaceful settlement on the civil war; yet, time and time again, political differences within the coalition prevented them from developing and implementing a unified and coherent strategy for ending the war.[34]

---

34. See Binaifir Nowrojee, "Joining Forces: United Nations and Regional Peacekeeping, Lessons from Liberia," *Harvard Human Rights Journal*, Vol. 18 (Spring 1995), pp. 129–152; George Klay Kieh, Jr., "The Obstacles to the Peaceful Resolution of the Liberian Civil Conflict," *Studies in Conflict and Terrorism*, Vol. 17, No. 1 (January–March 1994), especially pp. 102–105.

Indeed, the ECOWAS intervention created the very situation it hoped to prevent.[35] As Taylor escalated his attacks against the ECOMOG forces, ECOMOG increased its initial deployment from 3,000–17,000 troops. The intervention transformed a war that probably would have ended in a quick victory for Taylor into a protracted struggle that continued until 1995, when a peace agreement established a tenuous cease-fire. In August 1990, when ECOMOG intervened, an estimated 4,000–5,000 people had died in the Liberian war; by October 1994, an estimated 150,000 people had been killed.[36] The continuation of the war led to a proliferation of combatant groups, as remnants of the Doe regime reorganized and Taylor's forces splintered into competing factions, thus complicating the task of reaching a negotiated settlement.[37]

By turning the war into a protracted one, the ECOWAS intervention succeeded in spreading the fighting to other countries in the region. In August 1990, the conflict had generated an estimated 250,000–375,000 refugees; by October 1994, the war had produced an estimated 1.25 million refugees. Denied resources in Liberia, Taylor's forces invaded Sierra Leone and instigated a civil war there in February 1991.[38] Taylor's forces have also plundered parts of Guinea. In addition to becoming an active belligerent in the war, the intervention force has engaged in war profiteering and racketeering.[39]

This is not to say that a Taylor victory in 1990 would have created a

---

35. William J. Foltz, "Regional and Sub-Regional Peacekeeping in Africa," paper presented to the African Studies Association Annual Meeting, Orlando, Florida, November 1995, pp. 24–26.

36. The 1990 estimates can be found in Mark Huband, "Doe's Last Stand," *Africa Report*, Vol. 35, No. 3 (July–August 1990), p. 49, and Rick Wells, "The Lost of Liberia," *Africa Report*, Vol. 35, No. 5 (November–December 1990), p. 21. The estimate of 150,000 deaths is a common one; see Howard W. French, "War Engulfs Liberia, Humbling the Peacekeepers," *New York Times*, October 7, 1994, p. A4.

37. See Stephen Ellis, "Liberia 1989–1994: A Study of Ethnic and Spiritual Violence," *African Affairs*, Vol. 94 (April 1995), pp. 165–197.

38. William Reno attributes Taylor's invasion to the need for resources. Stephen Ellis argues that Taylor invaded Sierra Leone to punish it for participating in the ECOMOG intervention. Both considerations can be traced to the ECOMOG intervention, and both probably influenced Taylor's decision. See William Reno, "Reinvention of an African State," *Third World Quarterly*, Vol. 16, No. 1 (January 1995), pp. 109–120; Ellis, "Liberia 1989–1994," p. 170.

39. Herbert M. Howe, "ECOMOG and Its Lessons For Regional Peacekeeping," paper presented to the African Studies Association Annual Meeting, Orlando, Florida, November 1995, p. 22.

democratic Liberia. Taylor's behavior has confirmed that he seeks to maximize his personal wealth and that he has little regard for human rights. His forces have been involved in numerous atrocities and massacres. However, it is hard to imagine that a Taylor-led Liberia would have killed 150,000 civilians and forced 750,000 people to leave the country. Even if one fears that Taylor is a genocidal maniac, the ECOMOG intervention makes little sense. The settlement negotiated in July 1995 promises to end the war through elections; if Taylor wins, then all the intervention will have accomplished is a delay in Taylor's coming to power. If Taylor loses the election, it is likely that he will start fighting again. The intervention will have failed to end the war.

The crucial question is whether the ECOMOG experience discredits the whole idea of sub-regional peace enforcement in Africa. Peace enforcement operations in civil wars, even under optimal conditions, face almost impossible odds.[40] Sub-regional organizations might have advantages in carrying them out if they possess unity of purpose and common interests; if they embody regional norms of responsible conduct and good government that can be demanded of the warring parties; and if they have the capability and credibility to use force to defeat recalcitrant parties.

All of these things were lacking in the ECOMOG intervention in Liberia. The member states of ECOWAS disagreed over what was at stake and what would be a desirable outcome in Liberia. Nigeria, the largest and most powerful regional actor, had suspect motivations from the beginning. The organization, whose member states were mostly dictatorships, had no credibility in pushing an election as a solution to the conflict. Nigeria, led by a regime that came to power through a military coup and in existence as a state because it triumphed in a civil war, had no credibility when it came to urging parties to resolve their conflict peacefully. Moreover, because the Nigerian military was not accountable at home, it was not accountable for how it behaved in Liberia. As one scholar observes, "there is something suspect, indeed 'grotesque,' in the expectation that soldiers who subvert the rule of law in their own countries will respect, let alone establish, a law-based political authority in a foreign land."[41]

---

40. Stephen John Stedman, "The New Interventionists," *Foreign Affairs*, Vol. 72, No. 1 (Winter 1993), pp. 1–16.

41. Clement E. Adibe, *Managing Arms in Peace Processes: Somalia* (New York: United Nations Institute for Disarmament Research, Disarmament and Conflict Resolution Project, 1995), p. 105.

HUMANITARIAN INTERVENTION: THE CASE OF SOMALIA

Humanitarian intervention involves the use of military force to protect and feed civilians who are at risk from hostilities. In theory, it is possible to distinguish humanitarian interventions from peace enforcement operations because the former are impartial and do not seek to bring an end to the wars that cause the humanitarian problems. In practice, however, these distinctions are difficult to maintain. The tensions between these two types of intervention can be seen in the case of Somalia, where policymakers in distant national capitals and international bodies disagreed from the beginning about goals, strategies, and tactics.

A combination of drought and a two-year civil war that had disintegrated into fighting between twelve armed factions created a massive famine that by March 1992 had killed 300,000 Somalis. In July 1992, the International Red Cross estimated that seventy percent of Somalis were suffering from severe malnutrition. In September 1992, it predicted that 1.5 million Somalis were "threatened by imminent starvation."[42] Distribution of food was hindered by gangs and militia who commandeered relief supplies and intimidated and attacked humanitarian aid workers.

The United Nations responded in traditional fashion by attempting to work through the warring parties to gain their acceptance of a cease-fire, consent for peacekeeping troops, and protection for humanitarian food deliveries. From the beginning, mediation efforts were met with hostility by General Mohammed Farah Aideed, one of the contending warlords, whose base of support was in southern Mogadishu. Aideed's hostility was intensified by several UN gaffes that robbed the organization of its impartiality and undercut the effectiveness of Mahmoud Sahnoun, the Secretary-General's Special Representative.[43]

During the summer of 1992, Sahnoun attempted to mediate among the warring factions and consult with clan elders in the hope of bringing domestic pressure to bear on the warlords. Although Sahnoun claimed to be making progress, the death toll from starvation mounted. UN officials in New York suspected that Sahnoun was misreading the situation; they consequently bypassed him and authorized deployment of a force of 3,000 soldiers to assist humanitarian relief efforts.[44] This undercut

---

42. Ibid., p. 17.

43. Jonathan Stevenson, "Hope Restored in Somalia?" *Foreign Policy*, No. 91 (Summer 1993), pp. 138–154; Robert G. Patman, "The UN Operation in Somalia," in Ramesh Thakur and Carlyle Thayer, eds., *UN Peacekeeping in the 1990s* (Boulder, Colo.: Westview, 1995), pp. 90–92.

44. Patman, "The UN Operation in Somalia," p. 92.

Sahnoun's credibility with Aideed, who had demanded the right to approve any troop deployments to Somalia.

Sahnoun resigned in October 1992 and was replaced by Ismat Kittani, who promptly concluded that Aideed would oppose any troops sent to assist food deliveries. As the death toll continued to mount and Aideed's opposition to a UN force remained, nongovernmental organizations in the United States began to press for a forceful intervention to protect relief operations. Caught between a desire to address a major humanitarian disaster that had widespread television coverage and military advisers who feared protracted involvement in a civil war, U.S. President George Bush put forward a compromise: the United States, under the mandate of the United Nations and in conjunction with other nations, would intervene in Somalia in order to break the famine.

It was understood by Bush administration officials that simply protecting relief deliveries would be an ineffective palliative. They recognized that the United Nations would have to take over Somalia after this first step was taken. An administration official at one point hinted that the United Nations would create some kind of trusteeship to provide the long-term order that would be needed to rebuild the Somali state.[45] Bush quickly backed away from this idea, preferring an alternative formulation: that the U.S.-led force (known as the United Task Force, or UNITAF) would hand over power to a United Nations "peacekeeping force."[46]

The problem with this formulation, however, was that a UN peacekeeping force could only operate with the consent of the local parties. In Somalia, the warring parties did not give their consent, and there was no peace agreement to be implemented. The UN Secretary-General, Boutros Boutros-Ghali, recognized that any UN peacekeeping force would probably be seen by Aideed as an enemy. Boutros-Ghali therefore insisted that UNITAF use its impressive military capabilities to relieve the warring factions of their heavy weapons before it withdrew from Somalia. The United States, worried about possible casualties and the need to keep its mission simple, declined, insisting that disarmament went beyond the parameters of a humanitarian intervention.

From the beginning, however, UNITAF acted in more than a purely

---

45. Stephen John Stedman, "UN Intervention in Civil Wars: Imperatives of Choice and Strategy," in Donald C.F. Daniel and Bradd C. Hayes, eds., *Beyond Traditional Peacekeeping* (New York: St. Martin's, 1995), pp. 48–49.

46. John R. Bolton, "Wrong Turn in Somalia," *Foreign Affairs*, Vol. 74, No. 1 (January/February 1994), p. 60.

humanitarian capacity.[47] The head of the United States Liaison Office, Robert Oakley, attempted to mediate a political settlement early on in the conflict. In doing so, he publicly embraced two of the main warlords, Aideed and Ali Mahdi Mohamed, thus raising their standing in the eyes of some Somalis, but undercutting the legitimacy of the intervention in the eyes of Somalis who hoped that the warlords would be weakened by the international military action. Oakley's acceptance of Aideed reinforced the latter's intransigence toward the United Nations.

Violence in Somalia never was fully contained by UNITAF, nor was there any genuine commitment to negotiations among the warring parties during UNITAF's stay. Aideed knew that the U.S. presence would be short-lived and that he could outwait it. As the handover between UNITAF and the UN force, UNOSOM II, grew near, there were more and more signs that Aideed planned to test the new United Nations command.[48]

On June 5, 1993, the confrontation between Aideed and the United Nations came. His forces ambushed and killed twenty-four Pakistani peacekeepers during a pre-arranged inspection of a weapons facility. The United Nations, with U.S. support, decided to hold Aideed responsible. Between May and October of 1993, several pitched battles were fought between UN troops and Aideed's forces. By September, U.S. congressional opinion had turned against the Somalia intervention, and President Bill Clinton was questioned about U.S. involvement there. When Aideed's forces killed eighteen U.S. soldiers in a firefight in Mogadishu in October, Clinton announced that U.S. troops would leave Somalia in March 1994. Shortly afterwards, the United States reversed course and welcomed Aideed back into the negotiation process, going so far as to transport him to negotiations in Addis Ababa.

The United Nations stayed in Somalia for a year after the U.S. withdrawal. Stymied by the unwillingness of the Somalia warlords to make peace, it finally withdrew in March 1995.

The Somalia intervention raises important questions about the ability of humanitarian interventions to cope with Africa's problems. Some U.S. citizens who were involved with UNITAF, or who supported the decision to deploy it, claim that the intervention was purely humanitarian; that it created a secure environment for the delivery of food and prevented the starvation of 250,000 Somalis. They insist that the U.S.-led part of the intervention was a success, and that the intervention subsequently failed

---

47. Patman, "The UN Operation in Somalia," p. 94.

48. Walter S. Clarke, "Testing the World's Resolve in Somalia," *Parameters*, Vol. 23, No. 4 (Winter 1993–94), pp. 51–52.

because of the incompetence of the United Nations and the ambitions of Boutros-Ghali and the Clinton administration, who insisted that the United Nations must rebuild the Somali state.[49] Critics of the intervention insist that implicit in the decision to help feed starving Somalis was the imperative to rebuild Somalia, and that actions taken by UNITAF set up the United Nations for failure in the second phase of the intervention.[50] Indeed, the cheerleaders for the "purely humanitarian" intervention have vastly inflated the estimates of lives saved to congratulate a job half-done. The only existing scientific estimate of lives saved by the UNITAF intervention gives a range between 10,000 and 25,000, not the 250,000 or 500,000 asserted by the supporters of UNITAF.[51]

To evaluate the Somali intervention, two questions need to be considered. First, in the absence of a functioning state, how likely is it that Somalia will avoid war-related famine in the future? The answer is that the humanitarian intervention saved lives in the short term but did not solve the country's deeper problems. The intervention was more palliative than cure.

Second, did the intervention in Somalia interfere with actions that could have saved more lives elsewhere? There is a good case to be made that the intervention in Somalia had substantial opportunity costs. It contributed to the subsequent chaos in Rwanda in at least three ways. First, the Somalia operation was extremely expensive by UN standards and led to pressure to keep costs down in other UN peace operations. This indirectly contributed to the delay in approving, funding, equipping, and deploying troops for the UN mission in Rwanda — a mission that, because it had the consent of the warring parties and a framework provided by a negotiated peace agreement, had a much greater potential for success than Somalia. Second, the failures of the peace enforcement

---

49. Typical of this view are Bolton, "Wrong Turn in Somalia"; Chester Crocker, "The Lessons of Somalia," *Foreign Affairs*, Vol. 75, No. 3 (May/June 1995); and Robert Oakley and John Hirsch, *Somalia and Operation Restore Hope: Reflections on Peacemaking and Peacekeeping* (Washington, D.C.: U.S. Institute of Peace, 1994).

50. Clarke, "Testing the World's Resolve"; Ken Menkhaus, "Getting Out vs. Getting Through in Somalia," *Middle East Policy*, Vol. 3, No. 1 (1994), pp. 146–161.

51. For the estimate of 10,000–25,000, see Steven Hansch et al., *Excess Mortality and the Impact of Health Interventions in the Somalia Humanitarian Emergency* (Washington, D.C.: Refugee Policy Group and Centers for Disease Control and Prevention, August 12, 1994). For the figure of 250,000, see Crocker, "The Lessons of Somalia," p. 3. The figure of 500,000, asserted nowhere else and by no one else, is in Michael Mandelbaum, "Foreign Policy as Social Work," *Foreign Affairs*, Vol. 75, No. 1 (January/February 1996), p. 30.

operation in Somalia deterred most nations from attempting to stop the genocide in Rwanda.

More generally, the naive lesson that some U.S. citizens drew from Somalia — that one can draw a clear line between humanitarian motivation and political effect — led the United States to send its military to save Rwandan refugees, many of whom were responsible for the genocide and intent on continuing to fight the war from Zaire. The perversity of the humanitarian intervention in Rwanda is that nearly $1 billion were spent on relief that helped resurrect the capabilities of the Hutu aggressors, while only $69 million have gone to the new government of Rwanda for reconstruction and development.[52]

MEDIATION

Western states, with the participation of African regional organizations, have mediated the end of civil wars in Zimbabwe in 1979, Namibia in 1988, and Mozambique in 1992. Mediation also led to negotiated settlements in Angola in 1992, Liberia in 1993, and Rwanda in 1993, but all of these failed to be implemented.

Successful mediation and implementation has depended on the participation of non-African states and international organizations (the Commonwealth in Zimbabwe; the United Nations in Mozambique and Namibia). Western states possess resources to reward and punish parties that African states and regional organizations lack. The United Nations was instrumental in Namibia and Mozambique because it had the capability to carry out free and fair elections and to supervise the demobilization of troops and the cease-fires between the parties. It also was viewed as impartial by the warring parties.

As discussed in my chapter on negotiation and mediation in this volume, civil wars are rarely settled by negotiation. When they are, it is usually because the war in question has raged for several years and because the parties conclude that they cannot win a military victory. Often all of the regional parties to a conflict must similarly reassess the costs and benefits of the war.

A sense of hurting and urgency — that things can get worse if negotiations fail — plays a key role in driving antagonists in civil wars to settle. Actions taken to lower the level of violence in a war might actually dampen incentives for a settlement. This can put mediation at odds with humanitarian assistance. If food for civilians ends up feeding

---

52. Of the $69 million, $29 million was for repayment of debt incurred by the previous regime; see Barbara Crossette, "Send the Peacekeepers Home, A Ravaged Rwanda Tells U.N.," *New York Times*, June 8, 1995, p. A9.

armies, it may prolong conflict. Cease-fires may help civilians, but if they are used by armies to regroup, they may also prolong conflict. Both of these problems developed in Sudan, where humanitarian assistance was not connected in any way with a strategy for ending the civil war.[53]

PREVENTIVE DIPLOMACY
Preventive diplomacy attempts to resolve conflicts before they become violent. Preventive diplomacy depends on early warning, effective responses, and mobilization. Preventive action can be cheap and risk-free, if the conflicting parties are willing to listen to reasoned appeals for peaceful accommodation. If the parties in question are not willing to be persuaded, however, then preventive measures will have to be more forceful; external military intervention, in particular, can involve significant risks and costs.[54] Since preventive diplomacy depends on precise forecasts and crisp responses, it is a difficult task for regional organizations or coalitions to carry out. Many countries must agree on an assessment of the problem and on an appropriate course of action.

Africa's experiences with preventive diplomacy between 1991 and 1995 support these general points. In Southern Africa, concerted action by South Africa and Zimbabwe, acting in the name of the Southern African Development Community (SADC), defused an incipient civil war in Lesotho in September 1994 by quickly reversing a military coup.[55] Similarly, quick action by South Africa and Zimbabwe, in conjunction with the United Nations and Western diplomats, allayed a post-election crisis in Mozambique in October 1994, when rebel leader Afonso Dhlakama questioned the results and threatened to return to war. Both of these preventive actions succeeded because the conflicting parties were militarily weak, and because the states and organizations carrying out the prevention were militarily strong; the latter could consequently make credible threats. The multilateral coordination necessary for effective action was facilitated by the existence of regional norms of good governance. It was therefore easier for member states to identify potential crises, and forge a unified response.

Elsewhere in Africa, prevention has had mixed results. An OAU team sent to the Congo in 1993 is credited with creating a dialogue among

---

53. Francis Deng and Larry Minear, *The Challenges of Famine Relief: Emergency Operations in the Sudan* (Washington, D.C.: Brookings Institution, 1992).

54. Stephen John Stedman, "Alchemy For A New World Order," *Foreign Affairs*, Vol. 75, No. 3 (May/June 1995), pp. 14–20.

55. "The Lesotho Coup: A Lesson in Law," *Track Two*, Vol. 3, No. 4 (December 1994), pp. 16–21.

political opponents and defusing a volatile situation.[56] In Burundi, the international community has attempted, through the United Nations, Western diplomats, and the OAU, to prevent the simmering ethnic conflict between Hutu and Tutsi from boiling over into genocidal warfare. It is difficult to judge the effects of preventive regional and international actions in Burundi: ethnic violence and political instability have continued, but there has been no civil war or large-scale genocide.

The Burundi case suggests that effective responses are difficult to launch. Some believe that appropriate preventive actions should involve holding individual soldiers and militia leaders accountable for past atrocities. Others believe that tough actions may trigger escalation.[57] Some in the United Nations believe that the constant use of the word genocide in Burundi is doing more harm than good by raising people's fears to pathological levels.[58]

In the three most important candidates for state collapse in Africa — Kenya, Nigeria, and Zaire — preventive diplomacy has met with little success. Most analysts agree that the domestic politics of each of these countries could lead to dramatic civil violence with devastating implications for regional security.[59] The problem, however, is that there is no consensus on what outside powers should do to stave off such disasters. These three countries dominate their sub-regions and are led by power-hungry dictators who care little about the suffering of their people. All of these countries have friends among Western states, who benefit from trade with these regimes. Events in Somalia have perversely reinforced a sense of caution towards political change among policymakers in Wash-

---

56. I. William Zartman, "Guidelines for Preserving Peace in Africa," in David R. Smock and Chester A. Crocker, eds., *African Conflict Resolution: The U.S. Role in Peacemaking* (Washington, D.C.: U.S. Institute of Peace, 1995), p. 98.

57. For an argument for the need for past accountability, see Amnesty International, *Burundi: Time for International Action to End a Cycle of Mass Murder* (London: Amnesty International, May 1994), p. 10. For a more cautious evaluation that refers to issues of human rights in Burundi as "a political minefield," see Zdenek Cervenka and Colin Legum, *Can National Dialogue Break The Power of Terror in Burundi?* Current African Issues No. 17 (Uppsala, Sweden: Nordiska Afrikainstitutet, October 1994), p. 21.

58. The most prominent spokesperson for this view was Ahmedou Ould Abdallah, UN Special Representative in Burundi from 1993–95. See his op-ed, "Les Prophètes de Malheur," *Le Monde*, April 6, 1995, and his comments quoted in "Le Représentant de l'ONU au Burundi Accuse La Communauté Internationale," *Le Monde*, April 7, 1995.

59. For example, see Peter M. Lewis, "Nigeria: Domestic Crisis Challenges International Response," *SAIS Review*, Vol. 15, No. 2 (Summer–Fall 1995), pp. 17–38; J. Stephen Morrison, "Zaire: Looming Disaster After Preventive Diplomacy," *SAIS Review*, Vol. 15, No. 2 (Summer–Fall 1995), pp. 39–52; Gilbert M. Khadiagala, "Kenya: Intractable Authoritarianism," *SAIS Review*, Vol. 15, No. 2 (Summer–Fall 1995), pp. 53–73.

ington, London, and Paris; they seem to prefer the instability and slow collapse that they know to the effects of reform and leadership change that they do not know.

REGIONAL ORGANIZATIONS AND INSTITUTION-BUILDING

Several initiatives have been launched to build up the capabilities of African regional organizations to manage conflict. At the continental level, Africans have taken the first steps towards defining the norms of good governance and human rights to which African regimes are expected to adhere. The OAU has attempted to build on those norms what it calls a "mechanism for prevention, management, and resolution of conflict."[60] Other attempts to strengthen collective responses to conflicts are taking place at the sub-regional level, where efforts are under way to replicate the successes that Southern Africa has had in conflict management.

CONTINENT-WIDE INITIATIVES. Current efforts to create African norms and capabilities to manage conflict have their origin in the Kampala Document — a nongovernmental process of institution-building developed along the lines of the Conference on Security and Cooperation in Europe (CSCE, now OSCE, the Organization for Security and Cooperation in Europe).[61] In 1991, a group of prominent Africans, including various former heads of state, met in Kampala, Uganda, to discuss and endorse a "Conference on Security, Stability, Development, and Cooperation in Africa." The Kampala Document advocated regional cooperation and dialogue on security, human rights, and development issues. More importantly, the Kampala Document castigated African regimes for poor governance and identified the need for a set of norms to which African states should aspire: accountability, protection of human rights, transparency, and a commitment to development. The Kampala Document signaled the desire of key segments of African political affairs to tear away the veneer of sovereignty and self-determination under which Africa's leadership had hid.

In 1993, the OAU began to create the organizational basis for implementing the Kampala Document by calling into question its bedrock principles of sovereignty and non-interference in internal state affairs. At the same time, the OAU established a plan to create a system for provid-

---

60. *The OAU and Conflict Management in Africa: Chairman's Report of Joint OAU/IPA Consultation,* Addis Ababa, May 19–21, 1993.

61. African Leadership Forum, *The Kampala Document: Towards a Conference on Security, Stability, Development and Cooperation in Africa,* Kampala, Uganda, May 19–22, 1991.

ing early warning of impending internal conflicts and a capability for mediation and peacekeeping. The OAU proposed to create a separate department, staffed with experts on conflict resolution, that would report directly to the Secretary-General. In addition, special earmarked contingents of national armies would be made available for preventive deployments and peacekeeping.

The OAU's plan for developing a capability to prevent and manage conflicts is an attempt to adapt to the fact that Africa's conflicts are almost completely internal in nature and that they stem in many instances from bad governance. It is unlikely, however, that the plan will have much effect. Although it correctly recognizes that some kind of external interference in internal affairs will be necessary to prevent and resolve Africa's conflicts, the OAU is unlikely to have the resources or the will to overcome the resistance of powerful states such as Kenya, Nigeria, and Sudan, which brook no interference in their affairs. The OAU itself suffers from chronic financial problems; its members are currently $65 million in arrears. African acceptance of the norms on which the plan is predicated are weak. Indicative of this is that in May 1995, General Olusegun Obesanjo, a principal author of the Kampala Document, was arrested by the Nigerian military government for speaking out in favor of democracy.

SUB-REGIONAL ORGANIZATIONS. The success of SADC in managing conflicts in Lesotho and Mozambique in 1994, as well as its success in working toward another negotiated settlement to the Angolan civil war, has increased interest in sub-regional efforts to cope with Africa's internal conflicts. Both African and U.S. policymakers have favored strengthening the Inter-Governmental Authority on Drought and Development (IGADD) as a means of managing conflict in the Horn of Africa. There is also some support for providing higher levels of assistance to ECOWAS in West Africa.

Southern Africa has indeed produced remarkable results in the area of conflict management. In addition to its successes in conflict prevention and resolution, its members have begun to address the effects of civil war in the region by working together to stop the cross-border trade in light weapons. Southern Africa has gone further than any other region on the continent in establishing norms of democratic governance and developing common perceptions about threats to regional security.[62]

Southern Africa's successes, however, may not be transferable to other parts of Africa. Regional cooperation in Southern Africa is facilitated by

---

62. For a detailed discussion of the strengths and weaknesses of security cooperation in Southern Africa, see Ohlson and Stedman, *The New Is Not Yet Born*, chaps. 8 and 9.

the fact that the basic building blocks of the region — the individual states — are stronger than elsewhere in Africa. Equally important, all are currently committed to democratic governance. In West Africa and the Horn of Africa, states are weak and governance in the most important countries is atrocious. ECOWAS cannot become an effective mechanism for conflict management as long as Nigeria is governed by its military. IGADD cannot become an effective force for managing conflict until its members — Djibouti, Ethiopia, Kenya, Somalia, Sudan, and Uganda — become effective, responsive, internally responsible states.

Conclusions

Policymakers and analysts have put forward several recommendations for addressing Africa's internal wars and its proneness to violence. These include strengthening the ability of the OAU to conduct peace enforcement operations; building up sub-regional capabilities to manage conflict; and strengthening the ability of the international community to carry out peace enforcement operations and humanitarian interventions. These solutions have several common elements: they are high-profile, expensive, based on widespread desires for quick fixes for long-term problems, and completely at odds with African realities.

For example, some have urged the OAU to develop a peace enforcement capability.[63] This ignores the fact that ambitious interventions, such as the ECOWAS intervention in Liberia, are extremely costly, risky, and likely to complicate the prospects for conflict resolution. The OAU should not seek such a peace enforcement capability: it could increase the likelihood that Africans would find themselves in protracted civil wars.

Those who favor strengthening African sub-regional organizations seem to believe that Africa can overcome the coordination problems that continue to stymie more developed parts of the world.[64] Sub-regional and regional organizations are only as strong and virtuous as their member states. When regional organizations consist of weak states that are both dictatorial in nature and incapable of creating order within their own borders, then the prospects for regional conflict management efforts are exceedingly poor.

Finally, those who favor strengthening international capabilities for carrying out peace enforcement operations and humanitarian interven-

---

63. Herman Cohen, "African Capabilities for Managing Conflict: The Role of the United States," in Smock and Crocker, *African Conflict Resolution*, pp. 77–94.

64. Ibid.

tions must consider three facts. First, the international community has devoted and will continue to devote limited resources to Africa. Aid to Africa declined gradually in the first half of the 1990s. The proportion of gross domestic product allotted to developmental aid by donor countries has also declined, and the global competition for donor assistance has intensified because of the collapse of the Soviet Union.[65] Second, there is an intense competition for resources in Africa between countries and between types of assistance. Starting with the latter, funding for humanitarian assistance and for peacekeeping and peace enforcement has outpaced funding for sustainable development.[66] This, in turn, has affected the competition for resources between countries in Africa: those that are the most conflict-ridden receive more assistance than those that have implemented economic and political reforms and have achieved some measure of stability. Third, there is little that humanitarian interventions or peace enforcement operations can do in civil wars: the track records in Liberia and Somalia does not provide much basis for optimism.

Prescriptions for Africa's internal conflicts must be grounded in reality. There are profound limits to what international assistance can accomplish in civil wars. Africa's problems are long-term and their resolution will ultimately depend on economic development and the creation of regimes that are responsive to people and that have the capabilities to carry out the tasks that modern states are expected to perform.

Peace enforcement and humanitarian intervention, by drawing resources from African countries that have the potential to be self-sustaining, risk condemning all of Africa to collapse. If the international community is unwilling to increase development assistance to Africa, it should institute a policy of triage. Resources should go to countries that have a chance of becoming economically productive and politically stable. Assis-

---

65. "African Development Aid Faces Downturn," *Africa Recovery*, Vol. 8, No. 3 (December 1994), p. 12.

66. The United Nations Development Program reported that forty-five percent of UN assistance in 1992 was devoted to humanitarian emergencies, up from twenty-five percent in 1988. See "Emergencies Consuming Nearly Half of UN Assistance," *Africa Recovery*, Vol. 8, Nos. 1–2 (April–September 1994), p. 1. During the summer of 1994, Brian Atwood, administrator for the U.S. Agency for International Development (AID), reported that the United States was spending twice as much on disaster relief and peacekeeping as on long-term development assistance; see "Transcript of Remarks by AID Administrator Brian Atwood, June 26 at White House Conference on Africa." Finally, in May 1995, the World Food Program of the United Nations reported that due to humanitarian crises, it could only target twenty percent of its 1995 budget to long-term food production. The comparable figure for 1989 was sixty-six percent. See "Food Alarm As Disasters Swamp UN Aid Agency," *Guardian*, May 3, 1995, p. 7.

tance must aim to raise educational levels, develop economic and political infrastructures, and strengthen civil societies.

This does not mean that the plight of countries mired in civil wars should be ignored. Rather, emphasis should be placed on mediation, which involves modest costs and few risks; peacekeeping when agreements are reached; and reconstruction to help countries recover from the ravages of war. Adopting these priorities will allow suffering to continue while civil wars drag on, but it will ensure that international resources will be available to reinforce peace and security when wars end.

The future of Africa lies in the classrooms and playing fields of Lilongwe, Lusaka, Soweto, and countless other cities and villages, not in the peacekeeping fields of Liberia, the refugee camps of Zaire, and most certainly not in the halls of the OAU in Addis Ababa.

Chapter 8

Peacemaking and Violence in Latin America

Marc W. Chernick

The negotiated settlements in the early 1990s to armed insurgencies in El Salvador and Nicaragua were initial signs of a new conception of international intervention in Latin America. After thwarting earlier peace initiatives, the United States changed course at the end of the Cold War and supported internationally supervised negotiations to the Central American conflicts, then about to enter their second decade. The ensuing peace processes opened the door to constructive international involvement in the domestic politics of the war-divided region.

In Haiti, the international community restored democratic rule after a coup d'etat overthrew that Caribbean nation's elected president. For three years, economic sanctions were coordinated with diplomatic initiatives by the Organization of American States (OAS) and the United Nations (UN). The sanctions alone failed to dislodge the Haitian generals, however. The constitutional president, Jean-Bertrand Aristide, was restored to power in 1994 only after Washington made it clear that a U.S.-led military intervention was imminent. Even in a new era of multilateral diplomacy, the United States did not forswear military intervention in the hemisphere. Nonetheless, the rationale and intent of the intervention were remarkably different from those of earlier U.S. actions in the hemisphere. Using its troops as an advance guard for UN and OAS personnel, the United States deposed an unconstitutional military regime and restored a democratically elected government.

Multilateral actions have been very effective in resolving conflicts that had been internationalized by the Cold War, as in Central America, and in restoring democracy in Haiti. However, they have been considerably less effective in dealing with other problems — some old, some new.

The author would like to thank the Harry Frank Guggenheim Foundation for funding an individual research grant used in conducting the field research for this chapter.

Guerrilla wars have persisted in Colombia, Guatemala, and Peru. Peace efforts have been launched, but have been unsuccessful because these conflicts were not driven by the rivalries of the Cold War.

The new sources of violence in the region are ethnic mobilization, organized crime, and drug trafficking. In Colombia, Ecuador, Guatemala, Mexico, and Peru, guerrillas have taken up arms to demand more rights for indigenous populations long excluded from national politics. Ethnic movements in Latin America have, by and large, not adopted the secessionist platforms favored by many groups in the Balkans and the former Soviet Union. Ethnic movements in Latin America have operated *within* broader societal struggles for greater political participation. As a result, their campaigns have consistently found support in other sectors of their societies.

In Colombia and Peru, some insurgent groups have transformed themselves into major crime syndicates while maintaining radical political agendas. Other groups have simpler criminal and commercial agendas. Drug trafficking has spawned new and intense forms of violence, not just in Colombia and Peru, but throughout the Andes, in Mexico, and in other parts of Central and South America. Drug-related violence, which grew with the export boom in cocaine and heroin, is one of the most destabilizing forces in Latin America politics in the 1990s. Neither the United States nor the international community has developed adequate responses to these challenges.

This chapter begins with a brief review of the types of conflict and the evolution of outside intervention in the region from the enunciation of the Monroe Doctrine in the early nineteenth century to the onset of the Cold War in the middle of the twentieth century. The second section examines the Cold War era, focusing on the sources of internal conflict, the nature of outside intervention, and the unsuccessful regional efforts to end the conflicts in Central America in the 1980s.

The third section analyzes the successful peacemaking efforts that unfolded in the immediate aftermath of the Cold War. As national conflicts were disentangled from superpower proxy wars, peace became possible. Regional and international mediation played a decisive role in bringing these conflicts to an end. The democratic transitions in the region were also key: the starting point for negotiations in El Salvador and Nicaragua were agreements by all parties that power could be transferred only through elections and open, democratic competition.

The fourth section of this chapter will examine new sources of violence in the region together with new forms of outside intervention. A review of the region reveals that many countries are besieged by insurgencies and organized crime. Some of these conflicts might be settled through the type of multifunctional peace operations mounted in Central America in the early 1990s. The international community is already involved in the peace process in Guatemala, which is attempting to resolve the last of the Central American revolutionary conflicts.

Significantly, most of these small wars have not threatened to spill over into neighboring territories or draw in regional powers. The issue that has led to outside military involvement is the drug trade. Since 1989, the principal mission of the U.S. military in the hemisphere has been combating drug trafficking. The United States has negotiated new security agreements with drug-producing and transshipment nations. This military approach has failed. Moreover, it has sowed discord among U.S. allies in the region.

The chapter concludes by contrasting the successful multifunctional peace operations that were implemented in the Western hemisphere following the end of the Cold War with the failed policies that have been pursued to combat drug trafficking and other sources of internal violence in Latin America. The former represented a new form of involvement in the region's politics by the international community; the latter represented a return to the bilateral diplomacy and military approaches of the past. Against global trafficking operations, fully inserted into the flows of world trade and commerce, uncoordinated military activities in separate nations have been ineffective and destabilizing. Drug trafficking is the quintessential multilateral issue, affecting the economic and political integrity of dozens of nations. This chapter thus concludes with a series of recommendations for a new multilateral approach to the problem of drug trafficking and violence in post–Cold War Latin America.

From the Monroe Doctrine to the Cold War

Although Latin America contains many territorial disputes and national rivalries, it has experienced little inter-state war. The inter-American system — the network of mutual defense treaties and institutions that developed over the course of the twentieth century — was able to prevent or quickly settle most inter-state wars. The presence of a dominant regional power, the United States, also served to contain border conflicts and wars.

This is not to say that Latin America has been peaceful. If inter-state war was episodic and exceptional, internal violence was not. From the Mexican revolution (1910–17) to the Colombian *violencia* in the 1940s and 1950s, from the guerrilla insurgencies in Central America and the Andes in the 1980s to the Zapatista uprising in Mexico in the mid-1990s, Latin

America witnessed countless rebellions, insurgencies, coups d'état, and civil wars.

Some of these conflicts involved massive bloodletting, such as the Mexican revolution. Others involved only minor bloodshed or passed with little international commentary. With few exceptions, these conflicts did not involve neighboring states. The inter-American system success-fully prevented or limited intervention by neighboring powers. The one state unconstrained by these restrictions was the United States, which, as the hegemonic power in the region, became involved in both well-known and obscure conflicts.

In 1823, the United States unveiled the Monroe Doctrine, which authorized unilateral intervention in the hemisphere to prevent European powers from exploiting the vacuum left by Spain as it lost its colonies. In 1903, the Roosevelt Corollary to the Monroe Doctrine provided a new rationale for intervention: U.S. military force could be used to restore political stability when disturbances broke out in any Latin American or Caribbean nation.

The Roosevelt Corollary ushered in the age of "gunboat diplomacy." The United States subsequently put down insurrections in Cuba in 1906, 1912, 1917, and 1933. In 1912, U.S. marines landed in Nicaragua; they stayed until 1933. In 1914, U.S. marines occupied Veracruz, Mexico, for seven months in a disastrous attempt to influence the outcome of the Mexican Revolution. In 1915, U.S. troops began a nineteen-year occupa-tion of Haiti. A year later, U.S. forces landed in the Dominican Republic; they were not withdrawn until 1924.[1]

U.S. interventions in the Caribbean and Central America are occasion-ally depicted as minor actions aimed at seizing customs houses and protecting private property rights. This is inaccurate or, at best, incom-plete. Even in the early part of the twentieth century, the United States intervened elsewhere in the hemisphere principally for strategic reasons: the United States wanted unrestricted commerce through secure sea lanes bordered by nations with pro-U.S. governments.[2]

The onset of the Cold War in Latin America in the 1950s brought what was essentially a nineteenth-century policy of unilateral intervention into the twentieth century. The United States reaffirmed the basic principles of the Monroe Doctrine, prohibiting outside intervention in the Western hemisphere. The Soviet Union replaced Europe as the hostile, extra-hemi-spheric power in U.S. thinking.

---

1. Walter Lafeber, *Inevitable Revolutions: The United States in Central America* (New York: Norton, 1993), chap. 1.

2. Ibid.

Central America.

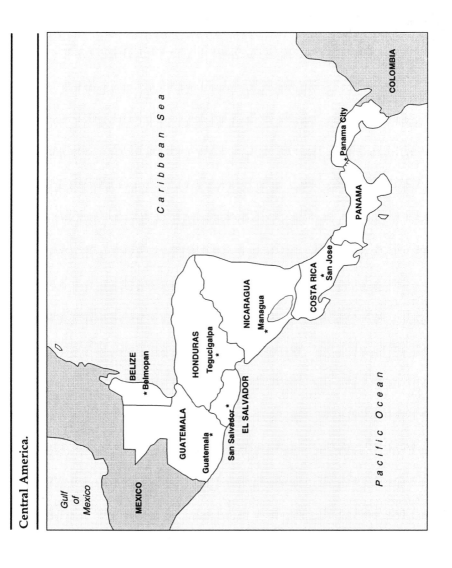

The Cuban Revolution of 1959 moved the issue of hemispheric security to the center of the U.S. foreign policy debate. Further, it provided the rationale for a massive reformulation of U.S. policy in the hemisphere. When Fidel Castro aligned Cuba with the Soviet Union, the United States developed a far-reaching strategy of regional security based on two conceptual and programmatic pillars: counterinsurgency and development assistance. These initiatives were to shape the politics of the region for the next thirty years.

The Cold War in Latin America

The Cold War in Latin America can best be understood by focusing on three dimensions of regional politics: internal conflicts; outside intervention by the U.S. and other actors; and the frustrated efforts at regional peacemaking in Central America during the final incendiary years of the Cold War. This section will carefully examine each of these areas. The analysis of peacemaking will look at the early, mostly failed, efforts of regional actors to promote a comprehensive settlement to the Central American wars through two peace initiatives, the Contadora and Arias Peace Plans, in the period before the fall of the Berlin Wall. These two peace plans, particularly the one headed by Costa Rican president Oscar Arias, were later to provide blueprints for peace in the post–Cold War world. What changed was the international context, particularly the position of the United States.

INTERNAL CONFLICTS DURING THE COLD WAR

The Cold War did not bring peace to Latin America. On the contrary, in almost every country in the region, guerrilla insurgencies influenced by Marxist thought emerged to challenge existing governments. The region's rugged mountains, sparsely inhabited rainforests and plains, and urban shantytowns were well-suited for irregular warfare. In two countries, Cuba and Nicaragua, guerrilla movements were able to organize a broad alliance of political groups and social classes, overthrow dictators, and take power. In a third, Chile, a coalition of leftist and Marxist parties took office by electoral means, only to be overthrown in a coup d'état with U.S. assistance three years later.

Ideas and ideology played a major role in fomenting armed struggle throughout the region. Marxism, Leninism, and Maoism had made deep inroads in the region by the middle of the twentieth century. Following the Cuban Revolution, Havana became a mecca for Latin American students and revolutionaries eager to replicate the experience of the Cuban

South America.

revolution in their homelands. Cuba provided training and assistance to many of these revolutionary groups.

In deeply Catholic Latin America, another new form of revolutionary thought emerged in the 1960s: liberation theology, based on a fusion of Marxist class analysis and the Second Vatican Council's "preferential option for the poor." The Second Vatican Council met from 1963 to 1965; its work was endorsed at the Latin American Bishops meeting in 1967 in Medellin, Colombia. In Latin America, the new church emphasis on the poor meant an historic re-orientation of the Catholic Church in the region away from its traditional alliance with the region's oligarchies. The church began to cast itself as a defender of the poor. Many priests and layworkers took the new theology as a license to become involved with community and political struggles. For some, liberation theology supported an involvement with revolutionary Marxist groups who also worked in the name of the poor and dispossessed. It was a potent mix. In Central America and Colombia, liberation theology was to profoundly influence established guerrilla groups, most notably the Sandinista National Liberation Front (FSLN) in Nicaragua and the National Liberation Army (ELN) in Colombia.[3] The latter, which still operates, has been led by Spanish priests since the 1980s.

Ideological and revolutionary religious politics found fertile ground in a continent undergoing massive social change. From the 1940s onward, Latin America urbanized at a rate not seen elsewhere in the developing or industrialized world. By the 1980s, the continent was principally urban, with swollen metropolitan areas forced to accommodate unceasing migrations from the countryside.[4] With only a few notable exceptions, shrinking rural populations were caught in semi-feudal arrangements. Most countries failed to implement serious agrarian reform.[5]

At the same time, decades of international development assistance had greatly expanded educational programs without providing sufficient employment opportunities for those who had advanced through the system. Universities became centers of revolutionary recruitment and

3. Donald C. Hodges, *Intellectual Foundations of the Nicaraguan Revolution* (Austin: University of Texas Press, 1986), pp. 268–288; Daniel H. Levine, *Popular Voices in Latin American Catholicism* (Princeton, N.J.: Princeton University Press, 1992).

4. Alejandro Portes and John Walton, *Urban Latin America: The Political Condition from Above and Below* (Austin: University of Texas Press, 1976).

5. Alain DeJanvry, *The Agrarian Question and Reformism in Latin America* (Baltimore, Md.: Johns Hopkins University Press, 1981).

training.[6] Latin America in the second half of the twentieth century witnessed decades of rural and urban protest as well as revolutionary insurgency.

In the 1960s, guerrilla insurgencies were mostly rural phenomena. By the 1970s, large urban guerrilla movements appeared, particularly in Argentina and Uruguay. Since then, notably in Colombia, El Salvador, and Peru, guerrilla insurgencies have established social bases in both the countryside and the shantytowns of the region's massive cities.

Some of these insurgencies were driven by the closed nature of national political systems and made possible by the existence of weak states. Colombia and Guatemala are the primary examples. Colombia developed an elite-dominated, two-party system that systematically excluded third parties. Guatemala was ruled by a succession of military rulers who excluded and repressed the large indigenous population. In both countries, the state had limited reach over much of its national territory. In both countries, insurrectionist movements were able to mobilize and organize disenfranchised populations in rebellions against state governments.

Although most of these insurgencies had domestic roots, combatants inevitably became caught up in Cold War politics. Indeed, the opening salvo of the Cold War in Latin America came in Guatemala in 1954, when the U.S. Central Intelligence Agency (CIA) overthrew a reformist government in the name of halting communism.[7] After the Cold War's end, guerrilla wars in El Salvador and Nicaragua were settled. In Colombia and Guatemala, however, they were not: in these countries, in particular, the domestic roots of conflict were deep.

INTERNATIONAL INTERVENTION DURING THE COLD WAR

The United States countered the revolutionary politics of the Latin American left, particularly after the Cuban Revolution in 1959, by providing extensive counterinsurgency assistance to governments in the region. On a few occasions, the United States deployed troops or created proxy armies.

U.S. policy was designed to prevent the rise of communism and the spread of Soviet influence in the hemisphere — to prevent "another

6. Timothy P. Wickham-Crowley, *Guerrillas and Revolution in Latin America: A Comparative Study of Insurgents and Regimes since 1956* (Princeton, N.J.: Princeton University Press, 1992), pp. 19–48.

7. Piero Gleijeses, *Shattered Hope: The Guatemalan Revolution and the United States, 1944–1954* (Princeton, N.J.: Princeton University Press, 1991).

Cuba," in the vernacular of the era. However, in a region that historically though often derisively has been referred to as the "backyard" of the United States, the geopolitical competition with the Soviet Union was asymmetrical. With the exception of Cuba, the Soviet Union gave only modest support to revolutionary groups or leftist governments. Even Cuba, which was active in training and supporting revolutionary groups for three decades, was unable to counter the overwhelming influence and military resources of the United States in the region.[8]

The one place where a second revolution triumphed was Nicaragua in 1979. However, the Nicaraguan revolution was won with matériel, financing, and logistical support provided by social democratic governments in Costa Rica and Venezuela, in addition to the support of the Cuban government. Moreover, it was won at a time when the United States reduced its support of the ruling Somoza government as part of the Carter administration's policy of promoting human rights.

The Cold War was therefore characterized by five forms of outside intervention in the internal conflicts of Latin America: Latin American support for insurgencies in other Latin American countries; Soviet assistance to Cuba and, on a reduced scale, to Nicaragua; deployment of U.S. troops; creation of U.S.-sponsored proxy armies; and extension of U.S. military assistance to local governments and training of local military and police forces.

Latin American states rarely intervened in the internal affairs of other states in the region. Cuba supported guerrilla movements throughout the hemisphere, especially in Colombia, El Salvador, and Nicaragua. Costa Rica and Venezuela supported the Sandinista guerrillas during the Nicaraguan revolution.

Direct Soviet intervention in the internal affairs of Latin American states was also minimal. The main exception was the Soviet Union's economic and military assistance to Cuba, which made possible Cuba's support of Latin American guerrilla insurgencies (as well as African insurgencies and governments). The Soviet Union's presence in Cuba was nonetheless a decisive influence on U.S. policy in the region during the Cold War.

U.S. troops were sent to the region on only two occasions during the Cold War: to the Dominican Republic in 1965, and to Grenada in 1983.[9]

---

8. Cole Blaisier, *The Giant's Rival: The U.S.S.R. and Latin America* (Pittsburgh, Penn.: University of Pittsburgh Press, 1983).

9. Abraham F. Lowenthal, *The Dominican Intervention* (Baltimore, Md.: Johns Hopkins University Press, 1994); Thomas Carothers, *In the Name of Democracy: U.S. Policy Toward Latin America in the Reagan Years* (Berkeley: University of California Press, 1991); Robert

In both cases, U.S. forces were withdrawn quickly once military and political objectives were met. The United States sought to legitimize its intervention in each case by invoking international and inter-American law. In both instances, the United States claimed that it needed to act to protect U.S. citizens caught in the zone of conflict. Also, in each case the United States claimed that it had uncovered communist conspiracies that threatened neighboring nations, thereby activating the provisions of the Inter-American Treaty of Reciprocal Assistance (the Rio Treaty).[10] In 1965, the United States sought and received official approval from the OAS and was able to call the invasion force an Inter-American Peace Force.

Proxy armies organized, trained, and financed by the United States constituted another form of outside intervention in Latin America. In 1954 in Guatemala, the United States engineered the overthrow of the reformist Arbenz government by creating a rebel army of former Guatemalan military officers. This was the model for the failed Bay of Pigs invasion in 1961. It was also the model for the Contra War in Nicaragua, a civil war that lasted for eight years, from 1982 to 1990.

U.S. military assistance and training programs were more common, especially in advanced South American countries such as Brazil and Chile. After the Cuban Revolution, the United States established close relationships with the armed forces in most countries of the region. Armies were trained and equipped to fight internal guerrilla wars; external warfare was de-emphasized.

In 1961, the United States and Latin American militaries developed a regional doctrine known as the National Security Doctrine that reflected their preoccupation with internal warfare. This doctrine called for combining irregular war against internal enemies with national programs to foster economic development and social welfare. It was based on the assumption that the region's immense poverty and social inequalities were breeding grounds for Marxist subversion, and therefore needed to be confronted for national security reasons.[11]

A. Pastor, *Whirlpool: U.S. Foreign Policy toward Latin America and the Caribbean* (Princeton, N.J.: Princeton University Press, 1992), chap. 8.

10. Henry P. Devries, *Cases and Materials on the Law of the Americas* (New York: Parker School of Foreign and Comparative Law, Columbia University, 1976), pp. 634–640.

11. Alfred C. Stepan, "The New Professionalism of Internal Warfare and Military Role Expansion," in Alfred C. Stepan, ed., *Authoritarian Brazil: Origins, Policies and Futures* (New Haven, Conn.: Yale University Press, 1973), pp. 47–68; Lars Schoultz, *National Security and U.S. Policy toward Latin America* (Princeton, N.J.: Princeton University Press, 1987); Francisco Leal Buitrago, *El Oficio de la Guerra* (Bogotá: Tercer Mundo Editores and IEPRI, 1994).

The National Security Doctrine, with its emphasis on internal warfare and economic development, brought U.S.-trained armed forces to the center of national politics in Latin America for several decades. In country after country, military institutions — as opposed to individual *putschist* officers of an earlier period — took power. The 1964 coup d'état in Brazil was the first "national security" coup. Similar coups followed in Chile (1973), Uruguay (1973), and Argentina (1976).[12] The new authoritarian regimes ruthlessly suppressed subversives, labor unions, political parties, student organizations, and others. Civil liberties were suspended; human rights were egregiously violated. In Argentina, over 9,000 people "disappeared."[13]

During the 1970s, U.S. national security policy was focused on the Southern Cone of South America. In the 1980s, the United States was preoccupied with communist revolutions in Central America. These brutal wars marked the final phase of the Cold War in the hemisphere. The regional peace initiatives that attempted to end these conflicts were the first signs of a new era.

REGIONAL PEACEMAKING

The Reagan administration took office only a year after the uprising in Nicaragua. It quickly vowed to prevent the spread of revolution in Central America by stopping strong insurgent movements in El Salvador and Guatemala with close ties to Cuba, Nicaragua, and the Soviet Union. President Reagan and his principal advisers let it be known, moreover, that they intended to "roll back" the Nicaraguan revolution.[14]

The escalation of war in Central America was predictable; the denouement was not. For the first time, a conflict in the Western hemisphere drew in regional and international actors committed to negotiations and peaceful settlements, despite the opposition of the United States to a regional peace process. The first attempt at peacemaking was launched when the leaders of four nations — Colombia, Mexico, Panama, and Venezuela — met on the small Panamanian island of Contadora in December 1983.

THE CONTADORA PEACE PROCESS. When the Contadora group first met, the Salvadoran guerrillas, one of the strongest insurgent movements ever

---

12. David Collier, ed., *The New Authoritarianism in Latin America* (Princeton, N.J.: Princeton University Press, 1979).

13. *Nunca Mas: Informe de la Comisión Nacional sobre la Desaparición de Personas* (Buenos Aires: Editorial Universitaria, 1984), p. 16.

14. Morris J. Blachman et al., eds., *Confronting Revolution: Security Through Diplomacy in Central America* (New York: Pantheon, 1986).

to appear in Latin America, were close to taking power. At the same time, the Sandinistas in Nicaragua were consolidating their revolution. The members of the Contadora Group believed that a U.S. invasion was imminent. They were concerned that armed intervention in Central America would prolong and escalate the conflicts; they feared that instability in Central America could spill over into their own countries. Colombia, long engaged in a border dispute with Nicaragua over the San Andres Islands and embroiled in a protracted guerrilla war of its own, was particularly concerned. Mexico, a traditional haven for Central American refugees, was also deeply worried about the regional implications of military escalation in Central America.[15]

For the populist-leaning Contadora presidents, the revolutionary insurgent groups in El Salvador and Guatemala, as well as the Sandinista government in Nicaragua, were seen as nationalist and reformist. They were more opposed to U.S. intervention than to the consolidation of leftist governments.

The Contadora group's principal aim was to prohibit all outside involvement in the region's wars. This would be accomplished through agreements to terminate all external military assistance to governments and insurgents in Central America. Foreign military bases would be closed, and foreign military advisers would be sent home.

The four presidents faced imposing odds. Throughout 1983 and 1984, U.S.-Nicaraguan relations deteriorated. Just six weeks after the Contadora group produced its first proposal, the Reagan administration sent an invasion force to Grenada. Some Reagan administration officials implied that Nicaragua was next. In the months that followed, a large force was assembled in Honduras and off the shores of Nicaragua as part of the most massive military exercise in the region's history; this force remained in place under different names for the next five years.[16]

Tensions rose in April 1984, when it was revealed that the CIA had mined Nicaragua's harbors. The Contadora proposals that followed contained stronger provisions for verification and democratization, a concession to the United States. However, it continued to insist that outside military assistance to the region must end. The United States continued to pressure its allies in El Salvador and Honduras to reject the treaty,

---

15. See Marc Chernick, "Colombia in Contadora: Foreign Policy in Search of Domestic Peace," in Robert Biles, ed., *Inter-American Relations: The Latin American Perspective* (Boulder, Colo.: Lynne Rienner, 1988), pp. 76–96; Terry Karl, "Mexico, Venezuela, and the Contadora Initiative," in Morris Blachman et al., *Confronting Revolution*.

16. William M. LeoGrande, "The United States and Nicaragua," in Thomas W. Walker, ed., *Nicaragua: The First Five Years* (New York: Praeger, 1985), pp. 442–444.

especially after Nicaragua announced that it was prepared to sign the agreement without further modifications.[17]

The Contadora initiative ultimately failed, although many of its provisions were adopted after the end of the Cold War. In the mid-1980s, however, the United States was not prepared to withdraw from Central America or revise its policy toward Nicaragua.

THE ARIAS PEACE PLAN.   By 1986, the Contadora leaders were no longer viable intermediaries. Costa Rica's president, Oscar Arias, consequently developed his own plan for peace. Significantly, Arias recognized and accepted U.S. military involvement in the region. The Arias plan, unlike the Contadora proposals, would allow the United States to continue to provide military assistance to regular armed forces in Central America.

But Arias, too, was committed to ending outside support of insurgent groups, especially U.S. funding of the Nicaraguan resistance, better known as the Contras. The Contra campaign threatened to draw Costa Rica into the conflict: under U.S. pressure, Arias's predecessors had allowed the Contras to use Costa Rican territory as a staging ground for attacks into Nicaragua. Settling the Nicaraguan conflict thus became a high priority for Arias. This meant finding a formula acceptable to the United States. Arias's proposal called for Nicaragua to hold open, fair, and internationally supervised elections in exchange for a U.S. agreement to halt all assistance to the Contras.[18]

The peace process was thus transformed from a Latin American diplomatic initiative to end outside intervention in the region to a more ambitious Central American effort to promote national reconciliation through elections and democracy. The complete plan, which Arias presented to the other Central American presidents in February 1987 in Esquipulas, Guatemala, provided a formula for ending insurgencies within a democratic framework. It called for countries plagued by civil wars to establish and implement a cease-fire; establish a National Commission for Reconciliation; extend a general amnesty to military officers and insurgents; begin a dialogue between the government and the insurgents; hold free and fair elections that involve former insurgents; and disarm and demobilize irregular forces. Three provisions of the plan were directed at external actors: foreign powers were to cut off all aid to irregular forces; Central American states were to deny use of their terri-

---

17.   See Jack Child, *The Central American Peace Process 1983–1991* (Boulder, Colo.: Lynne Rienner, 1992), chaps. 2, 3.

18.   Dario Moreno, *The Struggle for Peace in Central America* (Gainesville: University Press of Florida, 1994), chap. 4.

tory for attacks on neighboring countries; and effective international verifi-cation procedures for all phases of the agreement were to be established.[19]

The final version of the Peace Plan, known as Esquipulas II, was signed by the Central American presidents in August 1987. It was to be implemented in no more than ninety days. As it turned out, the settlement of the Nicaraguan conflict was to take another three years. In El Salvador, negotiations dragged on for another five years. In Guatemala, partial agreements were reached in 1994 and 1995, but final terms of a settlement remain elusive.

In short, the Arias Peace Plan provided a blueprint for peace that could be implemented only after the international and domestic changes brought about by the end of the Cold War had taken place. The plan required a commitment to peace and democratization that simply did not exist in 1987. The United States strongly backed the plans for elections in Nicaragua, but it was unwilling to cut its links with the Contras. As deadlines for demobilization came and went in the years that followed Esquipulas II, the United States continued to stall; at key moments when the U.S. Congress could have voted to suspend aid, the administration convinced congressional leaders to provide "humanitarian aid" to the Contras and keep pressure on the Sandinistas. Only after the Sandinistas were defeated at the polls in February 1990 did the United States finally agree to dismantle the Contra force — three years after Esquipulas II was signed.

The Post–Cold War Era in Latin America

Latin America shared in the euphoria that emerged in the immediate aftermath of the Cold War. After a decade of insurgencies and civil wars in Central America, the region welcomed the possibility of peace that the new era seemed to offer. Almost immediately, the Arias peace process was given new life. Moreover, the United Nations and the Organization of American States, reflecting a changed consensus in the international and inter-American communities, were now prepared to play a more active role in peacemaking and peacekeeping in the hemisphere. First in Nica-ragua and then in El Salvador, both multilateral bodies launched impor-tant missions designed to move the region from war to peace.

Beyond the impact of changing superpower politics, the Central American conflicts also benefited from a decade of democratization in

---

19. See "Peace Plan by Oscar Arias, 15 February 1987," and "Esquipulas II: Procedure for the Establishment of a Firm and Lasting Peace in Central America," reprinted in Moreno, *The Struggle for Peace*, pp. 184–198.

Latin America. By 1990, most of the region's governments were now under democratic rule. At the same time that the hemisphere's powers were focusing on promoting peace in Central America, they also began to rethink the role of democratic governance throughout Latin America and the Caribbean. For the first time, all members of the Organization of American States affirmed a commitment to democracy and called for immediate action in the event that constitutional rule was suspended in a member nation. This was a specifically inter-American position; it altered — at least conceptually — a longstanding regional emphasis on the inviolability of national sovereignty and an unswerving support for non-interventionism.

This section will first examine the peace processes in Nicaragua and El Salvador. It will conclude with a discussion of the regional trend toward democracy and the early decisions within the Organization of American States to consider various forms of multilateral interventionism in the name of fostering democratic governance.

PEACEMAKING MADE POSSIBLE

One of the first regions to feel the aftershocks from the events in Eastern Europe in 1989 was Central America. Peace processes that had been stalled were given new life as international tensions diminished and regional leaders reasserted themselves. The Arias Peace Plan had faltered principally because the United States was not prepared to back a settlement that left a hostile pro-Soviet state in Central America. The local parties to the conflict, moreover, were unwilling and unable to embrace negotiations and democratic participation as required by the Arias plan.

By 1989, changes occurring elsewhere in the international system facilitated the acceptance of Arias's proposals. First, the United States, as part of its reappraisal of its relationship with the Soviet Union, became more interested in ending the conflicts in Central America. Second, the collapse of communism in Eastern Europe had a dramatic effect on the left and Marxist insurgents throughout Latin America. Several groups, including those in Central America, began to reevaluate their positions on armed struggle and democracy. Finally, all sides became willing to experiment with Arias's novel formula for resolving internal conflicts in Latin America. In the immediate aftermath of the Cold War, the Organization of American States and the United Nations were invited into the region to help restore internal peace. Mounting multifunctional peace operations, these international organizations helped to mediate conflicts and to verify cease-fires. Further, international observers and advisers were sent to help adversaries address some of the underlying causes of conflict in the region.

UN and OAS special missions were sent to Nicaragua and El Salvador. In both countries, peacemakers followed the blueprint provided by the Arias plan. The critical steps for reaching peace in Nicaragua were the staging of fair and open elections, and the ending of external support for the armed opposition. The key developments in El Salvador were a fundamental restructuring of the security apparatus of the state, a downsizing of the military, and a purge of the police. Critical agreements also led to major reforms involving human rights, electoral participation, and land distribution. In both countries, UN and OAS missions became involved in verifying peace agreements, monitoring elections, supervising arms reductions, demobilizing troops, and implementing political and social reforms. The evolution of the peace processes in Nicaragua and El Salvador shows how civil wars can be settled through negotiation, outside mediation, and multifunctional peacemaking.

NICARAGUA.   The peace process in Nicaragua was in some respects less complex than its counterpart in El Salvador. In Nicaragua, peacemaking did not involve significant negotiations between the Sandinista government and the Contras. The main decisions to end the war were made by outside actors.

The Contras did not have the resources to fight on without the United States. Further, by 1988, the Sandinista army had regained control of almost all of its national territory. The Contras were penned into their bases in Honduras, and could mount only minor cross-border actions. For the Sandinista government, however, the continued existence of the Contras meant the continuation of a highly unpopular war which drained resources and support from the government.

The decisive question on which the whole peace process hinged was whether the United States would abide by the Central American request to suspend funding for the Contras as part of a broader process of Nicaraguan democratization. The answer was negative throughout 1987 and 1988. In 1989, following the inauguration of the Bush administration, U.S. policy became ambiguous. Unwilling to completely abandon the Contras and alienate many in his own party, President Bush worked out a compromise which provided $60 million in humanitarian aid to the Contras in the run-up to the Nicaraguan elections in February of 1990.[20]

The peace process came to depend on the holding of fair and open elections in Nicaragua. The United States would not cut off aid before

---

20. Cynthia Arnson, *Crossroads: Congress, the President, and Central America, 1976–1993* (University Park: Pennsylvania State University Press, 1993).

elections were held. The Contras would not disarm or demobilize. Honduras was unable to close Contra military bases because of U.S. pressure to keep them open.

The main area where progress was made, and proved to be critical, was the establishment of international verification and observer teams. The five Central American presidents formally requested international assistance from the United Nations and the Organization of American States, which created three special units: the Commission for Support and Verification (CIAV), which had separate OAS and UN units that oversaw the voluntary demobilization and repatriation of the Contras; the UN Observer Group in Central America (ONUCA), which was deployed mostly along borders; and the UN Observer Group for the Verification of Elections in Nicaragua (ONUVEN).

The CIAV units were established to assist the voluntary demobilization, repatriation, and relocation of the Contras from their camps in Honduras: CIAV-UN was responsible for the initial contacts in Honduras; CIAV-OAS was responsible for demobilization and resettlement inside Nicaragua. Once the disarmament process began following the elections, the OAS unit became the principal international body responsible for overseeing the full demobilization.

ONUCA's mandate was to verify the halt in arms shipments to the region's guerrilla forces, and to prevent cross-border actions that involved the use of one's state's territory as a base for armed aggression in another. ONUVEN, the UN election observance unit in Nicaragua, carried out the first UN-supervised election in a sovereign state that was not either partitioned or ending colonial rule.

In one of the most closely monitored elections in history, the Sandinistas failed at the polls. The social costs of the war, the economic hardships brought about by the U.S. embargo, and the great desire for peace among the Nicaraguan people were all factors that led to the Sandinista defeat. This became apparent only in retrospect: at the time, the loss was stunning. Public opinion polls and well-attended mass rallies had suggested that the Sandinistas would win easily.[21]

A broad opposition coalition strongly backed and openly financed by the United States won the elections.[22] The Sandinistas, though unprepared for defeat, accepted the verdict and agreed to work with the opposition

---

21. Carlos Sarti, "Las negociaciones políticas en Centroamerica," in Carlos Vilas, ed., *Democracia Emergente en Centroanmerica* (Ciudad del México: Universidad Autónoma de México, 1993), p. 348.

22. See Linda Robinson, *Intervention or Neglect: The United States and Central America Beyond the 1980s* (New York: Council on Foreign Relations, 1991), pp. 46–48.

in transferring power peacefully. However, they insisted that a peaceful transfer could only be achieved after the demobilization of the Contras. The new government of Violetta Chamorro immediately called on the Contras to lay down their arms.

The election results transformed the dynamics of the peace process. Most notably, the United States agreed to support the demobilization of the Contras under the terms of the Arias plan. The Contras did not participate in any significant way in this discussion: the United States simply told the Contra leadership that they had fulfilled their mission by forcing the Sandinistas from power, and that they could now disband as victors.

Five months after the elections and three months after the transfer of power, the last of the Contras handed in their weapons to the CIAV-OAS. Close to 23,000 Contras registered and received a few personal items in exchange for their weapons; 17,000 weapons were destroyed.[23]

EL SALVADOR. In September 1989, representatives from the government of El Salvador and the Farabundo Martí National Liberation Front (FMLN) began direct, face-to-face talks as stipulated under the Arias accords signed two years earlier. The guerrillas backed away from their earlier demands for power-sharing; they accepted elections as a legitimate path to power. Their agenda now focused on two main issues: reducing the size of the armed forces, and implementing constitutional and electoral reforms that would facilitate the transition of the FMLN from a guerrilla movement to a political party.[24] This in itself was a victory for those who had worked for peace in Central America. The Arias plan had advanced multi-party democracy as the accepted form of governance, specifically rejecting Nicaraguan or Cuban models. In 1989, the FMLN indicated for the first time its willingness to participate in fair and democratic elections, transforming its armed struggle into a political and electoral one.[25]

The idea of open elections stirred violent opposition. After a series of bombings and death threats aimed at the FMLN, in which the government denied being involved, the FMLN broke off further talks. Nine days later, the guerrillas launched their largest offensive of the war in an attack on San Salvador, the capital of El Salvador.

---

23. Child, *The Central American Peace Process,* p. 106.

24. Ibid., pp. 5–6.

25. Eliseo Francisco Ortiz Ruiz and Irene Sanchez, "El Salvador: La Contrucción de Nuevos Caminos," in Vilas, *Democracia Emergente en Centroamérica,* pp. 266–267.

Negotiations resumed only when the Central American presidents, meeting in Costa Rica, appealed to the United Nations to facilitate the resumption of talks. In January 1990, UN mediators began a round of shuttle diplomacy between the two parties to the Salvadoran conflict.[26] Six months after the FMLN attack on San Salvador, in April 1990, the government and the FMLN agreed to resume direct talks under UN supervision. In July, the two sides agreed to deploy a UN human rights observer team. In December, the United Nations authorized creation of the UN Observer Group in El Salvador (ONUSAL), which was deployed in mid-1991. ONUSAL was an extension of ONUCA, which consisted of teams that patrolled the borders of Nicaragua.

In January 1991, direct peace talks finally got under way in Mexico City. They came to a dramatic conclusion in the closing days of December 1991 at UN headquarters in New York. On December 29, President Bush dispatched six senior State Department officials to New York to negotiate directly with Salvadoran President Alfredo Cristiani. The United States had leverage: El Salvador was then the sixth largest recipient of U.S. aid in the world.[27] The United States had one message for Cristiani: it was time to end the war.[28] On December 31, UN Secretary-General Javier Perez de Cuellar's last day in office, an agreement was reached.

The importance of the UN mediation effort must be underscored. Peruvian diplomat Alvaro de Soto, the personal envoy of the Secretary-General during the talks, played a key role in pushing the negotiations forward. One of the wisest decisions made by de Soto was not to insist on implementation of a cease-fire as a pre-condition for negotiations. His position was that the peace talks should not be undermined or delayed with each skirmish, assassination, or bombing, as had happened in the past. This view was accepted by both parties to the conflict.[29]

The final document featured substantive agreements to democratize Salvadoran politics and society.[30] The New York agreements contained specific commitments to:

---

26. See Tommie Sue Montgomery, *Revolution in El Salvador: From Civil Strife to Civil Peace*, 2nd ed. (Boulder, Colo.: Westview, 1992), chap. 8.

27. Washington Office on Latin America (WOLA), *El Salvador: Is Peace Possible?* (Washington, D.C.: WOLA, April 1990), p. 21.

28. Montgomery, *Revolution in El Salvador*, pp. 224–226.

29. Comments made by Alvaro de Soto at the Woodrow Wilson Center for International Scholars, Washington, D.C., April 1995.

30. See *El Salvador Agreements: The Path to Peace* (United Nations Department of Public Information in cooperation with United Nations Observer Mission in El Salvador, May 1992).

- Reform, purge, and cut the military: these were the principal demands of the guerrillas and the greatest stumbling blocks to a settlement. The government agreed to purge the military of human rights violators; cut the size of the military by fifty percent; dismantle all counterinsurgency battalions, paramilitary forces, and autonomous intelligence units; and disengage the army from internal security functions.

- Abolish the National Guard, Treasury Police, and National Police: the agreements called for existing internal security agencies to be replaced by a new National Civilian Police. The new force would be comprised mainly of civilians who had not been involved in the conflict. The remainder would be comprised in equal measure of former FMLN and former members of the old National Police.

- Provide guarantees to the FMLN that would enable it to participate effectively in the electoral process: issues included ensuring the personal safety of the guerrillas as they openly campaigned and participated in the political process, and implementing reforms that would facilitate the conversion of the FMLN from a guerrilla movement to a viable political party. Access to the media was key in this regard.

- Create new institutions to implement the accords: the National Commission for the Consolidation of Peace (COPAZ) with joint government and opposition participation, and the Economic and Social Forum. The peace process deferred fundamental economic reforms by creating the latter agency to address the underlying social and economic problems seen to be at the root of the conflict.

- Institute a program of agrarian reform: the one economic issue that was addressed was land reform. An agreement to distribute land and provide access to rural services and credit was reached.

- Establish Truth: as in Argentina, Brazil, and Chile in the 1980s, a Commission on the Truth would be established to investigate and document past human rights abuses. In El Salvador, unlike the other cases, this commission would be an independent, international body, consisting of a three-member board appointed by the Secretary-General of the United Nations.

The agreements called for ONUSAL to play an expanded role in verifying all phases of the agreements. Effective immediately were provisions to separate and demobilize the combatants. The agreements requested the UN Secretary-General to increase the size of the ONUSAL deployment to meet the expanded mandate.

ONUSAL operated in El Salvador through April 1995. It oversaw the implementation of most of the agreements, particularly the restructuring of the armed forces and police.[31] Little progress was made in the distribution of land to former combatants, however. That said, ONUSAL's achievements were substantial. The United Nations demonstrated that it could create effective, multifunctional instruments for resolving internal conflicts.

DEMOCRATIZATION AND THE CENTRAL AMERICAN PEACE PROCESS

Peace in El Salvador and Nicaragua was brought about not only by international peacemaking facilitated by the end of the Cold War. It was also made possible by the growing acceptance of democratic forms of governance throughout much of Central and South America, a region that had previously lived for decades mainly under authoritarian rule.

The idea of democracy, once scorned on the left, came to have new value for those who suffered human rights abuses and infringements on their civil liberties in Brazil and the Southern Cone in the 1970s and 1980s.[32] The move toward respecting civil liberties, the rule of law, and democratic pluralism in Latin America was reinforced by the seismic changes that took place in Eastern Europe and the Soviet Union in the late 1980s and early 1990s.[33]

The Central American left was not exempt from these changes. It, too, became an active participant in the regional and international debate over the fall of communism in Eastern Europe and the Soviet Union. In 1989, the FMLN accepted for the first time the principle of representative democracy as the basis for ending the conflict in El Salvador. In Nicaragua, the Sandinistas accepted the idea of a fair, open, and internationally supervised election. When they lost the election, they ceded power. The importance of the transformation of ideology and politics in the region

---

31. Jack Spence et al., *The Salvadoran Peace Accords and Democratization: A Three Years Progress Report and Recommendations* (Cambridge, Mass.: Hemisphere Initiatives, March 1995).

32. See Francisco Weffort, "Why Democracy?" in Alfred Stepan, ed., *Democratizing Brazil: Problems of Transition and Consolidation* (New York: Oxford University Press, 1989), pp. 327–350.

33. See Steve Ellner and Barry Carr, *The Latin American Left: From the Fall of Allende to Perestroika* (Boulder, Colo.: Westview, 1993); Jorge Castañeda, *Utopia Unarmed: The Latin American Left after the Cold War* (New York: Knopf, 1993).

cannot be underestimated: the embrace of democracy contributed greatly to the move toward peace. The idea of democracy finally seemed to resonate in Latin America.

The left was not alone in beginning an ideological journey that ended with the acceptance of democratic forms of governance. Whereas the left in Latin America was influenced by external developments in Eastern Europe and the Soviet Union, changes in the views of the right came about principally because of pressure from the United States.

The Salvadoran right, for example, initially rejected the peace agreements; it relented only after the United States came out strongly in favor of a negotiated settlement. As a result, a democratic right emerged in Central America in the 1990s. In El Salvador, ARENA, a group known for its association with right-wing death squads, was transformed into a modern political party. An ARENA candidate won the presidency in 1990, and it was ARENA that negotiated peace with the FMLN. ARENA also beat the FMLN at the polls in 1994.

MULTILATERAL AND UNILATERAL INTERVENTION

The Organization of American States played an activist and independent role in ending the Central American wars. In the early 1990s, OAS member states moved guardedly but surely in favor of collective action to confront coups d'état and other violations of the constitutional order.[34]

The pressing question became one of instruments: with what would the OAS act to carry out its new commitment to democracy? Constitutional crises in Peru, Guatemala, and Haiti provided the first answers. In Peru (1992) and Guatemala (1993), elected presidents shut down congress and assumed dictatorial powers. In Haiti (1992), the president was overthrown in a conventional military coup d'état.

In response, the OAS convened the hemisphere's foreign ministers, who condemned the illegal actions. Their calls for collective action, however, were hortatory. Unlike the United Nations, the OAS charter has no provision for mandatory sanctions.[35] Instead, OAS diplomatic pressure isolated the three regimes, and the OAS called on member states to take further action. In the case of Haiti, for example, it called for a suspension of commercial and economic relations. That was the limit of OAS interventionism.

---

34. See Inter-American Dialogue (IAD), *The Organization of American States: Advancing Democracy, Human Rights and the Rule of Law. A Report of the Inter-American Dialogue Commission on the OAS* (Washington, D.C.: IAD, 1994).

35. Heraldo Muñoz, "The OAS's Comparative Advantage," in IAD, *The Organization of American States*, p. 32.

All three of these illegal seizures of power were nonetheless over-turned. In Peru, President Alberto Fujimori scheduled new elections seven months later, following strong pressure from the OAS and the suspension of most economic aid by the United States. In Guatemala, international pressure led to the resignation of the president, Jorge Serrano, after he failed to gain domestic support for his actions. Many observers believe that the actions of OAS envoys sent to Guatemala to meet with major domestic political actors contributed to Serrano's downfall.[36] In Haiti, the military ruled for over three years before it was deposed by a U.S. intervention force that restored the constitutional president. In this case, OAS condemnation was swift, but its role in overturning the coup was minimal.

These cases underscored the limits of the organization's "new inter-ventionism." The OAS was prepared to denounce the suspension of constitutional rule and initiate diplomatic activity to restore democracy. This distinguishes it from the United Nations, which has no mandate in its charter to maintain democracy. A regional consensus together with timely diplomatic initiatives and hortatory resolutions can be effective, as was seen in Guatemala.

However, the OAS does not control armies and has limited means to enforce compliance. Past uses of inter-American forces have been *ad hoc* and mostly unsatisfactory, such as in the Dominican Republic in 1965. In Central America, the CIAV-OAS mission used to demobilize the Contras in 1990 was a successful use of Latin American soldiers for a specific mission. However, there is still no OAS equivalent to the United Nations peacekeeping forces, or to the UN's ability to impose economic and military sanctions on individual states. Although the OAS has developed a consensus on promoting democracy, its member states are far from an agreement concerning the mandatory application of sanctions or force to restore democracy after constitutional rule has been suspended.

The case of Haiti demonstrated the shortcomings of the OAS. When President Aristide was overthrown in September 1991, the OAS immedi-ately called for the full restoration of democracy and the reinstatement of the Haitian president. The OAS then recommended that all member states suspend economic and commercial relations with Haiti. A year of resolu-tions and diplomatic initiatives proved to be ineffective. Economic sanc-tions were not uniformly applied.

In late 1992, the Bush administration brought the case before the United Nations, implicitly recognizing the limits of the OAS. In June 1993,

---

36. Viron Vaky and Heraldo Muñoz, *The Future of the Organization of American States* (New York: Twentieth Century Fund, 1993), pp. 26–27.

the UN Security Council declared Haiti a threat to regional peace and security. It then imposed a weapons and oil embargo on the Caribbean nation. Negotiations held on Governors Island, mediated by the United Nations, led to an agreement that would have restored Aristide to power and given amnesty to the generals who had seized power. The agreement soon broke down. In October, the Security Council approved a naval blockade of Haiti.

The Haitian impasse was resolved in September 1994, when the United States, supported by the UN Security Council, sent troops to overthrow the illegal military government and restore the constitutional president. Six months later, the United States handed over authority to UN peacekeepers and OAS special missions. Aristide was returned to power three years after being toppled; unilateral military action proved to be more decisive than three years of multilateral initiatives.

The Haitian case provides no clear guideline as to when and where the United States will act, and when and where it will not. For three years, the United States vacillated between isolationism and interventionism, unilateralism and multilateralism. When it did act, it was impelled mostly by domestic considerations: Washington was anxious to stop illegal immigration from Haiti. Moreover, African-American leaders began to denounce U.S. policy. By the fall of 1994, congressional and civil rights leaders were claiming that U.S. immigration policy was indifferent to the suffering of the people of Haiti.

The precedent nonetheless stands, and so does the principle of regional support for constitutional, representative democracy. What does this portend for the future? In general, the nations of the region continue to support an interventionist OAS. Meeting in Miami in December 1994, the hemisphere's heads of state (excluding Cuba) authorized an even greater role for the OAS in regional affairs. Promotion of democracy remains a high priority. However, as the post–Cold War world takes shape in Latin America, new issues such as combating drug trafficking and organized crime are beginning to crowd the agenda.[37]

New Internal Conflicts, New Forms of Intervention

The old forms of armed insurrection in Latin America as well as the Cold War challenges to democratic governance seem to have run their course. The last self-proclaimed, class-based insurgency — Sendero Luminoso in Peru, which launched its armed struggle in 1980 — was weakened in the

---

37. Organization of American States (OAS), *A New Vision of the OAS. Working Paper of the General Secretariat for the Permanent Council* (Washington, D.C.: OAS, 1995).

early 1990s by a harsh but intelligent counterinsurgency campaign. Sendero, moreover, showed a callous disregard for its peasant and indigenous supporters, and failed to gain the poor urban following that it eventually sought to recruit in replacement of its dwindling rural base. Though remarkably successful in challenging the Peruvian government and society for over a decade, Sendero's version of Maoist thought ultimately proved to be out of touch with most poor people's aspirations.[38] The rise and demise of Sendero closes a chapter on revolutionary warfare in Latin America that opened with the communist guerrillas in the Colombian mountains in the 1940s and 1950s, and then flowered in successive decades with the Cuban and Nicaraguan revolutions, and the formidable strength of the Salvadoran guerrillas in the 1980s.

What remains of the earlier revolutionary era is a still-standing, though chastened, Cuba. The collapse of the Soviet Union made Cuba geopolitically irrelevant, however. It also triggered a severe economic recession. The Cuban government survived by re-orienting its economy to compete more effectively in the new global economy. It opened its economy to foreign investment, promoted tourism, and stimulated traditional and non-traditional exports.

The enforcement of the U.S. economic blockade, principally compelled by the vocal Cuban-American community, has made Cuba's economic adjustment more wrenching. However, the United States stands alone in maintaining economic sanctions in Cuba. When Havana sought to reintegrate into the region's economy, it ended its support for Latin American revolutionary movements. The OAS had already rescinded its earlier endorsement of the embargo, and most Latin American nations have quietly resumed diplomatic and economic relations with Cuba. Foreign capital from Canada, Italy, Mexico, Spain, and elsewhere has kept the Cuban economy afloat.

Violent conflict in Cuba is still possible. If conflict breaks out, it would most likely draw in the United States in some form. However, by the mid-1990s, the worst of Cuba's economic crisis had passed. It appears that Cuba will enter the twenty-first century as just one more Caribbean nation, albeit with a better-trained and better-educated labor force than most.

The Cuban withdrawal of support for guerrillas and class-based national liberation movements in Latin America did not bring an end to armed insurrectionary movements in the hemisphere. Some armed oppo-

---

38. David Scott Palmer, ed., *Shining Path of Peru* (New York: St. Martin's, 1992).

sition movements, such as those in Colombia and Guatemala, persevered. At the same time, new guerrilla movements, such as the Zapatista National Liberation Army (EZLN) in the southern Mexican state of Chiapas, emerged with a new agenda for revolutionary action. More disturbingly, the post–Cold War world has witnessed new types of organized violence associated with the vertiginous rise of the drug trade in Latin America.

These new forms of violence almost immediately began to attract the attention of outside powers. In particular, beginning in the late 1980s, the United States initiated a major new effort to combat drug trafficking in the hemisphere. By 1990, with the Central American conflicts drawing to a close, U.S. assistance to the Andean region surpassed aid to the small Central American nations which had dominated U.S. policy in the region for a decade. In September 1989, the Bush administration launched a major new offensive against drug trafficking, calling it the number one national security threat facing the United States. President Bush vowed to go to the source to stop production and supply. Since then, U.S. military, intelligence, and anti-narcotics personnel have been redeployed throughout the region in a Sisyphean effort to stop the northward flow of cocaine, marijuana, and heroin.[39]

This section will look, first, at the rise of new forms of violence and rebellion in the Western Hemisphere. It will then analyze the ways in which outside powers are being drawn into these conflicts.

POST–COLD WAR INSURGENCY AND VIOLENCE

One of the most striking features about post–Cold War Latin America is the persistence of armed opposition groups. With the collapse of the Soviet Union, the crisis in Cuba, the electoral defeat of the Sandinistas and the negotiated settlement in El Salvador, some thought that the era of armed politics and guerrilla insurgencies in Latin America had passed.[40]

Much of the old left, from the FMLN in El Salvador to former guerrillas in Uruguay and Colombia, did re-evaluate their positions on democracy, particularly as their societies became more pluralistic and democratic. But by the 1990s, the left no longer could mobilize support

---

39. Bruce Bagley, "Dateline Drug Wars: Colombia: The Wrong Strategy," *Foreign Policy*, No. 77 (Winter 1989–90), pp. 154–171; Bruce Bagley, "Myths of Militarization: Enlisting Armed Forces in the War on Drugs," in Peter H. Smith, ed., *Drug Policy in the Americas* (Boulder, Colo.: Westview, 1992), pp. 129–150.

40. Castañeda, *Utopia Unarmed*.

as it once did. Decades of authoritarian repression, economic stagnation, labor union decline, and ideological crisis had marginalized many of the old parties. The collapse of socialism in Eastern Europe and the Soviet Union had left the region's communist parties adrift. The Manuel Rodriguez Patriotic Front, a guerrilla movement linked with the Chilean Communist Party, simply suspended its activities when the Pinochet dictatorship came to an end after seventeen years of rule.

Other guerrilla movements, however, continued with armed opposition. Some had roots in the Marxist liberation struggles of the Cold War period, such as the guerrillas in Colombia and Guatemala as well as the dissident faction of Sendero Luminoso, known as Sendero Rojo, in Peru. Each of these guerrilla movements, though, had substantially transformed their social bases, political positions, alliance networks, and funding sources. At the same time, other movements initiated armed actions: the Zapatistas in Mexico self-consciously reflect the social cleavages and political aspirations of the 1990s.

Three features distinguish Latin American guerrilla movements in the 1990s from insurgent movements in the Cold War period: new political strategies with respect to peace negotiations; new social bases among indigenous populations and other disenfranchised groups; and the mobilization of new resources involving criminal activity and drug trafficking.

NEW POLITICAL STRATEGIES IN GUATEMALA AND COLOMBIA. The guerrilla movements of the 1990s are political as well as military actors: peace processes have given insurgents a political stage and broadened the scope of their struggles. Colombian guerrillas have been negotiating with successive governments in Bogota since 1982. Guatemalan guerrillas, within the context of the Arias peace plan for Central America, first met with government negotiators in 1987. In each case, militarily weak (Guatemala) and politically weak (Colombia) guerrilla groups have attempted to negotiate broad agreements on issues that have national and international support, such as democracy, human rights, and halting oppression of minorities.

Guatemala was a signatory of the Central American peace accords, which committed the government to enter into a process of national reconciliation with its armed opposition groups. The Guatemalan guerrillas — the Revolutionary National Guatemalan Union (URNG), which joins the nation's two main guerrilla forces — had been severely repressed in the 1960s and were eventually pushed deep into Guatemala's highlands and rain forests. They gradually began to take up the cause of Guatemala's long-oppressed indigenous population. Unlike anywhere else in Latin America, the Guatemalan guerrillas turned their revolutionary struggle into a campaign for indigenous peoples.[41]

By the late 1980s, the insurgents were a severely battered fighting force with only a shadow of their earlier strength; they nonetheless persisted. Under the terms of the Central American peace accords, the government and guerrillas first met in Oslo in 1987. The United Nations designated several "friends" of the Guatemalan peace process: the governments of the United States, Mexico, Colombia, Norway, Spain, and Venezuela.

The United States was not providing significant amounts of military aid to the Guatemalan armed forces at that time. Because of major human rights abuses in Guatemala, most U.S. military aid had been suspended in the early 1980s, leaving only a small channel of covert CIA funding.[42] As a result, the Guatemalan military had considerable freedom of action.

Drawing on continued input from UN negotiators and the good offices of the "friends" of the Guatemalan peace process, the Guatemalan guerrillas and the government finally reached agreement on a framework for negotiations in April 1991. The framework is interesting because it calls for discussions on the broad structural, political, and social cleavages that plague Guatemalan society.[43]

After several years of negotiations, accords were ultimately reached in the following areas: human rights (signed in March 1994); the establishment of a commission to clarify past human rights violations (signed in June 1994); resettlement of groups uprooted by the conflict (June 1994); and the rights of the indigenous populations (March 1995). The pace of the negotiations has been slow, and implementation of the signed agreements has been incremental and partial. After eight years of talks, no agreement has been reached about ending the war itself.

However, this protracted process shows how the guerrillas, despite their weakened position, were able to seize on problems recognized by other members of society and use negotiations to redress them. Their political agenda has a large degree of national and international support,

---

41. Carol A. Smith, ed., *Guatemalan Indians and the State, 1545–1988* (Austin: University of Texas Press, 1990); Susan Jonas, *The Battle for Guatemala: Rebels, Death Squads and U.S. Power* (Boulder, Colo.: Westview, 1991).

42. "Death Threat Report Draws U.S. Response," *Washington Post*, April 15, 1995, p. A5; "Truth and Consequences: Rep. Toricelli Leaked the Goods on the CIA. Was It Loyalty or Betrayal?" *Washington Post*, April 17, 1995, p. C1.

43. *Documentos Basicos del Proceso de Paz* (Guatemala City: Fundacion Para la Paz, la Democracia y el Desarrollo (FUNDAPAZD), 1992).

even if the guerrillas themselves and their use of armed struggle might be of questionable legitimacy. Their political agenda has a wider resonance precisely because the government and certain government policies lack legitimacy. As a result, the negotiations have been used by both sides to re-establish their political legitimacy.

Because the Guatemalan guerrillas have embraced the broader regional agenda of democratization and cultural pluralism, foreign governments and nongovernmental organizations concerned with human rights and indigenous affairs have been drawn into the Guatemalan peace process. The United Nations, for its part, has been involved in verification matters. However, no outside power is pushing effectively for an end to the Guatemalan conflict; resolution of the armed conflict, though perhaps inevitable, will thus continue at an agonizingly slow pace.

The oldest Colombian guerrilla movement has its roots in the bloody civil war known as la Violencia, and dates back to the 1940s and 1950s. In the period following the Cuban Revolution, communist guerrillas formed the Revolutionary Armed Forces of Colombia (FARC), a pro-Soviet group linked with the Communist Party of Colombia. The second major group founded in this period was the ELN, a pro-Cuban group that became a Marxist-Christian group led by revolutionary priests who adhered to the liberation theology that swept the continent in the 1960s and 1970s.

By the 1980s, over half a dozen groups challenged Colombia's civilian regime, reflecting both the closed nature of Colombian politics and the absence of state control over large parts of the country. As in Central America, negotiations with the guerrillas were seen as a way to democratize the government and, equally critical, extend the geographic reach of the state. Unlike in Central America, however, outside powers or international organizations were not invited to participate in the peace process. The Colombian government viewed the insurgencies as a domestic issue, and it did not want international recognition extended to the guerrillas. The Colombian government negotiated with the different guerrilla movements on a bilateral basis, eventually leading to some partial successes and some major frustrations and failures.

The first round of negotiations, held from 1982–86, ended in spectacular failure: the April 19th Movement (M-19) seized the Palace of Justice in November 1985 to protest government actions. The takeover led to a fiery massacre that killed all of the guerrillas involved in the assault and half of the Supreme Court.[44] The second major round of negotiations, held

---

44. Ana Carrigan, *The Palace of Justice: A Colombian Tragedy* (New York: Four Walls, Eight Windows, 1993).

from 1989–90, proved to be more successful. Several groups, most notably the M-19, laid down their arms and formed political parties. The negotiating agenda was narrowly focused on implementing a cease-fire, providing amnesty, and transforming the guerrilla movements into viable political parties.

Although agreements were reached with four small groups, little progress was made in talks with the two large groups, the FARC and ELN, which had large armies and considerable influence in certain areas of the country. Their areas of control included the expanding agricultural frontier along the plains and the jungles that descended from the eastern slope of the Andes, as well as in some of the new urban shantytowns. The FARC and ELN demanded structural reforms in the social and economic spheres, and they denounced human rights abuses by the army and the government's paramilitary groups.

The FARC and ELN had few incentives to negotiate a final settlement: they were militarily secure, well-financed, and very influential at the local level. Over time, the FARC and ELN became a new type of opposition movement: they retained some of their political identify and agendas, but became deeply involved in criminal activity and illicit coca and opium poppy production.

In 1995, the Colombian government made overtures to the guerrillas in an effort to renew the stalled negotiations. For the first time, the government indicated a willingness to invite international mediators to participate in the talks. However, neither side seems able to negotiate while hostilities are under way. Each has used the peace process for political purposes and avoided serious bargaining. International mediation may be needed to advance the talks and create the necessary incentives for both sides to put an end to more than thirty years of guerrilla war.

NEW SOCIAL BASES IN MEXICO AND ECUADOR. For decades, the social base of most guerrilla movements in Latin America was organized around class-based oppression. In the 1990s, several guerrilla movements have emerged around the issues of ethnic or regional exclusion from national culture and politics. Insurgencies in Mexico and Guatemala consciously reflect ethnic cleavages and regional divisions. In Peru, Sendero Luminoso has roots in both ethnic and regional discrimination, although its insurgency is still articulated in class terms.

In parts of Latin America, indigenous people constitute forty to sixty percent of the total population.[45] With the decline of the left in Latin

---

45. According to the World Bank, indigenous people constitute 56.8 percent of Bolivia's population; 29.5 percent of Ecuador's; 43.8 percent of Guatemala's; 14.2 percent

American politics, indigenous movements have been able in some cases to fill the political vacuum that was left among intellectuals, peasants, and recent migrants to the cities.

These indigenous movements do not have separatist agendas. Instead, they are calling for a redefinition of the nation and fundamental political reform. Modernization theory had posited that economic development would create secular, integrated nations that would rise above the inequitable aspects of traditional society. In the 1990s, indigenous movements are calling for the recognition of multiple nations and ethnic groups within a common state. This may reflect the fact that, in some countries, indigenous populations are widely and unevenly distributed. Separatist agendas are consequently unrealistic.

Although these indigenous movements have sought legitimacy by advocating democratization, their means may be undemocratic. Just as the region's leaders and intellectuals were declaring the end of the era of armed insurgency, a previously unknown guerrilla movement, the EZLN, launched an armed struggle in southern Mexico. The uprising sent shock waves through Mexico, the United States, and the international financial community, all of which were anticipating implementation of the North American Free Trade Agreement (NAFTA).

The Mexican rebels adroitly inserted themselves into the politics of NAFTA. They launched their uprising on January 1, 1994, the day NAFTA formally took effect and began the process of linking the economies of Canada, Mexico, and the United States more closely. Just as Mexico was hoping to celebrate its entrance into the "First World," the Zapatistas revealed a Mexico that differed from the oasis of stability presented by proponents of the free trade agreement. One of the Zapatistas' demands was the suspension of NAFTA. They claimed that NAFTA would lead to further exploitation of their home region of Chiapas, one of the most impoverished areas of Mexico, but a zone rich in exportable natural resources.

Their principal demands centered on proposals to democratize Mexico. Theirs was an indigenous movement, they declared, which sought change through a broad democratic opening of the nation's political institutions. Their calls for democratic reform found support throughout Mexican society. The name of their movement evoked one of the peasant

---

of Mexico's; and 40.8 percent of Peru's. Ecuador and Bolivia are often considered to have a higher percentage of indigenous people. See Mary Lisbeth Gonzalez, "How Many Indigenous People?" in George Psacharopoulos and Harry Anthony Patrinos, eds., *Indigenous People and Poverty in Latin America: An Empirical Analysis* (Washington, D.C.: World Bank, 1994).

heroes of the Mexican Revolution, Emiliano Zapata. They declared that they were not Marxist, and that they were not interested in taking power.

Although the EZLN's proposals and ideology were novel in some respects, other elements of the situation in Chiapas were more familiar. Chiapas is a remote area with a large indigenous population. It is dominated by regional political bosses, and handicapped by an agrarian system that features unequal land tenure, sharecroppers, and landless peasants. In addition, the region is burdened by a large population of migrant workers from all over Mexico who settled newly cleared lands in the Lacandona Jungle. In these respects, Chiapas resembles guerrilla zones in Peru and Colombia.

The Zapatistas proved to be adept at mobilizing support from indigenous groups, international human rights organizations, and other nongovernmental organizations in North and South America and Europe. They were among the first insurrectionary movements to make widespread use of the Internet.[46] Under the glare of world attention, the Mexican government moved from confrontation to negotiations after twelve days of fighting.

The first round of negotiations between government and Zapatistas was mediated by the local Catholic Church. In these talks, the EZLN further defined themselves. Their main demand was for free and democratic elections, arguing that "democracy is a fundamental right of all indigenous and non-indigenous people." They called for new elections in the state of Chiapas, claiming that widespread fraud had made earlier efforts illegitimate. Other demands focused on cultural rights, including ending illiteracy in the indigenous communities, mandatory instruction in indigenous languages, and indigenous tribunals of justice designed to comply with local customs and traditions.[47]

After the fighting ended in a cease-fire, the EZLN acted more like a social movement than an armed militia. Its demands for democracy resonated with nation-wide frustration over the one-party system that has dominated Mexican politics since the 1930s. The EZLN's promotion of indigenous rights found support in indigenous communities throughout Mexico and, indeed, throughout Latin America.

Negotiations between the government and Zapatistas made little progress in 1994. Although the government launched a short counteroffensive in early 1995, for the most part the cease-fire has endured. More

---

46. Deedee Halleck, "Zapatistas On-Line," *NACLA Report on the Americas*, Vol. 28, No. 2 (September/October 1994), pp. 30–32.

47. *Zapatistas: Documents of the New Mexican Revolution, December 31, 1993–June 12, 1994* (New York, Autonomeida, 1994), pp. 238–243.

importantly, through their uprising, the Zapatistas effectively inserted themselves into national politics: they reshaped the political agenda, further eroded the government's legitimacy, and challenged the prevailing conception of representative democracy by emphasizing collective cultural and ethnic rights.

Mexico is not the only country in Latin America where the secular conception of the modern state has come under attack. Twice in the early 1990s, the indigenous population in Ecuador brought the government and economy to a standstill through massive strikes and blockades of major roads, stopping all transport and communication. Both times, the indigenous movement won major concessions on land, language, and political autonomy, although it failed to have the constitution amended to recognize Ecuador as a "multinational" state. Since the indigenous population in Ecuador is not geographically concentrated but interspersed with European, African, and mixed-raced populations throughout the country, the indigenous movement is not demanding geographical autonomy; rather, autonomy is conceived of in cultural and political terms.

Similar indigenous protests have occurred in Colombia and Bolivia. In Colombia, which has a much smaller indigenous population scattered throughout the country, the indigenous movement won special concessions in the new constitution in 1991. A special national voting district was created, guaranteeing a minimum of two indigenous seats in the Senate. Two years later, another special district was created for the African-Colombian communities.

The confrontation over the definition of the nation represents a major clash of ideas. Arms have been used, during the EZLN uprising, for example, but for most indigenous groups, arms remain symbolic. These are not groups with large stockpiles of sophisticated arms. In societies in which the dominant racial grouping is *mestizo* or "mixed blood," where the majority of the population carries some combination of European, indigenous, and African blood, there is no evidence that the emerging identity-based movements have led or will lead to "ethnic cleansing." However, these conflicts have the potential to become violent if the members of ethnic and indigenous communities remain second-class citizens, excluded from the national polity.

NEW RESOURCE BASES IN COLOMBIA AND PERU. In Guatemala, guerrillas successfully transformed their rebellion into an indigenous movement. In Colombia and Peru, guerrillas followed a different path into the 1990s.

Untethered from Soviet and Cuban support in the early 1990s, Colombian guerrillas turned to criminal activities to finance their war. This has become a key component of their insurgency, vastly amplifying practices that were always a part of the Colombian guerrilla experience. By the 1990s, Colombian guerrillas routinely engaged in kidnaping, extortion, burglary, and other criminal activities, blurring the distinction between insurgency and crime.

This trend has been facilitated by the development of the Andean region as the principal exporter of coca and coca's end product, cocaine. When demand sharply increased in the 1980s, the economies of the Andean nations — particularly Colombia, Peru, and Bolivia — were transformed. In Bolivia, which principally exports coca and coca paste to Colombia for processing into cocaine, the export boom gave rise to strong peasant movements that came to depend on the coca trade. Although the situation has created continuous conflicts with the government, which is under great pressure from the United States to repress the coca trade, the situation did not engender armed conflict. For the most part, disputes have been settled peacefully as both the government and the peasant unions have responded to competing national and international pressures. This was not the case in Peru and Colombia, which already had existing armed insurgencies. In these countries, the illegal commodity export booms were to completely reshape the dynamics of the armed conflict. Peru, like Bolivia, was integrated into the regional economy as a source of coca production. Colombia produced both coca and cocaine. In Peru, the coca trade helped sustain Sendero Luminoso. In Colombia, drug wealth benefited not only the guerrillas, but illegal armed groups associated with landowners, political bosses, and drug traffickers.

The Colombian guerrillas, particularly the FARC, became the principal authorities in some of the drug-producing regions of Caqueta, Guaviare, Putumayo, and elsewhere in the northern Amazon basin. Later, FARC troops took control of the opium-growing zones in the Central Andean highlands. This gave the FARC unprecedented sources of wealth, and allowed it to greatly expand its military activities in the early 1990s. It enabled the FARC to recruit and draw support from peasant coca and opium-poppy producers numbering in the hundreds of thousands.

Sendero Luminoso in Peru developed a similar relationship with peasant coca cultivators in the 1980s, particularly in the Upper Huallaga Valley.[48] In the 1990s, the main area of operations of Sendero Rojo is in the Upper and Central Huallaga, and in newer coca-producing zones along the Ene River.

Peasants in the drug cultivation zones of Colombia and Peru are usually internal migrants desperate for work. The drug trade has pro-

48. José E. Gonzales, "Guerrillas and Coca in the Upper Huallaga Valley," in Palmer, *Shining Path of Peru*.

vided an economic outlet: it has led to a large migration of workers and peasants into remote coca-producing zones, creating new boom towns beyond the effective control of the state.[49] Guerrillas have benefited from these dynamics: large numbers of people have moved into illegal activities in zones under their control.

The coca cultivators and their guerrilla patrons should not be confused with the "drug cartels," the large multinational organizations that refine the coca leaf and paste into cocaine and smuggle drugs into world markets. Most of the profits of the drug trade have gone into the hands of the cartels, not the guerrillas and peasant cultivators. These cartels operate, by definition, on the margins of the law. In Colombia, the Medellin cartel in the 1980s and the Cali cartel in the 1990s rose to challenge the state. These illegal multinational enterprises have invested in private armies which protect their interests and further their political influence.

The Colombian state in the 1990s is therefore faced with multiple armed challengers. The bipolar conflict between right and left, between the state and its guerrilla challengers, has become a multipolar conflict among the army, guerrillas, drug traffickers, and an array of paramilitary groups loyal to different masters. In Colombia, the state has at times been inclined to negotiate with the guerrillas. At other times, it has focused on coming to terms with the cartels.

As the distinction between traditional insurgencies and armed racketeering became blurred, efforts to negotiate peaceful settlements to guerrilla wars became considerably more complex. It is evident that negotiating a peace with the guerrillas will entail a commitment by the insurgents to withdraw from the drug trade. It will also entail a state commitment to finding an alternative form of subsistence for peasants whose livelihood depends on coca and poppy cultivation. These are not impossible goals, and are probably more feasible and less costly than dismantling the drug cartels. However, negotiating peace with the guerrillas without ending the drug trade would leave large numbers of growers and producers armed and beyond the control of the state.

This problem is not limited to Colombia. Drug-related violence has influenced politics in many Latin American nations, especially Mexico. In other countries, such as Brazil and Venezuela, drug-related and social violence are beginning to overwhelm the traditional institutions of

---

49. Catherine M. Conaghan and James M. Malloy, *Unsettling Statecraft: Democracy and Neoliberalism in the Central Andes* (Pittsburgh, Penn.: University of Pittsburgh Press, 1994), pp. 197–198.

authority. These challenges represent the gravest threat to security and stability in Latin America.

NEW MILITARY MISSIONS

The ground rules for outside intervention in Latin America have been altered quite dramatically by the end of the Cold War. There are now three rationales for military intervention in the internal affairs of another country: combating drug trafficking, the single most important military issue in the hemisphere; promoting democracy; and peacekeeping. The use of troops in promoting democracy and peacekeeping has already been examined. For the United States and other nations in the Caribbean and Latin America, combating drug trafficking has become the central military mission in the region.

Prior to 1989, the U.S. Department of Defense opposed using U.S. soldiers and matériel in drug enforcement operations. However, as Central America receded as a military concern, and in the face of declining budgets and diminished global missions, Secretary of Defense Richard Cheney decided in 1989 to involve the U.S. military in the war on drugs. Combating drug trafficking became the principal focus of U.S. military activities in the hemisphere.

The U.S. Southern Command in Panama became a frontline base in the post–Cold War world. In 1989, the Andean nations replaced Central America as the largest recipients of U.S. military aid in the region. President Bush announced an Andean strategy against drug trafficking that would initially channel $439 million to Colombia, Peru, and Bolivia. At the same time, U.S. military personnel were sent to the region: U.S. troops built and manned radar complexes in the jungles and along the coasts of Colombia; the U.S. Drug Enforcement Agency built a base in the Upper Huallaga Valley in Peru; U.S. Army specialists trained Andean soldiers and assisted in the fight against guerrillas based in drug cultivation zones.[50]

By fighting drug trafficking in countries with large guerrilla insurgencies, the United States once again became involved in counterinsurgency activities. After 1989, all U.S. military assistance to the Andes was dedicated to anti-narcotics missions; no funds were earmarked for pre-existing counterinsurgency programs. Once again, this time in Colombia and Peru, the United States became assigned to supporting local militaries in counterinsurgency wars. Even as the United States was trying to develop

---

50. Bagley, "Myths of Militarization."

civilian rule and respect for human rights in Latin America, U.S. drug enforcement policy in the Andean Region led Washington to strengthen relations with militaries which had some of the worse human rights records in the world.[51] Moreover, there was increasing evidence that military involvement in the drug wars was corrupting the military units assigned to these operations.[52] In Peru, the military was a principal supporter of President Fujimori's temporary suspension of democratic rule.

By the mid-1990s, the United States was engaged in anti-narcotics operations throughout Central America and the Caribbean. Mexico emerged as a major channel for Andean narcotics, and Mexican drug cartels became as formidable as their Colombian counterparts. The United States has consequently pressed the Mexican military into service in the drug war.

The results of the drug war have been meager. After half a decade of combating drug trafficking, there has been no decrease in the flow of cocaine from the Andean region.[53] In fact, the traffickers have also begun to export heroin, effectively diversifying their product line and market. The drug wars have, once again, reproduced the old tension between Latin America's desire for more multilateral decision-making and U.S. unilateralism. The drug war has generated more instability than stability.

Conclusions

The end of the Cold War made possible negotiated ends to entrenched guerrillas wars in Central America. Along the way, the international community gained valuable experience in ending civil wars. New multi-lateral instruments were created and tested; international organizations became involved in the domestic politics of several internally divided nations in ways that had no precedent in Latin America. At the same time, the international community was caught off balance by the persistence of older insurgencies and the emergence of new forms of violence in the region.

The experience accumulated in Central America, when adjusted to specific national conditions, will undoubtedly prove useful in settling other insurgent conflicts in the region. Ideas about restructuring political systems and converting armed conflicts into democratic competitions can

---

51. Americas Watch, *In Desperate Straits: Human Rights in Peru after a Decade of Democracy and Insurgency* (New York: Americas Watch Report, 1990).

52. WOLA, *Clear and Present Danger: The U.S. Military and the War on Drugs in the Andes* (Washington, D.C.: WOLA, 1991).

53. Comisión Andina de Juristas (CAJ), *Drogas y Control Penal en los Andes* (Lima: CAJ, 1994).

be effectively applied in other places. The prime candidates in Latin America are Colombia, Guatemala, Mexico, and Peru.

However, the multifunctional peace missions that worked within the framework of developing more democratic political regimes will be less effective in confronting the types of warfare waged by drug cartels and guerrilla crime syndicates. The drug trade involves the global movement of arms, drugs, goods, money, and people, but drug wars are mostly confined to domestic settings: Mexican drug lords assassinate Mexican officials; Colombian cartel leaders assassinate Colombian officials; private armies linked to the Cali cartel fight Colombian guerrillas over territory and politics. Overcoming the international drug trade and the violent national conflicts they foster will require a concerted effort at both the international and national level. In these particular conflicts, the operative ideas are not democracy and participation; they are justice and control.

LESSONS DRAWN FROM CENTRAL AMERICA

Democratic formulas proved to be powerful conflict-resolution tools in Central America. Their success was facilitated by a strong regional commitment to democracy. Negotiations also required the endorsement of the United States. However, once that support was forthcoming, a variety of measures and initiatives made peace more likely.

First, outside mediation played an important role in the peace process. Over several years, the outlines of a realizable peace in Central America took shape, involving commitments to democracy and national reconciliation. The acceptance of "international verification" (the preferred Latin American term) of the peace accords, or, in the case of El Salvador, of multifunctional peace operations, was critical in furthering the negotiations. Most participants concur that, left on their own, the government and the guerrilla negotiators would not have reached a final settlement.

Second, outside mediation was best undertaken by the United Nations. The Contadora and Central American initiatives laid the groundwork for peace in Central America, but local actors were not sufficiently disinterested to provide the necessary mediation or to exert pressure and interject ideas. The United Nations, which was seen as more impartial, was in a better position to move the negotiations forward in these respects.

Third, moving from a broad framework of regional principles to specific peace accords involved not only the resources of international organizations, but a sophisticated appraisal of national situations, the causes of conflict, and a vision of the future. This involved hard bargaining and considerable compromise, and would not have been possible without a major evolution in the political orientations of the combatants themselves. In El Salvador, the peace settlement focused on issues such as security, justice, democratic participation, and land. The settlement did not lead to the achievement of the great social goals originally proposed by leftist combatants. Rather, it established the framework for the construction of a democratic society. Both the right and the left came to accept this framework. However, in Nicaragua — with the exception of the agreements for the 1990 elections and the demobilization of the Contras — most of these issues were not specifically addressed after Esquipulas II. As a result, disputes continued to fester in each of these areas, particularly over the size of the military, national reconstruction, justice, and land for ex-combatants. In different national contexts, other reforms may be necessary. In Guatemala, the combatants have already defined the issues of indigenous rights and the return of refugees. These agreements are designed to be part of a larger package of democratization and structural reforms, similar to those negotiated in El Salvador.

As Guatemala slowly moves forward under UN mediation, the possibility of other negotiated settlements with armed and unarmed indigenous communities becomes more possible. It requires placing broader references to indigenous rights on to the regional agenda for democracy. How the conflicts in Guatemala and Mexico are resolved will likely shape the future regional and international responses to internal conflict in the hemisphere.

PROSPECTS FOR THE FUTURE

Latin America is now more democratic than it has ever been, but parts of the region will continue to be mired in conflict. The regional consensus on promoting democracy is still restricted to a formal conception of elections and disruptions of constitutional authority. As such, when the inter-American community pressured for the restoration of democratic governance in Guatemala and Peru in the early 1990s, its actions did nothing to address underlying problems of excess military authority, human rights violations and the exclusion of large sectors of the population from national life. Yet these are the principal sources of current and future conflicts and violence.

Moreover, the United Nations and the Organization of American States need to apply their considerable experience in conflict resolution to the issues of drug trafficking and organized crime. This will require the United States, which continues to control the agenda, to change its approach. The United States unilaterally fostered the militarization of the drug war; U.S. allies had little choice but to cooperate.[54] The United States

---

54. Ibid.

continues to use the levers of aid and trade to promote its own view of how these problems should be addressed.

The military approach, however, has failed to reduce the export of drugs from Latin America. It has failed to stem the flow of money and arms. When military force has been used at the national level, it has inflamed the problem: military action plays into the hands of guerrilla movements that find support among the coca and opium poppy–producing peasants. In some cases, U.S. policy has forced governments to confront indigenous populations resident in cultivation zones.

If the drug trafficking problem is to be addressed effectively, it needs to be reconceptualized. In the consuming nations, drug trafficking is a social problem; in Latin America, it is an economic and political issue involving violent criminal organizations, and displaced peasants and industrial workers drawn into the most lucrative area of the non-regulated economy. Defining drug trafficking as a simple national security issue has led to the indiscriminate use of force and counterproductive military strategies.

This problem must be confronted multinationally. No single country, not even the United States, has the resources or means to address the global dimensions and political ramifications of the drug trade. The United Nations and the Organization of American States could play a much greater role in combating drug trafficking. These multilateral organizations are better equipped to address the international dimensions of the problem, and to develop and implement a non-military approach to the problem. Drug-consuming nations need to develop effective treatment and rehabilitation programs. In producing nations, the emphasis should be on economic development and strengthened judicial systems. Police and intelligence operations need to be better coordinated at a multilateral level. To the extent that the drug trade has provided resources to guerrillas and private armies, a concerted international approach to stem the global commerce in narcotics will contribute to the diminution of these internal conflicts. In the context of such a demilitarized anti-drug strategy, the international community together with the region's governments could more effectively promote a negotiated settlement to the remaining guerrillas wars in the Andes, particularly in Colombia.

The nations of the hemisphere should build on the network of resources already in place in the inter-American and international systems. The peace operations in Central America and Haiti demonstrate that multilateral action in the Western hemisphere can be effective when there is a will among the member states to define political norms and conditions for peace — and to act.

Part II
International Engagement:
Instruments and Actors

Chapter 9

Political Accommodation and the Prevention of Secessionist Violence

Alicia Levine

The drive for self-determination is among the most pervasive and powerful forces in contemporary international politics. Ethnic groups in some seventy countries seek more political autonomy or states of their own.[1] Secessionist struggles, moreover, are often violent, as we have seen in Azerbaijan, Bangladesh, Ethiopia, India, Moldova, Spain, Sri Lanka, Turkey, the former Yugoslavia, and elsewhere. In some cases, however, political divorces have been reached through largely peaceful means. The Baltic states seceded from the former Soviet Union and Slovenia from Yugoslavia with comparatively little bloodshed. The Czech-Slovak divorce was peaceful. In still other cases — Belgium, for example — ethnic groups have decided to continue to live together under the auspices of a single state.

In this chapter, I first identify the conditions under which ethnic groups are most likely to make secessionist demands.[2] Ethnic geography is an obvious but extremely important factor: ethnic groups that are concentrated in specific regions are more prone to secessionist impulses than those scattered throughout a country. When groups are regionally concentrated, ethnic identities are strong, the costs of organizing politi-

The author would like to thank Matthew Evangelista, John Matthews, and John Mearsheimer for their helpful comments.

1. For a survey of self-determination movements, see the Appendix in Morton H. Halperin and David J. Scheffer, *Self-Determination in the New World Order* (Washington, D.C.: Carnegie Endowment for International Peace, 1992).

2. This chapter will focus on the secessionist demands of ethnic groups in multi-ethnic states. Secessionist movements, with few exceptions, define themselves in ethnic terms. Exceptions include some Siberian regions in Russia, which have economic motivations for seceding, the Lombard League in Italy, and the Southern states in the U.S. Civil War.

cally are comparatively low, and secession is more likely to be seen as feasible. Not all regionally concentrated groups seek states of their own, however. Political and economic discrimination against ethnic minorities plays a key role in leading groups to prefer self-government over existing arrangements. Broad institutional changes in a state's political and economic affairs can galvanize ethnic grievances and fuel separatist demands: ethnic groups are often blamed for political and economic setbacks and, in times of turmoil, they are more likely to have opportunities to seek self-rule.

Second, I identify the conditions that are most likely to lead to secessionist violence. The most volatile situations occur when central authorities fear that secession in one part of the country will lead to secessionist movements elsewhere, perhaps leading eventually to the collapse of the state; when separatist regions contain minority groups that will not accept new, local landlords; and when secessionist regions are vital to the security or prosperity of the states in question. Under these conditions, demands for regional autonomy and statehood generally lead to war. Unfortunately, these demographic conditions and security concerns are not easily changed; they are not amenable to easy political solutions. Other important factors — a lack of democratic institutions and external interference — are more amenable to control. External support for separatist regions generally makes violence more likely, conflicts more intense, and compromise more difficult. Curtailing third-party support for opposing parties, therefore, is one of the keys to controlling the level of violence in secessionist struggles.

Third, I develop concrete policy recommendations to address the problems posed by secessionist demands and secessionist conflicts. This is complicated because international actors have multiple and conflicting values with respect to these issues. On the one hand, they hope to promote political and economic justice for ethnic minorities, and they have a long-standing commitment to the principle of self-determination. On the other hand, policymakers value political stability and the sanctity of political borders. The best way around this dilemma is to devise ways for different ethnic groups to live together peacefully under the auspices of a single state. This is difficult, but not impossible. More widespread adoption of federalist arrangements would give regionally based groups more control over their own affairs. Proportional representation would give ethnic groups, whether they are regionally based or scattered throughout the territory of a state, more control over political and economic institutions and would make central authorities more responsive to minority concerns. Minority rights and equal treatment of all citizens should be enshrined as basic principles of good governance. Civic conceptions of nationalism should be promoted. Economic opportunities and prosperity should be equalized across ethnic groups. If these political and economic mechanisms fail and ethnic groups demand more in the way of self-determination, international powers should prevent neighboring states from giving military and economic support to warring parties. This will help keep escalation under control and make political settlements easier to reach.

What Causes Secessionist Demands?

Approximately 160 of the 180 or so states in the international system are ethnically heterogeneous, in the sense that ethnic minorities constitute more than five percent of the population.[3] But, as noted earlier, groups clamor for self-rule in some 70 countries; in the other 90, they do not.

Which groups are most likely to pursue secessionist agendas? Secessionist movements are most likely to develop when certain demographic, political, and economic conditions exist. This section delineates these conditions and discusses their interaction.

DEMOGRAPHIC CONDITIONS

Secessionist impulses are conditioned to a very great degree by ethnic geography — whether ethnic groups are concentrated in specific regions or scattered throughout the country. Secessionist demands are more likely to arise when ethnic groups are geographically concentrated. There are three reasons for this.

First, when an ethnic group is concentrated in a particular region of a state, ethnic identity is reinforced. When members of an ethnic group live together, they interact with other members of the group on a regular basis. They often speak the same language at work, home, and social events. Distinctions between members of the group and other groups — between "us" and "them" — intensify over time.

Second, secession is more likely to be seen as a feasible goal when members of an ethnic group are concentrated in one region of a state. Organizing political and military opposition to the central government is easier when an ethnic group is regionally concentrated. The costs of organizing against the central government are lower: resources and networks of supporters are easier to mobilize. If the region is populated mainly with members of one ethnic group, separatist movements will

---

3. See David Welsh, "Domestic Politics and Ethnic Conflict," in Michael E. Brown, ed., *Ethnic Conflict and International Security* (Princeton, N.J.: Princeton University Press, 1993), p. 45.

have little internal opposition to independence and will able to present a formidable challenge to the central government. Under these conditions, central governments find it both difficult and costly to neutralize secessionist challenges.

Third, minorities that are geographically concentrated are more likely to have political institutions of their own to draw on. Regions, provinces, and republics organize political activities along geographic lines; geographically concentrated ethnic groups can use these institutions to coordinate their political activities and mobilize their resources.[4] The French minority in Quebec can therefore challenge the Canadian state more effectively than the French minority in Newfoundland.

Most cases of secession based on ethnic claims are found in places where ethnic groups are concentrated in specific regions. For example, Czechoslovakia broke apart along administrative lines which coincided with ethnic divisions. Protestants lived throughout Ireland, but were concentrated in the north; only the north chose union with Britain in 1921. The Kurds have posed secessionist threats to Turkey, Iraq, and Syria because they are regionally concentrated in all three states. The Tamils of Sri Lanka are concentrated in the north and east, and hope for an independent state in this region. Geographically concentrated minorities have pressed for independence in many former Soviet and Yugoslav republics. Notably, the only secessionist threat posed by Russians in the Baltic states has been in the northeast corner of Estonia, where there is a large concentration of Russians.[5]

Conversely, when members of an ethnic group are scattered, secessionist demands are less likely to arise because ethnic ties are weaker and the probability of success is much lower. When an ethnic group is geographically scattered, organizing political and military resistance along regional or ethnic lines becomes very difficult if not impossible. The Roma of Central Europe do not pose secessionist threats to their host countries despite the fact that they are the objects of often-intense discrimination. The Catholics of Northern Ireland believe they have suffered under Protestant political rule, but because they are scattered throughout six counties, they have never demanded that one county secede from the rest. African-Americans are scattered throughout the United States; their agenda emphasizes civil rights and economic opportunities, not territorial autonomy.

---

4. Benedict Anderson, *Imagined Communities* (London: Verso, 1983) shows how institutions can create political and national identity.

5. See Philip Hanson, "Estonia's Narva Problem, Narva's Estonian Problem," *RFE/RL Research Report*, Vol. 2, No. 18 (April 30, 1993), pp. 17–23.

Secession remains an overwhelmingly ethnically defined enterprise.[6] Ethnic groups which are geographically concentrated and live in areas with regionally defined institutions are more likely to seek self-rule than groups which are scattered. However, the fact that secession is feasible does not mean it is probable.

POLITICAL CONDITIONS

Ethnic differences, by themselves, do not always generate secessionist movements. Nor does regional concentration lead inexorably to desires for self-government.

Problems in multiethnic states begin when one group dominates others. Unfortunately, discrimination based on ethnicity is often a way of life in multiethnic entities. In many cases, one ethnic group simply rules, as Russians and Serbs did in the former Soviet Union and the former Yugoslavia, respectively. In cases such as these, the ruling group is over-represented in every branch of the government: the executive, the legis-lature, the judiciary, the bureaucracy, the military, and the police. The language of the dominant group is used in all aspects of life, including governmental activities, economic affairs, and education. Other ethnic groups naturally resent the political and economic advantages members of the dominant group enjoy.

The European powers ruled their colonial empires by elevating some ethnic groups above all others.[7] This practice created ethnic tensions which, in the post-colonial era, have blossomed into secessionist move-ments. For example, by the end of British rule in Ceylon (Sri Lanka), the minority Tamil population was over-represented in the civil service and the professions. The majority Sinhalese deeply resented the fact that Tamils had better political and economic opportunities and, in the post-colonial period, passed a myriad of laws injurious to Tamils. Sinhalese governments restricted Tamil entry into the professions and educational institutions, made Sinhala the official state language, and encouraged Sinhalese to move to Tamil areas.[8] In response, the Tamils, by the late 1970s, demanded an independent state in the northern and eastern prov-inces of the country.

Moscow pursued similar policies in the republics of the former Soviet

---

6. For exceptions to the rule, see note 2.

7. See Donald Horowitz, *Ethnic Groups in Conflict* (Berkeley: University of California Press, 1985), pp. 149–184, 445–454.

8. See Sumit Ganguly, "Ethno-religious Conflict in South Asia," *Survival*, Vol. 35, No. 2 (Summer 1993), pp. 88–109; Marshall R. Singer, "Sri Lanka's Tamil-Sinhalese

Union, and these policies also fueled secessionist impulses. Moscow's explicit policy was to favor the titular nationality in each republic for education slots, factory jobs, and administrative posts in order to create an indigenous elite.[9] The result was that these titular nationalities were over-represented in party and state posts, as well as in the educational system and in the professions.[10] Other ethnic groups within the republics were denied comparable opportunities. Many of these minority groups were consequently eager to secede from their republics and become union-republics or autonomous republics. This would have elevated their status within the Soviet Union, and allowed the new titular nationality to benefit from Moscow's affirmative action policies. Funds and higher levels of investment from Moscow would have followed. For these reasons, Moscow was besieged with requests for regional autonomy from within the fifteen republics by the 1980s.

Much of the minority nationalism that developed in the republics and the successor states to the Soviet Union can best be understood in this light. For example, the Armenians of Nagorno-Karabakh wanted to join Armenia because Soviet Azerbaijan discriminated against them; the Armenians claimed that Baku prevented them from attaining higher education, blocked their attempts to travel to Armenia in order to obtain university training, and made insufficient investment in the region. Union with Armenia would end discrimination by the Azeris, and allow Armenians in Nagorno-Karabakh to enjoy more educational and economic opportunities.[11] South Ossetians and Abkhazis voiced similar complaints against Georgia; the former have tried to join the North Ossetians in the Russian federation, and the latter have demanded and fought for independence. The Gagauz minority in Moldova protested against discrimination in hiring and education during Soviet rule and demanded autonomy from Moldova after independence. Discriminatory Soviet

---

Ethnic Conflict: Alternative Solutions," *Asian Survey*, Vol. 32, No. 8 (August 1992), pp. 712–722; Amita Shastri, "Sri Lanka's Provincial Council System," *Asian Survey*, Vol. 32, No. 8 (August 1992), pp. 723–743.

9. Philip G. Roeder, "Soviet Federalism and Ethnic Mobilization," *World Politics*, Vol. 43, No. 2 (January 1991), pp. 202–222; Alexander Motyl, "The Sobering of Gorbachev: Nationality, Restructuring and the West," in Rachel Denber, ed., *The Soviet Nationality Reader: The Disintegration in Context* (Boulder, Colo.: Westview, 1992), pp. 576–578; David D. Laitin, "The National Uprisings in the Soviet Union," *World Politics*, Vol. 44, No. 1 (October 1991), pp. 139–177; Rasma Karklins, *Ethnic Relations in the USSR* (Boston: Allen and Unwin, 1968), pp. 142, 146, 219.

10. Roeder, "Soviet Federalism," pp. 204–205, 207–208, 212, 217.

11. Ibid., pp. 220–221.

policies have returned to haunt the successor states: many regions that grumbled in the Soviet era have mounted secessionist challenges against the new authorities.

Discrimination is often at the heart of secessionist impulses. It creates powerful incentives to change the status quo and can lead to demands for independent states. This is even more likely when ethnic minorities are geographically concentrated.

ECONOMIC CONDITIONS

Economic differences between regions often play key roles in the development of secessionist movements.[12] For example, some regions in a country might have more economic opportunities than others due to the presence of raw materials or the development of more advanced industry. Those who live in less-advantaged regions naturally resent their lack of economic opportunities. This can strain relations within states.

Paradoxically, economic concerns can lead both impoverished areas and wealthy regions to develop secessionist movements. Poor regions often point to inept or detrimental governmental policies as the causes of their economic plights, while wealthy regions resent subsidizing their poorer counterparts.

The breakup of Czechoslovakia illustrates the political consequences of uneven economic prospects. Before World War II, Bohemia and Moravia were industrializing, while Slovakia's economy was based on agriculture. Industry was first introduced to Slovakia after the war, and it was of the standard Soviet variety: large industrial plants, much of it geared to military production, supported entire towns and villages. When Soviet rule ended in 1989, Slovakia inherited a military industry that could not compete on the international market. Prague compounded the problem in 1990 when it decided to limit arms exports. This fueled resentment in Slovakia, where most of the nation's twenty-eight arms factories were located. More generally, Slovakian leaders believed that a rapid transition to a market economy, which Czech leaders favored, would benefit Czech regions and hit Slovakia hard. By the time of the June 1992 elections, evidence was accumulating that this was indeed happening. Unemployment in Slovakia was three times that in Moravia

---

12. See Horowitz, *Ethnic Groups in Conflict*, pp. 165–195, 229–288; Peter Gourevitch, "The Reemergence of 'Peripheral Nationalisms': Some Comparative Speculations on the Spatial Distribution of Political Leadership and Economic Growth," *Comparative Studies in History and Society*, Vol. 21, No. 3 (July 1979); Joseph Rudolph and Robert Thomson, "Ethnoterritorial Movements and the Policy Process: Accommodating Nationalist Demands in the Developed World," *Comparative Politics*, Vol. 17, No. 2 (April 1985); Roeder, "Soviet Federalism," pp. 196–232.

and Bohemia, and Western investment was flowing almost exclusively to Czech areas.[13] Slovakian leaders concluded that the pace of economic reform had to be slowed, and that they could do better economically on their own.

Similarly, Bangladesh's (East Pakistan's) secession from Pakistan was fueled by its deteriorating economic situation. Islamabad spent more on education, employment, and the civil service in the West than it did in the East, despite the fact that most of the population (fifty-six percent) lived in the East. In 1960, the West's per capita income was thirty-two percent higher than the East's; by 1970, the gap had grown to sixty-two percent.[14] This was a political time bomb. When Pakistan reverted to civilian rule in 1970, East Pakistan pushed for a loose federal system that would have given it greater control over its own economic affairs. Islamabad's refusal set in motion the events that led to Bangladesh's secession.

Regional economic differences also affect views in comparatively wealthy areas. A region which is economically robust in comparison to others might want to secede in order to discontinue support of its poorer counterparts. For example, Slovenia, with a per capita income three times higher than Serbia's, was the wealthiest of the Yugoslav republics.[15] If it had stayed in Yugoslavia, Slovenia would have had to subsidize other republics when market reforms were undertaken. Similarly, Czech regions had good reasons for appreciating Slovakia's demand for independence. Many Czechs felt that subsidizing Slovakia would drain the Czech economy. In addition, the Slovaks used their veto power in parliament to block the swift market reforms preferred by the Czechs. Czech leaders felt that their regions could more readily attract Western investment and do a lot better economically without Slovakia.[16]

The collapse of the Soviet Union was in part propelled by the wealthier republics, which demanded economic decentralization and pushed

---

13. As of June 1992, only five percent of Western investment in Czechoslovakia went to Slovakia. See William E. Schmidt, "Election in Czechoslovakia Will Be a Test of Tensions," *New York Times*, June 3, 1992, p. A3; John Tagliabue, "Arms Exports Bring Profits and Pain To Czechs and Especially to Slovaks," *New York Times*, February 19, 1992, p. A5.

14. Lee C. Buchheit, *Secession: The Legitimacy of Self-Determination* (New Haven, Conn.: Yale University Press, 1978), pp. 201–205.

15. Bogomil Ferfila, "Yugoslavia: Confederation or Disintegration?" *Problems of Communism*, Vol. 40 (July–August 1991), pp. 18–30.

16. Similarly, the development of oil fields off the coast of Scotland has strengthened the appeal of the Scottish nationalist movement. See William E. Schmidt, "With a New Fervor, the Scots Eye Independence," *New York Times*, March 3, 1992, p. A4.

nationalist agendas.[17] The Soviet system, in its drive for economic equality, transferred funds from the more developed to the less developed republics. By 1989, the five Central Asian republics were the only republics permitted to retain one hundred percent of the tax revenue collected within their borders. They also received subsidies from Moscow for education and industry. The wealthier republics subsidized these redistributive policies. The Baltic states, Armenia, and Ukraine were allowed to keep only fifty to seventy-five percent of the tax revenue they collected.[18] Not surprisingly, these redistributive policies created considerable resentment within the wealthier republics.

People in resource-rich regions also often conclude that they would be better off on their own. For example, the Katanga province of the Belgian Congo was extremely wealthy due to rich mineral deposits. Katanga had only thirteen percent of the Congo's total population, but it provided Belgium with sixty percent of the Congo's revenue. In return, however, Katanga received only twenty percent of the expenditures allocated for the colony.[19] After decolonization in 1960, Katangan leaders declared independence from Zaire, thinking that the province would be more prosperous on its own.

Raw materials are, in the mid-1990s, fueling separatist movements within the Russian federation. Control over natural resources can lead to enormous profits, now that the command economy is being replaced by a market-based one. As a result, there have been many struggles between Moscow and the regions over resource issues. This has been compounded by the fact that property rights remain uncodified in the Russian legal system. In addition, regions with exportable raw materials would like to make a rapid transition to a market-based economy, while industrial regions would prefer to go much more slowly; resource-rich regions prefer free trade, while industrial regions would like to see state subsidies continue. In many cases, these preferences have developed into struggles between Moscow and regional leaders for control over resources and the direction of economic policy.[20]

---

17. Roeder, "Soviet Federalism"; Mark Beissinger, "Demise of an Empire-State," in Crawford Young, ed., *The Rising Tide of Cultural Pluralism: The Nation-State at Bay?* (Madison: University of Wisconsin Press, 1993), p. 99.

18. Roeder, "Soviet Federalism," pp. 212–219.

19. Horowitz, *Ethnic Groups in Conflict*, pp. 255–288; Buchheit, *Secession*, p. 142.

20. See Jessica Eve Stern, "Moscow Meltdown: Can Russia Survive?" *International Security*, Vol. 18, No. 4 (Spring 1994), pp. 40–65, esp. pp. 44–50; Vera Tolz, "Regionalism in Russia: The Case of Siberia," *RFE/RL Research Report*, Vol. 2, No. 9 (February 26, 1993), pp. 1–9; and Matthew Evangelista's chapter in this volume.

For example, a struggle over economic resources is an important component of the dispute between Russia and Chechnya. Chechnya contains rich oil deposits, and strategic pipelines from the Caspian Sea to the Black Sea pass through its territory.[21] It therefore has compelling economic reasons, as well as ethnic and historical motivations, for seeking independence.

Economic interests are the driving forces behind the autonomy claims of mineral-rich Tatarstan and Siberia. Twenty-five percent of Russia's oil, coal, and copper deposits are in Tatarstan, whose gross national product is greater than those of Armenia, Estonia, Latvia, Lithuania, Moldova, Tajikistan, and Turkmenistan.[22] Tatarstan has already demanded the right to introduce its own currency and collect taxes, and it has passed laws prohibiting its citizens from performing military service outside of the region. Siberia contains ninety-nine percent of Russia's diamond deposits and a significant portion of its gold deposits. Siberia's conflicts with Moscow are struggles over ownership rights to these deposits. Secessionist movements are often galvanized when distributional policies are perceived as unfair and when political turmoil leads regional leaders to believe that they can take control over the resources found on their territories.

These kinds of economic considerations often drive autonomy and independence movements. Not surprisingly, political and economic discrimination often go hand in hand: groups that are barred from political participation, for example, are also apt to be subjected to economic deprivations of various kinds. This, of course, creates tremendous resentment against central authorities. In cases such as these, infusions of governmental funds might not be sufficient to solve the problem; political reforms of a more fundamental nature might be needed.

INSTITUTIONAL CHANGES

These ethnic, political, and economic factors are important background conditions which determine whether a region is a probable candidate for secession. Broad institutional changes — such as the collapse of colonial rule, the onset of democratization, the collapse of a federal state, or the transition to a market economy — are often the triggering mechanisms

---

21. See Jack F. Matlock, "The Chechen Tragedy," *New York Review of Books*, pp. 3–6; U.S. Central Intelligence Agency, "Instability and Pipelines in the Caucasus Region," Map No. 734957 2-95 (R00397).

22. Stern, "Moscow Meltdown," p. 62.

which convert political and economic grievances into actual demands for self-government.

Institutional changes alter the political and economic environment, and cause regional leaders to reassess the benefits of the status quo. First, institutional changes expose existing grievances and provide regional leaders with opportunities to voice their dissatisfaction. For example, after decolonization, mineral-rich Katanga took advantage of the weak post-colonial government to declare independence. In this case, decolonization did not create new interests; it simply permitted existing interests to be pursued at a lower cost. Similarly, when authoritarian regimes that discriminate against minority groups collapse, minority demands for special protection or autonomy often follow. For example, democratization permitted Bengalis in East Pakistan to protest Islamabad's rule.

Second, institutional changes can trigger independence movements by creating new interests. For instance, market reforms generally have different effects on regions with different kinds of industry. This was certainly the case in Czechoslovakia. Market reforms generally have great appeal to resource-rich regions: economic decentralization allows them to enter into contracts with foreign firms on their own, eliminating the central government as the middleman. Market reforms create new interests by making ownership the key to profit.

Similarly, the breakup of a political federation can create new political interests and independence movements.[23] For example, Yugoslavia was a delicately balanced, multiethnic federation in which the presidency rotated between republics. Before Croatia and Slovenia seceded in 1991, most Bosnians wanted to remain in Yugoslavia. After Croatia and Slovenia pulled out, however, life in a Serb-dominated Yugoslavia had little appeal for non-Serb Bosnians.[24]

Institutional changes often trigger movements for self-government. They provide opportunities to organize against central authorities, and they create new political and economic demands which cannot be met by existing political arrangements. Separatist movements often emerge in the midst of major political or economic upheavals.

---

23. I am indebted to Matthew Evangelista for pointing this out to me.

24. Misha Glenny, "Yugoslavia: The Great Fall," *New York Review of Books,* March 23, 1995, p. 58. In the 1990 Bosnian elections, no party ran on a platform calling for independence.

What Causes Secessionist Violence?

Violence is possible whenever multiethnic states break up. At a minimum, secession begets instability: different areas in a state are often so closely linked politically and economically that secession of a single region can disrupt the entire system. Moreover, important interests are always threatened by secessions. Powerful forces will consequently be inclined to use every instrument at their disposal to keep states together.

However, violence is more likely in some cases than others. First, demographic conditions are once again important. Violence is more likely if central authorities fear that secession in one part of the country will lead to secessionist activity elsewhere, leading to the eventual disintegration of the state. In cases such as these, central authorities have powerful incentives to react harshly whenever and wherever secessionism rears its head. Violence is also more likely if a secessionist region contains ethnic minorities opposed to new political arrangements. Second, violence is more likely if the separatist region is vital to the security or prosperity of the state in question. Central authorities are loath to give up control over regions that have great military or economic value. Third, secessionist disputes are more likely to become violent if the state in question lacks democratic institutions and traditions of civil discourse. Fourth and last, violence is more likely if neighboring states become involved. External interference, in the form of support for one or another of the opposing parties, makes escalation more likely and compromise more difficult.

Unfortunately, some important factors in the equation, particularly demographic conditions and security concerns, are hard to change. They do not lend themselves easily to political solutions. However, other factors, including democratic discourse and external interference, present more opportunities to those interested in preventing, managing, and resolving violent conflict.

DEMOGRAPHIC FACTORS

Demands for self-government often come in bunches. In the first half of the 1990s, for example, the Soviet Union, Yugoslavia, and Czechoslovakia have broken up, and some successor states have had to contend with secessionist movements of their own. This is no accident. Successful secessions can have powerful effects on people in other regions. They can also lead minority groups in new states to seek self-rule or affiliation with some other political entity.

Violence is likely, first of all, if central authorities fear that secession in one part of the country will have effects on and lead to secessionist campaigns in other parts of the country, or perhaps even throughout the country. The future of the state would then be in doubt. Central authorities who fear this prospect will be strongly inclined to react forcefully whenever a secessionist movement develops.[25]

In cases such as these, central governments often see little alternative to using military force. Granting more autonomy to a separatist region can be difficult from a constitutional standpoint and risky politically: other regions may then issue demands for more autonomy and new relationships with the central government. Instead of starting down this slippery slope, central authorities will be inclined to use military force when the first set of demands for autonomy or independence are made. They will hope to dampen centrifugal forces and deter other would-be secessionists from mobilizing.

Fears of secessionist chain reactions are naturally most pronounced in highly complex, multiethnic states. For example, since the collapse of the Soviet Union, Moscow has been deeply concerned about centrifugal tendencies within the Russian federation.[26] Central authorities fear that if even one region is allowed to leave the federation, nothing will stop others from following suit. Given that the federation consists of eighty-nine administrative-territorial units, including twenty-one ethnic republics (all of which have adopted declarations of sovereignty), and forty-nine provinces, Russia could unravel. The problem is compounded by the fact that President Boris Yeltsin and the parliament competed for support in 1992 and 1993 by promising more autonomy to the federation's regions.

The war in Chechnya can best be understood in these terms. Chechnya and Tatarstan have been the two ethnic republics most vocal about acquiring more autonomy or outright independence. Tatarstan, with its rich oil supplies, is located in the middle of the Russian federation; Chechnya is located on the edge of the Russian federation. In addition, six other ethnic republics surrounding Chechnya mark Russia's border in the volatile Caucasus region. Moscow's desire to discourage independence movements in Tatarstan, and in its border region in the Caucasus, undoubtedly played a big role in its decision to use military force in Chechnya in December 1994.

For similar reasons, India, perhaps the most heterogeneous country in the world, has reacted violently to secessionist movements in Punjab and in Kashmir. Indian leaders believe that acquiescing to demands for

---

25. See Stephen Van Evera, "Hypotheses on Nationalism and War," *International Security*, Vol. 18, No. 4 (Spring 1994), pp. 5–39, esp. p. 17.

26. Ann Sheehy, "Russia's Republics: A Threat to Its Territorial Integrity?" *RFE/RL Research Report*, Vol. 2, No. 20 (May 14, 1993), pp. 34–40.

more autonomy or independence would create massive, potentially life-threatening, problems for the Indian state down the road. Redefining New Delhi's relationship with Kashmir could lead to discussions about the constitutional status of every state in India.[27] This has hindered efforts to solve the Kashmir problem. By the same token, Bangladesh was battered by West Pakistan in 1970 because leaders in Islamabad worried that separatist movements in the West would pick up steam, should Bangladesh be granted more autonomy from the central government.

Ethnic geography is also a problem when secessionist regions contain ethnic minorities. Ethnic populations often spill over internal administrative boundaries, so that different nationalities are scattered among each other. As a result, separatist regions frequently contain their own minority groups, which may be opposed to independence. The problem is compounded by the fact that leaders of secessionist movements almost always invoke highly nationalistic and exclusivist arguments for self-government. This incendiary language is naturally threatening to minority groups living in the secessionist region, and often leads them to oppose the secessionist campaign. If the campaign is nonetheless successful, it often leads regional minorities to seek alternative political arrangements: independence; affiliation with another neighboring state; or reaffiliation with the former central government. Violence is often common in these situations, especially if there is a history of discrimination and repression among the groups in question.

For example, when the Soviet Union broke up, Georgia, Moldova, Azerbaijan, Armenia, and Estonia became independent states. Abkhazis, who had contested the fairness of the Georgian government for years, sought independence. Russians and Ukrainians living on the west bank of the Dniester River, with the support of the Russian 14th Army (which is based there), have declared independence from Moldova. The Gagauz have also sought to break away from the Moldovan government. Armenians in Nagorno-Karabakh sought to break away from Azerbaijan and link up with their ethnic brethren in Armenia. South Ossetians sought to break free from Georgia, but, unlike the Abkhazis, hoped to join with their ethnic brethren, the North Ossetians in the Russian federation, rather than form their own state. Russians in eastern Estonia would prefer to stay affiliated with Moscow. Similarly, Serbs in eastern Croatia sought to stay affiliated with Serbia after the breakup of Yugoslavia in 1991 and 1992.

---

27. Sumit Ganguly and Kanti Bajpai, "India and the Crisis in Kashmir," *Asian Survey*, Vol. 34, No. 5 (May 1994), p. 412; John F. Burns, "India Sends 2 Top Aides to Kashmir Over Ruined Mosque," *New York Times*, May 15, 1995, p. A3.

Violence is especially likely when ethnic groups accustomed to being part of the majority suddenly find themselves in the minority, or in the process of becoming a minority in a new state. For instance, before the outbreak of war in the Balkans in 1991 and 1992, Croatia was twelve percent Serbian and Bosnia was thirty-two percent Serbian; these Serbs were accustomed to being in a state with a Serb majority. The predominantly Tamil provinces of north and east Sri Lanka, which seek independence from Colombo, also have significant Sinhalese populations. Kashmir is one-third Hindu. Northern Ireland, which is mainly Protestant and which voted for union with Britain in 1921, is one-third Catholic.

These regional "minorities," used to being part of the majority, are often unwilling to support regional autonomy or independence, fearing that the new state will discriminate against them, or worse. These groups are inclined to seek support from the central government in thwarting regional independence movements. Because of their position in the old hierarchy, they often control police and military forces and can fight secessionist demands effectively. The ensuing wars frequently last for years.

Much of this came to pass during the breakup of Yugoslavia. In June 1991, Slovenia and Croatia declared independence from an increasingly nationalist, Serb-dominated Yugoslavia. At the time, Serbs constituted only two percent of the Slovenian population, but constituted twelve percent of the Croatian population. Furthermore, the Croatian government was nationalistic in deeply threatening ways: it used symbols from the Ustashe regime of the 1940s, which murdered close to 400,000 Serbs, and fired all Croatian Serbs from the police force, bureaucracy, and industry. Not surprisingly, Croatian Serbs opposed Croatian independence, and they confiscated the weapons of the Yugoslav army that were stored in Croatia during the independence campaign; Croatian Serbs also comprised a large portion of the Yugoslav Army's officer corps. War broke out several days after Croatia declared independence; Croatian Serbs formed an alliance with the Yugoslav army that stored and fought with considerable success against the new Croatian government.

Faced with the prospect of fighting two former republics at the same time, Belgrade chose to fight Croatia rather than Slovenia. The latter contained a small Serb minority and was less inclined to nationalist bombast. In addition, because Serbs comprised such a small portion of the Slovenian population, there was little opposition within the new country to the idea of an independent state. As a result, Slovenia would have been more difficult for Serbia to reconquer. In Croatia, however, a comparatively well-led and well-equipped army of Croatian Serbs was prepared to fight Zagreb.

MILITARY AND ECONOMIC FACTORS

A variety of military and economic concerns can lead a central government to use military force to thwart secessionist movements. To be more specific, central authorities are more inclined to use force to maintain control over a region if the region in question has great military or economic value.[28] If secession would threaten the security of the state, a violent response from central authorities is all but certain.

From a military standpoint, peripheral regions are often located near mountain ranges or waterways that provide natural barriers against invasion. Central authorities are loath to lose these forward defenses, particularly if the state lacks other natural lines of defense. Central authorities will in any event be disinclined to lose defensive buffer zones. Israel, for example, has found it difficult to relinquish the West Bank because the Jordan River and the Judean hills provide a natural obstacle to any army invading from the east.

Secession will also be firmly resisted if the region seeking independence contains vital raw materials, industry, or other economic assets. For example, newly independent Zaire could not survive without Katanga; the province, rich with raw materials, was the country's economic engine.[29] The Yugoslav Army's opposition to Bosnian independence can be partly explained by the fact that former President Josef Broz Tito moved sixty percent of Yugoslavia's military industry to the well-protected, mountainous terrain of Bosnia. And within Bosnia, most of this industry could be found in Muslim and Croat areas.[30] As noted earlier, one of the reasons Russia seeks to retain control over Chechnya is that vital Russian oil and gas pipelines cross Chechen territory.

Unfortunately, areas which contain important raw materials and which have other important economic assets are particularly inclined to seek independence, as discussed above. These are the regions that central

---

28. See John J. Mearsheimer, "Back to the Future: Instability in Europe After the Cold War," *International Security*, Vol. 15, No. 1 (Summer 1990), pp. 12–13; Jack Snyder, *Myths of Empire: Domestic Politics and International Ambition* (Ithaca, N.Y.: Cornell University Press, 1991), pp. 3–4, 10, 22–25; Michael Desch, "The Keys that Lock up the World: Identifying American Interests in the Periphery," *International Security*, Vol. 14, No. 1 (Summer 1989), pp. 100–108; Michael W. Doyle, *Empires* (Ithaca, N.Y.: Cornell University Press, 1986), pp. 146–148, 232–256; Robert Gilpin, *War and Change in International Politics* (Cambridge, U.K.: Cambridge University Press, 1981), chap. 3; Peter Liberman, "The Spoils of Conquest," *International Security*, Vol. 18, No. 2 (Fall 1993), pp. 125–153.

29. Buchheit, *Secession*, pp. 142–143.

30. Misha Glenny, *The Fall of Yugoslavia: The Third Balkan War* (London: Penguin Books, 1992), p. 150.

governments can least afford to lose; natural resources cannot be found everywhere, and factories and pipelines cannot always be replaced. Only changes in military technology render strategic territories less valuable. The more a state depends on a region for national security and prosperity, the more likely it is that central authorities will use military force to squash secessionist impulses.

POLITICAL FACTORS

Another factor that has a significant impact on the prospects for secessionist violence is the degree to which regional leaders can negotiate with leaders of the central government. This, in turn, depends to a very great degree on the presence of democratic institutions, flexible attitudes toward constitutional arrangements, and established traditions of civil discourse.

It is no accident that, while democracies have not always responded peacefully to separatist challenges, most peaceful secessions have involved democracies. Belgium, Canada, and Czechoslovakia, for example, have all addressed autonomy problems and independence claims through constitutional mechanisms. In democratic settings such as these, regional leaders can bring grievances to the attention of central authorities without resorting to violence. Constitutional and legal channels provide opportunities for regional leaders and central authorities to negotiate and seek mutually satisfactory political compromises.

When constitutional negotiations collapse and respect for democratic forms of governance breaks down, violence often follows. In Pakistan, constitutional negotiations broke down in 1970 because West Pakistan wanted to retain the system which had undercut the East's development. Islamabad's refusal to implement a federal system, which would have better represented the East's interests, led to the Bengali rebellion. The Indian government undermined the democratic process in Kashmir, which resulted in separatist violence in the late 1980s. The Indian government dismissed the locally elected government in Kashmir in 1984, and imposed central state rule; in 1987, New Delhi engaged in electoral fraud during the Kashmiri state elections.[31] Similarly, Stormont, the Northern Irish Parliament, was gerrymandered in 1969 to favor the Protestant majority. When the government, which did not adequately represent Catholic interests, suppressed the Catholic civil rights movement, violence ensued. In Sri Lanka, the majority Sinhalese imposed a new constitution in 1972, which lacked federal structures and which therefore

---

31. Ganguly and Bajpai, "India and the Crisis in Kashmir," pp. 404–405.

limited Tamil access to the central government. This was a watershed development that contributed greatly to the deterioration in Sinhalese-Tamil relations.

Limiting minority access to government institutions always produces resentment. It also gives the leaders of minority groups few legal ways of presenting grievances and negotiating with central authorities. Violence is often seen as the only option. The existence of democratic forms of governance does not guarantee that political and constitutional conflicts will be resolved peacefully. It does improve the odds, however. Minorities in general and regionally concentrated minorities in particular are more likely to be fairly represented in democratic systems.

EXTERNAL INTERFERENCE

External support for one of the opposing parties makes violence much more likely in secessionist disputes. Third-party support turns political struggles into violent conflicts by giving the weaker side the power to challenge the stronger. It also makes escalation more likely and de-escalation more difficult.

Third parties often hope to weaken their adversaries and shift regional balances of power in their favor by sending arms and advisers to secessionist groups in neighboring states. Nowhere has this dynamic been more obvious than in the former Soviet Union. For example, Moscow armed Abkhaz rebels in Georgia and provided support to Armenians in their war against Azerbaijan, thereby forcing the governments in Tbilisi and Baku to call on Russia for help. Moscow has taken similar steps in Moldova, using the 14th Army and Russian-speaking secessionists as political levers. As a result, all three states have reversed course and become members of the Commonwealth of Independent States (CIS). Fiercely independent Georgia has agreed to the deployment of Russian troops on its soil. Moscow has exploited internal disputes and encouraged separatist violence in places where political differences might have been solved more peacefully, in order to bring former republics back into the fold.[32]

Russia is not alone in arming insurgents and causing political quarrels to escalate into violence. Belgium, India, Pakistan, Iran, and Serbia, to name just a few, have taken similar steps for equally self-serving reasons. Belgium sent troops to the Congo after the leader of the Katanga province

---

32. For more discussion, see Matthew Evangelista's chapter in this volume. See also Celestine Bohlen, "Shevardnadze's Fight With Rebels Links His Fate to Georgia's Future," *New York Times*, October 3, 1993, p. A1; and Craig Whitney, "Worried Anew, Europe Asks How Best to Keep the Peace," *New York Times*, October 31, 1993, p. E5.

requested the former colonial power's help. India backed Bangladesh against West Pakistan in 1971, supplying guerrillas with arms and ammunition and allowing them to use Indian territory as a refuge. India also helped to arm and to train Tamil rebels in Sri Lanka, and allowed them to use India as a safe haven until 1989. Pakistan aided Sikh insurgents in their struggle against India in the early 1980s. Pakistan has also fueled the separatist violence in Kashmir, providing military and organizational support to certain groups. Iran armed Kurdish rebels in northern Iraq in the 1960s and the early 1970s. The Shah's rapprochement with Saddam Hussein in 1975 led to a cut-off of these supplies; the Kurdish secessionist movement subsequently stalled. The Islamic government in Tehran reestablished these lines of supply in the 1980s. Beginning in the late 1980s, Serbia supported rebel Serbs in Croatia and Bosnia. It helped create local Serb armies which made political compromise more difficult and fighting, when it came, more intense.

Third-party support for separatist groups also has corrosive effects on the prospects for political settlements. Because of third-party support, secessionist wars are more intense and last longer; this makes political compromise more difficult to reach. External support also leads opposing groups to radicalize their war aims, making compromise less likely.[33] Leaders of secessionist movements know that if a neighbor provides military aid, they have a better chance of prevailing. They are consequently less likely to accept offers short of full independence. It is not a coincidence that the most militant rebel group in Kashmir, for example, is the group armed by Pakistan. Furthermore, once separatist leaders make radical demands, it is hard for them to back down. This can create a spiral of violence. Under these circumstances, political compromise may be all but impossible.

It is important to note that, although third parties can easily intensify secessionist struggles, they have less leverage when it comes to forcing their clients to negotiate. Often, when third parties threaten to cut off support for rebel armies, they find that they have lost whatever control they once had over secessionist forces. Both Serbia and India have found themselves in this predicament.

External involvement in secessionist struggles can come in benign forms. For example, the West never recognized Stalin's absorption of the Baltic states into the Soviet Union, and was very clear on this point in its dealings with Moscow. The West's support for the independence of these

---

33. See Alexis Heraclides, "Secessionist Minorities and External Involvement," *International Organization*, Vol. 44, No. 3 (Summer 1990), pp. 341–378.

states undoubtedly played a role in the Kremlin's decision to allow them to secede from the Soviet Union in 1991.

Although external involvement in secessionist struggles can help bring about peaceful political settlements, this is often not the case. As we have seen, external intervention — especially if it comes in the form of military support for rebel factions from neighboring states that have regional agendas of their own — makes violence more likely and political settlements more problematic.

Preventing Secessionist Violence

Although ethnic and regional differences are pervasive features of intra-state politics, they are not uniformly destructive. What can be done to dampen secessionist impulses? In places where secessionist movements do develop, what can be done to make secessionist violence less likely and easier to control?

Some things, of course, cannot be easily changed, such as ethnic geography and the strategic value of territory, natural resources, and economic assets. Steps can be taken, however, to minimize the problems produced by these structural facts of life. I offer two main sets of recommendations.

First, one must address the root causes of secessionist movements if one is to dampen secessionist impulses. If ethnic groups feel that their political and economic interests are being looked after and their cultural rights are being respected by central authorities, they are less likely to seek states of their own. Several political and economic measures are the keys to dampening secessionist impulses. In states where ethnic groups are concentrated along regional lines, federal political arrangements should be implemented. In places where ethnic groups are intermingled, proportional representation is the key to political harmony. In all circumstances, central governments should take effective steps to protect minority rights. Civic conceptions of nationalism should be developed. On the economic front, central authorities must convince regional leaders that the central government is not hindering regional economic development. Central authorities should have regional leaders participate in regular, high-level discussions about economic matters, so there is no doubt about grievances being heard. Resource-rich regions should be given considerable control over the production and trade of regional products.

Second, when secessionist movements develop, the key to making violence less likely and more controllable is preventing neighboring states from aiding the opposing parties. This is an area where international powers and the international community can play constructive roles.

POLITICAL SOLUTIONS

As Donald Horowitz has pointed out, when it comes to ethnic conflict, "more is involved in the process of accommodation than the wishes of those in positions of formal authority."[34] Good will alone will not produce accommodationist majorities. The challenge is to design political systems which provide incentives for interethnic cooperation and accommodation, rather than division. The key is to ensure that ethnic minorities come to believe that their interests are being protected and advanced by existing political arrangements. My recommendations in this regard are threefold: federalism, in places where ethnic groups are concentrated in pockets; proportional representation, where they are intermingled; and minority rights safeguards and civic conceptions of nationalism, across the board.

FEDERALISM.   Federalism can dampen secessionist inclinations and is appropriate in two sets of circumstances: when ethnic groups are concentrated in regional clusters and when regional dissatisfaction stems from a lack of control over economic resources. Federalist arrangements work to dampen secessionism in four main ways.

First, regions and regional leaders have more political power in federalist systems. More important, regional authorities and parliaments control regional policies with respect to education, taxation, resource extraction, and maintenance of law and order — matters of great interest at a local level. With control over these important areas, regional politicians in federal systems have substantial constitutional powers.

Second, federalist systems have formal, constitutional mechanisms for communication and bargaining between regional leaders and central authorities. This gives the former legal ways of bringing their grievances to the attention of and influencing the latter. State-wide parliamentary bodies contain appropriate numbers of regional representatives, and in some cases, the federal presidency can rotate among regional leaders.

Third, federalist systems have regional governments, parliaments, bureaucracies, judiciaries, police forces, and educational systems. This creates jobs for local populations, and political opportunities for local politicians and elites.

Finally, federalism deflects hostility from the central government by creating new political institutions and political competition at the local level.[35] In federalist systems, local political struggles will naturally and inevitably develop: political parties will emerge and contest local

---

34. Horowitz, *Ethnic Groups in Conflict*, pp. 564–565.

35. This point is highlighted in ibid., pp. 601–628.

elections; individuals and groups will compete to secure positions in local bureaucracies. Political competition will take place primarily at a local level and *within* ethnic groups; ethnic groups may become divided in the process. These local power struggles lead to a healthy diffusion of political conflict and the creation of new political cleavages. The salience of state-wide, inter-group conflict is correspondingly reduced.

Federalism is particularly appropriate for states comprised of many regionally concentrated ethnic groups. Federalist systems allow for the formation of different coalitions on different issues, and prevent the same parties from contesting each other on every issue. When regions have different coalition partners on different occasions, political fault lines are less likely to develop. Regions A and B might support the same trade policy, while A and C advocate the same farm subsidies, and B and C promote the same immigration policy. When this happens, coalitions become forces for keeping states together, rather than ripping them apart.

Many multiethnic states have turned to federalism to deal with the challenges posed by separatist movements. In August 1995 and January 1996, the Sri Lankan government proposed a federal solution to the civil war between Sinhalese and Tamils. Moscow has offered more regional autonomy to Chechnya in an effort to bring the war there to an end. New Delhi is considering granting considerable local autonomy to several regions.

Unfortunately, federalism is difficult to implement. Major constitutional changes are always painful and costly. Some states will find it easier to repress a few ethnic groups than to rewrite a constitution. Moreover, in systems where there are only two distinct ethnic groups, the dominant group may see federalist compromises as caving in to the demands of the minority. There is, for example, considerable resentment among Anglophones toward separatist Quebecois in Canada, and among Romanians toward Hungarians in Transylvania.

Furthermore, central authorities worry that implementation of federalist arrangements will encourage regional leaders to push for more and more autonomy, and eventually complete independence: they fear that embracing federalism will make seccessionism more, not less, likely. Federalism, they fear, puts them on a slippery slope. There is no doubt that these risks exist. However, well-designed systems which give regional leaders a stake in the political system can weaken these centrifugal forces. State subsidies, economic interdependence, and rotating presidencies can work to keep federal systems together.

When ethnic groups are regionally concentrated and when regions are dissatisfied with their economic fortunes, federalism can dampen secessionist impulses. Federalism gives regional leaders more control over local political and economic affairs, and ensures that local interests are given a fair hearing by central authorities.

PROPORTIONAL REPRESENTATION. Minority populations often find that democratic institutions are unresponsive to their needs and interests. When majorities rule, minority groups are often ignored or, worse, actively discriminated against. Carefully designed electoral rules can address these problems and encourage moderation by providing incentives for cooperation between political parties and between groups. In particular, proportional representation allows for appropriate levels of minority representation in the central government; it ensures that minority groups will have influence in policymaking circles and legislatures. Proportional representation is essential when minorities are scattered throughout a state or region: federal arrangements cannot be used to safeguard minority interests when ethnic groups are intermingled in this manner.

In multiethnic societies in particular, proportional representation is superior to winner-take-all electoral systems.[36] In proportional systems, political parties receive seats in legislatures on the basis of their share of the popular vote; parties that come in second, third, and fourth overall are still represented. In winner-take-all systems, only the winning party gets a seat at the table. For example, a minority that constitutes fifteen percent of the overall population and organizes a political party of its own would receive around fifteen percent of the seats in the legislature in a proportional representation system, if all else is equal; in a winner-take-all system, it would not be represented at all.

Electoral and institutional arrangements have important consequences for political stability in multiethnic societies. As Donald Horowitz has observed, political parties in multiethnic societies tend to form along ethnic lines; this might be unfortunate, but it is a fact of life. Ethnic minorities consequently fare poorly in winner-take-all systems; they will never be represented in legislative or executive bodies. This gives minorities powerful incentives to oppose the status quo, but it denies them legal, peaceful ways of changing things. Political turmoil and

---

36. See Douglas W. Rae, *The Political Consequences of Electoral Laws*, rev. ed. (New Haven, Conn.: Yale University Press, 1971), pp. 88–92, 151–170; Juan J. Linz, "Transitions to Democracy," *Washington Quarterly*, Vol. 13, No. 3 (Summer 1990), pp. 143–164; Donald Horowitz, "Comparing Democratic Systems," *Journal of Democracy*, Vol. 1, No. 4 (Fall 1990), pp. 73–79; Horowitz, *Ethnic Groups in Conflict*, pp. 628–652.

violence often follow. Many post-colonial states in Asia and Africa, for example, plunged into ethnic warfare when it became clear that minorities would be permanently excluded from government.[37]

Proportional systems, however, base political representation on the percentage of votes received. An added bonus is that proportional voting rules tend to produce multi-party systems: there are incentives for forming new parties since it is fairly easy to achieve representation.[38] The result, in many cases, is that no one party receives a majority of the vote and that governments are coalitions of large and small parties. In such a system, a group that holds fifteen percent of the vote can do quite well. If it holds the swing vote, it can make or break coalitions and wield tremendous amounts of power. If different alliances are formed on different issues, cross-cutting cleavages help prevent ethnic polarization from developing.

Multiethnic coalitions have already appeared in the new democracies of Eastern Europe. The Hungarian party of Slovakia was included in the Slovakian government in 1994, and the Turkish party was included in the Bulgarian government in 1991.[39] Similarly, Labor governments in Israel have depended on the votes of Israeli Arabs; the Likud has also allied with Arab parties from time to time.[40] In proportional systems, small parties are not ignored.

Proportional systems thus have two peace-producing results. First, minorities are less likely to oppose the status quo because they are not permanently excluded from policymaking. Second, minorities have legal, peaceful means of addressing their grievances.

Some of the pacifying effects of proportional representation can also be temporarily produced by power-sharing arrangements. Ethnic conflict is regulated in power-sharing systems through four main mechanisms: governments are comprised of grand coalitions that contain all major ethnic groups; ethnic groups are represented in the executive, the bureaucracy, and other branches of government according to ethnic quotas; ethnic groups have veto power over major decisions; and ethnic groups have considerable autonomy in making decisions which pertain to their

---

37. Horowitz, *Ethnic Groups in Conflict*, p. 629.

38. A multi-party system is ensured by a small minimum percentage cut-off. See Dennis Mueller, *Public Choice II* (Cambridge, U.K.: Cambridge, University Press, 1989), pp. 215–222.

39. See Milada Vachudová's chapter on East-Central Europe in this volume.

40. Clyde Haberman, "Israel Suspends Its Plans To Seize Land in Jerusalem," *New York Times*, May 23, 1995, p. A1.

particular groups.[41] Because ethnic leaders are given high offices in government, they have an incentive to work together and bring interethnic stability to the state.

Although this might appear to be a promising recipe for producing social justice and political stability, power-sharing systems have three inherent flaws. First, ethnic leaders and ethnic groups are not always inclined to cooperate. Personal ambitions and radical group agendas might rule out accommodation and compromise, and bring power- sharing edifices crashing down.

Second, power-sharing arrangements tend to freeze ethnic quotas; power-sharing formulas can be built into the constitution of the state itself. This can lead to trouble when the relative size of ethnic groups changes over time. Changing quotas means redistributing political power, and this is always a volatile proposition. Those who have power are almost always unenthusiastic about giving it up. For example, Christians slightly outnumbered Muslims when the Lebanese National Pact was signed in 1943; high offices were handed out according to a strict formula based on these 1943 demographics. Because of different birth rates in different groups, Muslims eventually came to outnumber Christians, who refused to conduct censuses and change the system of political appointments. This was the underlying cause of the civil war that began in 1975.

Third and perhaps most importantly, power-sharing arrangements make ethnicity more, rather than less, important. In power-sharing systems, the tendency to form ethnic parties is strongly reinforced. Political cleavages form more sharply along ethnic lines. Ethnicity is the key to obtaining political appointments, jobs, educational opportunities, and economic subsidies. Individuals have incentives to identify themselves in ethnic terms, even if they are originally disinclined to do so. Politics at every level and in every arm of government is framed in ethnic terms. Ethnic polarization is unlikely to generate ethnic harmony in the long term.

In sum, proportional representation arrangements are clearly superior to winner-take-all systems, and they are also preferable to power-sharing systems. Proportional representation arrangements are more likely to lead

---

41. Arend Lijphart, *Democracy in Plural Societies* (New Haven, Conn.: Yale University Press, 1977), pp. 25–44. As Lijphart has recognized, various states have experimented with power-sharing. Some examples include Lebanon from 1943 to 1975, Malaysia from 1955 to 1969, and Cyprus, which toyed briefly with power-sharing arrangements from 1960 to 1963. Other states which have more successfully incorporated power-sharing elements include Belgium, the Netherlands, and Switzerland. The democratic South African Government is also a form of power-sharing where whites (through the National Party) are guaranteed certain ministries and have far more power in the parliament and the government than the twenty percent white minority would augur.

to the formation of fluid, multiparty systems where ethnicity is only one of several salient political forces. They are more likely to generate cross-cutting cleavages, and they can accommodate major governmental changes without re-writing constitutions and risking political upheaval. In proportional representation systems, ethnic groups can be protected without being exalted.

MINORITY RIGHTS AND CIVIC NATIONALISM. One of the keys to dampening secessionist impulses and preventing secessionist violence is safeguarding minority rights and promoting civic conceptions of nationalism. Ethnic groups will be less inclined to seek states of their own if they believe their rights will be protected and if they are not treated as second-class citizens. When ethnic groups do secede, minorities within these new states will be less inclined to opt out if they believe their rights will be respected and if second-class status is not in the offing.

Protecting the rights of minorities and promoting civic conceptions of nationalism are critical in all multiethnic states, whether minority groups are concentrated in particular regions or scattered throughout the country. Minorities should not be discriminated against in either political or economic affairs; they should have political, economic, and educational opportunities comparable to those of all other citizens. Freedom of speech and freedom of religion should be enshrined principles of government. Minority languages, customs, and cultures should be respected. Constitutional provisions or laws protecting minority rights should be instituted and energetically enforced. Minorities should be able to turn to police forces and the courts if and when problems develop.

More generally, political leaders should work to promote civic, rather than ethnic, conceptions of citizenship and nationalism.[42] Citizenship should be tied to where one lives and political loyalty, rather than ethnicity. In-group–out-group distinctions should not be emphasized in political discourse, and ethnic bashing should be condemned as a form of political rhetoric.

The Baltic popular fronts pursued these kinds of benign policies from 1987–91. During the formation of the Baltic independence movements, the fronts reached out to Baltic Russians. They published pro-independence newspapers in Russian, and forged links with the Russian community.[43]

---

42. See Jack Snyder, "Nationalism and the Crisis of the Post-Soviet State," in Brown, *Ethnic Conflict and International Security.*

43. Anatol Lieven, *The Baltic Revolution: Estonia, Latvia, Lithuania and the Path to Independence* (New Haven, Conn.: Yale University Press, 1993), pp. 188, 302; Saulius

These actions helped diffuse Russian opposition to Baltic independence.[44] Baltic leaders were extremely careful to engage rather than alienate Russian businessmen and industrial managers, the region's economic elite. Unfortunately, the spirit of civic nationalism and interethnic cooperation disappeared after independence; however, the moderate stance of the popular fronts was critical to the overall absence of Baltic Russian protest.

Ukrainian leaders also embraced civic nationalism in the dying days of the Soviet Union. Unlike their Baltic counterparts, they have managed to sustain this spirit, despite the fact that over twenty-two percent of the population is Russian and the eastern part of the country has strong cultural and economic ties with Russia. President Nursultan Nazarbaev of Kazakhstan has been extremely solicitous of his country's thirty-eight percent Russian minority, which is concentrated mainly near the Russian border.

Sustaining civic nationalism is never easy. Opportunistic or desperate politicians will always have incentives to play the nationalist card in order to improve their political positions. Moderate politicians can get pushed aside. Unfortunately, many political leaders prefer power to peace.

ECONOMIC SOLUTIONS

Economic discontent often creates powerful secessionist desires. To prevent secessionist movements from developing, central authorities should endeavor to equalize economic development across regions. They should also be sensitive to regional and ethnic complaints about economic discrimination. Regional leaders should be included in all discussions concerning anticipated changes in economic policy. Where appropriate, federal arrangements should be put into place, thereby allowing regional leaders to guide their own economic affairs.

There are, of course, no simple solutions to most economic problems. Providing subsidies to poor regions might address some problems there, but rich regions will inevitably resent giving more than they receive. The solution might be to promise rich regions more investment or more autonomy later on in exchange for paying a price in the short term. The

---

Girnius, "Unofficial Groups in the Baltic Republics and Access to the Mass Media," *Report on the USSR*, Vol. 1, No. 18 (May 5, 1989), p. 16.

44. Only one-third of the Baltic Russian population was opposed to Baltic independence. See for instance, Toomas Ilves, "Estonian Poll on Independence, Political Parties," *Report on the USSR*, Vol. 1, No. 22 (June 2, 1989), pp. 15–16. From 1989 to 1990, the percentage of Estonian Russians who supported republic status within the Soviet Union dropped from fifty-four percent to sixteen percent.

long-term viability of states which contain broad disparities between regions will depend on making adroit trade-offs such as these.

LIMITING EXTERNAL SUPPORT

Limiting the role of third parties is critical to limiting secessionist violence. Some secessionist movements are, in essence, created by neighboring states. It is hard to believe, for example, that the Abkhaz rebels would have been able to mount a successful military campaign against the numerically superior and better-armed Georgians if Russia had not thrown its considerable weight behind the Abkhaz cause. Neighboring states that arm and support would-be secessionists make secessionist violence more likely. When they replenish arsenals and raise expectations about winning, neighboring states intensify and prolong separatist wars.

International powers and the international community in general should therefore try to prevent neighboring states and third parties from providing arms and other forms of military support to aspiring secessionists and parties engaged in secessionist wars. Observer missions undertaken by the United Nations (UN) and regional security organizations should try to identify states that violate the principle of non-involvement. Strong sanctions should be imposed on states that do not comply with these guidelines.

THE ROLE OF INTERNATIONAL INSTITUTIONS

In theory, international institutions can play an important role in ensuring that states treat their minorities well. The United Nations and regional security organizations can offer to mediate conflicts. International financial institutions, such as the World Bank, can use their economic leverage to induce countries to respect minority rights and hold fair elections. Economic sanctions can be imposed on countries that violate individual and minority rights on a regular basis.

In practice, however, there are limits to what international institutions can do to turn despotic nationalists into liberal democrats. Although the international community has paid a fair amount of attention to the ways states treat individuals and minorities, it has limited leverage. Economic embargoes are often violated because some states in the system will have economic incentives to do so. The United Nations has military might only when member states provide it — which they rarely do. As a result, the United Nations is better at keeping peace agreements than inducing states to behave or compelling parties to put down their arms.

Rarely will a group of states have both an incentive and the power to ensure that states treat minority groups well. Western Europe's efforts with respect to Central and Eastern Europe stand out in this regard. Western Europe has a compelling strategic and economic interest in creating stable, peaceful, democratic states in the eastern half of the continent; they do not want ethnic violence to break out elsewhere in the region. They also have considerable leverage over their Central and Eastern European counterparts because the latter are anxious to join the European Union (EU) and the North Atlantic Treaty Organization (NATO). The current members of these organizations have made it very clear that if the Central and Eastern European states want to join Western economic, political, and military institutions they must be committed to democratic forms of governance and respectful of minority rights. Monitoring groups from the Organization for Security and Cooperation in Europe (OSCE, formerly CSCE, the Conference on Security and Cooperation in Europe) have investigated and publicized abuses, which gives Central and Eastern European states further incentives to behave.

Unfortunately, this type of constructive engagement is not likely to be duplicated in other parts of the world. Europe is unique in that states with a great interest in minority rights also have considerable economic, political, and military clout; they also have institutions capable of monitoring human rights developments.

Conclusions

In this chapter, I have tried to identify ways that will make it easier for ethnic groups to live together peacefully and equitably under democratic conditions. In many cases, political and economic reforms can address ethnic grievances, and make secession unnecessary.

However, there will inevitably be cases where legitimate minority grievances are not being addressed by central governments because authorities lack the will or capabilities (or both) to do so. When this happens, international powers and the international community will face a difficult choice. Although they will be inclined to do everything they can to prevent violence and maintain regional stability, refusing to help secessionists or preventing neighboring states from arming secessionists will reinforce an unjust status quo.

As Richard Betts has aptly remarked, the outside world should not confuse peace with justice.[45] Preventing secessionism and working to

---

45. Richard K. Betts, "The Delusion of Impartial Intervention," *Foreign Affairs*, Vol. 73, No. 6 (November/December 1994), p. 31.

bring wars to a quick end are defensible when just, durable political settlements can be envisaged. But political compromise and political solutions are not always possible. In these cases, limiting external support for secessionist movements may doom them to destruction and continued repression. This policy dilemma will not soon disappear.

Chapter 10

Negotiation and Mediation in Internal Conflict

Stephen John Stedman

When civil wars break out, diplomats often offer their services as mediators and urge the parties to negotiate. If initial peacemaking efforts fail, the international response is usually to try and try again. Between 1992 and 1995, the European Community (EC)/European Union (EU) and the United Nations (UN) toiled in vain to end the war in Bosnia. Ultimately, U.S. mediation produced an agreement that might end the war. When Russia invaded the breakaway republic of Chechnya in 1994, the European Union recommended a political settlement. In 1995, the United States quietly encouraged warring parties in Algeria to negotiate. Negotiation and mediation are favored even in cases of genocide: in Rwanda from April to June 1994, as extremist Hutu militias murdered 800,000 Tutsi and moderate Hutu, the United Nations and the United States appealed to the parties to return to peace talks.

Many policymakers see negotiation and mediation as panaceas. They assume that all civil wars are negotiable; that solutions can be found to address the needs of all warring parties; that leaders in civil wars are rational decision-makers who can be swayed by reason; and that negotiated settlements are morally preferable to military victory by one side. One analyst notes favorably that mediation has become the chief foreign policy tool of the United States in the post–Cold War era.[1]

Although negotiation and mediation are favored by many policymakers, critics tend to dismiss them in civil wars; negotiation and mediation are seen as doomed and often ethically unpalatable.[2] Civil wars are

---

1. Amitai Etzioni, "Mediation as a World Role for the United States," *Washington Quarterly*, Vol. 18, No. 3 (Summer 1995), pp. 75–87.

2. See Richard K. Betts, "The Delusion of Impartial Intervention," *Foreign Affairs*, Vol. 73, No. 6 (November/December 1994), pp. 20–33; Harrison Wagner, "The Causes of Peace," in Roy Licklider, ed., *Stopping the Killing: How Civil Wars End* (New York:

said to be immune to negotiation; the high stakes drive parties to fight to the finish. Political settlements only become possible after the parties exhaust themselves militarily — a process that takes years. Mediation, it is argued, can prolong civil wars by insisting on even-handed treatment of warring parties and interfering with the quest for unilateral victory. Typical is the assessment of Richard Betts, who disparages mediation "because it helps peacemaking most where peacemaking needs help least."[3]

Mediation in civil war is neither a panacea nor a placebo; it is a policy tool that is occasionally effective. Compared to military intervention, mediation seems weak and equivocating. Compared to preventive action, negotiating an end to a civil war that has already erupted seems belated. But unlike peace enforcement and conflict prevention, mediation in civil war has a proven track record. Between 1988 and 1994, negotiations brought five civil wars to an end — in El Salvador, Mozambique, Namibia, Nicaragua, and South Africa. With the exception of South Africa, formal mediation played a key role in ending those wars.

In order to improve their usefulness and appropriateness as a response to internal conflicts, a sophisticated understanding of the possibilities and limitations of negotiations and mediation efforts in civil wars needs to be developed. Mediators need to know the conditions that facilitate negotiation, the barriers that negotiations face, and how these barriers can be overcome more effectively.

In this chapter, I address five questions. First, why do few civil wars end through negotiated settlement? Second, what circumstances favor the negotiated settlement of a civil war? Third, how can third-party mediation support negotiation efforts? Fourth, why do some negotiated settlements of civil wars collapse during implementation? Fifth, how can international actors help parties implement civil war settlements more effectively?

The dynamics of civil war pose special challenges to those who would mediate and implement negotiated settlements. Civil wars tend to be total wars, where the parties believe that only a complete victory will allow them to survive. For mediation efforts to succeed, the parties in civil wars must come to fear the consequences of continued fighting more than they

---

New York University Press, 1993), pp. 235–268; Barbara F. Walter, "The Resolution of Civil Wars: Why Negotiations Fail," Ph.D. dissertation, University of Chicago, December 1994. For journalistic dismissals of mediation in civil war, see Victoria Brittain, "Even-handedness Leaves States Twisted," *Guardian Weekly*, April 23, 1995, p. 13; Edward N. Luttwak, "Perspective on the Balkans; They Haven't Given War a Chance," *Los Angeles Times*, August 8, 1995, p. B9.

3. Betts, "The Delusion of Impartial Intervention," p. 24.

fear the consequences of settlement — placing their security and well-being partially in the hands of former enemies. Fears about negotiated settlements can occasionally be assuaged by creative, capable mediation. Not all civil wars, however, can be ended through negotiation. Leaders in civil wars often suffer from powerful pathologies that prevent them from compromising. Mediators and implementers of peace agreements must distinguish between leaders who can be persuaded to make peace and those who cannot.

Barriers to Negotiated Settlements in Civil Wars

Negotiated settlements are much rarer in civil wars than in inter-state wars. Between 1900 and 1980, only fifteen percent of civil wars ended through negotiation; the remaining eighty-five percent were terminated by one side winning.[4] During the same period approximately fifty percent of inter-state wars ended through negotiation.[5]

Civil wars are more difficult to negotiate than inter-state wars for four reasons. First, political settlements in civil wars require the parties to disarm and form a single army and government. This creates intense security concerns: the parties will face worrisome military vulnerabilities.[6] Second, civil wars are often total wars, in which combatants come to believe that the character of their adversary is a cause of the war and that the only way to end the war is by eliminating their opponent. This creates survival stakes for the combatants, who fear that defeat will mean death. Third, civil wars are often fought by leaders who will accept nothing less than complete victory and complete control over the country in question. Fourth, even if the parties are fighting for limited aims, the rhetoric of total war increases risks and fears; those willing to contemplate negotiation must judge whether an opponent will be satisfied with less than complete victory.

---

4. Stephen John Stedman, *Peacemaking in Civil Wars: International Mediation in Zimbabwe, 1974–1980* (Boulder, Colo.: Lynne Rienner, 1991), pp. 4–9.

5. Paul Pillar, *Negotiating Peace: War Termination as a Bargaining Process* (Princeton, N.J.: Princeton University Press, 1983), pp. 16–26. Pillar's data set includes wars of the nineteenth and twentieth centuries; the estimate of fifty percent comes from wars fought between 1900 and 1980.

6. The application of the security dilemma to civil war comes from Walter, "The Resolution of Civil Wars," which provides the fullest elaboration of the problem in the literature. For other analyses that stress vulnerabilities in making peace in civil war, see Wagner, "The Causes of Peace"; Stedman, *Peacemaking in Civil War*, pp. 11–16.

SECURITY DILEMMAS

Negotiated settlements of civil wars are rare, first, because of the security dilemma that warring parties must overcome.[7] Civil war is structurally similar to international anarchy: the lack of an overarching authority leads the parties to seek self-help solutions to their security problems. As Barbara Walter argues, civil wars are difficult to negotiate because a political settlement to a civil war requires the parties to demobilize their soldiers, give up their arms, and create a unified state.[8] In the short term, the arrangements that lead to an end of hostilities are fraught with risks and dangers. If poorly organized and supervised, the integration of armed forces, the cantonment and disarming of soldiers, and the initiation and maintenance of cease-fires can provide opportunities for one side to take advantage of the settlement and seek complete victory.

In the long term, the parties must have confidence that their adversary will not gain a monopoly of power and use the coercive powers of the state against them. If elections are to be used to decide the postwar distribution of power, the parties must believe that the winner of the election will not take advantage of its position and eliminate the loser. Various constitutional arrangements can diffuse power among regions and institutions, and thereby reduce these risks. But constitutions do not in and of themselves provide security guarantees.

Even when parties are willing to compromise on their political goals, their fears of being vulnerable may prevent them from reaching a settlement. In the words of Harrison Wagner, "the problem in settling civil wars may therefore not be the absence of possible compromises, but the difficulty of finding a way of enforcing a compromise."[9]

Overcoming these security dilemmas is a necessary, but insufficient, condition for reaching agreements in civil wars. Considered alone, the security dilemma explanation of why settlements are rare in civil wars implies that all civil wars are negotiable, if only sufficient protections and assurances can be found to enable the parties to overcome their fears. This is misleading, however. Many parties in civil wars refuse to settle because

---

7. This section draws from Walter, "The Resolution of Civil Wars"; Wagner, "The Causes of Peace"; and Stedman, *Peacemaking in Civil War.* The concept of the security dilemma comes from Robert Jervis, "Cooperation Under the Security Dilemma," *World Politics,* Vol. 30, No. 2 (January 1978), pp. 167–213. For an application of the concept to ethnic conflict, see Barry Posen, "The Security Dilemma and Ethnic Conflict," in Michael E. Brown, ed., *Ethnic Conflict and International Security* (Princeton, N.J.: Princeton University Press, 1993), pp. 103–124.

8. Walter, "The Resolution of Civil Wars." As Walter observes, this is not a problem in those rare cases where parties agree to form separate states.

9. Wagner, "The Causes of Peace," p. 263.

they define their conflicts in all-or-nothing terms. In cases such as these, parties are not motivated by fear, but by base considerations, such as greed and thirst for power, or by lofty motives, such as justice.

PERCEPTIONS AND STAKES

Before parties can discuss security arrangements as part of a settlement, they must seek to resolve the issues over which they went to war in the first place. Scholars often assert that negotiations in civil wars are futile because the stakes are indivisible; that what is at issue is who will rule, which is said to be nonnegotiable.[10] For example, Richard Betts and Leslie Gelb claim that civil wars cannot be ended through negotiation "because the essential stake in such conflicts is indivisible: who will govern the country? Genuine coalition governments are possible only between parties whose differences are not fundamental and bitter enough to have put them at each other's throats in the first place."[11]

It is counterintuitive to assert that because civil wars are about issues of power and rule, they are thus less negotiable than inter-state wars. There are various ways to divide political power and resources in a country.[12] Indeed, one of the architects of the successful British mediation of the Zimbabwean civil war, Sir Robin Renwick, believed that if the conflict could be reduced "to the dimensions of a struggle for power," the parties would be more likely to settle.[13]

The pertinent question is why parties in civil wars seldom choose compromise solutions to the division of power. Part of the answer, as discussed above, is fear and mistrust. Part of the answer, as I will discuss shortly, is that some leaders will settle for nothing less than complete control over the country in question. But at least part of the answer has to do with how the parties perceive the issues at stake.

Civil wars often become total wars because the parties perceive that the character of their opponents is the cause of the war. If a warring party believes that the character of a leader (for example, Hitler's personality), a movement (for example, the aggressive nationalism of Naziism), or a

---

10. Pillar, *Negotiating Peace*, p. 24; Fred Iklé, *Every War Must End* (New York: Columbia University Press, 1971), p. 95; Leslie Gelb and Richard Betts, *The Irony of Vietnam: The System Worked* (Washington, D.C.: Brookings Institution, 1979).

11. Gelb and Betts, *The Irony of Vietnam*, p. 165.

12. See Donald Horowitz, *Ethnic Groups in Conflict* (Berkeley: University of California Press, 1985); Arend Lijphart, *Democracy in Plural Societies: A Comparative Exploration* (New Haven, Conn.: Yale University Press, 1977).

13. Robin Renwick, "The Rhodesia Settlement," unpublished paper, Harvard University, Center for International Affairs, 1981, p. 16.

people (for example, German militarism) is the cause of the war, then it will seek to end the war by eliminating or transforming that character. A fight to the finish emerges when at least one party believes that its survival is at stake — not just because it is vulnerable, but because it perceives the essence of a leader's, movement's, or group's character is hostile, threatening, and immutable.

Civil wars generate totalistic war aims for three reasons. First, civil wars tend to follow the failure of a ruler to meet limited demands for political change. When a ruler repeatedly refuses to meet limited demands, some within the opposition come to believe that incremental change is impossible and that the ruler must be replaced. Second, the refusal of a ruler to reform lends credence to ideological critique of the ruling regime: that the leader acts as he does because he represents a class, a culture, or ethnic group. The character of the regime is then seen by some as the cause of the war. So defined, the war cannot end unless the character of the regime — rooted in class, culture, or ethnicity — is transformed or the group itself is eliminated. Third, as ideological critiques of the ruling regime develop, the ruler becomes even more committed to monopolizing power, fearing that any reform will be a catalyst for revolution instead of a substitute for one.[14]

When ideology — based in class, religious, or ethnic belief systems — forms the basis for understanding conflict, the participants see different worlds, speak different languages, and often define the conflict as one between incommensurable principles. Groups produce sustaining myths that create "an image of 'others,' which is characterized by hostility, malevolence, suspicion, and mistrust."[15] Because these myths are often derived from events, a potent mix of "facts, myths, and distortions may become strongly and credibly linked over long periods of time in group consciousness."[16]

This does not rule out negotiation, but it means that political settlements to civil wars will depend on the willingness and ability of individuals to change their perceptions and definitions of conflict. This can happen even in the most entrenched conflicts: contrast the South Africa of 1995 to the South Africa of 1989, when a genocidal race war seemed

---

14. Samuel Huntington, *Political Order in Changing Societies* (New Haven, Conn.: Yale University Press, 1968), pp. 362–368.

15. Donald Rothchild and Alexander J. Groth, "Pathological Dimensions of Domestic and International Ethnicity," *Political Science Quarterly*, Vol. 110, No. 1 (Spring 1995), p. 71.

16. Ibid.

inevitable. Even when violent conflicts involve indivisible principles, parties can redefine their commitment to the violent pursuit of principle, thus rendering a negotiated settlement possible. This may be what has happened in Northern Ireland, where the Irish Republican Army (IRA) has reaffirmed its commitment to the unification of Ireland but stated that it is willing to forgo violence to attain its goal.

PATHOLOGIES OF LEADERSHIP

Totalistic perceptions and war aims render civil wars difficult to negotiate, but not impossible as long as perceptions, attitudes, and preferences can change. A key issue, then, is the capability of individuals to change deeply held views.

One school of conflict resolution assumes that all conflict derives from subjective evaluations of reality and argues that, since beliefs are malleable, all conflict is resolvable through problem-solving.[17] This goes too far, however. If some individuals are psychologically incapable of redefining a conflict and reordering their preferences, then their subjective evaluation of the conflict is fixed and becomes an objective aspect of the conflict. If such individuals are leaders of governments or rebel movements, then negotiated settlements are impossible unless these leaders are replaced. The perception that the character of a leader is a cause of war can be accurate.

Leaders in civil wars can suffer from pathologies that prevent them from changing their preferences. A leader's paranoia can render it impossible to assuage his fears of a negotiated settlement. For example, Emiliano Zapata feared a double-cross by authorities and was incapable of negotiating an end to the Mexican revolution.[18] A leader's drive for power can make compromise solutions impossible. Pol Pot, for example, was willing for tactical reasons to accept a peace agreement to end the civil war in Cambodia, but reneged when it became clear that it would not bring him back to power.[19] A leader's irrational attachment to principle can also make compromise solutions impossible. In the U.S. Civil War, Jefferson Davis's commitment to the South's independence was so strong

---

17. See John W. Burton, *Resolving Deep-rooted Conflict: A Handbook* (Lanham, Md.: University Press of America, 1987).

18. John Womack, *Zapata and the Mexican Revolution* (New York: Knopf, 1969).

19. See Trevor Findlay, *Cambodia: The Legacy and Lessons of UNTAC*, Stockholm International Peace Research Institute (SIPRI) Research Report No. 9 (New York: Oxford University Press, 1995).

that even after he lost his two main armies, he insisted the Confederacy should "carry on the war forever."[20]

Students and practitioners of conflict resolution may object to the argument that some leaders are incapable of compromise. The belief that someone is incapable of change — that their aggression is part of their character and not a product of their situation — reinforces the demonization of enemies that takes place in many civil wars and strengthens the view that compromise is simply impossible.

This objection is well taken; there are many instances where the incorrect characterization of an opponent foreclosed opportunities for negotiation. U.S. government beliefs that El Salvador's communists could never compromise because of their ideological convictions kept Washington from supporting negotiations for years. Similarly, the South African government's belief in the 1970s and 1980s that the African National Congress (ANC) was a communist, racist organization bent on the elimination of white society precluded possibilities for negotiation and compromise.

Ultimately, it is an empirical question whether some leaders hold fixed preferences and beliefs that are insensitive to costs and unresponsive to challenging information. Findings from cognitive psychology on the rigidity of attitudes support such a possibility.[21] The goals and behavior of individuals such as Pol Pot, Jonas Savimbi, and Ayatollah Khomeini seem consistent enough over time to allow for judgments concerning the malleability of their attitudes, beliefs, and preferences towards power and compromise.[22]

The preferences, beliefs, and attitudes of organized political movements, parties, and larger cultural groups is a more difficult issue. Do some parties or groups have an immutable desire for power? Is it a ridiculous exercise, as one analyst suggests, to look for moderate Islamic fundamentalists in Algeria?[23] Was it absurd to hope that the Khmer Rouge would transform itself into a peaceful, constitutional party willing to

---

20. Michael B. Ballard, *A Long Shadow: Jefferson Davis and the Final Days of the Confederacy* (Jackson: University Press of Mississippi, 1986), p. 136.

21. Robert Jervis, *Perception and Misperception in International Politics* (Princeton, N.J.: Princeton University Press, 1976).

22. Alexander George argues that if theories of conflict management are to be relevant to policymakers, scholars must examine the personalities of leaders. See his discussion of actor-specific behavioral models in *Bridging the Gap: Theory and Practice in Foreign Policy* (Washington, D.C.: U.S. Institute of Peace, 1993), pp. 125–131.

23. Edward G. Shirley, "Is Iran's Present Algeria's Future?" *Foreign Affairs*, Vol. 74, No. 3 (May/June 1995), pp. 28–44.

share or lose power through elections? Do various nationalist views in Bosnia make partition inevitable?

This is not as straightforward as it seems. Some of the most strident, dogmatic political parties and movements are capable of changing their beliefs. The National Party in South Africa openly sympathized with the Nazis in World War II, advocated white supremacy and the rigid separation of races, and instituted a totalitarian political program to put its vision into practice. By 1990, however, it had reversed its position on apartheid and defined its platform in terms of culture instead of race.

Likewise, cultural practices and ideas that seem permanent can be transitory. Cultures often have a wealth of traditions and beliefs that form the basis for their identities. Prevailing cultural practices and beliefs may reflect the interests of power holders who benefit from a particular conception of ethnicity.[24] The triumph of pathological forms of ethnicity or nationalism is more likely in times of rapid change and when gross economic and political inequalities exist.[25]

Political movements and parties are rarely unified on goals and beliefs; cultures often contain competing visions. As long as there are intragroup differences and as long as those who are willing to accept compromise solutions can influence group decision-making, then the preferences of a party or group are changeable. However, when individual leaders hold immutable preferences and are able to maintain strict discipline within the group, then the groups's preferences will be immutable until the leader is replaced.

In short, it is important to understand that the beliefs of some leaders and groups are malleable, and others are not.

THE RHETORIC OF TOTAL WAR

Some parties fight civil wars for limited goals; others fight for complete control over the country in question but can be persuaded to accept compromise settlements; still others will accept nothing short of total victory. Most parties, however, invoke the rhetoric of total war, denying the possibility or desirability of compromise and pledging to eliminate enemies — whether classes or ethnic groups — when they emerge victorious.

The rhetoric of total war creates two problems for negotiations. First, a leader who becomes willing to negotiate will find it difficult to signal

---

24. Gerard Maré, *Brothers Born of Warrior Blood: Politics and Ethnicity in South Africa* (Johannesburg: Raven Press, 1993).

25. Rothchild and Groth, "Pathological Dimensions," pp. 73–74.

new intentions if he has made repeated pledges to fight to the finish. A leader who hears moderate language from a formerly implacable foe will find it difficult to determine if it is sincere. If one eschews negotiation with an opponent who is sincere about making peace, then the war continues and the opportunity to end the war is squandered. If one reaches a settlement with an opponent who is insincere about making peace, then one risks making oneself vulnerable to an opponent who is looking for precisely such an advantage.

Second, the rhetoric of total war can create problems between leaders and followers. One reason for using the rhetoric of total war is that some followers like to hear it. Problems are therefore likely to arise when leaders who were formerly publicly committed to total victory enter into negotiations; they may be willing to compromise with their adversaries, but fear the reactions of their supporters. Factions opposed to compromise may continue to employ the language of total war and accuse their leaders of cowardice and treachery. Those leaders may make peace, only to find themselves under attack by former allies. For example, Michael Collins, the leader of the IRA, negotiated the partition of Ireland in 1921 and noted that he had likely signed his death warrant. In less than six months, his premonition came true: he was assassinated by former colleagues who felt he had betrayed the cause of Irish nationalism.

Such fears often drive leaders to talk peace in private and war in public. This is a dangerous balancing act, however: these leaders must contain the effects of invoking total war and persuade adversaries that their public belligerence is not representative of their true intentions.

The problem is that some people mean what they say. When Radio Mille Collines in Rwanda broadcast that Tutsi were enemies who had to be exterminated, it was not a mask for a complex political situation, but an accurate representation of the aspirations and preferences of the Presidential Guard in that country.

Unfortunately it is extremely difficult to discern the commitment of leaders and movements to their rhetoric. In 1979, some U.S. policymakers believed that if he came to power, Ayatollah Khomeini would moderate his plans for an Islamic revolution. Many Rhodesians believed that Robert Mugabe would carry out a socialist, racial revolution if he were to come to power. At least one analyst of the Cambodian peace process believed that the Khmer Rouge could be appeased because "the real Khmer Rouge military aim . . . is to force Phnom Penh to accept a comprehensive political settlement."[26] All of these judgments share one thing in common: they were wrong.

---

26. Stephen Morris, "Skeletons in the Closet," *New Republic*, June 4, 1990, p. 19.

Conditions Favoring Negotiated Settlements

There are enough similarities among negotiated settlements to civil wars to suggest some generalizations about the conditions that facilitate settlement. These facilitating conditions are tied to the moderation or absence of the characteristics of civil war discussed above.

FEARS ABOUT PEACE SETTLEMENTS

The four characteristics of civil war that hinder negotiated settlements are mutually reinforcing. The rhetoric of total war, perceptions of total stakes, and the possibility that one's opponent wants to dominate the country politically work together to intensify fears. Rational calculations of cost and benefit become distorted as perceptions of risk become magnified: parties overestimate the risks of settlement and underestimate the risks of continuing the war. The parties come to fear settlements more than they fear continued fighting.

Two factors contribute to a decision to sign a peace agreement. First, the greater the fear of what will happen if the war continues, the greater the willingness to reach a negotiated settlement. The prospect of greater pain and the impending loss of the resources needed to fight create pressures for negotiation. Second, the lesser the fear of the consequences of settlement, the greater the willingness to reach a negotiated settlement. Parties are more likely to sign an agreement if they believe that it will provide security.

In theory, these factors should be of equal importance in decisions on these matters; reducing the fear of settlement should be as important as increasing the fear of continued conflict. In practice, however, the latter is more important for four reasons. First, parties usually do not begin to explore the possibility of a negotiated settlement until their military alternatives are in doubt. Second, a sense of urgency — that things can get worse if negotiations fail — is often necessary for parties to reach agreement.[27] Third, perceptions about the battlefield can change quickly, but perceptions about the trustworthiness of an opponent change slowly. And fourth, military outcomes are usually easier to predict than political processes; the uncertainties associated with settlements generate caution. Thus, parties in civil wars seek agreements, not out of a desire for reconciliation and peace, but because military and political conditions compel them to stop fighting.

---

27. I. William Zartman, *Ripe for Resolution: Conflict and Intervention in Africa* (New York: Oxford University Press, 1985).

INCREASING THE FEAR OF CONTINUED CONFLICT. Concerns about the consequences of continuing to fight played important roles in all of the civil war settlements of the 1980s and 1990s. In Zimbabwe, the regime of Bishop Abel Muzorewa sought a settlement in 1979 because it believed that it was losing the war. Although Robert Mugabe believed that his Zimbabwe African National Union (ZANU) party would eventually win the war, he settled in part because his main patron, President Samora Machel of Mozambique, threatened to cut off his sanctuaries and supply routes.

A similar calculation prompted the warring parties in Cambodia to sign the Paris Peace Accords in 1991. The withdrawal of Vietnam from Cambodia created potentially dangerous problems for the Hun Sen government. At the same time, the withdrawal of Chinese support for the Khmer Rouge created grave doubts about the ability of the guerrilla movement to survive.[28]

In the case of Mozambique, the Mozambican National Resistance (RENAMO) signed the Rome peace accords in 1992 because a severe drought limited its ability to feed its soldiers and supporters, and it faced the loss of support of its main patron, South Africa.[29] The Mozambican government agreed to negotiate because its *de facto* sovereignty was limited to a small section of territory around the capital, Maputo. International donors and financial institutions, which kept the Mozambican government solvent and *de jure* sovereign, pushed it to seek a negotiated settlement.

Moscow's decision in early 1989 to stop sending arms to Central America "knocked the revolutionary perspective off balance" and prompted the Farabundo Marti National Liberation Front (FMLN) to reassess its military prospects and political demands in El Salvador.[30] A devastating guerrilla offensive in November 1989 undermined right-wing hardliners who believed that they could win a victory. Both sides were forced to recalibrate their prospects.[31]

---

28. Steven R. Ratner, *The New UN Peacekeeping: Building Peace in Lands of Conflict After the Cold War* (New York: St. Martin's and the Council on Foreign Relations, 1995), pp. 142–146, 158; and Findlay, *Cambodia*, pp. 3–4.

29. Cameron Hume, *Ending Mozambique's War: The Role of Mediation and Good Offices* (Washington, D.C.: U.S. Institute of Peace, 1994), p. 146; Witney W. Schneidman, "Conflict Resolution in Mozambique," in David R. Smock, ed., *Making War and Waging Peace: Foreign Intervention in Africa* (Washington, D.C.: U.S. Institute of Peace, 1993), pp. 233–234.

30. Terry Lynn Karl, "El Salvador's Negotiated Revolution," *Foreign Affairs*, Vol. 71, No. 2 (Spring 1992), pp. 151–152.

31. Ibid., p. 152.

Concerns about continued fighting can also be influenced by non-military considerations. In the case of South Africa, Nelson Mandela feared that a continuation of the war could endanger his leadership and bring to power a younger generation committed to a complete revolution. The decision of Gerry Adams, head of Sinn Fein (the political wing of the IRA), to denounce violence in Northern Ireland has been attributed to his concern that the IRA was becoming politically irrelevant among Catholics in Northern Ireland, who increasingly disdained violence.[32]

Leaders in civil wars vary greatly in their sensitivity to costs and aversion to risk. For example, Afonso Dhlakama, president of RENAMO, came to fear the consequences of the war in Mozambique only after fifteen years of fighting and more than one million deaths. In contrast, international sanctions and a low-level insurgency that killed several thousand people were enough to persuade F.W. de Klerk that South Africa had reached "a dead end street," where continued violence could lead to an all-out race war.[33]

Fears about the consequences of continued conflict explain an important aspect of most of the negotiated settlements mentioned above: with the exception of Cambodia, none was reached while a cease-fire was in place. In Angola, El Salvador, Mozambique, Nicaragua, and Zimbabwe, fighting continued while the parties negotiated. A cease-fire dampens the sense of urgency surrounding the situation and provides the warring parties with an opportunity to regroup and resupply troops in anticipation of further combat.

Finally, the fear of the consequences of continued conflict can be temporary. In the cases of Angola, Cambodia, El Salvador, Mozambique, and Zimbabwe in 1991, the warring parties negotiated when their patrons made it clear that they were willing to cut off military assistance. This contributed to negotiated settlements in all of these cases, but in the cases of Angola and Cambodia, two of the warring sides, National Union for the Total Independence of Angola (UNITA) and the Khmer Rouge, respectively, later resumed fighting: both developed black market sources of arms and supplies to replace the assistance provided by their former patrons.

---

32. Martha Crenshaw, "Decisions to Abandon Terrorism: A Preliminary Case Study of the IRA," paper delivered at the 1995 Annual Meeting of the American Political Science Association, Chicago, Illinois, August 31–September 3, 1995, pp. 6–7.

33. Thomas Ohlson and Stephen John Stedman, with Robert Davies, *The New Is Not Yet Born: Conflict Resolution in Southern Africa* (Washington, D.C.: Brookings Institution, 1994), p. 73.

REDUCING THE FEAR OF SETTLEMENT. In general, the fear of continued conflict triggers the search for a negotiated settlement; indeed, the fear of continued conflict can be enough to get leaders to sign a peace agreement.[34] The likelihood of reaching a negotiated settlement is increased, however, if the negotiations can reduce the fears of the participants about the prospective settlement.

Fears about settlements can be reduced in three ways: first, through the creation of detailed agreements; second, through external involvement in supervising, monitoring, verifying, and implementing the agreement; and third, through the creation of trust and mutual interest between the warring parties. Common to these processes is the ability of the warring parties to learn about the needs of their adversaries, various methods of addressing their own concerns, and why some solutions are inadequate.

When parties first agree to pursue negotiations in civil wars, their demands are often expressed in slogans: "one person/one vote," "group rights," "ethnic self-determination," "the proper legitimacy of the state," and "the need for law and order." Negotiations are needed to fill in the details that provide substance to the slogans. For example, a principle as simple and compelling as "one person/one vote" generated four years of negotiations in South Africa.

Addressing long-term fears requires agreement on the modalities and division of power and resources: will elections determine who will rule in the country? What kind of electoral system will be used? Will there be formal provisions for power-sharing? Will constitutional reform be part of the settlement? If so, will it be negotiated before or after an election? How will power be distributed regionally — through a federal or confederal arrangement? Will the performance and membership of state agencies — such as the police, judiciary, and military — be part of the negotiations?

Once the parties settle on the end point, process issues come to the fore. Parties must establish arrangements for establishing and monitoring a cease-fire. They must agree on whether demobilization and disarmament of soldiers will take place before or after an election. They must determine whether a new army will be established or whether elements of the rebel army will be incorporated into the government's existing army. Decisions must also be made about state authority during the transition, and the organization and monitoring of elections.

Successful settlements of civil wars have varied tremendously in their substantive answers to these questions. In South Africa, the parties agreed

---

34. Michael Doyle, *UN Peacekeeping in Cambodia: UNTAC's Civil Mandate*, International Peace Academy Occasional Paper Series (Boulder, Colo.: Lynne Rienner, 1995), p. 68; Findlay, *Cambodia*, pp. 49–50; Ratner, *The New UN Peacekeeping*, pp. 158–159.

on an interim government of national unity based on the principle of power-sharing; in El Salvador, Mozambique, Namibia, Nicaragua, and Zimbabwe, the combatants shunned power-sharing. In Zimbabwe, constitutional negotiations took place before elections; in South Africa and Namibia, parties agreed on broad constitutional principles but left the drafting of the constitution until after an election. South Africa put into place a weak federal system of government; Mozambique and El Salvador maintained centralized governments. In Mozambique and El Salvador, demobilization of guerrilla soldiers took place before elections; in Zimbabwe and South Africa, afterwards.

Negotiated settlements are facilitated by societal and regional contexts that create common frameworks for political solutions. Settlements in El Salvador, Nicaragua, and South Africa have been aided tremendously by societal and regional expectations that negotiations would ultimately lead to the institution of democratic forms of governance. Moreover, these expectations strengthen the prospects of sustaining democracy. Democracy requires that parties not know the results of elections beforehand; this creates an incentive for parties to participate in the hope of winning — a hope that was emphasized by mediators in Angola and Zimbabwe to induce the parties to settle. The problem, of course, is that elections have losers as well as winners. In established democracies, parties are certain that elections will continue to be contested in the future; this gives losers an incentive to accept electoral defeats. Although civil wars are destructive of the trust that is needed for parties to believe that their opponents will abide by their democratic obligations, organizations in civil society and regional organizations can help to create the expectation that democracy will continue in the future.

If the parties in civil wars can eliminate some of their mistrust and create a record of cooperation, negotiations are more likely to lead to peaceful settlements. In South Africa, a substantial amount of social capital was created during the negotiations by ANC and National Party efforts to solve various problems. But trust and confidence are not necessary conditions for settlements. In Angola, Cambodia, El Salvador, Mozambique, Namibia, Rwanda, and Zimbabwe, parties signed peace agreements while retaining grave suspicions about their enemies. An international role in monitoring and implementing agreements is crucial as a substitute for and possible creator of trust.

Warring parties have turned to the international community to provide troops to monitor and verify compliance of cease-fire, cantonment, and disarmament provisions; register and educate potential voters; carry out, monitor, and certify elections; investigate human rights violations; and train and re-educate police and military forces. External involvement can be minimal, as in South Africa, where the international community was asked to monitor political violence during the negotiations and elections, and observe the elections to ensure the freedom and fairness of the vote. Or it can be extensive, as in Cambodia, where the United Nations spent nearly $2 billion and sent nearly 20,000 soldiers and civilians to provide administrative support, carry out elections, protect human rights, repatriate refugees, assist with demining the countryside, and supervise and assist disarming and demobilizing the warring armies.

The international community can reduce fears by helping to build confidence that agreements will protect both sides and by enabling the parties to develop confidence in each other. The international community does not "guarantee" agreements in the sense that it will punish violators. As Steven Ratner notes, an international guarantee "literally guarantees nothing, but has political significance and some legal content."[35]

In some negotiated settlements, the parties maintained external alliances that could protect them if the agreement collapsed. In these cases, the fear of settlement was lessened by the knowledge that regional allies would provide help if needed. In the case of Zimbabwe, South Africa's military presence provided some assurance to the white regime, just as Mozambique, Tanzania, and Zambia (and indirectly, the Eastern Bloc countries) provided a security blanket for the Zimbabwean guerrillas. In the case of Namibia, South Africa's military might stood in reserve if South West African People's Organization (SWAPO) used the peace process to gain a tactical advantage in the war. In the case of Mozambique, the government could rely on the muscle of Zimbabwe and the new majority-ruled regime in South Africa if RENAMO resumed fighting. Indeed, during the election in October 1994, when RENAMO threatened to pull out of the peace agreement, South Africa and Zimbabwe pressured rebel leader Afonso Dhlakama into maintaining his commitment to the accords.

COMBATING TOTALISTIC PERCEPTIONS, STAKES, AND RHETORIC

Negotiated settlements are difficult to reach when the parties see the character of their opponents as a cause of the war, seek political domination, and use the rhetoric of total war. Four factors can help to facilitate settlements in the face of such problems.

First, warring parties can take actions to convince their opponents that they are willing to accept compromise solutions. Such actions are

---

35. Ratner, *The New UN Peacekeeping*, p. 49.

likely to be more credible if they are costly. Before formal constitutional negotiations began in South Africa, for example, the ANC signaled its desire to accommodate minorities by proposing proportional representation as the electoral system for the new constitution, even though a plurality system would have worked more to its advantage. In the Lancaster House negotiations on Zimbabwe, ZANU general Josiah Tongagara shared strategic information with the British and Rhodesians to signal his willingness to see a cease-fire implemented.

Second, the actions and language of leaders can play a key role in negating totalistic perceptions. Before his release from prison in 1990, Nelson Mandela spent four years talking with officials of the National Party in an effort to convince them that the ANC was not intent on racial domination. Between 1990 and 1994, Mandela constantly stated his desire to create a South Africa where whites, especially Afrikaaners, could prosper.

Third, peacemakers from the warring parties can create informal alliances to combat extremists who oppose peace. In El Salvador, "an unlikely tacit alliance emerged between ARENA [National Republican Alliance] and the FMLN [Farabundo Marti National Liberation Front] to overcome widespread skepticism about the prospects for peace and the opposition of hardliners."[36] In South Africa, the success of negotiations depended on the ability of two negotiators, Cyril Ramaphosa and Roelf Meyer, to present a unified front against attacks from extremists in their own parties who charged that they were compromising vital interests.

Fourth, negotiations can be facilitated if a civil society independent of the warring sides can create a lobby for peace, strengthen the standing of those who oppose the extremes, combat totalistic rhetoric, and encourage individuals from different groups and parties to interact and exchange views and information. Debate, dialogue, and access to information can play important roles in changing perceptions. In El Salvador and South Africa, the presence of independent organizations that could promote peace and discourage traditional racial and political stereotyping helped to reduce the fear of settlement among the warring parties. Such experiences stand in marked contrast to Rwanda and Angola, for example, where the media was controlled by the warring parties. Civil organizations, independent of the warring sides, were few in both countries and extremely vulnerable to attack by extremists.

---

36. Karl, "El Salvador's Negotiated Revolution," p. 159.

LEADERSHIP CHANGE

Often a change of leadership is necessary to produce a negotiated settlement. In the Mexican Revolution, circumstances favored a negotiated settlement, but Zapata could not bring himself to trust the Mexican government. After his death, Zapata's successor, Magaña, ended the war.[37] A negotiated settlement to the Zimbabwean civil war came only after Bishop Abel Muzorewa replaced Ian Smith as the chief negotiator for the Rhodesians. More recently, a negotiated settlement to South Africa's protracted insurgency was possible in part because F.W. de Klerk replaced P.W. Botha as president of South Africa.[38]

The Role of Mediators

International mediation can assist negotiations by influencing the subjective perceptions and the objective environment of the disputants. Mediation can intensify fears of continuing to fight and add to the sense of urgency surrounding deliberations. It can also lessen fears of settlement and provide a way for parties to test their perceptions about the character, aims, and needs of their opponents. To do these things effectively, mediation requires leverage, problem-solving abilities, strategy, and timing.

LEVERAGE

Leverage is the ability of the mediator to alter the objective environment of the disputants: in particular, the capacity of the parties to prosecute the war, the tangible rewards of choosing peace, and the provision of personnel and services to reduce the risks of settlement. Applying leverage to increase the fear of continued conflict is simple in theory, but difficult in practice. In theory, there are various options available to mediators to raise the costs of continuing a war, including imposing sanctions on one or all warring parties, selectively arming one of the parties, and using military force against recalcitrant parties. The more aggressive the action, however, the more it is likely to impose costs on and create risks for the mediator — principally, the risk that the mediator becomes an active belligerent in the conflict or inadvertently escalates the war.

This usually leads mediators to be more aggressive with the threat of military sanctions than with the actual use of military force. The effective-

---

37. Womack, *Zapata and the Mexican Revolution.*

38. Allister Sparks, *Tomorrow is Another Country: The Inside Story of South Africa's Road to Change* (New York: Hill and Wang, 1995), pp. 68–90.

ness of threats, of course, depends on their credibility. In 1979, the British government skillfully used the threat to recognize the Muzorewa regime (which implied providing military and financial assistance to the regime) to reach a settlement to the Zimbabwean civil war. Britain first won Muzorewa's support by promising him diplomatic recognition if he accepted the peace settlement and if the Patriotic Front declined. Once he accepted, Britain was in a strong position to gain Patriotic Front acceptance of the peace plan. Its threat worked because it was credible; no one doubted British Prime Minister Margaret Thatcher's willingness to follow through.

Elsewhere, threats have failed because the mediators in question lacked credibility. In Namibia, the Contact Group (Britain, Canada, France, Germany, and the United States) threatened South Africa with tough economic sanctions in 1979 if it continued to drag its feet in its negotiations with SWAPO. South Africa defied the Contact Group's threat because it knew that the group had been formed to prevent the imposition of sanctions. The same thing happened in Bosnia in August 1994, when a different Contact Group (Britain, France, Germany, Russia, and the United States) threatened severe repercussions, including lifting the arms embargo against the Bosnian government, if the Bosnian Serbs did not agree to peace terms. The Bosnian Serbs called the Contact Group's bluff, knowing that the group's *raison d'être* — the prevention of a split among its members — forestalled any policy that might escalate the war.

An alternative source of leverage is interference with the ability of disputants to fight by interdicting the supply of arms, ammunition, and other matériel. This usually requires working with regional patrons, who provide rebel movements and warring states with arms and other support. The Paris Peace Agreements on Cambodia succeeded in large part because of pressures brought by China, the Soviet Union, Thailand, and Vietnam on Cambodia's warring parties. To end the Zimbabwean civil war, Britain sought and received the cooperation of Mozambique, Tanzania, and Zambia in pressing the Patriotic Front to negotiate. The cut-off of Soviet assistance in Nicaragua and El Salvador pressured the Sandinistas and the FMLN to seek political settlements; at a crucial juncture in the Salvadoran peace process, a suspension of U.S. aid led the Salvadoran regime to make concessions.

It is difficult to tie the threat to terminate military assistance to fears of continuing to fight. Imposing an arms embargo on all warring parties can dampen the intensity of the war and lead to what I. William Zartman refers to as a grinding stalemate, where the combatants have the ability to continue the war at low levels and do not feel any urgency about reaching a settlement.[39] The threat to cut off military assistance is most effective when it is aimed at one recalcitrant party and holds the potential to alter the balance on the battlefield.

Leverage is more than a tool for intensifying fears or punishing recalcitrant parties. Donald Rothchild observes that several sources of leverage are aimed at rewarding parties who choose to pursue peace: purchase, or the payment of tangible resources to parties; insurance, or the provision of services and goods in order to reduce the fears of the parties; and legitimacy, or the recognition of the claims and status of warring parties.[40]

PROBLEM-SOLVING

Reducing the fears of settlement requires engaging the warring parties in problem-solving; that is, the development of practical solutions to their demands and needs. A prerequisite for problem-solving is facilitating communications between the parties, who often enter into negotiations with drastically different perceptions about the conflict and visions of peace. Mediators must constantly press combatants to address practical concerns and not voice objections in philosophical terms.

This does not necessarily mean that the mediator's task is to resolve misperceptions among the parties. Rather, the mediator must establish ways for the parties to test their perceptions about their opponents and, if warranted, then change their perceptions. The distinction is a small but important one, and it relates to the earlier discussion about the character of adversaries. If the roots of a conflict are misperceptions that the parties have about each other's intentions and aims, then resolving misperception is necessary. But this depends on the judgment of the mediator that the warring groups are in fact divided by misperceptions. If some leaders seek total power and unilateral victory, then the role of mediation should be to bring these aims into the open. One does that not by persuading the warring parties to that their conflict is mired in misperceptions, but by helping the parties test their judgments of character.

Problem-solving in civil war must address three issues. First, the warring parties need to create rules that will structure and govern their political interactions. Mediators can help by introducing the parties to various constitutional and electoral options. Second, the parties need to agree on how to manage the transition from war to peace. Mediators can

---

39. Zartman, *Ripe for Resolution*, pp. 265–266.

40. Donald Rothchild, "Managing Ethnic Conflict," chap. 12, unpublished manuscript, University of California at Davis, pp. 31–41.

assist the parties by pointing out issues that may arise in the course of a transition. Mediators can help the parties consider different methods of establishing cease-fires, of demobilization and disarmament, and military integration. Advice of this kind played an important part in ending Mozambique's civil war. Third, problem-solving must address the role of international actors in implementing agreements. On the one hand, mediators should use the prospect of international supervision to assuage the fears of combatants; on the other hand, it is vitally important for warring parties to understand that agreements must ultimately be self-enforcing.

In the short term, international observers can monitor and verify compliance; they can assist in carrying out elections, disarmament measures, and demobilization efforts. In the long term, international personnel will withdraw and the parties themselves must live with their agreements and make them work. Mediators should therefore attempt to socialize the warring parties and nurture a long-term peace process by emphasizing norms of responsibility and reciprocity.[41]

STRATEGY

If mediators are to be effective, they must have a strategy; that is, they must have preferred outcomes and ways of linking incentives and tactics to that outcome. Mediators must speak with one voice and be able to make credible threats and promises. They must also understand the demands of the parties, their vulnerabilities, and their internal politics if they are to develop influence over them.

The need to act in a unified, strategic manner can conflict with the need to acquire leverage over warring parties. Patrons of the warring parties may have the ability to pressure their clients, but they might have ideas about the terms of settlement that are at odds with those of mediators. For example, Britain and the United States found in 1976 that South Africa could be used to bring pressure on Rhodesian Prime Minister Ian Smith's regime in Zimbabwe. The price for using this leverage was that South Africa would not accept a negotiated settlement with Robert Mugabe, the leader of ZANU. In other cases, the regional patron may balk at penalizing its client. If regional patrons oppose the threats and promises made by mediators, the latter may lose credibility. For example,

---

41. Brian S. Mandell and Brian W. Tomlin, "Mediation in the Development of Norms to Manage Conflict: Kissinger in the Middle East," *Journal of Peace Research*, Vol. 28, No. 1 (January 1991), pp. 43–55; and Donald Rothchild, *Racial Bargaining in Independent Kenya* (London: Oxford University Press, 1973).

the unwillingness of Serbia in 1994 to go very far in punishing the Bosnian Serbs further undermined the credibility of the Contact Group.

The Bosnia case suggests that coercive mediation cannot work unless interested states in the region support the mediation effort.[42] If a decision is made to mediate a war, then outside powers must make sure that other policy initiatives also support the mediation process. However justifiable they might be on their own, war crimes trials and humanitarian interventions should be launched only if they advance the prospects for a negotiated settlement.

Bosnia also proves a well-known dictum about mediation — that the interests of the mediators place limits on possible solutions and effective strategies.[43] As discussed earlier, the political rationale for forming the Contact Group constrained its willingness to pursue the single strategy that might have ended the war: severe punishment of the Bosnian Serbs.

Because of the key role that strategy and coordination play in mediation, some scholars believe that the United Nations should not mediate civil wars. Saadia Touval, for instance, argues that the United Nations is organizationally incapable of pursuing coherent mediation strategies.[44] This is too harsh a judgment. In Somalia and Western Sahara, it is clear that the strategy of the UN mediator was confounded by actions taken by the UN Secretary-General in New York.[45] But in Bosnia, UN mediators were confounded more by the disparate policies of member states than by organizational problems in the United Nations.

When concerned member states reach a consensus on how to terminate a war, the United Nations can be an effective agent for bringing this about. In El Salvador, Alvaro de Soto, the UN Secretary-General's special representative, skillfully mediated between the warring factions and had the support of key countries when he needed to make promises. Indeed, an informal division of labor developed, whereby de Soto played the role

42. For more details, see Stephen John Stedman, "U.N. Intervention in Civil Wars: Imperatives of Choice and Strategy," in Donald C.F. Daniel and Bradd C. Hayes, eds., *Beyond Traditional Peacekeeping* (New York: St. Martin's, 1995), pp. 53–55.

43. See Saadia Touval and I. William Zartman, "Introduction: Mediation in Theory," in Saadia Touval and I. William Zartman, eds., *International Mediation in Theory and Practice* (Boulder, Colo.: Westview, 1985), pp. 7–17.

44. Saadia Touval, "Why the U.N. Fails," *Foreign Affairs*, Vol. 73, No. 5 (September/October 1994), pp. 44–57.

45. On Western Sahara, see William J. Durch, "Building on Sand: UN Peacekeeping in the Western Sahara," *International Security*, Vol. 17, No. 4 (Spring 1993), pp. 151–171. On Somalia, see Jonathan Stevenson, "Hope Restored in Somalia?" *Foreign Policy*, No. 91 (Summer 1991), pp. 138–154.

of the good cop, making and delivering on promises and earning the trust of the warring parties; the patrons of the warring sides played the role of the bad cop, threatening punishment when needed.

TIMING

Mediation should be timed to coincide with the moment when one or more of the combatants begins to fear the consequences of continuing the war. When mediation efforts are launched at the proper time, a skillful third party will add to the growing sense of urgency. For example, British mediators of the Zimbabwean civil war expertly cultivated the perception that Lancaster House was the warring parties' last chance to end the war through negotiations. If the conference failed, London implied, the result would be escalation and a bloody total war. This increased the pressure on the parties to stay at the negotiating table.

Mediation efforts should not be like buses that come along every fifteen minutes. Instead, they should be like the Lake Victoria ferry — one never knows if and when it is likely to pass by again. Warring parties are unlikely to fear the consequences of continuing to fight if they feel that mediation is always available as a fallback option. The international community must therefore resist the urge to mediate whenever and wherever there is war. Mediators must be willing to quit when the combatants are not sufficiently motivated to make peace. An unwillingness to quit leads the local parties to devalue the importance of mediation, encourages stubbornness, and delegitimizes the entire enterprise. Mediation under unpropitious circumstances can drive warring parties further apart, rather than bringing them closer together.

The Importance of Implementation

Between 1991 and 1994, settlements to four civil wars — in Cambodia, Liberia, Angola, and Rwanda — were successfully negotiated, only to fall apart during the implementation phase. When war resumed in the latter two cases, the levels of killing far surpassed the violence of the periods that preceded the settlements.

The reasons for implementation problems are directly related to the characteristics of civil wars. Since fear is high and trust is low among antagonists in civil wars, parties may fail to carry out their commitments because they believe their adversaries will take advantage of them. In some cases, leaders define conflicts in all-or-nothing terms, and their commitments to negotiated settlements are only tactical: they seek to weaken their opponents and strengthen themselves. If the agreement in question promises to bring them to power, they will of course be more likely to meet their stated obligations. However, if the agreement will reduce their power, they will be inclined to resume fighting. These problems are intensified if the warring parties are poorly organized; rogue factions may try to destroy the agreement by undermining its implementation.

Many international mediators assume that the signing of a peace agreement establishes that the warring parties have a mutual understanding of the stakes of implementation and a common desire for peace over war.[46] Moreover, military planning for implementing peace agreements is always based on best-case assumptions about the good faith of the warring parties.[47] These assumptions are profoundly misleading. Mediators must take into account the uncertainties inherent in the implementation phase of the process. Four major problems stand out.

First, the preferences of the warring parties are not always common knowledge. Signing a peace agreement does not prove that combatants prefer peace to war. They may sign in order to buy time and regroup, hoping to take advantage of the settlement, resume fighting, and gain complete victory.

Second, the payoffs from implementing an agreement are not always known; the costs and benefits associated with making peace or returning to war are often murky. Since many settlements use elections to establish political payoffs and since the outcomes of elections are often unknown, one cannot say that the players know for certain what the payoffs for peace will be. A party may agree to a settlement because it hopes or expects to win a subsequent election; if it loses, it may prefer to resume fighting.

Parties in civil wars have often misjudged the risks of returning to war. The Presidential Guard in Rwanda believed that, by taking advantage of the peace settlement, it could win a complete victory and forge a final solution to the country's ethnic war. Instead, within two months — while it directed the slaughter of approximately 800,000 civilians — its army was routed by a much smaller opponent. Its payoff for returning to war was being driven into refugee camps in Zaire. In Angola, Jonas Savimbi's UNITA launched a post-election offensive in 1992 and went from controlling nearly eighty percent of the country to likely military defeat.

Third, it is often unclear what the act of cheating means during the implementation phase of a settlement. In every civil war settlement

---

46. See Doyle, *UN Peacekeeping in Cambodia*, p. 82.

47. Findlay, *Cambodia*, p. 135.

achieved through 1995, there has been cheating on all sides. For example, a party may keep some soldiers out of cantonment areas as a precautionary move in case its opponent resumes fighting. A party may keep soldiers out of cantonment centers because they are useful for intimidating voters; it might want the settlement to go forward, but it might nonetheless cheat to improve its political position. A party may keep soldiers out of cantonment areas because its leader is waiting for the best moment to resume fighting in the hope of winning the war outright.

Fourth, many groups in civil wars lack organizational cohesiveness; this can make it difficult to attribute cheating to the group's leadership. During the implementation of the Lancaster House agreement in early 1980, Rhodesian special forces twice tried to assassinate Robert Mugabe, raising the issue of whether the forces had acted alone or under the command of their political bosses, who signed the peace agreement. In South Africa, violence perpetrated by police and rogue defense forces raised questions about the culpability of the de Klerk regime in efforts to undermine the peace settlement.

Some analysts argue that the international community should assess the will of the combatants before it agrees to implement a peace agreement in a civil war.[48] This assumes that the will of the parties to make peace is easy to ascertain. In practice, this is generally very difficult. In retrospect, for example, an observer might be able to say that the warring parties in Namibia and El Salvador wanted to make peace, but that was not clear at the time to the participants themselves or to third parties. In other cases, Zimbabwe in 1979 and Mozambique in 1992, it seemed clear that the parties lacked the will to make peace, but settlements were successfully implemented.

The Role of the International Community

In the short term, negotiated settlements of civil wars create dangerous periods of uncertainty and insecurity for the combatants. A key problem for antagonists (and third parties who attempt to oversee implementation of settlements) is imperfect information about the goals and character of their opponents. Are they sincere in wanting to make peace, or is their agreement a tactical maneuver? Even if all the relevant parties are sincere in wanting to make peace, their insecurity may lead them to pursue policies that are destructive of the mutual trust that is necessary for agreements to endure.

---

48. See Ratner, *The New UN Peacekeeping*, pp. 211–212.

Negotiated settlements provide opportunities for antagonists to reveal their true preferences. Implementation is the test of sincerity. But unless the implementation phase is designed and administered well, the failure of the parties to live up to their commitments may reflect inadequacies in the implementation framework rather than a lack of sincerity.

The task of assisting with the implementation of many peace settlements has fallen to the United Nations. Since 1989, the United Nations has attempted to implement settlements to civil wars in Angola, Cambodia, El Salvador, Mozambique, Namibia, Nicaragua, Rwanda, and Western Sahara. In doing so, it has tried to adapt its traditional approach to peacekeeping to a large set of tasks that were unanticipated when peacekeeping operations were first launched. Implementing negotiated settlements to civil wars falls between traditional peacekeeping and peace enforcement. It is similar to the former in that the warring parties have signed an agreement to stop fighting. But where traditional peacekeepers are asked to monitor the separation of contending armies, peace settlements to civil wars require the demobilization of forces and the creation of a unified army. Traditional peacekeeping worked because peace agreements between states involved static battle lines. Peace agreements in civil wars are inherently dynamic, and therefore are riskier and more difficult to monitor.

The United Nations can help implement peace settlements by addressing the uncertainties of the warring parties. By supplying information, monitoring and verifying compliance, and interpreting reluctance to meet obligations, it can help to clarify motives and reduce uncertainty about the preferences of the disputants. It can uphold rules of conduct and encourage compliance by punishing violations and rewarding cooperation. And it can try to raise the costs of going back to war by making appeals to regional and international sponsors.[49]

One misconception about the role of international actors in implementing peace settlements needs to be put to rest — that third parties enforce or guarantee agreements.[50] The idea that third parties protect disadvantaged parties or use military force to gain compliance distorts what has happened in successful implementation actions. If civil war had resumed in Zimbabwe, Britain and the Commonwealth would not have intervened to enforce the peace, nor did any of the participants expect this. If implementation of the El Salvador peace accords had broken

---

49. See Virginia Page Fortna, "Success and Failure in Southern Africa: Peacekeeping in Namibia and Angola," in Daniel and Hayes, *Beyond Traditional Peacekeeping*, p. 283.

50. See Walter, "The Resolution of Civil Wars."

down, neither the United Nations nor the United States would have intervened militarily to enforce the settlement.

Negotiated settlements of civil wars have, without exception, been self-enforcing; that is in part why they have been so rare. Although states may decide in the future to provide external enforcement for peace agreements, in the past they have shied away from doing so. Given the unwillingness of third parties to risk protracted military involvement in peace enforcement operations, the challenge for international policy-makers and policy analysts is to think of ways to convince disputants to honor their commitments in the absence of external coercion.

IMPLEMENTATION STRATEGIES

International actors have pursued three different strategies in trying to help implement settlements to civil wars. The first strategy, employed by Britain in implementing the Lancaster House agreement in Zimbabwe, strove to maintain a high degree of tension among the warring parties. Britain hoped that the antagonists would fulfill their obligations because they feared a resumption of fighting.[51]

The second strategy, employed by the United Nations in El Salvador and Mozambique, attempted to ease security concerns and build confidence between antagonists. The United Nations hoped that a grad-ual, phased implementation process would lead the parties to worry less about the consequences of the settlement. In Mozambique, the voluntary disarmament of the parties and the formation of a unified army was to take place before elections. In El Salvador, the demobilization and dis-armament of guerrillas and the purging of the armed forces of members who committed human rights violations were preconditions to the hold-ing of elections.

In 1994 and 1995, the United Nations employed a third strategy to implement the Lusaka peace accords on Angola. Drawing on the lessons learned by Jonas Savimbi's return to war in 1992, the United Nations established a phased implementation plan; UN peacekeepers would be deployed only after the parties met certain basic provisions of their agreement. The strategy was to make the parties demonstrate their good faith before investing UN resources in the implementation process.[52]

---

51. For a thorough discussion of the implementation of the Lancaster House accords, see Jeremy Ginifer, "Rhodesia/Zimbabwe Case Study," draft prepared for the United Nations Institute for Disarmament Research (UNIDIR) Project on Disarmament and Conflict Resolution, Geneva, Switzerland, June 1995.

52. Yvonne Lodico, "The United Nations Angolan Verification Mission (UNAVEM II) and Prospects for UNAVEM III," draft prepared for the Henry L. Stimson Center, March 1995.

Each strategy has risks and costs. The Lancaster House strategy was particularly risky because the vulnerability of the parties and their intense security concerns could have led either side to return to war. Moreover, the process was vulnerable to actors on both sides who wanted to return to war. Two assassination attempts were made on Robert Mugabe; if either had succeeded, it is unlikely that the guerrillas would have stayed committed to the settlement. It would not have taken much of a spark to re-ignite the war. Moreover, since the implementation plan did not include provisions for the demobilization and disarmament of the parties, it ensured that instability would continue to be a problem after the election and during the first years of the new regime.

The confidence-building strategy also has problems: it may reduce the sense of urgency that leads combatants to reach an agreement. It can also allow leaders to search for new ways of resuming the war, new sources of weaponry and support, and new opportunities for prevailing in combat. This is what happened in Angola in 1991–92 and Rwanda in 1993–94: the settlement interlude allowed combatants to regroup for war; the war then returned with unprecedented ferocity.

At first glance, it might appear that the reward strategy would help to address the problem of insincerity. It is problematic, however, in three respects. First, it asks parties to take high risks; outside troops are not part of the equation. Noncompliance, therefore, may be a function of fear more than insincerity. Second, if the parties in a civil war are willing to take bold risks for peace, they will not need peacekeepers as part of a confidence-building exercise. Third, although parties may take initial risks to get the United Nations to commit troops and personnel, their incentives to keep complying decrease over time as the incentives for the United Nations to stay involved increase. The reward strategy falls prey to what Michael Doyle refers to as the obsolescing bargain of UN peacekeeping: as long as few resources are committed, UN influence is high; as soon as the United Nations commits substantial resources and personnel, its influence wanes.[53] The need for the United Nations to justify high levels of investment increases the bargaining power of the warring parties.

IMPLEMENTATION PROBLEMS

The implementation of peace accords in civil wars must overcome several problems: parties who act as spoilers; incomplete adherence to agreements; lack of coordination between the mediators who design the

---

53. Doyle, *UN Peacekeeping in Cambodia*, pp. 82–83.

agreements and the United Nations, which has to implement them; lack of coordination among different UN bureaucracies that are involved in implementation; and the lack of international interest after agreements are narrowly implemented.

SPOILERS. The biggest problem by far in implementing peace accords in civil wars is getting parties who sign agreements to live up to their commitments. In Angola, Jonas Savimbi returned to war when he lost the first round of elections in 1992. In Cambodia, the Khmer Rouge reneged on the Paris Peace Accords almost immediately after signing them in 1992. In Rwanda, the Habyarimana government refused to implement key provisions of the Arusha Accords; when Juvenal Habyarimana finally took steps to proceed with the peace plan, he was assassinated by his own military, which then plunged the country into a genocidal civil war.

The United Nations, which was given the job of monitoring implementation of peace agreements in Angola, Cambodia, and Rwanda, seemed incapable of responding to clear signals that one or both of the parties in question were cheating. This can be explained in part by UN peacekeeping doctrine, which assumes that opposing transgressions makes UN operations vulnerable to charges of bias.

Mediators, who have a vested interest and substantial investment of time, energy, and honor in seeing settlements implemented, tend to interpret acts of noncompliance as being motivated by fear rather than insincerity. Even if they interpret motivations as malign and admit that insincerity is involved, they usually assert that the parties in question are trying to get better settlements, rather than attempting to destroy the settlements.

On the rare occasions when cheating is clearly recognized as such, the typical response by the international community is to reward the cheater — commonly referred to as appeasement. In Cambodia, the United Nations refused to stand up to Khmer Rouge and government violations of the peace accord, ignoring transgressions or using rewards to prompt compliance. And, as noted earlier, the United Nations and the United States responded to genocide in Rwanda by urging all parties to return to the negotiating table.

The Angolan example is a telling one. U.S. policymakers went to great lengths to blame everything but Savimbi's desire for power as the reason for the failure of the peace process. After Savimbi resumed fighting, a common sentiment in U.S. policy circles was that elections should not be used to terminate civil wars because elections provide few rewards to the losing party. Indeed, one State Department report went so far as to blame the "winner-take-all" electoral system in Angola as the cause of the collapse of the peace agreement, explaining that it was only natural for Savimbi to return to war when he received so little from the settlement.[54]

This kind of reasoning can be dismissed rather easily. Elections without power-sharing provisions were held in El Salvador, Mozambique, Nicaragua, and Zimbabwe — all cases where negotiated settlements were successfully implemented. Savimbi and UNITA received more from the Angolan settlement than any of the losing parties in El Salvador, Mozambique, Nicaragua, and Zimbabwe received in theirs. After the September 1992 Angolan elections, UNITA's share of seats in parliament was higher than that of any of the losing parties in El Salvador, Nicaragua, or Zimbabwe. Likewise, UNITA's representation on the general staff of the new Angolan army was greater than in any of the other cases, with the exception of Zimbabwe. Although UNITA lacked regional representation due to the highly centralized nature of the Angolan constitution, it should be pointed out that, with the exception of South Africa, none of these countries had federal constitutions that provided for regional governance.

In Angola, Cambodia, and Rwanda, appeasement was an ineffective and morally bankrupt policy. Appeasement cannot work if the target interprets appeasement as weakness. Critics of the UN operation in Cambodia believe that the failure of UN Special Representative Yasushi Akashi to challenge Khmer Rouge violations of the peace agreement "encouraged the Khmer Rouge to believe that it could get away with any abuse, no matter how blatant."[55] Moreover, the appeasement of the Khmer Rouge "gave the other Cambodian parties an incentive to violate provisions of the Accords."[56]

The odds against appeasement working are long because of the societal and cultural contexts operating in civil wars. By definition, societies at war are societies where the rule of law has broken down, where force has become the ultimate arbiter in disputes, and where accommodation can easily be interpreted as weakness.

To argue against appeasement is not to argue that the United Nations should automatically coerce violators of peace agreements. Rather, it is to argue that international military forces must be strong enough and determined enough to insist that local parties meet their obligations. If a party refuses to respect the terms of a peace accord, the United Nations should

---

54. Ann Reid, "Conflict Resolution in Africa: Lessons From Angola," *INR Foreign Affairs Brief* (Washington, D.C.: Bureau of Intelligence and Research, U.S. Department of State, April 6, 1993).

55. "Cambodia: Human Rights Before and After the Elections," *Asia Watch*, Vol. 5, No. 10 (May 1993), p. 7, cited in Findlay, *Cambodia*, p. 129.

56. Ibid.

call attention to the violation and establish that antagonists must adhere to rules. The willingness to take a tough line on violations must be established at the beginning of an operation, when the reputation of the mission is being formed. Once lost, credibility and legitimacy are extremely difficult to re-establish.[57]

An obstacle to establishing a tough approach to implementation is the operational code that UN bureaucrats bring with them. UN bureaucrats tend to see the world in a legalistic, not strategic, fashion.[58] They assume that local parties are acting in good faith to meet their obligations. The UN emphasis on the importance of maintaining a good working relationship with all parties can be a barrier to confronting recalcitrant civil war leaders effectively.[59]

INCOMPLETE ADHERENCE. Although civil wars were brought to an end in El Salvador, Mozambique, Namibia, Nicaragua, and Zimbabwe, many of the provisions of the peace accords were left unfulfilled in order to muddle through to an election. However, the failures to carry out all aspects of the accords have had dangerous implications for long-term stability in those countries. A failure to demobilize soldiers and provide them with financial means can lead to continuing political instability, as happened in Zimbabwe in the 1980s, or create large-scale banditry, a problem that has plagued Cambodia, El Salvador, and Mozambique. A failure to disarm factions and destroy stocks of weapons can create a thriving black market in small arms, which can prevent the establishment of law and order and destabilize other countries, a problem that has plagued Southern Africa.[60] A failure to address economic development problems can create new political grievances, which may incite new violence.

POOR COORDINATION BETWEEN MEDIATING AND IMPLEMENTING BODIES. The prospects for successful implementation of negotiated settlements could be improved by better coordination between those who mediate settlements and the United Nations, which implements them. In many cases,

---

57. See Findlay, *Cambodia*, pp. 131–132.

58. See Doyle, *UN Peacekeeping in Cambodia*, p. 82.

59. Ratner, *The New UN Peacekeeping*, pp. 200–202.

60. See Peter Batchelor, "Disarmament, Small Arms, and Internal Conflict: The Case of Southern Africa," and Chris Smith, "Light Weapons, Peacekeeping, Disarmament and Security: A Case Study of Southern Africa," drafts prepared for the UNIDIR Project on Disarmament and Conflict Resolution, Geneva, Switzerland, August 1995.

the warring parties have established timetables and logistical requirements that are impossible to meet. In Rwanda, UN approval of a mission
to implement the Arusha Accords came nearly three months after the
signing of the agreement. The number of soldiers sent to carry out the
mission was 2,500 less than the warring parties had expected. Their
deployment, moreover, was delayed until February 1994, six months after
the signing of the peace treaty.

In the case of Mozambique, the parties created an implementation
plan that called for the deployment of a large UN administrative and
military presence, which was to begin assisting the demobilization effort
in one month and carry out full demobilization, disarmament, creation of
a unified military, repatriation of over six million displaced persons, and
hold elections — all in one year's time. This was supposed to occur in a
country with little transportation or communication infrastructure. This
plan, negotiated without UN input, simply assumed that the United
Nations would be willing and able to meet these requirements. In the
event, the UN mandate for the mission in Mozambique was not approved
until two months after the peace agreement was signed; the first fully
operational contingent of troops arrived five months later. Similar stories
can be told about implementation of the peace accords in Angola and
Cambodia.

The international community's ability to assuage the fears of warring
parties depends on the quick arrival and establishment of the implementation force.[61] The United Nations must be kept aware of the demands
that will be made of it and plan accordingly; member states must quickly
authorize the resources and deployments needed to fulfill the mission;
and improvements must be made in contracting for delivery services.

POOR COORDINATION AMONG UN AGENCIES DURING IMPLEMENTATION.   The
peace treaties that have successfully ended civil wars in the 1990s have
been comprehensive documents that addressed a wide range of military,
political, social, and economic issues. Most have involved regional and
international participation. The tendency of the United Nations has been
to address these various components in an *ad hoc* way: peacekeepers have
been sent to build military confidence; relief workers have been sent to
address short-term humanitarian emergencies; development agencies
have helped to address long-term social needs; human rights advocates
have helped to educate people about the need to foster and protect
human rights; and representatives of international financial institutions

---

61. Findlay, *Cambodia*, pp. 113–116; Doyle, *UN Peacekeeping in Cambodia*, p. 83.

have tackled budgetary and monetary problems. What was lacking in many cases was effective coordination between and among these various activities and actors.

Alvaro de Soto, the UN negotiator of the Salvadoran peace accords, argues that in war-torn societies, international structural adjustment and stabilization policies often conflict with the implementation of peace plans in ways that keep both efforts from succeeding.[62] Peace settlements are more likely to succeed if money is provided to tackle the economic and social conditions that help produce civil war and political instability. Land transfers, demobilization efforts, military and police reforms, judiciary bodies, and militaries involve large expenses. Simultaneously, however, international financial institutions must attempt to create the fiscal discipline necessary for long-term economic growth. The problem, ultimately, is that neither peace nor economic development is independently sustainable.[63]

LACK OF ASSISTANCE. This double-barreled problem could be more readily overcome if the international community would sustain assistance to countries that successfully implement peace agreements. Donors are often willing to promise aid and assistance while peace agreements are being negotiated and implemented, but attention wanes and resources vanish when peace triumphs, usually signaled by the holding of elections. Between 1991 and 1994, for example, donors pledged nearly $1.7 billion to Cambodia; actual assistance delivered was $300–500 million.[64] In El Salvador, donors were quick to pledge support for the government's national reconstruction plan, but they have been slow in disbursing money. One year after the 1994 elections, the government had to appeal to donors to help meet a shortfall of approximately $158 million in financing for the peace accords.[65]

The sustenance of peace settlements depends on more than financial assistance from the international community. Drawing on the Cambodian experience, Trevor Findlay argues that international agencies should con-

---

62. Alvaro de Soto and Graciana del Castillo, "Obstacles to Peacebuilding," *Foreign Policy*, No. 94 (Spring 1994), pp. 69–83.

63. Ibid., p. 71.

64. William Shawcross, *Cambodia's New Deal*, Contemporary Issues Paper No. 1 (Washington, D.C.: Carnegie Endowment for International Peace, 1994), pp. 87–88.

65. Gobierno de El Salvador, *Avance de los Programs de Reinsercion* (San Salvador: Secretaria de Reconstruccion Nacional, February 1995), p. 5. I would like to thank Lael Parish for obtaining and translating this and other documents from El Salvador.

tinue long-term confidence-building programs long after elections bring the formal peace process to a close.[66]

Conclusions

The difficulties of negotiating civil wars, the conditions that lead to successful settlement, and the unpredictability that surrounds the implementation of agreements raise basic questions about the ethics and effectiveness of mediation as an international response to civil war. At least four issues require consideration: trade-offs between moderating the effects of war and the efficacy of bringing the war to an end; trade-offs between accountability for atrocities committed during the war and the pragmatic demands of mediation; trade-offs between the desire for parties to end their war through negotiation and the likelihood of successful mediation; and the obligations of mediators who make promises to warring parties.

As argued throughout this chapter, mediation in civil war is likely to be more successful when the parties come to fear the consequences of continued warfare. This means that international actors should do little to moderate the horrors of civil war. Although well-intentioned policies such as humanitarian intervention can lessen the costs and pain of war for civilians, they also strengthen the ability of the combatants to prolong the war. Food supplies delivered to civilians in Bosnia, Rwanda, Somalia, and Sudan have been used by armies to strengthen themselves. Safe havens in Bosnia have been used by Bosnian soldiers as supply depots and sanctuaries for launching attacks on Bosnian Serbs. An ethical standard must be used to evaluate how policies that lessen costs in the short term affect the chances of ending the war for good.[67]

Second, mediation is more likely to be successful when the fears of settlement are reduced. This means that punishing leaders and soldiers for war crimes might have to be sacrificed in some cases as the price for peace. In Angola, Cambodia, Mozambique, and Rwanda, the international community judged that stopping the fighting was of overriding importance. It was decided that certain provisions with respect to human rights and war crimes could be sacrificed. In Cambodia, holding

---

66. See Findlay, *Cambodia*, p. 169.

67. For the counterargument that short-term considerations of saving lives should take precedent over possible long-term solutions, see Saadia Touval, "Ethical Dilemmas in International Mediation," *Negotiation Journal*, Vol. 11, No. 4 (October 1995), pp. 333–337.

the Khmer Rouge accountable for its slaughter of millions in the 1970s was deemed less important than bringing the war to a close. In Mozambique, the price of a peace settlement was rewarding RENAMO for atrocities that it committed in the 1980s; it was a price the international community decided was worth paying.

The possibility of ending a protracted deadly war and the suffering it causes can warrant compromising even on important principles. However, sacrificing all norms of conduct to the altar of negotiated settlement robs the international community of a tool for bringing order to a conflict-ridden world. Moreover, the argument that pragmatism demands compromise cannot be defended in cases where the parties have demonstrated that they are not sincere in wanting to make peace — as in Angola, Cambodia, and Rwanda. In the latter case, after the Presidential Guard returned to war and organized the genocide of approximately 800,000 people, the United Nations and the United States continued to urge the parties to return to the negotiating table. No one seemed troubled by the ethical implications of asking victims of genocide to make peace with those who perpetrated the genocide. Nor did anyone pose the obvious question: if systematically killing approximately 800,000 people does not signal an unwillingness to negotiate, what would?

Morally defensible arguments can be made for both sides of the lives versus principle debate. The only truly unethical positions are to insist on a negotiated settlement when one of the parties has clearly rejected compromise and to veto a negotiated settlement on the grounds of principle, without then working to uphold the principle. In 1993, this occurred in the Balkans, when the United States rejected the Vance-Owen proposals because they violated the principle of not rewarding ethnic aggression. At the same time, the Clinton administration refused to fight for the principle of multinational tolerance in Bosnia. The war then continued for two and a half more years, until the Clinton administration mediated a settlement that went far beyond the Vance-Owen proposals in establishing ethnic partition and lessening the multinational basis of the Bosnian state.

In the absence of international willingness to uphold basic principles of decency and accountability in the conduct of civil war, the best that can be hoped for is to end the suffering and killing as quickly as possible. But this raises a third ethical issue: whether seeking a negotiated settlement is preferable to letting one side win. Roy Licklider argues that in civil wars fought over identity issues, negotiated settlements tend to be less stable than military victories; two-thirds of negotiated settlements fall apart within five years, and only twenty-one percent of wars that end in military victory see a resumption in fighting in the same time frame.[68] If one's goal is simply to end the war or to provide a basis for stability in a country devastated by civil war, it may be better for one side to win outright. The danger is that the winner will use its power to slaughter the losing side. Licklider observes that, in civil wars over identity issues, genocide was carried out in nineteen percent of military victories.[69] Licklider's research suggests that negotiated settlements of civil wars are worth pursuing. It also serves as a warning that if agreements are reached, the international commitment to peace must be sustained.

This raises a fourth ethical issue. In this chapter, I have argued repeatedly that the international community does not truly provide "guarantees" to parties who make peace. In case after case, however, mediators have used this term to assure combatants about international commitments, occasionally promising the warring parties insurance against betrayal.[70] Yet when confronted by insincerity, cheating, and aggression, the international community has not delivered, even in the face of genocide.

An ethical approach to mediation dictates that mediators not mislead parties on life and death matters. An ethical approach dictates that if third parties make security guarantees, they commit themselves to enforce, not merely monitor, the implementation of peace agreements.[71] Knowing what we know now about Rwanda, for example, it is clear that it would have been better off if its leaders had never toiled under the delusion that the international community would provide guarantees for the risky decision to make peace.

If the international community is not going to provide the resources and will needed to see the implementation of peace settlements through, it should not be in the business of mediating civil wars at all.

---

68. Roy Licklider, "The Consequences of Negotiated Settlements in Civil Wars, 1945–1993," *American Political Science Review*, Vol. 89, No. 3 (September 1995), pp. 681–690.

69. Ibid., p. 687.

70. For a prime example, see Hume, *Ending Mozambique's War*.

71. For an argument in favor of international peace enforcement of civil war agreements, see Walter, "The Resolution of Civil Wars," conclusion.

Chapter 11

Arms Limitations, Confidence-Building Measures, and Internal Conflict

Joanna Spear

This chapter is concerned with the role of weapons in internal conflict. The full life cycle of armaments is examined, from production and transfer, through deployment and use, to disarmament in the aftermath of internal conflicts. The main focus is on light weapons, which are defined as small arms, machine guns, grenades, land mines, artillery, shoulder-fired anti-tank weapons, and other forms of man- and truck-portable weapons. These are generally the weapons of choice in internal conflicts, which often feature guerrilla actions and counterinsurgency operations.

It is argued that the transformation of the international arms trade into a buyer's market, coupled with the permissive policies of many suppliers, means that states have, to a large extent, lost control of the trade in light weapons. This trade is no longer dominated by a few powerful suppliers. More than sixty states are now involved in the manufacture, sale, and transfer of light weapons. Moreover, a large sector of the market deals in second-hand weapons, and these transfers are increasingly in the hands of commercial firms, private arms dealers, and black marketers. The lack of state control over the market in light weapons has serious implications for potential efforts to prevent, manage, or resolve internal conflicts. The solution must be a concerted attempt to better regulate the international trade in light weapons. This will require both unilateral and multilateral measures designed to ensure that arms transfers are monitored, carried out with the full knowledge of state authorities, and are subject to international scrutiny to determine that transfers are not unnecessarily destabilizing.

In this chapter, five main facets of the relationship between arms and internal conflict are examined, beginning with a discussion of the

The author would like to thank the participants at the CSIA Workshop on Internal Conflict for their helpful comments on an earlier version of this paper.

relationship between arms and internal conflict and the ways in which arms transfers affect the likelihood and intensity of internal conflict. The second section reviews trends in the post–Cold War international arms trade, analyzes the emergence of a permissive arms market, and discusses the increased importance of the trade in light weapons. The third section looks at the opportunities for strategic manipulation of the arms trade through selective supply of weapons and the imposition of embargoes to prevent, manage, or resolve internal conflicts. The fourth section examines various initiatives designed to improve responsible control over the trade in light weapons. Two issues are given particular attention: the effort to strengthen national control over transfers of light weapons, and the efforts to extend the United Nations (UN) Arms Register to cover light weapons. This section then analyzes the prospects for establishing an early warning system that would alert states to destabilizing arms transfers. The fifth section concludes with an examination of some of the measures that can be taken to build confidence and security in situations where internal conflict is either a possibility or has already taken place.

It is the finding of this chapter that arms embargoes and the strategic supply of weapons are tools of policy best suited to different phases of the conflict cycle. Where the internal conflict is in a very active phase and one faction is in danger of being defeated (with all the genocidal consequences that this may entail), then strategic arms supplies to establish conventional deterrence are appropriate policy tools. By contrast, where the situation on the ground is one of stalemate, then an arms embargo is an appropriate policy tool. This would have the effect of removing the possibility of a new influx of conventional arms and changing the internal balance of power (and reigniting the conflict), and would therefore help to convince the parties that a negotiated settlement is the only way forward.

However, for either of these tools to be available to policymakers, the trade in light weapons must be brought back under state control. A range of unilateral and multilateral measures would be required to achieve this. Until this is accomplished, arms supplies cannot be successfully manipulated for policy ends.

The Relationship between Arms and Conflict

Surprisingly, the precise nature of the relationship between arms and conflict has been neglected by most analysts of international arms transfers. It is taken for granted that arms cause trouble. A closer study of this relationship is in order. Three aspects will be analyzed here: the role of arms as a proximate cause of conflict; the role of arms as a permissive factor exacerbating the likelihood of conflict; and the role of arms in the intensification of preexisting conflicts.

The literature on the security dilemma provides a useful account of the role arms can play in catalyzing conflict. The essence of the theory is that a state which arms in order to increase its security will decrease the security of other states, even if its intentions are defensive. This could trigger an arms race or a preemptive attack, thereby defeating the purpose of the first state's arms buildup.[1]

Security dilemmas can operate in intra-state situations as well. Indeed, in internal conflicts the dilemma can be even more acute because some of the factors that mitigate the dilemma in inter-state settings are not present. Robert Jervis has argued that the dilemma is lessened if the units involved are large, as they will feel less vulnerable. In internal conflicts, the parties are comparatively small, and they often have elevated threat perceptions. Similarly, it has been suggested that if the territorial boundaries of the conflict area are sufficiently large, buffer zones can be established to ameliorate the fear of surprise attack. This option is rarely available in internal conflicts.

Two other factors will affect the acuteness of the security dilemma in internal conflicts. First, the dilemma is lessened if the parties are happy with the status quo, and are therefore prepared to show benign intent and thus stabilize the situation. In internal conflicts, however, at least one of the parties is trying to overthrow the status quo, making the operation of the dilemma more intense. Second, in internal conflicts there are often no natural borders between the opposing groups; geography dictates that the security dilemma is unrelieved.

In internal conflicts that involve guerilla warfare, counterinsurgency, and other types of irregular operations, it is often difficult to distinguish between offensive and defensive strategies. This will exacerbate tensions between groups already suspicious of each other's military and political aims. Assessments of the balance of power between groups are made more difficult by the conditions that commonly prevail in internal conflicts: poor communications; a paucity of accurate information and intelligence; fear and loathing between opposing groups; and constantly changing battle lines. These factors make accurate and rational assessments of the military situation very difficult to reach. Worst-case thinking then takes over, leading to arms races and spirals of aggression.

Most internal conflicts involve light weapons, which are suitable for either offense or defense. However, given that a key feature of light

---

1. Robert Jervis, "Cooperation Under the Security Dilemma," *World Politics*, Vol. 30, No. 2 (January 1978), p. 169.

weapons is their mobility, they marginally favor the offense. This means that in internal conflicts where both sides are armed with light weapons, knowledge that the offense has advantages can lead to an acute form of the security dilemma; the dangers of preemptive attack can be very great.

Looking at the literature on the causes of war, it is clear that conflict may come about for a number of reasons, but among the most important catalysts are fear and opportunity. These are important motivators of internal conflict. Fear can derive from perceptions that an opposing group's (or ruling state's) military posture is offense-oriented and therefore threatening. These concerns may be heightened by patterns of arms supply that indicate that one's opponent is undertaking a significant buildup of offensive weapons. Opportunity is also an important motivator. A challenger group or ruling state may see a limited window of opportunity before its opponent receives new weapons or before reinforcements arrive. In these situations, either fear or opportunity may spur an attack.

It is certainly true that if parties to a conflict are bent on violence, arms and arms transfers will not be a crucial factor. The genocide in Rwanda in 1994 was largely perpetrated with very primitive weapons — machetes. Nevertheless, although weaponry is not always a cause of conflict, the presence of certain kinds of arms or changes (even anticipated changes) in arms balances may create a permissive atmosphere in which conflict becomes more likely. The presence of large numbers of light weapons in a region certainly makes the recourse to military means easy and more likely. Knowing that weapons are available may also make groups in dispute less likely to consider negotiation, arbitration, and other types of peaceful solutions to their grievances.

In addition, the availability of weapons is obviously important in determining both the duration and intensity of conflicts, once they are under way. The negotiated solutions to conflicts in Nicaragua, El Salvador, Mozambique, Namibia, and Cambodia were all facilitated by the fact that the parties involved had lost their major external sources of weaponry and military aid. Weapons supply can play a key role in perpetuating conflicts; cutting off this supply can facilitate their cessation.

The availability of weapons also affects the intensity with which conflicts are fought; the more accessible large amounts of weapons are, the more intense conflicts will be. In Uganda, the Lord's Resistance Army has been engaged in an insurgency since the late 1980s. For years the costs of the insurgency had been fairly low by international standards. This changed in April 1995, when the Army attacked a village in northern Uganda with newly acquired, sophisticated weapons. Using machine guns, mortars, and grenades (probably supplied by Sudan), the Army inflicted in one raid death and destruction equivalent to the levels it used to inflict in a year.[2]

Certain types of weapons can also intensify conflicts, either through the amount of destruction they cause (for example, when machine guns are introduced to a conflict previously fought with rifles, or heavy weapons into a conflict otherwise fought with light weapons), the lack of discrimination of the system (anti-personnel land mines make no distinction between civilians and combatants, and therefore increase the number of civilian deaths), or the longevity of the system (land mines can last for decades beyond the cessation of hostilities). Non-lethal supplies can also intensify conflicts. For example, night-vision equipment can make conflict an around-the-clock proposition.

If arms can act as either a proximate or permissive cause of conflict and perpetuate it once in progress, how can arms transfers affect the prospects for internal conflict? New arms transfers and the accumulation of arms purchases can affect the balance of power between groups within a state. Arms transfers may therefore be one of the "triggers" to internal conflict by spreading fear of the ways in which the newly obtained weapons might be employed.

In the run-up to an internal conflict, forms of arms racing often occur. Historically, however, it has been much easier for a state to obtain weapons than it has been for a sub-state group. It has been difficult for sub-state groups to engage in classic arms racing. However, this is becoming less true because of the emergence of a buyer's arms market.

Arms transfers to a state or sub-state group may also precipitate a preemptive attack by the opposing party. In addition, the easy availability of arms may lead a dispute between groups to become violent because the means of making war are present.

The importance of arms transfers does not stem solely from their role in precipitating violence: they can also play a role in widening conflicts. For example, if a recipient state collapses into chaos, its traditional supplier may feel obliged to enter the conflict to restore order and protect its allies. Other problems arise when the demand for weapons in one state is satisfied. The natural tendency of black market suppliers is to build on existing networks and to begin to send arms to other states in the region. An internal conflict in one state can destabilize an entire region. This

---

2. Gretchen Lang, "Insurgency's Toll Rising in Northern Uganda," *Boston Globe,* June 16, 1995, p. 2.

happened in and around Liberia, where civil war has had important regional repercussions.[3]

In sum, arms and arms transfers can play three roles in internal conflicts. First, arms can be the proximate cause of conflict because of the operation of an acute version of the security dilemma. An attempt by one group to enhance its security through arms acquisitions can lead other groups to stage preemptive attacks. Second, weapons can be one of the permissive factors that leads to an outbreak of conflict. Conflict can be exacerbated by the presence of weapons in the region. Finally, weapons and weapons transfers play important roles in determining the duration and intensity of conflict. For these reasons, management and manipulation of the trade in weapons is a potentially useful tool in preventing, managing, and resolving internal conflict.

Changing Patterns of Arms Supply

The state of the post–Cold War arms trade has important implications for the availability and affordability of the light weapons often employed in internal conflicts. Two trends have marked the emergence of a permissive buyer's market. The first change is a significant overcapacity in defense industries in both the East and West. With the end of the Cold War, there has been a steep decline in both military expenditure and defense procurement.[4] States wishing to preserve their defense industries are therefore aggressively seeking sales abroad. These problems are particularly acute in the former Soviet Union and Eastern Europe. There, the collapse of old political institutions combined with a desperate search for hard currency has led to a liberalization of the arms market.[5] The deregulation of the Soviet military-industrial complex has brought a range of new players into the international arms market, with private arms companies being established to represent newly independent enterprises.

The second change in the supply side of the market concerns stockpiles. In addition to having excess defense manufacturing capacities, many states also have significant stocks of excess weapons that were built up during the Cold War. These stockpiles are being sold to raise money

---

3. Howard W. French, "Long War Turns Liberia Into Core of a Spreading Blight," *New York Times*, May 25, 1995, p. A11.

4. Nicole Ball et al., "World Military Expenditure," Stockholm International Peace Research Institute (SIPRI), *SIPRI Yearbook 1994: World Armaments and Disarmament* (Oxford: Oxford University Press, 1994), pp. 389–454.

5. Charles C. Peterson, "Moscow's New Arms Bazaar," *Orbis*, Vol. 38, No. 2 (Spring 1994), pp. 277–292.

for the development and acquisition of more advanced weaponry.[6] This approach was first endorsed in the Conventional Forces in Europe (CFE) Treaty of 1990, which permitted a "cascade" of second-hand weaponry to approved recipients. These surplus weapons are nevertheless considered quite sophisticated by recipient states further down the arms hierarchy.

As a result, there is a glut of weapons for sale, and the international arms trade has become a buyer's market. Now that the Cold War is over, the arms trade has been depoliticized and is regarded primarily in commercial terms. The permissiveness of the market has at least four important effects on the relationship between weapons supply and internal conflicts.

First, the intense competition for sales has eroded the convention that arms are to be transferred only to governments. This convention was broken by the superpowers during the Cold War when weapons were transferred to favored insurgent groups. For example, the United States supported the Contra guerrillas in Central America and the *mujahidin* in Afghanistan, while the Soviet Union supported the Palestine Liberation Organization (PLO) in the Middle East and the Farabundo Marti National Liberation Front (FMLN) in El Salvador.[7] Despite these transgressions by the superpowers, the norm of not undermining governments was generally respected by middle-tier supplier states involved in less ideological, commercially oriented arms transfers. In the post–Cold War era, this convention is under sustained challenge. Strong demand for weapons from sub-state groups seeking autonomy has coincided with the depressed international arms market. The lure of new customers has proved irresistible. The arms market has consequently become both more permissive and less wedded to traditional notions of "legitimate" arms recipients. Table 11.1 provides a summary of sales to non-state groups in the first half of the 1990s.

Second, it used to be the norm that supplier states — unless they had a direct geostrategic interest in a dispute — would not provide weapons to states engaged in conflict. However, the norms are less clear *vis-à-vis* states engaged in internal conflicts. One of the justifications for not supplying weapons to states engaged in inter-state conflict was to avoid escalation. It might be assumed that such a rule should also apply to internal conflicts, and indeed some supplier states have adopted this approach. However, another norm that informed the rules of supply was

---

6.   Lora Lumpe, "Selling Old Weapons to Buy New," *Arms Sales Monitor*, No. 25 (April 30, 1994), p. 6.

7.   Barry M. Blechman, Janne E. Nolan, and Alan Platt, "Pushing Arms," *Foreign Policy*, No. 46 (Spring 1982).

Table 11.1. Weapons Supplies to Non-State Groups.

Supplier	Year	Recipient	Types of Weapons
Brazil	1988–92	National Union for the Total Independence of Angola (UNITA)	Regular supplies of small arms and light weapons
Portugal *Thwarted*	1991	Colombian Revolutionary Armed Forces	Large shipment of light weapons
Saudi Arabia	1991	*Mujahidin* guerrillas in Afghanistan	Several hundred Iraqi tanks (captured in Gulf War)
South Africa	1991–93	Christian militia in Lebanon	$3.4 million in light weapons
South Africa	1992–93	UNITA	At least twenty flights of weaponry
Russia (commercial firm) *Thwarted*	1993	Opposition forces in Sierra Leone	AK-47s, mortars, anti-tank rockets, grenades
Bulgaria and Hungary	1994	Opposition movement in Southern Yemen	Military equipment
France	1994	Hutu rebels in Zaire	Artillery, machine guns, assault rifles, ammunition
South Africa	1994	Hutu rebels in Zaire	Arms shipment; contents unknown
East European States	1994–95	Fundamentalist groups in Algeria	Anti-tank and anti-aircraft missiles
Russia (commercial firms)	1994–95	Chechen rebels	Light weapons and artillery
Russia	1995	UNITA	Light weapons
Sudan	1995	Lord's Resistance Army in Uganda	Machine guns, mortars, grenades, and ammunition

SOURCES: Terry Leonard, "Hutu Said to Receive Foreign Weapons," *Boston Globe*, May 30, 1995, p. 2; John Laffin, *The World in Conflict: War Annual 6* (London: Brassey's, 1994), p. 6; Ksenia Gonchar and Peter Lock, "Small Arms and Light Weapons: Russia and the Former Soviet Union," in Jeffrey Boutwell, Michael T. Klare, and Laura W. Reed, eds., *Lethal Commerce: The Global Trade in Small Arms and Light Weapons* (Cambridge, Mass.: American Academy of Arts and Sciences, 1995), pp. 121–122; Daniel Garcia-Pena Jaramillo, "Light Weapons and Internal Conflict in Colombia," in Boutwell, Klare, and Reed, *Lethal Commerce*, p. 110; Lucy Mathiak, "Light Weapons and Internal Conflict in Angola," in Boutwell, Klare, and Reed, *Lethal Commerce*, p. 90; Gretchen Lang, "Insurgency's Toll Rising in Northern Uganda," *Boston Globe*, June 16, 1995, p. 2; "South Africa Sold Missiles to Lebanese Militia," *Reuters*, January 18, 1995; David C. Morrison, "Small Arms, Big Trouble," *National Journal*, Vol. 27, No. 11 (March 18, 1995), p. 712; "Russia Probes Alleged Cyprus-Chechenya Arms Link," *Agence France Presse International News*, January 12, 1995; al-Tahir Hammad, "Military Containment Campaign Described," *Al-Watan Al'Arabi*, trans. in FBIS-NES, January 18, 1995, p. 16.

that of not getting involved in conflicts that might spread. Many suppliers apparently see this as being less of a danger with respect to internal conflicts. In any event, economic and market pressures, as discussed above, create powerful incentives to pursue all sales opportunities. The lack of clear and widely accepted norms on the transfer of weapons to states and groups involved in internal conflicts is leading to confusion and divergent policies. For example, after the Rwandan Patriotic Front (RPF) began its insurgency against the Rwandan Hutu government, Belgium banned all weapons transfers to Rwanda while France stepped up its transfers in support of the Hutu government.[8]

Third, the black market in arms, largely dormant since the 1930s, has revived.[9] This was presaged by the international community's increased use of the arms embargo as a political instrument.[10] The black market is controlled largely by non-state actors such as arms dealers and crime syndicates.[11] However, there is also illicit state activity in what is known as the "gray market." Much of this activity is a consequence of the deregulation of the military-industrial complex in the former Soviet Union and Eastern Europe, but many other supplier states are dabbling in the gray market, drawn by the lure of sales.[12]

The black market has evolved since the mid-1980s in ways that parallel the changes in the legal arms trade. There has been a deregulation of the market; new suppliers have entered the arena; and there have been changes in the way that deals are financed. Together, these changes have brought about a "disintegration of supply-side control," which renders the black market less amenable to management and restraint.[13]

---

8. Alain Destexhe, "The Third Genocide," *Foreign Policy*, No. 97 (Winter 1994–95), p. 11.

9. Edward J. Laurance, "Reducing the Negative Consequences of Arms Transfers Through Unilateral Arms Control," in Bennett Ramberg, ed., *Arms Control Without Negotiation: From the Cold War to the New World Order* (Boulder, Colo.: Lynne Rienner, 1993), p. 181.

10. Aaron Karp, "The Rise of Black and Gray Markets," *Annals of the American Academy of Political and Social Science*, Vol. 535 (September 1994), pp. 175–189.

11. Jess Guy, "Illegal Trafficking of Arms by Small Time Operators," in Peter Unsinger, ed., *The International Legal and Illegal Trafficking of Arms* (Springfield, Ill.: C.C. Thomas, 1989).

12. Ksenia Gonchar and Peter Lock, "Small Arms and Light Weapons: Russia and the Former Soviet Union," in Jeffrey Boutwell, Michael T. Klare, and Laura W. Reed, eds., *Lethal Commerce: The Global Trade in Small Arms and Light Weapons* (Cambridge, Mass.: American Academy of Arts and Sciences, 1995), pp. 121–122.

13. R.T. Naylor, "The Structure and Operation of the Modern Arms Black Market," in Boutwell, Klare, and Reed, *Lethal Commerce*, pp. 44–57.

Fourth, the increase in the number of arms suppliers, coupled with the end of strict alliance systems, has decreased the leverage that suppliers have over recipient states. Thus, one means by which internal conflicts were held in check during the Cold War has gone. In addition, the types of light weapons with which internal conflicts are often fought do not present great opportunities for the manipulation of training and spare parts supply — traditional forms of supplier leverage.

These changes in the international arms market are a consequence of the desperate search for sales by supplier states in the aftermath of the Cold War. This buyer's market is leading to "bidding wars" between supplier states. These contests for sales are eroding the minimal controls (based on notions of sovereignty and legitimacy) over the market that previously existed.

THE SCOPE OF THE TRADE IN LIGHT WEAPONS

To understand the implications of these developments for internal conflict, it is essential to understand the scope of the trade in light weapons in particular. Table 11.2 identifies the states known to manufacture light weapons or to produce them under license. This list is incomplete because knowledge about the light arms trade is sketchy. Nevertheless, it outlines the scope of the problem.

Although there has been a general decline in arms sales levels, the one area of the international arms trade that is said not to have been adversely affected by the end of the Cold War is the trade in light weapons.[14] Indeed, it has been asserted that there has been significant growth in the trade in light weapons.[15] However, there is currently little evidence to support this claim. Indeed, the U.S. Arms Control and Disarmament Agency (ACDA) provides evidence to the contrary. During the 1980s — a boom period in international arms transfers — the trade in munitions and small arms accounted for twenty-six percent of the global arms market. However, in the 1990s, the percentage of the arms market captured by small arms and munitions has fallen to thirteen percent.[16]

---

14. Michael T. Klare, "Awash in Armaments: Implications of the Trade in Light Weapons," *Harvard International Review*, Vol. 17, No. 1 (Winter 1994–95), p. 24.

15. Virginia Hart Ezell, "Small Arms Proliferation Remains Global Dilemma," *National Defense*, Vol. 79, No. 504 (January 1995), pp. 26–27; Stephen D. Goose and Frank Smyth, "Arming Genocide in Rwanda," *Foreign Affairs*, Vol. 73, No. 5 (September/October 1994), p. 91.

16. U.S. Arms Control and Disarmament Agency (ACDA), *World Military Expenditures and Arms Transfers 1991–1992* (Washington, D.C.: U.S. Government Printing Office [U.S. GPO], March 1994), p. 33.

Table 11.2. Small Arms Manufacturers.

Argentina	Finland	Philippines
Australia	France	Poland
Austria	Germany	Portugal
Bangladesh	Greece	Rep. of South Africa
Belgium	Hungary	Rep. of South Korea
Bosnia	India	Romania
Brazil	Iran	Russia
Burma	Iraq	Saudi Arabia
Bulgaria	Israel	Serbia
Canada	Italy	Singapore
Chile	Japan	Slovakia
China	Libya	Spain
Colombia	Malaysia	Sweden
Croatia	Mexico	Switzerland
Cuba	Namibia	Taiwan
Cyprus	Netherlands	Thailand
Czech Republic	Nicaragua	Turkey
DPR of Korea	Nigeria	United Kingdom
Denmark	Norway	United States
Dominican Republic	Pakistan	Venezuela
Egypt	Peru	Vietnam

SOURCES: *Arms Sales Manufacturing Project* (Washington, D.C.: Federation of American Scientists, 1994); *Jane's Intelligence Review,* September 1994, p. 429; Natalie J. Goldring et al., "Research Sources on the International Trade in Light Weapons," draft paper presented at the United Nations Institute for Disarmament Research (UNIDIR) Workshop on the Proliferation of Light Weapons in the Post–Cold War World, Berlin, May 4–5, 1995.

Moreover, small arms and munitions constituted a smaller percentage of a drastically reduced global market.[17] Thus, the available evidence on the trade in light weapons does not support the proposition that the trade in light weapons is growing.

How can we reconcile these conflicting accounts of the state of the international trade in light weapons? The key to this puzzle lies in the stockpiles of weapons built up by many states during the Cold War. Although the trade in *new* light weapons is in decline, there is a growing market in *second-hand* light weapons. Many of the light weapons produced by the superpowers and their allies during the Cold War were

---

17. A quick examination of the total international arms trade in the early 1990s shows that arms deliveries have declined by thirty-six percent from the record levels of the 1987–91 period, and arms transfer agreements (a less reliable measure) by fifty-five percent from the 1985 high-water mark. ACDA, *World Military Expenditures and Arms Transfers 1991–1992,* p. 8.

never fired in anger. In the 1990s, however, these weapons are being sold second-hand on the international market. The ACDA statistics cited above cover only the trade in new weapons. Indeed, the market in second-hand weapons is largely untracked, but of great significance to those interested in understanding internal conflicts.

Light weapons tend to be durable, which means that they tend to stay in service and on the market for a very long time — often decades. This was illustrated during the disarmament of factions in Mozambique following the 1992 Peace Accords. The quality of the weapons — mostly AK-47s — collected from the insurgents was not high. Nevertheless, these weapons cannot be considered obsolete because they are still effective tools in the types of irregular operations that internal conflicts often involve.

THE SUPPLY OF LIGHT WEAPONS

Scholars and analysts have identified four main routes through which light weapons transfers are made: government-to-government sales and aid; commercial sales; covert deliveries by governments; and black-market traffic.[18] In addition, light weapons — which by their very nature are portable and easily concealed — can be brought into states by refugees fleeing across borders. Illegal cross-border smuggling is common in many parts of the world. Theft from military and police forces is a growing problem, particularly in the former Soviet Union, as is the illegal sale of weapons by military or police forces.[19] The numerous means by which small arms and light weapons transfers can be made is an important indicator of the task faced when contemplating trying to choke off these sources of supply.

Knowledge about even the most prominent of these conduits is rudimentary. The government-to-government portion of the light weapons trade is not systematically tracked by either governments or international organizations.[20] Commercial sales are generally subject to even less scrutiny, with governmental involvement limited to providing export licenses and end-user certificates. Little is known about the black market in light

18. Klare, "Awash in Armaments," pp. 26, 75.

19. Vladimir Baranovsky, "Post-Soviet Conflict Heritage and Risks," in SIPRI, *SIPRI Yearbook 1993: World Armaments and Disarmament* (Oxford: Oxford University Press, 1993), p. 153.

20. Natalie J. Goldring et al., "Research Sources on the International Trade in Light Weapons," draft paper presented at the United Nations Institute for Disarmament Research (UNIDIR) Workshop on the Proliferation of Light Weapons in the Post–Cold War World, Berlin, May 4–5, 1995.

weapons. Although black market transfers require both licenses and end-user certificates, this is a trivial barrier because both are easily obtained.[21]

Although it is impossible to track the full extent of the black market, it is possible to identify weapons flows from one area to another. Light weapons, usually second-hand equipment provided by one of the super-powers to regional allies during the Cold War, are often traded by black marketers from areas where tensions have lifted to areas where tensions are growing. In the aftermath of the peace agreements in Mozambique and Namibia, for example, there has been an outflow of surplus weaponry to other states in Southern Africa.[22] This flow of arms is problematic for South Africa because it fuels crime and tribal disputes in the townships. Stinger missiles supplied in the 1980s by the United States to Afghan *mujahidin* forces have now been transferred to Iran, Qatar, and North Korea.[23]

One way of assessing the state of the black market in light weapons is by looking at the cost of these weapons. According to Samuel Cummings, president of Inter-Arms (the largest private arms supplier in the world), new AK-47s can be purchased for as little as $130, and new M-16s cost around $600.[24] In many regions of the world, the cost of second-hand light weapons is considerably lower. For example, in Swaziland an AK-47 can be purchased for as little as $6 and in Uganda for the price of a chicken. In Mozambique, rifles are being traded for one or two boxes of maize.[25] In Sarajevo, the black market in weapons is so well-established that "it is easier to buy a modern machine gun than a bar of Toblerone chocolate."[26] This is a clear indication that supply is meeting demand.

In sum, light weapons are plentiful, cheap, durable, and available through a variety of legitimate and illegitimate sources. Consequently, supplier leverage over the market is limited.

---

21. Naylor, "The Structure and Operation of the Modern Arms Black Market," p. 47.

22. *Facts on File*, Vol. 54, No. 2786 (April 21, 1994), pp. 272–273.

23. William D. Hartung, *And Weapons For All* (New York: HarperCollins, 1994), p. 126; "A CIA Effort to Recover Stingers in Afghanistan is Said to Go Awry," *Boston Globe*, March 7, 1994, p. 11.

24. Interview with Samuel Cummings, President of Inter-Arms, Voice of America, *Focus*, February 8, 1995.

25. Swadesh Rana, *Small Arms and Intra-State Conflicts*, Research Paper No. 34 (Geneva: UNIDIR, 1995), p. 5.

26. David C. Morrison, "Small Arms, Big Trouble," *National Journal*, Vol. 27, No. 11, (March 18, 1995), p. 712.

Supply-Side Manipulation of the Light Weapons Trade

Some have argued that the trade in light weapons could be manipulated in ways that would serve the goals of preventing, managing, or resolving internal conflicts.[27] How feasible is this? In this section, two options are assessed: imposition of arms embargoes, and strategic manipulation of weapons supplies. Implicit in each of these approaches is a theory about how conflicts are brought to an end. Advocates of arms embargoes believe that conflicts can be ended if the parties are denied the means with which to fight. Advocates of strategic manipulation believe that transferring weapons into arenas of conflict can re-establish balances and bring fighting to an end; at worst, it would ensure that all parties are able to defend themselves. Although these approaches might appear to be very different, they both seek a stalemate on the ground. Which approach is best depends upon the conflict in question.

ARMS EMBARGOES

What are arms embargoes expected to achieve? The best-case scenario is that they will lead to a military stalemate and a cessation of violence by denying the warring parties the means by which to prosecute the conflict. Embargoes are also initiated to prevent a state or sub-state group from pursuing a particular course of action (deterrence), or to change the behavior of a state or sub-state group (compellence). Embargoes also serve more instrumental goals. For example, an embargo may be imposed to prevent a conflict from spilling over into other states in the region. Embargoes are also seen as a way of avoiding more direct actions, such as military intervention.

What is the actual track record of UN arms embargoes? As of the mid-1990s, the record has not been impressive. If the aim was to end fighting by reducing the weapons available for waging war, then the embargo on the former Yugoslavia is obviously a failure. Similarly, the embargoes on the Angolan government and the National Union for the Total Independence of Angola (UNITA) did not end the fighting in this part of southwest Africa.

Have embargoes had any more success at deterring or compelling action? The case that is the most revealing is the embargo on South Africa. Despite being in place for some seventeen years, it would be hard to make a case that the embargo inhibited South Africa's ability to make war abroad or against its internal opponents, nor did it compel the South

---

27. See, for example, Richard Bernstein, "Security Council Stops Move to Arm Bosnians," *New York Times*, June 30, 1993, p. A6.

Table 11.3. UN Arms Embargoes.

Party Embargoed	Date Embargoed	Status
Korea	1951	Lifted
Rhodesia	December 1966	Lifted
South Africa	November 1977	Lifted
Iraq	August 1990	Ongoing
Former Yugoslavia	September 1991	Lifted
Angola	1991	Ongoing
Somalia	January 1992	Ongoing
Liberia	November 1992	Ongoing
Haiti	June 1993	Lifted
UNITA rebels in Angola	September 1993	Ongoing
Rwanda	May 1994	Lifted for one year in September 1995

SOURCE: Lori Fisler Damrosch, "The Civilian Impact of Economic Sanctions," in Lori Fisler Damrosch, ed., *Enforcing Restraint: Collective Intervention in Internal Conflicts* (New York: Council on Foreign Relations, 1993), pp. 274–315.

African government to move toward racial equality. The best case to be made is that the embargo increased the costs to the government of purchasing weapons. However, it certainly did not prevent the government from obtaining military hardware. Moreover, during the period of the embargo, the South African government built an impressive defense industry which earned $270 million per year in hard currency.

Significantly, all of the arms embargoes listed in Table 11.3 leaked: the embargo on the former Yugoslavia has been very porous;[28] the Haitian military received new tanks, weapons, ammunition, and uniforms while under embargo;[29] the Rwandan Hutu in exile continue to receive arms despite a UN embargo;[30] weapons flow freely into Liberia from neighboring states;[31] and there are allegations that the United States may have turned a blind eye to Iranian shipments of weapons to the Bosnian government.[32]

---

28. Aaron Karp, "Arming Ethnic Conflict," *Arms Control Today*, Vol. 23, No. 7 (1993), pp. 8–13.

29. Claudetter Antoine Werleigh, "Haiti and the Halfhearted," *Bulletin of the Atomic Scientists*, Vol. 49, No. 9 (November 1993), p. 23.

30. Terry Leonard, "Hutu said to Receive Foreign Weapons," *Boston Globe*, May 30, 1995, p. 2.

31. French, "Long War Turns Liberia Into Core of a Spreading Blight," p. 3.

32. "US Aware of Iranian Arms to Bosnia?" *Washington Post*, April 14, 1995.

In few of the cases where embargoes were imposed was there a parallel effort to stifle the supply of weapons from the black and gray markets. (Western policy on Angola is an exception.) This points to the twin problems of political will and the feasibility of staunching alternative sources of supply. The investment required to make embargoes work is often more than outside powers are prepared to make, particularly given that for many states the imposition of an embargo is an alternative to direct action. Indeed, active policing of an arms embargo might blur the boundary between non-intervention and intervention.

There are two major obstacles to achieving watertight arms embargoes: the illegal market, and existing stockpiles of weapons.

For an arms embargo to be comprehensive, more than sixty states known to manufacture small arms would have to agree to abide by it — a situation that is hard to imagine given the desperate search for overseas sales found at all tiers of the international arms market. To be effective, a comprehensive embargo would also require states to control the activities of the commercial firms and private arms dealers operating within their territories. Many states may be unable or unwilling to do this.

Since the mid-1980s, the black and gray markets have grown to meet the demands created by the imposition of arms embargoes by the United Nations. Therefore, for embargoes to be effective in the future there will have to be a significant crackdown on the black and gray arms markets to ensure that alternative sources of supply cannot substitute for legal sales. The lack of systematic tracking of illicit activity is a significant problem; however, effective monitoring is needed as a first step if enforcement is to be seriously contemplated.

The other major barrier to establishing effective embargoes is the stockpile problem: large quantities of many kinds of weapons were built up in many parts of the world during the Cold War. A state that has received significant amounts of weaponry in the past is in a good position to withstand an arms embargo for a number of years. This is especially problematic with respect to light weapons, which require minimal maintenance and few spare parts. In addition, if a state or sub-state group sees that an embargo is about to be put into place, it can neutralize international actions by building up arms stockpiles. This was UNITA's strategy vis-à-vis the Angola-Namibia Accords; by February of 1989, UNITA leader Jonas Savimbi claimed to have stockpiled a two-year supply of weapons.[33]

Given that embargoes take time to take effect, coalitions that impose

---

33. Lucy Mathiak, "Light Weapons and Internal Conflict in Angola," in Boutwell, Klare, and Reed, *Lethal Commerce*, p. 89.

them have to be prepared to hold together over a long period of time. In a post–Cold War world without the binding force of ideology, and given economic problems in many supplier states, this is a tall order. Moreover, the economic burdens of embargoes will fall more heavily on some states than on others. This may cause strains within embargo coalitions. In addition, the fear of losing sales to defectors is a big problem for coalition maintenance; the argument that "if we don't sell, others will" has long had a particular resonance in the arms trade.

It should be borne in mind that the imposition of an embargo against parties engaged in an internal conflict will have the effect of favoring the side that has access to the government's military stockpiles and industries. For example, in the former Yugoslavia, most defense industries and arms depots are on Serb territory. In cases such as these, embargoes might permit one side to win, rather than pushing both sides to a stalemate and a political settlement.

Despite their patchy record and inherent problems, embargoes may have in some cases increased the degree of difficulty experienced by states and groups seeking weapons. There is also value in having the United Nations put down markers that certain types of actions are unacceptable to the international community and will be punished. International powers may also appreciate having options between inaction and military intervention. Embargoes can have utility, but they need to be well-targeted (taking into account factors such as existing stockpiles and geography), and they should be employed only when they can make a positive difference.

STRATEGIC MANIPULATION OF WEAPONS SUPPLIES

A rather different form of action involves manipulating the strategic supply of weapons to prevent, manage, or resolve internal conflicts. For example, Barry Posen has suggested that in some cases it might be reasonable for external powers to provide groups with the wherewithal to defend themselves.[34] The feasibility of this will be quite situation-specific and depend on such factors as types of weaponry already deployed, numbers and positions of forces, the strength and deployment of opposition forces, the ability to get weapons to where they are needed, and the ability of local forces to actually use the weapons provided. The goal would be to establish a balance of conventional forces designed to ensure or restore deterrence (and thus avoid or end conflict). This would be most difficult to achieve, particularly if violence had already broken

---

34. Barry R. Posen, "The Security Dilemma and Ethnic Conflict," *Survival*, Vol. 35, No. 1 (Spring 1993), p. 44.

out. Moreover, what may look like a balance of forces to outside powers may be perceived very differently by local actors. External interference could lead to arms racing, preemptive attack, or both.

It is also true that many of the types of weapons that could be supplied to groups involved in an internal conflict would not be clearly defensive. For instance, to be of use in irregular warfare, weaponry needs to be mobile; such weapons could be regarded by the opposition as offensive. To avoid exacerbating security dilemmas, one would have to tie arms transfers to confidence and security building measures (CSBMs), such as weapons-free zones and notifications of troop movements. However, questions would remain as to whether states that had supplied arms to one side in a conflict could then be considered sufficiently neutral to assist in the implementation of CSBMs, and whether states and groups in conflict would permit intrusive CSBMs.

It is important to recognize that manipulating weapons supplies would not work in all situations. In many internal conflicts, lack of weapons is not the problem. In situations such as these, the only role of external manipulation would be to increase the sophistication of the weaponry available to one of the parties. However, rather than ensuring stalemate, increasing the sophistication of weaponry may lead to escalation, arms racing, and preemptive attacks. Moreover, it is not always the case that superior weaponry will either guarantee victory or stave off defeat. There is a tendency for military leaders to believe that having bigger and more advanced weapons will give them the deterrent or fighting edge they need. In internal conflicts, however, as Posen has suggested, factors such as motivation can provide the crucial edge that an injection of new weaponry will not overcome. Thus, rather than providing a deterrent to conflict, more advanced weapons may merely intensify conflict.

The provision of weapons could also lead to further external involvement in an internal conflict. This is particularly true if the weaponry supplied is highly sophisticated. A supplier state may find that after providing weapons intended to bring about a stalemate, new shipments have reached other groups, necessitating another round of transfers. An associated point is that the groups receiving weapons may not be able to use them without training.

For external manipulation of arms supplies to be effective, there has to be agreement among supplier states about the aims of such a policy. Just as embargoes can be broken by defectors, the effectiveness of attempts to manipulate arms supplies requires considerable cooperation. There would therefore have to be an international consensus about which side deserved external support, and this consensus would have to be maintained over time. Given the different political perspectives of the many supplier states, this will be hard to achieve in most instances; some states might choose to regard the initiation of a strategic supply policy as a "green light" to sell weapons to opposing forces. The problem of reaching international agreement on such a policy is exacerbated by the lack of control over the arms trade discussed previously.

A SELECTIVE SUPPLY-SIDE STRATEGY

As noted in the introduction to this section, each of these supply-side approaches carries with it a view of the best way to end conflict. I would argue that each approach is best suited to a different stage of the cycle of conflict.

Strategic manipulation of weapons supplies is more useful when the parties to a conflict are far from a military stalemate, but when there is a danger of one side losing outright. Moreover, as Stephen Stedman has pointed out, many conflicts have to intensify before they become ripe for resolution.[35] In cases such as these, sending arms to one side or the other might intensify the conflict in the short term while helping to solve it in the long term.

By contrast, arms embargoes are most useful in cases where the only way that fighting could continue would be through an injection of weaponry from outside suppliers. This implies that the conflict in question has raged for some time, and that a military stalemate has been reached.

In considering these two approaches, it is important to bear in mind that both the legal and illegal arms markets are now less amenable to supply-side controls. Therefore, effective utilization of arms transfers as a policy tool — either through supply or denial — will require a concerted effort to bring the trade in light weapons back under state control.

Initiatives to Manage and Control the Light Weapons Trade

The already formidable hurdles to controlling arms transfers are magnified when one looks at the trade in light weapons. Some of the reasons for this were outlined previously: the difficulties of monitoring the trade in light weapons, the many different sources of supply, the diverse means of transfer, the flourishing black and gray markets, and the desperation of many states and manufacturers to secure sales.

The justifications for imposing controls on light weapons can be placed into several categories. First, there are military concerns, for exam-

---

35. Stephen John Stedman, "Alchemy for a New World Order," *Foreign Affairs,* Vol. 74, No. 3 (May/June 1995), p. 20.

ple, that unregulated arms supplies may exacerbate security dilemmas and cause conflicts. Arms transfers may also threaten peacekeeping operations and make them more costly. Moreover, the availability of light weapons can trigger conflicts that might not otherwise become violent. Second, there are economic and political concerns. Supplies of light weapons reaching sub-state groups can increase the human and economic costs of intra-state conflict. Third, there are humanitarian concerns. Some types of light weapons — anti-personnel land mines, for example — inflict horrific injuries on both combatants and civilians.

Are these concerns sufficiently serious to lead to international attempts to restrain the light weapons trade? That is extremely doubtful, because the suppliers of light weapons are generally not directly affected by the problems they cause. However, there is a strong case to be made that the international trade in light weapons is spinning out of the control of states and that this is problematic, particularly if states wish to be able to employ supply-side tools such as arms embargoes or strategic shipments with any hope of success. There is a strong argument, in my opinion, for instituting measures designed to improve monitoring and management and therefore facilitate manipulation of the light weapons trade.

A key first step is to try and regain state control over the trade in light weapons. This involves instituting better management of the trade, both unilaterally and multilaterally. Once this has been achieved, it might be possible to manipulate arms transfers to serve foreign policy purposes and move toward positive controls on the light weapons trade. Several approaches to managing the light weapons trade — including tightening and extending the scope of national legislation and expanding the scope of international and regional transparency arrangements — need to be developed.

TIGHTENING NATIONAL CONTROLS OVER LIGHT WEAPONS TRANSFERS

Many states have statutory controls over the export of light weapons, but these controls tend to be loosely applied. This is in part because such transactions are often commercial, rather than government-to-government, endeavors, and are therefore merely licensed by the exporting state. As of 1995, there have been few attempts to tighten up national arms transfer legislation. Indeed, in the aftermath of the Cold War, the trend is running in the opposite direction, with states loosening restrictions to assist their manufacturers in the search for overseas sales.[36] Another factor

---

36. "Germany to Relax Arms Export Controls," *Arms Trade News*, January 1995, p. 3.

that has mitigated the attempt to control the light weapons trade is the difficulty of keeping track of these deals, which often involve a large number of small transactions. This does not mean that managing the light weapons trade is impossible, only that it requires more effort than governments have so far devoted to it.

If there were more effective national regulation of government-to-government and commercial sales, tightening of the procedures by which end-user certificates and export licenses were issued, and clear monitoring of certificates and licenses, the black market in light weapons would be severely curtailed. Better management of the light weapons trade would therefore permit states to once again use arms transfers as foreign policy tools.

The pronounced trend toward commercial sales rather than government-to-government transactions means that the former must be thoroughly scrutinized. For example, light weapons have been transferred from the United States to Rwanda — despite the UN arms embargo — because scrutiny of license requests is less exacting than that for government-to-government transfers.[37]

Given the continued utility of second-hand arms, it is necessary to ensure that the sale of stockpiles is both fully licensed and carefully monitored.[38] In addition, strict controls should be maintained by supplier states over the export of spare parts and ammunition. Recipients of Western economic aid who also manufacture ammunition could be threatened with aid cutoffs if they fail to control the export of ammunition.[39]

Greater attention should be paid to the human rights situations of would-be recipients when making decisions about arms that could be used within the state in question. To this end, there have been attempts in the United States and elsewhere to introduce a "code of conduct" with respect to arms transfers.[40] The utility of such approaches is that they bring legislatures into the arms transfer process. Governments and companies are likely to be careful to ascertain that sales that are subject to legislative scrutiny are acceptable. This will help to ensure that issues

---

37. "Private Arms Sales Twice DoD Deals," *Armed Forces Newswire Service*, April 10, 1995.

38. Linda Rothstein, "Y'all Come Down to the Missile Shoot," *Bulletin of the Atomic Scientists*, Vol. 49, No. 10 (December 1993), p. 4.

39. Christopher Smith, "Light Weapons — The Forgotten Dimension of the International Arms Trade," in *Brassey's Defence Yearbook 1994* (London: Brassey's, 1994), pp. 282–283.

40. Cynthia McKinney and Caleb Rossiter, "It's Time the US Stopped 'Boomerang' Arms Sales," *Christian Science Monitor*, May 23, 1995, p. 19.

such as human rights and the dangers of the weapons being used against civilians are considered before transfers are approved.

More restrictive measures include controlling or banning the sale of certain types of light weapons, either across the board or to states engaged in or considered to be susceptible to internal conflict. A selective approach such as this might be palatable to suppliers because few economic interests would be at stake. As a first step, supplier states could refuse to supply "force multipliers" — night-vision and intelligence-gathering equipment — to states likely to experience internal conflict. Suppliers could also curtail the supply of instruments of repression, such as handcuffs, cattle prods, and shackles.

Because of the large number of supplier states in the light weapons market, actions to restrain the light weapons trade have to be multilateral in order to be truly effective. However, there is still value in unilateral measures if they send a signal about the legitimacy of the actions being undertaken by the would-be recipient. If unilateral controls on weapons were connected with restrictions on aid, both economic and military, the signal would be even stronger.

In sum, few attempts are under way to increase government scrutiny over the arms trade in general; even less is being done *vis-à-vis* the light weapons trade. Because states have an interest in being able to manipulate weapons supplies for foreign policy reasons, they have an interest in improving management of the arms trade. Better management would enable governments to weed out dubious transfer deals and move toward selective controls over the arms trade.

THE UNITED NATIONS REGISTER OF CONVENTIONAL ARMS

Developing greater knowledge about the international arms trade is a necessary precursor to managing and controlling the trade more effectively. The most prominent multilateral initiative in this area is the UN Register of Conventional Arms. The UN Register is designed to give notice of destabilizing accumulations of arms, mitigate the effects of the security dilemma by reducing unnecessary suspicion, and inhibit arms transfers by opening up the process to public scrutiny. By promoting transparency, it also increases the difficulties involved in obtaining weapons illicitly; it therefore impinges on the black and gray arms markets.

As of 1995, the UN Register covers seven categories of weapons, but it excludes light weapons. Including light weapons in the UN Register would allow closer tracking of the trade in small arms and make it easier for the international community to detect military buildups. As international powers discovered after the Gulf War, individual transfer agreements that seemed perfectly innocuous take on a different meaning when seen in the context of other purchases.

There have been many calls for an extension of the UN Register to cover light weapons. UN Secretary-General Boutros Boutros-Ghali is among the advocates of this recommendation.[41] At the 1994 Arms Register Review Conference, a group of experts considered the case for including light weapons and land mines in the UN Register but was unable to reach a consensus on either point.[42]

Although the coverage the UN Register would provide would be far from perfect, extending it to cover light weapons would be an important beginning. This move would be more significant if it was accompanied by a decision to require reporting of domestic stockpiles, and therefore would begin to encroach on the second-hand market. Given the problems caused by the re-transfer of light weapons from Cold War arsenals, the UN Register would also have to cover re-transfers.

There has been some progress in multilateral initiatives designed to open up the arms transfer process to international scrutiny. This could lead to better management and eventual control of the trade. However, as of 1995 there is no agreement on the desirability of extending the UN Register to cover light weapons.

DEVELOPING AN EARLY WARNING SYSTEM FOR INTERNAL CONFLICT

UN Secretary-General Boutros-Ghali first suggested establishing an early warning system in his 1992 report, *An Agenda for Peace*.[43] The aim of an early warning system would be to alert the United Nations to situations where there was a danger of internal conflict breaking out, and thereby permit conflict prevention efforts to be launched.

Given the important role that arms can play in both catalyzing and sustaining internal conflicts, it would make sense to include information

---

41. "Small Arms Should be Curbed by UN Register," *Inter Press Service International News*, January 9, 1995.

42. Ambassador Hendrik Wagenmakers, "The UN Register of Conventional Arms: The Debate on the Future Issues," *Arms Control Today*, Vol. 24, No. 8 (October 1994), pp. 8–13; *Report on the Continuing Operation of the United Nations Register of Conventional Arms and its Further Development: Report to the Secretary-General*, UN General Assembly Document A/49/316, October 1994, para. 33.

43. Boutros Boutros-Ghali, *An Agenda for Peace*, A/47/277-S/24111 (New York: United Nations, June 1992).

on the transfer, deployment, or use of weapons in an early warning system. In addition to monitoring the activities of governments, this system should also monitor the purchase, deployment, and use of weapons by sub-state groups. Five categories of developments merit special attention.

PATTERNS OF ARMS PURCHASES. Monitoring arms transfers more systematically would help the international community to assess accumulations of weapons and their impact on the prospects for stability in the area. It would also help to assess the military priorities of states and sub-state groups by examining their purchases and the way in which weapons and troops were deployed. Because some weapons can be used for a variety of purposes, judgments would have to be made about specific transactions. For example, a Turkish request in 1994 to purchase U.S.-manufactured cluster bombs can be seen in two very different lights. Cluster bombs have great battlefield utility because they can pierce armor and start fires in combustible environments. However, they can also be employed as instruments of terror against civilians. Concern for the Kurdish population in Turkey has led Human Rights Watch to oppose this sale.[44]

Attempts by states or groups to obtain certain kinds of weapons — seen in the context of the external and internal threats they face — could be triggers for concern. For example, Algerian purchases of helicopters with night-vision equipment from France, Romania, and Russia and armored vehicles from Turkey have raised acute concerns in many quarters, given the Algerian government's stated aim of liquidating its Islamic opponents.[45]

There is some overlap between the types of weaponry useful in combating drug trafficking and fighting international crime syndicates on the one hand, and weapons suitable for prosecuting internal conflicts on the other. Sensitivity and judgment are therefore required in assessing patterns of arms purchases.

TYPES OF DEPLOYMENTS. As Michael Barnett has noted, "qualitatively different military procedures exist for meeting foreign threats as opposed to

---

44. Human Rights Watch Arms Project, "Human Rights Watch Calls for Denial of Cluster Bomb Sale to Turkey," press release, December 28, 1994.

45. al-Tahir Hammad, "Military Containment Campaign Described," *Al-Watan Al'-Arabi*, trans. in FBIS-NES, January 18, 1995, p. 16; "Algeria Rebellion Spurs Land Rover Buy," *Defense News*, May 15, 1995.

countering domestic opposition and civil strife."[46] It is therefore possible to analyze how governments deploy their military forces and, from this, to identify the types of threat they are arming against. For example, deployments in Algeria indicate that the government is preoccupied with an offensive campaign against insurgents. Helicopters with night-vision equipment and warplanes carrying napalm bombs have been deployed against rebel Islamic groups.[47]

The basing and positioning of troops is another important indicator of how states and sub-state groups view security threats. If a state's primary concern is an external threat, one would expect to see troops deployed near the border at risk. However, if troops are clustered in cities and away from borders, one can conclude that internal threats are considered primary. For example, in Burundi, following fighting between Hutu militias and the Tutsi army, the government decided to relocate an army barracks to an area north of the capital, Bujumbura, where Hutu militias were active.

FORMATION OF MILITIA GROUPS. In a well-regulated society facing no external threats, there is no role for militia groups. They tend to be created as extra-legal adjuncts to government activities. Their semi-independent status enables governments to distance themselves from militia activities, a useful device for avoiding responsibility for belligerent and illegal acts. Opposition groups and competing ethnic groups often form militias of their own. As Posen noted, although almost every society produces small numbers of people who are willing to engage in violence at any given moment, the rapid emergence of organized bands of particularly violent individuals is a sure sign of trouble.[48] Places where the formation of militias preceded violent internal conflicts include Burundi, El Salvador, Haiti, Nicaragua, Rwanda, and the former Yugoslavia.

TRAINING AND ARMING MILITIA GROUPS. A further step toward internal conflict is taken when militias, which had previously been acting in *ad hoc* fashion, are given some form of military training. Another serious step is taken when militias are provided with arms. Given that these groups are often employed by governments to complete tasks with which officials

---

46. Michael Barnett, *Confronting the Costs of War* (Princeton, N.J.: Princeton University Press, 1992).

47. al-Tahir Hammad, "Military Containment Campaign Described," p. 17.

48. Posen, "The Security Dilemma and Ethnic Conflict," p. 33.

do not wish to be associated, this can be a sign that state-sponsored violence against opposition groups is likely to intensify.

In Rwanda, for example, two Hutu youth militias were established, one as a wing of the Coalition for the Defense of the Republic (CDR) and one as a wing of the Mouvement Républicain National pour le Développement de la Démocratie (MRND). The latter group received military training and arms in 1993. These militias were involved in the slaughter of more than 2,000 people prior to the death of the Rwandan president, the ostensible cause of the 1994 genocide.[49]

Before the U.S. intervention in Haiti, the military regime distributed thousands of new M-16 rifles, Uzi sub-machine guns, and other weapons to the *attachés*, the civilian militias that work on behalf of the regime.[50]

ACTIVITIES OF MILITIA GROUPS.   There have been many reported incidents of armed aggression by militia groups. For example, in Bosnia there is clear evidence that armed Serb militias (the Panthers) have participated in the "ethnic cleansing" of the northeastern district of Bijeljina.[51] Prior to the onset of the full-scale genocide in Rwanda in 1994, there was a two-year campaign of mounting harassment and violence by government-organized Hutu militias against both moderate Hutu and members of the Tutsi minority.[52] In Burundi, there has been a steady escalation of violent attacks by Hutu militias against Tutsi civilians. At the same time, the Burundian (Tutsi) Army has acted in league with Tutsi militias in attacking unarmed Hutu civilians.[53]

South Africa under the system of apartheid saw collusion between the South African police and Inkatha Freedom Party militias. The police armed and trained both the militias and the secret hit squad, C10, and helped them carry out attacks on African National Congress supporters.[54]

---

49.   "Rwanda: An Existence Threatened," *Africa Research Bulletin*, Vol. 31, No. 5 (May 1–31, 1994), p. 11423; Alan Rake, "Operation Genocide," *New African*, No. 321 (July/August 1994), pp. 12–14.

50.   John Kifner, "U.S. Troops Receive Authority To Halt Haitian Police Beatings," *New York Times*, December 23, 1994, pp. A1, A12.

51.   Chuck Sudetic, "More 'Ethnic Cleansing' by Serbs is Reported in Bosnia," *New York Times*, July 18, 1994, p. 2.

52.   Robert M. Press, "UN Investigator Cites Preplanned Genocide in Rwanda," *Christian Science Monitor*, July 1, 1994, p. 7.

53.   Associated Press, "Thousands Slain in Burundi, Many By Troops, Group Says," *Boston Globe*, June 16, 1995, p. 8.

54.   "Inquiry Reveals Police Conspiracy," *Facts on File*, Vol. 54, No. 2786 (April 21, 1994), pp. 272–273.

THE UTILITY OF EARLY WARNING. Gathering information about developments in these five areas would help governments make reasonable decisions about arms transfers and licenses. Governments would also have a better idea of where internal conflict is likely. In this way, an early warning system could be a valuable adjunct to increased national and international oversight of arms transfers.

Confidence and Security Building Measures

When there are strong indications that internal conflict is likely, what can be done? Confidence and security building measures may play a role in preventing, managing, and resolving internal conflicts.

In pre-conflict situations, CSBMs may be able to mitigate the security dilemma and avoid the recourse to war. Perceptions of the opposition play a key part in intensifying the security dilemma, and CSBMs can help dampen threat perceptions. If fears of opposing groups are great, then confidence-building measures, brokered by a neutral authority and agreed upon by all parties, may make a difference. Useful steps might include establishing weapons-free zones and providing notification of troop movements.

However, it is unlikely that any state engaged in either a pre-conflict situation or an internal conflict would easily contemplate admitting that it was not in total control of its territory. Nor would it be inclined to allow infringements on its sovereignty, which intrusive confidence-building measures involve. A government may also reject mediation and CSBMs if they would prevent it from wiping out a troublesome secessionist movement. In fact, international involvement through the United Nations would confer legitimacy on opposition groups, which most states would want to avoid. It is also important to bear in mind that confidence can only be built if perceptions of belligerence are wrong; CSBMs will have no utility in situations where groups are genuinely aggressive and prone to violence. Indeed, in situations such as these, CSBMs can be dangerous.

Whereas examining the role of CSBMs in pre-conflict situations is somewhat speculative, CSBMs have an established track record in post-conflict settings. In these situations, the aim is to make the recourse to conflict both unnecessary and impossible. Two types of measures merit special attention: coercive disarmament and cooperative disarmament.

COERCIVE DISARMAMENT

In the first few years after the end of the Cold War, there was considerable interest in giving the United Nations an active role in solving internal conflicts. The concept of coercive disarmament was promulgated with this in mind. The failure of UN forces to disarm warring factions has since blunted the international community's enthusiasm for such actions.

When coercive disarmament efforts are undertaken, the outside forces involved cannot be regarded as neutral. Indeed, previous coercive disarmament efforts have been undertaken by intervention forces, such as the Indian force sent to Sri Lanka in the late 1980s. As the UN Secretary-General noted in *An Agenda for Peace*, missions engaged in these activities become peace-enforcement operations, and "the UN force then becomes a party to the conflict and must act as if it were at war."[55]

The most vigorous post–Cold War effort to engage in coercive disarmament took place in Somalia, which collapsed into chaos in 1991 with the fall of the Barré regime. The United Nations became involved in providing humanitarian aid to the country, but by late 1991 the situation was critical and over 4.5 million people were threatened with starvation. Clan warfare, widespread banditry, and looting severely hampered the delivery of humanitarian supplies.[56] The deteriorating situation led the UN Security Council to adopt Resolution 794, which authorized a Unified Task Force (UNITAF) to use force to provide "a secure environment for humanitarian relief operations."[57] The U.S.-led force numbered 35,000 and operated primarily in and around Mogadishu, the Somali capital.

During the Cold War, Somalia received significant amounts of weaponry, including small arms. In late 1991, before the Barré regime toppled, the United States supplied Somalia with 4,800 M-16 rifles, 448 TOW anti-tank missiles, 84 106-mm M40 recoilless rifles, 75 81-mm mortars, 24 50-caliber M2 Browning machine guns, and $9.5 million worth of ammunition.[58] It has been estimated that at least 100,000 weapons (including rifles and machine guns) left over from the Cold War ultimately fell into the hands of Somali teenagers.[59] These adolescents formed gangs aligned with different clan groups and extorted money from the relief agencies.[60]

---

55. Boutros-Ghali, *An Agenda For Peace*, p. 42.

56. United Nations Department of Public Information, "The United Nations and the Situation in Somalia," Reference Paper, May 1, 1994, pp. 1–6.

57. Ibid., p. 7.

58. Klare, "Awash in Armaments," p. 26.

59. Jonathan Stevenson, "Hope Restored in Somalia," *Foreign Policy*, No. 91 (Summer 1993), p. 138.

60. Colonel F.M. Lorenz, "Confronting Thievery in Somalia," *Military Review*, Vol. 74, No. 8 (August 1994), p. 47.

Most UN officials, aid agencies, and Somalis assumed that "providing security" would include disarming the warring factions.[61] However, the U.S.-led force pursued a more limited strategy.[62] UNITAF began to confiscate weapons at roadblocks, but a U.S. military spokesman made it clear that this was being done for self-defense.[63] When it became clear to U.S. forces that the Somali warlords did not intend to use these weapons against them, the United States discontinued the disarmament effort. Indeed, it appears that some weapons were actually handed back.[64] This led to an outcry from aid agencies. The disarmament effort recommenced after UN officials intervened, and attacks on UNITAF troops increased.

The way in which the United States went about this disarmament effort highlights the dilemmas inherent in the process. First, the United States gave notice to Somali factions that it intended to disarm them. This gave local militias time to move their weapons out of the range of U.S. forces. As a result, fighting spread into the countryside. As one Western relief worker noted, "These zones of security create zones of insecurity."[65] Second, the initial targets of the disarmament effort were bodyguards for aid agency workers, shopkeepers, and residents. This left much of the population unarmed and vulnerable whereas the warring gangs and militias that started the problem in the first place were left alone.[66] Finally, when UNITAF shifted its attention to disarming these groups, it was unable to carry out the operation in an even-handed manner.

In March 1993, UNITAF began to hand over its responsibilities to its successor, UNOSOM II.[67] Ironically, the United States, which had been unenthusiastic about disarming local militias, ensured that this was part of the mandate for the new force, which was both smaller than UNITAF

61. Rod Norland, Jeffrey Bartholet, and Jonathan Stevenson, "A Hurry-Up Offense," *Newsweek*, December 28, 1992, pp. 38–39.

62. Paul Claesson and Trevor Findlay, "Case Studies on Peacekeeping: UNOSOM II, UNTAC and UNPROFOR," SIPRI, *SIPRI Yearbook 1994*, p. 62.

63. Eric Ransdell, "Strangers in a Strange Land," *US News and World Report*, December 21, 1992, p. 65.

64. "The Right to Bear Arms," *Economist*, December 19, 1992, pp. 51–52; Martin Walker and Mark Husband, "US Reluctant to Disarm Gunmen," *Guardian*, December 17, 1992.

65. Norland, Bartholet, and Stevenson, "A Hurry-Up Offense," p. 39.

66. African Rights, "Operation Restore Hope: A Preliminary Assessment," May 1993, pp. 23–26.

67. United Nations Department of Public Information, *United Nations Peacekeeping: Information Notes*, Update: May 1994, DPI/1306/Rev. 3 (New York: United Nations, June 1994), p. 104.

and expected to operate over the whole country (rather than just around Mogadishu).[68] Somali groups, fearing that they would lose their weaponry and influence, attacked the UNOSOM II forces. In June 1993, twenty-four Pakistani peacekeepers were killed and fifty-four injured in a series of preemptive attacks by the forces of General Mohammed Farah Aideed.[69] Retaliatory attacks had little effect on the clan militias. After these debacles, UNOSOM's mandate was significantly narrowed and coercive disarmament was abandoned.

In retrospect, the UNITAF and UNOSOM II disarmament missions were partially successful. They got many heavy weapons off the streets and seized a significant number of small arms. However, this could have been achieved through negotiation rather than coercion. In any event, by 1994, the Somali factions were re-arming in anticipation of renewed hostilities.[70]

The United States applied the lessons it learned from Somalia to its 1994 operation in Haiti. Here, U.S. forces were extremely reluctant to engage in the types of coercive disarmament that provoked retaliation in Somalia.[71] Before the U.S. forces arrived in Haiti, the military regime had armed various militias. This meant that U.S. forces had to disarm not just the regular army and police force, but also the more elusive *attachés.* The lessons of Somalia loomed large, and the Clinton administration consequently refused to get involved in coercive disarmament, as demanded by UN officials.[72] The U.S. military has nonetheless confiscated more than 12,500 weapons, although it has not aggressively sought out arms caches.[73]

COOPERATIVE DISARMAMENT

To date, the record of cooperative disarmament is mixed. There are many examples of cooperative disarmament being undertaken, including the

---

68.   Claesson and Findlay, "Case Studies on Peacekeeping: UNOSOM II, UNTAC and UNPROFOR," pp. 65–66.

69.   United Nations Department of Public Information, "The United Nations and the Situation in Somalia," p. 13.

70.   Ibid., p. 24.

71.   Carla Anne Robbins, "Timid Globalism: The U.S. is Taking A Tentative Approach to Rebuilding Haiti," *Wall Street Journal,* February 23, 1995, p. A1.

72.   Edward Cody, "U.N. Leader Discounts GIs Quitting Haiti Soon," *Washington Post,* November 16, 1994, p. A20.

73.   Thomas Cardamone, "Buy-Back Program Nets Haitian Weapons," *Arms Trade News,* January 1995, p. 1.

largely successful cases of El Salvador, Mozambique, and Haiti. Among the failed efforts at cooperative disarmament are Angola and Cambodia.

One means of cooperative disarmament is use of a "buy-back" scheme whereby a person handing in a weapon is given money, goods, or land. Such schemes have had varying results. For example, the buy-back program in Mozambique seems to have been very successful, in part because the money, land, tools, and seed offered in exchange were considerably more valuable than the weapons concerned. More important, however, was the general war-weariness of the warring factions and the desire on all sides for peace.[74]

Cooperative disarmament was less successful in Haiti. By January 1995, the UN buy-back scheme had recovered 9,100 weapons.[75] These weapons tended to be older models, however, and many more weapons were known to be on the island.[76] A part of the reason for the limited success of the cooperative disarmament effort in Haiti was a failure to pursue parallel efforts at coercive disarmament. Civilians were unwilling to trade in their weapons because they knew that many bandits and *attachés* remained armed and dangerous.

In Angola, attempts at cooperative disarmament were hindered by the small size of the UN peacekeeping force there. With only 298 peacekeepers in the field, it was not possible to institute cooperative disarmament programs, let alone more aggressive disarmament efforts.[77] As a result, when the elections did not yield the victory that UNITA was expecting, it was able to resume fighting.[78] Another complication was that the timetable set for disarmament and the demobilization of forces was unrealistic.

A variant of cooperative disarmament is reversible or temporary disarmament, which involves temporary removal of weapons from parties to a conflict until a complete settlement can be arranged. Because it is cooperative, the outside forces guarding the weapons cannot stop factions from taking back their arms at any point along the way.

A prime example of this type of disarmament was the UN operation

---

74. Jim Wurst, "Mozambique Disarms," *Bulletin of the Atomic Scientists*, Vol. 50, No. 5 (September/October 1994), pp. 37–40.

75. Cardamone, "Buy-back Program Nets Haitian Weapons," p. 1.

76. "Haitians Worry About Security," *Associated Press*, February 1, 1995; Sylvie Kauffmann, "Haiti Begins to Grapple With a Spending Problem," *Le Monde*, February 7, 1995, reprinted in *Guardian Weekly*, February 19, 1995, p. 14.

77. Richard Bernstein, "Sniping is Growing at U.N.'s Weakness as a Peacekeeper," *New York Times*, June 21, 1993, pp. A1, A6.

78. "Major Armed Conflicts," SIPRI, *SIPRI Yearbook 1994*, p. 115.

in Croatia in 1992 (UNPROFOR I). The mandate was to consolidate the cease-fire around three UN Protected Areas (UNPA) and demilitarize them. This required the Yugoslav National Army (JNA) and the Croatian Army to withdraw and the local Territorial Defense Forces (TDFs) to be demobilized. The latter were Croatian Serb units disinclined to be disarmed. UNPROFOR I enjoyed an early success in that both sides withdrew their heavy weapons eighteen miles from the disengagement line and thus ensured that the cease-fire could not be easily broken.[79] However, the United Nations was unable to persuade the Croatian Serbs to comply fully with the demilitarization plan. When the JNA withdrew and the TDFs were demobilized, strengthened police and military organizations emerged in their place.[80]

UNPROFOR I forces made two separate attempts to canton the newly strengthened Serb "police" forces. However, on each occasion the situation seemed likely to become violent and the operation was suspended. An attempt to disarm Serb militia groups resulted in UN forces being surrounded and threatened. The UN's early success in taking control of Serb heavy weapons in mid-1992 was ultimately undermined in January 1993, when Croatia launched attacks on the south sector of Krajina and Serb forces "brushed aside UN troops and resumed possession of the heavy weapons."[81]

Because UN forces were weak, they were not able to impose their own timetable for returning weapons to their owners. Nor was UNPROFOR I able to deter the Croatian attacks that provoked the Serb seizure of UN-held weapons. The military weakness of the UN forces meant that they were powerless to prevent either a resumption of hostilities or rearmament.

Conclusions

It is clearly the case that the presence of arms is a necessary though not always sufficient condition for the precipitation of internal conflict. Arms can play three roles *vis-à-vis* internal conflict: as a proximate cause of conflict; as a permissive factor in the initiation of conflict; and as a means of sustaining and intensifying conflict.

---

79. Alan James, "The UN in Croatia: An Exercise in Futility?" *World Today*, Vol. 49, No. 5 (May 1993), p. 94.

80. United Nations Document S/24353, July 27, 1992, para. 7, cited in James, "The UN in Croatia," p. 94.

81. James, "The UN in Croatia," p. 94.

It therefore makes sense to try to manipulate the relationship between arms supply and internal conflict. As has been shown, however, the chances of successfully doing so have been undermined by the number of states that manufacture light weapons; the emergence of a permissive buyer's market; the proliferation of non-state sources of supply; the vast numbers of second-hand weapons now available; and the depoliticization and commercialization of the arms trade. As a result, states are no longer able to manage and manipulate the trade in light weapons to serve strategic goals.

Given the permissive and uncontrolled state of the international light weapons trade, there will probably be more internal conflicts in the future, stoked by the new and second-hand weapons flooding the market. If states are to avoid the negative consequences of further outbreaks of internal conflict, steps must be taken to manage the international trade in light weapons more effectively. The management measures — both national and international — discussed previously would begin the process of de-commercializing the arms trade and would help to institute effective management of the trade, mainly through opening up arms transfers to national and international scrutiny. This would enable states to once again use arms transfers as foreign policy tools.

If arms transfers are to be used in conflict management, one must recognize that internal conflicts and particularly civil wars have to reach stalemates before they can be successfully solved. In this type of situation, which is ripe for negotiated settlement, the denial of arms supplies can help propel the parties to compromise. Examples include Mozambique and El Salvador.

In some cases, it might be possible to manipulate supplies of weapons and thereby create a stalemate. Outside powers would supply weapons in order to re-establish conventional deterrence. This approach, however, is useful only in situations where one of the parties is at a significant military disadvantage and where there is a danger of it being defeated.

Because of the operation of the security dilemma and the nature of internal conflicts, conventional deterrence will generally be very difficult to re-establish. Putting more weapons into the theaters of conflict will generally intensify rather than dampen hostilities. This may nonetheless be a necessary step before the warring parties will decide that they are ready to negotiate a cease-fire. Strategic manipulation of weapons supplies can therefore serve two purposes: intensifying conflicts (and therefore bringing them closer to resolution) and ensuring that neither side suffers outright defeat. This is a high-risk approach, in part because of the uncontrolled nature of the arms trade but also because the costs of such a policy — in terms of lives lost — can be very great. The unpalatable truth is that supplying weapons to warring parties may prolong conflict, but this may be better than allowing an aggressor to triumph.

As this review of confidence- and security-building measures showed, coercive disarmament is both costly and risky. Attempts at temporary disarmament have also failed. The international community has had more success with cooperative disarmament, where the UN's role as a neutral party legitimizes and assists the process of war termination. In general, CSBMs and disarmament measures will work best when the parties to a conflict have reached a military stalemate.

Attempts to close down the arms trade altogether are problematic because they could have the effect of reinforcing the status quo. This makes sense if the priority — to use Goethe's analysis — is order over justice. However, if this means accepting the actions of the Hutu government in Rwanda, the Russians in Chechnya, the Algerian government's attacks on Islamic opponents, and China's hold on Tibet, then the costs of order may be too high.

Chapter 12

Economic Sanctions and Internal Conflict

Elizabeth S. Rogers

Can international coalitions use economic sanctions, or the threat of economic sanctions, to prevent, manage, or resolve internal conflicts?[1] If so, under what conditions will sanctions be most successful? What kinds of sanctions will be most successful and how should they be applied?

These are the questions this chapter addresses. Two recent developments lend them importance. First, the need to address the problems posed by internal conflicts has grown clearer as post–Cold War disorder has deepened, with wars unfolding in the former Yugoslavia, the Caucasus, the Middle East, Somalia, Sudan, Tajikistan, Liberia, and elsewhere. If uncontained, such conflicts could injure Western interests and those of other powers. Second, the U.S. public has grown increasingly leery of risking U.S. troops in overseas adventures. This often precludes the use of military force to dampen internal conflicts.[2] Can economic sanctions offer an alternative to force, serving as an instrument that allows interna-

The author would like to thank Rachel Bronson, John Chipman, Ivo Daalder, Sumit Ganguly, Brian Mandell, John Matthews, Steven Miller, Stephen Stedman, and Milada Vachudová for their thoughtful comments and suggestions on this chapter.

1. Economic sanctions involve the threat or use of economic punishment (e.g., trade embargoes, aid reductions or cutoffs, and asset-freezing) by one state or a coalition of states to produce a change in the political behavior of another state. Not included are military sanctions such as arms embargoes.

2. The limits of the U.S. public's tolerance for U.S. casualties were shown in Somalia in 1993, where a total of thirty U.S. combat deaths triggered a U.S. decision to withdraw. For more on this argument, see Harvey M. Sapolsky, "War without Killing," in Sam C. Sarkesian and John Mead Flanagin, eds., *U.S. Domestic and National Security Agendas* (Westport, Conn.: Greenwood, 1994), pp. 27–40.

tional powers to sustain or impose peace without exposing their troops to danger?

I advance six main arguments. First, economic sanctions could help to prevent, manage, or resolve internal conflicts in many cases. The historical record supports this conclusion: sanctions often worked when they were applied seriously and systematically. Past studies of sanctions understate their effectiveness by deriving their conclusions in part from cases of half-hearted or partial sanctions. If forceful sanctions are considered alone and are assessed against a reasonable standard of success, the record shows sanctions succeeding much more often than these studies suggest, and fairly often overall.[3] It follows that economic sanctions could be an effective tool for preventing or dampening internal conflicts.

Second, economic sanctions will enjoy more success in containing than in stopping or preventing internal conflicts. The control of internal conflict can be subdivided into three tasks: preventing the outbreak of civil wars; containing the international spread of civil wars after they have broken out (which falls under the heading of conflict management); and halting civil wars (or inter-state wars, if they have already spread). Economic sanctions will be most effective in the area of conflict management, somewhat effective with respect to conflict prevention, and least effective with regard to conflict resolution. However, sanctions could produce worthwhile results even in the area of conflict resolution, and should be applied toward all three goals.

Third, economic sanctions are often more cost-effective than military force. They are usually less effective than military options, but are also less costly and therefore are competitive alternatives to force.

Fourth, conditions are now more auspicious for using sanctions than they were during the Cold War. Most important, the collapse of the Soviet Union removed the "black knight" that broke Western sanctions in the past.[4] Sanctions are far more effective when applied by most or all major states. Before and during the Cold War, unanimity was seldom possible. Unanimity will be possible more often in the post–Cold War era. Hence, sanctions will be more effective.

---

3. Success should be measured by asking: would those who applied them be closer to their policy goals, farther from them, or at the same point if sanctions had never been imposed? Sanctions are successful if they bring these powers closer to policy goals.

4. Gary Clyde Hufbauer, Jeffrey J. Schott, and Kimberly Ann Elliott use the term "black knight" to refer to a power that counters another's sanctions by providing offsetting aid and trade to the target state. See their *Economic Sanctions Reconsidered*, Vol. I, 2nd ed. (Washington, D.C.: Institute for International Economics, 1991), p. 12.

Fifth, in order to succeed, post–Cold War sanctions efforts must be led by the United States. Sanctions cannot succeed without leadership by a great power, and the United States now stands alone as a superpower.[5]

Sixth, sanctions success requires that sanctioning governments (especially the U.S. government) fully commit to the enterprise. A full commitment entails several specific policies. The broadest possible range of sanctions should be applied early on. (Conversely, partial sanctions or slowly tightened sanctions should be avoided.) A broad international coalition must be assembled under U.S. leadership. Sanctions must be married to political programs that clearly frame what the international coalition wants local actors to do in order to have sanctions lifted. Finally, sanctions should be joined to strong declarations shaped to persuade target states or parties that the international coalition has the resolve to maintain sanctions until they comply.

If these policies are adopted, economic sanctions can often prevent or contain internal conflicts. If they are not adopted, sanctions will likely fail. Preventing, managing, and resolving internal conflicts are demanding tasks, and economic sanctions are not all-powerful. The key is getting U.S. leaders to fully commit to the enterprise.

I infer these conclusions from a worldwide survey of economic sanctions efforts since 1914. This record includes 130 cases: 115 instances of sanctions used by the United States and other powers from the pre–Cold War and Cold War eras (1914–89), and 15 post–Cold War (1989–95) cases. For sanctions imposed prior to 1989, I used the data compiled by Gary Hufbauer, Jeffrey Schott, and Kimberly Elliott.[6] I compiled data on 15 post–Cold War cases from press accounts.

A cursory look at this record suggests pessimistic conclusions, since most of these sanctions efforts failed. However, a closer look suggests the opposite. The track record includes many cases of half-hearted, partial, or unilateral sanctions, and sanctions efforts that were undercut by the Soviet Union during the Cold War. Such cases say little about the efficacy of U.S.-led multilateral sanctions firmly applied in the post–Cold War era. In very few of these 130 cases were the full range of economic sanctions actually employed.

---

5. Sanctions efforts by medium powers against very weak states can sometimes succeed, and thus form exceptions to this generalization.

6. See Hufbauer, Schott, and Elliot, *Economic Sanctions Reconsidered*, Vol. I, pp. 16–27. They warn that their list may omit some cases of sanctions imposed by small states (see Vol. 1, p. 4), but I believe it includes all major sanctions episodes involving great powers.

This chapter addresses the efficacy of U.S. and U.S.-led sanctions. I do not explore efforts led by other states or institutions in detail, because only U.S.-led efforts stand much chance of success in the post–Cold War era.[7]

The first section of this chapter assesses the track record of economic sanctions prior to 1989. The post–Cold War record is analyzed in the second section. The use of economic sanctions to prevent, manage, and resolve internal conflict is then discussed. The last section presents conclusions and policy recommendations.

Economic Sanctions, 1914–89

The literature on economic sanctions concludes that they have generally failed in the past. However, for two reasons, this is a poor guide to the future of economic sanctions, including sanctions imposed to prevent, manage, or resolve internal conflicts. First, the literature's conclusions rest in part on cases of sanctions applied half-heartedly; they therefore say little about what firmly applied sanctions could accomplish. Second, the Cold War produced many sanctions failures because the Soviet Union and the United States undercut each other's efforts — a problem that no longer exists. Thus, a direct extrapolation from the literature will underestimate the potential effectiveness of U.S.-led sanctions for conflict prevention, management, and resolution. We must infer our estimates of future effectiveness from this literature and from the empirical record on which it rests, since this is the starting point for assessing sanctions efficacy. However, we must adjust our conclusions to correct for the biases the record contains.

THE SANCTIONS RECORD

States have used economic sanctions often in the twentieth century. However, sanctions were never employed primarily to prevent, manage, or

---

7. Some might argue that the United Nations plays a major role in leading sanctions efforts, but this view rests on an overestimate of its autonomy from the great powers. When the United Nations acts, it acts as an arm of the great powers. In short, the concept of "UN-led sanctions" is a myth: sanctions led by great powers are implemented by the United Nations. Moreover, history records only five cases of sanctions implemented under the auspices of the United Nations: Rhodesia (1966), South Africa (1977), Iraq (1990), Yugoslavia (1991), and Libya (1992). Concurring with this view are Hufbauer, Schott, and Elliott, *Economic Sanctions Reconsidered*, Vol. 1, pp. 10–11.

Discussing and debunking the importance of international institutions in general is John J. Mearsheimer, "The False Promise of International Institutions," *International Security* Vol. 19, No. 3 (Winter 1994/95), pp. 5–49.

resolve internal conflict.[8] The lack of efforts in the past to prevent, manage, or resolve internal conflicts reflected U.S. Cold War foreign policy priorities: preventing communist expansion had a far higher priority than preventing or controlling internal conflicts. Thus, while we have extensive experience with economic sanctions, our experience with sanctions used for conflict prevention, management, or resolution is almost nil. We must therefore deduce the utility of sanctions for the latter purposes from our experience with their use for other purposes.

THE SANCTIONS LITERATURE

The literature on economic sanctions is small — far smaller than the writing on the use of military force — and dominated by the view that sanctions are ineffective.[9] Hufbauer, Schott, and Elliott conclude that

---

8. Some might argue that the sanctions imposed on North Korea in 1950 are an example of conflict resolution sanctions. However, under international law this was not an internal conflict, but rather a war between two sovereign states.

9. David Baldwin begins his analysis of sanctions by observing that "the two most salient characteristics of the literature on economic statecraft are scarcity and the nearly universal tendency to denigrate the utility of such tools of foreign policy." See David A. Baldwin, *Economic Statecraft* (Princeton, N.J.: Princeton University Press, 1985), p. 51. Henry Bienen and Robert Gilpin have likewise noted "the nearly unanimous conclusion of scholars that sanctions seldom achieve their purposes and more likely have severe counterproductive consequences." See Bienen and Gilpin, "An Evaluation of the Use of Economic Sanctions to Promote Foreign Policy Objectives, with Special Reference to the Problem of Terrorism and the Promotion of Human Rights," unpublished report prepared for the Boeing Corporation, April 2, 1979, p. 3.

Works concurring with this pessimistic view of the effectiveness of sanctions include James Barber, "Economic Sanctions as a Policy Instrument," *International Affairs*, Vol. 55 (July 1979), pp. 367–384; Bienen and Gilpin, "An Evaluation of the Use of Economic Sanctions"; C. Lloyd Brown-John, *Multilateral Sanctions in International Law: A Comparative Analysis* (New York: Praeger, 1975); Margaret P. Doxey, *Economic Sanctions and International Enforcement*, 2nd ed. (New York: Oxford University Press, 1980); Margaret P. Doxey, *International Sanctions in Contemporary Perspective* (New York: St. Martin's, 1987); Hufbauer, Schott, and Elliott, *Economic Sanctions Reconsidered*; James M. Lindsay, "Trade Sanctions as Policy Instruments: A Re-examination," *International Studies Quarterly*, Vol. 30, No. 2 (June 1986), pp. 153–173; Donald Losman, *International Economic Sanctions: The Cases of Cuba, Israel, and Rhodesia* (Albuquerque: University of New Mexico Press, 1979); Makio Miyagawa, *Do Economic Sanctions Work?* (New York: St. Martin's, 1992); Miroslav Nincic and Peter Wallensteen, "Economic Coercion and Foreign Policy," in Miroslav Nincic and Peter Wallensteen, eds., *Dilemmas of Economic Coercion: Sanctions in World Politics* (New York: Praeger, 1983), pp. 1–15.

For a collection of statements from political leaders and the popular press arguing that sanctions do not work, see M.S. Daoudi and M.S. Dajani, *Economic Sanctions: Ideals and Experience* (Boston: Routledge and Kegan Paul, 1983), Appendix II, pp. 178–188.

For dissents from the conventional wisdom, see Baldwin, *Economic Statecraft*;

sanctions worked thirty-four percent of the time between 1914 and 1989. They also conclude that the success rate has declined since the early to mid-1970s (to twenty-four percent for post-1973 cases, which comprise roughly half of the total), and that the success rate for U.S. efforts, while over fifty percent before 1973, fell to just seventeen percent after 1973.[10]

The thirty-four percent success rate that Hufbauer, Schott, and Elliott report is often cited to show the inefficacy of sanctions. However, a thirty-four percent success rate is low only if measured against a severe standard of expected performance.[11] It is more impressive if one bears in mind that sanctions cost the United States little to impose, involve little risk, and have not proved to be less successful than other foreign policy instruments — such as the use of force or covert action.[12]

The literature suffers from four additional biases that cause it to underestimate the effectiveness of sanctions. First, it uses too narrow a definition of success; partial success is coded as failure.[13] Sanctions can have three main foreign policy purposes: persuading the target to change its behavior; weakening the target, thereby leaving it less able to make trouble; and punishing the target, thereby deterring it and others from making trouble in the future.[14] The sanctions literature measures success against only the first of these three purposes (target compliance). It omits cases where sanctions successfully weakened or punished the target, thus

---

David A. Deese, "The Vulnerability of Modern Nations: Economic Diplomacy In East–West Relations," in Nincic and Wallensteen, *Dilemmas of Economic Coercion*, pp. 155–181. A useful review of the sanctions literature is Baldwin, Economic Statecraft, pp. 51–58.

10. Hufbauer, Schott, and Elliott, *Economic Sanctions Reconsidered*, Vol. I, pp. 93, 106–108. The post-1973 U.S. sanctions success rate is calculated from data in ibid., p. 108. In aggregate from 1914–90, the United States had a record of twenty-six successes and fifty-five failures — a thirty-two percent success rate.

11. Hufbauer, Schott, and Elliott classify as failures cases in which economic sanctions made a "minor contribution" to a "successful outcome," and instances when sanctions made a "modest contribution" to a "possibly positive outcome." See ibid., pp. 42–43.

12. Arguing that economic sanctions are often judged by a double standard when compared to other foreign policy instruments is Baldwin, *Economic Statecraft*, chap. 7, especially pp. 138–144.

13. Persuasively arguing that the pessimistic consensus on sanctions rests in part on a narrow definition of success is Baldwin, *Economic Statecraft*. He argues throughout that economic sanctions nearly always have multiple goals, and all should be considered when judging success.

14. Sanctions can also have other goals ancillary to internal conflict control. These include reassuring one's allies that one will stand by them in future crises, inflicting punishment for its own sake, raising an issue to prominence on the international agenda, and bolstering one's domestic image as tough and decisive.

it omits sanctions' debilitating effects and their future deterrent effects on the target or other states. Many sanctions are undertaken largely for these latter purposes. This omission therefore underestimates the effectiveness of sanctions as a foreign policy tool.

Second, the literature focuses on the ability of imposed sanctions to compel policy changes. The efficacy of threats of sanctions made to deter actions yet untaken has not been systematically studied. Hence, the literature asks if sanctions can achieve compellence, which is difficult, without asking if they can achieve deterrence, which is easier. The literature measures sanctions against a tough standard, since the threat of sanctions to deter yet-untaken acts will succeed more often than the imposition of sanctions to compel a policy reversal.

Third, the literature generalizes largely from cases of half-hearted, partial sanctions. Hence, it underestimates the effectiveness of strong, systematic sanctions. Most sanctions efforts to date have been partial; total economic sanctions have rarely been imposed.[15] Instances of partial sanctions include the many human rights, anti-terrorism, and nuclear proliferation sanctions imposed by the United States starting in the 1970s.[16] These three categories account for thirty-three of the forty-six cases (seventy-four percent) where U.S. economic sanctions were imposed

---

15. The United States imposed economic sanctions seventy-seven times during the Cold War, but only five of these cases involved total sanctions: those against North Korea (1950), North Vietnam (1954), Cuba (1960), Cambodia (1975), and Iran (1979). See Hufbauer, Schott, and Elliott, *Economic Sanctions Reconsidered*, Vol. I, pp. 9, 67. The United States has also imposed total sanctions three times since the end of the Cold War (against Iraq in 1990, Haiti in 1991, and Yugoslavia in 1992).

Sanctions succeeded in only four of these eight cases—specifically, the four most recent cases (Iran, Iraq, Yugoslavia, and Haiti), for a fifty percent success rate. However, this figure probably underestimates the success rate that comprehensive sanctions would produce in typical circumstances. In three of the four unsuccessful sanctions efforts (North Korea, North Vietnam, and Cambodia), the United States had less-than-average economic leverage with respect to the target state. Specifically, it had very little trade with any of these three states, and gave them no aid. Moreover, black knights (the Soviet Union and China) gave North Korea and North Vietnam offsetting aid. These conditions were not typical, and most targets of comprehensive sanctions in the future would find themselves in more vulnerable circumstances.

16. In all of these instances, U.S. economic sanctions grew out of congressional legislation. U.S. human rights legislation prevented U.S. foreign aid from going to governments that engaged in human rights abuses, but imposed no trade or financial penalties. Anti-terrorism legislation initially cut foreign aid and air travel to, and later cut exports to and imports from, countries supporting international terrorism; however, no financial sanctions were imposed. Nuclear non-proliferation legislation prevented U.S. foreign aid from going to countries working to acquire nuclear weapons, but did not impose trade or financial sanctions except for nuclear-related exports and imports. See Hufbauer, Schott, and Elliott, *Economic Sanctions Reconsidered*, Vol. II, 2nd

between 1973 and 1990, and largely account for the poor (seventeen percent) success rate that Hufbauer, Schott, and Elliott report for this period. This record is a poor predictor of the success rate of energetic sanctions. The literature's conclusions should be adjusted accordingly.

Fourth, the literature generalizes from pre–Cold War and Cold War cases — where clashing great powers were eager and able to undercut their opponents' sanctions. The presence of black knights made sanctions more likely to fail in that era.[17] Relations among the great powers have been more harmonious in the post–Cold War era, and may well remain so. If so, the experiences of earlier eras, which heavily color the sanctions literature, lead it to understate the likely effectiveness of sanctions in the post–Cold War era.

The sanctions literature contains one bias that cuts the other way, inflating the future effectiveness of sanctions for the prevention, management, or resolution of internal conflict. This bias stems from the fact that target states would probably offer less resistance to sanctions in some of Hufbauer, Schott, and Elliott's cases than in cases of sanctions imposed for conflict prevention, management, or resolution. In these latter cases, targets must be dissuaded from adopting or continuing war policies. Decisions for war are seldom made for minor reasons and are not easily overturned. Hence, sanctions for conflict prevention, management, and resolution may collide with more willful targets than sanctions imposed for other reasons. Thus, they may fail more often. However, it seems unlikely that this one bias is large enough to offset the other four biases noted above.

In short, the biases in the literature lead it to understate the likely effectiveness of post–Cold War sanctions undertaken for conflict prevention, management, and resolution.

U.S.-Led Sanctions Efforts after the Cold War

How have U.S.-led economic sanctions fared in the post–Cold War era? A sanctions optimist might expect that the disappearance of the Soviet Union, a perennial Cold War black knight, will enhance the prospects for success. A sanctions pessimist might expect that, without the alarming

---

ed. (Washington, D.C.: Institute for International Economics, 1991), pp. 327–329, 336–339, and 353–358.

17. Soviet undercutting of U.S. sanctions against Cuba and U.S. undercutting of Soviet sanctions against Yugoslavia illustrate this point.

specter of an enemy superpower, building and maintaining sanctions coalitions will be more difficult, thus decreasing their efficacy.[18]

Which view is correct? The post-1989 record is brief, but supports the optimistic view. No black knight has frustrated U.S.-led sanctions efforts since 1989, coalition problems have not developed, and U.S.-led sanctions have succeeded at a high rate when they have been firmly applied.

The United States has employed economic sanctions fifteen times since 1989. (See Table 12.1.) The U.S. government pursued most of these actions half-heartedly, but in three cases — Iraq, Haiti, and Yugoslavia — it made very determined efforts. The breadth of its tactics reflects its seriousness of purpose in these three cases: in each case the U.S. government sought broad international support for its campaign; used the full spectrum of economic sanctions (i.e., trade cutoffs, aid cutoffs, and financial sanctions); and used sanctions in conjunction with other policy instruments (e.g., military force or the threat to use force). These cases, in which the United States placed a high priority on success, are more revealing than other cases, since they show what sanctions can accomplish when they are seriously applied.[19]

LACK OF OPPOSITION

No determined sanctions-buster emerged in these three cases, or in any of the other twelve post–Cold War cases. In both Yugoslavia and Iraq, one might have expected Moscow to play the role of black knight. Russia and Serbia have historic ties based on culture and ethnicity. However, although Russia has given some diplomatic support to the Yugoslav position on Bosnia-Herzegovina, it has not undercut sanctions sponsored by the United Nations (UN). The Soviet Union also had an intermittent friendship with Iraq during the Cold War, but Moscow has supported UN-sponsored sanctions on Iraq and has not undercut them.

In some cases, China has come close to undercutting U.S.-led sanctions, but has not done so openly or aggressively. China sold M-11 missiles, or at least the technology to make them, to Pakistan; helped Algeria build a nuclear power plant; and assisted Iran's nuclear and chemical weapons programs.[20] China also blocked agreement on using economic

---

18. I thank Samuel Huntington for suggesting this argument.

19. I have also focused on the Iraqi, Haitian, and Yugoslav cases because U.S. goals in these cases included the prevention, management, and resolution of internal conflict.

20. Nicholas D. Kristof, "The Rise of China," *Foreign Affairs*, Vol. 72, No. 5 (November/December 1993), p. 71.

Table 12.1. Post–Cold War U.S. Economic Sanctions.

Year	Target State	Official Purpose	Type of Sanction	Result
1990	Iraq	Punish/reverse invasion of Kuwait	Aid, trade, financial	Ongoing but some success; sanctions damage Iraqi economy, weaken Iraqi military
1990	Pakistan	Halt nuclear program	Aid	Failure; nuclear program continues
1990	Guatemala	Reverse coup	Aid (trade threatened)	Success; coup reversed
1991	Jordan	Punish for pro-Iraq stance	Aid	Success; Jordan punished, later adopts friendly stance
1991	Yugoslavia	Support Croatian secession	Trade	Failure; Yugoslavia does not recognize Croatia
1991	Haiti	Restore Jean-Bertrand Aristide to power	Aid, trade, financial	Partial success; sanctions softened up Haitian elite
1991	Kenya	Improve human rights, compel elections	Aid	Partial success; elections held
1992	Peru	Reverse martial law	Aid	Success; elections held
1992	Libya	Punish for Pan Am 103 bombing; force extradition of suspects	Trade	Partial success; economic damage inflicted but no suspects are delivered
1992	Iran	Halt nuclear program	Trade	Failure; nuclear program continues
1992	Yugoslavia (Serbia & Montenegro)	Support Bosnian secession	Trade	Partial success; Bosnia recognized and Serb economy damaged
1993	Nigeria	Punish for annulment of elections	Aid	Ongoing; no new elections yet
1993	China	Punish for weapons exports to Pakistan	Trade	Success; PRC promises not to export in future
1993	Pakistan	Punish for import of weapons from China	Trade	Partial success; no new evidence of weapons imports
1994	Rwanda	Halt genocide	Financial	No result; sanctions applied too late

SOURCES: Compiled by author from press accounts.

sanctions to compel North Korea to halt its nuclear program.[21] However, China has not taken steps to undercut any U.S. or UN sanctions directly.

The absence of a powerful black knight in the post–Cold War world is a major development that should make sanctions much more effective.

CONTINUED COALITION COHESION

The emerging evidence does not support the proposition that international coalitions will be harder to form and maintain in the post–Cold War world, where there is no superpower enemy to rally against. When the United States has sought to create and preserve a tight coalition — in Iraq, Haiti, and Yugoslavia — it has succeeded. It achieved unprecedented levels of cooperation in its campaign against Iraq.[22] The United States and other Organization of American States (OAS) members cooperated effectively in imposing sanctions on Haiti. The United States and its North Atlantic Treaty Organization (NATO) allies have disagreed on Bosnian policy, but their disagreements have been over the use of NATO military forces, maintaining the arms embargo, and peace plans — not on economic sanctions policy. In short, when the United States has been serious about gaining and maintaining international cooperation for economic sanctions efforts, it has been able to do so.[23]

ASSESSING SUCCESS AND FAILURE IN IRAQ, HAITI, AND YUGOSLAVIA

The forgoing suggests that the conditions for employing economic sanctions are auspicious in the post–Cold War world. However, have post–Cold War sanctions efforts in fact produced results? Iraq, Haiti, and Yugoslavia may seem at first glance to be cases where sanctions have failed. Yet, in all three cases, economic sanctions had considerable impact.

In the Iraqi case, economic sanctions have crushed the Iraqi economy — Iraq's gross national product (GNP) has fallen by more than fifty percent since sanctions were imposed[24] — and weakened the financial

---

21. Nicholas D. Kristof, "China Opposes Sanctions in North Korea Dispute," *New York Times,* March 24, 1993, p. A8.

22. France, Russia, and China have favored lifting the sanctions on Iraq. As of late 1995, however, the United States has been able to keep the coalition together and get the necessary votes in the UN Security Council to maintain the sanctions. See "France Starts to Open the Doors," *Economist,* January 14, 1995, pp. 41–42; Barbara Crossette, "Iraq Hides Biological Warfare Effort, Report Says," *New York Times,* April 12, 1995, p. A8.

23. For more on international cooperation and economic sanctions, see Lisa L. Martin, *Coercive Cooperation: Explaining Multilateral Economic Sanctions* (Princeton, N.J.: Princeton University Press, 1992).

24. Iraq's GNP fell from $35 billion in 1989 to $15 billion in 1991 and $17 billion in

position of the Iraqi elite. Iraqi president Saddam Hussein has been forced to exhaust his large cash reserves secretly held in foreign banks.[25] Economic constraints have slowed the rebuilding of the Iraqi military and strengthened UN efforts to prevent Iraq from acquiring weapons of mass destruction.[26] They have also contributed to Iraq's decision to recognize Kuwait. Finally, the vast economic harm that sanctions have inflicted on Iraq serves as a powerful warning to other potential aggressors: it shows that a U.S.-led coalition can devastate an aggressor's economy.

Critics make two main observations to support their claim that sanctions have failed in Iraq. First, Saddam remains in power. Second, sanctions failed to induce Iraq to withdraw from Kuwait during the 1990–91 crisis. Their first argument measures sanctions against an unduly high standard of performance. National leaders who are firmly in power, as Saddam was in 1990, are very hard to unseat. Achieving their overthrow is perhaps the hardest task one could demand of sanctions. Economic sanctions have failed to overthrow Saddam, but military and covert action have also failed at the same task. The failure of economic sanctions to bring about Saddam's political demise means their success in Iraq is only partial. However, this should not obscure the successes they have achieved.[27]

The second observation, that sanctions failed to remove Iraq from Kuwait, is true but remains a weak indictment of sanctions efficacy

---

both 1992 and 1993. See International Institute for Strategic Studies (IISS), *The Military Balance, 1994–1995* (London: IISS, 1994), p. 129. The economic damage that sanctions inflict on targets is an indirect but nevertheless useful measure of their success. A target state may defy a sender's wishes even if it suffers economically, but the odds of compliance generally increase with the severity of the damage. Moreover, the damage that sanctions inflict directly measures their capacity to weaken the target (thereby reducing its capacity for mischief) or punish the target (thereby deterring it and others from future mischief). As discussed above, this can serve a valuable purpose.

25. Youssef Ibrahim, "Iraq Said to Sell Oil In Secret Plan to Skirt U.N. Ban," *New York Times*, February 16, 1995, p. A6.

26. UN monitor Rolf Ekeus described Iraq as in compliance with respect to nuclear and chemical weapons, but not biological weapons. Crossette, "Iraq Hides Biological Warfare Effort, Report Says."

27. It also bears mention that Saddam's overthrow is not a formal goal of the sanctions campaign. UN Security Council Resolution 687, passed in April 1991, required only that Iraq renounce all weapons of mass destruction—chemical, biological, and nuclear—and missiles with ranges above 150 kilometers, and that Iraq pay compensation and war reparations from the proceeds of future oil sales. See Alan Dowty, "Sanctioning Iraq: The Limits of the New World Order," *Washington Quarterly*, Vol. 17, No. 3 (Summer 1994), p. 180. Overthrowing Saddam became an informal U.S. sanctions goal shortly after the Gulf War.

because sanctions were not left in place long enough to accomplish the task. U.S. President George Bush decided not to wait to see if sanctions would work, but instead moved ahead with the military option six months into the crisis. Sanctions do not work overnight. During the Gulf crisis, sanctions advocates forecast that sanctions would take at least a year to force a change in Iraqi policy.[28] Sanctions were not given a full trial in Iraq and, therefore, cannot be judged a failure.

In Haiti, the United States got the policy outcome it wanted. President Jean-Bertrand Aristide is back in power. The question is whether or not economic sanctions contributed to this result. The case against sanctions is that sanctions were ineffective for three years and that the military junta stepped aside only when a U.S. military invasion was imminent.

In fact, sanctions were ineffective because they were first imposed in a tentative, half-hearted manner. The sanctions imposed in 1991 were partial, not total. Sanctions were targeted on Haitian elites only in the latter stages of the three-year confrontation.[29] Since the 1991 coup that ousted Aristide was sponsored by Haitian elites, sanctions would have to be targeted against the elites to bring about a policy change; this was a serious omission. Strong sanctions were imposed only in May–June 1994. Moreover, sanctions at first contained loopholes for U.S. businesses operating in Haiti, were loosened prematurely during the crisis before Haiti fully complied with U.S. and UN demands, and were accompanied by weak U.S. declarations and visible signs of U.S. irresolution.[30] In short,

---

28. See Gary C. Hufbauer and Kimberly A. Elliott, "Sanctions Will Bite—and Soon," *New York Times*, January 14, 1991, p. A17; and Les Aspin, "The Role of Sanctions in Securing U.S. Interests in the Persian Gulf," in U.S. Congress, House Committee on Armed Services, *Crisis In the Persian Gulf: Sanctions, Diplomacy and War*, Hearings Before the Committee on Armed Services, 101st Cong., 2nd sess., 1990, pp. 862–863.

29. Most strikingly, the financial assets of Haitian military leaders in the United States were not frozen until January 1994, more than two years into the crisis. See "U.S. Extends Economic Sanctions on Haiti," *New York Times*, January 28, 1994, p. A7.

30. The half-hearted and tentative nature of U.S. sanctions is reflected in the slow and meandering chronicle of their imposition. Shortly after Aristide's overthrow, in October and November of 1991, the United States suspended aid, trade, and all transactions with the Haitian government. OAS sanctions followed shortly. But in February 1992 the Bush administration created exemptions for U.S. businesses operating in Haiti. Only in June 1992 was the embargo broadened to deny U.S. ports to ships engaged in commerce with Haiti. Only in June 1993, nineteen months into the confrontation, did the United Nations impose an oil embargo on Haiti. This embargo was suspended in August after the Haitian junta signed the Governors Island Agreement; the embargo was reimposed in October 1993 when the junta reneged on the deal. Also in October 1993—two years into the confrontation—the United States froze the assets of forty-one government supporters. Only in January 1994 did the United States freeze the assets of members of the Haitian military and prohibit transactions with them.

sanctions were implemented in a very hesitating manner, especially in early phases of the crisis. Thus, it is not surprising that these sanctions were initially ineffective.

In the end, sanctions had an impact because they were toughened and targeted on Haitian economic and military elites. The junta's decision to step aside in September 1994 was undoubtedly triggered by the U.S. military forces on their way to Haiti, but economic sanctions had set the stage for their surrender by weakening their ability and their will to resist military action. Once sanctions were toughened to include a total trade embargo and a freeze of assets, they crippled the Haitian economy and hurt the elites.[31] This helped to convince Haiti's political elites to accept the idea of Aristide's return.[32] This, in turn, left the military leadership without its base of support, and unwilling to resist the U.S. invasion force. Economic sanctions made Haiti's military junta more willing to leave power peacefully when the United States threatened to use force.

Thus, despite being badly implemented at first, economic sanctions eventually injured the Haitian elites and thereby eased Aristide's restoration to power. These sanctions also serve as a powerful example that may deter militaries and elites elsewhere from considering anti-democratic coups.

The United States and the United Nations imposed aid, trade, and financial sanctions on Yugoslavia (Serbia and Montenegro) in 1992 with the goal of persuading it to rein in its Bosnian Serb clients and thus bring an end to the war in Bosnia.[33] These sanctions devastated the Yugoslav economy and helped to persuade Serbian leader Slobodan Milosevic to end his war for a "Greater Serbia." In late 1995, Milosevic accepted a

---

Commercial air service with Haiti was banned and financial transactions were further restricted only in June 1994. See Erin Day, *Economic Sanctions Imposed by the United States Against Specific Countries: 1979 Through 1992* (Washington, D.C.: Congressional Research Service, August 10, 1992), pp. 513–514, 523–525; "U.S. Extends Economic Sanctions on Haiti," *New York Times*, January 28, 1994, p. A7; Paul Lewis, "U.N. Again Imposes Sanctions on Haiti After Pact Fails," *New York Times*, October 14, 1993, p. A1; Heather M. Fleming, "Give Sanctions Time To Bite, Gray Tells Lawmakers," *CQ Weekly Report*, Vol. 52 (June 11, 1994), p. 1540.

31. Howard W. French, "Haiti's Poor Feeling the Pinch As Sanctions Ruin Economy," *New York Times*, November 15, 1993, p. A7; "Tightening the Stranglehold," *Economist*, August 6, 1994, p. 35.

32. "Sanctions Work," *Economist*, September 4, 1993, p. 41; Rick Bragg, "Many of Haiti's Elite Resign Themselves to Aristide's Return," *New York Times*, September 25, 1994, p. 16.

33. "Wide-ranging Sanctions Imposed Against Yugoslavia," *UN Chronicle*, Vol. 28, No. 3 (September 1992), pp. 5–12; Day, *Economic Sanctions Imposed by the United States Against Specific Countries*, pp. 425–428.

U.S.-brokered peace agreement reached in Dayton, Ohio, and pressed the Bosnian Serbs to accept it as well. Without the U.S.-UN sanctions, it seems very unlikely that the Serb side would even have considered the terms of the Dayton accord, let alone accepted them.[34]

Using economic instruments to end a war is extremely difficult. However, in this case, achieving peace has been made even more difficult because the United States has immoderate goals. Specifically, the United States has formally rejected a partition settlement, insisting that Bosnia must be maintained as a unitary state.[35] This requires the Bosnian Serbs to surrender sovereignty over all of their territory and abandon their goal of national independence — things they are very unlikely to do. The sanctions effort might have succeeded in achieving peace sooner if its goal had been more modest.

In short, economic sanctions have had a substantial impact on policy in Yugoslavia. Their failure to bring peace in Bosnia has been due mainly to U.S. political aims.

These three cases show that when a U.S.-led coalition has had the will to impose tough, comprehensive sanctions, it has achieved positive results. At a minimum, the economic damage done by these sanctions warns the world that the United States in coalition with other international powers can impose high economic costs on miscreant states and regimes. In addition, sanctions brought about important changes in the behavior of three targeted states. In the absence of sanctions, Saddam Hussein would have withheld his concessions on weapons of mass destruction, the Haitian elites would not have accepted Aristide's return, and Milosevic would not have pressured Bosnian Serbs to make concessions for peace.

In sum, economic sanctions work better than the academic literature or the conventional public wisdom suggests. The post–Cold War experience to date suggests that the prospects for U.S.-led sanctions are bright. No black knight has emerged to undercut sanctions efforts, and U.S.-led coalitions have remained cohesive. Sanctions are not surefire weapons, but they can help to bring about important changes in policy if they are firmly applied. They regularly work as well or better than other foreign policy instruments.

---

34. "Feeling the Pinch," *Economist*, October 8, 1994, pp. 54–55; Roger Cohen, "An Imperfect Peace," *New York Times*, November 22, 1995, p. A1.

35. David Binder, "U.S. Policymakers on Bosnia Admit Errors in Opposing Partition in 1992," *New York Times*, August 29, 1993, p. 10; Chuck Sudetic, "Clinton Writes to Reassure Bosnian Government of Support," *New York Times*, December 5, 1994, p. A12.

The Costs of Imposing Sanctions

Some skeptics argue that sanctions are poor foreign policy instruments because their use imposes exorbitant costs on sender states. According to this line of thinking, sanctions are not worthwhile: the price of success is excessive even if sanctions eventually succeed.[36] The high costs of sanctions make them less likely to succeed, because these costs weaken the senders' resolve. Seeing this, targets are emboldened to hold out, which further weakens the senders' will and eventually leads to the campaign's collapse. Finally, some critics argue that sanctions impose a moral cost on senders that outweighs their value.

In fact, the high economic costs that are cited by critics are largely mythical: sanctions seldom impose high economic costs on sender states. The case that costs are high has four shortcomings.

First, even the numbers used by skeptics do not indicate that economic costs to sender states are high. The National Foreign Trade Council, an anti-sanctions organization, has estimated that economic sanctions cost the United States $7 billion in lost exports to target states in 1987.[37] Even if this is true, $7 billion was only a very small fraction of U.S. gross domestic product (GDP) and total U.S. exports for 1987.[38] Moreover, the actual losses from these sanctions were undoubtedly lower because some portion of the exports not sent to sanctioned states were exported to other markets.

Second, many economic sanctions are cost-free to senders. Reducing or terminating bilateral foreign aid costs nothing, and will usually provide a net economic and domestic political gain. Similarly, financial sanctions, such as freezing assets and slowing or halting World Bank and International Monetary Fund (IMF) assistance impose almost no costs on senders. Even trade sanctions, which usually stir the greatest opposition,

---

36. On this argument, see Mary H. Cooper, "Economic Sanctions," *CQ Researcher*, Vol. 4, No. 40 (October 28, 1994), pp. 941, 943.

37. Gary Hufbauer, "The Impact of U.S. Economic Sanctions and Controls on U.S. Firms," report to the National Foreign Trade Council, April 1990, p. 23. The National Foreign Trade Council describes itself as an anti-sanctions organization. See Hufbauer, p. iii.

38. Total U.S. exports for 1987 were $250.4 billion and GDP was $4.46 trillion. Thus, $7 billion was 2.8 percent of total exports and 0.16 percent of GDP. Moreover, two-thirds of the $7 billion in losses resulted from Coordinating Committee for Multilateral Export Controls (COCOM) sanctions against the Soviet bloc, which have since been lifted. See Hufbauer, "Impact of U.S. Economic Sanctions," p. 44; IISS, *The Military Balance 1988–1989* (London: IISS, 1988), p. 18; U.S. Arms Control and Disarmament Agency (ACDA), *World Military Expenditures and Arms Transfers 1988* (Washington, D.C.: ACDA, 1989), p. 107.

can give an economic boost to domestic businesses by providing protection from foreign competitors. Hufbauer, Schott, and Elliott concluded that 85 percent of U.S. unilateral and U.S.-led economic sanctions produced a net gain to the senders or had little effect on the senders.[39]

Third, sanctions imposed with broad international support avoid the cost that businesses are most averse to paying: relative loss of market share to foreign competitors. When export restrictions are imposed, the pain and complaint level varies depending on whether the costs are relative or absolute.[40] Absolute costs occur when a sanctions effort has widespread support, such as the 1990 sanctions against Iraq. Under these conditions, firms lose business but do not lose market share to their foreign competitors because the competition is also participating in the embargo. Relative costs are incurred when countries impose unilateral sanctions or when only a small number of other states participate in the campaign. Under these conditions, businesses are likely to lose market share to foreign competitors.[41] However, with prospects for broad cooperation on sanctions efforts brightened by the Cold War's end, this problem will probably arise less often in the future.

Fourth, the costs to senders of imposing sanctions are far smaller than the costs of threatening or using force. Although sanctions cost the United States $7 billion in lost exports in 1987, the defense budget that year cost $283.5 billion.[42] It is also clear that the use of force has not been cost-free to the United States eighty-five percent of the time, as economic sanctions have been.[43] Moreover, sanctions do not risk U.S. lives.

---

39. Of the seventy-three cases involving the United States, forty-eight percent resulted in a net gain, thirty-seven percent had little effect on the sender, fourteen percent resulted in a modest loss to the sender, and only one percent (one case) caused a major loss to the sender. This single case was Iraq (1990), and the negative effects fell mainly on U.S. allies rather than the United States itself. Thus, the United States has never suffered a major economic loss from a sanctions effort. Data calculated from tables in Hufbauer, Schott, and Elliott, *Economic Sanctions Reconsidered*, Vol. I, pp. 84–90.

40. The concepts of relative and absolute costs are inspired by Joseph Grieco, who uses the concepts of relative and absolute gains to explain state behavior. See Joseph M. Grieco, *Cooperation Among Nations* (Ithaca, N.Y.: Cornell University Press, 1990).

41. This explains the growing U.S. corporate opposition to the COCOM sanctions in the 1980s. See Beverly Crawford, *Economic Vulnerability in International Relations: East-West Trade, Investment, and Finance* (New York: Columbia University Press, 1993), pp. 31–36; and Kevin F.F. Quigley and William J. Long, "Export Controls: Moving Beyond Economic Containment," *World Policy Journal*, Vol. 7, No. 1 (Winter 1989–90), pp. 175–178.

42. IISS, *The Military Balance 1988–1989*, p. 18.

43. A full comparison of the costs of economic sanctions and force requires assessing the cost of preparing to use each instrument and the actual cost of their use. Economic

Finally, some critics condemn sanctions because they hurt innocent civilians in the target country, and thus violate a moral proscription on injuring political innocents.[44] Two main points need to be made in response. First, injury to innocents is a real drawback to sanctions use. However, this cost should be measured against the benefits that sanctions provide. The value of avoiding injury to innocents is not an absolute, and should give way if the benefits of sanctions are greater. It is important to note that innocent civilians often welcome the imposition of sanctions against their countries when they share the goals of outside powers; Haiti is a case in point.[45] Sanctions should, of course, be targeted as much as possible at the government in question and its key supporters. Second, the alternative policy instrument — military force — would also, in most cases, cause significant and more grievous harm to ordinary citizens.

Implications for the Prevention, Management, and Resolution of Internal Conflict

What role can U.S.-led economic sanctions play in helping to prevent, manage, or resolve internal conflict in the future? How should they be applied? I argue that sanctions can be an effective instrument for controlling internal conflict, and should be used for that purpose far more than in the past. Sanctions are most likely to succeed when used to manage or contain internal conflicts, less likely to succeed when used to prevent conflicts, and least likely to succeed when used to resolve conflicts. When they are used, sanctions should be total and should be imposed early in

---

sanctions are usually far cheaper on both dimensions. Preparation for economic sanctions costs very little, requiring at most some stockpiling of goods. Preparation for force involves the cost of training, maintaining, and arming the military. Like sanctions, the cost of force will vary from case to case. For example, preparation for the Gulf War cost the United States $68 billion, and the war itself cost another $52 billion. Because of unique circumstances, the entire $52 billion was paid by allies. However, even this relatively cheap war cost the United States far more than the $7 billion total cost of all the economic sanctions in place during the year 1987. See Ann Markusen, "Mixed Messages: The Effects of the Gulf War and the End of the Cold War on the American Military-Industrial Complex," in John O'Loughlin, Tom Mayer, and Edward S. Greenberg, eds., *War and Its Consequences: Lessons from the Persian Gulf Conflict* (New York: HarperCollins, 1994), p. 165.

44. For more on this issue, see Lori Fisler Damrosch, "The Civilian Impact of Economic Sanctions," in Lori Fisler Damrosch, ed., *Enforcing Restraint: Collective Intervention in Internal Conflicts* (New York: Council on Foreign Relations, 1993), pp. 274–315.

45. See Pamela Constable, "Dateline Haiti: Caribbean Stalemate," *Foreign Policy*, No. 89 (Winter 1992/93), pp. 175–176, 183; "Still Embargoed," *Economist*, October 10, 1992, p. 54.

the conflict. The United States must win widespread cooperation from other states, and must show resolve to the target state. This, in turn, requires building domestic support for the sanctions policy, and clearly committing the relevant governments to maintaining the sanctions until the target complies with the demands being made of it.

USING SANCTIONS TO PREVENT INTERNAL CONFLICT

Outside powers could use economic sanctions to prevent internal conflicts if they could foresee impending civil wars and could pressure one or more colliding parties to adopt more peaceful policies. For example, governments could be pressured to adopt reforms that would defuse impending rebellions. Such reforms might include implementing democratic changes, granting autonomy to or sharing power with national minorities, land reform, redistribution of wealth, or refraining from disseminating hate propaganda. The sanctions that pressured South Africa to end apartheid could be considered a successful example of conflict prevention.

International financial institutions such as the World Bank and the IMF could tie economic assistance to a government's domestic policies — a procedure known as conditionality — for the same purpose.[46] Although not a traditional economic sanction, tying economic assistance to a government's domestic policies (e.g., respect for minority rights) is a way of using leverage to bring about peaceful political change.[47]

Sanctions efforts of this sort are worth attempting because conflict prevention is far easier than conflict resolution. If a conflict can be caught early, the effort required to avert it will be far less than the effort to halt it once it begins. The parties are not yet politically mobilized for war. Hence, they are more tractable.

There are, however, three serious impediments to using economic sanctions for conflict prevention. First, violent internal conflict is hard to predict. This makes it hard to identify cases where conflict prevention measures are needed. Second, the causes and preventives of internal

---

46. For an analysis of the issues surrounding conditionality by international financial institutions, see Wolfgang H. Reinicke, "Cooperative Security and the Political Economy of Nonproliferation," in Janne E. Nolan, ed., *Global Engagement: Cooperation and Security in the 21st Century* (Washington, D.C.: Brookings Institution, 1994), pp. 175–234.

47. Milada Vachudová argues, along similar lines, that the possibility of membership in the European Union and NATO has had a positive effect on the economic, social, and foreign policies of Central European countries. Thus, Western conditioning of membership in these institutions on political criteria such as maintaining democracy has dampened the potential for conflict in Central and Eastern Europe. For more on this argument, see Vachudová's chapter on East-Central Europe in this volume.

conflicts can be difficult to distinguish. For example, pressuring repressive regimes to reform can cause either peace or war, depending on the situation. The trick lies in knowing which situation one faces. U.S. pressures to reform sparked civil conflicts in both Nicaragua and Iran in the 1970s. Neither Anastasio Somoza Debayle nor the Shah Muhammed Reza Pahlavi ever enacted meaningful reforms, but the pressure to do so may have galvanized opponents by convincing them that the United States would not intervene to prop up the regime.[48] If sanctions are to be used for conflict prevention, a good understanding of the roots of internal conflict is needed in order to avoid such mistakes.

Third, it is difficult to impose sanctions against opposition groups and forces. In many cases, no clearly delineated borders separate the opposition from the government, making trade sanctions problematic. In addition, opposition groups are generally not direct recipients of foreign economic aid. This reduces outside leverage. Finally, freezing assets is often not an option because members of opposition groups are not wealthy enough to have assets in foreign banks, or because secrecy makes it difficult to identify those individuals whose assets should be frozen.

Thus, the prospects for using economic sanctions to prevent internal conflict are mixed. The fact that conflict prevention involves deterrence rather than compellence bodes well for success. The greatest difficulty with using sanctions to prevent civil conflict lies not with the power of the tool, but with the wisdom of its user. There are limits to our ability to recognize when civil war is imminent, and to distinguish the conditions in which pressure to reform will prevent war (as in South Africa) from the conditions in which pressure will trigger war (as in Nicaragua and Iran). To use sanctions effectively for conflict prevention in the future, excellent intelligence and a better understanding of the roots of war will be needed.

USING SANCTIONS TO MANAGE THE SPREAD OF INTERNAL CONFLICT

Outside powers can become involved in internal conflicts in two ways. First, outside powers can intervene in civil wars. Examples include the German and Italian interventions in the Spanish civil war, and the U.S. intervention in the Vietnamese civil war. Second, belligerents in civil wars can attack outside powers. Examples include Sandinista attacks on Honduras in the 1970s, and Vietnamese communist intrusions into Cambodia in the 1960s and 1970s.

---

48. Perhaps having learned from those experiences, the United States helped ease another dictator, Ferdinand Marcos, out of power in the Philippines without a civil war or a takeover by a hostile regime.

Hypothetically, economic sanctions can play a role in averting both kinds of problems. A coalition could avert the first scenario by threatening to sanction any outside powers that intervene in a civil war. It could avert the second scenario by threatening to sanction any belligerent in a civil war that attacks neighboring states.

Economic sanctions and the threat of sanctions are well-suited to efforts to limit outside intervention in civil wars. First, one is attempting to deter contemplated action rather than compel an actor to reverse steps already taken. Second, identifying the outside powers that might intervene in a civil war is relatively easy. The target of the threat (and of the sanction) would be clear.

Preventing belligerents from lashing out at neighboring states may be more difficult, because these belligerents are highly motivated, and therefore less likely to be swayed by sanctions or the threat of sanctions. However, even here a U.S.-led coalition may have leverage if its aid or trade is critical to a belligerent's war effort, or to its postwar rebuilding effort. If all else fails, a threat to assist the belligerent's enemies could deter it from attacking neighboring states.

USING SANCTIONS TO RESOLVE INTERNAL CONFLICT

Outside powers could adopt one of two strategies to terminate ongoing civil conflicts. One option is to choose a side and aid it in gaining a decisive victory. A second option is to coerce the parties to accept a compromise.[49] Regardless of which strategy the United States and its coalition partners adopt, using economic sanctions to end wars is difficult. First, the coalition members must reach agreement on a plan for peace — something they could not do with respect to Bosnia until the war was over three years old. Without a clear policy goal, no instrument, including economic sanctions, can be effective. Agreements on goals, however, can be difficult to forge. Second, even when a peace plan is in place, it can be difficult to verify compliance.[50] But unless one knows which party is in greatest breach of the plan, one will not know whom to sanction. Determining who should be targeted for sanctions is a problem that must be solved. However, this can be difficult. Third, ending wars is harder than preventing wars because compellence is harder than deterrence: it is

---

49. Discussing these options are Richard K. Betts, "The Delusion of Impartial Intervention," *Foreign Affairs*, Vol. 73, No. 6 (November/December 1994), pp. 20–33; and Barbara F. Walter, "The Resolution of Civil Wars: Why Negotiations Fail," Ph.D. dissertation, University of Chicago, 1994.

50. Bosnia is a case in point. It has often proven impossible to ascertain who first broke cease-fire agreements between Serbs and Muslims.

always harder to coerce actors to reverse policies already adopted than to eschew policies not yet embraced. Acts of war are among the hardest policies to reverse because the stakes are high and reversals leave elites politically exposed.

Finally, turning sanctions on and off, as iterated coercion of the parties may require — as one side, then the other, might need encouragement to comply with a peace plan — is problematic. The pain that sanctions produce can lag behind the imposition of sanctions by months or years. As a result, the sanctioner cannot locate the punishment close in time to the transgression, robbing the punishment of its deterrent effect. Turning sanctions on and off also allows the parties to stockpile goods while sanctions are not in effect. This will undercut the efficacy of future rounds of sanctions.

In sum, economic sanctions are less well-suited to the task of stopping wars than to conflict prevention. However, sanctions still have some prospects of success at this task, and often remain the best instrument for the job. The United States can impose sanctions at little cost. This cost is nearly always less than the cost of using military force. Hence, it is worthwhile to try using economic sanctions to resolve internal conflicts.

HOW TO APPLY ECONOMIC SANCTIONS

How should economic sanctions be applied in order to maximize their efficacy for conflict prevention, management, and resolution? Policymakers should embrace four main operating principles: imposing total sanctions, imposing sanctions immediately, obtaining the cooperation of all key states, and demonstrating resolve.

First, the full range of available economic instruments should be threatened and used. A combination of aid, trade, and financial sanctions is markedly more effective than any lesser combination. Iran (1979), Iraq (1990), Haiti (1991), and Yugoslavia (1992) are all cases where total sanctions produced positive results. When the United States and other international powers have shown the will to impose total sanctions, they have usually achieved results.

Second, total sanctions should be imposed as soon as decisions to impose sanctions are taken. A slow, incremental tightening of sanctions is far less effective. Incrementalism allows the target time to adjust and take steps (e.g., stockpiling supplies and moving money) that make sanctions less effective. Incremental sanctions may also cause the target to question the resolve of the United States and other coalition partners.

Third, in order to maximize the chances for success, the United States must acquire and maintain the cooperation of key states. The states whose cooperation is most necessary are the neighbors and major trading partners of the target. Not coincidentally, these are the states, in addition to the target, which are most likely to suffer from the imposition of economic sanctions. Therefore, gaining their cooperation may not be easy. However, it is possible to build a coalition if the United States and other powers provide carrots and sticks to induce cooperation from key states. Carrots could include compensation for the loss of revenue from trade with the target. Sticks could include threats to reduce aid or trade. Carrots will seldom induce perfect compliance — even if neighboring state governments cooperate, some smuggling is likely — but perfect compliance is not required. As Iraq and Haiti have demonstrated, a little leakage does not prevent sanctions from devastating the target's economy.

Fourth, the coalition must convince the target that it will continue to impose the sanctions until they are successful. This is extremely important because sanctions can take months, even years, to produce results.[51] Two steps are required to create this impression. First, if the United States leads the coalition, the U.S. government must commit itself, in a highly visible way, to maintaining sanctions until the target complies. Such a commitment will make a retreat more difficult. Second, the U.S. government must build broad domestic support for the sanctions policy. A lack of strong domestic support could lead the target to believe that it could wait out the sanctions. To do this, Washington must identify domestic interests that will be hurt by the sanctions in question. It then must decide to pay the political price of standing up to them, or persuade them not to work for the sanctions' repeal. This may involve providing compensation (political or economic) to offset the negative effects of the sanctions.

Conclusions

The conditions for using economic sanctions for conflict prevention, management, and resolution are generally auspicious and should remain so for the foreseeable future. Sanctions are better suited for these purposes than they were during the Cold War for two reasons. First, the Soviet black knight has vanished, and no replacement has emerged. This makes all Western uses of sanctions more likely to succeed. Second, there is a growing awareness in the United States and Western Europe that regional wars pose real costs and risks to the major industrial states. The world is consequently more willing to support U.S.-led efforts to prevent or contain such wars. One concern is that these conflicts will produce refugees

---

51. The average duration of sanctions coded as successes by Hufbauer, Schott, and Elliott was 2.9 years. See their *Economic Sanctions Reconsidered*, Vol. 1, p. 101.

who will head for the West. The war in Vietnam created a refugee crisis that is still not fully resolved. More recently, Haitian refugees forced the United States to deal with that country's political problems. The conflicts in Algeria and Bosnia have created refugee problems for Western Europe. These refugee crises have made Western powers more willing to act to stop the wars that produce them.

The United States has never used economic sanctions explicitly for preventing, managing, or resolving internal conflicts. It should do so. Sanctions are underrated, more effective than most analysts suggest, and they could be an effective damper on internal conflict. This conclusion clashes with the conventional view on sanctions, which holds that sanctions are seldom effective. However, past studies understate the effectiveness of sanctions by including cases of half-hearted sanctions and by defining success in narrow terms. Direct extrapolations from these studies would lead one to understate the likely success of U.S.-led sanctions in the post–Cold War era.

The efficacy of sanctions is also underrated because, unlike other foreign policy instruments, sanctions have no natural advocates or constituency. Business leaders dislike sanctions because they disrupt international commerce. Within the U.S. government, the State Department, the Central Intelligence Agency, and the Defense Department are natural advocates for diplomacy, covert action, and the use of military force, respectively. Economic sanctions have no equivalent champion. As a result, their successes go unreported while their failures are exaggerated by those with an interest in either avoiding the use of sanctions, or in using other instruments.

The main impediments to the success of economic sanctions stem from domestic political and intellectual concerns. The problem lies not with the weakness of the sanctions instrument — it is a strong and effective instrument, if wielded properly, firmly, and in a timely manner — but with the political indecisiveness and intellectual weaknesses of its users. To use sanctions for the prevention, management, and resolution of internal conflicts, we must develop a grasp of the roots of these wars, learn to predict their occurrence more accurately, and become better able to decide what solutions to impose. The United States and other international powers must also be willing to maintain sanctions for months or years if necessary, to stand up to (or buy off) domestic interests injured by sanctions, and to lead allies to cooperate. If these conditions are met, economic sanctions stand a good chance of producing results.

Chapter 13

Nongovernmental Organizations and Internal Conflict

Thomas G. Weiss

Two significant developments of the post–Cold War era come together in this chapter. The first is the growing willingness of the international community to address humanitarian emergencies within the borders of war-torn states. The language of the United Nations (UN) Charter with respect to state sovereignty is still intact, but humanitarian imperatives, especially since the imposition of safe havens for Kurds in northern Iraq in April 1991, have led governmental, intergovernmental, and non-governmental organizations (NGOs) to intervene more and more in essentially domestic matters. This was a major theme in the much-publicized reports of UN Secretary-General Boutros Boutros-Ghali, *An Agenda for Peace* and *Supplement to "An Agenda for Peace."*[1]

The second development is the growing number and enhanced profile of NGOs that attempt to mitigate suffering from internal conflicts. This is part of a larger development, the burgeoning of NGOs, which has injected new voices into international discourse.[2] In the 1970s and 1980s, and especially since the end of the Cold War, human rights advocates, gender activists, developmentalists, and groups of indigenous peoples have become more vocal and visible in contexts that were once thought

---

The author is grateful to William Durch, Larry Minear, and Colin Scott for helpful comments on earlier drafts of this chapter.

---

1. Boutros Boutros-Ghali, *An Agenda for Peace* (New York: United Nations, 1992), and *Supplement to "An Agenda for Peace": Position Paper by the Secretary-General on the Occasion of the Fiftieth Anniversary of the United Nations*, Document A/50/60, S/1995/1, January 3, 1995. These have both been republished as *An Agenda For Peace 1995* (New York: United Nations, 1995).

2. See Bertrand Schneider, *The Barefoot Revolution: A Report to the Club of Rome* (London: IT Publications, 1988).

to be the exclusive preserve of governments.[3] The Commission on Global Governance highlights the crucial contributions of NGOs and observes that "in their variety they bring expertise, commitment, and grassroots perceptions that should be better mobilized in the interests of better governance."[4]

Confusion persists about the precise definition of a "nongovernmental organization." Theoretical explorations are few in number[5] and specialized by sector, traditionally for economic and social development and more recently for the environment.[6] Moreover, much of the literature is legalistic and focuses on the formal relationships of those one thousand or so NGOs that have official UN consultative status.[7] This literature is inadequate and the legalistic approach, in particular, fails to explore the richness of NGO activity in response to internal conflicts.

There are numerous semantic alternatives to the term "nongovernmental organization" — private voluntary organizations, transnational social movement organizations, grass-roots social change organizations, and non-state actors. This chapter employs the term "NGO" because it is widely accepted (following the language of Article 71 of the UN Charter)

---

3. See Peter J. Spiro, "New Global Communities: Nongovernmental Organizations in International Decision-Making Institutions," *Washington Quarterly*, Vol. 18, No. 1 (Winter 1995), pp. 45–56.

4. Commission on Global Governance, *Our Global Neighbourhood* (Oxford: Oxford University Press, 1995), p. 254. One measure of the sea change that has occurred is that the Commission, composed almost entirely of former government officials and high-level officials from intergovernmental secretariats, devoted so much attention to non-governmental organizations.

5. Recent exceptions are Kathryn Sikkink, "Human Rights, Principled Issue-Networks, and Sovereignty in Latin America," *International Organization*, Vol. 47, No. 3 (Summer 1993), pp. 411–441; Ramesh Thakur, "Human Rights: Amnesty International and the United Nations," *Journal of Peace Research*, Vol. 31, No. 2 (December 1994), pp. 143–160; Thomas Princen, "NGOs: Creating a Niche in Environmental Diplomacy," and Matthias Finger, "NGOs and Transformation: Beyond Social Movement Theory," in Thomas Princen and Matthias Finger, eds., *Environmental NGOs in World Politics* (London: Routledge, 1994), pp. 29–66.

6. See John Clark, *Democratizing Development: The Role of Voluntary Organizations* (Hartford, Conn.: Kumarian, 1991); David Korten, *Getting to the 21st Century: Voluntary Action and the Global Agenda* (Hartford, Conn.: Kumarian, 1990); Michael Edwards and David Hulme, eds., *Making a Difference: NGOs and Development in a Changing World* (London: Earthscan, 1992); Lawrence Susskind, *Environmental Diplomacy: Negotiating More Effective Global Agreements* (New York: Oxford University Press, 1994).

7. See, for example, Open-Ended Group on the Review of Arrangements for Consultations with Non-Governmental Organizations, *General Review of Arrangements for Consultations with Non-Governmental Organizations*, Document E/AC.70/1994/5, May 26, 1994.

and because "non-state actors" include a host of transnational entities that should be deliberately excluded from this discussion, such as profit-making corporations, political parties, religious groups, banks, criminal organizations, terrorists, insurgents, and the media. Nongovernmental organizations are formal institutions that are intended to continue in existence; they are not *ad hoc* entities. They are or aspire to be self-governing on the basis of their own constitutional arrangements. They are private in that they are separate from governments and have no ability to direct societies or require support from them. They are not in the business of making profits. NGOs exist and operate beyond and beneath the states in which they are incorporated.

As part of the changing role of the state — indeed of its collapse in certain areas — and of alternative ways to address both local and global problems, NGOs are emerging as a critical set of institutions that are private in form but public in purpose.[8] Because they provide assistance and protect the rights of civilians caught in the throes of internal conflicts, they are worthy of analytical attention. Determining what they do well and what they should not do at all is a prerequisite to increasing the tensile strength of the international safety net under civilian victims of internal conflicts.

In this chapter, I analyze NGO efforts to mitigate life-threatening suffering from internal conflicts, a domain in which these institutions are increasingly important.[9] In the four sections of this chapter, I answer the following questions. First, where are NGOs situated among other humanitarian actors? Second, what roles do NGOs play? Third, what tasks do NGOs perform? Fourth, what are the most critical policy issues facing NGOs with respect to internal conflicts, and what policy recommendations are pertinent?

Humanitarian Actors

Eight types of actors constitute the core of the world's humanitarian safety net.[10] Three types come from inside conflict areas themselves — host governments, armed opposition groups, and local NGOs. Although

---

8.   See Lester M. Salamon and Helmut K. Anheier, *The Emerging Sector: An Overview* (Baltimore, Md.: Johns Hopkins University Institute for Policy Studies, 1994).

9.   See John Borton, "Recent Trends in the International Relief System," *Disasters*, Vol. 17, No. 3 (1993), pp. 187–201; John Borton, *NGOs and Relief Operations: Trends and Policy Implications* (London: Overseas Development Institute, 1994).

10.   See the longer discussion in Larry Minear and Thomas G. Weiss, *Mercy Under Fire: War and the Global Humanitarian Community* (Boulder, Colo.: Westview, 1995); Larry

they are critical, they are not discussed here because my focus is on responses by the international community. Unless specifically mentioned otherwise, the term "NGO" will be used only in reference to nongovernmental organizations based outside of the country in crisis (the "host country").

Five types of humanitarian actors are based outside conflict areas: the United Nations, donor governments, military forces that assume humanitarian tasks, the International Committee of the Red Cross (ICRC), and NGOs.

The United Nations is central to the world's responses to security and non-security crises in the post–Cold War world.[11] The UN system consists of several different humanitarian agencies sharing a common UN connection and staffed by international civil servants working under a common policy of recruitment and remuneration. The three major players in the humanitarian arena are juridically part of the United Nations: the UN Children's Fund (UNICEF), the World Food Program (WFP), and the UN High Commissioner for Refugees (UNHCR). Since 1992, UN humanitarian activities have been coordinated, at least on paper, by the UN Department of Humanitarian Affairs (UNDHA) and, in crisis areas, either by special representatives of the UN Secretary-General or by representatives of the UN Development Program. Other specialized agencies, for example, the World Health Organization and the Food and Agricultural Organization, are less relevant to this discussion because they normally concentrate on post-conflict problems.

The second type of outside actor, and in terms of resources the most important, consists of donor governments. They not only contribute resources to UN organizations and to NGOs, they also operate their own programs. The U.S. Agency for International Development (AID), to name just one, has traditionally been in the forefront of responses to natural and man-made disasters. Frequently, AID resources represent one-third to one-half of total governmental resources committed on a bilateral basis to humanitarian crises stemming from internal conflicts. In addition to having their own aid efforts, European governments in 1993 established a joint mechanism for aid, the European Community's Humanitarian Office (ECHO).

The third type of outside actor, outside military forces, has made

---

Minear and Thomas G. Weiss, *Humanitarian Politics* (New York: Foreign Policy Association, 1995).

11. See Thomas G. Weiss, David P. Forsythe, and Roger A. Coate, *The United Nations and Changing World Politics* (Boulder, Colo.: Westview, 1994).

significant contributions to humanitarian actions since the mid-1980s. During the Cold War, outside soldiers were occasionally mobilized to combat the consequences of natural disasters, but their contribution to the delivery of relief and the protection of human rights in war zones was limited to infrequent actions by UN peacekeepers.[12] However, beginning with the creation of safe havens for Kurds escaping Saddam Hussein's attacks in April 1991, outside military forces have assumed important responsibilities in Somalia, the former Yugoslavia, Rwanda, and Haiti. Outside military forces could of course be considered contributions by donor governments. But in the vast majority of humanitarian emergencies where they have been deployed since the end of the Cold War, they have done so under UN command, or at least under UN auspices. They thus could also be considered UN actions. However, given their distinct capacities and concerns, it is analytically useful to place them in a separate category.

The International Committee of the Red Cross, founded in 1864, is the fourth outside humanitarian actor. Based in Geneva, it seeks to assist and protect individuals in both international and "non-international" (ICRC terminology for internal) armed conflicts. As the custodian and monitor of the Geneva Conventions of 1949 and the Additional Protocols of 1977, the ICRC enjoys a special status in international law; it also enjoys an observer role in the General Assembly. As a hybrid organization with both governmental and private members, it is routinely supported by donor governments, which traditionally fund about 90 percent of its $500 million budget. The ICRC therefore belongs in a category by itself as the most visible private organization in armed conflicts.

The fifth and final pillar of the international community's humanitarian architecture is comprised of private relief groups, or NGOs. Some NGOs control programmatic resources that rival or dwarf those of many governments and UN agencies — for example, World Vision International, Save the Children, CARE, International Rescue Committee, Médecins Sans Frontières, Oxfam, and Catholic Relief Services. Others are far more modest in scale — for example, Norwegian People's Aid or the American Friends Service Committee. Some mount a range of activities in virtually all humanitarian crises, while others concentrate their energies on specific countries or continents, sectors, or population groups.

NGOs are effective and important because their energetic, low-overhead operations help victims that governmental and intergovern-

---

12. See Leon Gordenker and Thomas G. Weiss, eds., *Soldiers, Peacekeepers and Disasters* (London: Macmillan, 1991).

mental aid programs often fail to reach.[13] Their hallmarks are quick response and direct action. They are frequently on the front lines when less hardy humanitarians have departed or are reluctant to get involved. NGOs are also less bound by constraints with respect to state sovereignty. For example, they often set up cross-border operations when donor governments or UN organizations refuse to do so. NGO staffs typically are highly motivated and relatively unbureaucratic, although their work often suffers from a lack of professionalism, coordination, and follow-up.

NGO Types and Roles

Not every organization claiming to be an NGO fits the definition of a private organization that is transnational in scope and separate from government but active on humanitarian issues. There are three significant variations. The first two, government-organized NGOs and donor-organized NGOs, are excluded from detailed consideration in this chapter but are mentioned for the sake of completeness. The third, the quasi-NGO, is most pertinent.

Government-organized NGOs achieved notoriety during the Cold War because many owed their existence to communist governments of the Soviet bloc or authoritarian governments from the Third World. There was no difference between the "party lines" of these governments and such supposedly nongovernmental mouthpieces as unions and even United Nations associations. A few such NGOs in the West, particularly in the United States, functioned as a direct extension of a particular administration's foreign policy. During the 1980s, for example, a number of NGOs, including the International Rescue Committee, served as channels for U.S. government aid to refugees in Pakistan who were fleeing from the Soviet-backed Afghan government. In Central America, NGOs such as World Vision, World Relief, and the World Anti-Communist League assisted those fleeing from the "wrong" side in El Salvador (that is, from the Farabundo Marti National Liberation Front, or FMLN) and in Nicaragua (that is, from the Sandinista government). The residue from this past surfaced early in 1995, when various proposals were made to incorporate AID into the U.S. Department of State. Should this come to pass, it would be more difficult for NGOs taking resources from AID to argue that they are not instruments of U.S. foreign policy, because the helpful fiction of a somewhat independent source of financing would disappear.

A second type of special NGO is the donor-organized NGO. As two

13. See Brian H. Smith, *More Than Altruism: The Politics of Private Foreign Aid* (Princeton, N.J.: Princeton University Press, 1990).

observers have noted: "As donors become more interested in NGOs, they also find themselves tempted to create NGOs suited to their perceived needs."[14] Both governments and UN agencies have created and sustained such NGOs in, for example, Afghanistan and Cambodia. Because these are local NGOs from the country in crisis, they will not be discussed in detail here.

The third special type of NGO is the quasi-NGO. As already noted, the ICRC receives 90 percent of its operating budget from governments. Many Nordic and Canadian NGOs as well as a number of U.S. NGOs also receive the bulk of their resources from governments. The staffs of such organizations argue, for the most part justifiably, that their priorities dominate those of their donors. Many such organizations are therefore relevant for this discussion. Their services aim at internationally endorsed objectives and their operations are distinct from those of governments, even if their funding comes from governmental accounts. With more and more governmental and intergovernmental resources being disbursed through nongovernmental channels, these NGOs are becoming increasingly important. So, too, is their independence — their willingness to bite the hands that feed in order to make autonomous programmatic decisions.

Whatever their stripe, NGOs play two main roles: operational; and educational and advocative.

OPERATIONAL ROLES

At least part of the activities of most NGOs are operational in nature, involving the delivery of emergency relief. Operational NGOs are the most numerous type of NGO, have the easiest fund-raising tasks, and are central to international responses to internal conflicts in the post–Cold War world. The delivery of emergency humanitarian services is the most prominent item in most NGO budgets and the basis for the enthusiastic support that they receive from their donors. Many NGOs operate development programs, but they have become increasingly active in migration and disaster relief, which may be in total financial terms their most important activities.

In 1994 NGOs accounted for over 10 percent of total public development aid (some $8 billion). Their resources were greater than those of the UN system (excluding Washington-based financial institutions), and an ever-growing percentage of their resources, about half, was devoted to

14. David L. Brown and David Korten, *Understanding Voluntary Organizations: Guidelines for Donors*, Working Paper No. 258 (Washington, D.C.: World Bank, September 1989), p. 22.

emergency relief.[15] About one-quarter of U.S. development aid is being channeled through NGOs as of the mid-1990s, a figure that U.S. Vice-President Al Gore promised at the Social Summit in Copenhagen to increase to one-half by the end of the 1990s.

Bilateral and multilateral organizations are relying more and more on NGOs as sub-contractors. Some NGO managers are delighted with this trend: it will allow them to expand the scope of their activities. Others worry about being exploited by governments or intergovernmental organizations and losing their autonomy. The key to maintaining operational integrity is being a "partner" and not simply a "contractor." The former connotes authentic collaboration and respect for the autonomy of NGOs. Such relationships are rare, and it is difficult to imagine most NGOs enjoying them with large and powerful agencies.

EDUCATIONAL AND ADVOCATIVE ROLES

In addition to aiding the victims of humanitarian crises, many NGOs seek to educate and lobby their contributors, publics, and governments. Such NGOs seek primarily to influence citizens, whose voices are then registered through public opinion and bear fruit in the form of additional resources for NGO activities, as well as new governmental policies and on occasion enhanced international regimes. NGOs can reinforce the norms promoted by intergovernmental organizations through public education campaigns, which in turn can help hold states accountable to their international commitments.[16]

Western NGOs are under growing pressure from their partners in less-developed countries to educate contributors and Western publics about the origins of poverty and violence. NGOs that focus exclusively on education in their own countries are not numerous, but they exist. Many of the most effective educators are those with the credibility, knowledge, and convictions resulting from substantial operational experience. Examples are the educational efforts by Oxfam and Save the Children on the origins of poverty and injustice, which are linked to their campaigns to deal with the victims from wars in Bosnia and Somalia. Many NGOs that began with a focus on relief projects now place more emphasis on structural change and prevention through education. Two observers sum-

---

15. "NGOs and Conflict: Three Views," *Humanitarian Monitor*, No. 2 (February 1995), pp. 32–33.

16. See Jamie Leatherman, Ron Pagnucco, and Jackie Smith, *International Institutions and Transnational Social Movement Organizations: Challenging the State in a Three-level Game of Global Political Transformation*, Working Paper Series 5:WP:3 (Notre Dame, Ind.: Kroc Institute, Fall 1993).

marize the logic behind the shift away from relief projects: "Many of the causes of under-development lie in the political and economic structures of an unequal world . . . and in the misguided policies of governments and the multilateral institutions (such as the World Bank and the IMF [International Monetary Fund]) which they control. It is extremely difficult, if not impossible, to address these issues in the context of the traditional NGO project."[17]

Linked to education are the advocative efforts of NGOs working primarily in the corridors of governments and intergovernmental organizations. These organizations engage in discussions with decision-makers and their staffs in order to influence national and international policy. In seeking to inform or alter the policies of governments as well as governmental and intergovernmental agencies, NGOs engaged in advocacy seek to influence a wide variety of policymakers, not simply parliamentarians. Prominent examples in the humanitarian arena in the United States include the Lawyers' Committee for Human Rights, the Refugee Policy Group, Refugees International, and the U.S. Committee for Refugees. Although NGOs engaged in advocacy are important, they are not numerous and they often have great difficulty in raising funds.

In the past, a great deal of NGO advocacy has been directed against the official policies of governments and UN organizations. In the 1990s, however, many NGOs have moved toward institutionalizing what one observer has called a "full-fledged partnership with the governmental members of the United Nations."[18] Historically, NGOs have had some responsibility for treaty implementation, but they have begun to aspire to more direct involvement in treaty-making. When governments and international institutions are trying to decide upon the shape of actions in the face of humanitarian emergencies in war zones, the views of NGOs can be influential, as suggested by the international responses in northern Iraq, Somalia, Rwanda, Haiti, and Bosnia.

Both through formal statements in UN fora and through informal negotiations with international civil servants and members of national delegations, many NGOs seek to ensure that their views, and those of their constituencies, are reflected in international texts and decisions. They sometimes offer research and drafting skills, and provide scientific or polling data to support their positions.[19] First-hand reports and testi-

---

17. Edwards and Hulme, *Making a Difference*, p. 20.

18. Susskind, *Environmental Diplomacy*, p. 51.

19. See Cynthia Price Cohen, "The Role of Nongovernmental Organizations in the Drafting of the Convention on the Rights of the Child," *Human Rights Quarterly*, Vol. 12, No. 1 (February 1990), pp. 137–147.

mony from field staff can be powerful tools before parliamentary committees.

It is worth emphasizing the extent to which some NGOs have contributed more to international agenda-setting than many intergovernmental organizations or governments. For example, at the San Francisco Conference in April 1945, NGOs acted as "consultants" to the U.S. delegation and played a pivotal role in securing the inclusion of human rights language in the final draft of the UN Charter. They played a similar role in 1948 with respect to the formulation and subsequent ratification of the Universal Declaration of Human Rights. In fact, they have spurred action at each stage in the evolution of the human rights regime since the middle of the nineteenth century.[20]

NGO influence on governmental responses to internal conflicts varies from organization to organization and from case to case. There is no doubt, though, that NGO efforts can affect the timing and shape of international responses to internal conflicts. In the United States, for example, they helped to contribute to a supportive climate for President George Bush's decisions to violate Iraqi sovereignty on behalf of the Kurds and to respond to the crisis in Somalia. NGOs were unable to move the Clinton administration to act with respect to the genocide in Rwanda in April and May 1994, but they eventually were able to get the administration to help in Zaire and Tanzania. For three years, U.S. NGOs advocated a military invasion to restore the elected government of Reverend Jean-Bertrand Aristide in Haiti. In France, NGOs have launched and sustained an activist humanitarian policy, *le droit d'ingérence*, which became the official policy of François Mitterrand's government and which survives his departure.[21]

Organizations engaged in advocacy typically make public statements about problems that they have identified, seek to produce documents that can be circulated among decision-makers, and publicize the results of their research and monitoring efforts. Some are loud and theatrical; others are discreet and subtle, such as Médecins Sans Frontières or the International Committee of the Red Cross. In any event, it is clear that advocacy is a growing NGO activity.

---

20. See David P. Forsythe, *Human Rights and World Politics* (Lincoln: University of Nebraska Press, 1989), pp. 83–101, 127–159.

21. See Bernard Kouchner and Mario Bettati, *Le devoir d'ingérence* (Paris: Denoël, 1987); Bernard Kouchner, *Le malheur des autres* (Paris: Odile Jacob, 1991); and Mario Bettati, "Intervention, Ingérence ou Assistance?" *Revue Trimestrielle des Droits de l'Homme*, No. 19 (July 1994), pp. 308–358.

NGO Tasks in War Zones

As discussed in the preceding section, NGOs play significant roles in relief operations as well as in education and advocacy. Relief operations preoccupy policymakers involved with internal conflicts, and hence are the focus in this chapter. NGO efforts in the post–Cold War era are best understood in the context of their previous efforts in war zones.[22] The period of decolonization, which lasted through the mid-1980s, was particularly formative. The United Nations was constrained by the politics of the Cold War and a slavish interpretation of Charter Article 2 (7), which reduced its mandate to working with recognized governments and victims located within the territories under direct governmental control. Except for the ICRC, NGOs usually refrained from helping those in contested areas. Over time, individual NGOs as well as NGO coalitions began to mount limited cross-border operations. These operations were considered illicit in intergovernmental circles because they were not carried out with the consent of recognized governments in the target areas.

Examples from the twilight of the Cold War era illustrate the point. There was virtually no UN involvement in Eritrea and Tigray, where large cross-border operations were mounted by NGOs; the United Nations provided relief to the Ethiopian government through government-held territory. Similarly, cross-border assistance from Pakistan to *mujahidin*-held areas in Afghanistan came from NGOs; UNHCR, UNICEF, and WFP provided assistance to Afghan refugees in camps in Pakistan and to government-controlled areas in Afghanistan.

These cases illustrate the ability of NGOs to set new norms for international action. With the end of the Cold War in the late 1980s, cross-border operations gained *de facto* acceptance by donor governments and the UN system — at the expense of state sovereignty. Whereas previously the United Nations had not been inclined to provide help across borders without the permission of the relevant governments, in the late 1980s and early 1990s such UN action became commonplace. By the end of the 1980s, there were UN-mandated cross-border operations in southern Sudan, Eritrea, and Angola. In Bosnia, Somalia, and Rwanda in the early 1990s, the United Nations negotiated or secured access through

---

22. See Morris Davis, ed., *Civil Wars and the Politics of International Relief* (New York: Praeger, 1975); Randolph Kent, *Anatomy of Disaster Relief: The International Network in Action* (London: Puster, 1987); Mark Duffield and J. Pendergast, *Without Troops or Tanks: Humanitarian Intervention in Eritrea and Ethiopia* (Trenton, N.J.: Red Sea Press, 1994); Larry Minear et al., *Humanitarianism Under Siege: A Critical Review of Operation Lifeline Sudan* (Trenton, N.J.: Red Sea Press, 1991).

military force to raise funds and to orchestrate activities in civil war zones; NGOs carried out the bulk of actual relief efforts.

NGOs have not only increased in size and altered their approaches, they have also become more influential in internal conflicts. With the privatization of relief organizations and donor flexibility, virtually any NGO can now work in a war zone. Failed states, or states that are on the brink of collapsing, find it difficult to resist them. For example, in Rwanda in mid-1994, over one hundred NGOs were already conducting relief efforts. These groups are often the main purveyors of services and public welfare in times of crisis. They may also be the mainstays of local economies as primary sources of salaried employment, foreign exchange, and commercial contracting.

NGOs occasionally dwarf even major UN agencies. For example, World Vision International spent over $90 million in Mozambique in 1993 and approximately $90 million again in 1994, whereas the UN Development Program's total five-year budget is anticipated to be about $60 million. On a global scale, NGOs account for thirteen percent of all development assistance, a much larger amount than is being transferred through the UN system (not including Washington-based financial institutions). This figure is particularly striking since NGOs are also increasingly the conduit for funds allocated to UN organizations.[23] NGOs are filling a vacuum created by the absence of local authorities and the disinterest of governmental donors. As one critic has observed: "We are not far from a UN/NGO conglomeration taking over the running of a collapsed state."[24]

Some NGO representatives question their growing association with the United Nations and seek to distance themselves from what they see as the politicization of humanitarian action. But the problems associated with complex emergencies, the imperatives of resource mobilization, and the desire by governments to call upon the intergovernmental UN system mean that the vast majority of NGO activities in the future will resemble those of the first half of the 1990s.

The violence of the post–Cold War era has resulted in a dramatically increased demand for UN actions to address the threats from internal conflicts. This is not what the UN's founders intended, nor where

---

23. Open-Ended Group, *General Review of Arrangements for Consultations with Non-Governmental Organizations,* para. 16 and 28.

24. Marc Duffield, quoted in Royal Anthropological Institute, "International NGO's and Complex Political Emergencies: Perspectives from Anthropology," report from a session of January 9, 1995, p. 16.

previous UN involvement has been the most successful. UN efforts in the 1990s have been multifunctional, combining military, civil (including election and human rights monitoring, and police support), and humanitarian activities in often complex undertakings.[25] Demands on NGOs have gone up as well.

The functions of NGOs are "to serve underserved or neglected populations, to expand the freedom of or to empower people, to engage in advocacy for social change, and to provide services."[26] NGOs in complex emergencies therefore have contributions to make in six operational areas. Some of these are areas in which NGOs have comparative advantages, while others are tasks better accomplished by components of the UN system.

ASSESSMENT

A clear picture of the nature and extent of suffering is the point of departure for effective humanitarian action. In the age of satellites and CNN, a casual observer might wonder why it is difficult to figure out how many people are affected in a crisis and what kind of relief is needed. In many natural disasters — hurricanes, cyclones, floods, tidal waves, and the like — assessments can indeed be made quickly and accurately. In cases such as these, the governments of affected countries seek outside succor and hence facilitate information-gathering.

The task is more complicated in war zones. Humanitarian agencies push themselves to respond as quickly as possible to save lives. Assessments are driven by this concern as well as by institutional politics, fund-raising priorities, and the perceived need to keep fund-raising appeals simple. NGOs therefore place more emphasis in their public statements on the gravity of suffering in humanitarian crises than on the complex web of historical, social, economic, ethnic, and political forces that cause and complicate conflicts.

Moreover, political authorities in the countries concerned do not necessarily want the truth told. Both governments and insurgents alike have an interest in making sure that their side of the story is emphasized while the other's is underplayed. The United Nations is frequently responsible for making assessments in trouble spots; as an intergovernmental organization, it can be difficult for it to overrule governmental wishes

---

25. See Thomas G. Weiss, ed., *The United Nations and Civil Wars* (Boulder, Colo.: Lynne Rienner, 1995).

26. Kathleen D. McCarthy, Virginia Hodgkinson, and Russy Sumariwalla, *The Nonprofit Sector in the United States* (San Francisco: Jossey-Bass, 1992), p. 3.

to downplay or even ignore problems in insurgent-controlled areas. NGOs are less constrained by these governmental influences.

In addition to compensating for state-centric perspectives, NGOs contribute to international assessments of humanitarian emergencies by reaching needy populations in insecure and outlying areas. This has in the past provided useful counterpoints to official governmental and UN estimates. In an effort to make better and more systematic use of NGO coverage, officials from NGOs are now routinely members of UNDHA assessment teams.

Experience shows how important it is to have reliable information about the needs of victims in internal conflicts. In the chaos of civil wars, the task of establishing and monitoring human need remains complex, controversial, and critical; NGOs have critical roles to play in complementing information received from official and UN sources.

NEGOTIATION

Once the nature and severity of a crisis are known, humanitarians then confront another formidable task, negotiating access to those who require help. In the post–Cold War era, the United Nations plays a central role in this regard. But this is not without problems because the UN normally is in a better position to negotiate with governments than with insurgents. Moreover, if the UN Security Council decides to take coercive action under Chapter VII of the UN Charter, its efforts to negotiate with the representatives of the guilty party become problematic. Other intergovernmental organizations also have undertaken such negotiations: the North Atlantic Treaty Organization (NATO), the Western European Union (WEU), and the European Union in the former Yugoslavia; the Organization for Security and Cooperation in Europe (OSCE, formerly CSCE, the Conference on Security and Cooperation in Europe) in various parts of the former Soviet bloc; and the Commonwealth of Independent States (CIS) in former Soviet republics.

Nongovernmental organizations are unlikely to play major roles in such negotiations unless they are the only actors in a particular geographical area. However, they have helped or even taken the lead in some areas — for example, the Carter Center in Haiti and Bosnia, the Comunità di Saint 'Egidio in Mozambique, and the All Sudan Council of Churches in Sudan.[27]

---

27. See Cameron Hume, *Ending Mozambique's War: The Role of Mediation and Good Offices* (Washington, D.C.: U.S. Institute of Peace, 1994); Francis M. Deng and Larry Minear, *The Challenges of Famine Relief: Emergency Operations in the Sudan* (Washington, D.C.: Brookings Institution, 1992).

RESOURCE MOBILIZATION

Responding to humanitarian crises induced by internal conflicts requires enormous human and financial resources. For example, the 1994 costs of humanitarian relief in Rwanda were at least $1 billion, equal to 20 percent of the global emergency budget and 2 percent of total overseas development assistance.

Judgments about the availability of public and private resources figure prominently in decisions by various organizations about whether to become involved in humanitarian crises and at what level. All humanitarian organizations — those in the NGO sector even more than the UN system — raise funds to support specific relief efforts. This approach has the value of mobilizing a range of different constituencies, but continuous fund-raising appeals can confuse donors with multiple requests and try the patience of the public with constant claims for attention. Disjointed appeals from different organizations compound the problem; they place a premium on identifying activities in specific crises with particular agencies. This works against concerted strategies that maximize available resources or take advantage of substantive and geographic specializations.

Efforts at coordination and consolidation have been undertaken. In the mid-1980s, the Office of Emergency Operations in Africa mobilized resources for the UN system. More recently and less successfully, UNDHA has sought to do the same. Occasionally, NGOs pool efforts. However, the centrifugal forces operating here, such as the need to maintain independent financial bases, are powerful.

DELIVERY OF SERVICES

The provision of relief goods and services and the protection of human rights within war zones are important NGO tasks in humanitarian crises. This is the main thrust of NGO efforts in internal conflicts, and an area in which they have a significant comparative advantage. Donors, both governmental and intergovernmental, are increasingly relying upon NGOs in this regard.

During the Cold War, only a handful of private organizations operated in war zones, almost always led by the ICRC. Since the end of the Cold War, many more NGOs have become active while turmoil threatens not only local citizens but outside helpers. Part of the explanation for this is the nature of NGO fund-raising; another part is the proliferation of humanitarian tragedies; and still another is the increased use of outside military forces in humanitarian crises. As Secretary-General Boutros-Ghali wrote in January 1995: "this increased volume of activity would have strained the Organization even if the nature of the activity had remained unchanged."[28] The number of soldiers involved in UN peacekeeping operations has jumped from around seven thousand in the late 1980s to seventy to eighty thousand in the mid-1990s. The UN's peacekeeping budget approached $4 billion in 1995. These figures only hint at the financial and professional problems that now confront the United Nations.

The military performs two functions in the humanitarian arena: providing a secure environment and supporting with their logistics capabilities the work of humanitarian agencies or actually carrying out relief activities themselves.[29] Regular military involvement in UN humanitarian efforts in war zones is a phenomenon of the post–Cold War era, but the use of military forces for such purposes is not new.[30] The earliest recorded instances predate Alexander the Great. They continued in Europe through the Napoleonic Wars and into the twentieth century. In some cases, assistance was seen as a humane gesture to the vanquished, which was mixed with the desire to help secure loyalty from newly subject populations. Variations of this theme were played by colonial armies with assistance to the civil authority.

A quantum expansion of military activities in the humanitarian arena took place after World War II. The task of occupying Germany and Japan, as well as reconstructing as quickly as possible Europe's economic base, required new types of personnel within the armed forces: administrators, planners, developmentalists, and logisticians. At the time, there were relatively few international NGOs, and the UN humanitarian system was just in the process of being set up.

In the last half of the twentieth century, military assistance in natural disasters has become a normal extension of civil defense. Armed forces often possess an abundance of precisely the resources in shortest supply when disaster strikes: transport, fuel, communications, commodities, building equipment, medicines, and large stockpiles of off-the-shelf provisions. In addition, the military's "can-do" attitude, rapid response capabilities, and organizational capabilities are extremely useful in efforts to deal with acute, chaotic tragedies.

The end of the Cold War and the evaporation of much of the *raison*

28. Boutros Boutros-Ghali, *Supplement to "An Agenda for Peace,"* published in *An Agenda for Peace 1995* (New York: United Nations, 1995), para. 77.

29. A fuller discussion can be found in Thomas G. Weiss, "Military-Civilian Humanitarianism: The 'Age of Innocence' Is Over," *International Peacekeeping,* Vol. 2, No. 2 (Summer 1995), pp. 157–174.

30. See Frederick Cuny, "Dilemmas of Military Involvement in Humanitarian Relief," in Gordenker and Weiss, *Soldiers, Peacekeepers and Disasters,* pp. 52–81.

d'être for military spending by Washington, Moscow, and other powers have exerted considerable pressure on military establishments. The successful allied mobilization for the Gulf War and the subsequent use of military forces to create safe havens for the Kurds in northern Iraq — along with significant if less successful efforts in Somalia, Bosnia, Rwanda, and Haiti — have provided what both enthusiasts and critics see as a means for militaries to fend off efforts to reduce their infrastructure and personnel.[31] The proposals and conferences sponsored by the Canadian, Dutch, and Danish militaries provide evidence that this is not simply a concern for the largest powers.[32]

Whatever one's views about using military resources in humanitarian crises, the result is that virtually any international NGO can now be active in a war zone. The redefinition of civilian-military relations has made possible greater outside involvement in internal conflicts.

Although NGOs have become more active in war zones, they have been no more successful than other actors in dealing with the consequences of internal conflicts. Substantial numbers of field and headquarters staff from agencies working to alleviate suffering are less than enthusiastic about "humanitarian intervention" and "humanitarian war."[33] Many NGOs argue that humanitarian initiatives should be strictly consensual and premised on impartiality and neutrality; political authorities, it is said, must be persuaded to allow access to needy civilians. Intervention not only raises the level of violence and complicates the lives of humanitarians in the short run, it makes reconciliation more difficult in the long run.

However, with 1 in every 115 people on the planet forced into flight from war, military intervention may be the only way to halt genocide, massive abuses of human rights, and starvation.[34] Although many NGOs

---

31. See, for example, an extensive list in "Table 4: Possible Uses of Military Force for Humanitarian Missions in Complex Emergencies," from *Global Humanitarian Emergencies, 1995,* released by the U.S. Permanent Mission to the United Nations, January 1995, p. 19.

32. See Canadian Ministry of External Affairs, "Improving the UN's Rapid Reaction Capability: A Canadian Study" (February 1995); Dutch Ministry of Foreign Affairs, "A UN Rapid Deployment Brigade: The Netherlands Non-paper" (January 1995); and Danish Ministry of Defense, "A Multifunctional UN Stand-by Forces High-Readiness Brigade: Chief of Defence, Denmark" (January 25, 1995). See also Dick A. Leurdijk, "Proposals for Increasing Rapid Deployment Capacity," *International Peacekeeping,* Vol. 2, No. 1 (Spring 1995), pp. 1–10.

33. Adam Roberts, "Humanitarian War: Military Intervention and Human Rights," *International Affairs,* Vol. 69, No. 3 (1993), pp. 429–449.

34. See UN High Commissioner for Refugees (UNHCR), *The State of the World's*

are unlikely to endorse military action, their ability to deliver relief will occasionally, and perhaps often, depend on intervention by outside military forces.[35] When consent cannot be extracted from either local governments or insurgents, economic and military sanctions can be justified on both operational and ethical grounds to create and sustain access to civilians.

Rather than having NGOs suspend or drastically curtail relief and withdraw from active war zones, the international community can use force to guarantee access to civilians, protect aid workers, and disarm recalcitrant belligerents. In light of reservations in the capitals of troop contributors, however, even successful interventions — northern Iraq, Rwanda, and Haiti — are hard to sustain politically. It is preferable that access be negotiated and not seized, and that military intervention be a last resort.

COORDINATION

When a major human catastrophe strikes, a bewildering array of organizations — governmental, intergovernmental, and nongovernmental — responds. Although this sometimes works, confusion and waste often ensue. The normal reaction is to call for better "coordination."

The NGO community has sought to address this problem in both the development and humanitarian arenas. InterAction is a consortium of some 160 U.S.-based NGOs; it provides a forum to improve communications and promote joint undertakings. The Red Cross Disaster Steering Committee organizes regular monthly meetings in Geneva. The Geneva-based International Council of Voluntary Agencies (ICVA) plays a similar role for a range of northern and southern NGOs, as does the London-based Disaster Emergency Committee for British NGOs active in the humanitarian arena.

The altered nature of the coordination task in the new era, and of the new NGO role in it, is reflected in the UN secretariat's routine contacts and exchanges of information with NGOs. The United Nations Inter-Agency Standing Committee, which is chaired by the Undersecretary-General for Humanitarian Affairs, now has regular participation from InterAction, ICVA, the ICRC, and the International Federation of Red Cross and Red Crescent Societies (IFRC). Every four to six weeks,

---

Refugees 1993: The Challenge of Protection (New York: Penguin, 1993); UNHCR, *The State of the World's Refugees 1995: In Search of Solutions* (Oxford: Oxford University Press, 1995).

35. See Thomas G. Weiss, "Overcoming the Somalia Syndrome," *Global Governance*, Vol. 1, No. 2 (Spring 1995), pp. 171–187.

UNDHA in New York hosts meetings with the main U.S.-based NGOs, while the UNDHA office in Geneva and UNHCR organize similar meetings for European NGOs.

The United Nations and various donors have encouraged aggregation because it is easier to work with semi-structured consortia than with individual NGOs. Efforts to improve NGO coordination are needed to reduce duplication, ensure adequate geographical and sectoral coverage, and make more effective use of what are clearly limited resources. Improving coordination between and among the largest NGOs is especially important. There are not more than twenty NGOs in the United States and twenty in Europe that are involved on a regular basis in complex emergencies in a sufficient enough way to have a substantial impact on the ground. Although precise figures are hard to come by, it is estimated that "perhaps ten U.S. and another ten European NGOs receive seventy-five percent of all the public funds spent by NGOs in complex emergencies."[36]

STRATEGIC PLANNING

Long-range strategic planning is often overlooked by NGOs as they scramble to do what they do best — assist victims of humanitarian crises. No matter how acute the crisis, however, it pays to look beyond the emergency at hand. Analysts and practitioners agree that it is essential to think creatively about long-term reconstruction and rehabilitation issues.[37]

Another component of strategic planning is ensuring that humanitarian actions are not counterproductive in the long run. Humanitarian NGOs must take seriously the Hippocratic Oath and "do no harm." Rushing international food aid into a famine area may fend off starvation, but it may also undermine the incentives available to local producers. In Somalia in 1992 and 1993, for example, a very effective but counterintuitive strategy was to flood markets with food that was sold, not given away, in order to destroy the power of warlords, merchants, and hoarders. Bypassing local channels may expedite relief, but it may squander an opportunity to enlist local people and institutions in ways that can promote reconstruction. Commandeering outside troops to transport relief supplies and protect workers and civilians may get the job done quickly,

---

36.   Andrew Natsios, "NGOs and the UN in Complex Emergencies: Conflict or Cooperation," *Third World Quarterly*, Vol. 16, No. 3 (September 1995), pp. 406–407.

37.   See Mary B. Anderson and Peter J. Woodrow, *Rising from the Ashes: Development Strategies at Times of Disaster* (Boulder, Colo.: Westview, 1989).

but it may strengthen the status of nondemocratic institutions such as local armed forces.

Moreover, the changing nature of civil-military relations introduces the possibility — inconceivable to many humanitarians — that there may be situations where NGOs as well as UN organizations should not be involved. Difficulties constantly arise at the interface of civil-military humanitarianism because the objectives of politicians and humanitarians do not necessarily coincide; indeed, they are often in conflict. Political means, particularly the case of military forces, often collide with the humanitarian principles of neutrality and impartiality.

The politicization of humanitarian action in Bosnia and Somalia — or the perception of its politicization, which has the same impact — has altered humanitarian orthodoxy. The International Institute for Strategic Studies has suggested that civilians "should not embark on humanitarian operations where, over time, impartiality and neutrality are certain to be compromised," and that "if impartiality and neutrality are compromised, an ongoing humanitarian operation should be reconsidered, scaled down, or terminated."[38] This argument would have been anathema to NGOs only a few years ago, when humanitarians were guided by the imperative to respond to each and every man-made tragedy.

Development economists employ the term "negative externalities" when discussing the ways in which outside assistance may have unexpected and unhelpful consequences. Once calculated, such externalities can lead policymakers to decide against the implementation of what was previously seen as a sensible project. This notion should also be used by humanitarians. It is not always wise, or even helpful, to get involved in some crises.

Conclusions

NGOs are undoubtedly going to continue to play a critical, and probably increasing, role in the international community's responses to the humanitarian plights faced by victims of internal conflicts. What should that role be?

DETERMINING THE USE OF PUBLIC RESOURCES

In the first half of the 1990s, NGOs made significant contributions to UN operations in internal conflicts. Given their close working relations with community groups and their relatively low costs, the United Nations

---

38. International Institute for Strategic Studies, "Military Support for Humanitarian Operations," *Strategic Comments*, No. 2 (February 22, 1995).

should subcontract for more humanitarian services from NGOs, as it has increasingly done in Cambodia, Central America, Rwanda, Somalia, and the former Yugoslavia. In addition, governments and other donors should expand resources made available to private agencies and strengthen incentives to make better use of local NGOs.

Some NGOs are increasingly worried, however, about the extent to which resources for humanitarian relief are being subtracted from the resources devoted to economic development, and especially to the alleviation of poverty in poor countries.[39] As of the mid-1990s, over half of total U.S. assistance to Africa is accounted for by emergency aid, and, as mentioned earlier, close to half of NGO operational activities is devoted to humanitarian relief.

Internal conflicts are increasingly and openly brutal. UN peacekeeping and other multilateral military forces approved by the Security Council compete with development assistance rather than defense allocations. The policy challenge is to determine the most effective mix of military and humanitarian assets in complex emergencies; maintain the scarce resources that donor governments devote at present to poverty alleviation; and reduce inappropriate military spending. NGOs will be required to weigh in on these issues during future debates by the U.S. Congress and other Western parliaments.

HELPING THE MEDIA DO ITS JOB

Close cooperation between international relief agencies and the media is essential to prevent and contain the complex humanitarian emergencies that threaten to overwhelm the world's capacity to assist and to care for the victims of internal conflicts. The influence of the media in situations such as these is not new; the media influenced the international response to problems in Biafra in the late 1960s, Bangladesh in the early 1970s, and Ethiopia in 1974 and 1984. Nonetheless, the intensity of media coverage has changed with new technologies, and this undoubtedly influenced the international debates over northern Iraq, Somalia, and Rwanda.

There are, however, too many simplistic references to the "CNN factor" — the loose shorthand some use to convey the impression that Ted Turner and Rupert Murdoch are influential in shaping governmental, intergovernmental, and nongovernmental policy. Much more research is required to understand the interactions between and among the media,

39. See Judith Randel and Tony German, eds., *The Reality of Aid 94* (London: Actionaid, May 1994); Ian Smillie and Henny Helmich, eds., *Non-governmental Organisations and Governments: Stakeholders for Development* (Paris: Organisation for Economic Cooperation and Development, 1993).

policymakers, and humanitarians. Public opinion often influences decisions in Washington and other capitals, although probably less than is usually assumed.[40]

Nongovernmental organizations should develop more detailed strategies to work with the media to help educate publics and leaders in the industrialized world about the complexities of ethnonationalistic and religious wars. This will require NGOs to devote resources to activities other than raising funds for the latest emergency, which is more effectively done with poignant pictures of starving children than with more complicated messages. These fund-raising appeals convey an image of hopelessness and dependence that is not conducive to generating support for long-term investments or development aid.

LIVING WITH POLITICIZATION

A third and perhaps more pressing challenge for NGOs is confronting the "schizophrenia" of the UN system. Manipulation of well-meaning but naive NGOs by governments and insurgents occurs in every war, but new problems emerge when NGOs participate in multifunctional UN operations.[41] As in Iraq and Somalia, the work of humanitarian organizations in the former Yugoslavia has been politicized by its association with UN military and economic sanctions. The problem for NGOs is that the United Nations says in one breath that it wants to censure a regime and impose sanctions, but in the next breath it calls upon humanitarians to help cushion the plight of the vulnerable.

The ambivalence among NGOs toward the use of military coercion has been documented in all of the internal conflicts where outside military forces have been used. A similar ambivalence surrounds economic sanctions. Aid workers usually argue that sanctions cause much suffering to vulnerable groups such as women, children, and the elderly.

Learning to live with the duality of the UN system and with their own ambivalence about the politicization of aid in civil wars is a major challenge for NGOs. Given the violence on the ground in many internal conflicts, NGOs should consider concentrating their limited resources on

---

40.   See Jonathan Benthall, *Disasters, Relief and the Media* (London: Tauris, 1993). For a literature review, see David Hesmondhalgh, "Media Coverage of Humanitarian Emergencies: A Literature Survey," Overseas Development Institute, October 1993. See also Robert I. Rotberg and Thomas G. Weiss, eds., *From Massacres to Genocide: The Media, Public Policy, and Humanitarian Crises* (Washington, D.C.: Brookings Institution, 1996).

41.   See Gayle E. Smith, "Relief Operations and Military Strategy," in Thomas G. Weiss and Larry Minear, eds., *Humanitarianism Across Borders: Sustaining Civilians in Times of War* (Boulder, Colo.: Lynne Rienner, 1993), pp. 97–116.

what UNICEF calls the "silent emergencies" resulting from abject poverty rather than the "loud emergencies" of wars. This could be a rational and justifiable course of action. In purely cost-benefit terms, some thirty-five to forty thousand children perish daily from poverty-induced conditions that are ten to twenty times less expensive to address than similar conditions in war zones. If, however, they decide to remain active in civil wars, NGOs must accept that their wishes will often be subordinated to military and political considerations, from the United Nations and elsewhere.

THE COORDINATION DILEMMA

Perhaps the thorniest problems for NGOs involve the need for enhanced coordination. These coordination efforts are almost certain to be conducted under the auspices of the United Nations. As one aid administrator has noted: "The marriage of convenience between NGOs and the UN system in relief responses over time may become comfortable enough that *ad hoc* arrangements will work, even if a passionate love affair never occurs."[42]

The coordination problem, sizeable in efforts to alleviate suffering caused by natural disasters, is even more challenging in armed conflicts. Managers and field staff of humanitarian agencies favor coordination and donors insist upon it, but few NGOs wish to be integrated into joint undertakings. Many are reluctant to pay the costs — both in terms of human and financial resources as well as in lost autonomy and fundraising possibilities.

The coordination task has been complicated by UN military activities. Military organizations insist on caution and a hierarchical and disciplined structure that most NGOs are reluctant to endorse. The United Nations or one of its agencies is usually selected to be the "lead agency," but NGOs often prefer to keep their distance and work on their own. The ICRC is the clearest about its stance on the coordination issue; it shares information but does not allow its activities to be orchestrated by the United Nations or anyone else.

When humanitarian operations are initiated, careful thought should be given to the nature, structures, and costs of coordination. Managers frequently are unclear about their expectations for coordination and its claim on agency time and resources. These generalizations are perhaps more applicable to NGOs than to other actors because of their inclination to believe that "small is beautiful" and because of their intense commitment to organizational autonomy. The more effective orchestration of

---

42. Natsios, "NGOs and the UN in Complex Emergencies," p. 418.

NGO energy, creativity, and resources should be high on the international agenda. NGOs, for their part, must decide whether to cooperate or to pursue independent courses of action. Given the paucity of resources and the mushrooming demands for outside help, I would argue for more consolidation and more cooperation.

The current humanitarian system has too many moving parts. The professional cultures and approaches of the five main types of international humanitarian actors are quite different. Moreover, the divisions between individual organizations are immense. This is especially true with respect to NGOs. In 1994, the U.S. National Intelligence Council estimated that more than 16,000 NGOs were involved in responses to global humanitarian emergencies.[43] Although having a multiplicity of actors can be an asset, it is also a liability.

The indisputably worsening political climate throughout the Western world for mobilizing resources should jolt NGOs into reconsidering their ways. Rather than continuing to respond to crises in an *ad hoc* manner, they should take the lead in determining what they do best, and what they should not do at all. A clearer division of labor, common rules of procedure, enhanced professionalism, and greater accountability are urgently required and should be addressed by NGOs, individually and collectively. The policy challenge is to design a coordinated international delivery system that has greater coherence and effectiveness but does not undercut the vitality and the willingness to run risks that have often characterized NGO action at its best.[44]

LEARNING TO SAY NO

NGOs have earned a reputation for being more flexible, forthcoming, and caring than other members of the international humanitarian community. Whether an international NGO is small or large, focused or far-flung, its activities tend to concentrate on the practical needs of ordinary people. The prevailing grass-roots or people-to-people approach means that NGOs emphasize local links and endeavor to customize their activities to the communities that they seek to help. This distinguishes NGOs from most donor governments and many agencies in the UN system.

---

43. U.S. Permanent Mission to the United Nations, *Global Humanitarian Emergencies, 1994*, October 1994, p. 2.

44. For a discussion from the UN's point of view of the coordination issue, see Francesco Mezzalama and Siegfried Schumm, *Working with NGOs: Operational Activities for Development of the United Nations System with Non-Governmental Organizations and Governments at the Grassroots and National Levels* (Geneva: UN Joint Inspection Unit, 1993), Document JIU/REP/93/1. See also Thomas G. Weiss and Leon Gordenker, eds., *NGOs, the UN, and Global Governance* (Boulder, Colo.: Lynne Rienner, 1996).

NGOs also have weaknesses, of course. Their energy can lead to frenzy and confusion. Careful planning and evaluation are too rare. The desire to tackle the next emergency contributes to a lack of reflectiveness and a lack of institutional learning. Impatience with bureaucratic constraints reflects a naïveté about the highly political contexts in which NGOs increasingly operate. Some NGOs guard their independence so fiercely that they miss opportunities to work with like-minded institutions and thereby are unable to have a greater impact on humanitarian problems.

NGOs must take the lead in putting their own houses in order. They should refuse to get involved in a crisis if the task is either beyond their professional competence and means or if its successful completion will be ultimately counterproductive. They should determine when and where their efforts would truly make a difference. And they should collaborate whenever and wherever possible among themselves and with other appropriate governmental, intergovernmental, and military agencies.

Unlike states and intergovernmental organizations that are concerned about being drawn into internal conflicts, NGOs are more likely to react viscerally and jump in. Because their *raison d'être* is the alleviation of suffering, it is not so much geopolitics but humanitarian impulses that dominate their thinking. Moreover, NGOs need to be engaged in crises in order to raise money and to have long-term credibility. Although NGOs are generally hostile to the idea of analyzing when and where they should be active, recent experience suggests that more analyses and fewer impulsive reactions are in order. Médecins Sans Frontières and CARE, for example, withdrew from the Rwandan refugee camps in Zaire early in 1995 because, after reflection, they judged that their actions were strengthening the position of Hutu war criminals and decreasing the prospects for repatriation. Similarly, NGOs in Bosnia wonder if their humanitarian relief efforts have prolonged the war and become a substitute for meaningful political and military engagement.

When circumstances dictate, NGOs must learn to say to say "no." At a minimum, the limits imposed by finite resources might dictate ignoring a hopeless tragedy in one country in order to make a difference in another. When and where will NGOs be willing to say "no"? Under what conditions should they permit the use of relief and reconstruction assistance to support peace agreements? These potentially divisive questions should be debated by a broad spectrum of NGOs as they formulate *A Humanitarian Agenda* to complement the UN Secretary-General's *An Agenda for Peace*.

Chapter 14

The United States and Military Intervention in Internal Conflict

Ivo H. Daalder

The end of the Cold War and the success of the U.S.-led coalition in reversing Iraqi aggression in the Persian Gulf was heralded by U.S. President George Bush as the beginning of a "new world order." This new order, Bush suggested, "springs from hopes for a world based on a shared commitment among nations large and small to a set of principles that undergird our relations — peaceful settlement of disputes, solidarity against aggression, reduced and controlled arsenals, and just treatment of all peoples."[1] The conditions that made the new world order possible were, first, the absence, with the collapse of the Soviet Union, of any direct threat to the vital interests of the United States; and second, the ability and willingness of the United States, as the sole remaining superpower, to lead international efforts to combat threats to peace and security. Combined, these two factors made possible the promotion of core Western values such as democracy, market economics, and human rights through concerted international action, including the use of force.

That the new world order was not just rhetoric employed to justify U.S. action in the Gulf War became evident when the United States and its European allies deployed military forces to protect starving Kurdish refugees who had escaped the onslaught of Saddam Hussein's forces in northern Iraq. Operation Provide Comfort, as this action was called, set a number of important precedents. It suggested that the international community, working through the United Nations (UN) Security Council,

This chapter was written before the author joined the U.S. National Security Council staff in August 1995. It represents his personal views, not those of the Clinton administration.

1. President George Bush, speech at Air University, Maxwell Air Force Base, April 13, 1991.

now viewed the violent repression of human rights as a threat to international peace and security and would endorse (if not yet authorize) military intervention to address humanitarian crises. Within eighteen months, the UN Security Council made explicit what was still implicit in April 1991: acting under Chapter VII of the UN Charter, it authorized the "use of all necessary means" to deliver humanitarian assistance in Bosnia and to create a secure environment for feeding starving millions in Somalia.

Although public declarations about the new world order originally sprang from an inter-state conflict, the principal focus of action soon shifted to internal conflicts. Some of these conflicts had festered for years (in Cambodia, El Salvador, Angola, and Mozambique, for example), while others had emerged only in the aftermath of the Cold War (in the former Yugoslavia, Somalia, and Haiti). In each, however, the United Nations took the lead in attempting to address the underlying sources of conflict and to alleviate the humanitarian consequences of war. As a result, from 1988–92 the number of UN peacekeeping operations doubled from thirteen to twenty-seven, their combined cost tripled to over $3 billion, and the number of soldiers involved in peacekeeping operations quadrupled to 70,000.

Optimism about what the United Nations could and would do, however, soon foundered because internal conflicts proved to be more intractable than the proponents of the new world order had assumed. In Bosnia, the presence of 20,000 UN troops did little to end a vicious and deadly conflict. And in Somalia, although the initial intervention succeeded in alleviating widespread starvation, UN and U.S. troops were soon engaged in a direct confrontation with its most powerful warlord. These growing difficulties demonstrated that the United Nations was not capable of undertaking the difficult task of intervening in places where conflict was still raging. It lacked both the military muscle and the expertise necessary to deal decisively with recalcitrant factions. In addition, it adhered to a doctrine that eschewed forceful and preemptive enforcement efforts in favor of maintaining its much-vaunted neutrality in conflict. In short, the United Nations was capable and effective in situations where its role was to keep a peace agreed to by all parties, but not in those where the requirement was to make or enforce a peace that did not yet exist.

The realization that the United Nations was unable to meet the demands of an international environment in which internal conflicts were both deadly in nature and more numerous than during the Cold War confronted U.S. policymakers with a difficult choice. They could either intervene in the hope that others would follow suit and share the burden, or not intervene at all. Whereas the new world order had been premised on the belief that the United States would assume a leadership role in marshaling forces for multilateral interventions, it soon became evident that Washington was not willing to take on this role. The Bush administration refused to intervene in southern Iraq when Saddam Hussein's Republican Guards violently suppressed a Shi'ite uprising in the weeks following the Gulf War, and only very reluctantly agreed to deploy military forces in the north to protect fleeing Kurdish refugees. It left intervention in the former Yugoslavia to European states and rejected repeated requests to get involved militarily. Bush agreed to send U.S. forces to Somalia only after he lost the 1992 election.

Its rhetoric about "assertive multilateralism" to the contrary, the Clinton administration was no more interventionist than its predecessor. It, too, ruled out the deployment of ground troops in Bosnia in nearly all circumstances. Moreover, President Bill Clinton ordered the withdrawal of U.S. forces from Somalia when U.S. casualties increased. The administration also refused to act with respect to the genocide in Rwanda, other than sending humanitarian relief to the refugees in Zaire once the killings had ended. Finally, it hesitated for months about intervening in Haiti to restore democracy, although a U.S.-led invasion was ultimately authorized.

In this chapter, I seek to explain why the United States refused to take on the leadership role promised by the rhetoric of the new world order. Why, when U.S. political and military power was unquestioned and when the values it championed had garnered broad international consensus, did the United States decide to stand aside when internal conflicts directly threatened these values? Many argue that senior officials in the Clinton administration as well as the president himself are to blame. There is no doubt that U.S. policy toward Bosnia, Somalia, and Haiti in 1993–94 was confused, contradictory, and, at times, incompetent. But so was U.S. policy during the Bush administration. I argue that these problems were not due mainly to failings of individual decision-makers, but rather to a domestic political environment that discouraged the use of military force.

Three factors account for the growing U.S. reluctance to intervene militarily in internal conflicts. First, the conditions that made the new world order theoretically possible — especially the absence of a threat to vital U.S. interests — also ensured that the yearning to address long-festering domestic ills — including stagnating incomes, a mounting national debt, and a fraying social fabric — would become greater. The election of Clinton in 1992 underscored the idea that Bush's foreign policy success was not sufficient to win elections, whereas a commitment to domestic renewal evidently was. At a time when U.S. citizens were looking home rather than abroad, finding the political, human, and financial resources necessary to address internal conflicts would be difficult no matter who became the president or occupied senior policy positions.

Second, those who supported military intervention to deal with internal conflicts confronted formidable opposition from within the U.S. military. Facing declining budgets, few in the military hierarchy were willing to divert resources to humanitarian emergencies, particularly if doing so would expose U.S. troops to danger. Many also believed that overseas deployments for these purposes posed unacceptable risks to military readiness and training, and weakened the U.S. military's ability to fight in two major regional contingencies nearly simultaneously. In addition, the U.S. military regarded internal conflict as a type of conflict that the United States should avoid at all cost. The lesson that U.S. military leaders learned from Vietnam and Lebanon was that engagement in internal conflicts, especially if the objectives of the engagement were unclear and the forces deployed were limited, represented the type of open-ended commitment that could degenerate into a quagmire and lead to a loss of popular support. The Gulf War was the type of war the U.S. military wanted to fight: decisive force was employed in support of a clear objective and applied in overwhelming fashion, in order to minimize casualties and allow for a quick exit of U.S. forces. Internal conflicts shared none of these characteristics. They often lacked a clearly identifiable enemy, objectives were generally ill-defined, and decisive use of force was usually impossible. Absent a commitment to use overwhelming force, the military counseled that doing nothing would be preferable. Few political leaders would be willing to second-guess this advice.

Third, the question of military intervention in internal conflict became a major battle ground between the executive and legislative branches. In times of uncertainty about the direction and aims of U.S. foreign policy, Congress tends to be more assertive in foreign policymaking. This has been true in every postwar era, and it has been true in the wake of the Cold War. While Congress generally defers to the president on issues involving vital U.S. interests, it is more likely to object if interests are ambiguous or less than vital. The United Nations, peacekeeping, and U.S. military involvement in internal conflicts became major issues between the Congress and the president, especially after the UN mission in Somalia became increasingly controversial in the summer of 1993. Although congressional action was largely confined to passing non-binding resolutions and denying funds for particular UN missions, the net effect of congressional activism was to constrain the freedom of action of the president. Only by confronting Congress directly could Clinton have gotten his way, and this conflicted with his desire to save political capital for his domestic priorities.

In short, U.S. policy with respect to internal conflicts confronts a paradox: the factors that favor a leading U.S. role in addressing the security threats posed by internal conflicts — including the absence of a threat to vital U.S. interests and the possession of military and political power second to none — also allow for a greater focus on domestic problems, making risky and costly foreign engagements less likely. The United States is rapidly becoming "a self-deterred power": a country capable but unwilling to take the steps necessary to deal with the causes and consequences of internal conflict.[2] Although the short-term costs of U.S. detachment from the international scene are unlikely to be major, the long-term repercussions for international peace and security may well be profound. Left untended, internal conflicts can easily intensify in violence, enlarge in scope, and multiply in number. At a minimum, this will mean more suffering by an ever greater number of people. At some point, however, the disorder created by the proliferation of internal conflict will challenge important, if not vital, U.S. interests, either directly or by calling into question security commitments to critical allies.

The Reluctance to Intervene: Causes

The transformation of the international system in the wake of the Cold War has profoundly affected the U.S. debate about military intervention in internal conflicts. During most of the Cold War and especially before the defeat in Vietnam, the burden of proof regarding whether or not to intervene lay with those opposed to intervention. The global scope of the communist threat seemed to justify strong actions to defend freedom, no matter where the actions took place. After the end of the Vietnam War, the burden of proof began to shift to those favoring intervention. During the 1980s, traditional Cold War arguments justifying intervention could still be used, especially if action was quick and successful (as in Grenada) or conducted through surrogates (as in Angola and Afghanistan).[3] Since the collapse of the Soviet Union and the end of the Cold War, however, the burden of proof has been placed squarely on those who support intervention. The argument that intervention is justified in defense of vital national interests no longer has much credibility, since vital interests are generally unaffected by internal conflicts. The case for intervention is

---

2. Stanley R. Sloan, *The United States and the Use of Force in the Post–Cold War World: Toward Self-Deterrence?* (Washington, D.C.: Congressional Research Service, July 1994).

3. Stephen Solarz, "When to Intervene," *Foreign Policy*, No. 63 (Summer 1986), pp. 20–39.

therefore much more difficult to make, especially if the risks include the lives of U.S. soldiers.

In short, since internal conflicts now pose less of a challenge to U.S. interests, support for military intervention in these conflicts will never be automatic. At times, sympathy for the victims of conflict, especially if they are displayed on television screens in living rooms across the United States, will generate pressures to do something and result in support for a decision to intervene militarily. This was the case in Somalia, where pictures of starving children produced calls for action and guaranteed public support for an intervention. But in most cases, domestic political realities — including the public's inward focus, military opposition, and an assertive Congress — make intervention unlikely. These powerful domestic constraints account for the U.S. reluctance to intervene in internal conflicts.

THE PUBLIC'S INWARD FOCUS

Since the mid-1980s, the U.S. public has wanted its leaders to devote more energy to mounting problems at home. This predates the collapse of the Soviet Union; opinion poll data indicate that from the mid-1980s on there has been a growing sense that economic problems pose the greatest threat to U.S. security.[4] The end of the Cold War only strengthened this sentiment; this became evident in the 1992 election, when nearly 63 percent of those who voted cast their ballots for candidates whose campaigns were based almost exclusively on the need for change at home. Domestic concerns also dominated the congressional elections of 1994; foreign policy played no role in the Republican Party's stunning capture of both houses of Congress.

Some pundits and politicians have interpreted this inward focus as a sign of growing isolationism. Many conclude that this implies an unwillingness to expend resources or risk U.S. lives unless vital national interests are directly threatened. Neither assumption, however, is borne out by public opinion polling data. These data paint a more complicated picture of a U.S. public that is focused on developments at home but not in the grips of isolationism. Although support for the pursuit of many idealistic goals has dropped in the first half of the 1990s, there is latent support for the use of force to promote humanitarian aims so long as others are willing to share the burdens with the United States.

Contrary to what some claim, the U.S. public, having learned the bitter lessons of U.S. involvement in two world wars and one cold war,

---

4. Daniel Yankelovich, "Foreign Policy After the Election," *Foreign Affairs*, Vol. 74, No. 4 (Fall 1992), p. 5.

firmly rejects isolationism. Two-thirds of the U.S. public still believed in late 1994 that "it would be best for the future of the country if we take an active part in world affairs," a level of support comparable to that seen in the 1970s and 1980s.[5] At the same time, U.S. citizens believed that the principal objectives of foreign policy should be firmly tied to domestic concerns. Thus, among the four foreign policy goals supported by more than 70 percent of the public, three (stopping illegal drug trafficking, protecting American jobs, and controlling illegal immigration) related directly to the daily lives of U.S. citizens. Reflecting this domestic preoccupation, support for idealistic foreign policy goals has dropped precipitously since 1990. Thus, support for protecting weaker countries against foreign aggression dropped 33 points to 24 percent, support for promoting human rights dropped 24 points to 34 percent, and support for improving the standard of living of poor countries dropped 19 points to 22 percent. Support for helping to bring democracy to other countries, at 25 percent, remained low.[6]

If self-interest dominates the foreign policy priorities of the average U.S. citizen, this should not be taken to mean, as many observers often assume, that U.S. citizens favor the use of force only in very limited circumstances related directly to the defense of vital national interests.[7] In-depth surveys of U.S. opinion regarding the use of force and UN peacekeeping indicate that the U.S. public is less reluctant and more cosmopolitan in its views than is generally believed.[8] A majority of the public is likely to support the use of force in internal conflicts if three conditions are met.

First, the intervention must be sanctioned by or take place under the auspices of the United Nations, and the burdens of the action must be

---

5. John Rielly, "The Public Mood at Mid-Decade," *Foreign Policy*, No. 98 (Spring 1995), p. 78.

6. Ibid., pp. 81–82.

7. Andrew Kohut and Robert Toth make this point, although their data indicate that U.S. citizens favor the use of force in support of delivering humanitarian aid. See Andrew Kohut and Robert Toth, "The People, the Press, and the Use of Force," in Aspen Strategy Group, *The United States and the Use of Force in the Post–Cold War Era* (Queenstown, Md.: Aspen Institute, 1995).

8. A series of polls conducted from 1993–95 by the Program on International Policy Attitudes, jointly sponsored by the Center for the Study of Policy Attitudes and the Center for International and Security Studies at Maryland, demonstrated a surprising degree of public support for UN peacekeeping and multilateral intervention. See the succession of reports on U.S. attitudes toward intervention in Bosnia (dated May 15, 1993; May 4, 1994; and May 16, 1995), Somalia (October 26, 1993), and Haiti (August 22, 1994), and toward UN peacekeeping (March 7, 1994; April 27, 1995).

shared by others. A poll conducted prior to the intervention in Haiti demonstrated a 30-point gap in support between a unilateral U.S. action (supported by 24 percent) and a UN action that included U.S. troops (54 percent). The importance of burden-sharing was demonstrated by polls on the possible deployment of U.S. ground troops to Bosnia during the first half of 1994, which found a 16.5-point gap in support between a unilateral U.S. intervention (43.3 percent support) and a multilateral action that included U.S. troops (59.8 percent).[9]

Second, there must be a clear humanitarian objective. This becomes clear when one considers U.S. views of the operation in Somalia. In retrospect and despite U.S. casualties, 82 percent of the public approved of the UN mission in Somalia to deliver food, though a 46 percent plurality thought it was a mistake to have tried to end the civil war.[10] More generally, while a majority of U.S. citizens (52 to 41 percent) favored using force to "prevent famines and mass starvation" in Africa, Asia, and Latin America, a similar majority (51 to 41 percent) opposed using force "to restore law and order if governments break down" in these regions.[11]

Third, there must be a commitment to act decisively and in a relatively short period of time. The attachment to decisiveness is demonstrated by U.S. opinion towards the UN operation in Bosnia. Although an April 1995 poll indicated that the public was clearly frustrated with the UN operation, it found that only 29 percent wanted UN forces to withdraw while 50 percent wanted to see them get tougher. Moreover, 87 percent favored the use of force "when aid convoys are attacked or obstructed," 65 percent "to defend civilians in safe havens," and fully 64 percent favored following through on a UN threat to "intervene with a large military force to stop ethnic cleansing," even if this meant the deployment of 150,000–300,000 troops, one-third of them from the United States.[12]

These polling data indicate that, contrary to the commonly-held view, the U.S. public will support U.S. intervention in internal conflicts under

---

9. Steven Kull and Clay Ramsay, *U.S. Public Attitudes on U.S. Involvement in Haiti* (College Park, Md.: Program on International Policy Attitudes, August 1994), p. 5; Steven Kull and Clay Ramsay, *U.S. Public Attitudes on U.S. Involvement in Haiti* (College Park, Md.: Program on International Policy Attitudes, May 1994), p. 13.

10. Steven Kull, *Americans on UN Peacekeeping* (College Park, Md.: Program on International Policy Attitudes, April 27, 1995), p. 6.

11. Kohut and Toth, "The People, the Press, and the Use of Force," p. 155.

12. Steven Kull, *Americans on Bosnia: A Study of U.S. Public Attitudes* (College Park, Md.: Program on International Public Attitudes, May 1995), pp. 1–3. Regarding a favorite alternative to the UN operation in Bosnia, lifting the arms embargo, 51 percent opposed this move while 40 percent favored it. Ibid., p. 6.

certain conditions. At the same time, given its inward focus, there is no sign that the U.S. public is clamoring for action on the part of the United States or even the United Nations to deal with the causes and consequences of internal conflicts. This suggests that support for U.S. mil- itary intervention in internal conflict is unlikely to be automatic. Rather, those favoring intervention will have to build their case by obtaining UN authorization and participation by other countries, underscoring the humanitarian reasons for intervening, and ensuring that the objectives of the operation can be achieved in a relatively short period of time.

MILITARY OPPOSITION

The U.S. military's perspective on the question of intervention in internal conflicts has been shaped by two major conflicts: the ignominious defeat in Vietnam and the stunning victory in the Persian Gulf.[13] The former suggested that certain types of combat situations should be avoided at all costs: internal conflicts where the political and military objectives of the intervention are unclear, and where there is likely to be a preference for the gradual use of force. The lessons learned from Vietnam were applied in full in Operation Desert Storm, and the result was the decisive defeat of Iraq. Given this historical record, a new orthodoxy has arisen around the critical questions of how and when to use force. This orthodoxy has produced a deep-seated skepticism about U.S. military involvement in internal conflicts, especially if the objectives of the operation in question are not clearly defined and the means available are limited in either scope or application. The new orthodoxy places an overriding emphasis on being able to fight and win "the nation's wars," which are defined as major, regional, inter-state conflicts. As a result, in the competition for financial and human resources, the U.S. ability to participate in peace operations or interventions in internal conflicts tends to lose out to the need to be prepared to carry out other, more traditional missions.

THE NEW ORTHODOXY: DECISIVE FORCE. The core concept of the new orthodoxy is "decisive force." The absence of decisive force in Vietnam and its full application in Desert Storm account for its inclusion as a key strategic principle in the January 1992 National Military Strategy. Its

---

13. In ascribing a single view to the "U.S. military," I do not mean to imply that all members of the armed forces think alike on this or any other question. There are many who reject the dominant view of how and when the United States should use force, and a growing number of people in the military believe that there is a role in military doctrine and force planning for the full spectrum of peace operations. Nevertheless, the perspective on the use of force described below remains the dominant view within the U.S. military and, especially, in the higher echelons of the Joint Chiefs of Staff.

definition was based squarely on U.S. military experiences in these two conflicts:

Once a decision for military action has been made, half-measures and confused objectives extract a severe price in the form of a protracted conflict which can cause needless waste of human lives and material resources, a divided nation, and defeat. Therefore, one of the essential elements of our national military strategy is the ability to rapidly assemble the forces needed to win — the concept of applying decisive force to overwhelm our adversaries and thereby terminate conflicts swiftly with a minimum loss of life.[14]

The prevailing view in the U.S. military is that the use of military force should be guided by four principles.[15]

First, force should only be used as a last resort. It should be used only after diplomatic and economic solutions have been tried and have clearly failed. Even during the run-up to the Gulf War, many U.S. military leaders (including General Colin Powell, the Chairman of the Joint Chiefs of Staff, and General Norman Schwarzkopf, the U.S. commander in the Gulf) favored waiting for economic sanctions to work over going to war.[16]

Second, force should only be used when there is a clear-cut political objective. It should not be used to achieve vague political objectives. This was a key lesson that the U.S. military took away from the war in Vietnam as well as from the Marine deployment in Lebanon, neither of which had clear political objectives and both of which ended in disaster.

Third, force should only be used when there is a clear end point to the military engagement. This implies that the objectives to be achieved through the use of force are clearly measurable, as in "end the Iraqi occupation of Kuwait," so that troops can be brought home as soon as the objective has been achieved. It means avoiding the use of force for

---

14. *National Military Strategy of the United States* (Washington, D.C.: U.S. Government Printing Office [U.S. GPO], January 1992), p. 10.

15. For a good summary of the new orthodoxy, see Les Aspin, "The Use and Usefulness of Military Force in the Post–Cold War, Post-Soviet World," address to the Jewish Institute for National Security Affairs, Washington, D.C., September 21, 1992. The person most directly identified with these views is Colin Powell, Chairman of the Joint Chiefs of Staff from 1989–93. His most succinct statement on the issue is Colin Powell, "U.S. Forces: Challenges Ahead," *Foreign Affairs*, Vol. 71, No. 5 (Winter 1991/92), p. 38. Powell's views mirror closely the six tests for the use of force first laid out in 1984 by then–Defense Secretary Caspar Weinberger. (Powell was Weinberger's chief military aide at the time.) See Weinberger, "The Uses of Military Power," speech to the National Press Club, Washington, D.C., November 28, 1984.

16. See Michael Gordon and Bernard Trainor, *The General's War: The Inside Story of the Conflict in the Gulf* (Boston: Little Brown, 1994), pp. 129–132, 149.

unclear political objectives such as providing warring parties an incentive to negotiate or demonstrating U.S. military strength.

Fourth, force should only be used in a decisive fashion. The goal must be to use force decisively so that the engagement can be ended quickly and with minimal loss of life. This requires not gradual escalation but the use of overwhelming force — another key lesson from Vietnam.

Together, these four principles distill the key lessons that the U.S. military learned from the Vietnam and Gulf Wars. Left unstated, though implicit in the new orthodoxy, are two political principles with respect to the use of force. One principle is that the use of force should be reserved for situations in which vital U.S. interests are at stake. Powell did not make this explicit, because determining which interests are vital and which are not is properly left to political authorities. Since the decisive use of force will by definition be costly, it follows that only the defense of vital interests would warrant resort to force. The second principle is that the use of force be supported by the U.S. public and its representatives, another key lesson derived from Vietnam. It is assumed that a decision to use force in defense of vital interests will enjoy public and congressional support, particularly if the use of decisive force promises to bring hostilities to an end quickly and with minimal risk to U.S. lives.

Given the success of the decisive force doctrine in the Gulf, it should not be surprising that its main tenets have had a major influence on the development of U.S. military strategy and force planning in the postwar period. The Bottom-Up Review (BUR), completed in September 1993, argues that the United States should have conventional forces sufficient to engage in two major regional contingencies (MRCs) "nearly simultaneously."[17] Why major regional contingencies — in the Persian Gulf, Northeast Asia, or elsewhere — should be seen as the most likely military contingencies is not at all clear. What is clear, however, is that the doctrine of decisive force is most applicable in these circumstances, which is one reason why they form the basis for future force planning. (Another reason is that planning for two MRCs justifies a massive force and a large defense budget at a time when there are no clear threats to vital U.S. interests.) The BUR recognized the importance of contingencies in which the use of force is more likely — including internal conflict and peace operations — but considered force planning and training for these missions to be secondary activities. This point was made with abundant clarity by General Powell when he introduced the results of the BUR in September 1993:

---

17. Les Aspin, *The Bottom-Up Review: Forces For a New Era* (Washington, D.C.: Department of Defense, September 1993).

Let me begin by giving a little bit of a tutorial about what an armed force is all about. Notwithstanding all of the changes that have taken place in the world, notwithstanding the new emphasis on peacekeeping, peace enforcement, peace engagement, preventive diplomacy, we have a value system and a culture system within the armed forces of the United States. We have this mission: to fight and win the nation's wars. . . . Because we are able to fight and win the nation's wars, because we are warriors, we are also uniquely able to do some of these other new missions that are coming along — peacekeeping, humanitarian relief, disaster relief — you name it, we can do it . . . But we never want to do it in such a way that we lose sight of the focus of why you have armed forces — to fight and win the nation's wars.[18]

DECISIVE FORCE AND INTERNAL CONFLICTS.   The central role played by the doctrine of decisive force in U.S. military thinking and planning has profound implications for the country's ability to intervene in internal conflicts. As a practical matter, the priority placed on fighting two regional wars severely limits the personnel, matériel, and financial resources available for conducting limited interventions and peace operations. Especially at a time of shrinking resources, actual or proposed peace operations have inevitably competed with the requirement to maintain forces at the level of readiness necessary for conducting two MRCs nearly simultaneously. Proposals for every new mission — intervention in Bosnia, the delivery of humanitarian relief to Rwanda, or actual intervention in Haiti — have invariably been accompanied by complaints from the military that the operation in question would reduce military readiness or deprive the armed forces of the training and equipment needed to "fight and win the nation's wars."[19] Unless the military leadership can be persuaded (or is told) that some internal conflicts engage U.S. interests directly, policy-makers considering intervention are likely to face strong opposition from the Pentagon.

---

18.   Cited in a prepared statement by Colonel Harry G. Summers, Jr., U.S. House of Representatives, *U.S. Participation in United Nations Peacekeeping Activities,* Hearings before the Subcommittee on International Security, International Organizations and Human Rights of the Committee on Foreign Affairs, 103rd Cong., 1st sess., September 21, 1993, pp. 114, 116. That Powell's concern is shared by his successor, General John Shalikashvili, was made clear a year later when Shalikashvili complained shortly before the U.S. intervention in Haiti, that "my fear is we're becoming mesmerized by operations other than war and we'll take our mind off what we're all about, to fight and win our nation's wars." See "Shalikashvili: Focus Remains on Warfighting, Not Peacekeeping," *Defense Daily,* September 2, 1994, p. 354.

19.   See, for example, Bradley Graham, "Pentagon Officials Worry Aid Missions Will Sap Military Strength," *Washington Post,* July 29, 1994, p. A29; Eric Schmitt, "Military's Growing Role in Relief Missions Prompts Concerns," *New York Times,* July 31, 1994, p. 3; Eric Schmitt, "Pentagon Worries About Cost of Aid Mission," *New York Times,* August 5, 1994, p. A6.

Aside from these practical difficulties, the military's embrace of decisive force also poses doctrinal obstacles to intervention in internal conflicts. The doctrine of decisive force is based on a classic, inter-state war scenario in which political objectives are clear, and in which force can be applied in overwhelming fashion against easily identifiable and clearly separated combatants. The absence of these conditions in most internal conflicts makes the application of this doctrine highly problematic. In other words, the doctrine of decisive force is relevant primarily under conditions that rarely obtain, and is largely irrelevant to those circumstances that are most common in the post–Cold War period.[20] This is why its critics have termed this doctrine an "all-or-nothing" approach to the use of force, arguing that its advocates either insist on using overwhelming force or, failing that, do nothing.[21] The record indeed shows that since the Gulf War, the U.S. military leadership has opposed intervening in internal conflicts as a general rule. It has supported intervention only if the United States is committed to using overwhelming force.

In Iraq, both Powell and Schwarzkopf opposed the use of force to stop attacks on civilian Shi'ites by Saddam Hussein's forces in the weeks immediately following the end of the ground war. These attacks were conducted by armor and troops from Iraq's Republican Guards, which had escaped the clutches of the U.S. forces, and by armed helicopters, which had been given explicit permission by Schwarzkopf during the cease-fire negotiations to fly fully armed. Despite the presence of hundreds of thousands of U.S. troops and complete air superiority over the skies of Iraq, President Bush followed the military's advice and did nothing. The military leadership also opposed sending U.S. troops to help Kurds suffering from an assault by Iraqi forces in the north. Dramatic television footage combined with concerted pressure from France, Britain, and Turkey led Bush to overrule the Pentagon, and some 10,000 U.S. troops were sent to northern Iraq in April 1991 to establish a safe area.[22]

In the former Yugoslavia, senior Bush administration officials were reluctant to intervene militarily, preferring to leave the diplomatic and

---

20. See Andrew J. Bacevich, "The Limits of Orthodoxy: The Use of Force After the Cold War," in Aspen Strategy Group, *The United States and the Use of Force*, pp. 185–189.

21. See, for example, Aspin, "The Uses and Usefulness of Force"; Jim Hoagland, "Sarajevo Guns: How Sarajevo Will Reshape U.S. Strategy," *Washington Post*, August 9, 1992, pp. C1–C2; Edward Luttwak, "Toward Post-Heroic Warfare," *Foreign Affairs*, Vol. 74, No. 3 (May/June 1995), pp. 109–122. See also Christopher Gacek, *The Logic of Force: The Dilemma of Limited War in American Foreign Policy* (New York: Columbia University Press, 1994), especially chaps. 1, 8–10.

22. See Gordon and Trainor, *The General's War*, pp. 454–457; and Tom Mathews, "A Quagmire After All," *Newsweek*, April 29, 1991, pp. 23–25.

military effort to the European Community and the United Nations. When the war in Bosnia escalated in the summer of 1992 and pressure mounted on the administration to launch limited air strikes against Serb heavy weapons indiscriminately attacking cities around Bosnia, Powell took the unusual step of publicly criticizing those favoring action. In a *New York Times* op-ed article, Powell argued: "Decisive means and results are always to be preferred, even if they are not always possible. So you bet I get nervous when so-called experts suggest that all we need is a little surgical bombing or a limited attack. When the desired result isn't obtained, a new set of experts then comes forward with talk of a little escalation. History has not been kind to this approach."[23] Powell's forceful opposition to intervention in Bosnia was never overcome, even by the Clinton administration, which was at least rhetorically more committed to intervention than its predecessor. In part because of the military's opposition, Clinton ruled out the use of U.S. ground troops for any purpose other than enforcing a peace agreement or helping to evacuate UN peacekeepers. That decision effectively undercut forceful military action in Bosnia, because countries with troops on the ground retained a veto over any action designed to punish aggression or help bring the conflict to an end.[24]

It was in the case of Somalia that the central role of U.S. military views regarding intervention in internal conflicts became fully apparent. For months in 1992, mid-level officials in the State Department proposed the deployment of U.S. forces to secure the delivery of food, much of which was sitting on the docks of Mogadishu, the Somali capital. It was only when the Joint Chiefs of Staff suggested that this was a mission that the U.S. military could perform that intervention became a serious option.[25] Operation Restore Hope was fully consistent with the doctrine of decisive force: nearly 30,000 U.S. troops were dispatched on a limited mission to secure supply routes for food deliveries. It was expected that the operation would take no more than two to three months and that it would not involve U.S. forces in the disarmament of local warlords. Instead, the

---

23. Colin Powell, "Why Generals Get Nervous," *New York Times*, October 8, 1992, p. A35. See also Michael R. Gordon, "Powell Delivers a Resounding No on Using Limited Force in Bosnia," *New York Times*, September 28, 1992, pp. A1, A5.

24. For further analysis, see Ivo H. Daalder, "Fear and Loathing in the Former Yugoslavia," in this volume.

25. On the decision to intervene, see Don Oberdorfer, "The Path to Intervention," *Washington Post*, December 6, 1992, pp. A1, A35; Maryann Cusimano, *Operation Restore Hope: The Decision to Intervene in Somalia* (Washington, D.C.: Pew Case Studies in International Affairs, 1995).

essential task of building peace by resolving the underlying causes of starvation was to be left to a new UN peacekeeping mission, to be launched after U.S. forces had departed. The U.S. role was limited to getting food to people and creating a secure environment in which the UN peacekeepers could operate. In short, Operation Restore Hope fulfilled the requirements of the reigning orthodoxy: the application of overwhelming force, clear and limited objectives, and an early exit of U.S. forces.

In the case of Rwanda, where 800,000 people were slaughtered and millions fled to Zaire and Tanzania within the space of just three months in 1994, the U.S. military's perspective coincided with that of other officials in the Clinton administration and members of Congress: this was seen as a situation in which the United States had no direct interest and it was therefore best handled by African countries working through the United Nations. The genocide in Rwanda occurred at a time when interest in and support for humanitarian intervention among senior U.S. officials had reached a low point. Still fresh was the debacle in Somalia, where the mission had gone badly off track in mid-1993 and thirty Americans had lost their lives in battles with one of the reigning warlords. To the lessons of Vietnam and Beirut were added the lessons of Mogadishu, which counseled that military intervention in an internal conflict for humanitarian purposes should be left to others. France eventually did intervene in Rwanda, setting up safe zones that provided shelter for many hundreds of thousands of people. In July 1994, the United States sent 2,350 soldiers as part of a humanitarian airlift to Zaire, where many of the refugees were dying from cholera and other disease. But for the hundreds of thousands of Rwandans who had already been massacred, these actions came too late.

The experience in Somalia also had a profound effect on U.S. policy toward Haiti. As in each previous internal conflict where intervention was contemplated, the U.S. military opposed an invasion, fearing a repeat of the debacle in Somalia. The civilian leadership in the White House and the State Department eventually overruled the Pentagon, which then set out to formulate the requirements for an intervention force: 20,000 troops to invade and secure the country, a mandate with limited objectives, and a clear exit strategy. In addition, the mandate for the UN Mission in Haiti (UNMIH), which would take over from the U.S. force once a stable and secure environment had been created, was also limited. It did not include many of the nation-building tasks that had doomed the UN operation in Somalia. The U.S.-led multinational force was assigned the task of bringing about the departure of the military junta in Haiti, restoring the legitimate government, and creating a secure and stable environment.

This was to be accomplished within six months. UNMIH's mandate was limited to professionalizing the Haitian armed forces, creating a new police force, and establishing an environment conducive to free and fair elections.

Although the operation in Haiti has been successful in many respects, it is far from clear that this experience will provide a new model for intervention in internal conflict. The U.S. military leadership never supported the invasion of Haiti, though they fully and professionally implemented the decision and policy of the commander-in-chief. The circumstances in Haiti were also unique in a variety of ways, including its proximity to U.S. shores and the constant attempts by thousands of Haitians to enter the United States. The U.S. response to Rwanda is likely to be more typical, not just because of the military's opposition to intervention in most internal conflicts, but also because an increasingly assertive Congress has taken steps to make future decisions to intervene more difficult.

AN ASSERTIVE CONGRESS

Relations between the executive and legislative branches on foreign affairs have always been contentious; indeed, the Constitution created, "an invitation to struggle for the privilege of directing American foreign policy."[26] But the debate between the two branches in the post–Cold War period, especially on issues such as peacekeeping and intervention in internal conflicts, has been particularly fractious. On a wide variety of issues, Congress has challenged the Clinton administration: it has threatened to cut off funding for U.S. forces in Somalia and Rwanda, demanded prior congressional authorization for the deployment of U.S. troops to Bosnia and Haiti, denied administration requests to use Defense Department funds to pay UN peacekeeping assessments, and proposed far-reaching restrictions on U.S. participation in and funding for UN peacekeeping operations. These efforts — even when unsuccessful — shaped the administration's internal deliberations and strengthened the hands of those who were reluctant to intervene.

In one sense, the acrimonious debate between Clinton and Congress on peacekeeping and intervention issues reflected simple partisan differences. Republicans have accused the administration of a slavish devotion to multilateralism and a consequent neglect of U.S. national interests; Clinton has castigated the Republican-controlled Congress for embracing isolationism. Real differences also separated Clinton and Congress —

---

26. Edward S. Corwin, *The President: Office and Powers, 1787–1957* (New York: New York University Press, 1957), p. 171.

over Bosnia policy and whether or not to lift the arms embargo, over sending troops to Haiti, over funding for UN peacekeeping. But these differences were magnified by partisan rhetoric that obscured the very large areas of agreement that existed, including a shared reluctance to intervene in most internal conflicts.

Although partisanship inevitably produces rhetorical fire, the fractured nature of debate between Clinton and Congress on foreign policy and, especially, on questions relating to peacekeeping and intervention, cannot be explained entirely or even largely by partisan differences. The underlying structural development was growing congressional assertiveness. For example, when the Democrats controlled both branches of government in 1993–94, sixty percent of the contested votes on national security issues that the Clinton administration lost concerned peacekeeping and intervention issues.[27] The reason for this is the end of the Cold War, which brought an end to the consensus that had existed on security issues in the U.S. body politic, elevated the importance of domestic and economic issues, and stimulated partisanship.[28] The result was a growing Congressional willingness to challenge the president on a wide variety of issues relating to U.S. policy toward internal conflict.

The most important change produced by the end of the Cold War was the collapse of the consensus that had existed in the United States on the nature of the international security environment and the threats and opportunities it offered. For decades, the threat of Soviet communism had been the organizing principle of U.S. foreign policy, clarifying both vital interests and strategies to counter threats to those interests. When the Soviet Union collapsed, a debate unfolded about what interests were truly vital, what threats to those interests existed, and what new opportunities for promoting these interests might have been created. As a result, the foreign policy debate has become more fractious within the nation at large. This, in turn, has affected the debate within Congress and between the executive and the legislative branches. Under these circumstances, Congress is less likely to defer to the president and more likely to challenge his preferences. This is especially true in cases where there is profound disagreement over the extent to which national interests are

---

27. Jeremy Rosner, *The New Tug-of-War: Congress, the Executive Branch, and National Security* (Washington, D.C.: Carnegie Endowment for International Peace, 1995), p. 66, n. 7. Rosner defines a "contested vote" as a roll-call vote on an issue in which the administration had declared a position.

28. On the effect of these changes on executive-congressional relations, see Rosner, *The New Tug-of-War;* James Lindsay, "Congress and the Use of Force in the Cold War Era," in Aspen Strategy Group, *The United States and the Use of Force,* pp. 71–110.

engaged. Peacekeeping and intervention in internal conflict are such issues.

A second result of the end of the Cold War is the growing attention paid to domestic and, especially, economic issues. Much of the U.S. foreign policy debate in general, and the debate on peacekeeping in particular, takes place within this larger domestic political context. The focus is more and more on the economic impact of particular foreign policy initiatives, rather than on the merits of the issues themselves. Driven by a desire to balance the federal budget, available funds for national security and international affairs have shrunk precipitously since the end of the Cold War. In the competition for scarce resources, policy initiatives that do not enjoy widespread support often fall victim to the need to reduce spending. Such, indeed, has been the case with funding for peacekeeping, humanitarian assistance, and military intervention. The U.S. Congress has slashed the Clinton administration's requests to pay rising UN peacekeeping assessments, rejected a proposed formula of shared responsibility between the Defense and State Departments for funding future peacekeeping operations, cut off funding for U.S. troop deployments in Somalia and Rwanda, and proposed that the United Nations reimburse the United States for voluntary contributions to UN-authorized operations.

Finally, the end of the Cold War has elevated the role of partisan politics in foreign policy, repeating a pattern often seen in the immediate aftermath of a major war. Jeremy Rosner has observed that following major wars, control of the presidency and Congress often changes hands and disproportionate numbers of new members are sent to Congress.[29] The presidency changed hands in 1992, and control of both houses of Congress shifted from the Democrats to the Republicans in 1994. In addition, 110 new representatives and 11 senators were elected in 1992; another 86 new House members and 11 senators took office in 1995. This was the largest number of new members to take office since the congressional elections of 1946 and 1948. Although changes such as these need not result in partisan debates over foreign policy, they are more likely to do so if there is no consensus on the nature of the security environment and if the economy takes center stage.[30] As noted earlier, both of these conditions obtained in the wake of the Cold War. Partisan foreign policy debates followed.

These broad trends have produced a more assertive Congress, which

---

29. For details, see Rosner, *The New Tug-of-War*, chap. 3.

30. Rosner, *The New Tug-of-War*, pp. 20–42.

since at least 1993 has attempted to shape U.S. policy on intervention in internal conflicts. Congressional activism has taken a number of forms.[31] Through floor speeches, hearings, and new legislation, members of Congress have sought to frame the debate about intervention. A good example was congressional unease about the direction of U.S. policy toward Somalia in 1993. Senator Robert Byrd used his considerable rhetorical skills on the floor of the Senate to question the continuing presence of U.S. forces in Somalia at a time when few in the public, in the Congress, or at the higher levels of the administration were paying much attention to developments there. When four U.S. soldiers were killed in August in fighting with the Somali warlord Mohammed Farah Aideed, Byrd called for the withdrawal of U.S. forces, introducing a binding resolution to this effect in early September. From that point on, public opinion increasingly turned against the U.S. mission in Somalia. When seventeen U.S. Army Rangers were killed in a failed ambush of Aideed's headquarters on October 3, the public and congressional reaction was to call for the immediate withdrawal of U.S. troops. With the terms of debate largely set, the administration subsequently proposed withdrawing U.S. troops from Somalia, albeit in six months rather than immediately.

Congressional activism has also come in the form of non-binding resolutions and proposed procedural changes that have reduced the Clinton administration's room to maneuver. For example, Congress passed non-binding resolutions in September 1993 demanding that the administration report on the status of U.S. forces in Somalia within one month and seek congressional authorization by November 15 for continuing the deployment. Similar resolutions were passed concerning U.S. intervention in Bosnia and Haiti, with Congress insisting that the president seek prior congressional authorization for sending U.S. forces to either place. For the first time since the end of the Vietnam War, Congress passed resolutions that cut off funding for the deployment of U.S. troops abroad (in Somalia and Rwanda), although it did so only after the administration had decided to withdraw U.S. forces anyway. Finally, Congress adopted provisions requiring consultation with Congress prior to votes in the UN Security Council on new peacekeeping missions, and restricting the use of funds reimbursed by the United Nations for Pentagon activities in support of UN-authorized peacekeeping operations.

Although Congress rarely acts to prohibit or direct specific actions on the part of the president (since doing so would imply that Congress was taking full responsibility for U.S. policy, something members are loath to

---

31. Lindsay, "Congress and the Use of Force in the Post–Cold War Era," especially pp. 82–88.

do), indirect forms of congressional assertiveness influence the policy-making process in important ways. In considering what course of action to take, the administration has to anticipate the likely congressional reaction and adapt its proposed policy accordingly. This may involve changes in the way a policy is publicly presented, or it can completely foreclose certain options. The former occurred in the case of Haiti, while the latter appeared to have been decisive in administration deliberations concerning what to do about the genocide in Rwanda. In the case of Haiti, though the administration was committed to sending troops despite clear congressional opposition, the president decided at the last minute to send a high-level presidential delegation to Port-au-Prince in an effort to convince his critics that invasion was truly the option of last resort. In the case of Rwanda, the administration ruled out direct intervention to stop the massacre, believing (correctly) that Congress would have vigorously opposed the use of U.S. forces. In fact, the administration was careful not to endorse a new UN mission to Rwanda, hoping to convince Congress that its policy towards UN peacekeeping would be more selective and cost-effective than in the past.

In short, while the power of initiative on questions relating to military intervention remains squarely in the hands of the president, the executive branch invariably anticipates and responds to the legislative branch in deciding what to do. This has, more often than not, led to a reluctance to intervene in internal conflicts.

The Reluctance to Intervene: Official Policy

U.S. reluctance to intervene in internal conflicts has been reflected in policy toward the conflicts in Iraq, Bosnia, Somalia, and Rwanda. This reluctance is manifested in the official U.S. policy statement on these matters, Presidential Decision Directive 25 (PDD-25), a public summary of which was released in May 1994.[32] This directive contained the first comprehensive policy statement on questions relating to peacekeeping and intervention in conflicts that did not affect vital U.S. interests — that is, the vast majority of conflicts in the post–Cold War era. Although PDD-25 represented a significant departure from the policy promulgated by the Bush administration in late 1992 — especially in terms of its stated willingness to contribute the full range of U.S. military capabilities to multilateral peace operations — its development during the first year of

---

32. *The Clinton Administration's Policy on Reforming Multilateral Peace Operations* (Washington, D.C.: Bureau of International Organizational Affairs, Department of State, May 1994).

the Clinton administration was nevertheless influenced by the constraints on U.S. intervention that were discussed previously.[33] This was evident from the document's defensive tone and from the absence of a positive vision for the role of multilateral peace operations in dealing with the threats posed by internal conflicts. In addition, its emphasis on burden-sharing as a critical contribution of UN peacekeeping, its endorsement of clear and precise limits on future UN peacekeeping operations and possible U.S. participation therein, its elaborate restatement of long-standing policy regarding command and control of U.S. forces in multilateral operations, and its deliberate emphasis on the importance of consultation with Congress and the U.S. public — all reflected an appreciation of the constraints any policy on intervention in internal conflicts would inevitably face.

Whereas drafts of PDD-25 completed in mid-1993 contained detailed statements of how an expanded commitment to multilateral peace operations could advance national interests, its public presentation nearly a year later was defensive in tone and lacked the enthusiasm of earlier administration statements on the subject. Announcing the completion of the administration's review in February 1994, Clinton's national security adviser, Anthony Lake, stressed: "Let us be clear: peacekeeping is not at the center of our foreign or defense policy. Our armed forces' primary mission is not to conduct peace operations but to win wars." Lake went on to emphasize the limits of multilateral peace operations: "Can the UN build nations for others? No. Can we let the UN become a dumping ground for conflicts that the warring parties themselves lack the will to resolve? No. Do UN peace operations always benefit the American people? No. Should we then throw away an often useful foreign policy tool in a fit of frustration? Of course not."[34] This defensiveness came through in the public summary of PDD-25. The Clinton administration stressed that multilateral peace operations should "be placed in proper perspective among the instruments of U.S. foreign policy." This meant that in "improving our capabilities for peace operations, we will not discard or weaken other tools for achieving U.S. objectives." Nor would the United States support creation of a standing UN army or earmark specific U.S. military units for participation in UN operations. Finally, to underscore

---

33.   For more details on the development of Bush and Clinton administration policies, see Ivo H. Daalder, "Knowing When to Say No: The Development of U.S. Peacekeeping Policy in the 1990s," in William J. Durch, ed., *UN Peacekeeping, American Policy and the Uncivil Wars of the 1990s* (New York: St. Martin's, 1996).

34.   Anthony Lake, "The Limits of Peacekeeping," *New York Times*, February 6, 1994, sec. IV, p. 17.

the point, the administration emphasized that "it is not U.S. policy to seek to expand either the number of UN peace operations or U.S. involvement in such operations."[35]

Having stressed what the United States would not do, the administration went on to say how support for and reform of multilateral peace operations would serve U.S. interests. Here, the emphasis was on the ways in which multilateral operations could ease the burdens on the United States. It suggested that in the post–Cold War world, multilateral peace operations can be "a cost-effective tool to advance American as well as collective interests in maintaining peace in key regions and create global burden-sharing for peace." It was therefore in the U.S. interest "to strengthen UN peacekeeping capabilities and to make operations less expensive and peacekeeping management more accountable." At times, the administration continued, peace operations will "offer the best way to prevent, contain, or resolve conflicts that could otherwise be more costly and deadly. In such cases, the U.S. benefits from having to bear only a share of the burden." Noting that being able to "invoke the voice of the community of nations on behalf of a cause we support" was also beneficial, the administration suggested that U.S. participation in multilateral operations could serve U.S. interests by persuading "others to participate in operations that serve U.S. interests" and enabling the United States "to exercise influence over an important UN mission, without unilaterally bearing the burden."[36]

Domestic constraints on U.S. involvement in internal conflicts were also evident in the Clinton administration's development of specific guidelines for voting on and participating in UN peace operations. In some important respects, the guidelines demonstrated a stronger rather than weaker commitment to peace operations. For example, the administration's guidelines did not stipulate that intervention should only be considered as a last resort, suggesting instead that "the political, economic and humanitarian consequences of inaction by the international community" be weighed. In addition, the administration's guidelines predicated U.S. support for and participation in peace operations on a determination

---

35. *The Clinton Administration's Policy on Reforming Multilateral Peace Operations*, p. 3. Earlier drafts had expressed support for the "rapid expansion" of UN operations, welcomed a greatly expanded U.S. role in peacekeeping, and committed the United States to supporting these operations "politically, militarily, and financially." Cited in Barton Gellman, "Wider U.N. Police Role Supported," *Washington Post*, August 5, 1993, p. A1.

36. *The Clinton Administration's Policy on Reforming Multilateral Peace Operations*, pp. 1–2.

that these operations advance general, rather than vital, U.S. interests. Finally, the administration's guidelines defined threats to or breaches of international peace and security — the key to UN Security Council action — in very broad terms: "international aggression; urgent humanitarian disaster coupled with violence; [or a] sudden interruption of established democracy or gross violation of human rights coupled with violence or threat of violence."[37]

In other instances, however, the Clinton administration's guidelines reflected input from the U.S. military, including its concern that decisive force be used whenever military action is taken. For example, the guidelines emphasized the need for clear exit strategies, insisting that an "operation's anticipated duration is tied to clear objectives and realistic criteria for ending the operation," and that the "role of U.S. forces is tied to clear objectives and an endpoint for U.S. participation." In addition, the guidelines drew specifically on the doctrine of decisive force with respect to operations that were likely to involve combat:

- there exists a determination to commit sufficient forces to achieve clearly defined objectives;

- there exists a plan to achieve those objectives decisively;

- there exists a commitment to reassess and adjust, as necessary, the size, composition, and disposition of our forces to achieve our objectives.

Finally, the administration noted that "large scale participation of U.S. forces in a major peace enforcement mission that is likely to involve combat should ordinarily be conducted under U.S. command and operational control or through competent regional organizations such as NATO [the North Atlantic Treaty Organization] or *ad hoc* coalitions."[38]

In general, the Clinton administration's policy toward multilateral peace operations was based on a realistic appraisal of what the U.S. domestic political system could bear. It accepted the fact that the U.S. public, while perhaps engaged internationally, would place primary emphasis on developments at home, a policy preference shared by President Clinton. The administration did not make a forceful case for engagement internationally or for the need to intervene militarily in internal conflicts.

---

37. Ibid., p. 4.

38. Ibid., pp. 4–5, 9.

Moreover, it sought to accommodate rather than counter the U.S. military's opposition to intervention in such conflicts. This grew out of both the president's record on Vietnam and the confrontation in early 1993 between the White House and the Pentagon over the issue of gays in the military; this meant that the Clinton administration would be more sensitive to military views than others might have been. Finally, with an ambitious domestic agenda in mind, the administration sought to avoid a confrontation with Congress over foreign policy and peacekeeping; it wanted to save its political capital for domestic initiatives.

In accommodating rather than challenging these domestic political constraints, the Clinton administration's policy on multilateral peace operations represented an evolutionary rather than revolutionary change from the policy developed late in the Bush administration. Therefore, it did not go as far as some had hoped and others had feared. Although Clinton's policy rejected the development of a UN standing army or earmarking specific U.S. units for UN operations, it did for the first time commit the United States to participate in multilateral operations with the full range of military forces at its disposal, rather than merely providing "unique" capabilities, as had previously been the case. Clinton also clarified when and how U.S. troops could be placed under the operational control of a UN or foreign commander. At the same time, it was clear that Clinton would not support a host of new peacekeeping ventures or commit U.S. forces to a large number of operations. To the contrary, in the first test case, involving the genocide in Rwanda, the administration used its new guidelines to slow the UN response, arguing that the operation proposed by the UN Secretary-General did not have a clear mandate and that forces and financing had not yet been identified.[39] At the same time, the guidelines did prove a useful checklist for the Haiti operation, especially with respect to the limited but realistic mandate of the UN mission that followed the U.S.-led invasion.

The Reluctance to Intervene: Consequences and Remedies

Since the end of the Cold War, the domestic debate on the U.S. role in internal conflicts and, especially, on whether or not to intervene militarily, has focused primarily on the costs of intervention: the risk of U.S. casualties; the financial burden of launching and sustaining large peacekeeping operations; the effect on the morale and readiness of U.S. military forces; and the diversion of attention and energy from pressing problems

---

39. See Douglas Jehl, "U.S. Showing New Caution On U.N. Peacekeeping Mission," *New York Times*, May 18, 1994, pp. A1, A6.

at home. These costs are real and, given the absence of a threat to vital U.S. interests, they help explain U.S. reluctance to intervene in internal conflicts. Indeed, their prominence in the debate is underscored by the fact that even those who deplored the absence of a more forceful U.S. stance in conflicts such as Bosnia have often proposed alternative courses of action that minimized attendant costs. The most popular alternative to the Clinton administration's policy of supporting the UN humanitarian operation in Bosnia was to lift the arms embargo on Bosnia unilaterally and perhaps launch limited airstrikes. Few suggested sending 100,000 or more U.S. troops to halt and reverse Serb aggression.[40]

The costs of inaction, including costs to humanitarian and other important U.S. interests, tend to be ignored or downplayed.[41] In the short run, the costs of inaction are primarily humanitarian and fall principally on the victims of internal conflicts — on the Tutsi massacred by Hutu, the Somalis deprived of food by warlords, the Shi'ites hounded by Republican Guards, the Muslims "cleansed" by Serbs, and the Chechens bombed by Russian security forces. In the long run, however, internal conflicts can affect important U.S. interests. Left untended, internal conflicts can spread, affect the well-being of neighboring states, and threaten regional stability, all in ways that can damage U.S. interests. For example, the conflict in Bosnia could spread to Kosovo, Macedonia, and beyond to encompass major parts of the Balkans, at which point U.S. interests would be very much at stake. Similarly, U.S. interests would be affected if conflicts in the Russian littoral were to have a negative effect on political developments inside Russia, perhaps by strengthening the hands of nationalist forces in Moscow that demand military action abroad and suppression of democratic dissent at home.

At times, it may be necessary to limit the costs of inaction by intervening directly in an internal conflict. Indeed, past interventions in internal conflicts have been justified on precisely this basis. Humanitarian interests led the United States to intervene in northern Iraq and Somalia, and to launch a large relief operation in Rwanda. A combination of

---

40. Important exceptions are Senator Richard Lugar and General William Odom. See Katherine Seelye, "Many in Congress Reluctant to Widen U.S. Role in Bosnia," *New York Times,* June 2, 1995, pp. A1, A10, for Lugar's view; William Odom, "Send in Ground Troops, and A Lot of Them," *New York Times,* May 31, 1995, p. A21.

41. It should be noted that the Clinton administration's directive on peace operations includes the following among the factors to be considered in deciding whether to support new operations: "The political, economic, and humanitarian consequences of inaction by the international community have been weighed and are considered unacceptable." See *The Clinton Administration's Policy on Reforming Multilateral Peace Operations,* p. 4.

humanitarian and other interests (principally an interest in containment) help to explain the few forceful actions taken in Bosnia. And the intervention in Haiti was justified by important interests such as U.S. support for democracy in the Western hemisphere and the need to stem the refugee flow to U.S. shores.

As these actions indicate, it is sometimes possible to overcome the reluctance to intervene even in cases where vital interests are not at stake and, instead, to use force to defend lesser interests.[42] However, even when the reasons for intervention are clear and persuasive, deciding how to intervene still poses a major problem, one that helps to account for the reluctance to intervene in such cases. Debates on how to intervene have been dominated by a particular view on the use of force, a view that tends to conflict with the more limited interests that are often at stake. The Pentagon's insistence on using decisive force suggests that the aim of using force should always be to win, and to win decisively. This tends to rule out limited means. As General Powell argued in opposing those who favored resorting to air strikes in Bosnia: "As soon as they tell me it's limited, it means they do not care whether you achieve a result or not. As soon as they tell me 'surgical,' I head for the bunker."[43] In other words, if the interests at stake in a conflict are limited and the only means to achieve them involve the use of decisive force, the result will probably be a decision not to intervene. That is why the military has nearly always opposed intervening in internal conflicts.

Can military force be used in alternative, less decisive ways that are more in accordance with the interests at stake in most internal conflicts? The answer, clearly, is yes.[44] The key is limiting one's objectives to something short of all-out victory, more in line with the interests at stake. For

---

42. This is reflected in the Clinton administration's National Security Strategy, which suggests that there are three categories of national interests that might merit the use of force. The first involves vital interests; the second consists of important, but not vital, interests, which are defined as those that "affect importantly our national well-being and the character of the world in which we live"; the final concerns are humanitarian interests. See *A National Security Strategy of Engagement and Enlargement* (Washington, D.C.: The White House, February 1995), p. 13.

43. Cited in Michael R. Gordon, "Powell Delivers a Resounding No on Using Limited Force in Bosnia."

44. See, for example, Aspin, "The Uses and Usefulness of Force"; Richard Haass, *Intervention: The Use of American Military Power in the Post–Cold War World* (Washington, D.C.: Carnegie Endowment for International Peace, 1994), chap. 5; Jane Holl, "We the People Here Don't Want No War: Executive Branch Perspectives on the Use of Force," in Aspen Strategy Group, *The United States and the Use of Force*, pp. 120–126; and Luttwak, "Toward Post-Heroic Warfare."

example, if the interests involved are purely humanitarian, the objective of an intervention could be to control the level and intensity of violence rather than to end the war altogether. This might involve only limited use of force.

For example, one response to the genocide in Rwanda could have been setting up clearly demarcated safety zones in part of the country, as indeed the French did, albeit very late in the conflict. The objective would not have been to end the conflict or even to halt the killing altogether, but to offer a safe zone for people who either lived in the region or could reach it on their own accord.

In Bosnia, the establishment of heavy weapons exclusion zones around safe areas offered a way to limit the scope of Serb violence against civilian populations. Of course, the integrity of the zones depended on a credible threat of military action and, if necessary, military enforcement. The former led to the creation of a weapons exclusion zone around Sarajevo in February 1994 and a marked improvement in living conditions in the city; the absence of the latter in May 1995 led to the breakdown of the concept, which was only re-established again in September 1995, after the decisive military intervention of NATO. If the aim of intervention in Bosnia had been to put a stop to the use of artillery against cities, an early, sustained, but patient air campaign designed to find and destroy artillery and other heavy weapons near population centers would have been possible, particularly in a setting where the United States possessed complete air superiority.

If limited interests dictate limited involvement, then military forces should be used in limited ways. The use of military force does not have to be decisive or aimed at victory, though advocates of the decisive force doctrine are right to insist that one should have a clear political and military objective. However, one's objective should not be determined by rigid ideas about how to use force, as is the practice in the Pentagon and, to a lesser degree, in the U.S. foreign policy establishment in the 1990s. Instead, one's objective should be determined by the interests involved. If these interests are limited, as they usually are in internal conflicts, then the manner in which force is used should be similarly limited.

Internal conflicts often challenge only limited U.S. interests, principally humanitarian ones. Given the nature of U.S. domestic politics in the post–Cold War era, the absence of a challenge to important, let alone vital, national interests will lead to inaction more often than not. This is understandable and, in many instances, correct. There will be cases, however, where either the humanitarian consequences of conflict or the long-term costs to other interests will obligate the United States to take action, possibly even military action. In such cases, U.S. policymakers should have the ability to use military forces in a limited manner, tied to specific though limited objectives. The U.S. military leadership, however, prefers an "all or nothing" approach with a strong bias in favor of the latter. Since an insistence on using decisive force in internal conflict will almost always lead to inaction, internal conflicts are likely to fester, proliferate, and, ultimately, undermine U.S. national interests.

Chapter 15

The United Nations and Internal Conflict

Chantal de Jonge Oudraat

The United Nations (UN) was established in 1945 "to maintain international peace and security."[1] The UN Security Council was given primary responsibility for maintaining and restoring peace and security, and its decisions were made binding. To enable the Council to take effective action, each member of the United Nations was to make national armed forces available to the Council. This was one of the keys to the system of collective security and enforcement envisioned in the UN Charter.

For decades, however, this system was crippled by two problems. First, Security Council decisions had to be supported by all five permanent members of the Council — China, France, the Soviet Union, the United Kingdom, and the United States — and these five states rarely reached a consensus on international peace and security issues during the Cold War. Conflicts abounded, but Chapter VII enforcement actions (actions with respect to threats to the peace, breaches of the peace, or acts of aggression — including economic sanctions, military embargoes, and the use of force) were few and far between. Second, effective action was impaired because national military forces were never made available to the Council in the way envisioned in the Charter.

Non-coercive instruments were consequently brought into play. Some of these instruments — most notably, peacekeeping operations — were not provided for in the Charter, but were developed over time in response to specific conflict situations. Peacekeeping operations were initially seen as crisis control instruments: the idea was that they would dampen regional conflicts and keep them from escalating into U.S.-Soviet confrontations. This was the best the United Nations could do given the virtual impossibility of getting the five permanent members of the Security

---

1. See *Charter of the United Nations*, Article 1 (1).

Council, known as the P-5, to arrive at a consensus and invoke Chapter VII enforcement measures.

With the end of the Cold War, the main political obstacle to Chapter VII actions seemed to have disappeared. Many thought that the United Nations would at last be able to uphold the principles enunciated in 1945 and become an effective guarantor of international peace and security. In the euphoria of those early post–Cold War years, some hoped that the Security Council would henceforth be able to bring into play the full range of enforcement measures provided for in the Charter. Many new peacekeeping operations were launched in the late 1980s and early 1990s, and some of these operations were remarkably ambitious and complex. In a departure from past practice, most of these operations were launched in response to intra-state conflicts.

It was against this background — the new and fundamentally different international environment, the unique and formidable challenges posed by intra-state conflicts, and the expanding array of UN operations — that the Security Council, in January 1992, requested that the UN Secretary-General, Boutros Boutros-Ghali, prepare a report on "ways of strengthening . . . the capacity of the United Nations" with respect to peace and security issues.[2] Boutros-Ghali's June 1992 report, *An Agenda for Peace*, called for an expanded UN role in this area, and sparked an international debate on these issues.[3] This debate is far from closed.

This chapter analyzes UN efforts to prevent, contain, and resolve internal conflicts (as opposed to inter-state conflicts such as the Iraqi invasion of Kuwait).[4] It will seek to answer the following questions: what is the legal framework for UN action, and how has this framework evolved over time? How has the end of the Cold War affected the relationship between and among the main actors within the UN system — the Security Council, the General Assembly, and the Secretary-General? To what extent and in what ways do financial constraints impinge on the scope for UN action? What instruments does the United Nations have at its disposal to counter threats to peace and security, and how has the utilization of these instruments evolved? Under what conditions are these instruments most likely to be used, and under what conditions are they most likely to be used effectively?

---

2. See UN Security Council Document, S/23500, January 31, 1992.

3. See *An Agenda for Peace*, Report of the Secretary-General, A/47/277 or S/24111, June 17, 1992.

4. For further discussion of the distinction between intra-state and inter-state conflicts and the focus of this analytic undertaking, see Michael Brown's introductory chapter to this volume.

In this chapter, it is argued that the UN Charter gives the Security Council tremendous latitude to deal with threats to international peace and security. Indeed, it is entirely up to the Security Council, which has re-emerged since the end of the Cold War as the dominant voice within the United Nations, to determine if a particular problem constitutes a threat to international order. If it determines that a threat does exist, it has a variety of options. This chapter identifies and discusses seven main instruments at its disposal: humanitarian assistance; fact-finding; traditional peacekeeping; multifunctional peacekeeping; economic sanctions and arms embargoes; judicial enforcement measures; and use of military force.

Whether or not the Security Council takes action with respect to an internal or intra-state conflict depends on two main factors: the extent to which the conflict in question poses a threat to regional peace and security; and the political wishes of the members of the Security Council, particularly the P-5. Looming over these policy decisions is the UN's financial crisis, which poses a severe challenge to its effective functioning.

In general, it is a mistake to think of "the United Nations" as an independent political actor with respect to peace and security issues: it would be more accurate to think of the United Nations as a policy instrument of the organization's member states. Except for limited actions undertaken by the Secretary-General, such as fact-finding and mediation efforts, member states, led by the P-5, determine when and whether action will be taken.

This chapter begins with a short review of the legal framework for UN actions and highlights some of the legal issues that dominate the current debate. It then discusses the changing organizational dynamics within the United Nations, and the organization's financial situation.[5] This is followed by an assessment of the seven main instruments available to the United Nations and activities that have been undertaken in each of these areas. This chapter concludes with a discussion of the conditions under which the United Nations is most likely to take action, and the conditions under which it is most likely to take effective action.

---

5. This chapter will not dwell on organizational and administrative problems or the many reform proposals that have been put forward with respect to these issues. For more on those questions, see, for example, Erskine Childers and Brian Urquhart, *Renewing the United Nations System* (Uppsala, Sweden: Dag Hammarskjöld Foundation, 1994); W. Andy Knight, "Beyond the UN System? Critical Perspectives on Global Governance and Multilateral Evolution: A Review Essay," *Global Governance*, Vol. 1, No. 2 (May–August 1995), pp. 229–253.

The Legal Framework

The United Nations was established as an organization of equal and sovereign states with the goal of ensuring and developing peaceful and friendly relations between states.[6] When states join the United Nations, they promise to refrain from the threat or use of force in a manner that would be inconsistent with the principles of the UN Charter.[7] They also confer on the Security Council responsibility for the maintenance of international peace and security, and empower it to act, using military force if necessary, in response to any "threat to the peace, breach of the peace, or act of aggression."[8] They agree, furthermore, to accept and carry out the decisions of the Security Council.[9] Council decisions, therefore, are binding on all members of the organization.

What constitutes a "threat to the peace, breach of the peace, or act of aggression" is not defined in the Charter because the great powers, particularly the United States and the Soviet Union, wanted to maintain control over UN decisions in this area on a case-by-case basis: precise, formal definitions would have impinged on the P-5's political control of the organization.[10] Although internal conflict was not a main concern of the founders of the United Nations, the UN Charter gives the Security Council the authority to disregard the general principle of non-intervention in the domestic affairs of states if a threat to international peace and security exists.[11] The Council, in short, has tremendous latitude to decide if a particular problem poses a threat to peace and security, and to take whatever action it deems appropriate.

Once the Council has determined that a situation poses a threat or potential threat to peace and security, it may resort to either the conciliatory measures outlined in Chapter VI of the Charter or the coercive

---

6. See *Charter of the United Nations*, Article 2 (1).

7. See ibid., Article 2 (4). States are permitted to use armed force for self-defense; see Article 51.

8. See ibid., Article 24, 39, and 42.

9. See ibid., Article 25.

10. The General Assembly has attempted to define "aggression," while recognizing that the Security Council alone has the authority to determine whether or not an act of aggression has taken place. See A/res/3314 (XXIX), December 12, 1974.

11. See *Charter of the United Nations*, Article 2 (7): "Nothing contained in the present Charter shall authorize the United Nations to intervene in matters which are essentially within the domestic jurisdiction of any state or shall require the Members to submit such matters to settlement under the present Charter; but this principle shall not prejudice the application of enforcement measures under Chapter VII."

enforcement measures outlined in Chapter VII. Its decisions on these matters are political decisions: they depend on creating a consensus on the Council, especially among the P-5, and on the means available to execute decisions. Decisions to use military force under Chapter VII, for example, can only be implemented if member states are willing to place national military forces at the disposal of the Council.

The Security Council, however, has never been equipped with the armed forces envisioned in the Charter. Article 43 of the Charter stipulates that all member states are to make armed forces available to the Security Council, on its call and in accordance with special agreements between the Council and individual states. These agreements were never negotiated. As a result, armed forces have been made available to the Council only on a voluntary, case-by-case basis. The Council is totally dependent on the inclinations of individual states. The Charter's Chapter VII enforcement provisions have consequently been undercut.

Since the end of the Cold War, the UN's level of activity in security affairs in general and intra-state security problems in particular has increased dramatically. This has unleashed a vigorous debate concerning the status of such legal principles as sovereignty and non-intervention in the domestic affairs of states. One school of thought maintains that the passage of UN Security Council Resolution 688 (1991) authorized a multinational intervention in northern Iraq and helped establish a new legal norm, a norm that would subordinate the prerogatives of national sovereignty to human rights principles. Those who subscribed to this line of thinking saw this as a good thing: they saw sovereignty as a concept of diminishing relevance in a world plagued by global concerns ranging from environmental pollution to economic underdevelopment. They also believed that states should not be allowed to hide behind the shield of sovereignty when gross violations of human rights were taking place on their territory or when civil wars raged. It was argued that international intervention could be justified in cases such as these on humanitarian grounds.[12] A second school of thought maintained a more traditional view of state sovereignty and the question of humanitarian intervention. Proponents of this school did not see a "right of humanitarian intervention" emerging, nor did they see steps in this direction as desirable.[13]

---

12. See, for example, Laura W. Reed and Carl Kaysen, eds., *Emerging Norms of Justified Intervention* (Cambridge, Mass.: American Academy of Arts and Sciences, 1993); Jarat Chopra and Thomas G. Weiss, "Sovereignty is no Longer Sacrosanct: Codifying Humanitarian Intervention," *Ethics and International Affairs,* Vol. 6 (1992), pp. 95–118.

13. A close reading of Resolution 688 (1991) shows that it was driven by security concerns, not humanitarian considerations, and that it did not authorize the multina-

Several problems have plagued this debate. First, some have confused the right to receive humanitarian assistance with an obligation to provide humanitarian assistance: the former exists; the latter does not. Modern humanitarian law and the General Assembly resolutions on humanitarian assistance adopted in 1988 and 1991 reaffirm that people in need have a right to receive humanitarian assistance, but they do not obligate states or international bodies to provide it.[14]

Similarly, the right to receive humanitarian assistance — assistance that is provided through peaceful means and is aimed at the victims of a humanitarian disaster — has often been confused with a right of humanitarian intervention — a forceful action and an obligation to punish those who have behaved unlawfully. The confusion lies in the fact that the right to receive humanitarian assistance is a legal notion, while intervention is a political matter. If carried out under the authority of the UN Security Council, force can be used legally for humanitarian purposes. Whether states will take action, however, depends entirely on political, not legal, considerations. Recent practice suggests that forceful humanitarian actions are still viewed with trepidation by the great powers. Indeed, the 1991 intervention in northern Iraq was triggered by security concerns, not humanitarian considerations. Similarly, the great powers have been reluctant to use force in Bosnia even though the humanitarian consequences of the war there are well-known. The great powers, in short, have not yet accepted the idea that a "right of humanitarian intervention" exists.

The debate over state sovereignty and the principle of non-intervention in the domestic affairs of states is far from new and far from over. Although reasonable people disagree about how the United Nations and the international system should evolve with respect to these questions, it seems clear that the state remains the main actor in international peace and security affairs and that states will continue to attach great importance to their sovereignty and independence. These views are not confined to the great powers: many developing countries are deeply concerned about UN involvement in internal conflicts and about the debates over humanitarian intervention and the universality of human rights.

Although the United Nations is based on the principle of sovereign

---

tional military intervention that followed (Operation Provide Comfort), contrary to what some contend.

14. See UN General Assembly Resolution 43/131 of December 8, 1988; 45/100 of January 29, 1991; 46/182 of December 19, 1991; and 48/57 of December 1993. See also Report of the Secretary-General, *Strengthening the Coordination of Emergency Assistance of the United Nations*, A/49/177, June 21, 1994.

equality of states, sovereignty and independence have never been absolute, rigid concepts. They have evolved over time, as has application of the UN Charter to peace and security problems. One suspects that, although the end of the Cold War marked a major transformation in some aspects of inter-state politics, changes in the UN's legal framework — or, more accurately, interpretations of that framework — will continue to be, as they have been in the first few years of the post–Cold War era, evolutionary rather than revolutionary in nature.

The Organizational and Financial Setting

Although the UN Charter envisioned the Security Council as the dominant body within the organization and an active force in international peace and security affairs, the Council was ineffectual throughout most of the Cold War era. It was paralyzed by Cold War politics: any one of the five permanent members of the Council could prevent it from taking action in any particular case, and one or another of the five often did. The General Assembly, although technically subordinate to the Council on peace and security issues, had a higher profile than the Council on many issues for many years.

The end of the Cold War has revitalized the Security Council and returned it to its rightful place at the top of the UN hierarchy. As mentioned in the previous section, the Council is the main organ of the United Nations with respect to peace and security issues. It is composed of fifteen members, the five permanent members and ten non-permanent members elected for two-year terms on a rotating basis (five are elected each year). Decisions of the Security Council on all non-procedural matters need nine affirmative votes, including the support of all five permanent members of the Council.

Although the end of the Cold War removed key obstacles from the Security Council's path, important problems remain. First, the five permanent members of the Council still have different national interests and different perspectives on issues ranging from Bosnia to Iraq to the Spratly Islands. A consensus does not always exist among the P-5 and this, of course, limits what the Security Council can do. Second, although each of the five permanent members of the Council can veto UN action, and has a denial capacity, only the United States has the resources needed to carry out a major military enforcement operation. For the United Nations to take forceful action, the United States must be willing to take the lead. The United States, however, is reluctant to become involved in coercive enforcement operations: it has little interest in becoming "the world's policeman."[15] The ability of the Security Council to take effective, forceful action is therefore limited.

The end of the Cold War and the re-emergence of the Council has weakened the role of the General Assembly. The influence of non-aligned countries in the United Nations has consequently diminished. However, the General Assembly still has primary responsibility for activities in the social and economic fields. Many conflicts have social and economic roots; the General Assembly's efforts to promote social and economic development and human rights can therefore indirectly dampen conflict and contribute to international peace and security. Moreover, if the Security Council decides that a particular conflict is not a threat to international peace and security and hence not an appropriate candidate for Council action, the General Assembly can fill the void and take the lead, at least at a declaratory level.[16]

The role and responsibilities of the UN Secretary-General have changed dramatically since the end of the Cold War. The United Nations has seen a great increase in complex peacekeeping operations, and the Secretary-General is responsible for overseeing these activities. In addition, Boutros-Ghali has been very active in trying to place peace and security problems on the UN's agenda, and trying to bring conflicts in various parts of the world to an end.

The Secretary-General's power remains limited, however. He is the chief administrative and executive officer of a large organization, but the United Nations itself is an instrument of the organization's member states: states decide; the Secretary-General implements. The fact that the United Nations is an organization of 184 equally sovereign but not equally important states gives the Secretary-General some room to maneuver, but his capacity to act is extremely limited if the P-5 agree on a

---

15. For a discussion of U.S. attitudes on these matters, see Ivo H. Daalder's chapter on the United States and military intervention in this volume.

16. Article 11 of the UN Charter stipulates that the General Assembly may discuss questions relating to the maintenance of international peace and security, and make recommendations on these issues. However, problems that require action are to be referred to the Security Council. Article 12 of the Charter states that the General Assembly is not to make recommendations on problems under consideration by the Council. However, this provision has not kept the Assembly from urging the Security Council to lift the arms embargo on Bosnia; see A/res/47/121. Finally, mention should be made of the Uniting for Peace Resolution, 377 (V) of November 1950, whereby the General Assembly reserved the right to substitute itself for the Council in cases where the latter is not able to discharge its responsibilities. This resolution, however, has never been invoked.

particular course of action or if the interests of one of the members of the P-5 are engaged.

The Secretary-General is also constrained by a lack of resources and by the UN's financial difficulties. Although the United Nations has always had resource and financial problems, these problems have become especially acute since the end of the Cold War. It is no exaggeration to say that, in 1995, the United Nations is in the midst of a financial crisis.

This financial crisis stems from three main sources. First, UN peacekeeping activities have increased exponentially since the late 1980s. This has obvious financial implications. In 1990–91, for example, peacekeeping operations consumed seventeen percent of the UN's budget; in 1992–93, they took up fifty-three percent of the organization's budget.[17]

Second, most member states are far behind in making their mandatory financial payments to the United Nations. As of September 1994, for example, only 17 of the organization's 184 member states had met their financial obligations in full and on time. Over two-thirds of the contributions to the UN's peacekeeping account were outstanding.[18] The United States and Russia have been the two biggest deadbeats, although the latter has an economic crisis of its own as an excuse. (See Table 15.1 for a list of the top ten deadbeats.) To put things in perspective, the UN's regular and peacekeeping budgets total $7–8 billion per year — roughly equal to three percent of the budget for the U.S. Department of Defense.

Third, most of the financial burden for both the regular and peacekeeping budgets is being borne by just a few members of the organization. (See Table 15.2 for a list of the top ten contributors to the UN's regular and peacekeeping accounts.) For example, the United States, Japan, Germany, and France are responsible for fifty-four percent of the UN's regular budget and sixty-two percent of the peacekeeping budget. A mere fifteen countries pay ninety percent of the peacekeeping budget. This has led many people, particularly in the United States, to argue that these financial burdens should be distributed more equally. It is worth noting, of course, that big financial contributors have great influence, particularly on the Security Council and on peace and security issues.

Many U.S. politicians, Democrats and Republicans alike, argue that the United Nations needs to streamline its bureaucracy and conduct its affairs more effectively and more efficiently. Reform, they say, is sorely

---

17. See *Financial Report and Audited Statements for the Biennium Ending 31 December and Report of the Board of Auditors,* Vol. II: *United Nations Peace-keeping Operations,* A/49/5, August 3, 1994.

18. See *Report of the Secretary-General on the Work of the Organization,* A/49/1, September 2, 1994.

Table 15.1. Top Ten Deadbeats in Millions of U.S. Dollars (as of November 15, 1995).

Country	Owes UN Regular Budget	Country	Owes UN Peacekeeping Budget
1. United States	414.4	1. United States	847.4
2. South Africa	61.1	2. Russia	477.3
3. Ukraine	42.6	3. Ukraine	185.9
4. Yugoslavia	10.8	4. France	107.1
5. Belarus	10.4	5. South Africa	57.7
6. Iran	9.5	6. Belarus	48.2
7. Azerbaijan	7.7	7. Italy	48.0
8. Kazakhstan	7.5	8. Germany	22.0
9. Georgia	6.9	9. Spain	19.4
10. Argentina	5.2	10. China	16.8
Subtotal	576.1	Subtotal	1,829.8
Total for all UN member states	645.5	Total for all UN member states	2,038.1

SOURCE: Report of the Secretary-General, *Improving the Financial Situation of the United Nations*, A/50/666/Add.2, November 28, 1995, p. 9.

Table 15.2. Biggest Contributors to UN Accounts by Percentage (1995 scales of assessment).

Country	Supposed to Contribute to the UN's Regular Budget	Supposed to Contribute to the UN's Peacekeeping Budget
1. United States	25.00	31.15
2. Japan	13.95	14.00
3. Germany	8.94	8.98
4. France	6.32	7.88
5. Russia	5.68	7.08
6. United Kingdom	5.27	6.57
7. Italy	4.79	4.81
8. Canada	3.07	3.08
9. Spain	2.24	2.25
10. Netherlands	1.58	1.59
Total	76.84	87.39

SOURCES: Office of the UN Secretary-General, February 1995; General Assembly, *Report of the Committee on Contributions*, A/49/11, July 26, 1994.

needed, and the United States will hold back on its financial contributions until serious reforms are instituted. Some, particularly from the conservative wing of the Republican party, believe that U.S. contributions to the United Nations should be slashed.

There is no doubt that institutional reform is needed at the United Nations.[19] There is also no doubt that the UN's financial crisis puts severe limits on what the organization can do with respect to peace and security problems. Unless states start paying their dues on time and in full, management reforms will be moot: the United Nations will be crippled.

The Instruments

The United Nations has at its disposal seven main instruments to deal with the problems posed by internal conflicts: humanitarian assistance; fact-finding; traditional peacekeeping; multifunctional peacekeeping; economic sanctions and arms embargoes; judicial enforcement measures; and the use of military force.[20] (Tables summarizing when these instruments have been used since 1945 can be found in the annex to this chapter.)

The first four of these instruments — humanitarian assistance, fact-finding, traditional peacekeeping, and multifunctional peacekeeping — are effective only when the consent of the relevant parties is obtained. Indeed, they have been highly problematic in cases where some parties object to the operation in question, or if consent is withdrawn. The other three instruments — economic sanctions and arms embargoes, judicial enforcement measures, and the use of military force — are coercive in nature. Most of these seven instruments are versatile and can be used for conflict prevention, conflict management, or conflict resolution. Fact-finding, for example, can be carried out before, during, or after a conflict. Similarly, troop deployments can be used to help prevent, contain, or resolve a conflict. The only instrument that is well-defined in this respect is multifunctional peacekeeping, which clearly operates best after the fighting has stopped and a peace agreement has been signed.

---

19. The UN's organizational problems and proposed reform measures are beyond the scope of this chapter. See note 5.

20. Although they will not be examined in detail in this chapter, one should note that the United Nations engages in a wide variety of other activities that have an impact on the prospects for peace and security. These activities include economic development efforts, human rights efforts, arms control and disarmament efforts, and the provision of various other technical and advisory services. For an overview of these activities, see Adam Roberts and Benedict Kingsbury, eds., *United Nations, Divided World: The UN's Role in International Relations*, 2nd. ed. (Oxford: Clarendon, 1993).

HUMANITARIAN ASSISTANCE

As we have seen in many parts of the world, internal conflicts often involve disruptions of food production and distribution channels, human rights abuses, and direct attacks on civilian populations, producing horrifying numbers of casualties and refugees. Since the end of the Cold War, many humanitarian assistance efforts have been launched to deal with the problems created by internal conflicts and civil wars, and many of these operations have been carried out under battlefield conditions. In a great number of cases, humanitarian relief supplies have been seized by warring factions and used as political weapons. In some, relief personnel have been attacked. Although humanitarian assistance efforts are generally seen as non-political by distant powers and international bureaucrats, they are often seen as deeply political by local belligerents: humanitarian efforts can affect the balance of power on the ground.

The right to receive humanitarian assistance in armed conflicts, including intra-state conflicts, was recognized in the 1949 Geneva humanitarian law conventions as well as in the 1977 Protocols to the Geneva conventions.[21] UN General Assembly resolutions in 1988 and 1991 gave a new impetus to this principle, and widened its scope to include natural disasters and other emergency situations.[22] These resolutions also called on all states to facilitate such assistance. The norm of humanitarian assistance based on the principles of impartiality and neutrality is hence well-established.

However, in places where governmental authority and civil society have broken down, respect for humanitarian law has often evaporated. These kinds of situations have posed formidable problems for humanitarian organizations.[23]

First, they have been obligated to protect their personnel and relief supplies. In many cases, relief organizations have tried to do this themselves, entering into negotiations with local leaders to obtain access to troubled areas and to obtain guarantees of safety for relief personnel. This

---

21. See Article 3, common to all four 1949 Geneva conventions, which concerns internal conflicts.

22. See note 14.

23. Within the UN Secretariat, the key actors are the Department for Humanitarian Affairs (DHA) and the Emergency Relief Coordinator. The other main organizations within the UN system are: the UN High Commissioner for Refugees (UNHCR); the United Nations Children's Fund (UNICEF); the World Food Program (WFP); and the UN Development Program (UNDP). An Inter-Agency Standing Committee (IASC), composed of the heads of the humanitarian agencies, including the International Committee of the Red Cross (ICRC), addresses coordination issues.

has often meant negotiating with a number of mutually hostile groups. The situation on the ground in other cases has been so volatile that humanitarian operations had to be suspended. The Security Council has become involved in some cases, not because it believed in a right of humanitarian intervention, but because it believed that humanitarian problems posed threats to international peace and security.

However, in three instances in the early 1990s — Bosnia, Rwanda, and Somalia — the Council made the provision of humanitarian assistance the primary task of peacekeeping operations. It even authorized its peacekeeping forces to protect humanitarian relief convoys and populations in need with "all necessary means," including the use of military force. However, as events unfolded in all three countries, the United Nations failed to protect vulnerable populations and fulfill its humanitarian promises: its leading members lacked the will to address the root causes of the conflicts and to use force decisively; they simply treated the humanitarian symptoms of strife, and did so in a half-hearted manner. The UN's credibility consequently suffered. Equally important, the Security Council's impotence helped to undermine respect for the principles of humanitarian law. Its actions in these cases were not just ineffective, they were in important respects counterproductive.

Second, faced with increasing demands for humanitarian assistance and a growing range of operations, UN relief organizations have been forced to coordinate activities among themselves and between UN agencies and the many nongovernmental organizations (NGOs) present in the field.[24] A number of institutional reforms were implemented in the United Nations in the early 1990s with this in mind, including the establishment within the UN Secretariat of a Department of Humanitarian Affairs (DHA) and the appointment of an Emergency Relief Coordinator. Much more needs to be done, however. Decades of bureaucratic rivalry are not easily overcome, and a great deal of waste and incompetence remains endemic in many UN organizations.[25]

More generally, the humanitarian crises of the 1990s have revealed that several decades of development efforts have failed: as of 1994, over thirty million people were in need of humanitarian assistance of one form or another.[26] State structures, economic systems, and civil societies have

---

24. For more on the activities of NGOs in this context, see Thomas G. Weiss's chapter on nongovernmental organizations in this volume.

25. For a highly critical discussion of the United Nations, see Rosemary Righter, *Utopia Lost: the United Nations and World Order* (New York: Twentieth Century Fund, 1995).

26. See *Strengthening the Coordination of Emergency Assistance of the United Nations.*

collapsed or are in danger of collapsing in many parts of what we would like to think of as the developing world. These development problems have important implications for regional peace and security. Humanitarian assistance may treat some of the symptoms of these problems, but reformulated development efforts that will address the structural roots of instability and conflict more effectively are needed.

FACT-FINDING

Launching a fact-finding mission is often a first step that the United Nations takes to help prevent, manage, or resolve conflicts. The idea is to provide a detailed, impartial report on the issues in dispute.[27]

Fact-finding missions come in many forms. Some come at the initiative of the state or states in question. Others come at the initiative of the Security Council, the General Assembly, or the Secretary-General. Any of these UN actors can conduct a fact-finding mission, but all fact-finding missions to the territory of a state require an invitation from or the consent of the state or states that are being examined. Some missions consist of a single person; others are larger undertakings.

The mandates of fact-finding missions also vary. Some try to determine the causes of a conflict, while others examine the role of neighboring powers in a conflict. Many investigate human rights abuses. Some fact-finding missions are launched before violence breaks out, and are therefore conflict prevention efforts. Others are launched during conflicts, and can be seen as conflict management or conflict resolution measures.

Fact-finding missions with respect to internal conflicts have become much more common since the end of the Cold War. Their mandates have ranged from general assessments of conflict situations (e.g., Tajikistan and Uzbekistan), to investigations of reports of ethnic cleansing (e.g., Georgia) and genocide (e.g., Rwanda). Fact-finding missions frequently lead to other UN initiatives, such as good offices missions, mediation efforts by the Secretary-General or other authorized officials, peacekeeping operations of various kinds, and the employment of coercive instruments, including arms embargoes, economic sanctions, judicial actions, and the use of military force.

However, assessing the impact of fact-finding missions is very difficult. Many of these missions are carried out under conditions of confidentiality, and their findings are not always publicized. Fact-finding missions carried out before violence breaks out have considerable potential

27. See General Assembly Resolution 46/59, *Declaration on Fact-Finding by the United Nations in the Field of the Maintenance of International Peace and Security*, December 9, 1991.

as conflict prevention measures. The role of the Secretary-General in this context should not be underestimated. Similarly, fact-finding missions carried out after a conflict has broken out can be useful in gathering information for subsequent conflict management and conflict resolution efforts.

Although there has been a great deal of discussion about strengthening the UN's fact-finding missions, including early warning capabilities, efforts to move in this direction have faced three main obstacles.

First, although member states have publicly urged the Secretary-General to do more in the areas of fact-finding and preventive diplomacy, they have serious reservations about his acquisition of more influence — especially with respect to security issues.[28] Investing the UN Secretariat with independent means of information-gathering would greatly strengthen the position of the Secretary-General, and have therefore been resisted. For example, attempts by the Secretary-General to transform the close to 130 UN Information Centers around the world into UN embassies that could provide the Secretariat with independent sources of information were opposed by member states. It was said that this would infringe on the sovereignty of states and constitute meddling in the domestic affairs of states. The Secretary-General's proposals were ultimately shelved. Peacekeeping operations, however, cannot be conducted without intelligence-gathering and early warning capabilities. Although member states often provide intelligence to the United Nations, this is not the same thing as having independent intelligence assets. The United Nations remains, and will probably continue to remain, handicapped in this regard.

Second, the UN's financial crisis has impinged on the Secretary-General's ability to develop fact-finding and early warning capabilities. Appropriately trained staff are in short supply. Hardware, including computers and communications equipment, is inadequate. Even low-cost ventures, such as sending a special envoy or a small fact-finding team to a troubled area, are frequently curtailed because of budgetary constraints. In January 1995, the Secretary-General proposed establishing a small $25 million preventive diplomacy account that he could draw on at his discretion.[29] Whether the General Assembly or the Security Council will follow up on this suggestion remains to be seen.

Third, UN efforts to develop more robust early warning capabilities are hampered by the nature of the UN system — a semi-feudal patchwork of bureaucracies and independent agencies over which the Secretary-

---

28.   See Boutros Boutros-Ghali, *Supplement to "An Agenda for Peace": Position Paper of the Secretary-General on the Occasion of the Fiftieth Anniversary of the United Nations,* A/50/60 or S/1995/1, January 3, 1995.

29.   See ibid.

General has limited control. Coordination within the Secretariat, between UN headquarters and field operations, and among agencies is undercut by bureaucratic rivalry and competition. Many UN programs and agencies are funded by voluntary contributions from member states and have independent, intergovernmental governing boards: they are fiefdoms unto themselves. The Secretary-General's efforts since 1993 to strengthen the coordinating role of the Department of Political Affairs are steps in the right direction but much more needs to be done. A truly interdepartmental, interagency approach is required.

TRADITIONAL PEACEKEEPING

As noted earlier, peacekeeping operations were not provided for in the UN Charter. They were developed during the Cold War to control conflicts between states. The main concern was that regional conflicts might draw in the great powers and lead to a superpower confrontation.

A traditional peacekeeping force is a military force positioned between two or more disputants. It is deployed with the consent of the relevant local parties, and its main mission is to monitor an agreed-upon cease-fire. In such an operation, peacekeepers are authorized to use force in self-defense and to deter small-scale attacks, but they do not have any significant coercive capabilities or enforcement authority. Traditional peacekeeping operations are normally accompanied by diplomatic efforts to resolve the underlying political conflict, and they are usually authorized by the Security Council.[30]

As far as internal conflicts are concerned, traditional peacekeeping operations can help bolster peace processes in a number of ways. First, they can monitor the cantonment and separation of warring factions. The UN peacekeeping missions in Cyprus (UNFCYP), Georgia (UNOMIG), and the initial deployment of the United Nations Protection Force (UNPROFOR) in the former Yugoslavia are examples. Second, peacekeeping forces can monitor and verify the withdrawal of foreign troops from a conflict zone. Examples include the UN operations in the Congo (ONUC), which oversaw the withdrawal of Belgian troops from the region; Angola (UNAVEM I), which oversaw the withdrawal of Cuban troops; and Afghanistan (UNGOMAP), which oversaw the withdrawal of Russian troops. Third, peacekeeping forces can monitor the cessation of aid to irregular forces and insurrectionist movements. Examples include the UN missions in Lebanon (UNOGIL) and Yemen (UNYOM). Fourth, peacekeeping forces can help ensure that the territory of one state is not

---

30. See note 16.

used for attacks on others. Cases where UN forces sought to do this include Yemen (UNYOM), Lebanon (UNIFIL), Central America (ONUCA), and Tajikistan (UNMOT). Fifth, peacekeeping forces can help discourage one state or party from attacking another. The preventive deployment of UN troops in Macedonia (UNPREDEP) was designed with this in mind.[31]

During the Cold War, traditional peacekeeping operations were deployed in four internal conflict situations: the Congo, Cyprus, Lebanon, and Yemen. These operations were successful from the standpoint of preventing a superpower confrontation from developing. However, they failed to keep hostilities from breaking out again locally. One could therefore say that these operations were fairly successful as conflict control measures, but not as conflict resolution efforts, which they were never intended to be.

Since the end of the Cold War, the need to avoid confrontations between Washington and Moscow has of course diminished. However, traditional peacekeeping operations remain useful instruments for the prevention, containment, and resolution of conflicts, including internal conflicts. They have the greatest promise in cases where the P-5 have interests (but not antagonistic interests), and in cases where the political conditions for resolving the conflict in question or deploying multifunctional peacekeeping personnel do not exist. Traditional peacekeeping forces have played useful roles in dampening the post–Cold War conflicts in Angola, Central America, and Tajikistan, for example.

One should keep in mind, however, that peacekeeping forces are deployed because two failures have already taken place.[32] First, diplomatic efforts to keep a conflict from actually breaking out have failed. Second, the Security Council has failed to carry out its responsibilities effectively. Indeed, traditional peacekeeping forces have often been de-

31. For details on peacekeeping operations, see the relevant Security Council documents as well as reference papers published by the UN Department of Public Information. See also: United Nations, *The Blue Helmets: A Review of United Nations Peace-keeping*, 2nd. ed. (New York: United Nations, 1990); United Nations Institute for Disarmament Research (UNIDIR), "Peace-keeping, Peace-making, Peace Enforcement," *UNIDIR Newsletter*, No. 24 (December 1993); Mats R. Berdal, *Whither UN Peacekeeping?* Adelphi Paper No. 281 (London: International Institute for Strategic Studies [IISS], 1993); Lori Fisler Damrosch, ed., *Enforcing Restraint: Collective Intervention in Internal Conflicts* (New York: Council on Foreign Relations, 1993); Donald C.F. Daniel and Bradd C. Hayes, eds., *Beyond Traditional Peacekeeping* (New York: St. Martin's, 1995); William J. Durch, ed., *The Evolution of UN Peacekeeping: Case Studies and Comparative Analysis* (New York: St. Martin's, 1993).

32. See Serge Sur, "The Jack of All Trades of International Security," *UNIDIR Newsletter*, No. 24 (December 1993), pp. 3–4.

ployed in places where more powerful military forces with coercive, Chapter VII mandates were needed. The UN deployment in the former Yugoslavia, for example, has experienced many problems for this reason. Traditional peacekeeping forces, in short, are often deployed under challenging circumstances. This should be taken into account when one assesses their track record.

MULTIFUNCTIONAL PEACEKEEPING

Multifunctional peacekeeping operations were developed by the United Nations to address the complex problems posed by intra-state and regional conflicts and to take advantage of the political opportunities that emerged after the end of the Cold War. With the end of the U.S.-Soviet competition for global influence, Moscow and Washington disengaged from regional conflicts in various parts of the world. Reduced levels of superpower patronage made peace settlements more likely in Central America, sub-Saharan Africa, and Southeast Asia, for example. Although peace settlements had become more likely, they still faced formidable obstacles. Years of civil war had made combatants deeply mistrustful of one another, and many countries needed to be completely reconstructed politically and economically. The United Nations was uniquely well-suited to play the role of impartial monitor and facilitator of reconstruction and rehabilitation efforts.

Traditional peacekeeping operations and multifunctional peacekeeping operations are similar in that they both depend on the full consent of the local parties, the use of force is basically limited to self-defense, and they have limited coercive or enforcement capabilities. However, they differ in three important respects.

First, traditional peacekeeping forces can be deployed once a cease-fire is reached, but multifunctional peacekeeping operations can only be launched after a comprehensive peace agreement has been reached. Multifunctional operations are strictly post-conflict undertakings.

Second, traditional peacekeeping operations concentrate mainly on military problems — monitoring cease-fires and keeping combatants separated, for example — whereas multifunctional peacekeeping operations seek to address a wide range of military, political, and economic problems. Multifunctional operations often include a traditional peacekeeping element, but they also help to demobilize armed forces and collect weapons; monitor the provisions of political settlements; design and supervise constitutional, judicial, and political reforms; organize and monitor elections; train local police; monitor potential human rights problems; and help to promote economic recovery and economic development.

Third, traditional peacekeeping operations are military undertakings that involve few civilians, whereas multifunctional peacekeeping operations involve a wide range of military and civilian personnel. In some multifunctional operations, separate organizational elements are set up for electoral, human rights, and humanitarian issues, for example. Most multifunctional operations have large numbers of people involved in the maintenance of law and order, and the training of local police forces.

Two main problems have plagued multifunctional peacekeeping operations. First, the scope and complexity of these operations have left ample room for organizational and administrative mishaps: inadequate planning; incompetent and poorly trained personnel; equipment shortages; ineffective communications between the field and UN headquarters; and insufficient financial resources. The lines of command between the UN Secretariat and specialized humanitarian and development agencies have not always been clear, and interagency coordination has often been flawed.

Second, in some cases, local parties have not been serious about implementing political settlements and making peace: they have used peace agreements as tactical devices that enable them to rest, recuperate, reorganize, and then re-launch military offensives. Multifunctional peacekeeping operations work only when the local parties genuinely seek peace and enter into agreements in good faith. Under these circumstances, the United Nations can help the former combatants overcome their mutual mistrust, monitor the implementation of the agreement, and help reconstruct political and economic institutions. Its function is to serve as an impartial observer, facilitator, and tripwire. If non-compliant behavior is observed, the United Nations can blow the whistle, thereby alerting all concerned that violations of the agreement have taken place. However, except for unintentional and minor breaches of the peace that can be dealt with by the military or police elements of the peacekeeping force, multifunctional operations have limited coercive or enforcement capacities: they cannot force the parties to live up to the terms of the agreement. Multifunctional peacekeeping operations are not trusteeships.

It follows, therefore, that the United Nations needs to be extremely careful to ensure that local parties are acting in good faith and that they are serious about making peace before launching multifunctional operations. Otherwise, the United Nations might find itself drawn into open hostilities. Its authority, credibility, and effectiveness will be greatly undermined as a result.

When faced with violations of the Paris Accords in Cambodia, the temptation to use force to induce parties into compliance or to punish them for non-compliance was avoided. When the Khmer Rouge refused to allow its troops to be cantoned and disarmed, UN peacekeepers treated this as a fact of life — a problem that had to be worked around. Some critics have called UN behavior in Cambodia spineless, and advocated a more forceful response to non-compliant actions.[33] In the Cambodian case, however, this would have required a change in UNTAC's mandate, which UN member states were not willing to make.

The UN peacekeeping operation in Angola has been criticized on similar grounds. Some have said that the United Nations should have taken steps to punish Jonas Savimbi when he re-initiated hostilities after the September 1992 electoral triumph of his opponents. However, it is not at all clear what the United Nations could have done above and beyond what it subsequently did: the Security Council imposed an arms and oil embargo on Savimbi and his União Nacional para a Independência Total de Angola (UNITA) cohorts in October 1993; the number of UN military observers in Angola was reduced, and restored only after new assurances were received from Savimbi that UNITA would comply with the terms of the brokered agreement.[34]

This shows the importance of securing a viable peace agreement in the first place. Once the framework of a political settlement has been concluded, a number of steps can be taken to minimize compliance problems. If the United Nations is to assist in implementing the agreement, it should help draft the implementation provisions of the accord. Its technical expertise and experience may enable it to devise creative and effective verification protocols, involving, for example, reporting, inspection, and consultation mechanisms. Verification and monitoring tasks should not be left entirely to the United Nations, however. Indeed, it would be very useful to involve former belligerents in verification and monitoring activities. Providing them with independent verification capabilities would be worthwhile. In sum, anticipating implementation problems is one of the keys to successful multifunctional peacekeeping operations.

ECONOMIC SANCTIONS AND ARMS EMBARGOES

The adoption of mandatory economic sanctions and arms embargoes under Chapter VII of the UN Charter has increased dramatically since the

---

33. For accounts and rebuttals of these criticisms, see Trevor Findlay, *Cambodia: The Legacy and Lessons of UNTAC* (Oxford: Oxford University Press, 1995), pp. 128–133.

34. For more details on the UN's operation in Angola, see Stephen John Stedman, "UN Intervention in Civil Wars: Imperatives of Choice and Strategy," in Daniel and Hayes, *Beyond Traditional Peacekeeping*, pp. 57–58.

end of the Cold War.[35] During the Cold War, the United Nations imposed mandatory sanctions only twice: against Rhodesia in 1966 and against South Africa in 1977.[36] Since 1990, mandatory Chapter VII sanctions and embargoes have been imposed eight times, six in the context of internal conflicts: in the former Yugoslavia in 1991 and 1992; in Somalia in 1992; in Liberia in 1992; in Angola in 1993; in Haiti in 1993 and 1994; and in Rwanda in 1994.[37]

The increased utilization of Chapter VII measures is a reflection of several broad developments: the end of Cold War antagonisms between Washington and Moscow; the revitalization of the UN Security Council; and the Security Council's willingness to address threats to international peace and security in a more resolute and forceful manner. However, it is also a reflection of the particular problems posed by internal conflicts. Many policymakers hope that arms embargoes will reduce weapon flows and the horrific levels of violence often found in civil wars. In addition, arms embargoes and economic sanctions are seen as vehicles for exerting influence over belligerents when one does not want to send one's own troops into the fray.

Arms embargoes and economic sanctions are most likely to be effective under two sets of circumstances. First, when a government has been taken over by a clearly illegitimate group, it will be comparatively easy to build an international consensus around the idea of imposing mandatory sanctions on the junta in question. This was the case, for example, in Haiti. Second, when a neighboring state is actively and opening meddling in the affairs of another and exacerbating a conflict, it will be comparatively easy to build an international coalition against the offending party (because it is violating the non-interference principle) and it will be comparatively easy to target the offending party (because it is a state, as opposed to a faction or some other poorly defined entity). This was the case, for example, with respect to Serb intervention in Bosnia.

However, the use of these instruments is likely to be problematic with respect to internal conflicts for a number of reasons. First, arms embargoes will often have a limited effect on the level of violence in civil wars because these wars are usually fought with small arms and light weapons

---

35. For more on arms embargoes and economic sanctions, see Joanna Spear's chapter on arms limitations and confidence-building measures and Elizabeth Rogers's chapter on economic sanctions, both in this volume.

36. See UN Security Council Resolution 232 (1966) of December 16, 1966 and Resolution 418 (1977) of November 4, 1977.

37. For more details, see the annex to this chapter.

— mortars, machine guns, rifles, machetes, and the like. The international trade in light weapons such as these is extremely difficult to regulate, especially since much of this trade is conducted on the black market.[38]

Second, economic sanctions can hurt innocent people or countries that have important trading relationships with the target state. This problem was foreseen by the drafters of the UN Charter: Article 50 gives states the right to consult with the Security Council if they will suffer unduly from sanctions imposed on another country. The increase in Chapter VII sanctions makes this problem less of a theoretical one. Since most internal conflicts are taking place in the developing world and most sanctions are consequently being applied there, it follows that developing countries — countries that can ill afford additional economic burdens — will often have to pay these collateral costs.

The willingness of developing countries to comply with sanction regimes will depend to a great degree on steps the United Nations might take and mechanisms it might establish to reduce these costs. UN efforts to get the International Monetary Fund and the World Bank to address these problems have thus far not received a very enthusiastic response.[39] Hence, in January 1995, Secretary-General Boutros-Ghali proposed setting up a body that would assess the likely impact of sanctions on both the target country and other countries before sanctions are imposed; monitor implementation of economic sanctions; measure the effects of sanctions, which would enable the Security Council to fine-tune them and maximize their impact while minimizing collateral damage; ensure the delivery of humanitarian assistance to vulnerable groups; and explore ways of assisting states that suffer collateral damage and evaluating claims submitted by such states under Article 50 of the Charter.[40]

The Secretary-General's proposal deserves support. A more equitable system of burden-sharing needs to be devised: the P-5 and other industrialized countries can bear the collateral costs of economic sanctions more easily than developing countries. Looking at it purely from a pragmatic standpoint, something needs to be done if the great powers want to use economic sanctions on a more regular basis: developing countries will be unable or unwilling to bear collateral costs if burdens are not redistributed. Sanctions regimes will be more likely to fall apart under these circumstances.

Third and more generally, ensuring compliance with embargoes and

38. See Spear's chapter on arms limitations.

39. See Boutros-Ghali, *Supplement to "An Agenda for Peace."*

40. Ibid.

sanctions is difficult. Although the Security Council sets up sanctions committees to monitor the implementation of such measures and assess their effectiveness, it has to rely on reports from member states, which might not have the information needed and which might not be inclined to divulge all of their intelligence. The Security Council, moreover, has no real enforcement mechanism other than the use of military force, a blunt instrument that is likely to be used rarely and only in the case of egregious violations.

Finally, it needs to be emphasized that arms embargoes and economic sanctions will be most effective when they are embedded in a comprehensive political strategy for conflict prevention, conflict management, and conflict resolution. Their effectiveness will also be enhanced when the specter of the use of military force is present.

JUDICIAL ENFORCEMENT MEASURES

The idea of creating an international criminal court as an instrument for peace and security has been discussed by the General Assembly and the UN International Law Commission at regular intervals ever since 1946.[41] The possibility of establishing an international criminal court was also anticipated in the 1948 Genocide Convention. However, apart from the Nuremberg and Tokyo tribunals, no international body has been set up to try crimes under international law.

The failure to establish an international criminal tribunal may be attributed to both Cold War politics and the profound aversion of states to allow a foreign body to adjudicate with respect to acts committed on their territories, and to seeing their own nationals called before a jurisdiction other than their own. The end of the Cold War eliminated one of these obstacles; however, it was the genocidal slaughter in the former Yugoslavia and in Rwanda that gave new impetus to the idea of establishing an international criminal court.

The Security Council's frustrations with respect to the former Yugoslavia and Rwanda led it to create an *ad hoc* international criminal tribunal for the former in 1993 and for the latter in 1994.[42] By establishing these tribunals as enforcement measures under Chapter VII of the UN Charter — an unprecedented development — the Security Council sidestepped the problems associated with creating a permanent international criminal

---

41. See the report of the International Law Commission, UN General Assembly document, A/49/10, July 1994.

42. The Yugoslav tribunal was created by UN Security Council Resolution 808 (1993) of February 22, 1993; its statute was adopted by UN Security Council Resolution 827 (1993) of May 25, 1993. See Report of the Secretary-General, S/25704, May 3, 1993. Its

court through a treaty. It was able to move quickly, and it didn't need the consent of the relevant states and parties: Chapter VII resolutions are binding on all member states.[43]

The tribunals have three main tasks: to prosecute and try persons responsible for serious violations of international humanitarian law; to deter further crimes; and to contribute to the restoration and maintenance of peace. The Yugoslav tribunal was authorized to adjudicate: (1) grave breaches of the 1949 Geneva Conventions, such as willfully killing or causing great injury to wounded soldiers, prisoners of war, or civilians; torture; unlawful deportation; or taking civilians hostage; (2) violations of the laws or customs of war, such as wanton destruction of cities or villages; attacks on undefended civilian populations; and destruction of institutions dedicated to religion, charity, or education; (3) genocide, defined as crimes committed with the intent of destroying in whole or in part a national, ethnic, racial, or religious group; (4) crimes against humanity, defined as inhumane acts such as murder, torture, or rape, committed as part of a widespread or systematic attack against any civilian population on national, political, ethnic, racial, or religious grounds. The Rwandan Tribunal was authorized to adjudicate serious violations of humanitarian law in the latter two of these areas as well as violations of Article 3 of the Geneva Conventions, which pertains to intra-state armed conflicts. Violations of this article include attacks on persons who take no active part in hostilities, including acts such as murder, torture, the imposition of collective punishments, the taking of hostages, acts of terrorism, rape, enforced prostitution, and pillaging.[44]

The tribunals are subsidiary organs of the Security Council. The initial task of investigating allegations of offenses and obtaining evidence falls on a prosecutor, who is nominated by the Secretary-General and appointed by the Security Council. Judges are elected by the General Assembly from a list submitted by the Security Council. The international tribunals do not monopolize criminal jurisdiction on these issues, mean-

---

seat is in the Hague, the Netherlands, and it is authorized to investigate crimes committed since January 1991. The Rwandan tribunal was created by UN Security Council Resolution 955 (1994) of November 8, 1994; its statute can be found in an annex to this resolution. The Rwandan tribunal is based in Arusha, Tanzania, and it is authorized to investigate crimes committed between January and December 1994.

43. This was particularly important in the case of the former Yugoslavia; Serbia's rejection of the tribunal's jurisdiction is therefore null and void from a legal standpoint. The new Tutsi-run Rwandan government had asked the Security Council to establish a tribunal with respect to crimes committed in Rwanda in 1994.

44. See the statutes of the tribunals cited in note 42.

ing that national courts can also adjudicate with respect to war crimes and crimes against humanity. However, the international tribunals may intervene if they determine that national courts are shielding criminals from investigation and prosecution.

The establishment of these tribunals has been met with a fair amount of skepticism. The capacities of the tribunals to bring to justice those who violated humanitarian law in the former Yugoslavia and Rwanda are limited. Although Chapter VII resolutions are legally binding on all member states of the United Nations, this does not necessarily mean that cooperation will be forthcoming. Indeed, much will depend on the extent to which authorities in the former Yugoslavia and the neighboring states of Rwanda are willing to provide evidence to international investigators and hand over indicted persons. Providing these tribunals with the necessary financial resources is also essential. The fitful interest and ambivalent support of the main advocates of the tribunal, namely France and the United States, is not very reassuring in this respect. Another major problem is that the legal requirement to bring war criminals to justice is in conflict with the political requirement to bring conflict to an end: leaders in the former Yugoslavia will be unwilling to agree to peace settlements if legal indictments are sure to follow.

In this connection, the fact that the tribunals are prohibited from conducting trials *in absentia* is deplorable. Upholding the principles of humanitarian law and justice is more important than political expediency because of the magnitude of the atrocities in these cases.[45]

Although these tribunals clearly face problems, they may nonetheless play important roles in promoting reconciliation in war-torn countries. By attributing war crimes to specific individuals rather than blaming entire groups, they may make it easier for people to end hostilities and rebuild civil societies. The establishment of these tribunals, as imperfect as they may be in bringing to justice those responsible for war crimes, should also be hailed as important precedents in the defense of humanitarian law and human rights. They are small but important steps in the right direction. The stakes are high, and not just for the former Yugoslavia and Rwanda.

USE OF MILITARY FORCE

The ultimate enforcement instrument at the disposal of the United Nations is the use of military force under Chapter VII of the UN Charter.

---

45. A compelling case in favor of *in absentia* trials is made by Ruth Wedgwood, "War Crimes in the Former Yugoslavia: Comments on the International War Crimes Tribunal," *Virginia Journal of International Law*, Vol. 34, No. 2 (Winter 1994), pp. 267–275.

In the first half of the 1990s, the Security Council authorized the use of force with respect to several internal conflicts: Bosnia, Haiti, Rwanda, and Somalia.[46]

Three conditions must be met if the Security Council is to use military force effectively under Chapter VII of the Charter. First, none of the five permanent members of the Council can oppose the use of force: any one of the five can veto a Security Council resolution authorizing military action. It is extremely important, moreover, for most of the P-5, and particularly the United States, to actively support the military action in question. Unfortunately, this has rarely happened: China and Russia have been bystanders in Bosnia, Haiti, Rwanda, and Somalia; France, the United Kingdom, and the United States have lacked determination or consensus in Bosnia, Rwanda, and Somalia. Different interests and differences of opinion have not been washed away by the end of the Cold War. These differences have undercut and will continue to undercut the UN's ability to use force effectively. Developing a consensus among the P-5 is not a given, and will have to be done on a case-by-case basis.

Second, if military force is to be used effectively, the Security Council must identify and enunciate clear and consistent political objectives. This was done in Haiti; Operation Restore Democracy has consequently been a success. This was not done in Bosnia, Rwanda, and Somalia, where UN missions have been markedly less successful. The Security Council authorized Operation Turquoise in Rwanda, which was led by France, and Operation Restore Hope in Somalia, led by the United States. Although these operations were successful in terms of establishing a secure environment for the delivery of humanitarian relief, they did not address the political roots of the conflicts that created the humanitarian crises. Nor did they provide a long-term presence. Chaos returned when UN forces withdrew.

The case of Somalia is especially instructive in this context. In 1992, Somalia began to disintegrate. Civil war, drought, and famine began to claim hundreds of thousands of lives. The United Nations estimated that out of a total population of 8 million, 4.5 million people were at risk, including 1 million children. Efforts by the United Nations to help the parties negotiate a cease-fire and reconcile were unsuccessful. The level of violence in the country made the delivery of humanitarian assistance virtually impossible. UN Secretary-General Boutros-Ghali harangued the West, which was preoccupied with Bosnia, for ignoring the Horn of Africa. Finally, in December 1992, U.S. President George Bush offered to

---

46. For more details, see the annex to this chapter.

send a U.S.-led force to Somalia to create a secure environment for the delivery of humanitarian relief.

Problems regarding the purpose of the mission rapidly surfaced. The United States saw the operation in Somalia as a short-term proposition with limited, humanitarian objectives. Boutros-Ghali saw it as the beginning of a long-term undertaking with much more ambitious political objectives: he wanted the international force to disarm the warring factions in Somalia and lay the groundwork for rebuilding the country. This difference of opinion became a real problem in May 1993 when the United States handed over command of the force to the United Nations; the United States withdrew some of its military forces from Somalia at that point.[47] Once the United Nations assumed command, Boutros-Ghali's vision of the mission took over and its political objectives became more ambitious. However, this took place at the precise moment when military capabilities were diminishing. The result was a mismatch between growing objectives and shrinking capabilities. Disaster after disaster followed on the ground. The United States withdrew the last of its troops from Somalia in March 1994, and the UN operation was shut down in March 1995.

The case of the UNPROFOR operation in the former Yugoslavia is more complex, but it reinforces the same point: having a clear and consistent political objective is a prerequisite to the effective use of military force. Initially, UNPROFOR was a traditional peacekeeping operation. It was deployed in Croatia in February 1992 with the aim of containing the conflict that arose from the disintegration of the former Yugoslav Republic. War broke out in Bosnia the following month, but Secretary-General Boutros-Ghali concluded that the main condition for deployment of a UN peacekeeping force — obtaining the consent of all the relevant parties — was not met in Bosnia.[48] The situation in Bosnia rapidly deteriorated, and it was clear that Serbia was providing assistance to Bosnian Serbs engaged in ethnic cleansing and in attacks on Sarajevo and other cities, towns, and villages. Seeing this as a form of aggression on another state, the Security Council subsequently decided to impose wide-ranging economic sanctions on Serbia. The situation in Bosnia nonetheless continued to deteriorate. In August 1992, the Security Council invoked Chapter VII of the UN Charter, and authorized UNPROFOR to use force in Bosnia.[49] UNPROFOR's mandate, though, was not to restore the peace, but to protect

---

47. In terms of nomenclature, UNITAF became UNOSOM II at this point.

48. See UN Security Council document S/23900, May 12, 1992.

49. See UN Security Council Resolution 770 (1992) of August 13, 1992.

humanitarian convoys against attack.[50] The UN's position became more complicated in April and May 1993, when the Security Council designated "safe areas" in Bosnia and authorized the use of North Atlantic Treaty Organization (NATO) air power to deter attacks against these areas.[51] Boutros-Ghali and others worried that using NATO air power to suppress Bosnian Serb air defenses would be seen as a hostile act that would take UNPROFOR beyond the limits of a peacekeeping operation and make it a party to the conflict.[52] Attacks of this kind eventually took place, and UNPROFOR's position became increasingly murky and difficult as time went by. At various points in the conflict, Bosnian Serbs took UN peacekeepers hostage to deter further NATO action.

The third condition that has to be met if the United Nations is to use force effectively under Chapter VII of the Charter is that sufficient military forces have to be made available to the Security Council. The fact that the Council lacks military forces it can call upon, as provided for in Article 43 of the Charter, severely limits its ability to act. Although this does not preclude action, it makes UN operations totally dependent on the willingness of states, especially the P-5, to make troops available at a particular point in time. The United States is key: it alone has the firepower, transport, command and control, communications, intelligence, logistics, and power projection capabilities needed for large-scale operations.

Decisions to contribute troops to UN operations will inevitably be based on idiosyncratic calculations about costs, benefits, and risks, and will be heavily influenced by domestic politics. An important consideration for many states will be the nature of the command and control arrangements for the operation in question. Many countries, particularly the United States, will insist on retaining operational command over their own troops, especially whenever combat is likely. France, for example, retained command over French troops involved in Operation Turquoise in Rwanda; the United States did the same with respect to U.S. troops

---

50. Boutros-Ghali has gone to great lengths to emphasize the "non-enforcement" character of UN troops on the ground in Bosnia. The only enforcement action in Bosnia was undertaken by NATO aircraft in connection with the no-fly zone. See Boutros-Ghali's report, S/1995/444, May 30, 1995; UN Security Council Resolution 816 (1993) of March 31, 1993.

51. See UN Security Council Resolution 819 (1993) of April 16, 1993 and Resolution 824 (1993) of May 6, 1993, which designated Bihac, Gorazde, Srebrenica, Tuzla, and Zepa as safe areas. Resolution 836 (1993) of June 4, 1993, authorized UN ground troops to use force in self-defense and NATO to use airpower in support of UNPROFOR.

52. See Boutros-Ghali's report, S/1995/444, May 30, 1995.

involved in Operation Restore Democracy in Haiti. The UN bureaucracy has begun to accept this as a fact of life.[53]

What many people think of as "UN enforcement actions" and "UN military operations" have been and will continue to be actions authorized by the UN Security Council but carried out by individual states or groups of states. Whether or not these kinds of operations will be launched, therefore, will depend to a significant degree on the extent to which state interests are engaged by particular problems. In many trouble spots, the interests of distant powers will not be engaged, and the prospects for UN-authorized military action will be extremely slim. One can argue, however, that because the P-5 have a special status within the United Nations and a special responsibility for maintaining international peace and security, they have a special obligation in this area.

The Prospects for UN Action

A large number of internal conflicts have taken place since the end of the Cold War.[54] The United Nations has taken action in some cases, but not others. Its actions have been successful in preventing, containing, and resolving conflicts in some cases, but not in others. What explains these patterns? More specifically, under what conditions is the UN Security Council likely to take action with respect to an internal conflict? Under what conditions is UN Security Council action likely to be successful in preventing, containing, or resolving a conflict? It is to these questions that we now turn.[55]

Two main factors influence the course and content of UN actions with respect to internal conflicts: the extent to which the interests of one or more members of the P-5 are engaged; and the extent to which the conflict in question poses a threat to international peace and security.

The interests of a member of the P-5 are likely to be engaged if an internal conflict takes place on or near the territory of a P-5 member; takes place in a region of strategic or economic importance to a P-5 member; threatens or involves a formal ally of a P-5 member; or threatens or involves a party to whom a P-5 member has close historical, ideological, or political ties.

An internal conflict is more likely to be seen as posing "a threat to

---

53. Ibid.

54. For an overview of active conflicts, see Table 1 in Michael Brown's introductory chapter to this volume.

55. The focus will be on major UN actions, defined as UN Security Council actions.

international peace and security" — a key phrase in the UN Charter — if it involves neighboring states in one way or another. Internal conflicts can involve neighboring states in a variety of ways. They can send large numbers of refugees streaming into neighboring states. The territory of neighboring states can be used as bases or sanctuaries for rebel groups, or for the shipment of arms, supplies, and money to rebel groups; cross-border military operations and interdiction campaigns often result. In addition, neighboring states can become involved in internal conflicts in more direct ways: they can intervene for legitimate national security reasons; they can intervene to protect ethnic brethren; and they can support insurrectionists or intervene militarily for purely opportunistic reasons.[56] An internal conflict can also pose a threat to regional peace and security if it threatens to lead to violence elsewhere in the region. In short, an internal conflict is more likely to be seen as posing a threat to international peace and security if it is not contained within the territory of the state from whence it sprang, i.e., if it has become a regional security problem. A conflict is less likely to be seen as a threat to international peace and security if it is contained within the territory of a single state, i.e., if it remains an internal as opposed to a regional problem. As we have seen in many parts of the world, internal conflicts often become regional problems.[57]

In addition, an internal conflict can be seen as posing a threat to international peace and security if it engages the interests of more distant powers. Internal conflicts can have international ramifications if they threaten access to strategic resources such as oil, if they take place in a strategically significant part of the world, or if they engage alliance commitments, for example. Finally, an internal conflict can be seen as a threat to international peace and security if it involves serious violations of international humanitarian law.[58]

THE LIKELIHOOD OF UN ACTION

The likelihood that the United Nations will take action with respect to any given internal conflict is a function of two main factors: the extent to which the interests of one or more of the members of the P-5 are engaged

---

56. For a fuller discussion of the ways in which states can become involved in nearby internal conflicts, see Michael Brown's introductory and concluding chapters to this volume.

57. For more details, see chapters 1–8 in this volume.

58. For a fuller discussion of the international ramifications of internal conflicts, see Michael Brown's introductory and concluding chapters to this volume.

in the case in question; and the extent to which the conflict is believed by the P-5 to constitute a threat to international peace and security. A two-by-two matrix can help us visualize the four logical possibilities. (See Table 15.3.)

UN action is most likely (Box 1 in the matrix) if an internal conflict has become a regional security problem *and* P-5 interests are engaged. UN action is somewhat less likely (Box 2) if the conflict constitutes a regional security problem but does not engage P-5 interests. UN action is even less likely (Box 3) if the conflict is largely contained within the territory of a single state, even if it does engage P-5 interests. UN action is least likely — in fact, highly unlikely — (Box 4) if a conflict is contained within the territory of a single state and does not engage P-5 interests in any major way.

The "internal versus regional" question is key because of the way the UN Charter looks at internal affairs, on the one hand, and international peace and security problems, on the other. Article 2 (7) of the Charter prohibits the United Nations from intervening in matters which are "essentially within the jurisdiction" of a state, unless the Security Council determines that enforcement measures under Chapter VII need to be taken to maintain or restore international peace and security. Although the Security Council can define "threats to international peace and security" as it chooses, it will find it easier to categorize an internal conflict as an international problem if the conflict is not contained within the territory of a single state, if it involves neighboring states in one way or another, or if it has significant regional or international ramifications. For these reasons, the "internal versus regional" character of a conflict is key in determining the likelihood of UN action.

The interests of the P-5 are also important, however. Whether or not the Security Council takes action with respect to any given problem

Table 15.3. The Likelihood of UN Action.

P-5 Interests	Internal Conflict	
	Contained	Not Contained
Yes	3	1
No	4	2

depends to a very significant degree on one or more members of the P-5 taking the diplomatic lead and one or more of the P-5 bearing the costs of diplomatic, economic, or military action. If P-5 interests are engaged, diplomatic initiatives and Security Council action are more likely.

Two caveats have to be interjected at this point. First, it has to be stressed that these generalizations apply only to the post–Cold War era. During the Cold War, the P-5 rarely agreed on security issues, and the Security Council was consequently paralyzed. As far as the United Nations was concerned, inaction was the rule. The defining feature of the post–Cold War era is that international politics is no longer dominated by the East-West geostrategic competition. Although the members of the P-5 naturally have different national interests and different perspectives on security issues, cooperation is far more likely with respect to security problems in various parts of the world. As a result, the United Nations has been much more active in peace and security affairs: a new pattern of activity has emerged since the late 1980s.

Second, these generalizations do not automatically apply if the territory of a P-5 member is involved. The permanent members of the Security Council of course have a high level of "interest" in what happens on their own territories, but they also have vetoes over Security Council actions. This means that the United Nations cannot take action with respect to the internal conflicts in Chechnya, French Polynesia, Northern Ireland, and Tibet, for example, unless the relevant member of the P-5 wishes the United Nations to become involved. The same applies for the spheres of influence of P-5 members: the United Nations took action in Tajikistan and Haiti, for example, only because Russia and the United States, respectively, supported the idea.

We can test the validity of these propositions about the likelihood of UN action by examining recent real-world cases. More specifically, we can look at the internal conflicts that are currently taking place around the world, categorize them in terms of whether they are largely contained within the territory of a single state and the extent to which they engage P-5 interests, and note if the UN Security Council has taken action in each case. We can also examine recent and current UN missions for patterns of activity. These cases can then be plotted onto our two-by-two matrix, with the caveat that it is difficult to categorize complex events in simple binary terms. (See Table 15.4.)

As we can see, UN action is indeed most likely when an internal conflict has regional ramifications and when P-5 interests are engaged: since the end of the Cold War, UN Security Council actions have been or are being undertaken in eleven of sixteen cases that fit this description (Box 1). In the remaining five cases (Algeria, Azerbaijan, Colombia, Israel,

Table 15.4. Internal Conflict and UN Action.		
	Internal Conflict	
P-5 Interests	Contained	Not Contained
Yes	(3) *Haiti Moldova Russia/Chechnya United Kingdom/Northern Ireland	(1) *Afghanistan Algeria Azerbaijan *Bosnia *Cambodia Colombia *Croatia *Cyprus *El Salvador *Georgia *Iraq Israel *Lebanon *Nicaragua *Tajikistan Turkey
No	(4) Bangladesh Egypt Guatemala Indonesia/East Timor Iran Kenya Peru Philippines *Somalia	(2) *Angola Burma *Burundi India/Kashmir *Liberia *Mozambique *Namibia Pakistan *Rwanda Sierra Leone Sri Lanka Sudan *Western Sahara

SOURCES: Current internal conflicts are taken from Table 1 in Michael Brown's introductory chapter in this volume; UN actions are taken from the annex to this chapter.
* Major UN actions have been taken in these cases.

and Turkey), unilateral actions to help dampen conflict have been taken by at least one member of the P-5.

UN action is somewhat less likely when internal conflicts have regional dimensions but do not engage P-5 interests: UN actions have been or are being undertaken in seven of thirteen cases of this type (Box 2). In one other case, a UN peacekeeping mission (UNGOMIP) has been in place since 1949 to dampen Indian-Pakistani tensions over Kashmir. Low-level UN actions are being carried out by the Secretary-General or the General Assembly in most of the remaining cases.

UN action is even less likely when internal conflicts are largely contained within the territory of a single state, even if P-5 interests are engaged: in this sample, UN Security Council action was taken in only one of four cases (Box 3). Unilateral P-5 actions have been taken with respect to the other three (in Moldova, Russia/Chechnya, and the United Kingdom/Northern Ireland). In the one case where a UN Security Council operation was launched (Haiti), it had the full blessing of the P-5 member whose interests were engaged (the United States). And in this case, it should be noted, a refugee problem provided a "threat to international peace and security" pretext for UN action.

Finally, UN action is least likely, and indeed quite rare, when internal conflicts are largely contained within the territory of a single state and when they do not engage P-5 interests: in recent years, UN Security Council action has been undertaken in only one of nine cases (Box 4). The fact that a UN mission was sent to Somalia can be explained by the magnitude of the humanitarian crisis there and the intense media coverage of this humanitarian disaster. However, although humanitarian concerns and moral imperatives were enough to get a UN operation launched in this case, they were not enough to sustain it.

This leads us to a more systematic examination of the conditions under which UN operations are most likely to be successful.

THE PROBABILITY OF SUCCESS

The probability that the United Nations will take effective action with respect to an internal conflict is also a function of P-5 interests and the "internal versus regional" character of the conflict in question. Once again, a two-by-two matrix can help us visualize the possibilities. (See Table 15.5.)

UN actions are most likely to be successful (Box 1) if the conflict in question engages the interests of one or more members of the P-5 and if it is largely an intra-state matter. If the interests of the P-5 are engaged, UN operations are more likely to be led effectively and with determination; provided with the requisite diplomatic, financial, and military resources; and sustained over time. Internal conflicts are always difficult problems to solve, but they are more manageable if they are largely confined to the territory of a single state and if neighboring states are not deeply involved; internal conflicts are more difficult to contain and

Table 15.5. The Probability of Successful UN Action.		
	Internal Conflict	
P-5 Interests	Contained	Not Contained
Yes	1	2
No	3	4

resolve when third parties and additional sets of interests and objectives are part of the war and peace equation.

UN actions are less likely to be successful if P-5 interests are engaged but the conflict in question involves neighboring states (Box 2). The fact that P-5 interests are engaged means that determined UN action is possible, but regionalized conflicts are harder to resolve than contained conflicts. UN actions are even less likely to be successful if the conflict in question does not engage P-5 interests, even if it is largely an intra-state matter (Box 3). The problem might be comparatively manageable, but vigorous, sustained action is unlikely in the absence of a highly motivated P-5 state. Finally, UN actions are least likely to be successful when neither condition is met, i.e., when a conflict has become regional in character but nonetheless does not engage P-5 interests (Box 4).

We can test the validity of these propositions by examining recent and current UN Security Council actions, categorizing them according to the two variables that frame our analysis, and plotting them onto our two-by-two matrix. (See Table 15.6.)

Recent experience on the whole confirms our analytic expectations. The conflict in Haiti (Box 1) engaged U.S. interests because of its proximity and because it generated a refugee problem. Although these refugees gave the Haitian case a regional dimension, the conflict itself was confined almost entirely to Haiti. The UN operation to Haiti was successful in ousting the junta, restoring Jean-Bertrand Aristide to power, and laying the groundwork for elections and reconstitution of democratic processes and civil society. Progress has inevitably been uneven and much remains to be done, but the mission as a whole has been successful in accomplishing what it set out to do.

A number of cases engage P-5 interests but have become regional problems (Box 2). Some UN operations conducted under these conditions

Table 15.6. Outcomes of UN Actions.		
	Internal Conflict	
P-5 Interests	Contained	Not Contained
Yes	(1) Haiti (+)	(2) Afghanistan (0) Bosnia (0) Cambodia (+) Croatia (0) Cyprus (+) El Salvador (+) Georgia (+) Iraq (+) Lebanon (0) Nicaragua (+) Tajikistan (+)
No	(3) Somalia (–)	(4) Angola (0) Burundi (–) Liberia (–) Mozambique (+) Namibia (+) Rwanda (–) Western Sahara (0)

NOTE: (+) denotes success; (–) denotes failure; (0) denotes mixed outcome.

have nonetheless been successful. The UN mission in Cambodia has helped to stabilize and rebuild a ravaged country, and has marginalized the Khmer Rouge; China's new, constructive attitude toward the conflict in Cambodia has been key. The UN forces in Cyprus, Georgia, and Tajikistan have helped to keep adversaries apart and to maintain cease-fires. The UN guards in northern Iraq have shielded Kurds from Iraqi aggression and provided them with a measure of political autonomy; stringent UN Security Council constraints on the whole of Iraq and the continued engagement of U.S. military forces have been key in this case. The multifunctional UN operation in Central America has played a major role in bringing peace to El Salvador and Nicaragua; U.S. engagement has played a key role here as well.

Other UN operations that have operated under these conditions have had mixed outcomes. The UN peacekeeping force in Afghanistan success-fully oversaw the withdrawal of Soviet troops from the country, but limited UN efforts since then have been unsuccessful in bringing the civil war to an end. The UN force in Lebanon has had no success in bringing about the withdrawal of Israeli troops from southern Lebanon, restoring peace, or re-establishing Lebanese government authority over the country. However, it has contributed to stability in the region and been quite effective from a humanitarian point of view. UN forces in Bosnia and Croatia have helped with the delivery of humanitarian assistance, mainly in the former, but have been ineffective as conflict control and conflict resolution instruments: ethnic cleansing and genocidal slaughter have continued unabated. Progress was made in the peace process only when the most powerful presence on the Security Council, the United States, decided that important national interests were at stake and took the diplomatic lead.

The UN mission to Somalia was conducted under less auspicious circumstances: it was largely confined to Somalia itself, but it did not engage the interests of any member of the P-5 (Box 3). As noted earlier, the UN mission to Somalia was driven by humanitarian impulses. The fact that the war in Somalia did not have major implications for regional security and did not engage important P-5 interests explains why the UN mission there ultimately failed: the great powers lacked determination and a willingness to pay even moderate costs.

Finally, a number of UN operations have been conducted under most inauspicious conditions: when regional conflagrations have been met by P-5 disinterest (Box 4). Not surprisingly, many of these UN efforts have failed miserably — in Burundi, Liberia, and Rwanda. UN operations elsewhere in Africa — Angola, Mozambique, Namibia, and Western Sahara — have had better-than-expected success, but these are special cases. Namibia and Western Sahara have stabilized because regional powers have begun to play constructive roles. The conflicts in Angola and Mozambique were driven to a very great degree by the Cold War competition between the Soviet Union and the United States. Once the Cold War ended, the geostrategic fuel that fed these fires disappeared.[59] In fact, peace in Angola and Mozambique became possible because the superpowers *lost* interest in this part of the world.

If the foregoing analysis is correct, UN actions are most likely to take place when internal conflicts involve neighboring states and have become regional problems, but they are most likely to be successful when conflicts are bottled up. In other words, the UN Security Council is more likely to take action when problems are difficult, risks are high, and failure is

---

59. Political reforms in South Africa removed another source of external aggravation.

entirely possible; and predisposed to do nothing when the chances of success are greater.

Conclusions

Internal conflicts pose tremendous challenges to those charged with maintaining international peace and security. The United Nations has a range of suitable instruments available at its disposal, but it is important to remember that the United Nations itself is simply an instrument in the hands of its member states, particularly the P-5. When "the United Nations" fails to take action, it is really the P-5 that has failed. When a UN operation stumbles or falls flat, one should look first to the P-5 and other key member states to see if they have provided the leadership, determination, and resources needed to get the job done. In all too many cases, they have not. The United Nations has organizational weaknesses, to be sure, but one should not blame it for the failings of others.

Since the late 1980s, the United Nations has compiled a fairly successful track record in many respects. It has had notable successes in El Salvador, Haiti, Mozambique, Namibia, and Nicaragua, for example. Policymakers in national capitals would be wise to build on these successes. The United Nations can be an effective and cost-effective instrument. Whether or not national leaders will employ the United Nations more aggressively in the future remains to be seen. If they are inclined to do so, they should take several steps.

First, member states must resolve the UN's financial crisis. It will be impossible for the organization to take timely, effective action to deal with peace and security problems in the future if it is crippled by resource constraints.

Second, member states must devise a strategy for dealing with the humanitarian consequences of internal conflicts. In many cases, humanitarian relief cannot be delivered because of an insecure environment, and a secure environment cannot be created without the delivery of humanitarian assistance. This vicious circle has proved to be difficult to break. If international powers are serious about dealing with these problems and upholding international order, they will have to revisit the question of using military force in humanitarian crises. In an ideal world, the creation of a UN military force would circumscribe the difficulties the United Nations currently has in dealing with these kinds of crises. It is highly unlikely, however, that member states will agree to the creation of such a force.

Third, more attention should be devoted to helping countries rebuild law enforcement capabilities when police forces have collapsed or been corrupted. Dealing effectively with these law and order problems is one of the biggest challenges the United Nations faces in post-conflict settings.

Fourth and more broadly, a more holistic approach to development and security problems is needed: economic development and regional stability often go hand in hand, as do economic stagnation and collapse and political chaos. UN development efforts, which do not have a good track record, need to be reconceptualized. International development consortiums made up of traditional donor states, governmental and non-governmental development and humanitarian organizations, regional organizations, and international financial institutions need to develop "mini-Marshall Plans" to get sputtering or free-falling economies back on track. Stronger commitments need to be made to economic and social justice, human rights, and good governance. Peace and security are not just military problems.

Annex to Chapter 15: The United Nations and Internal Conflict, 1945–95

The tables in this annex indicate when and where UN instruments were used with respect to internal conflicts. One instrument, humanitarian assistance, is not included because it comes in many forms and is extended to a vast number of countries.

SOURCES: Reports of the Secretary-General on the Work of the Organization; *United Nations*, The Blue Helmets: A Review of United Nations Peace-keeping, *2nd. ed. (New York: United Nations, 1990); United Nations Institute for Disarmament Research (UNIDIR), "Peace-keeping, Peace-making, Peace Enforcement,"* UNIDIR Newsletter, *No. 24 (December 1993); William J. Durch, ed.,* The Evolution of UN Peacekeeping: Case Studies and Comparative Analysis *(New York: St. Martin's, 1993).*

The United Nations and Internal Conflict: Africa.

Country	Start of Current Hostilities[a]	Fact-finding[b]	Traditional Peacekeeping	Multifunctional Peacekeeping	Economic Sanctions; Arms Embargoes[c]	Use of Force[c]	Judicial Enforcement Measures[c]
Angola	1975, 1992		UNAVEM I 1989–91	UNAVEM II 1991–95 UNAVEM III 1995–present	UNSC Res. 864 (1993): Arms Embargo against UNITA		
Burundi	1972, 1993	Special Envoy: 1993, 1995. Missions: March–April 1994, August 1994, February 1995.					
Liberia	1989			UNOMIL[d] 1993–present	UNSC Res. 788 (1992): Arms Embargo		
Mali	1990	Mission: 1994					
Mozambique	1978			ONUMOZ 1992–94			
Namibia	1966[e]			UNTAG 1989–90[f]			
Rhodesia (now Zimbabwe)	1965[g]				UNSC Res. 232 (1966): Economic sanctions, Lifted in 1979		
Rwanda	1990	Mission: February 1995		UNAMIR 1993–present[h]	UNSC Res. 819 (1994): Arms Embargo, Lifted in 1995	UNSC Res. 929 (1994): Operation Turquoise, June–July 1994	UNSC Res. 955 (1994): International Tribunal

Sierra Leone	1991	Special Envoy: 1995			
Somalia	1990	Mission, Special Envoy: 1992	UNOSOM I 1992–93	UNSC Res. 733 (1992): Arms Embargo	UNSC Res. 794 (1992): UNITAF, December 1992–May 1993 UNSC Res. 814 (1993),[i] 837 (1993)[j]
			UNOSOM II 1993–95		
South Africa		Mission: 1992		UNSC Res. 418 (1977): Arms Embargo, Lifted in 1992	
Western Sahara	1976[k]	MINURSO 1991–present			
Zaire (formerly the Congo)		Special Envoy: 1993	ONUC 1960–64		UNSC Res. 161 (1961)[l]

[a] See Table 1 by Michael Brown in the introductory chapter of this volume.

[b] This column includes major fact-finding missions launched since 1991 by the Security Council, the General Assembly, and the Secretary-General, as well as major mediation and good offices efforts, including the dispatch by the UN Secretary-General of Special Envoys (Representatives). Special Envoys (Representatives) that are part of a traditional or multifunctional peacekeeping operation are not listed.

[c] This column lists the relevant UN Security Council Resolutions (UNSC Res.). Unless otherwise indicated, these resolutions made explicit reference to Chapter VII.

[d] This mission was carried out in cooperation with the Military Observer Group (ECOMOG) of the Economic Community of West African States (ECOWAS).

[e] In 1966, the UN General Assembly revoked South Africa's authority to administer the Territory of Namibia and declared it to be the direct responsibility of the United Nations. That same year SWAPO was recognized by the Assembly as the sole and authentic representative of the Namibian people.

[f] The settlement was signed in 1978. However, it took 11 years before the UN Transition Assistance Group could be deployed. Namibia became an independent state in March 1990.

[g] In November 1965, Rhodesia declared independence.

[h] A traditional peacekeeping operation was first deployed in Uganda in June 1993. UNOMUR was to observe the border between Uganda and Rwanda. The turn of events in Rwanda in 1994 would, however, prevent UNOMUR from fully implementing its mandate. The operation was terminated in September 1994.

[i] Resolution 814 authorized use of force in conjunction with disarmament efforts in Mogadishu.

[j] Resolution 837 reaffirmed Resolution 814 and authorized UNOSOM to apprehend criminal elements. Resolution 885 (1993) suspended the apprehension of criminal elements.

[k] This is the year in which Spain relinquished control over Western Sahara to Morocco and Mauritania, and when the Frente POLISARIO proclaimed the independent Saharan Arab Democratic Republic.

[l] Resolution 161 (1961), which authorized the use of force, did not explicitly refer to Chapter VII.

The United Nations and Internal Conflict: Asia.

Country	Start of Current Hostilities[a]	Fact-finding[b]	Traditional Peacekeeping	Multifunctional Peacekeeping	Economic Sanctions; Arms Embargoes	Use of Force	Judicial Enforcement Measures
Afghanistan	1978, 1992	Special Mission, Good Offices: 1994. OSGA: 1995[c]	UNGOMAP 1988–90				
Bougainville	1988	Special Envoy, Good Offices: 1994 and 1995					
Burma (Myanmar)	1948	Good Offices: 1994					
Cambodia	1975	UNMLT: 1993–94; Special Envoy: 1994		UNAMIC 1991–92; UNTAC 1992–93			
Indonesia (East Timor)	1975	Good Offices: 1994–present					

[a] See Table 1 by Michael Brown in the introductory chapter of this volume.

[b] This column includes major fact-finding missions launched since 1991 by the Security Council, the General Assembly, and the Secretary-General, as well as major mediation and good offices efforts, including the dispatch by the UN Secretary-General of Special Envoys (Representatives). Special Envoys (Representatives) that are part of a traditional or multifunctional peacekeeping operation are not listed.

[c] Office of the Secretary-General in Afghanistan.

The United Nations and Internal Conflict: The Middle East.

Country	Start of Current Hostilities[a]	Fact-finding[b]	Traditional Peacekeeping	Multifunctional Peacekeeping	Economic Sanctions; Arms Embargoes	Use of Force	Judicial Enforcement Measures
Iraq	1980		UN Guards Contingent 1991–present[c]				
Lebanon	1957		UNOGIL 1958 UNIFIL 1978–present				
Yemen	1962, 1994	Special Envoy: 1994	UNYOM 1963–64				

[a] See Table 1 by Michael Brown in the introductory chapter of this volume.

[b] This column includes major fact-finding missions launched since 1991 by the Security Council, the General Assembly, and the Secretary-General, as well as major mediation and good offices efforts, including the dispatch by the UN Secretary-General of Special Envoys (Representatives). Special Envoys (Representatives) that are part of a traditional or multifunctional peacekeeping operation are not listed.

[c] Strictly speaking, this is not a peacekeeping operation. Following Operation Provide Comfort (April 1991), the United Nations negotiated an agreement with Iraq to deploy a contingent of 500 police officers. See also Resolution 678 (1998) adopted under Chapter VII, which authorized Operation Desert Storm (January–April 1991). The conditions for the cease-fire were laid down in Resolutions 687 (1991) and 715 (1991). An arms embargo and economic sanctions were imposed by Resolution 661 (1990) and is still in force.

The United Nations and Internal Conflict: Europe.

Country	Start of Current Hostilities[a]	Fact-finding[b]	Traditional Peacekeeping	Multifunctional Peacekeeping	Economic Sanctions; Arms Embargoes[c]	Use of Force[c]	Judicial Enforcement Measures[c]
Cyprus	1963	Good Offices: 1994–present	UNFICYP 1964–present				
Georgia	1991	Mission: 1992–93	UNOMIG 1993–present				
Tajikistan	1992		UNMOT 1994–present				
Yugoslavia[d]	1991	Special Envoy: 1991	UNPROFOR 1992–95		UNSC Res. 713 (1991): Arms Embargo, Lifted in 1995		UNSC Res. 808 (1993); 827 (1993): International Tribunal[e]
Bosnia-Herzegovina	1992		UNPROFOR 1992–95		UNSC Res. 713 (1991): Arms Embargo, Lifted in 1995	UNSC Res. 770 (1992)[f] 816 (1993)[g] 836 (1993)[h] 958 (1994)[i]	UNSC Res. 808 (1993); 827 (1993): International Tribunal[e]
Croatia	1991		UNPROFOR 1992–95 UNCRO 1995–present		UNSC Res. 713 (1991): Arms Embargo, Lifted in 1995	UNSC Res. 958 (1994)[i]	UNSC Res. 808 (1993); 827 (1993): International Tribunal[e]
Macedonia	1991		UNPROFOR 1992–95 UNPREDEP 1995–present		UNSC Res. 713 (1991): Arms Embargo, Lifted in 1995		UNSC Res. 808 (1993); 827 (1993): International Tribunal[e]

Serbia and Montenegro	1991	UNSC Res. 713 (1991): Arms Embargo; 757 (1992): Economic Sanctions; 787 (1992): Expanded Sanctions; Embargo and Sanctions lifted in 1995	UNSC Res. 808 (1993); 827 (1993): International Tribunal[e]
Slovenia	1991	UNSC Res. 713 (1991): Arms Embargo; Lifted in 1995	UNSC Res. 808 (1993); 827 (1993): International Tribunal[e]

a See Table 1 by Michael Brown in the introductory chapter of this volume.

b This column includes major fact-finding missions launched since 1991 by the Security Council, the General Assembly, and the Secretary-General, as well as major mediation and good offices efforts, including the dispatch by the UN Secretary-General of Special Envoys (Representatives). Special Envoys (Representatives) that are part of a traditional or multifunctional peacekeeping operation are not listed.

c This column lists the relevant UN Security Council Resolutions (UNSC Res.). Unless otherwise indicated, these resolutions made explicit reference to Chapter VII.

d Yugoslavia broke up in 1991.

e As a concession to Russia and China no mention was made of Chapter VII in Resolution 808 (1993). However, Resolution 827 (1993), which adopts the statute of the tribunal, does make explicit reference to Chapter VII.

f Resolution 770 (1992) authorized the use of force to facilitate humanitarian efforts.

g Resolution 781 (1992) established a no-fly zone over Bosnia and Herzegovina, but did not mention Chapter VII. Resolution 816 (1993) authorized the use of force to enforce the no-fly zone.

h Resolution 836 (1993) authorized the use of air power to deter attacks against safe areas and to support UNPROFOR.

i Resolution 958 (1994) extended close air support of UNPROFOR into Croatia.

The United Nations and Internal Conflict: Latin America.

Country	Start of Current Hostilities[a]	Fact-finding[b]	Traditional Peace-keeping	Multi-functional Peacekeeping	Economic Sanctions; Arms Embargoes[c]	Use of Force[c]	Judicial Enforcement Measures
Central America[d]	1970s		ONUCA 1989-92[e]				
Dominican Republic	1965		DOMREP 1965-66				
El Salvador	1970s	Good Offices, MINUSAL: 1995-present		ONUSAL 1991-95			
Guatemala	1968	Observer: 1990; Mediator: 1994; Human Rights Mission (MINUGA): 1994-95; Special Envoy: 1995.					
Haiti	1991	Special Envoy: 1990. Human Rights Mission (MICIVH): 1993-present[f]		UNMIH 1993-present[g]	UNSC Res. 841 (1993): Oil and Arms Embargo. Lifted in 1993. UNSC Res. 873 (1993): Reimposes Oil and Arms Embargo. UNSC Res. 917 (1994): Expanded Sanctions (All sanctions and embargoes other than UNSC Res. 841 (1993) were lifted in 1994.)	UNSC Res. 940 (1994): Operation Restore Democracy, September 1994-March 1995.[h]	

a See Table 1 by Michael Brown in the introductory chapter of this volume.

b This column includes major fact-finding missions launched since 1991 by the Security Council, the General Assembly, and the Secretary-General, as well as major mediation and good offices efforts, including the dispatch by the UN Secretary-General of Special Envoys (Representatives). Special Envoys (Representatives) that are part of a traditional or multifunctional peacekeeping operation are not listed.

c This column lists the relevant UN Security Council Resolutions (UNSC Res.). Unless otherwise indicated, these resolutions made explicit reference to Chapter VII.

d Central America here includes Costa Rica, El Salvador, Guatemala, Honduras, and Nicaragua.

e The UN also deployed the United Nations Observer Mission to Verify the Electoral Process (ONUVEN) in Nicaragua in 1989.

f The General Assembly also sent an Election Monitor Observer Mission (ONUVEH) in 1990–91.

g In March 1995, UNMIH took over from the Multinational Force which had led Operation Restore Democracy.

h Resolution 940 (1994) authorized the use of force to facilitate the departure of the military junta.

Chapter 16

Collective Security Organizations and Internal Conflict

Dan Lindley

In this chapter, I assess the ability of collective security organizations to prevent, manage, and resolve internal conflict. To do this, I answer four sets of questions. First, what are the inherent strengths and weaknesses of collective security organizations in preventing, managing, and resolving conflicts? What are their inherent advantages and disadvantages, compared to lone states, *ad hoc* coalitions, and alliances? Second, what special problems does internal conflict pose for peacemakers in general and collective security organizations in particular? How does internal conflict complicate enforcement, peacekeeping and other operations in which collective security organizations engage? Third, what is the record of collective security organizations — including the League of Nations, the United Nations (UN), and regional security organizations — in carrying out these activities? Fourth, what recommendations flow from this analysis?

I offer these answers. First, collective security organizations have the following advantages. Due to their broad charters, non-exclusive memberships, and due process provisions, collective security organizations tend to possess greater impartiality, legitimacy, and moral authority than individual states, *ad hoc* coalitions, and alliances. These assets enhance the effectiveness of collective security organizations in peacekeeping, in conflict mediation, and in multifunctional peace operations. The main disadvantages of collective security organizations are that they have no organic military capability and little economic clout. They depend on the power and backing of their member states, and this can vitiate their

The author wishes to thank Rachel Bronson, Ivo Daalder, Bill Durch, Trevor Findlay, Sumit Ganguly, Jennifer King, John Mearsheimer, the MIT New Directions in Security Studies Working Group, Taylor Seybolt, Joanna Spear, Katherine Tucker, and Stephen Van Evera for their helpful comments.

impartiality, legitimacy, and moral authority. Large memberships, the burdens of due process, and the need to reach consensus may lead to organizational paralysis, especially if tensions are high among the great powers. When collective security organizations operate with the prior consent of the parties engaged in a conflict, they take advantage of their impartiality and minimize the need to use coercive force. This allows collective security organizations to play to their strengths and mitigate their weaknesses.

Second, internal conflicts pose special problems for collective security organizations. It is hard to mobilize international responses when borders have not been violated, and it is hard to keep peace along unclear borders. Potential interveners also have to contend with irregular military forces, and the prospect of fighting guerilla wars. Internal conflicts may be hard to mediate if local leaders include hate-mongers, if local leadership is divided, or if the factions view the fight as a zero-sum war for control of the country. These factors also make it hard for collective security organizations to gain consent from the parties for humanitarian, peacekeeping, or other peace operations.

Third, collective security organizations have compiled a mixed record in their attempts to prevent, manage, and resolve conflicts. In their ideal form, collective security organizations are designed to use force to defeat aggression wherever it arises in the system. However, collective security organizations have poor track records with respect to enforcement. In most of the wars that have begun since the creation of the League of Nations, combatants have not been worried about intervention by the League, the United Nations, or any other collective security organization. The League's failures to confront the invasions of Ethiopia and Manchuria loom large in the history of collective security because the League considered intervention in both cases and then failed to take effective action. Although the United Nations reversed North Korea's invasion of South Korea and the Iraqi invasion of Kuwait, the United States bore the brunt of the burden in both cases and deserves most of the credit for leading the international response to aggression.

The League and the United Nations have been more successful with traditional peacekeeping, mediation, and multifunctional peace operations. Most of the UN's traditional peacekeeping missions during the Cold War helped to preserve peace. The United Nations has also had several successes in the post–Cold War era, helping to end internal wars and sponsor elections in Mozambique, El Salvador, Namibia, and Cambodia. There have been failures as well, of course. The missions in Bosnia and Somalia had trouble mustering and using coercive force; they did not bring much leverage to mediation efforts; they tried to be impartial and punish aggressors at the same time; and they had trouble gaining and maintaining the commitment of member states and troop contributors. Most importantly, the UN operations in Bosnia and Somalia show the dangers of intervention when the consent of the parties has not been obtained or is lost over the course of the mission. In short, collective security organizations are useful, low-cost instruments that have good track records in some respects and problematic records in others.

Finally, this chapter makes two recommendations. The first is straight-forward: the United Nations and other collective security organizations should play to their strengths. They should engage in peacekeeping, mediation, and multifunctional operations when they enjoy the consent of the parties and can act with impartiality. Since they have trouble using coercive force and often fare poorly in situations where they lack consent, collective security organizations, as a general rule, should avoid operations that require more than minimal use of coercive force.

Second, ethnonationalist hate-mongers catalyze many internal conflicts. In areas where this is taking place, collective security organizations should launch information campaigns to promote human and minority-group rights, rebut incorrect or selective historical claims, and introduce wider and calming perspectives to the political debate. The United Nations has already begun to acquire experience in this area, having conducted extensive information campaigns that helped bring about elections in Namibia and Cambodia. It should build on this experience and use information campaigns to confront ethnonationalist hate-mongering.

Comparative Advantages and Disadvantages

Compared to lone states, *ad hoc* coalitions, and alliances, collective security organizations often possess greater impartiality, legitimacy, and moral authority. These advantages derive from the mandates, non-exclusive memberships, and decision-making procedures of collective security organizations.

First, the principal mandate of a collective security organization is to control conflicts among its members. In theory, if a war breaks out, a collective security organization is supposed to identify the aggressor or aggressors and then band its members together to defeat the aggression.[1] In practice, however, collective security organizations rarely resort to war

---

1. This is the theoretical ideal, but not all collective security organizations strive for it. The Organization of African Unity, for example, has no provision for the use of force in its charter. Indar Jit Rikhye, *The Theory and Practice of Peacekeeping* (London: C. Hurst and Company for the International Peace Academy, 1984), p. 151.

to defeat aggression and the roles they play are usually more modest: serving as fora to discuss security concerns; repositories and implementing bodies for treaties and international laws; and mechanisms for peacekeeping and mediation. Nonetheless, collective security organizations are not directed against specific threats, and they have broad mandates to confront security problems wherever they arise. This distinguishes collective security organizations from alliances and *ad hoc* coalitions, and gives them a reputation for impartiality that helps them to carry out peacekeeping, mediation, and other kinds of tasks.

Second, the non-exclusive memberships of collective security organizations give them legitimacy in the same way universal suffrage gives democracies legitimacy. The more that citizens participate in the functioning of their governments, the more legitimately these governments can claim to speak for their citizenries. The United Nation's membership includes almost every state on earth, while the membership of the Organization for Security and Cooperation in Europe (OSCE, formerly CSCE, the Conference on Security and Cooperation in Europe) spans over fifty European and Eurasian countries from Russia to Portugal.[2]

Third, decision-making in collective security organizations involves lengthy debate, consensus-building, and due process. This adds to their legitimacy and lends moral authority to their decisions. When large numbers of states consider a decision and when each decision faces many procedural hurdles, the probability that the decision is arbitrary and capricious is reduced. Collective security organizations also derive moral authority from their roles as developers, codifiers, and repositories of international law.

Their legitimacy and moral authority help collective security organizations mediate conflicts, carry out peacekeeping missions, and facilitate good offices missions (mediation efforts by the Secretary-General or other authorized officials). When a conflict gets on the agenda of a collective security organization, the "spotlight effect" can spur member states to action, and can give mediators more leverage and peacekeepers more power. By publicizing the lack of response to the famine in Somalia, UN Secretary-General Boutros Boutros-Ghali "publicly embarrassed the UN Security Council and Washington into action."[3] Their legitimacy and moral authority also help collective security organizations identify and

---

2.   Inis L. Claude, Jr., "Collective Legitimization as a Political Function of the United Nations," *International Organization,* Vol. 20, No. 3 (Summer 1966), pp. 367–376; David D. Caron, "The Legitimacy of the Collective Authority of the Security Council," *American Journal of International Law,* Vol. 87, No. 4 (October 1993), pp. 552–588.

3.   Jeffrey Clark, "Debacle in Somalia: Failure of the Collective Response," in Lori

punish aggressors. Although war crimes trials are rare and have usually been conducted by the victors of wars, the United Nations is a natural forum for such trials. In May 1993, the UN Security Council established a tribunal with respect to the wars in the former Yugoslavia; the tribunal's first indictments were handed down in late 1994.[4] The United Nations has also played an important role in authorizing and legitimizing economic sanctions and arms embargoes, especially since the end of the Cold War. Although collective security organizations rarely go war to counter aggression, the UN's involvement in and authorization of the Korean and Gulf Wars helped mobilize international and domestic support for these operations.

The principal disadvantages of collective security organizations are that they have no military capabilities of their own and little economic clout. They depend on the sometimes fickle political, military, and financial backing of member states. Individual states, coalitions, and alliances are better able to wield military and economic power. They have more resources to draw on, they have relatively streamlined decision-making procedures, and they also tend to be more highly motivated because they usually use their clout in response to direct security threats. In contrast, the broad mandates of collective security organizations require their members to deal with a wide range of conflicts, many of which do not engage the interests of all members.

The qualities that give collective security organizations advantages also generate disadvantages. Their large memberships impose collective action problems, and due process can become cumbersome. If tensions are high, consensus among member states may be hard to reach. Superpower tensions caused gridlock in the United Nations during the Cold War, when the United States and the Soviet Union routinely vetoed each other's resolutions in the Security Council. Bloc politics had similar effects in the General Assembly.

The distribution of international power can impinge on the impartiality, legitimacy, and moral authority of collective security organizations in the following ways. First, whether power is explicitly concentrated in a security council or whether a collective security organization operates by consensus, some states are more influential than others. This adversely affects the organization's reputation for impartiality. If a collective security organization acts only at the behest of its most powerful members,

Fisler Damrosch, ed., *Enforcing Restraint: Collective Intervention in Internal Conflicts* (New York: Council on Foreign Relations), p. 206.

4. "Justice without Victors," *Economist*, January 7, 1995, p. 44.

its mandate narrows, it becomes a tool of the powerful, and its actions will reflect the biases of these states. This is inevitable, but is more problematic in some cases than others. The intervention of the Economic Community of West African States (ECOWAS) into Liberia, for example, was highly problematic. The intervention was dominated by Nigeria, ECOWAS took sides in the conflict, and the conflict was consequently aggravated. Obtaining the consent of the warring parties serves as a filter that helps establish impartiality no matter what the impetus for involvement.

Second, institutions can be adapted to reduce collective action problems, but often at the expense of legitimacy. The United Nations concentrates most of its security functions in its Security Council. The Security Council is run by the "permanent five" (the United States, Russia, China, Great Britain, and France), each of whom wields a veto. This arrangement impinges on the legitimacy of the United Nations because it grants control of the most important functions to a few great powers.[5] This structure will not prevent paralysis if great-power tensions are high, but it does reduce collective action problems. In contrast, the OSCE operates on the basis of consensus. While maximizing legitimacy, this often inhibits action and reduces the scope of the organization's initiatives. The OSCE has recently tried to reduce collective action problems by delegating some functions to small numbers of states and modifying the consensus rule for some issues.[6] The Organization of American States (OAS) requires a two-thirds majority for major decisions, an arrangement that makes decisions comparatively easy to reach. Finally, anything that introduces bias or reduces legitimacy also reduces the moral authority of the organization in question. Moral authority is vitiated if a collective security organization seems to be speaking or acting on behalf of only one or some members.

There is no way to isolate collective security organizations from the influence of their most powerful members. Collective security organizations have little inherent power, and they require the political, economic, and military backing of their members to succeed. However, missions that receive prior consent from warring parties take advantage of organizational impartiality, obviate the need for massive force, and tend to reduce

---

5. Caron, "The Legitimacy of the Collective Authority of the Security Council."

6. Adam Daniel Rotfield, "Europe: Towards a New Regional Security Regime," in the *SIPRI Yearbook 1994* (Oxford: Oxford University Press for the Stockholm International Peace Research Institute (SIPRI), 1994), pp. 223–233; Konrad J. Huber, "The CSCE and Ethnic Conflict in the East," *RFE/RL Research Report*, Vol. 2, No. 31 (July 30, 1993), pp. 30–36.

the need for expensive coercive leverage. Consent helps collective security organizations play to their strengths and avoid their weaknesses.

The Special Problems Posed by Internal Conflicts

Internal conflicts have several qualities which make them more difficult for collective security organizations to handle than inter-state conflicts.[7] In their most ambitious enforcement role, collective security systems are supposed to lead their members in a counterattack against any country that forcibly crosses a border. Crossing a border is a simple and clear threshold; it defines aggression and helps catalyze international responses. Internal conflicts often lack this clear threshold because they occur within countries and because hostile groups may be intermingled. Ambiguity and debate about the identity of the aggressor can stall international responses and can render actions ineffective. In addition, states are often reluctant to intervene in the internal affairs of other countries.

Intermingled groups and ill-defined borders and front lines also complicate traditional peacekeeping. Peacekeeping missions implement and maintain negotiated cease-fires and thereby improve the climate for further peace talks. If the lines between hostile groups are unclear, it is difficult to define the status quo, and harder to negotiate cease-fires. Unclear borders are harder to patrol and more permeable, increasing the likelihood of cease-fire violations and reducing faith in the monitoring capability of peacekeeping forces. The importance of ill-defined borders varies; it depends on whether the conflict in question is a secessionist struggle or a fight over control of the central government, on whether geography helps define or obscure the lines, on how intermingled the combatants are, and on how seriously committed they are to a cessation of hostilities. The border problem makes peacekeepers all the more useful,

---

7. This analysis is based on Richard K. Betts, "The Delusion of Impartial Intervention," *Foreign Affairs*, Vol. 73, No. 6 (November/December 1994), pp. 20–33; U.S. Department of the Army, *FM 100-23: Peacekeeping Operations* (Washington, D.C.: U.S. Department of the Army, December 1993), pp. 12–14; Paul Diehl, *International Peacekeeping* (Baltimore, Md.: Johns Hopkins University Press, 1993); Charles Dobbie, "A Concept for Post–Cold War Peacekeeping Operations," *Survival*, Vol. 36, No. 3 (Autumn 1994), pp. 121–148; Alan James, "Internal Peacekeeping: A Dead End for the UN?" *Security Dialogue*, Vol. 24, No. 4 (December 1993), pp. 359–368; Alan James, "International Peacekeeping: The Disputants' View," *Political Studies*, Vol. 28, No. 2 (June 1990), pp. 215–230; Barry R. Posen, "The Security Dilemma and Ethnic Conflict," in Michael E. Brown, ed., *Ethnic Conflict and International Security* (Princeton, N.J.: Princeton University Press, 1993), pp. 103–124; Stephen Van Evera, "Hypotheses on Nationalism and War," *International Security*, Vol. 18, No. 4 (Spring 1994), pp. 5–39.

but it also raises the military requirements of peacekeeping operations and reduces the prospects for success.

The problems posed by unclear borders and front lines can be reduced by forming "safe areas" and by containing the conflict. Safe areas overcome the lack of borders by creating them. The French did this successfully when they intervened in Rwanda, establishing a line that encompassed and protected hundreds of thousands of Hutu. The UN "safe areas" in the former Yugoslavia have been far less effective because the Bosnian Serbs are well-armed. Although borders or front lines may be hard to discern in internal conflicts, there may be a clear border around the country in turmoil. If so, peacekeepers may have a useful role to play in containing internal conflicts. Peacekeepers stationed along international borders could deter irredentist forces from joining in; prevent fighting from spilling over into neighboring countries, thereby reducing the incentive for neighbors to intervene; and disarm refugees as they cross borders.

Internal conflicts are often fought by irregular military forces; this creates several political complications. Irregular forces are harder to distinguish from civilians than uniformed troops. Thus, the use of military force against irregulars entails the risk of fighting a guerilla war and of harming civilians, risks most politicians and military leaders are loath to take. Irregular forces are also harder to detect and identify as they move about; they can make even clear borders permeable. Finally, irregular forces are more likely to consist of or evolve into splinter groups. Splinter groups may wreck negotiations by engaging in terror campaigns or refusing to abide by negotiated agreements. This is even more likely to occur if a group's central leadership is divided.

Internal conflicts are often galvanized by leaders who come to power through ethnonationalist hate-mongering, divisively manipulating nationalism and glorifying their own group while debasing others.[8] Conflicts driven by hate-mongering are hard to stop. If hate-mongers negotiate with an enemy that they have maligned in order to gain power, they threaten their own power base. Negotiations are therefore less likely to take place, and they are less likely to be successful due to the intense levels of distrust on all sides. Politicization of ethnic differences and hate-mongering exacerbate the zero-sum nature of internal conflicts,

---

8. Ethnonationalist hate-mongering embodies what Stephen Van Evera calls "self-glorifying, self-whitewashing, and other-maligning" nationalist mythmaking. Van Evera notes that such mythmaking can lead to policies that aim to annex diasporas and oppress minorities. See "Hypotheses on Nationalism and War," pp. 12–15, 26–30.

leaving little room for compromise and making power-sharing highly problematic.

A further complication is that internal conflicts often involve groups that have weak leaders, or divided leadership factions. This complicates negotiations, makes negotiators vulnerable to being undercut, and encourages the emergence of splinter groups. As Canadian General Lewis MacKenzie, former commander of the UN peacekeeping forces in Sarajevo, has observed:

You can sit down and negotiate with those people and come up with some really good contracts. . . . The trouble is, they're never executed. Half-way down the chain of command, you run up against one of these war lords that says, "This is my area. . . . I don't care what [Bosnian President Alija] Izetbegovic says. This is my terrain, and thou shalt not pass." . . . when the out-of-control elements receive instructions they like, they follow through. . . . But as soon as they get something they do not like — for example, you watch it on television.[9]

Military force can be more effective against weak leaders, but this consideration may be outweighed by the difficulties listed above.

Hate-mongers and leaders with tenuous power are not unique to internal conflicts. However, they are frequent elements in internal conflicts, making cease-fires and consent more difficult to secure and hurting the prospects for peacekeeping and mediation missions. This suggests that mediation and peacekeeping in internal conflicts are more likely to succeed the more the warring parties resemble independent states. Mediation and peacekeeping will tend to be easier if the groups are less interspersed, and if they have independent governing structures and economies.[10]

The Track Record of Collective Security Organizations

In their efforts to prevent, manage, and resolve conflicts, the League of Nations, the United Nations, CSCE/OSCE, ECOWAS, and other collective security organizations have launched several different types of operations: enforcement operations; traditional peacekeeping operations;

---

9. Testimony of Canadian General Lewis MacKenzie, former Commander of the UN Peacekeeping Forces in Sarajevo, before the U.S. Senate Armed Services Committee, *Situation in Bosnia and Appropriate U.S. and Western Responses,* 102nd Cong., 2nd sess., August 11, 1992, pp. 52–53.

10. Donald L. Horowitz, *Ethnic Groups in Conflict* (Berkeley: University of California Press, 1985), pp. 580–584.

mediation efforts; and multifunctional peace operations, which often involve peacekeeping, mediation, sponsorship of elections, and a host of other activities.

Overall, the track record of collective security organizations is mixed, but better than many people believe. Problems with UN missions in Bosnia and Somalia have obscured the successes in Cambodia, Central America, and Namibia, as well as in many of the traditional peacekeeping missions during the Cold War. Collective security organizations have encountered problems when they have compromised their impartiality and lost the consent of the parties to the conflicts in question. Decision-makers have, from time to time, forgotten that whereas enforcement operations by definition do not enjoy the consent of the warring parties, traditional peacekeeping operations, mediation efforts, and multi-functional peacekeeping operations depend on the acquisition and maintenance of consent. Peacekeeping operations that have coercive elements or begin to engage in coercion and enforcement are accidents waiting to happen.

PEACE ENFORCEMENT

Enforcement involves using military force to end or reverse aggression. In rare, extreme cases, the members of collective security organizations have waged all-out war to defeat aggressors and reverse aggression. The Korean and Gulf Wars are the only two instances of this full-blown realization of collective security. Force, or the threat of force, is usually used in more measured ways.

In the Korean and Gulf Wars, the United Nations provided international legitimization for what were essentially U.S.-led wars: the United States urged the United Nations to authorize the use of force against North Korean and Iraqi aggression, and it provided most of the military forces needed to carry out the mission. UN authorization was nonetheless crucial because it helped the United States form and maintain coalitions and mobilize domestic support for the wars. These kinds of all-out enforcement operations have been and will probably continue to be completely dependent on the leadership and military contributions of a superpower.

In three cases where force was used in more measured ways, the United Nations authorized others to act on its behalf: France was authorized to intervene in Rwanda, and the United States led multilateral interventions in Somalia and Haiti. In a fourth Chapter VII enforcement mission, the second United Nations Operation in Somalia (UNOSOM II), the United Nations itself assumed operational control over the mission. The United Nations combined the two approaches in the former Yugoslavia by authorizing member states and regional organizations (the North Atlantic Treaty Organization [NATO], in particular) to assist the UN Protection Force (UNPROFOR).[11]

The operations in Rwanda and Haiti were successful because goals were clear and French and U.S. forces were large enough to deter challenges. In Rwanda, the Hutu slaughter of Tutsi was catalyzed by the death of the country's president, a Hutu, in a plane crash on April 6, 1994. This genocidal assault prompted the Uganda-based Tutsi Rwandan Patriotic Front (RPF) to invade Rwanda. This, in turn, generated massive streams of Hutu refugees. On June 23, France launched Operation Turquoise, which created a safe zone in southwestern Rwanda that protected hundreds of thousands of Hutu refugees both in the zone and beyond it in Zaire. Although the French action saved many lives, it mainly protected the Hutu perpetrators, not the Tutsi victims, of the Rwandan genocide. French forces, moreover, did not disarm Hutu in the safe zone.[12] Similarly, neither U.S. forces, which arrived in July to help alleviate the appalling conditions in the refugee camps in Zaire, nor the short-lived UN Assistance Mission for Rwanda (UNAMIR) took steps to disarm Hutu murderers or militia. This may help to set the stage for a Hutu re-invasion from the safe zone and refugee camps in Zaire.[13]

The crisis in Haiti began in September 1991 when its democratically elected president, Jean-Bertrand Aristide, was ousted in a coup led by General Raoul Cedras. The human rights abuses of the Cedras regime led many Haitians to flee to the United States. One barrier to ending Haiti's political turmoil was that Cedras and Aristide refused to talk to each other; the United Nations and the Organization of American States served as go-betweens and mediators. The United States, Canada, France, and Venezuela also facilitated negotiations and put pressure on both parties. In June 1993, the UN Security Council authorized an oil and arms embargo on Haiti. This spurred Cedras to accept the Governors Island

---

11.   Pamela L. Reed, J. Matthew Vaccaro, and William J. Durch, *Handbook on United Nations Peace Operations*, Handbook No. 3 (Washington, D.C.: Henry L. Stimson Center, April 1995), Boutros Boutros-Ghali, *Supplement to "An Agenda for Peace": Position Paper of the Secretary-General on the Occasion of the Fiftieth Anniversary of the United Nations*, A/50/60, S/1995/1, January 3, 1995, pp. 28–29.

12.   Alain Destexhe, "The Third Genocide," *Foreign Policy*, No. 97 (Winter 1994–95), p. 11; Alan Rake, "France and Africa: A New Chapter," *New African* (November 1994), pp. 13–14; *Economist*, "Who Will Save Rwanda?" June 25, 1994, p. 13; *Economist*, "The French in Rwanda," July 2, 1994, p. 39; *Economist*, "Zone of Influence," July 9, 1994, p. 42.

13.   "Massacres, 'Mindless Violence and Carnage' Rage in Rwanda," *UN Chronicle*, Vol. 31, No. 3 (September 1994), pp. 15–20. R.A. Dallaire and B. Poulin, "UNAMIR:

Agreement, which called for Cedras to step down in exchange for amnesty. Cedras subsequently backed out of the agreement. The United Nations then reimposed sanctions, and eventually gave the United States authorization to lead a military intervention to restore Aristide to power. In September 1994, with U.S. military forces about to descend on Haiti (when sixty-one planes were literally in the air), Cedras agreed to step down. U.S. forces entered Haiti peacefully.[14]

In contrast, the UN operation in the former Yugoslavia has failed in important respects. In early 1992, UNPROFOR was deployed to protect three UN Protected Areas in Croatia. The main goal of the UN mission was to mitigate the ravages of war by trying to protect pockets of civilians and deliver humanitarian aid. By mid-1995, the number of Protected Areas had multiplied and the number of UN peacekeepers had grown from a few hundred to twenty-two thousand in Bosnia and nearly forty thousand throughout the former Yugoslavia.[15] NATO had conducted eight air strikes in support of UNPROFOR and against Serb forces.[16] A wide array of steps were taken to try to end the war: high-level conferences were held and prominent mediators were sent to the region; belligerents were expelled from multilateral organizations; arms embargoes and economic embargoes (ranging from oil products to all trade) were imposed; a naval blockade and air exclusion zones were established; artillery pieces were placed under UN control; cease-fire lines were drawn; and traditional peacekeeping operations were launched. The UN Security Council passed sixty resolutions concerning the war, approximately twenty of which enlarged previous mandates.[17]

Fighting in Croatia and Bosnia nonetheless continued. The main

---

Mission to Rwanda," *Joint Forces Quarterly*, No. 7 (Spring 1995), pp. 66–71; Donatela Lorch, "U.N.-Rwanda Ties Sour As Mandate Nears End," *New York Times*, May 21, 1995, p. 8.

14. Ian Martin, "Haiti: Mangled Multilateralism," *Foreign Policy*, No. 95 (Summer 1994), p. 80; Robert Greenberger, Michael Frisby, and Jose de Cordoba, "Dodging the Bullet: An Invasion of Haiti is Averted by Accord to Restore Aristide," *Wall Street Journal*, September 19, 1994, p. A1; U.N. Security Council Resolution 940 (1994), which cites Chapter VII in authorizing the intervention.

15. Randolph Ryan, "Constraints Test UN's Troops," *Boston Globe*, May 2, 1995, p. 1.

16. Roger Cohen, "NATO Jets Bomb Arms Depot at Bosnian Serb Headquarters," *New York Times*, May 26, 1995, p. A1.

17. Mats Berdal, "United Nations Peacekeeping in the Former Yugoslavia," in Donald C.F. Daniel and Bradd C. Hayes, eds., *Beyond Traditional Peacekeeping* (New York: St. Martin's, 1995), pp. 228–247; "Croatia Takes on the Serbs," *Economist*, May 6, 1995, p. 47; Lawrence Freedman, "Why the West Failed," *Foreign Policy*, No. 97 (Winter 1994–95), p. 59; Ryan, "Constraints Test UN's Troops"; United Nations Department of

failing of the UN mission was that it tried to be impartial and coercive at the same time. Mediation efforts failed because the United Nations was neither impartial nor truly coercive; over thirty cease-fires were broken. Outside powers tried to do the impossible: punishing the Serbs while not angering them. The limited air strikes that were launched often resulted in counterattacks on UN peacekeepers. Other uses of force were similarly ineffective. NATO's air forces, dominant in the Gulf War, failed to stop over three thousand violations of the no-fly zone. In parts of Bosnia, fifty percent of the food aid fell into the hands of soldiers, and because of continued fighting "only twenty percent of planned relief reached its destination" in early 1994.[18] UN sanctions broadened Serbian President Slobodan Milosevic's power base by giving him an enemy to rail against and by preventing outside information from reaching Serbia.[19]

Missions that attempt to deliver humanitarian aid into war zones do not try to end wars; they try to mitigate the tragic consequences of war — famine, malnutrition, and disease. However, relief aid is often perceived by one, both, or all sides as helping other combatants. As a result, humanitarian missions rarely enjoy the consent of the warring parties. Military force is often needed to insure the safe delivery of aid. Humanitarian missions, in short, often become coercive undertakings.

The UN and UN-authorized missions[20] in Somalia, for example, attempted to deliver humanitarian aid into war zones. Civil war in Somalia broke out in 1991, following the ouster of President Siad Barré. Political chaos, conflict between warlords, and roving bandits prevented deliveries of food aid and led to mounting death, starvation, and disease. By early 1992, 300,000 people were dead and hundreds of thousands more were threatened by starvation. In mid-1992, the United Nations launched

---

Public Information, "The United Nations and the Situation in the Former Yugoslavia," Reference Paper, March 15, 1994.

18. Åge Eknes, "The United Nations' Predicament in the Former Yugoslavia," in Thomas G. Weiss, ed., *The United Nations and Civil Wars* (Boulder, Colo.: Lynne Rienner, 1995), p. 122.

19. "End-of-Year Cease-Fire Signed, Further Negotiations Urged," *UN Chronicle*, Vol. 32, No. 1 (March 1995), pp. 30–34; Berdal, "United Nations Peacekeeping in the Former Yugoslavia," p. 233; Roger Cohen, "Serbs, Meeting With Carter Agree to Bosnian Cease-Fire," *New York Times*, December 20, 1994, p. A1; Cohen, "NATO Jets Bomb Arms Depot at Bosnian Serb Headquarters"; Michael R. Gordon, "Pulling Punches: NATO Hits Serbs But Not Too Hard," *New York Times*, November 22, 1994, p. A14; Susan L. Woodward, "Yugoslavia, Divide and Fail," *Bulletin of the Atomic Scientists*, Vol. 49, No. 9 (November 1993), pp. 24–27.

20. The United Nations has direct control over UN missions. It authorizes states or other organizations to act on its behalf in UN-authorized missions.

UNOSOM I, sending fifty observers and five hundred security personnel to monitor a cease-fire and escort aid deliveries. However, consent from the warring factions was evanescent. The five hundred UN soldiers arrived but could not be deployed in the field, and were robbed and fired upon. Delivery of aid dwindled. Even though warehouses were full, one thousand to three thousand people died each day.[21] U.S. President George Bush prompted the UN Security Council to act under Chapter VII. Resolution 794, passed in December 1992, authorized member states to "use all necessary means to establish . . . a secure environment for humanitarian relief operations in Somalia."[22]

The U.S.-led Unified Task Force (UNITAF) began to put troops on the ground on December 9, and eventually involved 38,000 troops, 25,800 from the United States. Although UNITAF overwhelmed local forces and got aid flowing again, there was confusion from the beginning about the extent of UNITAF's mandate — especially over whether the militia of the various clans should be disarmed. UNITAF handed the mission over to UNOSOM II in May 1993, and international forces in Somalia were reduced to 28,000. UNOSOM II stepped up UNITAF's limited disarmament efforts, which continued to be directed primarily at the forces of Mohammed Farah Aideed.

In response, Aideed took to the airwaves to denounce both the UN mission and its leaders. On June 5, Somali forces, shielded by women and children, savagely killed twenty-four Pakistani troops and wounded another fifty-four. The Security Council quickly authorized the arrest and punishment of those responsible for the ambush. For the United States and the United Nations, this meant going after Aideed. On June 12, the U.S. Air Force destroyed Aideed's radio station and UN troops raided his headquarters. Aideed escaped, the conflict escalated, and in the eyes of many Somalis, the United Nations had become another faction in the war. On October 3, two U.S. helicopters were shot down. In the ensuing fight to rescue those on board, eighteen U.S. soldiers and hundreds of Somalis were killed. The hunt for Aideed was subsequently called off, and negotiations resumed. U.S. and UN troops scaled back their operations until their respective withdrawals in 1994 and 1995.[23]

---

21. United Nations Department of Public Information, "The United Nations and the Situation in Somalia," Reference Paper, May 1, 1994, p. 5; Clark, "Debacle in Somalia," in Damrosch, *Enforcing Restraint*, p. 205.

22. United Nations Department of Public Information, "The United Nations and the Situation in Somalia," p. 7.

23. Gary Anderson, "UNOSOM II: Not Failure, Not Success," in Daniel and Hayes, eds., *Beyond Traditional Peacekeeping*, pp. 267–281; Clark, "Debacle in Somalia" in

Although the U.S. and UN efforts saved many Somali lives, these missions went horribly wrong. Their aims grew ever wider, and they consequently lost whatever consent they had from local Somali factions. The intervenors then found the costs of disarming and governing the country too high, their missions were scaled back and eventually terminated, and the long-term prospects for Somalia remained largely unchanged.

Collective security organizations should be wary about forceful intervention in internal conflicts. Enforcement operations are most likely to succeed when they have clear mandates and when they represent the will — backed up with sufficient force — of the great powers. In the Korean and Gulf enforcement actions, the missions were clear, the intervenors were determined, and forces were robust. Missions that use force in more measured ways can succeed, but are much trickier. If limited missions lack clear political goals and clear mandates, they face serious problems. As in Bosnia, intervenors may think they can be both impartial and coercive. However, one cannot be both at the same time. In Somalia, the scope and character of the mission changed over time, becoming more coercive even as forces grew smaller. Muddled thinking is especially costly when military force is being used: operational confusion, death, and defeat often follow.

TRADITIONAL PEACEKEEPING

Traditional peacekeeping operations, which always have the consent of the combatants, help to implement cease-fires. These missions separate combatants, patrol borders or lines of disengagement, and thereby help to deter hostile parties from re-engaging in combat. A promise to deploy peacekeeping troops can help warring parties to agree on a cease-fire, but peacekeepers are not generally deployed until after a cease-fire has been negotiated. Maintenance of buffer zones and monitoring of troop movements can reduce misperceptions and dampen escalatory tendencies. Thus, by overseeing compliance with cease-fires, peacekeeping increases transparency and builds confidence between hostile parties. This can help disputants negotiate a more lasting peace.

It is important to keep in mind that traditional peacekeeping missions always operate with the consent of the local parties, while enforcement operations involve the coercive use of military force. Traditional

---

Damrosch, *Enforcing Restraint;* Debarati G. Sapir and Hedwig Deconinck, "The Paradox of Humanitarian Assistance and Military Intervention in Somalia," in Weiss, *The United Nations and Civil Wars;* United Nations Department of Public Information, "The United Nations and the Situation in Somalia," pp. 151–172.

peacekeeping operations, therefore, generally cost less and incur fewer casualties than their coercive counterparts.

The United Nations has been fairly successful at peacekeeping, although much of its experience was accumulated during the Cold War in inter-state disputes. Two-thirds (about sixty-five percent) of the UN's traditional peacekeeping missions have helped to end or to limit conflict. Of the UN's seventeen main operations, there were eleven successes (approximately sixty-five percent), two mixed outcomes (around twelve percent), and four failures (about twenty-four percent).[24] Table 16.1 summarizes these results.

The biggest problem with traditional peacekeeping is that it depends on the consent of the warring parties, and thus can only make a modest difference in resolving conflicts. Most of the failures listed in Table 16.1 were caused by a failure to secure the consent of all local parties before deploying forces, or by a loss of consent after deployment. Although loss of consent normally marks the end of a peacekeeping operation, it can also serve a useful purpose by signaling the onset of hostilities. For example, when Egypt asked the United Nations Emergency Force (UNEF I) to leave the Sinai-Gaza armistice line in 1967, this signal helped Israel to conclude that an attack was imminent.[25] Decisions to ask peacekeeping forces to withdraw may help the international community to identify oppressors. Leaders who agree to a settlement and then back out make themselves appropriate targets for sanctions and other coercive measures.[26]

Some peacekeeping missions have been criticized for creating stalemates and prolonging conflicts. Peacekeeping, it is said, can create an environment in which there is little pressure to negotiate. The most

---

24. Principal sources used in creating this table were Diehl, *International Peacekeeping;* William J. Durch, ed., *The Evolution of UN Peacekeeping: Case Studies and Comparative Analysis* (New York: St. Martin's, 1993); Alan James, *Peacekeeping in International Politics* (New York: St. Martin's, 1990); Rikhye, *The Theory and Practice of Peacekeeping;* United Nations, *Blue Helmets: A Review of United Nations Peacekeeping* (New York: United Nations Department of Public Information, 1990); United Nations Department of Public Information, *United Nations Peacekeeping: Information Notes,* Update: December 1994, DPI/1306/Rev. 4 (New York: United Nations, March 1995); David W. Wainhouse, *International Peace Observation: A History and Forecast* (Baltimore, Md.: Johns Hopkins University Press, 1966).

25. Mona Ghali, "United Nations Emergency Force I," in Durch, *Evolution of UN Peacekeeping,* pp. 124–125; James, *Peacekeeping in International Politics,* pp. 220–223; Indar Jit Rikhye, Michael Harbottle, and Bjorn Egge, *The Thin Blue Line: International Peacekeeping and Its Future* (New Haven, Conn.: Yale University Press, 1974), pp. 58–70.

26. Stephen John Stedman, "UN Intervention in Civil Wars: Imperatives of Choice and Strategy," in Daniel and Hayes, *Beyond Traditional Peacekeeping,* pp. 58–60.

prominent case cited by critics in this regard is the UN Force in Cyprus (UNFICYP) mission in Cyprus, although the UN Disengagement Observer Force (UNDOF) and the UN Military Observer Group in India and Pakistan (UNMOGIP) are occasionally criticized on these grounds as well. These critiques are unconvincing. Although stalemates are frustrating, war is worse. UNFICYP still deals with hundreds of incidents each year, ranging from cease-fire violations to crowd control.[27] This suggests that UNFICYP still contributes to peace. Some contend that withdrawal of UN troops would force the parties to contemplate the costs of war and lead them into serious negotiations. This proposition was tested in April 1992, when the UN Security Council told the island's Greek and Turkish leaders to settle their dispute or risk termination of the UNFICYP mission. This was a credible threat because several countries were thinking of pulling their troops out of the UN operation. However, in a February 1993 election that was seen as a referendum on a UN peace plan for Cyprus, the Greek side elected an opponent of the plan. The Turks had already rejected the plan. The UN force has since been cut almost in half, and a settlement to the conflict is no closer.[28]

The ECOWAS operation in Liberia, known as the ECOWAS Monitoring Group (ECOMOG), offers a cautionary tale about peace operations conducted by regional collective security organizations. In August 1990, Nigeria led twelve thousand ECOMOG troops into Liberia, hoping to negotiate a cease-fire and separate the warring factions. The Liberian rebel leader, Charles Taylor, attacked the ECOMOG force, and cease-fires have routinely fallen apart ever since. Originally intended to be peacekeepers, ECOMOG's forces became combatants, but they did not have enough firepower or political and financial backing to impose a settlement on the Liberian factions. The ECOMOG force came from neighboring states that were not entirely disinterested parties. This created disputes within ECOMOG, and helped foster perceptions of bias that hurt the mission. The war in Liberia continues, and has so far killed 150,000 people, driven over one million people from their homes — causing a crisis in Guinea,

---

27. United Nations Department of Public Information, *United Nations Peacekeeping: Information Notes*, Update: May 1994, DPI/1306/Rev. 3 (New York: United Nations, June 1994), p. 9.

28. "Greek Cypriot President, Backer of Island Unity, Faces Runoff Vote," *Boston Globe*, February 8, 1993, p. 2; "Greek Cypriots elect foe of reunification," *Boston Globe*, February 15, 1993, p. 4; Diehl, *International Peacekeeping*, pp. 95–106; Durch, "Getting Involved: The Political-Military Context," in Durch, *Evolution of UN Peacekeeping*, p. 30; James, *Peacekeeping in International Politics*, pp. 234–236; Paul Lewis, "U.N. Warns That Time Is Running Out on Cyprus," *New York Times*, April 12, 1992, p. 13; United Nations, *United Nations Peacekeeping: Information Notes*, May 1994, pp. 8–12.

Table 16.1. UN Traditional Peacekeeping Operations.

Mission	Outcome
UN Special Committee on the Balkans (UNSCOB), 1947–51; investigated outside support for guerillas in Greece	Success
UN Truce Supervision Organization (UNTSO), 1948–present; monitors cease-fires along Israeli borders	Failure[a]
UN Military Observer Group in India and Pakistan (UNMOGIP), 1949–present; monitors cease-fire in Jammu and Kashmir	Mixed[b]
UN Emergency Force (UNEF I), 1956–67; separated Egyptian and Israeli forces in Sinai	Success
UN Observation Group in Lebanon (UNOGIL), 1958; monitored infiltration of arms and troops into Lebanon from Syria	Failure
UN Operation in the Congo (ONUC), 1960–64; restored civil order	Mixed
UN Temporary Executive Authority/UN Security Force (UNTEA/UNSF), 1962–63; implemented cease-fire, kept order and administered West New Guinea pending transfer to Indonesia from Dutch	Success
UN Yemen Observation Mission (UNYOM), 1963–64; monitored infiltration into Yemen via Saudi border	Failure
UN Force in Cyprus (UNFICYP), 1964–present; maintains order; beginning in 1974, monitors buffer zone	Success
UNEF II, 1973–79, see above	Success
UN Disengagement Observer Force (UNDOF), 1974–present; monitors separation of Syrian and Israeli forces on Golan Heights	Success
UN Interim Force in Lebanon (UNIFIL), 1978–present; establishes buffer zone between Israel and Lebanon	Failure
UN Good Offices Mission in Afghanistan and Pakistan (UNGOMAP), 1988–90; monitored Soviet pullout from Afghanistan	Success
UN Iran-Iraq Military Observer Group (UNIIMOG), 1988–91; monitored cease-fire in Iran-Iraq war	Success
UN Angola Verification Mission (UNAVEM I), 1989–91; monitored Cuban pullout from Angola	Success
UN Observer Group in Central America (ONUCA), 1989–92; monitored compliance with Esquipulas II agreement; demobilized Nicaraguan contras	Success
UN Iraq-Kuwait Observer Mission (UNIKOM), 1991–present; monitors buffer zone after Gulf War	Success

NOTES: This table includes almost every traditional peacekeeping operation. Missions were excluded from the table if their principal mandate had little to do with traditional peacekeeping (implementing a peace accord, monitoring a buffer zone) and more to do with election monitoring or civil administration; if there was insufficient information available about the operation; or if they are ongoing and an assessment could not be made. The Mission of the Representative of the Secretary-General in the Dominican Republic (DOMREP, 1965–66) was excluded because it was not really a peacekeeping mission (James, *Peacekeeping in International Politics*, p. 59). The UN India-Pakistan Observation (UNIPOM) was excluded because it was merely an "administrative adjunct" of UNMOGIP (United Nations, *Blue Helmets*, p. 164). UNSCOB was included because Durch included it in his survey of peacekeeping operations (Durch, *Evolution of UN Peacekeeping*). The mini-summaries of each mission in the left-hand column are taken or adapted from Durch, pp. 8, 10; and Reed, Vaccaro, and Durch, *Handbook on United Nations Peace Operations*, No. 3, pp. A-2–A-3.

Most of the cases have been studied by a number of scholars. Except where noted, a mission was judged a success or a failure if a consensus of the studies so judged. "Successes" range from providing a figleaf for the Soviet withdrawal from Afghanistan, to the case of UN Iran-Iraq Military Observer Group (UNIIMOG) which probably kept the war from flaring up anew. Some successes, the UN Emergency Force (UNEF I) for example, kept the peace for a number of years and were therefore modestly successful even though the mission ended as war broke out between Israel and Egypt. "Failures" also cover a wide range of events. Brian D. Smith, "The UN Iran-Iraq Military Observer Group," in Durch, *Evolution of UN Peacekeeping*, pp. 253–254; James, *Peacekeeping in International Politics*, pp. 170–174; and United Nations, *Blue Helmets*, p. 333.

[a] Analysts were sharply divided on this mission, with Mona Ghali writing that it "unequivocally failed" (*Evolution of UN Peacekeeping*, p. 98), James writing that it was "enormously valuable" (*Peacekeeping in International Politics*, p. 156), and Wainhouse writing that with "limitations, UNTSO . . . performed indispensable functions" (*International Peace Observation*, p. 272). I find Ghali's arguments compelling.

[b] This mission was a success prior to the 1971 war, and a failure thereafter.

inspiring a rebellion in Sierra Leone, and spreading arms and turbulence throughout West Africa.[29]

Compared to the United Nations, regional collective security organizations are even less likely to confront conflicts with adequate military force and financial and political backing. Although it has little organic power, the United Nations counts among its members all of the world's richest and most powerful states — something not true of most regional organizations. Further, regional organizations such as ECOWAS, the Organization of African Unity (OAU), and the OAS are physically closer to the conflicts they are likely to confront, increasing the probability that members are influenced by political, economic, ethnic, and other ties. The United Nations's worldwide membership neutralizes some of these sources of bias.

MEDIATION

The impartial character of collective security organizations helps them convene negotiations, mediate disputes, and propose solutions to conflicts that would be rejected had they come from more biased sources. Collective security organizations can also help national leaders legitimize outcomes within their countries. Although collective security organizations can play very useful roles in mediating disputes, they lack political, economic, and military leverage — crucial factors in most mediation efforts. For example, the U.S. efforts to mediate the Egyptian-Israeli conflict have been successful because the United States has given billions of dollars in aid to the two sides and because the United States has considerable leverage over each party.

Two scholarly studies of mediation conclude that it succeeds somewhere between fifteen and twenty-two percent of the time. A study of two hundred and eighty-four attempts to mediate international disputes concluded that full settlements were reached in five percent of the cases, partial settlements in nine percent, and cease-fires in eight percent. Mediators ranged from collective security organizations to individual states. Breaking down the results even further, this study concluded that media-

---

29. Howard W. French, "Long War Turns Liberia Into Core of a Spreading Blight," *New York Times*, May 25, 1995, p. A11; W. Ofuatey-Kodjoe, "Regional Organizations and the Resolution of Internal Conflict: The ECOWAS Intervention in Liberia," International Peacekeeping, Vol. 1, No. 3 (Autumn 1994), pp. 261–302; Stephen P. Riley, "Intervention in Liberia: Too Little, Too Partisan," *World Today*, Vol. 49, No. 3 (March 1993), pp. 42–43; Thomas Sotinel, "Liberia Fails to Emerge from the Twilight," *Le Monde*, March 29, 1995, reprinted in *Guardian Weekly*, April 9, 1995, p. 14; David Wippman, "Enforcing the Peace: ECOWAS and the Liberian Civil War," in Damrosch, *Enforcing Restraint*, pp. 156–203.

tion is much less likely to succeed when the conflict in question revolves around ideology (ten percent success) or political independence (eleven percent) than when it focuses on territory (twenty-three percent) or borders (twenty-seven percent). This study lends support to the argument that the stakes in ideological disputes and struggles for self-determination are more absolute and less amenable to compromise than those involving territory. The fact that struggles for self-determination are difficult to resolve is particularly relevant here.[30]

A study that examined the sixty-eight civil wars of the twentieth century concluded that fifteen percent of those that ended were resolved through negotiation; sixty percent ended in capitulation or elimination of one of the warring parties.[31] The fact that mediation efforts have been more successful in inter-state disputes than internal conflicts is consistent with the arguments made earlier in this chapter about the problematic nature of the latter.

However, internal conflicts are not impossible to resolve, just more difficult. Collective security organizations have played important roles in resolving conflicts by successfully carrying out good offices missions and other mediation efforts. As a general rule, collective security organizations should try to maintain their impartiality — one of their main strengths — while getting other parties to apply leverage. This will better enable them to accomplish with mediation what they do with peacekeeping: help parties to do what they want to do anyway.[32]

MULTIFUNCTIONAL PEACE OPERATIONS

Multifunctional peace operations are comprehensive efforts to implement settlements to conflicts. These missions are often costly and complex because they usually involve peacekeeping, delivery of humanitarian aid, sponsorship of elections, policing, civil administration, and rebuilding infrastructure and institutions. These operations usually have the full

30. Jacob Bercovitch, J. Theodore Anagnoson, and Donnette L. Wille, "Some Conceptual Issues and Empirical Trends in the Study of Successful Mediation in Relations," *Journal of Peace Research*, Vol. 28, No. 1 (February 1991), pp. 10, 13–14.

31. Stephen John Stedman, *Peacemaking in Civil War: International Mediation in Zimbabwe, 1974–1980* (Boulder, Colo.: Lynne Rienner, 1991), pp. 4–12.

32. Cameron Hume, "Perez de Cuellar and the Iran-Iraq War," *Negotiation Journal*, Vol. 8, No. 2 (April 1992), pp. 173–174; Farouk Mawlawi, "New Conflicts, New Challenges: The Evolving Role for Non-Governmental Actors," *Journal of International Affairs*, Vol. 46, No. 2 (Winter 1993), pp. 398–399; Giandomenico Picco, "The U.N. and the Use of Force," *Foreign Affairs*, Vol. 73, No. 5 (September/October 1994), pp. 14–18; I. William Zartman and Saadia Touval, "International Mediation: Conflict Resolution and Power Politics," *Journal of Social Issues*, Vol. 41, No. 2 (1985), pp. 27–45.

consent of the local parties, but the necessities of policing and the general complexity of the missions often lead to at least some use of force. Seven of the fifteen UN peace operations initiated since 1990 have been multifunctional, i.e., those in Angola, Rwanda, Western Sahara, Cambodia, El Salvador, Haiti, and Mozambique. Of these, the latter four have so far been successful — a success rate of fifty-seven percent.[33]

Multifunctional operations are more costly than humanitarian relief or peacekeeping operations because they are complex undertakings. Although they are often successful, they are riskier than simpler humanitarian or peacekeeping operations. Consent can erode and casualties mount, but an intervenor's financial and human investment can make a decision to withdraw difficult. In some cases, it is wise to withdraw if consent evaporates. But the case of the UN Transitional Authority in Cambodia (UNTAC), discussed below, shows that it is possible to face these difficulties, persevere, use flexible and innovative tactics, and succeed.

Some multifunctional operations are discussed elsewhere in this volume, and the difficulties encountered by collective security organizations when they launch coercive or humanitarian aid operations without consent are discussed above.[34] The sponsoring of elections and the fostering of democratic institutions is therefore the focus of the discussion here.

A defining feature of UN activities in the 1990s is that most of its peace operations have included efforts to promote democracy, usually through sponsorship or supervision of elections. In 1994, for example, the United Nations assisted with elections and helped foster democracy in twenty-one countries; in 1988 the corresponding figure was zero.[35] This is a dramatic measure of the post–Cold War political environment. When the UN Security Council voted to allow a U.S.-led invasion of Haiti, Resolution 940 passed by a vote of twelve to zero, with Brazil and China abstaining. Even Cuba voted in favor of the resolution, which included language about restoring democracy and holding free and fair legislative elections in Haiti.[36]

Elections can help settle conflicts by giving groups a peaceful way to allocate power. External, impartial actors can sponsor and monitor elec-

---

33. Reed, Vaccaro, and Durch, *Handbook on United Nations Peace Operations*, No. 3, pp. 2–3, A-4–A-5.

34. For more discussion of UN multifunctional peace operations, see Chantal de Jonge Oudraat's chapter in this volume.

35. United Nations Secretary-General, *Supplement to "An Agenda for Peace,"* p. 8.

36. "Digest" and "Documentation" sections of *International Peacekeeping*, Vol. 1, No. 4 (Winter 1994), pp. 485, 499–502.

tions, making them more free and fair. By certifying the validity of election results, outside actors can calm the suspicions of the contending groups. By promoting political transparency and building confidence, collective security organizations can help hostile parties seek peaceful solutions to their conflicts.

The UN mission to Cambodia, UNTAC, was a multifunctional operation that culminated in elections. UNTAC's mandate was to implement the October 1991 Paris Agreement between the four principal factions in Cambodia. Under the terms of the agreement, Cambodia became a virtual trustee of the United Nations. UNTAC's mandate gave it responsibility for functions ranging from policing to controlling finances. UNTAC was also supposed to separate and demobilize opposing local military forces, clear mines, monitor the withdrawal of foreign military forces, monitor and enforce human rights policies, repatriate refugees, repair the country's infrastructure, and organize elections. The latter included everything from voter education to protection of polling places. UNTAC involved twenty-two thousand UN peacekeepers and other personnel, and cost approximately $2 billion. Following the May 1993 elections, a new government formed and assumed responsibility for running the country. It remains to be seen whether democracy will endure, but UNTAC certainly helped to end the civil war. The election also gave international legitimacy to Cambodia's new government, which made the extension of foreign aid possible once again.

Although UNTAC's disarmament efforts were less than successful, the elections were a conspicuous success. Ninety-six percent of the eligible voters were registered, ninety percent of those registered voted, and violence at the polling stations was minimal. In addition to the resolve of the Cambodians, three principal factors explain this success. First, the United Nations persevered in the face of intimidation, deadly attacks on UN units, and other pre-election violence that killed over two hundred Cambodians. The United Nations employed a variety of tactics to counter these problems, including adjusting UNTAC's mandate, deploying mobile military patrols, arresting troublemakers, and disseminating anti-propaganda. Second, although they vowed to obstruct the election, the Khmer Rouge were unwilling or unable to do so, for reasons that have yet to be explained. Third, UNTAC undertook an unprecedented information and anti-propaganda campaign that explained to the Cambodians how elections worked and why they were important. This effectively countered anti-UNTAC and anti-democracy propaganda. The most important message of the campaign stressed the secrecy of the ballots. A key part of the information campaign was the establishment of Radio UNTAC which, at its peak, broadcast fifteen hours a day and was the most popular station in the country.[37]

Elections can only take place with the consent of the opposing parties. A big problem, therefore, is the possibility that one side or another will reject the results of the election. This can happen in two ways. The first is outright rejection of the election. This happened in Angola in 1992, when Jonas Savimbi rejected the results of the UN-monitored election and resumed fighting. Second, parties reject elections when sponsors or monitors appear to be or actually are biased. This happened to the League of Nations in 1921. Both Germany and Poland claimed Upper Silesia, and a plebiscite was to be held to settle the dispute. The Interallied Plebiscite Commission sent in to keep the peace and monitor the voting had 11,500 French and 2,000 Italian troops; the French openly sided with the Poles. This led the Poles to think that they would win, so when they lost, they rejected the results. More troops from other countries had be to sent in, and France's relations with Germany, Italy, and Britain were damaged. A Japanese member of the League ultimately proposed a plan that resolved the dispute.[38] These cases show that elections sometimes provoke further violence, but this is not the fault of outside observers as long as they remain impartial. The United Nations has generally done a commendable job of maintaining its impartiality when monitoring elections.

OVERVIEW OF THE HISTORICAL RECORD

Collective security organizations have a mixed track record in using the tools at their disposal to prevent, manage, and resolve conflicts. Coercive operations work best when all-out wars are waged. Coercive operations may still succeed when force is used in more measured ways, but they involve risks: mandates can be vague, or become more ambitious over

---

37. See Michael W. Doyle and Ayaka Suzuki, "Transitional Authority in Cambodia," in Weiss, *The United Nations and Civil Wars*, pp. 127–150; Trevor Findlay, *Cambodia: The Legacy and Lessons of UNTAC*, SIPRI Research Report No. 9 (Oxford: Oxford University Press for SIPRI, 1995); Janet E. Heininger, *Peacekeeping in Transition: The United Nations in Cambodia* (New York: Twentieth Century Fund Press, 1994); Steven R. Rattner, "The United Nations in Cambodia: A Model for Resolution of Internal Conflicts?" in Damrosch, *Enforcing Restraint*, pp. 240–273; James A. Schear, "Beyond Traditional Peacekeeping: The Case of Cambodia," in Daniel and Hayes, *Beyond Traditional Peacekeeping*; United Nations, *The United Nations and Cambodia, 1991–1995*, United Nations Blue Book Series, Vol. II (New York: United Nations, 1995), pp. 245–266; conversations with John C. Brown, a Ph.D. Candidate in MIT's Department of Political Science, who is currently writing a dissertation on Cambodia.

38. Wainhouse, *International Peace Observation*, pp. 33–35; and F.P. Walters, *A History of the League of Nations* (London: Oxford University Press, 1952), pp. 145–146.

time. The risk-intolerant political climate, especially in the United States, therefore makes limited coercive operations highly problematic. Traditional, consensual peacekeeping operations, on the other hand, have been at least moderately successful sixty-five percent of the time, and they involve far fewer risks. Mediation helps settle conflicts somewhere between fifteen and twenty-two percent of the time. Most multifunctional operations have succeeded. In short, collective security organizations fare better in some respects than others. Traditional peacekeeping operations, mediation efforts, and multifunctional peace operations stand out as low-risk, cost-effective instruments.

Recommendations

The forgoing analysis provides the basis for two main policy recommendations. First, the United Nations and other collective security organizations should play to their strengths. This would be a banal recommendation were it not for the fact that collective security organizations frequently fail to recognize their limitations. Second, collective security organizations should oppose ethnonationalist hate-mongering with information campaigns of their own.

PLAY TO STRENGTHS
The comparative strengths of collective security organizations are their impartiality, legitimacy, and moral authority. Operations that rely on the consent of the local parties — traditional peacekeeping, mediation, and multifunctional missions involving elections — take advantage of these attributes. Collective security organizations should therefore emphasize these missions, and should generally eschew riskier and more costly coercive missions.

Traditional peacekeeping operations, mediation efforts, and multifunctional peace operations will succeed some of the time, and they are comparatively inexpensive. The United Nations spent a little over $3.5 billion on seventeen peacekeeping operations in 1994, averaging just over $200 million per operation. The United States contributes thirty-one percent of the UN peace operations budget, or about $1 billion per year. In 1994, that represented 0.45 percent of the Department of Defense budget, 0.086 percent of the Federal Budget, and 0.0159 percent (less than 2/100ths of one percent) of the Gross Domestic Product.[39]

---

39. Eric Schmitt, "House Votes Bill to Cut U.N. Funds for Peacekeeping," *New York Times*, February 17, 1995, p. A1; Office of the President of the United States, "A Time for Peace. Promoting Peace: The Policy of the United States," (Washington, D.C.: The

The primary weakness of the United Nations and other collective security organizations is their difficulty in mustering and sustaining coercive force. Some coercive missions fail because they try to be coercive and impartial at the same time. Others fail because they gradually take on coercive assignments for which they are not equipped. Failure is especially likely if an organization's leading powers are indecisive about getting involved in a conflict, and pass the responsibility for handling the conflict to the organization, but then fail to give the organization the resources or forces needed to deal with the problem. This is what has happened in Bosnia, where what is sometimes characterized as a UN failure is really a failure of the great powers who make decisions at the UN Security Council.

Every peace operation risks failure and most also risk lives. Coercive missions generally heighten these risks. One cannot know *a priori* when coercion will work because much depends on the willpower and resolve of the local combatants. However, one's own resolve and interests in a conflict are somewhat easier to determine. Coercive missions in areas of peripheral interest should be avoided unless the humanitarian imperatives are powerful enough to create and sustain strong political support for the operation.

NEUTRALIZE HATE-MONGERS

One of the most prominent proximate causes of internal conflict is ethno-nationalist hate-mongering. Compared to many structural causes of conflict, hate-mongering is tractable. It is usually carried out by elites determined to maintain or elevate their political positions. Hate-mongering tends to be most effective when countries have a history of ethnic conflict or when they are experiencing political or economic turmoil.

Compared to fixing an economy or partitioning large intermingled populations, it is easy to provide information that can counter this kind of ethnic propaganda.[40] Information campaigns can break news monopolies, reveal the outside world's views and actions, promote the idea of minority-group rights, sponsor debates, and rebut incorrect or selective

---

White House, February, 1995), pp. 9–10, 21–22; Boutros-Ghali, *Supplement to "An Agenda for Peace,"* p. 4; and information provided by the Project on Peacekeeping and the United Nations, sponsored by the Council for a Livable World Education Fund.

40. For arguments about manipulating nationalism, see Timothy M. Frye, "Ethnicity, Sovereignty and Transitions from Non-Democratic Rule," in *Journal of International Affairs*, Vol. 45, No. 2 (Winter 1992), pp. 599–623; Ernst B. Haas, "Nationalism: An Instrumental Social Construction," *Millennium: Journal of International Studies*, Vol. 22, No. 3 (Winter 1993), pp. 505–545.

historical claims. Collective security organizations, which have helped to develop and codify human rights (the CSCE's Helsinki Final Act and the UN's Universal Declaration of Human Rights, for example), are well-suited to carry out these kinds of information campaigns.

Ethnonationalist hate-mongering has been one of the driving forces behind many internal conflicts. In Rwanda, for example, Hutu-controlled broadcasts from Radio Mille Collines encouraged the massacre of Tutsi and spurred their exodus from the country. In a country with few media outlets (even fewer after Tutsi journalists were killed) and little outside information, Hutu filled the radio waves with exhortations to "extermi-nate the rats."[41] "The children must also be killed" and the "graves are still half-empty"[42] — these were the battle cries of the Rwandan genocide. Radio Mille Collines also denounced the UN's Assistance Mission for Rwanda (UNAMIR). The UN Secretary-General, the Paris-based group Reporters Without Borders, and independent analysts have all noted the influence of this hate-mongering radio station on events in Rwanda.[43]

In the former Yugoslavia, Serbian President Slobodan Milosevic came to power on a platform that called for creation of a "Greater Serbia." The need for a Greater Serbia was justified in large part by claims that Serbs living outside of Serbia proper were endangered. In 1988 and 1989, huge rallies were staged across Serbia to protest a non-existent genocide and atrocities against Serbs in Kosovo. According to Serb mythology, the world has always been out to get the Serbs, Muslims trade Serb women to Arab sheiks, and Sarajevo has not been under siege. Reinforcing the alleged danger posed by Germany, a Serbian information ministry pamphlet warned that "a Germany stretching from the Adriatic to the Volga is becoming a reality."[44] A group of Serb journalists asked other journalists at a 1992 conference in Germany: "Why aren't you broadcast-ing to Serbia? Don't you realize that Milosevic . . . controls the media? You wouldn't believe the stories they do to whip up ethnic hatred and to justify their genocidal policies."[45] Milosevic's media monopoly allowed him to shape public opinion with "astonishing efficacy and speed," and

---

41. "Rwandan Journalists Aided Massacres, Press Group Says," *Boston Globe*, November 3, 1994, p. 20.

42. Destexhe, "The Third Genocide," p. 8.

43. "Report of the UN Secretary-General on the Situation in Rwanda," S/1994/640, May 31, 1994, reprinted in *International Peacekeeping*, Vol. 1, No. 2 (Summer 1994), pp. 222–223; "Massacres, 'Mindless Violence and Carnage' Rage in Rwanda," p. 20.

44. Roger Thurow and Tony Horwitz, "Hostile Forces: Paranoid and Vengeful, Serbs Claim Their War Is to Right Old Wrongs," *Wall Street Journal*, September 18, 1992, p. 1.

45. Quoted in Sudarsan V. Raghavan, Steven S. Johnson, and Kristi K. Bahrenburg,

he succeeded in convincing the Serbs that UN sanctions were uncon-
nected to his policies.[46]

Ethnonationalist leaders (and revolutionaries) recognize the importance of the media, and are therefore quick to seize control of media
outlets when they come to power. Outside powers, including collective
security organizations, have generally done a poor job in launching anti-
propaganda efforts. The Council of Europe took months to set up a Radio
Boat to broadcast into the former Yugoslavia. However, it had a feeble
signal, and in a move revealing a need for better coordination between
international organizations, the Serbs persuaded the International Tele-
communications Union to shut it down. U.S. Senator Carl Levin argued
that the United States should deploy its specially equipped aircraft to
override Serb television and radio, and broadcast "unfiltered news, evidence of ethnic cleansing by the Serbs, even the text of UN resolutions
and news of world opinion" into Serbia. The U.S. government, however,
found operating the aircraft too costly. Although the United States and its
Western allies officially supported broadcasting into the former
Yugoslavia, they did not take concrete action.[47] More generally, the United
States has cut Radio Free Europe's budget and privatized some of its
branches. Voice of America and the U.S. Information Agency are under
siege from budget-cutters, despite increased shortwave listenership in
South Asia and Africa. (Half of the world's 600 million shortwave radios
are in Africa and Asia.)[48]

Information and anti-propaganda campaigns can be effective. During
the Cold War, the West continually broadcast into Eastern Bloc countries.

---

interview of Malcolm S. Forbes, Jr., "Sending Cross-Border Static," *Journal of International Affairs*, Vol. 47, No. 1 (Summer 1993), p. 78.

46. Stan Markotich, "Government Control over Serbia's Media," *RFE/RL Research
Report*, Vol. 3, No. 5 (February 4, 1994), pp. 38–39. See also V.P. Gagnon, Jr., "Ethnic
Nationalism and International Conflict: The Case of Serbia," *International Security*,
Vol. 19, No. 3 (Winter 1994/95), pp. 130–166; Misha Glenny, "Yugoslavia: The Re-
venger's Tragedy," *New York Review of Books*, August 13, 1992, pp. 3, 38–43.

47. Quote from questions that Senator Levin submitted for the record, following
testimony of Frank Wisner, Undersecretary of Defense for Policy, Senate Committee on
Armed Services, Subcommittee on Coalition Defense and Reinforcing Forces, *International Peacekeeping and Peace Enforcement*, 103rd Cong., 1st sess., July 14, 1993, S. Hrg.
103-353, p. 71. See also Senator Carl Levin, "Use Propaganda Weapon: Broadcast Truth
of War to Bosnian Population," *Defense News*, June 27–July 3, 1994, p. 24; Marlene
Nadle, "Fight the War With Words — At Least," *New York Times*, July 12, 1993, p. A17.

48. David Binder, "Shortwave Radio: More Preachers, Less Propaganda," *New York
Times*, August 28, 1994, sec. 4, p. 6; Craig Whitney, "U.S. Packs Up to Move Radio Free
Europe and Radio Liberty," *New York Times*, August 21, 1994, p. 12.

By breaking control of the locally censored press, these broadcasts provided useful news about such things as the existence and successes of dissidents. When Lech Walesa led Poland's Solidarity movement, he knew that Western broadcasts would spread news of labor strikes in Gdansk across the country. Czechoslovak President Vaclav Havel and Hungarian President Arpad Guncz also maintained that Western broadcasting helped to free their countries. News from the outside undermined government-sponsored news agencies, and undermined confidence in governments themselves. Constant Eastern bloc attempts to jam Western broadcasts also testified to the influence of these broadcasts.[49]

More recently, media exposure helped curb some human rights abuses in Bosnia. According to General MacKenzie:

> . . . wherever the media goes, a lot of the serious violations of human rights either move away or stop. The media was the only major weapon system I had. Whenever I went into negotiations with the warring parties, it was a tremendous weapon to be able to say: "Okay, if you don't want to do it the UN's way, I'll nail your butt on CNN in about 20 minutes." That worked, nine times out of ten.[50]

News of Serb concentration camps enraged the world and led the Serbs to open the camps to UN and Red Cross inspectors and to free some of the prisoners.[51]

The United Nations has been accumulating experience with media missions since 1947, when UN Special Committee on the Balkans (UNSCOB) was ordered to monitor radio broadcasts in the Balkans. In 1958, a monitoring mission in Jordan may have led to the shutdown of hate-mongering Radio Free Jordan broadcasts.[52] Information campaigns have been important parts of many recent UN operations. In Cambodia and Namibia, the United Nations explained to people why they should vote. Not only did UN staff take to the presses and airwaves, they also sent teams of actors and puppeteers into the countryside. In Namibia, the United Nations promoted elections on radio and television, and with post-

---

49. Raghavan, Johnson, and Bahrenburg, "Sending Cross-Border Static"; Kevin J. McNamara, "Reaching Captive Minds with Radio," *Orbis*, Vol. 36, No. 1 (Winter 1992), pp. 23–40.

50. General Lewis MacKenzie, "Military Realities of UN Peacekeeping Operations," *RUSI Journal*, Vol. 138, No. 1 (February 1993), p. 23.

51. Charles William Maynes, "Containing Ethnic Conflict," *Foreign Policy*, No. 90 (Spring 1993), p. 18.

52. Wainhouse, *International Peace Observation*, pp. 224–226, 388, 573.

ers, stickers, leaflets, cartoons, and videotapes. In August 1994, the United Nations was working with the U.S. National Security Agency (NSA) to try to locate a mobile arm of the Hutu radio station Mille Collines (which started broadcasting a day after the original Mille Collines was unplugged). Like its parent station, the mobile station had been hate-mongering and harassing the United Nations. If the NSA had found the station, UN forces would have tried to jam, broadcast over, or otherwise stop it.[53]

Article 39 of the UN Charter specifies that it is up to the Security Council to determine the existence of threats to international peace and to formulate responses. The Security Council has complete discretion to define hate-mongering in a conflict as a threat to international peace and security. The great powers, through the United Nations, clearly have the legal right and the power to take action against hate-mongering, if they are so inclined.

Fortunately, international information campaigns need not be expensive. Although international campaigns could use many different media outlets, from dropped pamphlets and cassettes to radio and television, the costs of constructing and operating radio stations are illustrative. The upper bounds of those costs are suggested by U.S. estimates for establishing a Radio Free China — a huge task. The estimated cost of construction and startup was $110 million, with annual operating expenses of around $34 million. UN information campaigns would be focused on specific, geographically limited areas, and would therefore cost far less to operate than the BBC's worldwide service ($295 million per year), or the U.S. broadcasting effort into the Eastern Bloc during the Cold War ($200 million per year). The United Nations could also cut costs if it bought or received donated time from other stations. Donations are not unrealistic. Private Japanese donors gave nearly 300,000 radios to Cambodians to help Radio UNTAC spread its word. The United Nations already receives donated airtime from stations as diverse as Radio Beijing and Radio Cairo for its politically innocuous public information broadcasts. To put these costs in context, the United Nations spent an average of $212 million on each of its seventeen peace operations in 1994.[54]

---

53. See Ingrid A. Lehmann, "Public Perceptions of U.N. Peacekeeping: A Factor in the Resolution of International Conflicts," *Fletcher Forum*, Vol. 19, No. 1 (Winter/Spring 1995), p. 116; Paul Quinn-Judge, "US Tries to Find Rwanda Radio," *Boston Globe*, August 27, 1994, p. 2; Keith Spicer, "Propaganda for Peace," *New York Times*, December 10, 1994, p. 10.

54. Binder, "Shortwave Radio"; Schear, "Beyond Traditional Peacekeeping: The Case

There are several potential objections to information campaigns. First, it might be said that they will interfere with governance, thus violating the target country's sovereignty. This may be true, but it is also true that the UN Security Council can override the non-interference principle if it determines that international peace and security are threatened. Second, it might be said that information campaigns will reduce the UN's impartiality and impinge on its ability to negotiate with target countries. This may be true in some cases, but it is also true that negotiations and mediation efforts often continue with parties on the receiving end of harsh sanctions. In fact, like sanctions, information campaigns might increase the UN's leverage in negotiations with targeted governments. Third, it might be said that information campaigns will be difficult to implement. This is unlikely to be a problem. Information campaigns will require less international cooperation than economic sanctions and arms embargoes; they do not require major financial sacrifices and are immune to "sanctions runners."

In short, international information and anti-propaganda campaigns are sorely needed. They are also legal, inexpensive, easy to implement, and effective. They should play a much more prominent role in international efforts to prevent, manage, and resolve internal conflicts.

Conclusions

The end of the Cold War generated considerable optimism about the potential of the United Nations and other collective security organizations to create what George Bush called a "new world order." The end of the Cold War has also seen the United Nations and other collective security organizations try to prevent, manage, and resolve a large number of internal conflicts — conflicts that are difficult to deal with under the best of circumstances, but which pose particular problems for collective security bodies. The United Nations, as we know too well, has experienced all sorts of problems in Bosnia and Somalia. However, the United Nations has had considerable success in other parts of the world, e.g., Cambodia, El Salvador, Mozambique, Namibia, and Nicaragua, and these successes should not be overlooked.

Overall, collective security organizations have a mixed track record.

---

of Cambodia," p. 257, in Daniel and Hayes, *Beyond Traditional Peacekeeping;* Hans N. Tuch, "The Case Against Radio Free China," *Foreign Service Journal,* Vol. 69, No. 7 (July 1992), p. 24; Boutros-Ghali, *Supplement to "An Agenda For Peace,"* p. 4; "Cross-Frontier Broadcasting," *Economist,* May 2, 1992, pp. 21–24.

Wise policymakers will play to their strengths — traditional peacekeeping, mediation, and multifunctional peace operations — and add information and anti-propaganda campaigns to the list of actions that collective security organizations perform well and should execute regularly. When they operate with an appreciation of their inherent strengths and weaknesses, collective security organizations can provide very useful policy tools that offer good returns on the money and other resources invested in them.

Part III
Conclusions

Chapter 17

The Causes and Regional Dimensions of Internal Conflict

Michael E. Brown

In this book, we have analyzed three main sets of issues: the causes of internal conflict; the regional dimensions of internal conflict; and international efforts to deal with the problems posed by internal conflict.

First, we have conducted an investigation into the causes of internal conflict, distinguishing between the permissive conditions that make violence more likely and the proximate causes of such violence. We have examined problems in eight important regions of the world — the Balkans, East-Central Europe, the former Soviet Union, South and Southwest Asia, Southeast Asia, the Middle East and North Africa, sub-Saharan Africa, and Latin America — including places where violence has broken out as well as places where it has not. This provides a solid empirical foundation and a good comparative platform for the development of some general arguments about the causes of violent intra-state disputes.

Drawing on these regional studies, I argue that the proximate causes of internal conflict are poorly understood by most observers. Most major internal conflicts are triggered by internal, elite-level actors — to put it bluntly, bad leaders — contrary to what policymakers, popular commentary, and the scholarly literature on the subject generally suggest. Mass-level forces are important, but mainly in terms of creating the underlying conditions that make conflict possible. Bad leaders are usually the catalysts that turn potentially volatile situations into open warfare. External forces occasionally trigger internal conflict, but the deliberate actions of neighboring states — bad neighbors — are more important in this regard than mass-level "contagion," "diffusion," or "spillover" effects. This is also contrary to what one would conclude from reviewing popular commentary and the scholarly literature on the subject.

Second, we have examined the regional dimensions of internal conflict, distinguishing between the effects of internal conflicts on neighboring states and the actions of neighbors with respect to these conflicts.

These broad categories, moreover, can be broken down into several distinct kinds of effects and several distinct kinds of actions.

My main argument with respect to the regional dimensions of internal conflicts is that few such conflicts are hermetically sealed; the vast majority affect or involve neighboring states in one way or another. Internal conflicts almost always have implications for regional stability. Furthermore, although neighboring states can be the innocent victims of internal conflicts, they are often active contributors to military escalation and regional instability. This challenges the view of many policymakers, journalists, and scholars on these matters.

Third, we have analyzed international efforts to address the problems posed by internal conflicts, examining different tasks (conflict prevention, conflict management, conflict resolution), policy instruments (humanitarian assistance, fact-finding, mediation, confidence-building measures, traditional and multifunctional peacekeeping operations, arms embargoes and arms transfers, economic sanctions and inducements, judicial enforcement measures, and the use of military force) and key international actors (states operating either unilaterally or multilaterally, international organizations, and nongovernmental organizations [NGOs]).

Our collective assessment is that the track record of international efforts in this area is mixed. However, we prefer to think of the glass as being half-full: policy options *do* exist, and these options, in our view, have not been optimally utilized. The key lies in understanding the problems different kinds of actions face and the conditions under which different kinds of actions are most likely to be effective.

I will endeavor to develop these arguments and make some concrete policy recommendations in this book's two concluding chapters. In this chapter, I will focus on the causes and regional dimensions of internal conflict, which are intertwined issues. In the next, I will examine the track record of international efforts to deal with the problems posed by internal conflict, and offer some policy recommendations.

The Causes of Internal Conflict

The widely held view in policymaking and journalistic circles about the causes of internal conflicts — that they are driven by the "ancient hatreds" many ethnic groups have toward each other — is pervasive but simplistic and ultimately unsatisfying. It is certainly true that historical grievances, long-standing grudges, and deep-seated desires for revenge have played important roles in many of the internal conflicts that have raged across the landscape of the post–Cold War world — in the former Yugoslavia, Rwanda, Chechnya, and Sri Lanka, for example. But it is also true that many other groups — Ukrainians and Russians, Czechs and Slovaks, French-speaking and English-speaking Canadians, Maori and Pakeha in New Zealand — have historical grievances, ethnic grudges, and less than benign images of each other, but they have abstained from killing each other in large numbers over recent political disputes. In addition, many internal conflicts are not driven by ethnic grievances at all, but by power struggles, ideological crusades, and criminal agendas. In short, the "ancient hatreds" explanation for the causes of internal conflict cannot account for significant variation in the incidence and intensity of such conflict. It is not a good explanation of why conflicts break out and escalate in some areas, but not in others.

Political philosophers and social scientists have pondered the causes of internal conflicts for years, and have advanced our knowledge in important ways. More specifically, they have identified four main clusters of factors that make some places more predisposed to violence than others: structural factors such as weak states, security concerns, and ethnic geography; political factors such as discriminatory political institutions, exclusionary national ideologies, inter-group politics, and elite politics; economic/social factors such as widespread economic problems, discriminatory economic systems, and economic development and modernization; and cultural/perceptual factors such as patterns of cultural discrimination and problematic group histories.

The scholarly literature on internal conflict has three great strengths and three corresponding weaknesses. First, it is impressive in its discussion of the permissive conditions that make some places prone to violence, but it is weak when it comes to identifying the proximate causes of internal conflict. Second, the literature gives considerable attention to the structural, political, economic, social, cultural, and perceptual forces that operate on a mass level, clearly favoring mass-level explanations of the causes of internal conflicts, but it has much less to say about the roles played by elites and leaders in instigating violence. Third, the scholarly literature has much to say about the forces at work within countries, but it is less illuminating with respect to external forces. Attention has generally focused on mass-level "contagion" or "diffusion" effects, whose causal mechanisms are poorly specified. The roles played by neighboring states in triggering conflicts have by and large been ignored. As a result, several important sets of factors have received insufficient attention.

In trying to explain the causes of internal conflict, we must be careful to avoid three analytic traps. First, although more thought needs to be given to the proximate causes of internal conflict, the permissive conditions that make violence more likely should not be set aside. We need to think about how these two sets of factors interact, and how they can be integrated into a more comprehensive framework for analyzing these issues. Second, although more thought needs to be given to the roles played by elites and leaders in instigating violence, the role of other factors that influence mass behavior cannot be ignored. Here, too, we need to think about how these two sets of factors interact, and how they can be integrated into a more comprehensive analytic framework. As Donald Horowitz has observed, we need a theory that integrates elite-level and mass-level factors. To put it more prosaically, we need to answer two questions: how do leaders lead? And why do followers follow?[1] Third, although the catalytic role that external forces — neighboring states, in particular — can play needs to be defined more carefully, we cannot leave internal factors out of the equation. Again, our goal should be the development of an analytic framework that integrates these two sets of factors in a comprehensive package.

The danger, more generally, lies in failing to recognize that internal conflict is a complex phenomenon. There are several different types of internal conflict, each activated by different sets of factors.[2] This means that, by definition, no single-factor explanation, such as "ancient hatreds," will be able to account for everything. The problem with "ancient hatreds" theorizing is not that historical grievances are irrelevant but that a single factor is said to be responsible for a wide range of developments. To put it in more formal methodological terms, a single independent variable is said to govern a wide range of dependent variables. This is asking a lot of any one variable or factor. It would therefore be a mistake to replace this particular single-factor explanation with another, one based on "economic discrimination," for example.[3] By the same token, we should not try to come up with a single list that ranks factors in order of

---

1. Donald L. Horowitz, *Ethnic Groups in Conflict* (Berkeley: University of California Press, 1985), p. 140.

2. Indeed, although we could classify internal conflicts in any number of ways — according to type of antagonists or level of violence, for example — the most useful way to categorize conflicts is in terms of their causes.

3. It must be emphasized that the best scholarly studies of internal conflict are powerful precisely because they do not rely on single-factor explanations. Instead, they try to weave several factors into a more complex argument. See, for example, Samuel P. Huntington, *Political Order in Changing Societies* (New Haven, Conn.: Yale University Press, 1968); Jack Snyder, "Nationalism and the Crisis of the Post-Soviet State," in Michael E. Brown, ed., *Ethnic Conflict and International Security* (Princeton, N.J.: Princeton University Press, 1993), pp. 79–101; Barry R. Posen, "The Security Dilemma and Ethnic Conflict," in Brown, *Ethnic Conflict and International Security*, pp. 103–124; Stephen Van Evera, "Hypotheses on Nationalism and War," *International Security*, Vol. 18, No. 4 (Spring 1994), pp. 5–39; Ted Robert Gurr and Barbara Harff, *Ethnic Conflict and World Politics* (Boulder, Colo.: Westview, 1994), chap. 5.

importance. A simple rank-ordering exercise will fail to capture the complexity of the phenomenon we are trying to explain.[4] Instead, we need to think in terms of identifying several main types of internal conflicts and the sets of factors that cluster together and bring about different types of conflicts.

I will develop four main arguments in the next few sections of this chapter. First and most generally, the proximate causes of internal conflict are poorly understood. Important factors — the roles played by domestic elites and neighboring states, in particular — have been neglected by most studies of this issue. The starting point for understanding the proximate causes of internal conflict is developing a comprehensive framework that includes all relevant factors and organizes them in a useful way. I will argue that, in theory, internal conflicts can be triggered by any one of four sets of proximate causes: internal, mass-level factors (bad domestic problems); external, mass-level factors (bad neighborhoods); external, elite-level factors (bad neighbors); or internal, elite-level factors (bad leaders).

Second, the scholarly literature on the causes of internal conflict emphasizes the importance of the first two sets of factors: internal, mass-level factors such as economic development and modernization; and external, mass-level factors, which are usually characterized as "contagion" or "diffusion" effects. I will argue that, when one categorizes all active, major internal conflicts according to the four-part framework just outlined, one observes different patterns. Major conflicts are rarely triggered by "contagion" effects or bad neighborhoods. Major conflicts are occasionally triggered by external forces, but the deliberate, malicious actions of neighboring states — bad neighbors — play a more prominent role than mass-level phenomena. Although many internal conflicts are triggered by internal, mass-level factors, the vast majority are triggered by internal, elite-level factors. In short, bad leaders are the biggest problem.

Third, I will argue that there are three main types of internally-driven, elite-triggered conflicts: ideological conflicts, which are driven by the ideological convictions of one or more of the parties to the conflict; criminal assaults on state sovereignty, which are driven primarily by the economic motivations of drug barons; and power struggles between and

---

4. For a discussion of the problems of theorizing in this area, see Harry Eckstein, "Introduction: Toward the Theoretical Study of Internal War," in Harry Eckstein, ed., *Internal War: Problems and Approaches* (New York: Free Press, 1964), pp. 1–32; Walter Lacquer, "Diversities of Violence and the Current World System," in *Civil Violence and the International System*, Adelphi Paper No. 83 (London: International Institute for Strategic Studies [IISS], 1971), pp. 9–16; Milton J. Esman, *Ethnic Politics* (Ithaca, N.Y.: Cornell University Press, 1994), pp. 266–267.

among competing elites, which are driven mainly by personal, political motivations. Of the three, raw power struggles are far and away the most common.

Fourth, power struggles are most likely to lead to widespread violence when three conditions are met: political elites are vulnerable; group histories are antagonistic; and domestic economic problems are mounting. When all three factors are present, permissive conditions and active catalysts come together, and the potential for violence is great.

PROXIMATE CAUSES OF INTERNAL CONFLICT

The existing literature gives us a running start at developing a framework for analyzing the proximate causes of internal conflict because it provides us with a well-rounded set of twelve structural, political, economic/ social, and cultural/perceptual factors that predispose some regions to violence. If we assume that each of these twelve underlying factors can play a more catalytic role if rapid changes take place in the area in question, then we also have a list of twelve possible proximate causes of internal conflict. (See Table 17.1.)

In brief, states are especially prone to violence if state structures are collapsing due to external developments (such as sharp reductions in international financial assistance or sharp declines in commodity prices), internal problems (new, incompetent leaders or rampant corruption), or some combination of the above. Under these circumstances, states are increasingly unable to cope with societal demands.[5] When state structures weaken or when new states are created out of the rubble of a larger entity, groups have a heightened sense of potential security problems. They are more likely to take measures to protect themselves which, in turn, are more likely to generate fears in other groups. In situations such as these, security dilemmas are especially intense and arms races are especially likely. Changing military balances or fears about possible adverse developments make arms racing and conflict escalation difficult to control.[6] Demographic changes brought about by birthrate differentials, migration, urbanization, or sudden influxes of refugees can aggravate ethnic problems and further complicate the picture by changing the domestic balance of power.

Political transitions brought about by the collapse of authoritarian rule, democratization, or political reforms also make states particularly

---

5. See I. William Zartman, "Introduction: Posing the Problem of State Collapse," in I. William Zartman, ed., *Collapsed States: The Disintegration and Restoration of Legitimate Authority* (Boulder, Colo.: Lynne Rienner, 1995), pp. 1–11.

6. See Posen, "The Security Dilemma and Ethnic Conflict."

Table 17.1. The Underlying and Proximate Causes of Internal Conflict.

Underlying Causes	Proximate Causes
Structural Factors	**Structural Factors**
Weak states	Collapsing states
Intra-state security concerns	Changing intra-state military balances
Ethnic geography	Changing demographic patterns
Political Factors	**Political Factors**
Discriminatory political institutions	Political transitions
Exclusionary national ideologies	Increasingly influential exclusionary ideologies
Inter-group politics	Growing inter-group competitions
Elite politics	Intensifying leadership struggles
Economic/Social Factors	**Economic/Social Factors**
Economic problems	Mounting economic problems
Discriminatory economic systems	Growing economic inequities
Economic development and modernization	Fast-paced development and modernization
Cultural/Perceptual Factors	**Cultural/Perceptual Factors**
Patterns of cultural discrimination	Intensifying patterns of cultural discrimination
Problematic group histories	Ethnic bashing and propagandizing

prone to violence.[7] The emergence and rise of exclusionary national ideologies, such as ethnic nationalism and religious fundamentalism, can be destabilizing as well. The emergence of dehumanizing ideologies, which literally deny the humanity of other ethnic groups, is particularly dangerous because it is often the precursor to genocidal slaughter.[8] The rise of new groups or changes in the inter-group balance of power can intensify inter-group competition and anxieties, making political systems more volatile.[9] The emergence of power struggles between and among elites can be particularly problematic, because desperate and opportunistic

7. See Edward D. Mansfield and Jack Snyder, "Democratization and the Danger of War," *International Security*, Vol. 20, No. 1 (Summer 1995), pp. 5–38.

8. On ethnic nationalism, see Snyder, "Nationalism and the Crisis of the Post-Soviet State." On dehumanizing ideologies, see Helen Fein, "Explanations of Genocide," *Current Sociology*, Vol. 38, No. 1 (Spring 1990), pp. 32–50; Leo Kuper, *Genocide: Its Political Use in the Twentieth Century* (New Haven, Conn.: Yale University Press, 1981), chap. 3.

9. See Joseph Rothschild, *Ethnopolitics: A Conceptual Framework* (New York: Columbia University Press, 1981); Charles Tilly, *From Mobilization to Revolution* (Reading, Mass.: Addison-Wesley, 1978); Horowitz, *Ethnic Groups in Conflict*; Gurr and Harff, *Ethnic Conflict and World Politics*; Van Evera, "Hypotheses on Nationalism and War."

politicians are particularly prone to employing divisive ethnic and nation-alistic appeals.[10]

Potentially catalytic economic and social problems include mounting economic difficulties, intensifying resource competitions, growing economic inequities and gaps, and fast-paced development and modern-ization processes.[11] Industrialized countries, countries attempting to make the transition from centrally-planned to market-driven systems, and developing countries generally have to contend with different kinds of problems, but they are all susceptible to economically and socially induced turmoil.

Finally, states are especially prone to violence if discrimination against minorities intensifies or if politicians begin to blame some ethnic groups for whatever political and economic problems their country may be experiencing. Ethnic bashing and scapegoating are often precursors to violence.[12]

Creating lists of possible underlying and proximate causes of internal conflict is a useful starting point for analyzing these issues, but it does not take us far enough. Since we are primarily interested in the sources and origins of violence, it follows that we should pay special attention to the proximate causes of conflict — the catalytic factors that transform potentially violent situations into deadly conflicts.[13] However, this list of twelve possible proximate causes does not distinguish sharply between elite-level and mass-level factors. It is incomplete, moreover, because it does not take into account the catalytic role that neighboring states and developments in neighboring states can play in triggering violence.

---

10. See V.P. Gagnon, Jr., "Ethnic Nationalism and International Conflict: The Case of Serbia," *International Security*, Vol. 19, No. 3 (Winter 1994/95), pp. 130–166; Human Rights Watch, *Playing the "Communal Card": Communal Violence and Human Rights* (New York: Human Rights Watch, 1995); Warren Zimmerman, "The Last Ambassador: A Memoir of the Collapse of Yugoslavia," *Foreign Affairs*, Vol. 74, No. 2 (March–April 1995), pp. 2–20.

11. See, for example, Sandy Gordon, "Resources and Instability in South Asia," *Survival*, Vol. 35, No. 2 (Summer 1993), pp. 66–87.

12. See Snyder, "Nationalism and the Crisis of the Post-Soviet State," pp. 92–93; Posen, "The Security Dilemma and Ethnic Conflict," p. 107; Van Evera, "Hypotheses on Nationalism and War," pp. 8–9; Donald Rothchild and Alexander J. Groth, "Pathological Dimensions of Domestic and International Ethnicity," *Political Science Quarterly*, Vol. 110, No. 1 (Spring 1995), pp. 69–82.

13. Since many permissive conditions or underlying factors are present in most cases where violence does break out, we will find it easier to identify different types of conflicts and classify cases if we focus our attention for the moment on proximate causes. This is not to say that underlying factors or permissive conditions are unimportant, only that they can be most usefully integrated into the equation later on.

Table 17.2. The Proximate Causes of Internal Conflict.		
	Internally-driven	Externally-driven
Elite-triggered	Bad leaders	Bad neighbors
Mass-triggered	Bad domestic problems	Bad neighborhoods

I argue that internal conflicts can be categorized according to whether they are triggered by elite-level or mass-level factors;[14] and whether they are triggered by internal or external developments. There are, therefore, four main types of internal conflicts, and they can be depicted in a two-by-two matrix. (See Table 17.2.) Put another way, internal conflict can, in theory, be triggered by any one of four sets of proximate causes.

First, conflicts can be triggered by internal, mass-level phenomena, such as rapid economic development and modernization or patterns of political and economic discrimination. To put it more prosaically, they can be caused by "bad domestic problems." The conflicts in Punjab and Sri Lanka are examples, the former being galvanized by rapid modernization and migration and the latter by long-standing patterns of political, economic, and cultural discrimination.[15] Another example is the conflict over Nagorno-Karabakh, which was triggered by problematic ethnic geography and patterns of discrimination highlighted by the breakup of the Soviet Union.[16]

The proximate causes of a second set of conflicts are mass-level but external in character: swarms of refugees or fighters crashing across borders, bringing turmoil and violence with them, or radicalized politics sweeping throughout regions. These are conflicts caused by the "contagion," "diffusion," and "spillover" effects to which many policymakers,

---

14. The utility of the distinction between elite-level and mass-level factors has been noted by others. See Renée de Nevers, *The Soviet Union and Eastern Europe: The End of an Era*, Adelphi Paper No. 249 (London: IISS, 1990), pp. 27–29; Stuart J. Kaufman, "An 'International' Theory of Inter-Ethnic War," *Review of International Studies*, Vol. 22, No. 2 (April 1996), pp. 149–171.

15. See Sumit Ganguly's chapter on South and Southwest Asia in this volume.

16. See Matthew Evangelista's chapter on the former Soviet Union and Alicia Levine's chapter on secessionist violence, both in this volume.

analysts, and scholars give much credence.[17] One could say that such conflicts are caused by "bad neighborhoods." The expulsion of radical Palestinians from Jordan in 1970 led many militants to resettle in Lebanon, where Muslim-Christian tensions were already mounting. This, one could argue, was the spark that ignited the civil war in Lebanon in 1975.

The proximate causes of a third set of conflicts are external but elite-level in character: they are the results of discrete, deliberate decisions by governments to trigger conflicts in nearby states for political, economic, or ideological purposes of their own. This only works, one must note, when the permissive conditions for conflict already exist in the target country; outsiders are generally unable to foment trouble in stable, just societies. Such conflicts, one could say, are caused by "bad neighbors." Examples include the Soviet Union's meddling in and subsequent 1979 invasion of Afghanistan, which has yet to emerge from chaos, and Russian meddling in Georgia and Moldova in the 1990s.[18] Another example is Rhodesia's establishment of the Mozambican National Resistance (RENAMO) in 1976 to undermine the new government in Mozambique.[19]

The proximate causes of the fourth and final type of internal conflict are internal and elite-level in character. Variations include: power struggles involving civilian (Georgia) or military (Nigeria) leaders; ideological contests over how a country's political, economic, social, and religious affairs should be organized (Algeria, Peru); and criminal assaults on the state (Colombia). To put it in simple terms, conflicts such as these are triggered and driven by "bad leaders."

PATTERNS OF INTERNAL CONFLICT

Most scholars seem to think that the first two types of conflicts — those triggered by internal, mass-level developments and by external, mass-level developments — are far more common than the latter two — those driven by elite-level forces either internal or external to the state in

---

17. See, for example, John A. Vasquez, "Factors Related to the Contagion and Diffusion of International Violence," in Manus I. Midlarsky, ed., *The Internationalization of Communal Strife* (London: Routledge, 1992), pp. 149–172; Ted Robert Gurr, *Minorities at Risk: A Global View of Ethnopolitical Conflicts* (Washington, D.C.: U.S. Institute of Peace, 1993), pp. 132–135. For a thoughtful review of the literature on contagion and diffusion effects, see Stuart Hill and Donald Rothchild, "The Contagion of Political Conflict in Africa and the World," *Journal of Conflict Resolution*, Vol. 30, No. 4 (December 1986), pp. 716–735.

18. On Afghanistan, see Sumit Ganguly's chapter on South and Southwest Asia, in this volume. On Moldova and Georgia, see Matthew Evangelista's chapter on the former Soviet Union, in this volume.

19. I thank Stephen Stedman for suggesting this illustration.

question. This is reflected in the existence of a massive literature on internal, mass-level forces such as modernization and a robust literature on "contagion," "diffusion," and "spillover" effects.[20] Elite-level factors — bad leaders and bad neighbors — have received comparatively little attention.[21]

To test this line of thinking and develop a better sense of the types of internal conflicts that plague the world today, we can attempt to classify all major, active conflicts in terms of these variables and plot these cases onto our two-by-two matrix.[22] This is not a simple task, but neither is it impossible.[23] (See Table 17.3.)

Six main propositions are suggested. First, the idea that internal

---

20. On the former, see my introductory chapter to this volume. On the latter, see Hill and Rothchild, "The Contagion of Political Conflict."

21. For some studies that have examined the role of elites in instigating violence, see note 10.

22. A "major" conflict is defined as one in which at least 1,000 people have been killed. For a list of major, active internal conflicts, see Table 1 in my introductory chapter to this volume.

23. Several caveats have to be noted. First, there is no doubt that multiple forces are at work in most cases, particularly in terms of generating the permissive conditions that make conflict possible and likely. For this exercise to succeed, we will have to focus on the proximate causes of violence and try to identify the critical factors that push potentially violent situations across the line and transform them into deadly confrontations.

Second, to be sustained over time, internal conflicts need both leaders and followers: without the former, mass action lacks focus and eventually dies out; without the latter, one has little more than conspirators in a cafe. This makes it difficult to classify cases according to a binary, either/or framework. However, it should be possible in most cases to make a reasoned judgment and identify the key catalytic factors that led to the onset of violence.

Third, sorting out internal and external factors is also difficult. As noted above, neighboring states cannot trigger internal conflicts unless trouble is already brewing. The key here is identifying cases in which external actors were responsible for initiating violence that otherwise would not have taken place. We must also be careful to distinguish between external meddling that sparks violence and meddling that takes place after a conflict has already begun; the latter is very common.

Fourth, analysis is complicated because some countries are plagued by multiple conflicts; Colombia, Georgia, India, and Indonesia are examples. Different conflicts in the same country might have different proximate causes. Some conflicts, moreover, have mutated and become more complex over time: political movements in Burma, Colombia, and Peru, for example, have turned to drug trafficking to finance their activities; several class-based conflicts in Latin America have taken on ethnic agendas since the end of the Cold War; and power struggles in the former Yugoslavia and Rwanda, for example, have become ethnic holocausts. Not surprisingly, most if not all raw power struggles are misrepresented by those involved in the contests and characterized in nobler terms — as ethnic, religious, or ideological crusades.

Table 17.3. The Proximate Causes of Major, Active Internal Conflicts.

	Internally-driven	Externally-driven
Elite-triggered	Algeria Angola Bosnia Burma Burundi Cambodia Colombia Croatia Egypt Guatemala Indonesia (East Timor, Irian Jaya) Iran Iraq Kenya Liberia Peru Philippines Russia (Chechnya) Rwanda Somalia Sudan Tajikistan Turkey	Afghanistan Georgia Moldova
Mass-triggered	Azerbaijan (Nagorno-Karabakh) Bangladesh (Chittagong Hills) India (Punjab, Kashmir) Israel Pakistan (Sindh) Sri Lanka United Kingdom (Northern Ireland)	Sierra Leone

conflicts are driven more by mass-level forces than by elite-level forces seems to be off target. Elite-level forces are often the proximate causes of internal conflicts. This does not mean that mass-level factors are unimportant, only that their role in triggering violence is less prominent than many postulate.

Second, the idea that internal conflicts are often triggered by external forces also seems to be off target. In this sample of active conflicts, violence was triggered by internal factors in the vast majority of cases. Although internal conflicts often have important regional implications and often involve neighbors who jump in once hostilities are under way, they are almost always triggered by internal forces of one kind or another.

Third, the widely held view that internal conflicts are often triggered by external "contagion" or "spillover" effects is particularly suspect. In this sample of active internal conflicts, only one — the civil war in Sierra Leone — was triggered by "spillover effects" from a neighboring state. And one could argue that this war was not triggered by mass-level forces, but by Liberian rebel leader Charles Taylor, a bad neighbor if there ever was one, who invaded Sierra Leone in order to plunder its diamond mines and fund his militia.[24] This suggests that, although internal conflicts can generate a wide range of military, economic, and political problems in neighboring states, they rarely trigger new, massive blood-lettings.[25]

Fourth, to the extent that external forces are responsible for triggering internal conflicts, the deliberate acts of neighboring states — bad neighbors — seem to be more important than mass-level "spillover" effects. However, it is important to note that all three of the conflicts in this sample that were triggered by neighboring states — Afghanistan, Georgia, and Moldova — were sparked by Moscow. If we set aside these conflicts on the grounds that problems involving the former Soviet Union might be special cases, this type of internal conflict also appears to be comparatively rare.

Fifth, most of the conflicts that were triggered by internal, mass-level forces were driven by ethnic strife born out of unfortunate ethnic geography and decolonization. These ethnic problems were intensified by historical grievances, perceived patterns of political, economic, and cultural discrimination, and, in some cases, the effects of economic development and modernization. Although leaders played roles in every conflict, one could argue that these ethnic conflicts were likely to erupt regardless of who was at the helm.

Sixth and last, most major, active internal conflicts were triggered by internal, elite-level forces. This is clearly contrary to what most scholars would argue about the causes of internal conflicts. Although mass-level

---

24. See Stephen Stedman's chapter on sub-Saharan Africa in this volume.

25. One can hypothesize that internal conflicts are most likely to lead to turmoil in neighboring states when ethnic groups straddle international borders, and when empires break up. On the former, see Gurr, *Minorities at Risk*, pp. 132–135. On the latter with respect to the collapse of Soviet power in Eastern Europe, see de Nevers, *The Soviet Union and Eastern Europe*, pp. 27–29. Much also depends on the stability on the neighboring states in question; see Hill and Rothchild, "The Contagion of Political Conflict."

factors are clearly important underlying conditions that make some places more predisposed to violence than others, and although neighboring states routinely meddle in the internal affairs of others, the decisions and actions of domestic elites often determine whether political disputes veer toward war or peace. Leaving elite decisions and actions out of the equation, as many social scientists do, is analytically misguided. It also has important policy implications: under-appreciating the import of elite decisions and actions hinders conflict prevention efforts and fails to place blame where blame is due.

INTERNALLY-DRIVEN, ELITE-TRIGGERED CONFLICTS
The proximate causes of many internal conflicts are the decisions and actions of domestic elites, but these conflicts are not all driven by the same domestic forces. There are three main variations: ideological struggles, which are driven by the ideological convictions of various individuals; criminal assaults on state sovereignty, which are driven primarily by the economic motivations of drug traffickers; and power struggles between and among competing elites, which are driven by personal, political motivations.[26] Admittedly, these compartments are not water-tight. It is nonetheless important to make these distinctions, however rough they might be: there are several, distinct motivational forces at work here — several identifiable proximate causes of internal violence. It is important to have an appreciation of the multifaceted nature of the problem, particularly if one is interested in enhancing international efforts to prevent, manage, and resolve conflict.

IDEOLOGICAL CONFLICTS. First, some internally-driven, elite-triggered conflicts are ideological struggles over the organization of political, economic, and social affairs in a country. Some ideological struggles are defined in economic or class terms; others are fundamentalist religious crusades guided by theological frameworks. Ideological struggles over how political, economic, and social affairs should be organized have not gone away with the end of the Cold War, but they have tended to take on new forms. Class-based movements with Marxist agendas have faded from the scene in many parts of the world, including Southeast Asia, the

---

26. As noted above, this kind of exercise is inherently problematic. Some conflicts have mutated over time and have more than one distinguishing characteristic. Most power struggles are characterized by those involved in politically convenient ethnic or ideological terms. Many of these conflicts have powerful ethnic dimensions. These problems make analysis difficult, but not impossible. For further discussion, see note 23.

Middle East, Africa, and Latin America, although some rebels in Colombia and Peru have remained largely true to form. Some rebel movements — in Guatemala, for example — have mutated and taken on the political agendas of indigenous peoples and ethnic minorities. In many places — Afghanistan, Algeria, Egypt, India, Iran, Sudan — conflicts have formed around new secularist-fundamentalist fault lines. These ethnic and fundamentalist movements draw on many of the same sources that impelled class-based movements in the Cold War era — patterns of political, economic, and cultural discrimination, and widespread dissatisfaction with the pace and equitability of economic development — but they are channeled in different directions. In other words, many of the underlying causes of these conflicts are the same, but their proximate causes have changed.

CRIMINAL ASSAULTS ON STATE SOVEREIGNTY. Second, some internally-driven, elite-triggered conflicts are in effect criminal assaults on state sovereignty. In several countries in Asia and Latin America, in particular, drug cartels have accumulated enough power to challenge state control over large tracts of territory. This is certainly true in Afghanistan, Brazil, Burma, Mexico, Tajikistan, and Venezuela, for example. In Colombia, most notably, state sovereignty has been directly challenged by drug barons and their criminal organizations.[27] This problem shows no sign of abating. A related problem is that, with the end of the Cold War and consequent reductions in financial support from Moscow and Washington, many ethnic groups and political movements have turned to drug trafficking to finance their activities. This is true, for example, of various groups in Colombia and Peru.[28] In addition to its other pernicious effects, drug trafficking complicates the nature of the conflicts in question and therefore makes conflict management and resolution more difficult.

POWER STRUGGLES. Third, some conflicts are in essence power struggles among competing elites. Of the three types of internally-driven, elite-triggered conflicts outlined here, raw power struggles are clearly the most common. Some are sustained government campaigns to repress ethnic minorities and democratic activists. This would seem to be a fair characterization of the conflicts in Burma, Cambodia, Guatemala, Indonesia, Iraq, and Turkey, for example. Government repression is a prominent

---

27. For a detailed discussion of drug-related problems in Latin America, see Marc Chernick's chapter in this volume.

28. Ibid.

feature of other conflicts as well, but power struggles are particularly intense and the "ethnic card" is played very aggressively. Examples abound: Angola, Bosnia, Burundi, Croatia, Kenya, Liberia, the Philippines, Russia/Chechnya, Rwanda, Somalia, and Tajikistan.

One type of power struggle is particularly prominent and particularly pernicious: it accounts for the slaughter in Rwanda and the former Yugoslavia, and has played a role in the conflicts in Azerbaijan, Burundi, Cameroon, Chechnya, Georgia, India, Kenya, Nigeria, Romania, Sri Lanka, Sudan, Togo, Zaire, and elsewhere.[29] The starting point is a lack of elite legitimacy, which sooner or later leads to elite vulnerability. Vulnerabilities can be brought about by weakening state structures, political transitions, pressures for political reform, and economic problems. Those who are in power are determined to fend off emerging political challengers and anxious to shift the blame for whatever economic and political setbacks their countries may be experiencing. In cases where ideological justifications for staying in power have been overtaken by events, they need to devise new formulas for legitimizing their rule. Entrenched politicians and aspiring leaders alike have powerful incentives to play the "communal card," embracing ethnic identities and proclaiming themselves the champions of ethnic groups.[30]

This produces a shift in the terms of public discourse from civic nationalism to ethnic nationalism and to increasingly virulent forms of ethnic nationalism. Ethnic minorities are often singled out and blamed for the country's problems, and ethnic scapegoating and ethnic bashing become the order of the day. When power struggles are fierce, politicians portray other ethnic groups in threatening terms, and inflate these threats to bolster group solidarity and their own political positions; perceived threats are extremely powerful unifying devices.[31] When leaders have control over the national media, these kinds of campaigns are particularly effective: a relentless drumbeat of ethnic propaganda can distort political discourse quickly and dramatically. Political campaigns such as these undermine stability and push countries towards violence by dividing and radicalizing groups along ethnic fault lines. In the former Yugoslavia, Serbian leader Slobodan Milosevic and Croatian leader Franjo Tudjman rose to power by polarizing their societies even though Serbs and Croats had previously coexisted peacefully for decades.

---

29. See Human Rights Watch, *Playing the "Communal Card."* See also Stephen Stedman's chapter on sub-Saharan Africa in this volume.

30. See Human Rights Watch, *Playing the "Communal Card."*

31. See Esman, *Ethnic Politics*, p. 244.

WHY DO FOLLOWERS FOLLOW?   It is easy to understand why desperate and opportunistic politicians in the midst of power struggles would resort to such tactics. For many politicians, tearing their countries apart and causing thousands of people to be killed are small prices to pay for staying in or getting power. The more interesting question is: why do followers follow? Given that politicians all over the world employ ethnic appeals of one kind or another, why do these appeals resonate in some places but not in others? Why do large numbers of people follow the ethnic flag in some places at some times, but not others?

The survey in this book of several dozen conflicts in eight regions of the world suggests that two factors are particularly important in this regard: the existence of antagonistic group histories; and mounting economic problems. If groups have negative histories of each other and especially if they see themselves as victims of other, aggressive communities, inflated ethnic threats seem plausible. If economic problems such as unemployment and inflation are mounting and resource competitions are intensifying, ethnic scapegoating is more likely to resonate and more people are likely to accept a radical change in a country's political course, including armed confrontation. In short, the emergence of elite competitions might be the proximate causes of conflicts in places like the former Yugoslavia and Rwanda, but hostilities escalate only because of the existence of other underlying problems or permissive conditions — problematic group histories and economic problems.

It appears that all three factors — irresponsible leaders driven by intensifying elite competitions; problematic group histories; and economic problems — must be present for this kind of conflict to explode. Russians and Ukrainians, for example, have had to contend with collapsing economies and standards of living, and many Ukrainians do not have benign historical images of Russians. However, Ukrainian politicians have by and large refrained from making the kinds of nationalistic appeals that have caused trouble elsewhere. They undoubtedly recognize that provoking a Russian-Ukrainian confrontation would not bode well for their own positions as leaders of an independent state. Some Russian politicians have been far less responsible in this regard, but their nationalistic appeals have not yet taken over the Russian national debate. Whether or not nationalistic and pseudo-nationalistic politicians remain confined to the margins of the Russian political debate is certainly one of the keys to its future and to the stability of a large part of the world.

A few parts of the world have experienced economic turmoil and power struggles, but have been blessed with homogeneous populations and few internal ethnic problems. Finland, for example, has experienced a sharp economic decline since the late 1980s but has not experienced interethnic strife because minorities are few and small and because inter-group relations are relatively harmonious. Similarly, Poland has gone through a complete political and economic transformation since 1989, but it has few minorities and few inter-group problems: nationalistic appeals have no audience. Poland's hotly contested 1995 presidential election was consequently fought along ideological lines.

Other parts of the world have deeply troubled ethnic histories and leaders who have not hesitated to do whatever was necessary to get and keep power, but they have been spared massive bloodlettings because of their comparatively rosy economic pictures. Much of Southeast Asia — Malaysia and Thailand, for example — experienced considerable turmoil during the Cold War, but are quite stable today because of the economic boom that has swept most of the region. Indonesia has had to contend with simmering conflicts in East Timor, Irian Jaya, and Aceh, but these conflicts have not escalated dramatically, nor has the country as a whole splintered into dozens or hundreds of ethnic fragments, as it might have.[32] Much of this can be traced to a track record of sustained economic growth, which gives even relatively disadvantaged groups incentives to avoid conflict and destruction of a system that is bringing more and more economic benefits to increasing numbers of people.

One can also point to East-Central Europe, which has experienced more than its share of turmoil in the past and which is not blessed with leaders steeped in the principles of Jeffersonian democracy, but which has nonetheless avoided the carnage that has consumed the former Yugo-slavia a few hundred miles to the south. East-Central Europe has been comparatively peaceful even though every country in the region has been going through a political transition of the most profound sort; elites have been jockeying for position ever since 1989. If one had to choose one reason for East-Central Europe's stability, one would point to its compara-tively good economic performance and its comparatively good economic prospects. The fact that the states of this region have a good chance of joining the European Union at some point in the not-too-distant future gives people powerful incentives to ignore nationalistic appeals and not to rock the boat. This point is driven home with even greater force when one looks at differences within the region: nationalistic appeals have been less successful in Hungary, which has an ethnic diaspora but one of the region's strongest economies and one of the region's best chances of

---

32. See Trevor Findlay's chapter on Southeast Asia in this volume.

joining the European Union quickly, than in Romania, which has struggled economically.[33]

Economic developments have also marked important turning points in the Middle East and Africa. The Middle East experienced considerable domestic turmoil in the 1950s and 1960s, when weak states were unable to meet societal demands, but less instability in some places in the 1970s and 1980s, when high oil prices and high levels of foreign aid from the United States and the Soviet Union gave governments more largesse to spread around. Potential opposition forces were pacified and, in essence, bought off. The fact that oil prices and foreign assistance levels have declined sharply in the 1990s does not bode well for the region's future.[34]

Much of sub-Saharan Africa has experienced similar problems for similar reasons. Many governments in West, Central, and East Africa were able to hold their heads above water in the 1970s and 1980s — even though they were riddled with ethnic problems and run by corrupt, incompetent leaders — because they received substantial amounts of financial support from two external sources: the superpowers and Western Europe; and international financial institutions such as the International Monetary Fund (IMF) and the World Bank. In the late 1980s, however, two things happened: the Cold War ended and international financial institutions changed their ways of thinking about how financial assistance would be handed out. Direct aid from Washington and Moscow dried up, and most aid from Western Europe was redirected to Central and Eastern Europe. In addition, international financial institutions threatened to withhold aid unless governments overhauled their corrupt political systems and ineffective economic systems. This placed many leaders in Africa between a rock and a hard place: if they overhauled their patronage systems they would lose the support of their domestic constituencies and subsequently lose power; if they told the IMF and the World Bank that they would not implement political and economic reforms, they would not get financial assistance from abroad, their governments and economies would collapse, and they would lose power anyway. Many leaders in West, Central, and East Africa failed to resolve this dilemma and consequently threw their countries into turmoil in the late 1980s and early 1990s.[35] Nigeria, which had substantial oil reserves, suffered similar financial setbacks when oil prices dropped and its gov-

---

33. See Milada Vachudová's chapter on East-Central Europe in this volume.

34. See Rachel Bronson's chapter on the Middle East and North Africa in this volume.

35. See Stephen Stedman's chapter on sub-Saharan Africa in this volume.

ernment mismanaged the country's oil income. Although parts of Africa — Southern Africa, in particular — have stabilized since the end of the Cold War, much of the continent has moved in the other direction.

This points to how precarious Russia's position is. Russia is a country with a deeply xenophobic worldview; it is comprised of dozens of ethnic groups, many of whom have spent centuries despising each other; with the breakup of the Soviet Union, many Russians now live as minorities in other, contiguous states; and the Russian economy has been in a free-fall since the mid-1980s. The fact that rabid nationalistic appeals have not yet taken over Russia's political debate is a minor miracle, attributable in large part to Boris Yeltsin's reluctance to go down this path and his willingness to use force to squelch his opposition. However, there are good reasons for fearing that more formidable nationalists will enter the picture, leaders not burdened with Vladimir Zhirinovsky's self-crippling tendencies.[36] Given Russia's continuing economic crisis and its deeply troubled ethnic picture, the emergence of powerful nationalistic politicians could be the spark that ignites a highly combustible mixture. The key to defusing this situation — and a lever over which outside powers have at least some control — is turning Russia's economy around.

Some scholars downplay the importance of economic factors in bringing about internal conflict;[37] I argue that they can be key in this context. Although Karl Marx was off target in thinking that class struggles were the be-all and end-all of conflict, he was right in pointing to the economic dimensions of political turmoil. It is ironic that this should come out in a study of post–Cold War conflicts, in the aftermath of the collapse of communist rule in Eastern Europe and the former Soviet Union and in conjunction with communism's declining appeal in most of the developing world.

The Regional Dimensions of Internal Conflicts

Although neighboring states and developments in neighboring countries rarely trigger all-out civil wars, almost all internal conflicts involve neighboring states in one way or another. The vast majority of internal conflicts have important implications for regional stability.

---

36. See Michael Spector, "Army Hero Enters Russian Race, Posing a Big Threat to Reformers," *New York Times*, December 29, 1995, p. 1.

37. See Milton J. Esman, "Economic Performance and Ethnic Conflict," in Joseph V. Montville, ed., *Conflict and Peacemaking in Multiethnic Societies* (Lexington, Mass.: Lexington Books, 1990), pp. 477–490; Ted Robert Gurr, "Peoples Against States: Ethnopolitical Conflict and the Changing World System," *International Studies Quarterly*, Vol. 38 (1994), pp. 347–377.

The conventional wisdom about the regional dimensions of internal conflict relies heavily on crude analogies to diseases, fires, floods, and other forces of nature: conflicts are said to "spill over" from one place to another and spread like virulent infections, deadly poisons, or wildfire, depending on the imagery preferred by the speaker or writer in question. This way of thinking about the regional dimensions of internal conflict is deeply entrenched in policymaking and journalistic circles, and it also influences scholarly work in this area.[38] Indeed, many scholars frame this problem as a "contagion" problem, as noted above.[39]

This way of thinking about the regional dimensions of internal conflict is simplistic at best and dangerous at worst. It is simplistic because it sees things moving in only one direction: from the place where conflict began to neighboring states, which are characterized as the passive, innocent victims of trouble elsewhere. This line of thinking is dangerous, moreover, because forces of nature — rather than the acts of leaders and governments — are blamed for the spread of turmoil and conflict. The implication is that these forces of nature are beyond anyone's control: there is little or nothing distant powers can do about these problems. It is certainly true that there is little distant powers can do about some things, but it is irresponsible and dangerous to suggest that every aspect of every conflict is completely uncontrollable. Many problems are the products of discrete decisions made by identifiable individuals and nearby governments not necessarily immune to international pressure.

The first thing we must do to advance analytic clarity in this area is distinguish between the effects of internal conflicts on neighboring states and the actions that neighboring states take with respect to these conflicts. Then, we need to identify and isolate different problems in each area. (See Table 17.4.)

THE EFFECTS OF INTERNAL CONFLICTS ON NEIGHBORING STATES
The effects of internal conflicts on neighboring states fall into five main categories: refugee problems, economic problems, military problems, instability problems, and war.

---

38. See, for example, "Clinton's Words: 'The Promise of Peace'," *New York Times*, November 22, 1995, p. A11; Warren Christopher, "No Troops, No Peace," *New York Times*, November 27, 1995, p. 15; Ralph R. Premdas, "The Internationalization of Ethnic Conflict: Some Theoretical Explanations," in K.M. de Silva and R.J. May, eds., *The Internationalization of Ethnic Conflict* (London: Pinter, 1991), p. 10.

39. See note 17.

Table 17.4. The Regional Dimensions of Internal Conflicts.

The Effects on Neighboring States	The Actions of Neighboring States
Refugee problems	Humanitarian interventions
Economic problems	Defensive interventions
Military problems	Protective interventions
Instability problems	Opportunistic interventions
Inter-state war	Opportunistic invasions

REFUGEE PROBLEMS.   As we have seen in virtually every part of the world, internal conflicts often involve direct, deliberate attacks on civilians, and they consequently generate numbers of refugees that have to be counted in tens and hundreds of thousands. The conflicts in Afghanistan, Angola, Azerbaijan, Bosnia, Iraq, Israel, Liberia, Rwanda, Somalia, Sri Lanka, Sudan, and Turkey have each displaced over one million people.[40] At a minimum, refugees pose heavy economic burdens on host countries, the vast majority of whom have severe resource constraints. It is unfortunate but true that refugee problems fall most often on the states least able to take on new economic burdens. In addition, refugees can generate serious security problems. Fighters often mingle with refugee populations, using refugee camps for rest, recuperation, recruitment, and reorganization; offering sanctuary to refugees can therefore invite military reprisal, thereby drawing host countries into the conflict. If refugees flee to neighboring countries where large numbers of their ethnic brethren live, their plight can lead their compatriots to become more radicalized. Political instability can follow.[41] One striking example of this is in Central Asia, where refugee flows back and forth across the border between Afghanistan and Tajikistan have contributed to instability problems in both countries. One can also point to the Middle East, where Israel's occupation of the West Bank during the 1967 war led large numbers of Palestinians to flee to other parts of Jordan. The creation of new refugee populations combined with a growing radicalization in certain parts of the Palestinian community led to the Jordanian civil war of 1970 and the subsequent expulsion of radical Palestinian groups. Many of the latter

40. Although some of these refugees are internally displaced, many have crossed international frontiers. For estimates of refugees in different parts of the world, see Table 1 in my introductory chapter to this volume.

41. See Gil Loescher, *Refugee Movements and International Security*, Adelphi Paper No. 268 (London: IISS, 1992).

resettled in Lebanon and helped trigger yet another civil war a few years later.

ECONOMIC PROBLEMS. Internal conflicts can also disrupt the close economic ties that neighboring states often have, damaging regional interests in important ways. Trade, transportation, communication, manufacturing, finance, and access to raw materials can all be disrupted by armed hostilities. The wars in Azerbaijan and Chechnya, for example, have interfered with oil deliveries from the Caspian Sea. The wars in Afghanistan and Tajikistan have completely disrupted trade in Central Asia, blocking off centuries-old trade routes for conventional goods and commodities, and driving many groups into drug trafficking. If international powers become worried about the stability of a region as a whole, foreign investment and trade can be cut back or cut off. This has become a problem for parts of Africa, which many international investors have written off as too risky.

MILITARY PROBLEMS. Internal conflicts can create military problems for neighboring states. Four main problems stand out. First, the territory of neighboring states can be used to ship arms and supplies to rebel groups.[42] Pakistan, Tajikistan, and Iran have served as logistical conduits for Afghan rebels, as has Thailand for Karen rebels fighting in Burma. Arms for the Tamil Tigers in Sri Lanka have passed through the Indian state of Tamil Nadu.

Second, the territory of neighboring states can be used by rebel groups as bases of operations or sanctuaries.[43] Karen rebels in Burma have sought sanctuary with and established bases near their Karen brethren in Thailand. Kurdish rebels in Turkey have used northern Iraq as a base of operations.

Third, rebel groups can launch attacks in neighboring states, either to strike at their adversaries indirectly or to attract regional and international attention to their cause. Insurgents in Irian Jaya, for example, have attacked Indonesian consulates in Papua New Guinea. Former Indian Prime Minister Rajiv Gandhi was assassinated by a Tamil Tiger suicide bomber in retaliation for India's deployment of a peacekeeping force in

---

42. When this is done with the permission of the neighboring state, it would be more accurate to describe that neighbor as an active, interventionist actor, as opposed to a passive, innocent victim. The actions of neighboring states with respect to internal conflicts will be discussed in more detail momentarily.

43. See note 42.

Sri Lanka in the late 1980s, which Gandhi oversaw as head of India's government at the time.

Fourth, when the territory of neighboring states is used for arms shipments or military bases, hot-pursuit operations and interdiction campaigns often follow. Israel invaded Lebanon in 1982 and has launched strikes on southern Lebanon on any number of occasions since then to stop Palestinian attacks on northern Israel. Burmese pursuit of Karen rebels into Thailand has led to direct clashes between Burmese and Thai military forces. A striking example of this took place in early 1995, when Turkey launched a massive attack on rebel Kurd positions in northern Iraq.

INSTABILITY PROBLEMS. This leads to the more general question of how an internal conflict in one place can generate instability in another. The scholarly literature on this question is unsatisfying because it relies heavily on discussions of "contagion," "diffusion," and "spillover" effects that obscure more than they illuminate.[44] What we need is a clear understanding of the mechanisms that transmit instability from one place to another, and the conditions under which this is most likely to happen. It does not help — indeed, it hinders understanding — to suggest that these mechanisms are bacteriological, mechanical, or hydraulic in character.

Political instability can be generated in several ways, and some of these mechanisms have already been identified. Refugees can radicalize ethnic populations and provoke turmoil. They also impose economic costs on host countries; these costs can be politically controversial and can weaken host governments. Internal conflicts can also generate economic problems of a more general sort, and, as we have seen in many places around the world, economic problems often play important roles in outbreaks of civil strife. In addition, rebel activities in neighboring states can undermine state control over its territory and provoke military clashes.

However, as discussed in the previous section on the causes of internal conflicts, problems such as these rarely cause new intra-state wars on their own. Of the thirty-five or so major internal conflicts in the world today, only one (in Sierra Leone) was triggered by refugee, economic, or military problems crashing across international borders. It does not follow, however, that the effects of internal conflicts on neighboring states are unimportant. These problems often trigger minor conflicts and significant amounts of bloodshed. In addition, they often contribute to tur-

44. See note 17.

moil that is already brewing for other reasons. Internal conflicts are most likely to spark conflicts in neighboring states when ethnic groups straddle formal international frontiers: divided ethnic groups are particularly effective conflict transmitters.[45] The conflicts in Burundi and Rwanda have been difficult to resolve precisely because interconnected ethnic problems bounce back and forth between the two.[46]

INTER-STATE WAR. Thus far, the discussion has focused on the ways in which an internal conflict in one place can lead to internal problems in neighboring states. One final set of problems needs to be examined, and that involves the ways in which internal conflicts can lead to inter-state hostilities. Some possibilities have already been mentioned: hot-pursuit operations and interdiction campaigns can lead to inter-state military clashes when one government is trying to root out rebels in a neighboring state, and the neighboring state in question seeks to defend its territory and sovereignty.

Another problem that has implications for neighboring states is the emergence of aggressive nationalism. Internal conflicts can lead warring parties to adopt increasingly radicalized, belligerent platforms; aggressive nationalism can develop and become directed not just at internal rivals, but external actors. Neighboring states are the most likely targets of intensifying nationalistic crusades.

A final problem is diversionary war: leaders beset by domestic problems occasionally lash out against neighboring states to divert attention from problems at home.[47] In cases such as these, neighboring states can be the passive, innocent victims of deliberate actions taken elsewhere.

THE ACTIONS OF NEIGHBORING STATES
The actions that neighboring states take with respect to internal conflicts also fall into five main categories, defined mainly in terms of motivations: humanitarian interventions, defensive interventions, protective interventions, opportunistic interventions, and opportunistic wars. "Interven-

---

45. This contention is supported by quantitative studies of this question. See Gurr, *Minorities at Risk*, pp. 132–135.

46. See Stephen Stedman's chapter on sub-Saharan Africa in this volume.

47. Some leaders beset by internal turmoil become aggressive and launch diversionary wars; others feel vulnerable and concentrate on winning the war at home, fearing that starting an inter-state war would weaken them further. A systematic examination of the conditions that push leaders in these two directions is needed, but is beyond the scope of this study. For a general discussion of this issue, see Geoffrey Blainey, *The Causes of War* (New York: Free Press, 1973), chap. 5.

tions" in this context should be thought of broadly: they include diplomatic initiatives, extending economic assistance or employing economic sanctions, extending military assistance of one kind or another to either rebel or government forces, and sending military forces directly into the fray. Many interventions are complex in that they involve a range of activities and actions. They are also complex in that states usually act for a variety of reasons, and true motivations are often hidden behind diplomatic smokescreens and spin-control exercises. It is nonetheless possible to make some broad, analytically useful distinctions among different kinds of actions.

HUMANITARIAN INTERVENTIONS.   First, in some cases neighboring states are driven to take action for humanitarian reasons. As we have seen in all too many parts of the world, internal conflicts usually cause tremendous amounts of humanitarian suffering. In some cases, regional powers take action aimed at relieving humanitarian distress and restoring peace and security in their neighborhoods. Their intentions are comparatively benign and altruistic. The efforts of the leaders of Colombia, Costa Rica, Mexico, Panama, and Venezuela to bring peace to El Salvador, Guatemala, and Nicaragua in the 1980s and early 1990s are good examples. The mediation efforts and military deployments made by the Economic Community of West African States (ECOWAS) in Liberia in the 1990s are another.[48] It is important to note, however, that regional powers always have national interests at stake in situations such as these: regional powers can never launch purely altruistic initiatives because they always have selfish reasons for wanting to see peace and stability restored to their particular corners of the globe. Although Latin American leaders wanted to see an end to humanitarian suffering in El Salvador, Guatemala, and Nicaragua, they also wanted to put an end to these conflicts and keep these wars from spreading for national security reasons. Similarly, West African states had powerful selfish reasons for wanting to keep the Liberian civil war contained and trying to bring it to an end. Nigeria had an interest in extending its influence in the region. However, it seems fair to say that the actions of these Latin American and West African states were driven to some degree by humanitarian motivations.

DEFENSIVE INTERVENTIONS.   Second, neighboring states often launch "defensive interventions" designed to bring cross-border problems (such as refugee flows or military assaults) to an end, to keep wars from

---

48.   On Latin America, see Marc Chernick's chapter in this volume; on sub-Saharan Africa, see Stephen Stedman's chapter.

spreading, or, more ambitiously, to bring wars to an end. In cases such as these, the motivations of regional powers fall under the general heading of self-defense. Examples abound: Israel invaded Lebanon in 1982 to neutralize Palestinian forces operating there, as noted above; South African defense forces attacked Botswana, Mozambique, and Zimbabwe on various occasions in the 1980s to root out military units of the African National Congress (ANC);[49] India sent peacekeeping forces to Sri Lanka in the late 1980s; the United States sent military forces to Haiti in 1994 because Haitian refugees were swarming to Florida; Turkey sent 30,000 troops into northern Iraq in early 1995 to destroy rebel Kurd forces based there.

PROTECTIVE INTERVENTIONS.　Third, leaders in neighboring states occasionally launch "protective interventions" designed to protect or assist ethnic brethren involved in hostilities elsewhere. In cases such as these, neighboring states take actions that cannot be characterized as purely defensive from an international legal standpoint, although intervenors always argue that they are simply "defending" their brethren. Serbia's decision to attack Croatia in 1991 was justified on these grounds, as was Serbian and Croatian intervention in Bosnia. Middle Eastern states have justified their support for Bosnian Muslims on these grounds as well. The Armenian intervention in the war between Azerbaijan and Armenian secessionists in Nagorno-Karabakh was also a protective intervention. Many Russians have agitated for Russian intervention in states carved out of the former Soviet Union for protective reasons: ethnic Russians in non-Russian lands now find that the jackboot is on the other foot.[50]

OPPORTUNISTIC INTERVENTIONS.　Fourth, neighboring states often launch "opportunistic interventions" designed to exploit internal turmoil elsewhere, advance their political, economic, and military interests, and improve their regional positions. By supporting insurgents involved in hostilities against a regional rival, a neighboring state can keep its rival preoccupied with internal affairs and perhaps weaken it over time. Leaders in the neighboring state might hope, more ambitiously, that its rival can be dismembered or forced to the brink of collapse. Regional rivals often support insurgents in each other's countries, substituting

49. South Africa's motivations were not entirely defensive and its actions far from benign, as discussed in Stephen Stedman's chapter on sub-Saharan Africa in this volume.

50. For a discussion of the factors that influence decisions to launch protective interventions, see Rothschild, *Ethnopolitics*, chap. 6.

rebel proxies for direct inter-state warfare.[51] Support activities include providing financial assistance; weapons and communications equipment; manpower, training, and leadership; logistical assistance; and bases and sanctuaries. Examples of opportunistic interventions are plentiful: South Africa actively aided insurgents in Mozambique and Angola in the 1980s, to retaliate for the latter's support of the African National Congress and to weaken their respective governments; Angola and Zaire have also engaged in mutually destructive exercises of this type, as have Sudan and Uganda;[52] Pakistan has supported insurgents in the Indian province of Punjab, and India has supported insurgents in the Pakistani province of Sindh;[53] Honduras provided a base of operations for Nicaraguan "contras" in the 1980s.[54] Neighboring states almost inevitably characterize their opportunistic actions in self-serving humanitarian, defensive, or protective terms.[55]

Neighboring states can also intervene to prop up friendly governments and help keep mutually troublesome rebels under control. Uzbekistan's deployment of troops to Tajikistan would fall under this heading, for example.

OPPORTUNISTIC INVASIONS. Fifth and last, neighboring states take advantage of the momentary weakness caused by internal turmoil to launch an invasion of a rival. Internal conflicts create windows of opportunity for neighboring states, which they often exploit. The difference between an "opportunistic intervention" and an "opportunistic invasion" is mainly a matter of degree and form: in the former, neighboring states support rebel forces and engage in proxy wars while trying to maintain an innocent public facade; in the latter, they launch full-scale military assaults using

---

51. See Stephen Stedman's chapter on sub-Saharan Africa in this volume.

52. Ibid.

53. See Sumit Ganguly's chapter on South and Southwest Asia in this volume.

54. See Marc Chernick's chapter on Latin America in this volume.

55. As discussed in the previous section of this chapter, neighboring states occasionally provide the spark that leads potentially volatile disputes across the violence threshold and into armed confrontation. In cases such as these, neighboring states can be characterized as the proximate causes of the conflict in question. Russia's activities in Georgia and Moldova are examples. In this section, we are looking at cases where neighboring states take advantage of conflicts that have already become openly violent. The distinction is subtle but important: in the former, neighboring states are responsible for triggering violence; in the latter, they take advantage of violence that has broken out and are responsible for escalation. In both cases, neighboring states are motivated by national interests and driven by opportunistic calculations.

their own forces and make a less credible pretense about their intentions. Examples of opportunistic inter-state invasions include the Syrian invasion of Jordan during the latter's civil war in 1970. Vietnam's invasion of Cambodia in 1978 had defensive and protective elements, but was also driven by opportunistic calculations. The Iraqi invasion of Iran in 1980, in the aftermath of the overthrow of the Shah, also fits into this category.

Policy Implications

My discussion of the causes of internal conflict has three main policy implications. First, conflict prevention efforts should be guided by a two-track strategy. One track should be a series of long-term efforts aimed at the underlying conditions that make violent conflicts more likely. Particular attention should be paid to economic problems, distorted group histories, and patterns of political, economic, and cultural discrimination. A second track should focus on the proximate causes of internal conflict, the catalytic factors that turn potentially violent situations into deadly confrontations.

Second, conflict prevention efforts need to take into account the fact that internal conflicts can be triggered by any one of four sets of proximate causes: internal, mass-level forces; external, mass-level forces; external, elite-level forces; and internal, elite-level forces. Different kinds of conflict prevention efforts will be needed in each case. No single set of preventive actions will suffice.

Third, conflict prevention efforts should focus very aggressively on the decisions and actions of domestic elites, who are usually responsible for sparking internal conflicts. Ambitious individuals will always aspire to power; the challenge is to keep power struggles from exploding into civil wars. Those interested in conflict prevention need to think systematically about ways of neutralizing the ethnic bashing, ethnic scapegoating, hate mongering, and propagandizing that are often the precursors to violence.

One of the policy implications that leaps out of our survey of internal conflicts in eight regions of the world is that few if any internal conflicts are hermetically sealed: the vast majority have important regional dimensions and implications of one kind or another. This is true even in geographically isolated places, such as the Philippines.[56] Therefore, policymakers in North America and Western Europe should not be allowed to

---

56. Muslim insurgents in Mindanao received support from Malaysia. See Trevor Findlay's chapter on Southeast Asia in this volume.

argue, as they often do, that internal conflicts elsewhere are isolated problems that have no international ramifications. If regional stability matters, so do internal conflicts.

Another broad implication is that, although neighboring states can be the innocent victims of turmoil in their regions, they are often active contributors to violence, escalation, and regional instability. Hot-pursuit operations, cross-border interdictions, defensive interventions, protective interventions, opportunistic interventions, and opportunistic invasions are common. The conventional wisdom about the regional dimensions of internal conflict — problems "spill over" from one place to another in a unidirectional manner that is no one's fault and beyond anyone's control — is misleading. Problems come from two directions — from the places where conflicts originate and from neighboring states — and they are often the products of discrete, deliberate decisions taken by leaders and governments. The "no-fault" view of how internal conflicts become regional problems — favored by many policymakers, journalists, and scholars — would have us believe that this is a process driven by forces of nature or by "conflict" itself. Instead, we should place blame squarely where blame is due: bad neighbors are a big problem, much bigger than conventional thinking would lead us to believe.

This is important because conflicts usually become much harder to control and resolve once neighboring states become involved. Escalation becomes easier and more likely, de-escalation becomes harder, and conflict resolution harder still. The introduction of additional sets of interests and additional resources into the equation intensifies escalatory dynamics: wars become hotter, and they last longer.[57]

One of the implications of this analysis is that distant powers and the international community in general are not as helpless as the conventional wisdom would have us believe. Internal conflicts are usually triggered by domestic elites, not mass unrest or some uncontrollable form of domestic or regional mass hysteria. Bad leaders and bad behavior are discrete problems that can be identified and targeted for action. Similarly, the regionalization of internal conflicts is not an inexorable process always beyond human control: it can often be traced to discrete, deliberate decisions and acts made by one regional actor or another. These decisions and acts are not necessarily immune to international pressure: they mark

---

57. For a discussion of how third party interests complicate internal conflicts, see I. William Zartman, "Internationalization of Civil Strife: Temptations and Opportunities of Triangulation," in Midlarsky, *The Internationalization of Communal Strife*, pp. 27–42. See also Alicia Levine's chapter in this volume.

moments when distant international powers can try to use their leverage and influence the course of events.

Implications for the Study of Internal Conflict

It should go without saying that the frameworks and propositions out-lined above do not constitute the final word on this tremendously complex subject. First, the distinctions among different kinds of underlying and proximate causes need to be sharpened if we are to refine our classification of conflicts according to these causes. Second, it is entirely possible that other types of conflicts driven by different combinations of factors will be identified as more work is done in this area. Third, the sample of cases used here is limited in that it includes only active, major conflicts. Inactive conflicts and less deadly conflicts should also be examined. Unfortunately, the universe of internal conflict cases is large. Fourth and finally, one of the keys to advancing knowledge in this area will be the production of detailed case studies carefully focused on the proximate causes of internal conflicts, and more specifically, on the precise moments when political disputes become violent confrontations. Most case histories lack a sharp analytical focus, and the theoretical literature on this subject, as noted above, tends to focus on the permissive conditions of internal conflicts, not the proximate causes of violence. The regional dimensions of internal conflicts also need to be examined more closely on a case by case basis. In short, much more work needs to be done.

Chapter 18

Internal Conflict and International Action

Michael E. Brown

Internal conflict is widespread, and often causes tremendous amounts of human suffering, posing serious threats to regional and international security along the way. The debate over international responses to the problems posed by internal conflict is framed by two main questions: first, what *can* the international community — broadly defined to include sovereign states, international organizations, and nongovernmental organizations (NGOs) — do to prevent, manage, and resolve internal conflicts? Second, what *should* the international community do with respect to these problems? Our primary focus in this book is on the first of these questions, although we have some things to say about the second as well.

International efforts to prevent, manage, and resolve internal conflicts face formidable obstacles. The forces that drive internal conflicts are many and powerful. When civil wars break out, escalation is easy, de-escalation is hard, and conflict resolution is harder still. Internal conflicts are often seen by the warring parties as high-stakes, zero-sum competitions where group survival hangs in the balance. Security dilemmas, arms races, and escalatory spirals are particularly intense. Civilians are often involved as both combatants and targets of terrorist attacks. Attacks on civilian populations, increasingly vengeful attitudes, mounting sunk costs, and power-hungry leaders combine to make compromise, settlement, and reconciliation difficult. Renegade groups and troops are often hard to control, making negotiations difficult and agreements complicated.

Moreover, international actors interested in conflict prevention, management, and resolution find that collective action problems are especially formidable in cases such as these. Aggressors are hard to identify. Short-term operational objectives are hard to define, and long-term political objectives can be close to impossible to divine. Different international actors often have radically different perceptions of problems, fundamentally different interests at stake, and wildly different ideas about what should be done and who should do it. In addition, those who would band together to deal constructively with internal conflicts always have to contend with the thorny issue of state sovereignty: they have to determine if the conflict in question poses a threat to international peace and security, and therefore merits violation of the principle of non-interference in the domestic affairs of others.

The starting point for assessing international efforts to deal with these problems is differentiating between different tasks, instruments, and actors. First, we need to distinguish between three main tasks: conflict prevention, conflict management, and conflict resolution. Second, we need to distinguish between different kinds of policy instruments. Ten main policy instruments have been analyzed in this book: humanitarian assistance; fact-finding; mediation; confidence-building measures; traditional peacekeeping operations; multifunctional peacekeeping operations; the manipulation of arms supplies through embargoes and transfers; the utilization of economic levers, including sanctions and aid; judicial enforcement measures; and the use of military force. Third, we need to distinguish between three main types of actors: independent states; international organizations, including the United Nations (UN) and regional organizations; and nongovernmental organizations.

My analysis of these issues focuses first on conflict prevention, then on conflict management, and finally on conflict resolution. I draw on the discussions of various policy instruments and international actors found elsewhere in this volume, and fold them into this framework as appropriate. My aim is to analyze the different kinds of problems that crop up in each area, and identify the conditions under which different kinds of international actions are most likely to succeed. This provides a foundation for developing some policy recommendations. I conclude with a discussion of several policy dilemmas that complicate international efforts to prevent, manage, and resolve internal conflicts.

I develop six general arguments about what the international community can and should do, as well as three clusters of specific arguments about conflict prevention, conflict management, and conflict resolution.

The first of my general arguments is that the problems posed by internal conflict are formidable, but options for international action do exist. Second, internal conflicts are complex, so actions taken to address these problems have to be multifaceted. There is no simple solution to the internal conflict problem. Third, internal conflicts have deep roots, so long-term efforts will be needed if prevention, management, and resolution efforts are to succeed. There are no quick fixes to these problems. Fourth, internal conflict is widespread and international resources are limited, so difficult choices will have to be made about when and where to act. This means, in effect, addressing some problems and ignoring others — triage. Fifth, the international community should favor actions that have high probabilities of success and low costs. This would be a banal thing to say but for the fact that the international community often does precisely the opposite. The goal should be building a track record of success that lends credibility to international undertakings.

Sixth, internal conflicts fall into two basic categories as far as international actors are concerned: cases where local parties are willing to work for peace and give their consent to international involvement; and cases where they are not. There is a sharp line between cases where local authorities have given their consent to international intervention and cases where they have not. It is imperative for intervenors to know if they are engaged in cooperative or coercive exercises. Operations that have the approval of local authorities have higher probabilities of success and lower costs than their coercive counterparts, and should therefore be given a higher priority. This does not mean that coercive actions should never be undertaken: coercive actions are indeed warranted when important interests are engaged or when moral outrages, such as genocide, are being committed. Under these conditions, international action should be undertaken even if local parties have not given their consent to international involvement, and will have to be coerced to change their behavior. In cases such as these, there is still a lot the international community can do to prevent or end violence, but the costs of action are higher and the probabilities of success are lower because international powers are in the coercion business. Coercive actions should therefore be undertaken selectively, with great care, and with great determination.

My first cluster of more specific arguments has to do with conflict prevention. I argue that conflict prevention should be the international community's top priority because keeping disputes from becoming violent in the first place is key: once the violence threshold is crossed, escalatory dynamics intensify and reconciliation becomes much more difficult. Conflict prevention efforts, moreover, are low-cost undertakings that enjoy a high probability of success precisely because they do not have to contend with societies polarized by bloodshed. A two-track strategy is needed to address both the underlying, permissive conditions that make conflict likely and the proximate causes or triggers of violence itself. More emphasis should be placed on sustained, long-term efforts to address the permissive conditions of internal conflicts, such as patterns of discrimination, economic problems, and problematic group histories. These efforts should be complemented, when necessary, by focused, short-term emergency responses to head off impending violence.

Second, conflict management efforts aimed at limiting violence once it has broken out should be undertaken selectively. As a general rule, crisis management efforts should be launched sooner rather than later, before violence escalates to high levels. In addition, the international community should endeavor to keep internal conflicts from becoming regional conflicts. The regionalization of internal conflict complicates the picture and makes violence more difficult to control. International actors contemplating intervention should distinguish between cases where the local parties are ready to stop fighting and seek outside assistance, and cases where warring groups are determined to continue fighting. The international community should concentrate its efforts on the former: there is a lot it can do to limit and end fighting when it has the consent and cooperation of the parties on the ground. It can also take effective coercive actions, but coercion is riskier and more expensive, and should only be employed when important interests are at stake or when crimes against humanity, such as genocide, are being committed.

Third, conflict resolution efforts should be guided by a simple principle: help those who would help themselves. Since the end of the Cold War, the international community has helped to resolve conflicts in El Salvador, Mozambique, Namibia, and Nicaragua, places where adversaries were weary of war, ready to make peace, and eager for international assistance. It has had less success in Angola, Liberia, and Somalia, places where warlords and would-be leaders continue to contend for power through armed violence. There is a lot that the international community can do to help people who want to make peace. Its chances for success are greatest when international efforts are multifaceted and when they are sustained over time. Just as Rome was not built in a day, war-torn societies cannot be rebuilt overnight.

The Importance of Conflict Prevention

The idea of conflict prevention has a lot of intuitive appeal: conflict management and conflict resolution clearly have to contend with far more inflammatory situations. Conflict prevention, however, is far from simple.[1] Conflict is, after all, inherent in political, economic, and social life, even if violent conflict is not. Conflict, broadly defined, cannot be

---

1. See Stephen John Stedman, "Alchemy for a New World Order: Overselling 'Conflict Prevention'," *Foreign Affairs*, Vol. 74, No. 3 (May–June 1995), pp. 14–20. For other views, see Michael S. Lund, "Underrating Preventive Diplomacy," *Foreign Affairs*, Vol. 74, No. 4 (July–August 1995), pp. 160–163; John Stremlau, "Antidote to Anarchy," *Washington Quarterly*, Vol. 18, No. 1 (Winter 1995), pp. 29–44.

extinguished, only controlled. In addition, as noted above, the forces that drive and trigger internal conflicts are many and powerful. Unfortunately, social scientists have not yet developed a full-fledged theory of the causes of internal conflict. As a result, we do not have a fully developed strategy for preventing such conflicts.

In this volume, I have endeavored to develop a framework for analyzing the causes of internal conflict that takes us a step closer to developing a full-fledged theory of internal conflict.[2] This analytical framework, I would argue, provides a corresponding framework for action. It suggests three broad guidelines for international actors interested in preventing internal conflicts.

ADOPT A TWO-TRACK STRATEGY

First, if it is useful to distinguish between the permissive conditions and proximate causes of internal conflict, it follows that those interested in conflict prevention should have a two-track strategy. One track should be a series of sustained, long-term efforts focused on the underlying problems that make violence likely. The other track should be a series of more aggressive efforts focused on the proximate causes of internal conflicts — the triggers that turn potentially violent situations into armed confrontations.

Both tracks need to be pursued. Long-term efforts to address the permissive conditions of internal conflicts are relatively low-cost, low-risk undertakings, but they tend to be neglected by policymakers in national capitals and international organizations who are inevitably preoccupied with the crisis *du jour*. At the same time, the catalytic factors responsible for triggering violence — often in places where bloodshed could be avoided — merit careful attention and vigorous action.

PLACE MORE EMPHASIS ON UNDERLYING PROBLEMS AND LONG-TERM SOLUTIONS

A second guideline is that long-term efforts aimed at the underlying problems that make violence likely need to be given more emphasis and made more effective. This is easier said than done. If a simple formula existed for dealing with these problems, the world would be a more tranquil and happier place than it currently is.

Some factors are difficult or impossible to change, such as the military or economic value of a potentially secessionist region or the fear that secessionism in one region will lead to the unraveling of a multiethnic

---

2. See my introductory chapter and Chapter 17 in this volume.

state.[3] Ethnic geography and demographic patterns are other factors that are not particularly manipulable.

To the extent that they change at all, the underlying factors that predispose some places to violence change slowly. This means that international efforts to influence events will have to be long-term undertakings. International actors will have to be willing to live without immediate gratification; this is a lot to ask of politicians. If international actors are to address deep-seated structural, political, economic, and cultural problems effectively, they will have to be willing and able to commit for the long haul and they will have to be willing to set aside requirements for having "exit strategies." Fortunately, these kinds of undertakings are comparatively low-cost, low-risk efforts: they are usually political, economic, and diplomatic ventures, and they do not involve sending large numbers of troops into all-out civil wars.

As I have discussed elsewhere in this book, the permissive conditions of internal conflict include security problems, political factors, economic/social factors, and cultural/perceptual factors.[4] This suggests that international efforts to address the root causes of internal conflict will have to be multifaceted in character. Efforts will have to be undertaken in each of these areas.

REDUCE SECURITY CONCERNS. Security concerns and arms races contribute to instability and the potential for violence. One way to reduce the uncertainties that often drive arms races is to promote transparency. International actors should encourage local parties to make prior public declarations about arms acquisitions and military movements. Weapon-free buffer zones should be established. International monitors should be deployed to potentially volatile places to help implement transparency and confidence-building agreements. Promoting transparency will not help when groups have malign intentions toward one another, but it will dampen escalatory spirals when groups are driven to strengthen themselves by fears of the unknown. The challenge will be convincing governments that they face these kinds of instability problems and that they should agree to outside involvement in domestic security matters.[5]

---

3. See Alicia Levine's chapter on the prevention of secessionist violence in this volume.

4. See my introductory chapter and Chapter 17 in this volume.

5. See Joanna Spear's chapter on arms limitations and confidence-building measures in this volume.

OVERTURN PATTERNS OF POLITICAL DISCRIMINATION. When people feel that existing political arrangements are unjust and incapable of being changed peacefully, the potential for violence increases dramatically. There are a number of steps that can be taken to ameliorate these problems. If ethnic groups are distributed along regional or provincial lines, central authorities should be encouraged to embrace federalism and grant more autonomy to provincial governments. This will give groups more control over their own affairs, and dampen resentment toward the status quo.[6] Regardless of how ethnic groups are distributed, people need to be assured that they have proper access to the levers of governmental power and that their interests are properly represented in the halls of government. Electoral systems based on proportional representation have clear advantages over winner-take-all systems, and should therefore be promoted. Formal power-sharing systems, with positions allocated according to strict formulas, intensify ethnic identifications and should be discouraged. They might work in the short term, but they will inevitably come under pressure in the long term as group demographics change.[7] Human rights should be formally integrated into the constitutional and statutory pillars of state, and they should be aggressively and fairly implemented. The emergence of exclusionary national ideologies, whether they are based on ethnic or religious identifications, should be actively discouraged.[8]

International actors can help promote peaceful political change by extending technical advice about constitutional and electoral reforms, for example. They can also exert considerable influence by linking financial assistance and the development of closer economic ties to political reforms — that is, by making financial aid and economic relationships conditional. They can also link membership in international economic, military, and political institutions to domestic political reforms. This has worked fairly well in East-Central Europe, where states are eager to join the European Union (EU) and the North Atlantic Treaty Organization

---

6. See Alicia Levine's chapter on preventing secessionist violence in this volume. Ted Robert Gurr observes that granting more political autonomy to regional and provincial governments has helped to dampen conflict in the West and the developing world; see Gurr, "Peoples Against States: Ethnopolitical Conflict and the Changing World System," *International Studies Quarterly*, Vol. 38 (1994), pp. 347–377. For a dissenting view, see Milada Vachudová's chapter on East-Central Europe in this volume.

7. See Alicia Levine's chapter on preventing secessionist violence in this volume.

8. See ibid. See also Jack Snyder, "Nationalism and the Crisis of the Post-Soviet State," in Michael E. Brown, ed., *Ethnic Conflict and International Security* (Princeton, N.J.: Princeton University Press, 1993), pp. 79–101.

(NATO), and are willing to do whatever is necessary to improve their chances of being offered early admission to Western institutions. International actors face two main challenges in this regard. First, they have to brace themselves to meddle in the domestic political affairs of others, which is always a matter of great delicacy. Second, they have to promote change without undermining stability: reform is good, but instability is bad. This is a fine line to walk because change always involves upsetting the status quo.[9]

PROMOTE ECONOMIC DEVELOPMENT, OPPORTUNITY, AND JUSTICE.   A country's economic situation and economic prospects have tremendous implications for its potential for violence.[10] Rising levels of unemployment and inflation, declining standards of living, and grim economic prospects intensify resentments, polarize societies, and make people more receptive to ethnic and nationalistic appeals. Patterns of economic discrimination and growing economic inequities only make bad situations worse. The importance of the economic roots of internal conflict cannot be underestimated: if international actors are serious about preventing internal conflict and civil war, they have to do more than treat the military dimensions and military manifestations of the problem; they have to address the economic sources of conflict in troubled societies. What this means, in practice, is paying more attention to economic development and doing a better job of promoting economic development in industrializing and non-industrialized societies in particular.

Developing a formula for global economic development is beyond the scope of this book. However, resource competitions and land reform are problems that merit special attention, as are the general problems of ending endemic corruption and extending economic and educational opportunities more equitably throughout societies. International actors can help promote economic reforms the same way they can help promote political reforms: by extending technical assistance; by linking financial assistance and economic relationships to the implementation of reforms; and by linking membership in international organizations and institutions to reforms. States, international financial institutions, and other international organizations should work together to develop "mini-Marshall Plans" for countries in need of special economic attention.[11]

---

9. See Edward D. Mansfield and Jack Snyder, "Democratization and the Danger of War," *International Security*, Vol. 20, No. 1 (Summer 1995), pp. 5–38.

10. See Chapter 17 in this volume. See also the regional studies in Part I of this volume.

11. See Chantal de Jonge Oudraat's chapter on the United Nations in this volume.

NGOs should devote more of their resources to these "silent emergencies," as opposed to *post hoc* responses to crises that have already exploded into violence and chaos.[12] The dilemma international actors face in this area is the same one they face with respect to political reform: reform is good, but change can be destabilizing. The challenge is to promote gradual, peaceful change without undermining stability.

ADDRESS CULTURAL AND PERCEPTUAL PROBLEMS. Finally, international actors need to address the cultural and perceptual factors that lead some countries towards violence. This means working to overturn patterns of cultural discrimination by safeguarding rights with respect to language, religion, and education. This also means working to revamp the distorted histories groups often have of each other. Governments could be asked to enter into international dialogues about group histories and to publish foreign criticisms of school curricula and textbooks.[13] Scholars and teachers should be brought into these dialogues. Pernicious group histories play important roles in galvanizing internal conflicts, and they need to be given much greater attention in conflict prevention circles.

NEUTRALIZE THE PROXIMATE CAUSES OF INTERNAL CONFLICT

A third guideline is that those interested in conflict prevention should pay more attention to the proximate causes of internal conflict. Internal conflicts can be triggered by any one of four clusters of proximate causes: internal, mass-level factors; external, mass-level factors; external, elite-level factors; and internal, elite-level factors. Conflict prevention efforts therefore need to be multifaceted. No single approach will suffice. However, most internal conflicts are triggered by domestic, elite-level forces, and most of the conflicts that fall into this category are raw power struggles. It follows that international actors interested in conflict prevention should focus on this problem area.

TACKLE DOMESTIC PROBLEMS. Conflicts triggered by internal, mass-level factors — bad domestic problems — are often driven by ethnic strife.[14] The key to negating pressures for ethnic violence is overturning perceived patterns of political, economic, and cultural discrimination. When tension

---

12. As Thomas Weiss points out, this will be very hard for most NGOs to do because crisis-response efforts are the linchpins of their fund-raising campaigns. See his chapter on NGOs in this volume.

13. See Stephen Van Evera, "Hypotheses on Nationalism and War," *International Security*, Vol. 19, No. 4 (Spring 1994), p. 37.

14. See my discussion in Chapter 17 in this volume.

is building, violence is looming, and distrust is mounting, international actors can help defuse potentially explosive situations by international-izing the dialogue and injecting impartial observers and mediators into the equation. Fact-finding missions can be launched to help identify the origins of specific problems, human rights monitors can help ensure that injustices do not go unnoticed, and election monitors can help guard the integrity of political processes. Ethnic bashing and scapegoating in the media can be countered by international organizations and the inter-national media, thereby helping to promote less emotionally charged debates.

ISOLATE BAD NEIGHBORHOODS. Conflicts triggered by external, mass-level forces — bad neighborhoods — are sparked by waves of refugees or troops crashing across international borders, bringing turmoil and vio-lence with them.[15] The fact that a war is already under way in the immediate vicinity means that conflict prevention efforts have already failed in that part of the world. Waves of refugees and motley gangs of renegade troops are hard to deter or control because they lack effective leadership. The international community can try to prevent refugee prob-lems from becoming regional problems by setting up refugee camps and safe areas in the country where violence first started. To be effective, however, international actors will have to move quickly and convince refugees that safe areas are genuinely safe. This will not be easy to do, given the international community's track record in Bosnia and Iraq. Preventive military deployments are another option.

DETER BAD NEIGHBORS. Internal conflicts triggered by external, elite-level forces — bad neighbors — would seem to be easier to prevent. Specific actions can be proscribed, potentially troublesome governments can be identified, and a wide range of coercive actions can be threatened or taken with respect to renegade states. The preventive military deployment in Macedonia, for example, undoubtedly helped to discourage Serbia from causing trouble in that part of the Balkans.[16] States are powerful actors, however, and they can therefore be difficult to dissuade, especially if leaders believe important national interests are at stake. Deterring bad neighbors from causing trouble in nearby states is particularly difficult when the neighbors in question are large and powerful. Russia, for

---

15. Fortunately, internal conflicts are rarely sparked by these kinds of problems. See ibid.

16. See Ivo Daalder's chapter on the former Yugoslavia and the Balkans in this volume.

example, clearly played a key role in triggering conflicts in Georgia and Moldova, but it was hard to influence because of its size, its position on the UN Security Council, and its firm conviction that Georgia and Moldova were part of its sphere of influence.

CO-OPT OR CONFRONT BAD LEADERS. Finally, conflicts that are triggered by internal, elite-level forces — bad leaders — come in several forms: some are driven by ideological motivations; some by criminal motivations; and many by raw power struggles.

The taproot of ideological strife is political, economic, and social distress, and conflict prevention efforts have to start by addressing these underlying problems. Ideological movements, whether they are based on political/economic or political/religious principles, are guided by leaders who almost always have political agendas and political aspirations of their own. The key to keeping these kinds of struggles from turning violent might be accommodating rebel leaders in coalition or provincial governments. Accommodation and co-optation are probably the most viable alternatives to confrontation.

Conflicts driven by the aspirations of criminal organizations and drug lords are another matter. In cases such as these, governments cannot cede political power or grant even a small measure of political legitimacy to their adversaries without compromising their own integrity and legitimacy. The key to dealing with these kinds of problems is forging multinational coalitions to weaken and eventually crush criminal operations. Part of the effort should be directed at providing alternative sources of income for the peasant populations that cultivate coca and opium out of economic need.[17] Drug trafficking is a global problem, so international efforts will have to be selective. They should focus first and foremost on those places where criminal organizations pose serious challenges to state sovereignty. Colombia is at the top of this list.

Conflicts triggered by power struggles between opportunistic and desperate politicians are common, and should therefore receive special international attention.[18] Since economic problems make escalation and violence more likely, emergency economic relief packages should be part of the equation when tensions rise and danger looms. Cynical campaigns to mobilize ethnic support, polarize ethnic differences, and blame other ethnic groups for whatever troubles a country may be experiencing are often responsible for inciting violence and leading countries into all-out

17. See Marc Chernick's chapter on Latin America in this volume.

18. See my discussion in Chapter 17 in this volume.

civil wars. It follows that international actors interested in preventing these conflicts from becoming violent and escalating out of control should endeavor to neutralize hate-mongers and their propaganda. At a minimum, this means launching international information campaigns and anti-propaganda efforts to ensure that reasoned voices can be heard and alternative sources of information are available in political debates. In more extreme cases, when leaders call for the extermination of their adversaries or entire ethnic groups, as in Rwanda in 1994, more forceful measures will be called for. Radio and television stations can be jammed or destroyed, and leaders can be captured by international military forces and brought before international tribunals. Taking coercive action is a big step, but some situations — such as calls to commit genocide or slaughter — should lead to forceful international action.

Many internal conflicts are triggered by self-obsessed leaders who will do anything to get and keep power. They often incite ethnic violence of the most horrific kind for their own political ends. If the international community is serious about preventing internal conflicts, it needs to think more carefully about the kinds of political behavior that should be proscribed and the kinds of actions it will be willing to take to steer or even seize control of domestic political debates. These are extremely difficult problems, both intellectually and politically, but they have to be confronted if international actors are to prevent the deadliest internal conflicts.

The Challenge of Conflict Management

Once violence breaks out and fighting begins, escalation becomes much more difficult to control. Security concerns and arms races intensify, and attacks on civilians can spiral out of control. Compromise and settlement become more difficult. Conflict management is more challenging than conflict prevention, and should therefore be undertaken more selectively and with even more care. The costs and risks can be high. I would recommend the following three guidelines.

ACT EARLY TO KEEP VIOLENCE FROM ESCALATING
First, international actors worried about emerging internal conflicts should act sooner rather than later. Internal conflicts often begin with limited clashes that escalate only gradually.[19] Put another way, a window of opportunity for crisis management exists even after violence breaks

---

19. See Gurr, "Peoples Against States," pp. 365–366.

out. The longer international actors wait, the more intense conflicts become, and the more difficult conflict management becomes. International actors have a wide range of policy instruments at their disposal, including cooperative instruments such as mediation and the deployment of traditional peacekeeping forces, and coercive instruments such as arms limitations and embargoes, economic sanctions, and the use of military force.

Unfortunately, international motivations to take action are weakest in the early stages of internal conflicts, when levels of violence are low and windows of opportunity are open. Motivations to take action increase as levels of violence increase, but rising levels of violence also make conflict management efforts more difficult. In other words, international motivations to act are weakest when options are strongest, and motivations to act are strongest when options are weakest.

KEEP INTERNAL CONFLICTS FROM BECOMING REGIONAL CONFLICTS

Second, international actors interested in conflict management should strive to keep internal conflicts from becoming regional conflicts. Internal conflicts usually become more difficult to control and to resolve when neighboring states become involved. Additional sets of interests are injected into the equation, and additional resources are made available to combatants. Fighting often intensifies, and negotiations almost always become much more complicated.[20]

This means addressing two problems. First, it means working to minimize the impact of internal conflicts on neighboring states, including refugee problems, economic problems, military problems, and instability problems. These kinds of problems often lead neighboring states to launch defensive or protective interventions.[21] Second, international actors should work to discourage neighboring states from engaging in opportunistic acts of aggression, such as supporting rebel forces in order to influence the regional balance of power or launching opportunistic invasions.[22]

There are reasons for being optimistic about the international community's ability to take effective action in this area. The problems that internal conflicts pose for neighboring states are easy to identify, even if they are not all easily solvable. The actions that neighboring states should be discouraged from taking are also easy to identify. In addition, the UN

---

20. See Alicia Levine's chapter on preventing secessionist violence and my Chapter 17, both in this volume.

21. See the discussion in Chapter 17 in this volume.

22. Ibid.

Charter provides a legal foundation for taking action to maintain international peace and security. Also, international actors are dealing with established governments in neighboring states, and governments can be engaged and influenced in ways that amorphous political movements and rebels groups cannot. If necessary, the full array of international policy instruments can be brought to bear on troublesome or potentially troublesome neighboring states, including threats to use economic sanctions and military force. Economic sanctions have a good track record since the end of the Cold War,[23] and preventive military deployments, such as the dispatch of an international force to Macedonia, seem to have had some deterrent value.

One important problem needs to be noted, however. International powers and neighboring states often meddle in the affairs of others by supplying light weapons and other arms to rebel groups. Since the end of the Cold War, the international trade in arms in general and light weapons in particular has become increasingly unregulated. If the international community is to discourage regional meddling in internal conflicts, it must re-establish control over the international arms market. This means improving intelligence and monitoring capabilities, cracking down on the black and second-hand markets, and establishing more effective national and multilateral control over the transfer of arms. None of this will be easy to do, but progress in each area will be necessary if the international community is to exert influence over the flow of arms between and within regions.[24]

FAVOR COOPERATIVE OVER COERCIVE ACTIONS

Third, it is essential for international actors contemplating intervention to distinguish between two fundamentally different kinds of problems: cases where the local parties are ready to stop fighting and are receptive to international involvement; and cases where they are not. The track record of international efforts to bring fighting to an end is good in the former, bad in the latter, and truly awful when the line about the terms of international engagement is blurred.

During the Cold War, peacekeeping operations were usually deployed to monitor cease-fires, and they were almost always deployed with the consent of the relevant local parties. These operations

---

23. See Elizabeth Rogers' chapter on economic sanctions in this volume.

24. For more discussion, see Joanna Spear's chapter on arms limitations and confidence-building measures in this volume.

consequently enjoyed a high rate of success.[25] It was understood that there was a sharp line between these kinds of undertakings and the coercive operations launched under Chapter VII of the UN Charter.

This line began to blur in 1992, when UN Secretary-General Boutros Boutros-Ghali suggested that future peacekeeping operations might not depend on the consent of all local parties.[26] The UN-authorized missions to Somalia and the former Yugoslavia that followed were deeply troubled exercises mainly because the line between consent and coercion was blurred. UN humanitarian operations in these two countries were presented as impartial efforts to relieve human suffering, but they were seen quite differently by local leaders who correctly understood that humanitarian relief had implications for the local balance of power. International efforts to put pressure on local leaders and open the way for humanitarian supplies failed, first, because international actors insisted on pretending that they were not engaged in coercion and, second, because they did not have sufficient forces on the ground to engage in effective coercion. In fact, the deployment of lightly armed units to escort humanitarian relief convoys was counterproductive: UN peacekeepers became pre-positioned hostages. This completely undercut international efforts to bring fighting to a quick end.[27]

UN officials, to their credit, have learned from these mistakes, and by 1995 it was again an article of faith in UN circles that there was a sharp line between cooperative and coercive undertakings.[28] Some scholars and analysts continue to argue, however, that there is a gray area between cooperation and coercion, and that a "third option" or "middle option" exists.[29]

---

25. See Chantal de Jonge Oudraat's chapter on the United Nations and Dan Lindley's chapter on collective security organizations, both in this volume.

26. See Boutros Boutros-Ghali, *An Agenda for Peace: Preventive Diplomacy, Peacemaking, and Peacekeeping* (New York: United Nations, June 1992), p. 11.

27. See Ivo Daalder's chapter on the former Yugoslavia and the Balkans and Thomas Weiss's chapter on NGOs, both in this volume.

28. See Boutros Boutros-Ghali, *Supplement to "An Agenda for Peace": Position Paper of the Secretary-General on the Occasion of the Fiftieth Anniversary of the United Nations,* S/1995/1, January 1995, paras. 33–35; Shashi Tharoor, "United Nations Peacekeeping in Europe," *Survival,* Vol. 37, No. 2 (Summer 1995), pp. 121–134; Shashi Tharoor, "Should UN Peacekeeping Go 'Back to Basics'?" *Survival,* Vol. 37, No. 4 (Winter 1995–96), pp. 52–64. See also Charles Dobbie, "A Concept for Post–Cold War Peacekeeping," *Survival,* Vol. 36, No. 3 (Autumn 1994), pp. 121–148.

29. See Adam Roberts, "The Crisis in UN Peacekeeping," *Survival,* Vol. 36, No. 3 (Autumn 1994), pp. 93–120; Donald C.F. Daniel and Bradd C. Hayes, "Securing

My view is that the new thinking at the United Nations is correct: cooperative and coercive operations are fundamentally different kinds of undertakings, and it is essential for international actors to keep these two kinds of activities separate. The UN-authorized missions to Bosnia and Somalia ran into trouble because whatever consent had once been given began to evaporate when mission objectives expanded and international actors began to engage in more and more coercion. Consent and coercion are mutually exclusive: by definition, one cannot agree to be coerced. Trying to mix the two makes no sense conceptually, is problematic operationally, and counterproductive politically. Trying to have it both ways will make it much harder to secure consent and engage in cooperative conflict management exercises in the future: warring parties will be less inclined to agree to international deployments if international peacekeepers are seen as the thin edge of a coercive wedge. International actors in general and the United Nations in particular need to restore their reputations for doing what they say — no more, no less.

It is certainly true that peacekeeping operations often engage in coercion at a tactical level (against renegade elements or in the context of monitoring a cease-fire), in the course of policing activities (to stop looting), and in self-defense. However, this kind of coercion takes place with the consent of local leaders and usually within the framework of a cease-fire agreement. There is a big difference between this kind of "tactical" coercion and "strategic" coercion designed to secure an agreement from local leaders, change their political goals, or change the correlation of local military forces. Tactical coercion is normal and acceptable. Attempting to engage in strategic coercion with lightly armed peacekeepers deployed under misleading or obsolete pretenses is deeply problematic, as we have seen in the Horn of Africa and the Balkans.

This is not to say that international actors should eschew coercion, only that they need to distinguish between cooperative and coercive undertakings and be prepared to play hardball when they are engaged in the latter. Coercion *can* work, and the international community has many coercive policy instruments at its disposal. Arms supplies can be offered or arms embargoes can be imposed on one party or another.[30] Economic

Observance of UN Mandates Through the Employment of Military Forces," manuscript, March 1995; Donald C.F. Daniel and Milton E. Miles, "Is There a Middle Option in Peace Support Operations? Implications for Crisis Containment and Disarmament," paper prepared for the UN Institute for Disarmament Research (UNIDIR), November 1995; Adam Roberts, "From San Francisco to Sarajevo: The UN and the Use of Force," *Survival*, Vol. 37, No. 4 (Winter 1995–96), pp. 7–28.

30. See Joanna Spear's chapter on arms limitations and confidence-building measures in this volume.

sanctions can be powerful sources of leverage, especially when one is dealing with central governments, neighboring states, and other easily identifiable and targetable actors.[31] Military force can be threatened or used and, contrary to current thinking in the U.S. Department of Defense, it can be used in limited ways in support of limited objectives: safe areas can be established and protected; heavy-weapon exclusion zones can be established and enforced; and air power can be directed at specific targets such as arms depots, communications and transportation links, military bases, and forces in the field.[32]

Successful coercion depends on several things. First, international actors must recognize and admit that they are engaging in coercion: they should not delude themselves or try to delude their publics into thinking that threatening to use military force, for example, will be seen as a form of cooperative engagement. Coercion is not aimed at "conflict": it is aimed at governments, groups, and individuals who will see threats and coercive acts as forms of aggression. Second, international actors need to be clear about both their long-term political objectives and their short-term operational objectives. This is one of the reasons why coercion worked in Haiti and failed in Bosnia. UN mandates, which should be secured whenever possible, should be clear on these counts as well. Third, coercive actions need to be pursued with great political determination and with sufficient resources. When military forces are involved, this might mean deploying large numbers of heavily armed troops guided by clear and liberal rules of engagement. Lightly armed peacekeepers should not be sent out to wage war, or into situations where they might reasonably be expected to engage in open combat. It is reckless and irresponsible to place peacekeepers in such jeopardy.[33]

Although coercion can work, the international community should emphasize cooperative conflict management actions over their coercive counterparts. Cooperative actions — such as sending mediators to help negotiate cease-fires and sending peacekeepers to help monitor cease-fires

---

31.   See Elizabeth Rogers' chapter on economic sanctions in this volume.

32.   I concur with Ivo Daalder, who argues that the Pentagon's all-or-nothing approach to the use of force limits U.S. military intervention to cases where vital interests are engaged. This puts the cart before the horse. National interests should define policy objectives, and policy objectives should determine how force is used. If interests and objectives are limited, one should be able to use force in a limited way. If one is unable to use force in a limited way for doctrinal reasons, then bureaucratic dogma is damaging national interests. See Daalder's chapter on the United States and military intervention in this volume.

33.   See Chantal de Jonge Oudraat's chapter on the United Nations and Dan Lindley's chapter on collective security organizations, both in this volume.

— are relatively low-cost, low-risk undertakings that have high rates of success. They should be the mainstays of international efforts in this area. Coercion is more expensive and riskier, and should be employed only when important interests are at stake or when crimes against humanity, such as genocide or the deliberate slaughter of civilians, are being committed. The international community should engage in these kinds of high-cost, high-risk undertakings only when the stakes are high and only when it is determined to see a serious campaign through to the bitter end.

The Potential for Conflict Resolution

The end of the Cold War has led to the resolution of a number of conflicts — in El Salvador, Mozambique, Nicaragua — driven in large part by the geostrategic competition between Washington and Moscow. The international community, under the aegis of the United Nations, has played an active and important role in helping to bring these conflicts to an end. It has also helped to end the conflicts in Haiti, Namibia, and South Africa, which were not driven by Cold War dynamics, and it has helped to dampen tensions in Cambodia, Iraq, Tajikistan, and Western Sahara.

Conflict resolution is an enormously tricky proposition: it is hard for people to lay down their arms, rebuild ravaged political and economic systems, reconstruct civil societies, and reconcile when large amounts of blood have been spilled and vengeance has come to dominate political discourse. There are, however, reasons for being hopeful about the prospects for conflict resolution in some parts of the world, and about the ability of the international community, through the United Nations, to facilitate these conflict resolution processes.

HELP THOSE WHO WOULD HELP THEMSELVES

The international community's resources are not unlimited, and difficult decisions will inevitably have to be made about where and when to try to lend a helping hand. The guiding principle should be: first, help those who would help themselves.

When people are determined to keep fighting, there is little the international community can do to bring hostilities to an end unless it is willing and able to impose peace. This means employing coercive instruments with a heavy hand, and in most cases this probably means unleashing a massive, crushing military blow followed by the imposition of an international trusteeship under the supervision of the United Nations. These are bound to be exceedingly expensive, open-ended operations. It is therefore highly unlikely that the international community will be inclined to go down this path. It did not do so in either Somalia or

Rwanda, where humanitarian crises were intense and local military forces were comparatively weak.

Given that the international community has limited resources to devote to peace processes and a limited tolerance for pain, it makes sense for international efforts to be concentrated in places where combatants are tired of fighting, ready for peace, and looking for help. There is a lot that the international community can do to help resolve conflicts and make peace under these conditions, when it has the full consent and cooperation of the local parties. It can provide humanitarian assistance to refugees and others in need.[34] It can launch fact-finding and mediation missions to help resolve outstanding political differences. Traditional peacekeeping forces can help keep former adversaries apart while cooperative disarmament efforts get under way. Multifunctional peacekeeping operations, which will be discussed in more detail below, can help with political and economic reconstruction. The track record of international efforts in post-conflict settings such as these is good: again, there is a lot international actors can do to help people who genuinely want to make peace.[35]

The key is making sure that one is dealing with people who genuinely want peace. Most people want peace, of course, but on their own terms. When they agree to peace settlements and elections, leaders of factions often assume that electoral triumph is in the offing. Problems can arise when elections turn out in unexpectedly unsatisfying ways: peace settlements that were attractive when high office appeared to be part of the package are much less attractive when it is not. When this happens, leaders can conclude that resuming the fight in the bush or the jungle is preferable to being a political non-entity. This is what happened in Angola after the September 1992 elections, which Jonas Savimbi lost. The challenge for international actors is to make sure that local parties are acting in good faith, and that local leaders fully understand the potential ramifications of the peace process.

CO-OPT OR NEUTRALIZE MILITANTS

A serious problem in many conflicts is the intransigence of militants and radicals who are unwilling to compromise and settle for anything less

---

34. Humanitarian assistance efforts can be highly problematic (indeed, counterproductive) when international actors are simultaneously trying to coerce local parties, as discussed above. This problem is side-stepped in post-conflict settings, when the consent of all local parties has been given.

35. See Chantal de Jonge Oudraat's chapter on the United Nations and Dan Lindley's chapter on collective security organizations, both in this volume.

than total victory. This problem is particularly acute but far from unique in the Middle East, where extremists in both the Israeli and Palestinian communities bitterly oppose the peace process. Similar problems have stymied peace initiatives in Sri Lanka, where Tamil and Sinhalese radicals have rejected proposals for the establishment of a federal system, and in Northern Ireland, where Catholic and Protestant extremists are wary of peace initiatives.

There is no simple solution to this problem. If most people, as well as top leaders in the relevant communities, want peace and accept the provisions of whatever peace plans are on the table, then international actors are operating in a fundamentally cooperative setting. This gives them a lot of latitude to help moderates deal with militants, forcefully if need be.

A two-track strategy is needed. One track should be co-optation: undercutting popular support for militants by implementing political and economic reforms that address broad-based societal problems; marginalizing militants by bringing more and more fringe elements into the political and economic mainstream; and subverting militant movements by offering political and economic inducements to group leaders. Co-optation was successful in El Salvador, where former adversaries on the battlefield are now electoral rivals.

The second track, if needed, should be an aggressive campaign of neutralization: cutting off arms and logistics from neighboring states; and search-and-capture or search-and-destroy missions. Taking forceful action against militants and extremists is mainly the responsibility of national leaders, but there is much international actors can do to help if they have the blessing of the local political establishment.

The key in the long term is developing political and economic systems that are open and fair, and promoting civic nationalism and the development of civil societies through education. If progress is made in these areas, then there are reasons for being hopeful about co-opting and marginalizing militant fringe elements. El Salvador, as noted above, has made dramatic headway in just a few years. However, if political and economic reforms fail, it will probably be impossible to eliminate confrontation and violence from political discourse.

LAUNCH MULTIFACETED UNDERTAKINGS

As I have discussed at some length in this book, the forces that drive internal conflicts are complex. It follows that, if conflict resolution efforts are to be successful in the long run, they will have to be multifaceted undertakings.

The United Nations has launched a number of multifunctional

peacekeeping operations since the end of the Cold War. The UN missions in Cambodia, El Salvador, Haiti, Mozambique, Namibia, and Nicaragua are the most prominent examples. As noted above, these wide-ranging operations have a fairly good track record, and offer some useful lessons for the future.

Ideally, international efforts to help resolve internal conflicts will address four sets of problems. The first order of business must be to bring military hostilities to an end and address attendant military and disarmament problems. Cease-fires have to be negotiated, implemented, and monitored. International mediators and peacekeeping forces can be tremendously helpful in this regard. Military adversaries then have to be persuaded to hand in their arms; buy-back schemes have been successful in El Salvador, Haiti, and Mozambique. Over time, rebel military forces and militia have to be demobilized, and national military forces, including appropriate representation from all relevant ethnic and political groups, have to be reconstituted. The key to continued progress is addressing the security concerns that former adversaries will inevitably have as disarmament and demobilization processes unfold.[36] International actors can help to reassure local parties by monitoring these processes carefully and promoting transparency.

Second, international actors can help with political reconstruction. In the short term, this means helping to establish transitional governments, as well as fair and effective police forces and courts. In El Salvador, Nicaragua, South Africa, and elsewhere, the United Nations has helped to organize and supervise elections. The United Nations can also provide technical expertise with respect to constitutional reforms, the creation of federal systems, the establishment of human rights safeguards, and the like.

Third, international actors can — and indeed, must — help with the long and difficult problem of economic reconstruction and the promotion of economic development. Many countries torn apart by internal conflict were in poor economic shape to begin with; years of war only made matters worse. As noted above, "mini-Marshall plans" involving the international development organizations, regional organizations, and multinational corporations will generally be needed.[37]

Finally, international actors will have to help with the complex problem of rebuilding civil societies. This can involve activities ranging from the repatriation of refugees to the creation or re-creation of a free and fair

---

36. See Joanna Spear's chapter on arms limitations and confidence-building measures in this volume.

37. See Chantal de Jonge Oudraat's chapter on the United Nations in this volume.

press to the founding of schools. As I have discussed elsewhere in this chapter, getting groups to come to terms with the distorted and pernicious aspects of their histories and inculcating the values of compromise and tolerance in political and social discourse are among the most important problems war-torn countries face. In short, education is one the keys to long-term political stability. This is surely an area where the international community can make a difference.

MAKE LONG-TERM COMMITMENTS

One of the most depressing aspects of internal conflict is its recurring nature. In place after place, from Angola to India to Zaire, conflicts sputter to a halt, only to start up with renewed fury years or decades later. Internal conflict seems to go in a state of suspended animation from time to time, but it never goes away.

Conflict resolution is not easy, and it cannot be brought about in months or even a year or two. Conflict resolution is a long-term process, and if international actors are to contribute in useful ways to this process, they have to be willing, able, and prepared to make long-term efforts. Consider the magnitude of the problems most countries face in the aftermath of civil war: state structures have to be rebuilt; legal institutions and police forces have to be reconstituted; political institutions and electoral processes have to be re-established; industrial and agricultural activities have to be re-launched; communication and transportation systems have to be reconstructed; schools have to be re-opened; and so on.

The goal should be creation of a lasting peace that would allow international actors to walk away at some point: peace would be self-sustaining. This is not an impossible dream, but it most certainly is not a short-term proposition. Politicians in Western capitals who need immediate gratification and crave regular diplomatic triumphs need not apply. This is a job for serious international actors capable of making long-term commitments to deep-seated problems.

Enduring Dilemmas

What should the international community do about internal conflicts? The central dilemma confronting the international community is that peace, order, and stability are not the only values policymakers should seek to maximize. Political, economic, and social justice are equally important, and these two sets of values are not always in perfect harmony. Although policymakers should try to prevent conflicts as a general rule, they should not necessarily work to keep oppressed peoples from rising up against totalitarian leaders who will not accept peaceful political change. Although policymakers should try to keep armed conflicts from escalating as a general rule, they should not work to keep arms from people who have been attacked by others or who are being slaughtered in large numbers. And, although policymakers should try to resolve conflicts quickly, this becomes complicated when aggressors have the upper hand, which they often do. Under these conditions, bringing a war to a quick conclusion might not be compatible with bringing it to a just conclusion.[38]

The challenge, of course, is to promote both sets of values — peace, order, and stability, on the one hand; political, economic, and social justice, on the other — at the same time. The best way to do this is for the international community to devote more effort to political and economic development and the broadening and deepening of civil societies. Internal conflict is not just a military problem: it is fundamentally a political, economic, and social problem. Addressing the military manifestations of internal conflict means dealing with the political, economic, and social roots of organized violence.

Put another way, the international community needs to place more emphasis on sustained, long-term efforts to prevent conflicts. They are comparatively low-cost, low-risk undertakings: they produce a lot of non-bang for the buck. Particular attention should be paid to political and economic development in troubled and potentially troubled parts of the world. In more concrete terms, this means working more aggressively to ensure that individuals and groups need not fear for their survival or security; overturn patterns of political, economic, and cultural discrimination; promote proportional representation in political and governmental affairs; establish and implement human rights safeguards; dampen the development of exclusionary national ideologies, whether they are based on ethnic or religious identifications; extend the benefits of economic prosperity and educational opportunities more equitably across societies; and work to develop civil societies by addressing the pernicious effects of distorted group histories and by promoting the values of compromise, conciliation, consensus, and tolerance. As Stephen Stedman has argued, the promotion of peace will, in the long run, depend more on what happens in the classroom than on the peacekeeping field.[39]

---

38. See Alicia Levine's chapter on the prevention of secessionist violence and Joanna Spear's chapter on arms limitations and confidence-building measures, both in this volume.

39. See Stephen Stedman's chapter on sub-Saharan Africa in this volume. For a concurring opinion, see Chantal de Jonge Oudraat's chapter on the United Nations in this volume.

This does not mean that focused responses to emerging crises should be eschewed, only that they need to be complemented by sustained efforts to address underlying problems.

This leads to yet another policy dilemma. Although the international community's best bets for peace and justice are long-term conflict prevention efforts, the moral concerns and national interests of international actors are engaged most acutely when people are being killed or displaced in large numbers — that is, when an intense war is under way. In other words, the international community's motivations to act are strongest when the options for taking effective action are weakest.

Although the international community should devote more effort to long-term conflict prevention, there are cases where aggressive conflict management and conflict resolution efforts should be undertaken to deal with particularly horrifying levels of violence. Sadly, as we have seen in Bosnia, Rwanda, and all too many other places, the international community is often disinclined to take firm action even when moral outrages are being committed, international values are being trampled, and national interests, indirectly and even directly, are engaged. Ever since 1945, well-meaning people have piously proclaimed that "never again" would the international community stand by and allow genocide to take place. Yet in 1994, the international community did precisely that while 800,000 people were slaughtered in Rwanda over a three-to-four month period. It is not possible, moreover, for the international community to plead ignorance about what was happening in Central Africa in 1994. The Rwanda genocide received extensive coverage in the international media, including televised footage of mutilated bodies piled high or floating in streams, rivers, and lakes. Furthermore, it was clear very early on in the crisis that this was an orchestrated, politically motivated campaign, not a spontaneous eruption of mass ethnic hysteria.[40]

The leaders of powerful states, who ignored UN Secretary-General Boutros-Ghali's repeated pleas for action, are particularly culpable — none more so than the upper echelon of the Clinton administration. White House and State Department officials tried to pass off an orchestrated campaign of slaughter as mass hysteria, when they knew better, and they pretended that they lacked the capacity to take action, when they were spending $250 billion per year on military capabilities, including in particular long-range power-projection capabilities. They even went so far as to instruct administration spokesmen to avoid using the word "genocide," fearing that this would push them into taking actions they

---

40. See Keith Richburg, "In Rwanda, 'Highly Organized' Slaughter," *International Herald Tribune*, May 9, 1994, p. 1.

dreaded for domestic political reasons.[41] The United States intervened only when the Rwandan Patriotic Front (RPF), a Tutsi force, drove the Hutu militia and thousands of Hutu refugees into Zaire. White House and State Department officials argued that the ensuing refugee crisis was a humanitarian problem that merited the deployment of U.S. military forces, even though this meant coming to the aid of those responsible for perpetrating genocide.

My case for international action in cases such as these is not based solely on moral or humanitarian considerations — although I believe that the moral case for acting is compelling and sufficient when genocide is being committed, as it was in Rwanda and Bosnia, and when international powers have the capacity to take effective action, which they clearly did in both of these cases. Even in cases where the direct national security interests of few states are engaged, such as the Rwandan genocide, internal conflicts can undermine principles of international law and order that all well-meaning states have an indirect interest in maintaining and developing.

This brings us to a final policy dilemma. In conflicts such as these, the costs of international action are easy to measure and they have to be paid immediately: they include the financial costs of economic sanctions and military deployments; the risks to troops placed in harm's way; and the domestic political risks that policymakers might have to run. The costs of inaction are much harder to measure and are usually realized only in the long term: they include damage to core political values, international norms of behavior, international law and order, and regional and international stability. It is important to remember that almost all internal conflicts have regional dimensions, implications for regional security, and implications for international order. Internal conflicts are rarely self-contained pockets of turmoil. The costs of inaction are therefore real, as is the moral diminishment that attends inaction in the face of slaughter. Unfortunately but inevitably, the costs of action receive more attention than the costs of inaction in policymaking debates. Politicians invariably focus on the calculable, short-term costs that they will have to bear as political figures. Statesmen worry more about the long-term costs to national and international security that accumulate only with the passing of time — but true statesmen are few and far between.

---

41. See Douglas Jehl, "Officials Told to Avoid Calling Rwanda Killings 'Genocide'," *New York Times,* June 10, 1994. See also Holly J. Burkhalter, "The Question of Genocide: The Clinton Administration and Rwanda," *World Policy Journal,* Vol. 11, No. 4 (Winter 1994), pp. 44–54.

Suggestions for Further Reading

The Causes and Consequences of Internal Conflict: General Works

Anderson, Benedict, *Imagined Communities: Reflections on the Origins and Spread of Nationalism* (London: Verso, 1983).

Aya, Rod, "Theories of Revolution Reconsidered: Contrasting Models of Collective Violence," *Theory and Society*, Vol. 8, No. 1 (July 1979), pp. 1–38.

Betts, Richard K., "The Delusion of Impartial Intervention," *Foreign Affairs*, Vol. 73, No. 6 (November–December 1994), pp. 20–33.

Brown, Michael E., ed., *Ethnic Conflict and International Security* (Princeton, N.J.: Princeton University Press, 1993).

Bull, Hedley, "Civil Violence and International Order," in *Civil Violence and the International System*, Adelphi Paper No. 83 (London: International Institute for Strategic Studies [IISS], 1971), pp. 27–36.

Chazan, Naomi, ed., *Irredentism and International Politics* (Boulder, Colo.: Lynne Rienner, 1991).

Cohan, A.S., *Theories of Revolution* (New York: Wiley, 1975).

De Silva, K.M., and R.J. May, eds., *Internationalization of Ethnic Conflict* (London: Pinter, 1991).

Eckstein, Harry, ed., *Internal War: Problems and Approaches* (New York: Free Press, 1964).

Esman, Milton J., "Ethnic Actors in International Politics," *Nationalism and Ethnic Politics*, Vol. 1, No. 1 (Spring 1995), pp. 111–125.

Esman, Milton J., ed., *Ethnic Conflict in the Western World* (Ithaca, N.Y.: Cornell University Press, 1977).

Esman, Milton J., *Ethnic Politics* (Ithaca, N.Y.: Cornell University Press, 1994).

Esman, Milton J., and Shibley Telhami, eds., *International Organizations and Ethnic Conflict* (Ithaca, N.Y.: Cornell University Press, 1995).

Evans, Gareth, "Cooperative Security and Intra-State Conflict," *Foreign Policy*, No. 96 (Fall 1994), pp. 3–20.

Fein, Helen, "Explanations of Genocide," *Current Sociology*, Vol. 38, No. 1 (Spring 1990), pp. 32–50.

Gagnon, V.P., Jr., "Ethnic Nationalism and International Conflict: The Case of Serbia," *International Security*, Vol. 19, No. 3 (Winter 1994/95), pp. 130–166.

Goldstone, Jack A., "Theories of Revolution: The Third Generation," *World Politics*, Vol. 32, No. 3 (April 1980), pp. 425–453.

Gurr, Ted Robert, *Minorities at Risk: A Global View of Ethnopolitical Conflicts* (Washington, D.C.: U.S. Institute of Peace Press, 1993).

Gurr, Ted Robert, "Peoples Against States: Ethnopolitical Conflict and the Changing World System," *International Studies Quarterly*, Vol. 38 (1994), pp. 347–377.

Gurr, Ted Robert, *Why Men Rebel* (Princeton, N.J.: Princeton University Press, 1970).

Gurr, Ted Robert, and Barbara Harff, *Ethnic Conflict and World Politics* (Boulder, Colo.: Westview, 1994).

Helman, Gerald and Steven Ratner, "Saving Failed States," *Foreign Policy*, No. 89 (Winter 1992/93), pp. 3–20.

Heraclides, Alexis, "Secessionist Minorities and External Involvement," *International Organization*, Vol. 44, No. 3 (Summer 1990), pp. 341–378.

Hill, Stuart, and Donald Rothchild, "The Contagion of Political Conflict in Africa and the World," *Journal of Conflict Resolution*, Vol. 30, No. 4 (December 1986), pp. 716–735.

Horowitz, Donald L., *Ethnic Groups in Conflict* (Berkeley: University of California Press, 1985).

Human Rights Watch, *Playing the "Communal Card": Communal Violence and Human Rights* (New York: Human Rights Watch, 1995).

Huntington, Samuel P., "Civil Violence and the Process of Development," in *Civil Violence and the International System*, Adelphi Paper No. 83, (London: IISS, 1971).

Huntington, Samuel P., *Political Order in Changing Societies* (New Haven, Conn.: Yale University Press, 1968).

Kuper, Leo, *Genocide: Its Political Use in the Twentieth Century* (New Haven, Conn.: Yale University Press, 1981).

Little, Richard, *Intervention: External Involvement in Civil Wars* (Totowa, N.J.: Rowman and Littlefield, 1975).

Luard, Evan, ed., *The International Regulation of Civil Wars* (London: Thames and Hudson, 1972).

Maynes, Charles William, "Containing Ethnic Conflict," *Foreign Policy*, No. 90 (Spring 1993), pp. 3–21.

Midlarsky, Manus I., ed., *The Internationalization of Communal Strife* (London: Routledge, 1992).

Montville, Joseph V., ed., *Conflict and Peacekeeping in Multiethnic Societies* (Lexington, Mass.: Lexington Books, 1990).

Newman, Saul, "Does Modernization Breed Ethnic Political Conflict?" *World Politics*, Vol. 43, No. 3 (April 1991), pp. 451–478.

Nordlinger, Eric A., *Conflict Regulation in Divided Societies* (Cambridge: Harvard University, Center for International Affairs, 1972).

Rosenau, James N., ed., *International Aspects of Civil Strife* (Princeton, N.J.: Princeton University Press, 1964).

Rothchild, Donald, and Alexander J. Groth, "Pathological Dimensions of Domestic and

International Ethnicity," *Political Science Quarterly,* Vol. 110, No. 1 (Spring 1995), pp. 69–82.

Rothschild, Joseph, *Ethnopolitics: A Conceptual Framework* (New York: Columbia University Press, 1981).

Rule, James B., *Theories of Civil Violence* (Berkeley: University of California Press, 1988).

Samarasinghe, S.W.R. de A., and Reed Coughlin, eds., *Economic Dimensions of Ethnic Conflict* (London: Pinter, 1991).

Smith, Anthony D., *The Ethnic Origins of Nations* (New York: Basil Blackwell, 1986).

Smith, Anthony D., *The Ethnic Revival in the Modern World* (New York: Cambridge University Press, 1981).

Smith, Anthony D., *National Identity* (London: Penguin, 1991).

Tilly, Charles, "Does Modernization Breed Revolution?" *Comparative Politics,* Vol. 5, No. 3 (April 1973), pp. 425–447.

Van Evera, Stephen, "Hypotheses on Nationalism and War," *International Security,* Vol. 18, No. 4 (Spring 1994), pp. 5–39.

Von Hippel, Karin, "The Resurgence of Nationalism and Its International Implications," *Washington Quarterly,* Vol. 14, No. 4 (Autumn 1994), pp. 185–200.

Walt, Stephen M., "Revolution and War," *World Politics,* Vol. 44, No. 3 (April 1992), pp. 321–368.

Waltz, Kenneth N., *Man, the State and War: A Theoretical Analysis* (New York: Columbia University Press, 1959).

Weiner, Myron, "Peoples and States in a New Ethnic Order?" *Third World Quarterly,* Vol. 13, No. 2 (1992), pp. 317–333.

Zartman, I. William, ed., *Collapsed States: The Disintegration and Restoration of Legitimate Authority* (Boulder, Colo.: Lynne Rienner, 1995).

The Former Yugoslavia

Banac, Ivo, *The National Question in Yugoslavia* (Ithaca, N.Y.: Cornell University Press, 1985).

Cohen, Lenard, *Broken Bonds: The Disintegration of Yugoslavia* (Boulder, Colo.: Westview, 1993).

Djilas, Aleksa, "A Profile of Slobodan Milosevic," *Foreign Affairs,* Vol. 72, No. 3 (Summer 1993), pp. 81–96.

Gagnon, V.P., Jr., "Ethnic Nationalism and International Conflict: The Case of Serbia," *International Security,* Vol. 19, No. 3 (Winter 1994/95), pp. 130–166.

Goodby, James, "Peacekeeping in the New Europe," *Washington Quarterly,* Vol. 15, No. 2 (Spring 1992), pp. 153–171.

Minear, Larry et al., *Humanitarian Action in the Former Yugoslavia: The UN's Role 1991–1993,* Occasional Paper No. 18 (Providence, R.I.: Watson Institute for International Studies, 1994).

Newhouse, John, "Dodging the Problem," *New Yorker,* August 24, 1992, pp. 60–71.

Newhouse, John, "No Exit, No Entrance," *New Yorker,* June 28, 1993, pp. 44–51.

Steinberg, James, "Yugoslavia," in Lori Fisler Damrosch, ed., *Enforcing Restraint:*

Collective Intervention in Internal Conflicts (New York: Council on Foreign Relations, 1993), pp. 27–76.

Weller, Marc, "The International Response to the Dissolution of the Socialist Federal Republic of Yugoslavia," *American Journal of International Law,* Vol. 86, No. 3 (July 1992), pp. 569–607.

Wijnaendts, Henry, *Joegoslavische Kroniek: Juli 1991–Augustus 1992* (Amsterdam: Thomas Rap, 1993).

Zametica, John, *The Yugoslav Conflict,* Adelphi Paper No. 270 (London: IISS, 1992).

Zimmerman, Warren, "The Last Ambassador," *Foreign Affairs,* Vol. 74, No. 2 (March/April 1995), pp. 2–20.

East-Central Europe

Baldwin, Richard, *Toward An Integrated Europe* (London: Centre for Economic Policy Research (CEPR), 1994).

Banac, Ivo, ed., *Eastern Europe in Revolution* (Ithaca, N.Y.: Cornell University Press, 1992).

Cuthbertson, Ian, and Jane Liebowitz, *Minorities: The New Europe's Old Issue* (Boulder, Colo.: Westview, 1993).

Graubard, Stephen, ed., *Eastern Europe . . . Central Europe . . . Europe* (Oxford: Oxford University Press, 1993).

Freedman, Lawrence, ed., *Military Intervention in European Conflicts* (Oxford: Blackwell, 1994).

Karp, Regina Cowen, ed., *Central and Eastern Europe: The Challenge of Transition* (Oxford: Oxford University Press, 1993).

Miall, Hugh, ed., *Minority Rights in Europe: Prospects for a Transnational Regime* (London: Royal Institute of International Affairs, 1994).

Rollo, Jim, and Alasdair Smith, "EC Trade with Eastern Europe," *Economic Policy,* No. 16 (April 1993), pp. 140–181.

Schöpflin, George, *Hungary and Its Neighbors,* Chaillot Paper No. 7 (Paris: Western European Union (WEU) Institute for Security Studies, May 1993).

Smith, Alasdair, and Helen Wallace, "The New European Union: Towards a Policy for Europe," *International Affairs,* Vol. 70, No. 3 (July 1994), pp. 429–444.

Whitefield, Stephen, ed., *The New Institutional Architecture of Eastern Europe* (London: Macmillan, 1993).

The Former Soviet Union

Allison, Roy, *Peacekeeping in the Soviet Successor States,* Chaillot Paper No. 18 (Paris: WEU Institute for Security Studies, November 1994).

Arbatov, Alexei G., "Russia's Foreign Policy Alternatives," *International Security,* Vol. 18, No. 2 (Fall 1993), pp. 5–43.

Aron, Leon, and Kenneth M. Jensen, eds., *The Emergence of Russian Foreign Policy* (Washington, D.C.: U.S. Institute of Peace, 1994).

Baranovsky, Vladimir, "Conflict Development on the Territory of the Former Soviet Union," *SIPRI Yearbook 1994* (London: Oxford University Press, 1994), pp. 169–203.

Hill, Fiona, and Pamela Jewett, *Back in the USSR: Russia's Intervention in the Internal Affairs of the Former Soviet Republics and the Implications for United States Policy Toward Russia* (Cambridge, Mass.: Strengthening Democratic Institutions Project, John F. Kennedy School of Government, Harvard University, January 1994).

Klimenko, Vladimir, "A Tale of Two Countries," *Mother Jones* (July/August, 1993), pp. 54–57.

Porter, Bruce D., and Carol R. Saivetz, "The Once and Future Empire: Russia and the 'Near Abroad'," *Washington Quarterly*, Vol. 17, No. 3 (Summer 1994), pp. 75–90.

Shenfield, Stephen D., "Armed Conflict in Eastern Europe and the Former Soviet Union," in Thomas G. Weiss, ed., *The United Nations and Civil Wars* (Boulder, Colo.: Lynne Rienner, 1995), pp. 31–48.

Stern, Jessica Eve, "Moscow Meltdown: Can Russia Survive?" *International Security*, Vol. 18, No. 4 (Spring 1994), pp. 40–65.

Tadjbakhsh, Shahrbanou, "The Bloody Path of Change: The Case of Post-Soviet Tajikstan," *Harriman Institute Forum*, Vol. 6, No. 11 (July 1993), pp. 1–10.

Wallander, Celeste, ed., *The Sources of Russian Conduct after the Cold War* (Boulder, Colo.: Westview, 1995).

South and Southwest Asia

Brass, Paul, *The Politics of India Since Independence* (Cambridge, U.K.: Cambridge University Press, 1994).

Cohen, Stephen P., *The Indian Army* (Berkeley: University of California Press, 1971).

Cohen, Stephen P., *The Pakistan Army* (Berkeley: University of California Press, 1984).

Ganguly, Sumit, "Ethno-Religious Conflict in South Asia," *Survival*, Vol. 35, No. 2 (Summer 1993), pp. 88–109.

Ganguly, Sumit, *The Origins of War in South Asia*, 2nd ed. (Boulder, Colo.: Westview, 1994).

Ghosh, Partha, *Conflict and Cooperation in South Asia* (New Delhi: Manohar, 1989).

Gupta, Jyoti Bhusan Das, *Jammu and Kashmir* (The Hague: Marinus Nijoff, 1968).

Hoffmann, Stanley, *India and the China Crisis* (Berkeley: University of California Press, 1990).

Manor, James, ed., *Sri Lanka in Change and Crisis* (New York: St. Martin's, 1993).

Nasr, Seyyed Vali Reza, *The Vanguard of the Islamic Revolution* (Berkeley: University of California Press, 1994).

Rizvi, Hasan-Askari, *Pakistan and the Geostrategic Environment* (New York: St. Martin's, 1993).

Rubin, Barnett R., *The Fragmentation of Afghanistan* (New Haven, Conn.: Yale University Press, 1994).

Rubin, Barnett R., *The Search for Peace in Afghanistan: From Buffer State to Failed State* (New Haven, Conn.: Yale University Press, 1995).

Sisson, Richard, and Leo Rose, *War and Secession: India, Pakistan and the Creation of Bangladesh* (Berkeley: University of California Press, 1990).

Weinbaum, Marvin G., *Pakistan and Afghanistan* (Boulder, Colo.: Westview, 1994).

Southeast Asia

Acharya, Amitav, *A New Regional Order in South-East Asia: ASEAN in the Post–Cold War Era*, Adelphi Paper No. 279 (London: IISS, 1973).

Alagappa, Muthiah, "The Dynamics of International Security in Southeast Asia: Change and Continuity," *Australian Journal of International Affairs*, Vol. 45, No. 1 (May 1991).

Brown, David, *The State and Ethnic Politics in Southeast Asia* (London: Routledge, 1994).

Hewison, Kevin, Richard Robinson, and Garry Rodan, eds., *Southeast Asia in the 1990s: Authoritarianism, Democracy and Capitalism* (St. Leonards, U.K.: Allen & Unwin, 1993).

Keyes, Charles F., The *Golden Peninsula: Culture and Adoption in Mainland Southeast Asia* (Honolulu: University of Hawaii Press, 1985).

Lyon, Peter, *War and Peace in South-East Asia* (London: Oxford University Press, 1969).

Mack, Andrew, and John Ravenhill, eds., *Pacific Cooperation: Building Economic and Security Regimes in the Asia-Pacific Region* (St. Leonards, U.K.: Allen & Unwin, 1994).

Schwarz, Adam, *A Nation in Waiting: Indonesia in the 1990s* (Boulder, Colo.: Westview, 1994).

Segal, Gerald, *Rethinking the Pacific* (Oxford: Clarendon, 1990).

Singh, Daljit, ed., *Southeast Asian Affairs 1994* (Singapore: Institute of Southeast Asian Studies, 1994).

Steinberg, David Joel, *In Search of Southeast Asia: A Modern History* (Honolulu: University of Hawaii Press, 1989).

The Middle East and North Africa

Bar-Simon-Tov, Yaacov, *Linkage Politics in the Middle East: Syria Between Domestic and External Conflict, 1961–1970* (Boulder, Colo.: Westview, 1983).

Esman, Milton J., and Itamar Rabinovich, *Ethnicity, Pluralism, and the State in the Middle East* (Ithaca, N.Y.: Cornell University Press, 1988).

Faour, Muhammad, *The Arab World After Desert Storm* (Washington, D.C.: U.S. Institute of Peace, 1993).

Gause, F. Gregory III, "Revolutionary Fevers and Regional Contagion: Domestic Structures and the Export of Revolution in the Middle East," *Journal of South Asian and Middle Eastern Studies*, Vol. 14, No. 3 (Spring 1991), pp. 1–23.

Harff, Barbara, "Minorities, Rebellion and Repression in North Africa and the Middle East," in Ted Robert Gurr, ed., *Minorities at Risk: A Global View of Ethnopolitical Conflicts* (Washington, D.C.: U.S. Institute of Peace, 1993), pp. 217–251.

Hourani, A.H., *Minorities in the Arab World* (New York: Oxford University Press, 1977).

Hudson, Michael C., *Arab Politics: The Search for Legitimacy* (New Haven, Conn.: Yale University Press, 1977).

Khoury, Philip S., and Joseph Kostiner, eds., *Tribes and State Formation in the Middle East* (New York: I.B. Tauris, 1991).

Luciani, Giacomo, ed., *The Arab State* (Berkeley: University of California Press, 1990).

McLaurin, R.D., ed., *The Political Role of Minority Groups in the Middle East* (New York: Praeger, 1979).

Migdal, Joel, *Strong Societies and Weak States: State-Society Relations and State Capabilities in the Third World* (Princeton, N.J.: Princeton University Press, 1988).

Parsons, Anthony, *Prospects for Peace and Stability in the Middle East,* Conflict Studies No. 262 (London: Research Institute for the Study of Conflict and Terrorism, June 1993).

Sub-Saharan Africa

Callaghy, Thomas M., and John Ravenhill, *Hemmed In: Responses to Africa's Economic Decline* (New York: Columbia University Press, 1994).

Davidson, Basil, *The Black Man's Burden: Africa and the Curse of the Nation-State* (New York: Times Books, 1992).

Deng, Francis, and I. William Zartman, eds., *Conflict Resolution in Africa* (Washington, D.C.: Brookings Institution, 1991).

Licklider, Roy, ed., *Stopping the Killing: How Civil Wars End* (New York: New York University Press, 1993).

Modelski, George, "International Settlement of Internal War," in James N. Rosenau, ed., *International Aspects of Civil Strife* (Princeton, N.J.: Princeton University Press), pp. 122–153.

Ohlson, Thomas, and Stephen John Stedman, *The New Is Not Yet Born: Conflict Research in Southern Africa* (Washington, D.C.: Brookings Institution, 1994).

Rothchild, Donald, and Naomi Chazan, eds., *The Precarious Balance: State and Society in Africa* (Boulder, Colo.: Westview, 1988).

Sandbrook, Richard, *The Politics of Africa's Economic Recovery* (Cambridge, U.K.: Cambridge University Press, 1992).

Smock, David, ed., *Making War and Waging Peace: Foreign Intervention in Africa* (Washington, D.C.: U.S. Institute of Peace, 1993).

Stedman, Stephen John, "UN Intervention in Civil Wars: Imperatives of Choice and Strategy," in Donald C.F. Daniel and Bradd C. Hayes, eds., *Beyond Traditional Peacekeeping* (New York: St. Martin's, 1995), pp. 40–63.

Touval, Saadia, "Why the UN Fails," *Foreign Affairs,* Vol. 73, No. 5 (September/October 1994), pp. 44–57.

Zartman, I. William, *Ripe for Research: Conflict and Intervention in Africa,* 2nd ed. (New York: Oxford University Press, 1989).

Latin America

Aguilar Zinson, Adolfo, "Negotiation in Conflict: Central America and Contadora," in Nora Hamilton, ed., *Crisis in Central America* (Boulder, Colo.: Westview, 1988), pp. 97–115.

Arnson, Cynthia, *Crossroads: Congress, the Reagan Administration and Central America* (New York: Pantheon, 1989).

Castañeda, Jorge G., *Utopia Unarmed: The Latin American Left after the Cold War* (New York: Alfred A. Knopf, 1993).

Chernick, Marc, "Negotiated Settlement to Armed Conflict: Lessons from the Colombian Peace Process," *Journal of Interamerican Studies and World Affairs,* Vol. 30, No. 4 (Winter 1988/89), pp. 53–88.

Child, Jack, *The Central American Peace Process 1983–1991: Sheathing Swords, Building Confidence* (Boulder, Colo.: Lynne Rienner, 1992).

Fundacíon para la paz, la democracia y el desarrollo, *Documentos basicos del proceso de paz* (Guatemala City: Fundapazd, 1994).

Garcia Duran, Mauricio, *De la Uribe a Tlaxcala: Procesos de Paz* (Santa Fe de Bogotá: CINEO, 1992).

Garcia Sayan, Diego, *Coca, Cocaina y Narcotrafico: Laberinto en los Andes* (Lima: Comisíon Andina de Juristas, 1989).

Gonzales, Fernan E., *Violencia en la Regíon Andina: El Caso Colombia* (Santa Fe de Bogotá: CINEO, 1993).

Harvey, Neil et al., *Rebellion in Chiapas* (San Diego: Center for U.S.-Mexican Studies, University of California at San Diego, 1994).

Moreno, Dario, *The Struggle for Peace in Central America* (Gainesville: University of Florida Press, 1994).

Montgomery, Tommie Sue, *Revolution in El Salvador: From Civil Strife to Civil Peace*, 2nd ed. (Boulder, Colo.: Westview, 1992).

Organization of American States (OAS), *A New Vision of the OAS,* Working Paper of the General Secretariat for the Permanent Council, April 1995.

Palmer, David Scott, *Shining Path of Peru* (New York: St. Martin's, 1992).

Psacharopolous, George, and Harry Anthony Patrinos, *Indigenous People and Poverty in Latin America* (Washington, D.C.: World Bank, 1984).

Smith, Peter H., ed., *Drug Policy in the Americas* (Boulder, Colo.: Westview, 1992).

Van Cott, Donna Lee, ed., *Indigenous Peoples and Democracy in Latin America* (New York: St. Martin's, 1994).

Political Accommodation and the Prevention of Secessionist Violence

Buchheit, Lee C., *Secession: The Legitimacy of Self-Determination* (New Haven, Conn.: Yale University Press, 1978).

Glenny, Misha, *The Fall of Yugoslavia: The Third Balkan War* (London: Penguin, 1992).

Halperin, Morton, and David Scheffer, *Self-Determination in the New World Order* (Washington, D.C.: Carnegie Endowment for International Peace, 1992).

Hannum, Hurst, *Autonomy, Sovereignty, and Self-Determination: The Accommodation of Conflicting Rights* (Philadelphia: University of Pennsylvania Press, 1990).

Horowitz, Donald, *Ethnic Groups in Conflict* (Berkeley: University of California Press, 1985), chap. 6.

Kampelman, Max M., "Secession and the Right to Self-Determination: An Urgent Need to Harmonize Principle and Practice," *Washington Quarterly,* Vol. 16, No. 3 (Summer 1993), pp. 5–12.

Posen, Barry R., "The Security Dilemma and Ethnic Conflict," in Michael E. Brown, ed., *Ethnic Conflict and International Security* (Princeton, N.J.: Princeton University Press, 1993), pp. 103–124.

Premdas, Ralph R., S.W.R. de A. Samarasinghe, and Alan B. Anderson, *Secessionist Movement in Comparative Perspective* (London: Pinter, 1990).

Shehadi, Kamal S., *Ethnic Self-Determination and the Break-Up of States*, Adelphi Paper No. 283 (London: IISS, 1993).

Van Evera, Stephen, "Hypotheses on Nationalism and War," *International Security*, Vol. 18, No. 4 (Spring 1994), pp. 5–39.

Watson, Michael, *Contemporary Minority Nationalism* (London: Routledge, 1990).

Williams, Colin H., *National Separatism* (Cardiff: University of Wales Press, 1982).

Negotiation and Mediation in Internal Conflict

Licklider, Roy, ed., *Stopping the Killing: How Civil Wars End* (New York: New York University Press, 1993).

Modelski, George, "International Settlement of Internal War," in James N. Rosenau, ed., *International Aspects of Civil Strife* (Princeton, N.J.: Princeton University Press, 1964), pp. 122–153.

Stedman, Stephen John, *Peacemaking in Civil War: International Mediation in Zimbabwe, 1974–1980* (Boulder, Colo.: Lynne Rienner, 1991).

Stedman, Stephen John, "UN Intervention in Civil Wars: Imperatives of Choice and Strategy," in Donald C.F. Daniel and Bradd C. Hayes, eds., *Beyond Traditional Peacekeeping* (New York: St. Martin's, 1995), pp. 40–63.

Touval, Saadia, "Why the UN Fails," *Foreign Affairs*, Vol. 73, No. 5 (September/October 1994), pp. 44–57.

Barbara F. Walter, "The Resolution of Civil Wars: Why Negotiations Fail," Ph.D. dissertation, University of Chicago, 1994.

Zartman, I. William, *Ripe For Resolution: Conflict and Intervention in Africa*, 2nd ed. (New York: Oxford University Press, 1989).

Arms Limitations, Confidence-Building Measures, and Internal Conflict

Arms Project of Human Rights Watch and Physicians for Human Rights, *Landmines: A Deadly Legacy* (Washington, D.C.: Human Rights Watch and Physicians for Human Rights, 1993).

Boutwell, Jeffrey, Michael T. Klare, and Laura W. Reed, eds., *Lethal Commerce: The Global Trade in Small Arms and Light Weapons* (Cambridge, Mass.: Committee on International Security Studies, American Academy of Arts and Sciences, 1995).

Destexhe, Alain, "The Third Genocide," *Foreign Policy*, No. 97 (Winter 1994/95), pp. 3–17.

Goose, Stephen D., and Frank Smyth, "Arming Genocide in Rwanda," *Foreign Affairs*, Vol. 73, No. 5 (September/October 1994), pp. 86–96.

Karp, Aaron, "Arming Ethnic Conflict," *Arms Control Today*, Vol. 23, No. 7 (September 1993), pp. 8–13.

Klare, Michael T., "Awash in Armaments: Implications of the Trade in Light Weapons," *Harvard International Review*, Vol. 17, No. 1 (Winter 1994/95), pp. 24–26, 75–76.

Stevenson, Jonathan, "Hope Restored in Somalia," *Foreign Policy*, No. 91 (Summer 1993), pp. 138–154.

Wurst, Jim, "Mozambique Disarms," *Bulletin of the Atomic Scientists,* Vol. 50, No. 5 (September/October 1994), pp. 36–39.

Economic Sanctions and Internal Conflict

Baldwin, David, *Economic Statecraft* (Princeton, N.J.: Princeton University Press, 1985).

Chayes, Antonia Handler, and Abram Chayes, "Regime Architecture: Elements and Principles," in Janne E. Nolan, ed., *Global Engagement: Cooperation and Security in the 21st Century,* (Washington, D.C.: Brookings Institution, 1994), pp. 65–130.

Damrosch, Lori Fisler, "The Civilian Impact of Economic Sanctions," in Lori Fisler Damrosch, ed., *Enforcing Restraint: Collective Intervention in Internal Conflicts* (New York: Council on Foreign Relations, 1993), pp. 274–315.

Day, Erin, *Economic Sanctions Imposed by the United States Against Specific Countries: 1979 Through 1992* (Washington, D.C.: Congressional Research Service, August 10, 1992).

Elliott, Kimberly, and Gary Hufbauer, "'New' Approaches to Economic Sanctions," in Arnold Kanter and Linton Brooks, eds., *U.S. Intervention Policy for the Post–Cold War World: New Challenges and New Responses* (New York: American Assembly, 1994), pp. 132–158.

Hendrickson, David, "The Democratic Crusade: Intervention, Economic Sanctions and Engagement," *World Policy Journal,* Vol. 21, No. 4 (Winter 1994/95), pp. 18–30.

Hufbauer, Gary, "The Impact of United States Economic Sanctions and Controls on U.S. Firms," a report to the National Foreign Trade Council, April 1990.

Hufbauer, Gary, Jeffrey Schott, and Kimberly Anne Elliott, *Economic Sanctions Reconsidered,* 2nd ed., 2 vols. (Washington, D.C.: Institute for International Economics, 1990).

Kaempfer, William, and Anton Lowenberg, *International Economic Sanctions: A Public Choice Perspective* (Boulder, Colo.: Westview, 1992).

Leyton-Brown, David, ed., *The Utility of International Economic Sanctions* (New York: St. Martin's, 1987).

Martin, Lisa, *Coercive Cooperation* (Princeton, N.J.: Princeton University Press, 1992).

Miyagwa, Makio, *Do Economic Sanctions Work?* (New York: St. Martin's, 1992).

Renwick, Robin, *Economic Sanctions* (Cambridge, Mass.: Harvard University, Center for International Affairs, 1981).

Rodman, Kenneth A., "Sanctions at Bay? Hegemonic Decline, Multinational Corporations, and U.S. Economic Sanctions Since the Pipeline Case," *International Organization,* Vol. 49, No. 1 (Winter 1995), pp. 105–137.

Nongovernmental Organizations and Internal Conflict

Borton, John, *NGOs and Relief Operations: Trends and Policy Implications* (London: Overseas Development Institute, 1994).

Davis, Morris, ed., *Civil War and the Politics of International Relief* (New York: Praeger, 1975).

Edwards, Michael, and David Hulme, eds., *Making a Difference: NGOs and Development in a Changing World* (London: Earthscan, 1992).

Kent, Randolph, *Anatomy of Disaster Relief: The International Network in Action* (London: Puster, 1987).

Korten, David, *Getting to the 21st Century: Voluntary Action and the Global Agenda* (Hartford, Conn.: Kumarian, 1990).

McCarthy, Kathleen D., Virginia Hodgkinson, Russy Samariwalla et al. *The Nonprofit Sector in the Global Community* (San Francisco: Jossey Bass, 1992).

Minear, Larry, and Thomas G. Weiss, *Mercy Under Fire: War and the Global Humanitarian Community* (Boulder, Colo.: Westview, 1995).

Randel, Judith, and Tony German, eds., *The Reality of Aid 94* (London: Actionaid, 1994).

Schneider, Bertrand, *Barefoot Revolution: A Report to the Club of Rome* (London: IT Publications, 1988).

Smith, Brian H., *More Than Altruism: The Politics of Private Foreign Aid* (Princeton, N.J.: Princeton University Press, 1990).

Spiro, Peter J., "New Global Communities: Nongovernmental Organizations in International Decision-Making Institutions," *Washington Quarterly*, Vol. 18, No. 1 (Winter 1995), pp. 45–56.

Thakur, Ramesh, "Human Rights: Amnesty International and the United Nations," *Journal of Peace Research*, Vol. 31, No. 2 (December 1994), pp. 143–160.

Weiss, Thomas G., ed., *NGOs, the UN, and Global Governance* (Boulder, Colo.: Lynne Rienner, 1996).

Weiss, Thomas G., ed., *The United Nations and Civil Wars* (Boulder, Colo.: Lynne Rienner, 1995).

The United States and Military Intervention in Internal Conflict

Blackwill, Robert D., "A Taxonomy for Defining U.S. National Security Interests in the 1990s and Beyond," in Werner Weidenfeld and Josef Janning, eds., *Europe in Global Change: Strategies and Options for Europe* (Gütersloh, Germany: Bertelsmann Foundation, 1993), pp. 100–119.

Berdal, Mats R., "Fateful Encounter: The United States and UN Peacekeeping," *Survival*, Vol. 36, No. 1 (Spring 1994), pp. 30–50.

Betts, Richard K., "The Delusion of Impartial Intervention," *Foreign Affairs*, Vol. 73, No. 6 (November/December 1994), pp. 20–33.

The Clinton Administration's Policy on Reforming Multilateral Peace Operations, PDD-25, The White House Press Office, May 1994.

Daalder, Ivo, *The Clinton Administration and Multilateral Peace Operations*, Draft Pew Case Study, (August 1994).

Daniel, Donald C.F., and Bradd C. Hayes, eds., *Beyond Traditional Peacekeeping* (London: Macmillan, 1995).

Reisman, W. Michael, "Peacemaking," *Yale Journal of International Law*, Vol. 18, No. 1 (Winter 1993), pp. 415–422.

U.S. Congress, *U.S. Participation in United Nations Peacekeeping Activities*, Hearing before the Subcommittee on International Security, International Organizations, and Human Rights of the Committee on Foreign Affairs, U.S. House of Representatives, 103rd Cong., 1st sess. (Washington, D.C.: U.S. Government Printing Office [U.S. GPO], June 24, September 21, and October 7, 1993).

U.S. Congress, *International Peacekeeping and Peace Enforcement,* Hearings before the Subcommittee on Coalition Defense and Reinforcing Forces of the Committee on Armed Services, U.S. Senate, 103rd Cong., 1st sess. (Washington, D.C.: U.S. GPO, July 14, 1993).

U.S. Department of the Army, *Field Manual 100-23: Peace Operations,* December 1994.

The United Nations and Internal Conflict

Arend, Anthony Clark, and Robert J. Beck, *International Law and the Use of Force* (London: Routledge, 1993).

Berdal, Mats R., *Whither UN Peacekeeping?* Adelphi Paper No. 281 (London: IISS, 1993).

Cot, Jean-Pierre, and Alain Pellet, eds., *La Charte des Nations Unies, Commentaire article par article,* 2nd ed. (Paris: Economica, 1991).

Damrosch, Lori Fisler, ed., *Enforcing Restraint: Collective Intervention in Internal Conflicts* (New York: Council on Foreign Relations, 1993).

Dupuy, René-Jean, ed., *Le développement du rôle de Conseil du sécurité: The Development of the Role of the Security Council.* Hague Academy of International Law Workshop, The Hague, July 21–23, 1992 (Dordrecht: Martinus Nijhoff, 1993).

Durch, William J., ed., *The Evolution of UN Peacekeeping: Case Studies and Comparative Analysis* (New York: St. Martin's, 1993).

James, Alan, *Peacekeeping in International Politics* (New York: St. Martin's, 1990).

Lowe, Vaughan, and Colin Warbrick, eds., *The United Nations and the Principles of International Law* (London: Routledge, 1994).

Reed, Laura W., and Carl Kaysen, *Emerging Norms of Justified Intervention* (Cambridge, Mass.: American Academy of Arts and Sciences, 1993).

Roberts, Adam, and Benedict Kingsbury, eds., *United Nations, Divided World: The UN's Role in International Relations,* 2nd ed. (Oxford: Clarendon, 1993).

Ronzitti, Natalino, *Rescuing Nationals Abroad and Intervention on the Grounds of Humanity* (Dordrecht: Martinus Nijhoff, 1985).

United Nations, *The Blue Helmets: A Review of United Nations Peace-Keeping* (New York: United Nations, 1990).

United Nations Institute for Disarmament Research (UNIDIR), "Peace-keeping, Peace-making, Peace Enforcement," *UNIDIR Newsletter,* No. 24 (December 1993).

Weiss, Thomas G., David P. Forsythe, and Roger A. Coate, *The United Nations and Changing World Politics* (Boulder, Colo.: Westview, 1994).

White, N.D., *Keeping the Peace: The United Nations and the Maintenance of International Peace and Security* (Manchester, U.K.: Manchester University Press, 1993).

Collective Security Organizations and Internal Conflict

Bercovitz, Jacob, J. Theodore Anagnoson, and Donnette L. Wille, "Some Conceptual Issues and Empirical Trends in the Study of Successful Mediation in Relations," *Journal of Peace Research,* Vol. 28, No. 1 (February 1991).

Betts, Richard K., "Systems for Peace or Causes of War? Collective Security, Arms Control, and the New Europe," *International Security,* Vol. 17, No. 1 (Summer 1992), pp. 5–43.

Betts, Richard K., "The Delusion of Impartial Intervention," *Foreign Affairs*, Vol. 73, No. 6 (November/December 1994), pp. 20–33.

Diehl, Paul, *International Peacekeeping* (Baltimore, Md.: Johns Hopkins University Press, 1993).

Downs, George, ed., *Collective Security Beyond the Cold War* (Ann Arbor: University of Michigan Press, 1994).

Durch, William, ed., *The Evolution of UN Peacekeeping: Case Studies and Comparative Analysis* (New York: St. Martin's, 1993).

Haas, Ernst B., "Regime Decay: Conflict Management and International Organizations, 1945–1981," *International Organization*, Vol. 37, No. 2 (Spring 1983), pp. 189–256.

James, Alan, *Peacekeeping in International Politics* (New York: St. Martin's, 1990).

Kupchan, Charles A., and Clifford A. Kupchan, "Concerts, Collective Security, and the Future of Europe," *International Security*, Vol. 16, No. 1, (Summer 1991), pp. 114–161.

Rikhye, Indar Jit, *The Theory and Practice of Peacekeeping* (London: C. Hurst and Company for the International Peace Academy, 1984).

United Nations Secretary-General, *Supplement to "An Agenda for Peace": Position Paper of the Secretary-General on the Occasion of the Fiftieth Anniversary of the United Nations*, A/50/60, S/1995/1, January 3, 1995.

Van Evera, Stephen, "Primed for Peace: Europe After the Cold War," *International Security*, Vol. 15, No. 3 (Winter 1990/91), pp. 7–57.

Wainhouse, David W., *International Peace Observation: A History and Forecast* (Baltimore, Md.: Johns Hopkins University Press, 1966).

Walters, F.P., *A History of the League of Nations* (London: Oxford University Press, 1952).

Contributors

Michael E. Brown is Associate Director of the International Security Program, Managing Editor of *International Security,* and Director of the Project on Internal Conflict at the Center for Science and International Affairs (CSIA) at the John F. Kennedy School of Government, Harvard University. Before taking up his current position in January 1994, he was Senior Fellow in U.S. Security Policy and Editor of *Survival* at the International Institute for Strategic Studies (IISS) in London. He is editor of *Ethnic Conflict and International Security* (Princeton University Press, 1993), and author of *Flying Blind: The Politics of the U.S. Strategic Bomber Program* (Cornell University Press, 1992), which won the Edgar Furniss National Security Book Award.

Rachel Bronson is a pre-doctoral Research Fellow at CSIA and a doctoral candidate in political science at Columbia University. Her dissertation explores the relationship between domestic instability and foreign policy decisions in the Middle East.

Marc W. Chernick is Acting Director of the Latin American Studies Program and Assistant Professor of Political Science at the School of Advanced International Studies, Johns Hopkins University. In 1992–94, he was Visiting Professor at the National University of Colombia in Bogotá and Visiting Researcher at the Institute of Peruvian Studies in Lima, where he conducted comparative research on political violence, drug trafficking, and state responses to these problems in Colombia and Peru.

Ivo H. Daalder is Associate Professor at the School of Public Affairs and Director of Research at the Center for International and Security Studies (CISSM) at the University of Maryland. He has received a Council on Foreign Relations International Affairs Fellowship, and is spending 1995–96 working on peacekeeping issues as a member of the National Security Council Staff. He has been a Research Fellow at CSIA and the IISS, and his most recent publications include *Cooperative Arms Control: A New Agenda for the Post–Cold*

War Period (CISSM, 1992), and (with Terry Terriff) *Rethinking the Unthinkable: New Directions for Nuclear Arms Control* (Frank Cass, 1993).

Matthew Evangelista spent 1993–95 as a Research Fellow at CSIA. He plans to join the faculty of Cornell University's Department of Government. He is the author of *Innovation and the Arms Race: How the United States and the Soviet Union Develop New Military Technologies* (Cornell University Press, 1988) and articles in journals such as *International Security*, *World Politics*, and *International Organization*.

Trevor Findlay is Project Leader on Peacekeeping and Regional Security at the Stockholm International Peace Research Institute (SIPRI). He is a former Australian diplomat and a former Senior Research Fellow at the Peace Research Centre, Australian National University, Canberra, where he was founding editor of the quarterly journal *Pacific Research*. He is the author of *Nuclear Dynamite: The Peaceful Nuclear Explosions Fiasco* (Brassey's Australia, 1990), *Peace Through Chemistry: The New Chemical Weapons Convention* (Peace Research Centre, 1993), and *Cambodia: The Legacy and Lessons of UNTAC* (Oxford University Press, 1995).

Sumit Ganguly is Professor of Political Science at Hunter College of the City University of New York and a member of the South Asian Institute at Columbia University. He is the author of *The Origins of War in South Asia*, 2nd ed. (Westview, 1994) and has just completed a book on the roots of the secessionist insurgency in Kashmir.

Chantal de Jonge Oudraat was, from 1981–94, a Senior Research Associate at the United Nations Institute for Disarmament Research (UNIDIR) in Geneva, where she was founder and editor of *The UNIDIR Newsletter*. She is currently a Research Affiliate of CSIA, and is writing a book on the United Nations.

Alicia Levine received her Ph.D. from the University of Chicago. In 1994–95, she was a post-doctoral Research Fellow at the John M. Olin Institute for Strategic Studies at Harvard University. During the 1995–96 academic year, she was a Fellow at the Center for International Security and Arms Control at Stanford University. She plans to take a post as Assistant Professor of Political Science at Johns Hopkins University.

Dan Lindley is a pre-doctoral Research Fellow at CSIA and a Ph.D. candidate in political science at the Massachusetts Institute of Technology. He is examining the Concert of Europe and the United Nations in his dissertation, "Transparency and Security Regimes." Before coming to MIT, he worked at the Center for Defense Information, the Federation of American Scientists, and the Brookings Institution.

Elizabeth S. Rogers is a post-doctoral Research Fellow at CSIA. From 1991–95, she was an Instructor and Assistant Professor of Political Science at Case Western Reserve University. In 1994–95, she was a post-doctoral Research Fellow in the Economics and National Security Program at the John M. Olin Institute for Strategic Studies, Harvard University.

Joanna Spear was a post-doctoral Research Fellow at CSIA in 1993–95. In her permanent position, she is Director of the Graduate Program in International Studies and Lecturer in Politics at the University of Sheffield. Her publications include *Carter and Arms Sales: Implementing the Carter Administration's Arms Transfer Restraint Policy* (Macmillan, 1995) and *Restraining the Trade in Conventional Weapons* (MIT Press, forthcoming).

Stephen John Stedman is Associate Professor at the School for Advanced International Studies (SAIS), Johns Hopkins University. His publications include *Peacemaking in Civil War: International Mediation in Zimbabwe, 1974–1980* (Lynne Rienner, 1991) and (with Thomas Ohlson) *The New Is Not Yet Born: Conflict Resolution in Southern Africa* (Brookings Institution, 1994).

Milada Anna Vachudová is a pre-doctoral Research Fellow at CSIA and a DPhil. candidate in International Relations at St. Antony's College, University of Oxford, where she was a Marshall Scholar for three years. Her work experience includes writing for the RFE/RL Research Institute and teaching at the Central European University.

Thomas G. Weiss is Associate Director of Brown University's Thomas J. Watson, Jr. Institute for International Studies and Executive Director of the Academic Council on the United Nations System. Formerly an official at the United Nations, his latest publications include an edited volume, *The United Nations and Civil Wars* (Lynne Rienner, 1995), and an overview of recent emergencies (with Larry Minear), *Mercy Under Fire: War and the Global Humanitarian Community* (Westview, 1995).

INDEX

Center for Science and International Affairs

Graham T. Allison, Director
John F. Kennedy School of Government
Harvard University
79 JFK Street, Cambridge MA 02138
(617) 495-1400

The Center for Science and International Affairs (CSIA) is the hub of research and teaching on international relations at Harvard's John F. Kennedy School of Government. CSIA seeks to advance the understanding of international security and environmental problems with special emphasis on the role of science and technology in the analysis and design of public policy. The Center seeks to anticipate emerging international problems, identify practical solutions, and encourage policymakers to act. These goals animate work in each of the Center's four major programs:

- The International Security Program (ISP) is the home of the Center's core concern with international security issues.

- The Strengthening Democratic Institutions (SDI) project works to catalyze international support for political and economic transformations in the former Soviet Union.

- The Science, Technology, and Public Policy (STPP) program emphasizes public policy issues in which understanding of science, technology, and systems of innovation are crucial.

- The Environment and Natural Resources Program (ENRP) is the locus of interdisciplinary research and environmental policy issues.

Each year CSIA hosts a multinational group of approximately 25 scholars from the social, behavioral, and natural sciences. Dozens of Harvard faculty members and adjunct research fellows from the greater Boston area also participate in CSIA activities. CSIA also sponsors seminars and conferences, many open to the public; maintains a substantial specialized library; and publishes a monograph series and discussion papers. The Center's International Security Program, directed by Steven E. Miller, publishes the CSIA Studies in International Security, and sponsors and edits the quarterly journal *International Security*.

The Center is supported by an endowment established with funds from the Ford Foundation and Harvard University, by foundation grants, by individual gifts, and by occasional government contracts.